SINGULAR ENCOUNTERS

SINGULAR ENCOUNTERS

NAIM ATTALLAH

QUARTET BOOKS
LONDON NEW YORK

First published in Great Britain by
Quartet Books Limited 1990
A member of the Namara Group
27/29 Goodge Street, London W1P 1FD

British Library Cataloguing in Publication Data
Singular encounters.
1. Celebrities – Biographies – Collections
I. Attallah, Naim
920.02

ISBN 0–7043–2768–6

Phototypeset by Input Typesetting Ltd, London
Printed and bound in Great Britain by BPCC Hazell Books Ltd,
Aylesbury, Bucks

FOR RAMSAY

CONTENTS

FOREWORD

In 1986 my book *Women* was published after a year's effort spent interviewing 318 remarkable women whose common denominator was achievement. I felt enriched by the experience, but when the excitement of publication subsided, I became dejected. Clearly I needed a new preoccupation, another book in which to immerse myself. Since writing is a solitary pursuit, I preferred, once again, to be stimulated through the medium of the interview. A suitable challenge had to be found. What about men? Would the sort of men I had in mind agree to talk to me?

I was very apprehensive, perhaps due largely to my upbringing: no public school grounding, very little exposure to masculine conviviality – factors which have always left me feeling curiously detached in male society, despite being gregarious at heart. Nevertheless I began in earnest. Letters were written and, in most cases, replies were received. Initially I was disappointed because it seemed that people were being over-cautious. They wanted to know more about the project, about the company in which they would appear, and whether this was to be some sort of companion volume to my *Women* book. I could elaborate on the project, define the shape the book was to take, but it was difficult to speculate on those likely to take part.

My enthusiasm grew when my first interview was arranged. It was with Richard Ingrams, whom I considered to be a complex and contradictory character. If it went well, the project was likely to gain impetus from the outset. As it turned out it was a success. Indeed I am indebted to Richard Ingrams for encouraging others to take part in the book just at the point where I needed to feel that some substantial progress was being made. Auberon Waugh came next, and thereafter one agreement to be interviewed followed another. The eventual choice of people included is by design a rare miscellany. I wanted the book to entertain as well as inform, so that it might appeal to the general reader. To have

achieved this on a broader scale, I would have needed to interview at least fifty people, an impossibility within the confines of a single volume. I believe there is enough material here, however, to engage the interest of a wide and varied audience.

My objective in *Singular Encounters* is to lay before the reader the experience and thoughts of various men from whom we can perhaps learn something about ourselves and the times in which we live. To have written about their lives would have been the more creative challenge, had it been done in the traditional biographical form. That is a form which has great merit, especially when the author is a man of wisdom and talent. His views and perceptions may then re-create the lives of others through interpretation and comment, through elegant writing and fine composition. I preferred, however, the fusion or intertwining of interviewer and subject.

In framing my questions, I did not want to emulate the rigid approach of the sociologist, but rather to adopt one which was more free-ranging and conversational, although similar questions would sometimes reappear in different interviews. I aimed always for a simplicity and directness of approach in order to prompt a response that came from the heart as well as the head. My role was that of a catalyst. I set out to be as invisible as possible. Only where my interjections helped to create a vivid flow or turn in the conversation, or point the sense, have they been retained in the editing. Questions appear only when it was felt they helped with the final structuring of an interview, and in some cases they have been totally omitted. This method has produced a variety of approach which matches the individualities of the persons concerned.

The people who are the subjects of this book articulate their own views in their own distinct manner and style. I feel it is always much more compelling to hear a story at first hand, without the possibility of misunderstanding on account of authorial distortion. Clever writers have a way with words and frequently take a certain amount of liberty with what is factual and what is not.

I took up the challenge of *Singular Encounters* because I am interested in people, in what they do and what draws them to do it. It is an interest which I hope the reader will find amply rewarded in the pages that follow.

SIR HAROLD ACTON

Harold Acton was born in 1904 and educated at Eton and Christ Church, Oxford. He enjoyed a long friendship with Evelyn Waugh and was a fond admirer of Edith Sitwell and Gertrude Stein. He spent seven years in Peking where he lectured in English at the University of Peking and became a devotee of Chinese classical theatre. He served in the RAF during the Second World War, chiefly in the Far East where he worked in Intelligence. He is a prolific author, believing his best publications to be history books, in particular *The Bourbons of Naples*. He was awarded the CBE in 1965 and has lived alone for many years in La Pietra, a magnificent Renaissance villa in Tuscany.

On the subject of beauty, you have written that those who philosophize most loudly and persistently about it seldom have intrinsic taste. Is beauty purely subjective?

I fear it is. In my case I've been privileged: born in Florence and surrounded by beautiful things with a father who was a painter and collector and whose friends were art historians, art critics. I think of Offner, whose centenary will be celebrated very soon, and Berenson, and Herbert Horne, who bequeathed his collection to Florence – his palace is now a museum – and Stibbert, another Englishman who lived not far from where I do. All these men were collectors and I imbibed something of that atmosphere when I was young. There were many beautiful villas, all full of treasures.

The British community was then predominant, though it's been ebbing now for some time, ever since just before the last war. People gave up their houses and went back to live in England. I suppose that really they were scared away by fascism. Life was made very unpleasant for them by the young blackshirts, you know, so they started to retreat, to leave their lovely houses in the Italian countryside. One or two, like Lord Lambton, have in more recent times bought properties here in beautiful situations near Siena, Signa, Pistoia, all around here. In fact some parts of Tuscany are today quite Anglicized, you might say. Young English historians and art critics like John Fleming and Hugh Honour live near Lucca and write well on Italian painting, and those are the few who remain. Formerly every other Englishman here was an art historian or collector or painter. It was like a kitchen of the arts.

You have said that your most valued experiences have been aesthetic. Could you elaborate?

A single visit to Florence can answer that question, though Florence is

suffering from new horrors. There is an appalling lack of architectural taste today. It's rather sad, this degradation of architecture in Italy which I don't think applies in the same way in England. Incidentally, where England is concerned, I do think Prince Charles is very enlightened. Aren't we lucky to have a prince who takes an interest in architecture. It's unique. After all, architecture in England has always been very important, but lately people have closed their eyes to the horrors that have arisen in London. Prince Charles is absolutely right to point it out. Of course, good architects do exist, but Prince Charles is in revolt against the vulgarization of everything. He's a man of taste. I don't think the Duke of Edinburgh cares two hoots. As for the Queen, she has other things to think of.

Are there any objective, or at least non-subjective, criteria for beauty?

Yes, I think there are. The French, after all, have Versailles, and they have so many marvellous buildings which are perfectly proportioned in every sort of style. They have the classical tradition of remarkable taste, but unfortunately, as soon as the *petite bourgeoisie* takes over, then it becomes grotesque. French taste has gone down the drain. Even their painting is now very poor. Only think what they used to be in the eighteenth century.

The whole question of taste is very difficult because taste is so personal, so private a thing, but I think that a person who has a certain classical education is entitled to some say in matters of taste. Classical education is the background. I'm afraid there is also natural bad taste, and bad taste is more general than good taste. When I see the garish, the obvious, the bright, the sexy, all of that appals, alas.

In your memoirs you say: 'In spirit I remain a nomad, a restless and nostalgic ex-pat.' Is this still true?

The older I get the more true it seems. With age I feel that I am more devoted to travel in search of art, of international art, not limited to English or Italian. I've always been drawn, for instance, to Chinese art. I also like their drama, which I have translated with L. C. Arlington, and I have translated popular Chinese plays which are immensely artistic and beautiful in performance. Unfortunately China today is too different from the China I knew in the seven happy years I lived in Peking. I have no particular yearning to return under the present régime, but all the same I'm haunted by the happy years I lived there just before the war.

All the accounts that friends bring me of China today are rather depressing, but I love the country and I like the people. Wherever I went, whether in the north, to Honan and Hoonan, or all the way south

to Hong Kong, I always got on well with the Chinese. I feel homesick sometimes for China, but I know it's been transformed under Mao Tse-tung. How could it be otherwise? When I was there, there were still the remains of the Imperial Manchu dynasty. I met several who were talented painters, Prince P'u Ju P'u Hsin-yu, for instance, a cousin of the ex-emperor, who was a very talented poet and painter and who I think eventually fled to Japan. I don't expect he's alive now, but I knew him well and his palace was not far from where I had a house in Kung Hsien Hutung. He painted a portrait of me, which I haven't got because I left everything behind in Peking, expecting to go back after the war, but of course the revolution changed all those expectations. Instead I returned to Italy where I was born, and here I have remained: all my eggs in one basket.

You wrote about your early years: 'I cannot remember thinking of myself as a child for I was as embarrassed by children then as I am now and whined when I was referred to as one of the species.'

I've always been uncomfortable with children and they're uncomfortable with me. I don't know why, but I never felt at ease with children, and, of course, if you're surrounded by works of art then you're always terrified that they're going to break them; and those children that I know will immediately go towards a little statue and *Crash!*, within a moment the statue is down and in smithereens on the floor. Children are very destructive, particularly English children, though I don't think I was ever destructive as a child. I was always rather careful. I had a natural instinctive love of art and so was always extremely careful of everything in this house. I never played with the statues or the paintings I admired. Quite early in life I became attached to Italian art. I used to go to the galleries, which children would not normally do nowadays, and would feast in the Pitti and the Uffizi and the different churches of Florence.

I don't know that I could say I had a very happy nature. I enjoyed Florence, I enjoyed Italy, so when I was at school in England I was very homesick for Italy. I never settled happily in the English atmosphere. Not when I was a child, at any rate. Oxford was another matter. Those days in England were very exciting.

There were the three Sitwells, for instance, all of them publishing, and reciting their poems to music composed by William Walton. They, too, had a place here in Florence at Montegufoni, a huge palatial structure about fifteen miles on the way to Siena. It was bought by Sir George Sitwell, the father, and there they stayed for many years. Sir Osbert Sitwell lived there after Sir George's death, and continued to write, and I think his work, which is detailed and beautifully written,

will be more appreciated in the future for the history of our time and the figures he knew in the arts. Sacheverell Sitwell, too, woke people up to appreciate the baroque and his book on Italian Baroque is still excellent. Of course, baroque has now come to be generally understood and appreciated, but the Sitwells were voices crying a little in advance of the present success.

Of all the literary people you knew during your Oxford days, you speak with special fondness of Edith Sitwell and Gertrude Stein.

Both of them in their ways were poets. Edith Sitwell is probably underestimated as a poet today, but she brought new life, new colour into the English language with *Façade*, set to music so beautifully by Walton. Gertrude Stein was playing pranks with the English language, but as recited by her, her portraits of human beings sounded rather imposing. Anybody who reads them, and reads them in her slow American voice, will see how they were very sharp portrayals of artists and people she knew. She was in Florence at a time when Mabel Dodge lived at the Villa Curonia here, and she did a portrait that doesn't make sense from a logical point of view but which is somehow a creative abstract portrait of Mabel Dodge. I think it is quite extraordinary how she managed it. In terms of abstract language, her portraits of people are really rather good. Nobody else has done it; she's unique. Her first book, *Three Lives*, is still a rather remarkable work, not especially exciting but successful as a literary experiment.

You once said, 'Most novels are confessions in disguise; most "confessions", like Rousseau's, are novels in disguise.' Where did your poetry fit into such a scheme of things? Did you see your early poetry as confessional or were you aware that others might view it as such?

I think all poetry is confessional. It seems to me that the poet unburdens himself of his dreams, of his subconscious, and I'm sure that my poems, which I never look at nowadays, were really subconscious confessions that had to come out in one way or another. Though I'm a Roman Catholic, I don't think they ever came out in the confessional. They had to come out in more elaborate ways and they came out in verse.

You said of writing that you wanted to pour honey from your hive, but what people wanted was gall and wormwood. Were you ever tempted to compromise?

I was never so tempted. All the poets around me, such as Auden, Spender and others whose names I forget, were left-wingers producing poems of protest. There will always be poems of protest, but poetry should take other forms, should not be limited. Poems of protest have

existed since Dante, you might say, but I'm not at all politically minded, and I take the view that politics and poetry do not combine. I suppose Byron with his love of Greece was politically minded, but it is not something you find very often at the heart of the English tradition. Among Italian poets – Leopardi and Carducci – you do, but in English poetry I don't think it's ever that important. With the English, in poetry as in painting, it is nature that is all-important. My poetry was just colour and rhythm, and it was joyful, but as I now realize, it had no depth. It was no more than the exuberance of youth, and every young man has a poetic mood. I was just trying to express my *joie de vivre*, which is nothing to be ashamed of. The older I grow the more I admire the quality in other people.

You once called Cyril Connolly a treacherous Irishman on the grounds that he was a hundred per cent homosexual at school, slept with everyone, then turned against those who remained so.

Well, Connolly was personally *antipatico* to me. He laid down the law, a little dictator surrounded by yes-sayers, all of whom agreed with him, though it also has to be said that he did a good job editing the magazine *Horizon*. When we were contemporaries at Eton I used to get very irritated with his dictatorial manner. He was rather a bully, and he was entirely homosexual, then he changed over to the women and never stopped. He discovered the girls rather late in life, and then it was one after another. A treacherous Irishman is what he was, and I didn't care much for him.

You sometimes make Eton sound like one of the 'cities of the plain'.

Oh, no. It was the most innocent place. No cities of the plain there. In fact a sharp eye was kept on the morals of the Etonians by the housemasters, so they could not stray, though I suppose subconsciously there was a good deal of homosexuality.

Your friendship with Evelyn Waugh spanned many years. Did you admire him as a man and writer equally?

I admired his writing far more than I admired his character, but he was a delightful, warm-hearted, hot-tempered personality such as you rarely find today. He was a man of extreme views and a convert to Catholicism, and a passionate convert at that, which is also rather rare nowadays. He was a deeply religious person, but his gifts were not really in the most serious vein. His gifts were humorous and I think his best novels are the least serious. For instance, *Decline and Fall*, his first novel, dedicated to myself, is still I think one of the most brilliant of English

light novels. He got a little more serious towards the end, and he lost somehow the light touch, so rare in English literature. Not many people have that light touch. Evelyn Waugh was a master of prose as well; he wrote very good English. That's another thing that is rare nowadays: good, sound, logical English.

I wouldn't say Waugh was depressing as a person. He was rather more depressed than depressing because he saw the way the world was going and it didn't appeal to him at all. But he had a heart of gold and I was really very fond of him. I was best man at his first wedding, a marriage which went badly, alas. I'm afraid he married a rather superficial lady who flirted with others and he couldn't stand it. He was very old-fashioned, expected his wife to be loyal and faithful to him. He couldn't stand the strain of her going off on her own. He was a proud man and he was very loyal as a friend. We stayed friends till the day he died and he's one of the few friends I've never quarrelled with. I'm also a friend of his son Bron.

Towards the end of his life, Evelyn became a kind of recluse, except that he loved his family, and loved to be in the company of his devoted wife, surrounded by his children. He didn't care to join literary societies, but liked to stand on his own. He was independent. There's too much nowadays of congregating in these literary societies, of people blowing their own trumpets, but Evelyn was dignified about all of that.

It has been said that characters in Brideshead Revisited *are based on your own character. Do you find the idea flattering or provoking?*

I think it very flattering, but I don't recognize any character in *Brideshead* connected with myself. He's taken little traits from me in one of the characters, certain physical traits so that people confuse me sometimes with that particular character, but I don't think it was in his mind. A novelist has to take everything in his experience and use it. That's why we respond. If we felt a novelist's work was false, we wouldn't admire it, unless his fiction were absolutely farcical and fantastic, and Evelyn's is only farcical up to a certain degree. There is a seriousness underlining all his fiction.

Max Beerbohm and Somerset Maugham seem to have belonged in quite separate worlds, but you knew them both. Were they at all alike?

They were not very alike, except that they belonged to the same period in a sense, Beerbohm being very much a figure of the 1890s, a sort of dandy of that era who survived into the present century. Maugham, too, had all the mannerisms of a man of the nineteenth century: very formal and living in the South of France in sumptuous splendour. He was not a modern; he didn't really change with the century. He had

this stutter, poor man, which only vanished on certain occasions. When he had to speak in public he stopped stammering, but in private life it was embarrassing because he took a long time to come out with any sentence. Pathetic. He used to stay here next to us before he went to the South of France.

As for being an admirer of his writing, I would have to answer yes and no. I think he's a first-rate novelist. *Of Human Bondage* is a book that will last, and there are a lot of things he wrote that exactly struck the mood of the moment.

Is there any foundation in the rumour of a rift between you and Gore Vidal?

It's a fabrication. He's not exactly one of my heroes, far from it, but he is in a way a very amiable young man, though very naïve. He thinks himself sophisticated, but he's really very simple. If there's any disagreement, it's entirely on his side not on mine. I live, as you see, in a totally different atmosphere. He was in Rome, I think, for a time, used to turn up here occasionally, but I have very little in common with him. He's not an aesthete, not by any means. The arts don't mean much to him. He's an embryo politician and all his ambitions are towards the Senate in the United States. He's a fish out of water here in Florence. We have never quarrelled on my side. On his, I do believe he bears me ill-will. I'm very sorry for it because to me he is just like an American sophomore. I can't say I take him seriously as a writer.

You have dismissed most English novelists as preachers who mistake their vocation.

Lately they have tended to preach less. I don't think, for instance, that Somerset Maugham was much of a preacher and the Bloomsbury writers, Virginia Woolf – or even Aldous Huxley – did not preach much. But the Victorians were eminently preachers. If you pick out any Victorian novelist, you find they have a tendency to speak from a pulpit, to address an imaginary public.

If I were to have my reading confined to one English novelist I should say Dickens because I think he was a man of overall breadth of view and knowledge of society. Though his language is very dated, it is very vital English. As you read him you are still living in a sort of Victorian present. Thackeray is also remarkable, but I feel he is more of the past. I don't feel he is as alive as Dickens is today.

As for the English being a literary nation, I find the claim exaggerated. I fear they're not literary. They do not buy literary works, they want something different. Nowadays it's sex, sex and lively fashion magazines. The stress of modern life drives them to the frivolous by contrast, it seems to me.

On the subject of religion, you write that the Protestant faith has much misery to answer for. Why single out the Protestant faith?

I think it could be said of many religions, but as a Roman Catholic I remain firm in seeing all around me in this country how religion lives among the people and how it is the inspiration, the joy and the philosophy of the Italians that has kept them going for centuries. I feel a stronger Catholic here than anywhere else, though it is always a delight, a joy to me when I go to England to find that Westminster Cathedral is full. I can't say I'm deeply religious, but I believe religion is essential to us and that without it we lose our bearings. It is extremely important for us to have a faith if we're fortunate enough. I cannot imagine being without faith, I cannot imagine the purpose of life in that case.

After a good long life, my faith is stronger than ever. My belief is in the Church and in our wonderful Pope. I have the greatest admiration for him. He is a heroic man. I'm very happy to have been with a Polish squadron during the war. They were all deeply religious: heroic boys, but deeply pious. If you went to Mass in Blackpool it was all Poles at that time. They sang beautifully, and in their voices you could hear their faith ringing out. It was quite splendid, an inspiration, and wherever I've been – even in India – the Catholics were always far more vocal than the Protestants. I wouldn't want to make any sort of comparison, but it was a great inspiration. There's only one faith for me. It's in the Church of Rome.

Of course the Pope is a traditionalist. The Church is traditional, it has to be. We can't revolutionize what Our Lord has preached in the past, we can't change his words. I freely admit, though, that I was saddened by the abandonment of the Tridentine rite. The strength of the Church is in the old Tridentine.

Do you believe in sin?

I believe rather in weakness than in sin, though certain politicians make me believe seriously in sin. If one turns to politics, one has to admit that there are evil people about.

Can you think of any really honest and straightforward politician?

I remember at Oxford how the young men who were going in for politics and the Union were very shallow, very superficial. They were only ambitious for themselves. I stayed aloof from all those brilliant geniuses who were passing all their exams with top marks, double firsts and all that, then disappearing into the House of Commons. We've heard nothing of them since. Those with the biggest reputations at that time have vanished. Roger Hollis is still known, perhaps, though he

was a scandalous fellow, a traitor. I also met Guy Burgess, but I prefer to forget him. A boorish sort of fellow, not an intellectual. He was nothing. I don't know why people talked about him. He had a talent for making a noise, that's all.

Speaking of politicians, I did admire Churchill. He was an outstanding person who also wrote well. He was enlightened, the sort of universal man who can be admired anywhere in the world. He was a great draughtsman and he could also paint. Some of his earlier work will endure, I'm sure, but then he became experimental. The desire always to be young, always to experiment, always just to beget children has been, in my view, a great loss in art. Instead of clinging to his own natural talent for beautiful draughtsmanship and colour, Churchill turned his back on his talent, and, like several other painters today, though they don't realize it, was led astray by the critics. I think the wish to be modern at all costs, to alarm, to shock, to startle is the trouble, whereas great painters in the past were not thinking about startling anybody, they were just devoted to their vision and to trying to interpret it in a way others could share. I don't believe anybody can share the visions of Picasso, or even Matisse.

The political animal is something very foreign to me, though, because I have lived in a world of aesthetics, of love of the arts, which it seems to me is natural to anybody born in Florence. Although a good many Englishmen born here were not as interested in the arts as you might expect, generally speaking all the English who were here had one foot in the art world.

Did you ever live in Italy under fascism?

The atmosphere was too unpleasant for me, so that was when I went off to China. But whenever I came back in those years I could feel this rather unpleasant atmosphere of coercion, and many of my English friends sympathized with fascism, thinking it very splendid and dramatic. It's hard to believe now, but they were taken in by the show, by the theatrical element. My parents were here under fascism. I paid them a visit and found the atmosphere very bellicose at that time. It wasn't something that could be said of the Italians in general, because they were peace-loving and didn't want war at all, but the people one met – journalists, writers – were all very bellicose and attracted to Nazism. The Germans had tremendous influence. My parents were both in prison for a short time before getting away to Switzerland.

Eventually I felt I couldn't sit there in Peking any longer, enjoying life while Britain was at war. I had to do my duty in some way and so went back to England and joined the RAF. I didn't fly because my vision and my age were against me – I was already in my thirties. They

took me because of my knowledge of Chinese and things Oriental after living in China for seven years. The war was also by then being fought in the Far East, and so I was sent off there after a period at various air stations to pick up the methods. I was in Intelligence, so called. The people I met were all very brilliant, but I never give those years a thought today. Now that I'm eighty-five years old, it's strange to think of how I was once restricted to air stations in England as an interrogating Intelligence officer, listening to the crews who had been bombing Germany when they arrived back absolutely worn out from their sorties.

Have you ever been a romantic?

I've been an admirer of Schiller, of the romantics, and so on. I think we've all gone through a romantic phase, particularly in youth.

Did you ever fall in love?

Oh, yes, I think we all did, but I suppose I haven't got the depth of character to fall desperately in love, like so many of my friends. No, I never had that. I suppose I must be a cold-blooded fish, really – more mental than physical.

Certainly it occurred to me to marry. I was proposed to many times, but I lived in China then and it would have been very inconvenient. I liked to be an independent bachelor in Peking, having my choice of friends and of girl-friends. I preferred my freedom. I'm happy now. I'm an old bachelor, but I don't suffer from solitude. I sometimes regret that I never chose such and such a person, but I have many particularly good friends here.

I spent a long time with a Chinese woman, which was a very happy time, except when I had to leave, of course, but you couldn't continue for ever. It was a rewarding relationship. The Chinese have such an exquisite old civilization and Chinese women have a wonderful instinct for affection. They're warm hearted, and I like everything about their figures: very graceful and unhairy. I don't like a lot of hair, so they appealed to me. If I had married I would have married a Chinese. So I was living with a Chinese girl for many years, and happily because I was never disturbed; no scenes, no jealousy, nothing of that sort. They had another tempo. With an Italian woman it would be a series of scenes and life would become impossible. I know, because I have so many Italian friends.

I never felt any regret at the lack of an heir. I'm leaving everything to New York University. I don't think Oxford would look after it properly, and anyway, they haven't got the money. I offered it all to Oxford first, but met with such little response that I changed my mind. So everything goes to New York University and they will take the villa

over and use it as a centre for Italian studies. My father didn't like the idea at all. I discussed it with him before he died and he, of course, would have preferred me to marry and have children, but I never had that desire. I never had a feeling for children and family. Even my mother didn't have much feeling of that kind, and I think she agreed with me fundamentally. She always preferred the place to be lived in by people who appreciated the arts.

Do you feel you had to forsake the pleasures of the flesh for the sake of art, or can the two go together?

They can go together, of course, but the pleasures of the flesh were very small in my case. They are an important part of life, but they didn't dominate me in the way they dominate so many people. Talking of Maugham, he was always in the hands of some dreadful creature. Gerald Hackston, for instance, who dominated him, or his wife, whom he hated. In my case I have nothing of that sort, thank God. No hatreds. I feel I have chosen wisely to be my own master and to leave everything to a university that can enjoy it and use it. After all, Florence will continue to be the capital of the arts. It's bound to be. It always has been since the Medici.

Have you ever been attracted to erotic art?

As a juvenile I was rather interested in certain Beardsley drawings and others appealed to me. I still think Beardsley is a very good draughtsman, but on the whole I think that art should rise above the erotic.

How do you see the relationship between art and morality? Presumably the two can never be separated.

Many artists have been considered deeply immoral. Art is to me beyond morality. If you start moralizing then art disappears. It becomes a sort of preaching.

Throughout your memoirs you display an irritation with and contempt for critics, especially for art critics.

I think that many art critics are would-be painters. They are disappointed and frustrated and consequently their frustration is brought out in their criticism of others. That's my opinion, particularly in England where many of the critics I have known personally have been painters on the sly who have had no success and no chance of success and consequently have been bitter about others. I am afraid it is a weakness of human nature to be like that, but it is a sad thing that most of the critics are failed painters.

Literary critics are larger, broader. I'm not capable of judging, for instance, modern poetry, because I'm rather indifferent to what I see in the way of poetry today, but on the whole I consider that our literary critics are excellent. I read the *Spectator* every week with pleasure for its admirable, clear, well-written criticism. It's an excellent journal, and the *New Statesman* and others of high quality compare well with any publication of the past. The late Victorian publications seem rather heavy-going now if we try to look through them, but still they contain some very good criticism.

Are scholarly work and critical explanations the most helpful ways of making art available?

No. I don't think people pay much attention to the critics. The critics don't possess much weight any longer. In the days of Ruskin, of course, it was quite different.

What about Bernard Shaw?

He was a very loud, able and brilliant critic, but I think he was somehow deeply inhuman. I met him once at a public meeting. He had a most beautiful voice and great charm of manner, there's no doubt about it, but I think he was fundamentally a eunuch. I don't think he had any sex. That's my own private view. He was married, of course, but I don't think he was a marrying man. He was all brain and, in spite of the beard, I don't think he was very virile. At least, that was my own personal impression.

Why inhuman? Well, I think that of people entirely given to politics and the stage and boosting themselves. He was a tremendous egocentric, the best propagandist for himself that ever was.

You say of Charles Loeser: 'He would question every objet d'art *until it vouchsafed an answer.' What sort of an answer, and in what way does one question an* objet d'art? *You go on to speak of the way Loeser would interpret a great master's drawing. What is it to interpret a drawing?*

Oh dear, very difficult. Loeser had an impeccable eye. He was one of the first people to collect Cézanne and he used to tell his servants or his ignorant cook to come in, and he would ask them, 'Do you feel that is a landscape?' And they'd say, *'Si, si.'* 'My cook knows more about it than I do,' he would say. 'She has the eye, she is unspoilt, untutored. I am unfortunately a Harvard graduate with too much education to be able to see properly.' Of course, he was exaggerating, but still, there was a certain amount of truth in it. He was a very original man.

At the beginning of your memoirs you write: 'Peace and goodwill towards men will only be brought about by individuals like myself.' Can you elaborate?

It's a very conceited statement. I'm rather shocked that I ever wrote it. But I think that people like us, who are only interested in culture and history, do perhaps a little more for the general public than is recognized and yet we are dismissed by journalists as decorative people on the fringe. In fact we influence people far more than they're ready to admit. That's my opinion.

It sometimes seems that high art must necessarily be a restricted pleasure. Do you think the taste of the connoisseur can ever really coincide with the larger, more democratic taste, if you like?

It can't coincide, but it's a guide. The connoisseur must guide taste and most people pay attention to the connoisseur when they know he's genuine. They may laugh at him to begin with, but they follow. They laughed at Whistler, but his 'Ten O'Clock Lecture' is a wonderful piece of prose, quite apart from the fact that the message had a great influence.

What do you think an aesthetic emotion is? Is it really distinguishable from other sorts of feelings?

Oh, yes. It's the most difficult thing to put into words. Aesthetic emotions require a Walter Pater, who wrote his book on the Renaissance with great difficulty over many years. It was a product of careful thought, and we cannot suddenly express that in a few words. Think of the aesthetic philosophers in Germany and in Italy. They are rather long winded and obscure, and it's very difficult to tone that down to the level of popular understanding. Very difficult – though I think that the average person confronted with a great statue can tell the difference between that and, say, the sort of abstract stuff that is supposed to be a statue now. I think the average man or woman in England can respond immediately to a genuine work of art, a fine Niobe or an Apollo and Marsyas. I think it is extraordinary that the public tolerates the sort of thing that I see very often being put up in London. In my day we'd have tarred and feathered those statues, but they've even spread to Italy. It's a blight.

Some literary artists like Oscar Wilde and T. S. Eliot have seemed to allow art to border on the trivial by saying that all art is useless, as Wilde did, or by calling it a superior entertainment, as Eliot did. What are your feelings about this?

I think they're both very mistaken. I think art is an essential to civilized life, to our private existence. I cannot conceive of an existence without

art. But alas, in many places, in industrial cities in the North of England, people manage to live without it very well, but still it's a severe loss to them. If they had beautiful things to look at, it would inspire them to do even better work. But art in England has always been a small group of people, wealthy, old families with an interest in painting or architecture. It's never been open to the masses, unfortunately, and we have suffered accordingly.

You quote Andrew Marvell's lines, 'My love is of a birth so rare/As 'tis for object strange and high,/It was begotten by Despair/Upon Impossibility.' Why did these lines seem to you to explain the otherwise inexplicable?

Marvell was a man of profound vision and of deep spirituality which is rare in the poetry of that period. But it seems to me that these lines are modern and can convey that twilight of the consciousness which is so seldom expressed nowadays.

Over the centuries many hundreds of men and women have devoted their lives to music or painting or dance. Does such a devotion in itself give value to their art?

Certainly. It must give value to their art, if they are devoted in the real, true sense of the word. Pavlova, until she was quite old, was still dancing. I remember seeing her when she was about to retire. She was still the most graceful sylph-like figure one could possible dream of. She was exquisite, and that's a triumph of art.

You record in your memoirs the fate of works of art at the hands of the Germans in Florence. You describe, for example, an 'Adoration of the Magi' being used as a tablecloth and stabbed with a knife. At the same time you praise the Germans and say that in courage and fortitude they were certainly our peers. Why did they behave so badly, do you think?

Well, unfortunately, that's a sort of racial thing that they have inherited: the rough, primitive instincts which have been glorified by certain great geniuses like Wagner. Wagner glorifies the coarsest instincts in *The Ring*. It's a sign of strength they feel, this great love of their own strength, their own power. It's quite a good thing in a way from the point of view of art, because that is the way good art is produced, but also, alas, bad art.

Why do you think that art seems not to affect people's behaviour as one might hope? Both the Germans and the Japanese seem to have been capable of terrible savagery concurrently with an appreciation of the subtlest effects of art.

That's a very strange point, yes. The Japanese can certainly be split

personalities. I've never quite understood their Buddhism; it's not like the Buddhism of the Indians, not contemplative. Everything that they do has got to be active in a hysterical sort of way. They are very peculiar, the Japanese, very peculiar people. The women in Japan, I should say, are superior to the men. They are people of very refined taste: the way they dress, the way they paint, the poems they write. Many of the best novels written in Japan are written by women, such as *The Tale of Genji.* The Japanese are full of surprises, because the women are so refined and elegant and the men fundamentally so crude and rough. They believe strongly in virility, of course, and virility is mixed up with militarism. They occupied Peking when I was there and behaved appallingly. I have no great love of the Japanese male.

It's very difficult to say anything definite about Germans because they are so different from each other. Germany's a land of individualists. People think that they are all together, all followers of Bismarck, Hitler or whatever it is, but they're not. Germans are strongly individual characters. You can see that in their music, in their philosophy, in their works of art.

The journey to your home in Tuscany has become a kind of pilgrimage for many. Are you happy to end your days in Florence, or do you ever feel like coming home?

I was born here, so my home is here. I feel Florentine and I'm an honorary citizen of Florence, and all my life-long friends, my closest associations are with Florentines. I left for China because of *fascismo* and China was my next love, but of course in view of what's happened there, its worse even than *fascismo* was here. So I could never think of going back or living as I did in Peking in a private house, surrounded by Chinese.

What was it that drew you to China initially? You say you felt strangely at home there.

I always loved Chinese art. The Chinese written character is in itself a very beautiful thing, a work of art, and their cooking is a very important element in civilization. I think people who feed well are on the side of the angels. It's very important that people should eat decent food, properly cooked, and the Chinese do. It's strongly in their favour. And their poetry is sung. When I was there, they would sing their poems. The effect was so very striking. Unlike our poets. We can hardly say that they sing.

I understand that the Chinese do not distinguish between an original work of art and an exact copy. Is that the best approach?

Their tradition is so strong that they go on painting in the same style as they did in the fifteenth century. Landscape artists, for instance, continue to paint in the style of the fifteenth-century Ming dynasty. It may be a sort of limitation to talent. I don't think that always remaining so traditional is such a good thing. The great artists have always broken with tradition. Turner, for instance, with his billowing seas and all that, broke with the tradition of the eighteenth-century landscape in his landscapes. That's the way art should be: alive. Start with the tradition, but then break it; rules have got to be broken.

How can we really enter into the appropriate frame of reference to allow us to respond properly to work in an alien tradition, like that of China?

I feel there's too much emphasis on the word alien. I think it's exaggerated. A Chinese artist can appreciate a drawing by Michelangelo and Michelangelo would appreciate a good landscape by some eighteenth-century Chinese. Art is a republic, not a monarchy.

Writing about China, you say: 'Behind the broad main streets were networks of alleys, rather slummy, with their mounds of refuse and mongrel dogs.' Did you not find this public indifference distressing?

The back streets were full of families all living together, crowded, but not really squalid, because they had a certain dignity. The Chinese lived in a very agreeable way. I wouldn't have minded joining one of those households.

You also record that in the average year, 29,000 corpses, the bodies of overworked young mill-workers, were gathered on the streets. Didn't your knowledge of this interfere with your admiration of China?

I think all countries have something of that kind, you know. It's not publicized, but I think it's not so extraordinary. It happens everywhere.

Do you think there is anything left in Communist China of what originally drew you to the country?

The landscape remains, and they have protected a good many of their old monuments, I imagine, and from what I hear the Forbidden City in Peking remains the same. But the spirit perhaps has gone, as people are unified by Marxism. I can't believe that that suits the Chinese, not the Chinese I knew, who were very independent and individual. But I never think of China now. I try not to think of it because I was extremely happy there and saw it *couleur de rose.*

What is it like to smoke opium?

I never became an addict, but I occasionally joined a Chinese friend and smoked a pipe and very much enjoyed it. It seemed to clear my mind and allowed me to forget about the tiresome irritations of life. I found it soothing. And I think that the danger of opium is grossly exaggerated. I have known many people who have smoked it for years who are now old, and yet in spite of their age are flourishing.

You give an account of a visit to an astrologer in Calcutta. Do you, or did you, believe in such things?

Oh, yes, I believe in these things. I don't begin to understand it, but that it exists and that it has existed for centuries and is very strong in India there is no doubt at all. I feel that the Indians have got another sense for astrology which we lack here. Our lives are so different from theirs in that way. We can't keep pace with that strange other-worldliness.

You wrote that a book of memoirs should concentrate on all that is vital and attempt to recapture the moments of exultation and delight. Is there no place for a recollection of sadder times?

I don't think that sadness adds to other people's vitality, and I'm all in favour of vitality. The sad, the gloomy, the depressing are life-diminishing, and I'm for the life-enhancing. So much is life-diminishing nowadays that we must return to the National Gallery and the Louvre to refresh ourselves. In all our lives we have had sad, not to say tragic times, especially during the world wars. One is surrounded by tragedy, but man is helpless against that sort of tragedy.

I would say I have been fortunate in my own life. I've been privileged to live here in Florence in a fifteenth-century villa with a garden surrounded by statues by well-known sculptors. If I were unhappy it would be a crime. But I do have a horror of death, an absolute horror of it. I enjoy life so much that I would really not welcome death at all. So many friends of mind commit suicide or threaten it. I just don't understand. Life is so wonderful, there's so much more to discover. We're given these blessings, and living here in Florence I'd be mad to wish to die.

I don't consider my work to be of much importance, but I don't think I have done yet what I have it in me to do, which is to write a good short story. But if I were to live my life again, I think I would do the same things again. I would write, I would edit magazines at Oxford. I don't think I could have chosen another path. My only regret is that I didn't write better, that I haven't done more with a flow of imagination. But you can't force that. It is something you are born

with. Otherwise I have nothing but thankfulness for the life I have enjoyed.

What fortifies you nowadays against life's disappointments?

It's a very difficult question, but with age I enjoy the beauty of landscapes, scenery and architecture more perhaps than ever, and that keeps me alert and optimistic in my outlook, but otherwise I'm afraid I don't really enjoy the present moment. It's only through art that I exist: through my love of the arts. I have no belief of any kind in my genius. No, that is a part of youth. In youth we're all geniuses. When one is young one has a spirit, but it grows rather feeble as the years pass. Now I find myself rather disappointed with life. I suppose that is a part of creeping age, of getting feebler with the years and becoming mentally not quite so alert. I don't really feel so buoyant as I used to. I used to be very active, particularly when I was at Oxford, editing *Oxford Poetry* and surrounded by very talented poets like Peter Quennell and Robert Graves, and a great many distinguished dons like Beazley, the greatest authority on Greek vases in the world, and Gow on the plough, famous also as a Greek scholar. It seemed like a Renaissance when I was at Oxford, but that Renaissance didn't last.

LORD ALEXANDER QC

Born in 1936, Robert Alexander was educated at Brighton College and King's College, Cambridge. He was called to the Bar (Middle Temple) in 1961 and became a Queen's Counsel in 1973. His briefs have included Ken Livingstone's bid to maintain fair fares on London Transport, Mrs Thatcher's ban on trade unions at GCHQ and Jeffrey Archer's libel action against the *Star* newspaper. He was created a life peer in 1988 and relinquished his position on the Takeover Panel in October 1989 when he was appointed chairman of the National Westminster Bank. He is married to a barrister and has two sons and a daughter by a previous marriage.

Your origins were relatively humble, your parents had to make sacrifices for your schooling and education. Were you conscious at the time of there being different social classes, hence different opportunities?

I was well aware that the opportunities that were given me were opportunities which were hard earned by my parents. They actually did go without things so I could be educated. I was equally well aware in the area in which we initially lived, Stoke-on-Trent, and to a lesser extent when we moved south, that these opportunities weren't available to many people. But at that time there were also the grammar schools, and many parents who weren't able to send children to schools such as the one I went to, could send their bright children to grammar schools. I might easily have gone to a grammar school, and I'm sure I would have received a very good education.

Both my parents were immensely supportive. My father, who himself left school at fourteen or fifteen, was dedicated to my receiving the best education possible and becoming a member of a profession. He had been very well served by a solicitor at one stage of his life when he was establishing his filling station, and, unlike many sections of the population, he had a high regard for lawyers as a group. So when I decided to turn to law, he encouraged me. My mother was also an intelligent person, perhaps without the same single-minded drive towards education for her sons that my father had, but giving considerable and generous backing to it.

Would you say your upbringing and parental influence stood you in good stead for what you were to make of your life, or did you feel set apart from your family?

I felt a great affection for my parents. I knew they wanted me to succeed, to make something of my life, to have high educational standards and

good values. Indeed, my father showed his concern for that in stressing the importance of dressing correctly and neatly, making certain that shoes were clean, making sure everything about one was as he would like to see – worthy of respect. Inevitably, however, the education they gave me was one they'd not had themselves, and therefore they couldn't share it. They could not appreciate what I read in history, what I read in literature, so although there was affection and gratitude, it wasn't easy to have shared interests as I grew older. But they remained immensely enthusiastic about and proud of my progress. They were very understanding.

When you were at Cambridge, you apparently felt diffident about speaking in union debates. Yet public speaking was to be pivotal to your chosen profession. When did your talent for public speaking emerge?

Certainly not at university. I had done some public speaking at school, in a small group, in debates, in preparing essays to be spoken; and I had won poetry-reading prizes. But in the larger arena of Cambridge, as someone who was conscious of being very tall, thin and rather angular, not particularly socially accomplished and feeling that others around were much more sophisticated with perhaps a dazzling ability, I didn't feel able to walk into the spotlight of that large stage. I never spoke in the Union then, and I would have found it almost impossible to get to my feet with an audience of that size. I decided to become a lawyer at the end of my second year at university. I was reading English, but didn't feel I had the talent to be a dramatist, nor the inclination to be a journalist, and I knew I didn't want to be a schoolteacher. I liked what I'd heard of the disciplined approach of the law. I enjoyed English literary criticism where it appeared to be particularly logical in its analysis, and was attracted by the way in which Dr Leavis wrote, even though he was not particularly well regarded in my own college, King's.

When I changed over to the law, I did so with a view to becoming a solicitor, but at the back of my mind somewhere was the nagging interest in the Bar. I read the biographies of all the great advocates of the past – Marshall Hall, Isaacs, Birkenhead, Birkett, Hastings, Carson – and I became fascinated by their careers, the challenges and particularly perhaps their early careers when they were breaking through to become successful. That decided me to attempt the Bar myself. I was encouraged by my Cambridge tutor, Kenneth Polack, who was a law tutor at King's College. He was the first law tutor they'd had for many generations and had himself just done a pupillage at the Bar. He encouraged me to believe that the Bar was changing in the sense that it was perhaps becoming open to people without private money. So I decided to make

an attempt at the Bar without having any clear view in my own mind whether I would be good at that form of public speaking.

From the first time I stood up in court, it seemed to go reasonably well. I didn't feel overawed by arguing a case prepared from a brief where the court was the forum, where the purpose was representing the client, where there was something clear to say which was the argument of the case. At that stage it went well in that I enjoyed the speaking element and seemed able to marshal and present the arguments reasonably. That was the only form of public speaking I did for many years, and for a long time I felt very diffident about anything approaching, for example, an after-dinner speech.

Your style as a barrister was not flamboyant, not thundering, not at all like the image of Rumpole. What exactly was it that attracted you to the Bar?

I liked the challenge of representing a client in a case which would often be difficult. The satisfaction that clearly came from doing it to your best ability, and winning, was immense. I was fascinated by the advocacy, for example, of Isaacs and Birkett, and, of course, by the standards of their time some of those were not flamboyant. They would seem flamboyant by our standards, but Isaacs, for example, set a quite different approach to advocacy from Carson or Marshall Hall – much quieter, much more logical in terms of presentation, and perhaps a forerunner of the modern manner. I got the greatest satisfaction in cases which were not obviously jury cases, but civil cases or appeal cases, where the critical part of the case would be the court's questions. In a real sense, this would be the central area. You would have done the preparatory work, have laid it out before the court; you would have got into the details of the argument. But then the argument had to be tested by what classicists would call the Socratic dialogue, and it was that area where I found I could react well to the questions, could put forward the answers in a way that seemed reasonably convincing. In other words, I had some facility for thinking on my feet.

Our legal system has always been adversarial, so doesn't that make for certain difficulties, such as that the truth will not necessarily prevail because victory is a function of successful rhetoric?

I don't accept that the adversarial system is contrary to truth and makes success dependent on rhetoric. I've never been able to work out in my own mind what percentage of cases would have the same result whatever the advocacy, and what percentage is either won or lost by advocacy, but I suspect the latter occasions are comparatively few. I also believe that the adversarial system evolved as a very effective way of seeking to get at the truth of the issues raised before the court. There are

obviously limitations. In a criminal case the judge and jury only look at the issues which the prosecution and defence put before them. They don't have any roving commission of their own. My own main concern about the adversarial system is that, although it may lead to a just result, it's a very slow and expensive way of getting to a result. This is a concern that I had at the Bar, and still have now I have left the Bar. The problems of delay and cost are central. The wheels of God grind slowly, but they grind sure; the same can be said of the legal system, but that isn't too much of a consolation to those for whom the delay is unacceptable or who can't afford to ride in the carriage. For those reasons I would particularly like to see a situation where the system was altered in four ways.

First, I would like to see a greater balance between written and oral work. They've carried it too far in the United States where, in much appellate work, there is very little oral advocacy and not enough time for questioning; but they have not carried it far enough in this country where there ought to be a considerable amount of the case put before the judge in writing. He should then be granted proper time to read it as part of his working day. I found when I was arguing a case that the most tedious part would be introducing the court to the documents – the affidavits or written evidence. It seemed absurd that all this process had to be done orally. Sometimes it was said that it was important it should all be done in open court so that justice could be seen to be done. Sometimes it was said that you couldn't necessarily trust the judges to read the material unless it was read out to them aloud. But overall our system has to develop, and of course it is to some extent already developing towards a greater balance between written and oral argument. This evolution has farther to go.

The second feature that I think is very important is that there should be a greater interplay between the judge and those presenting the case right from the outset; that from the moment a case is started it should become part of a particular judge's list; that he should have the computerized facilities to monitor its progress, and should be able to inquire whether it was not coming forward speedily. This actually happened for a time when Sir John Donaldson was chairman of the Industrial Relations Court during the short-lived 1971 Trade Union and Labour Relations Act. The judge should be able, at these early stages, to look at the issues which have been raised by the parties and should be able to say that a particular issue looks a rather barren one, and hear brief argument on it and guide the advocates for the parties towards what really matters. The advocates should make certain that they get to grips with the real issues, that there are not unnecessary documents put before the court, nor unnecessary witnesses called. I think that the Bar is very good at advising people when it's sensible to settle a case before going

to court. What I don't think it's always as good at is pruning the issues that actually go before the court when the case is contested. A bit of a lead has to come from the judiciary.

The third area – and this is much more controversial, and it may be that it's theoretical and fanciful – is that I wonder, as we approach the twenty-first century, if people are going to expect a different form of duty to be discharged by a lawyer. At the moment the lawyer has a duty to represent his client to the best of his ability. That means that if his client, for some reason, isn't in a hurry to have the case tried, then the lawyer has no obligation to put pressure on his client. I think that possibly the function of the lawyer is increasingly going to move towards being a reconciler, a problem-solver, and that the more we can get away from what is the adversarial conflict, the more we will ultimately meet society's expectations as they develop. The gladiatorial element will then be minimized. But, of course, it would need a great deal of working out, it will only come to pass gradually and it will require changing attitudes from society. Nor, in saying this, am I being critical of the approach currently adopted by the legal profession. It is societal expectations which must shape their future role.

The fourth area where I think our system has to develop is informal dispute resolution. We must find a way of offering people an alternative system whereby they can have their dispute brought speedily before an arbitrator who is in a position to do his or her best: to look at the material, hear some evidence and say, I think the result should be this. Otherwise you may get a denial of justice. You may get a denial where a defendant does not respond to a demand for payment and puts forward an arguable defence, gains time, and the plaintiff suffers very much in the meantime. I've heard of one situation in the present economic turndown where a constructor has gone into receivership undoubtedly owing money, and can't continue trading until the litigation is concluded. You may also get a denial of justice where someone does not pursue their rights because the process is unaffordable. The importance of being able to find a quick and fair solution in this situation is very great. The Americans are working on alternative dispute resolution. I hope we will do more in this country.

I think those four areas are very much more important than what is coming out of all the populist conflict about the legal profession that the government has initiated over the past year. It's been applauded by the public and the media because they believe that what's being suggested will reduce delay and reduce cost. In fact, the principal changes to the structure of the legal profession will not reduce delay, will not reduce cost.

Why do you think people are so suspicious of members of the legal profession?

It's difficult this, isn't it? Whichever group you're in in society, you frequently see that the public perception of it is not particularly high. I don't think the public perception of politicians is particularly high, nor the public perception of journalists, which is influenced by invasion of privacy and unnecessary trivialization. I don't believe that the public perception of bankers, which is my new occupation, is uniformly high either. As a lawyer, it's important not to think that yours is the only section of society which is under attack. But throughout history lawyers have not been a popular group. Chaucer made fun of his lawyer, who was rather busy, rather pompous, very keen on the fees and had a bustling image, pretending he was busier than he actually was. Shakespeare didn't have a wonderfully kind view of lawyers either. What causes it?

First, I don't think people like being involved with the law. There's rarely any particular profit in it; it's solving a dispute at a cost. If, for example, you are involved in a criminal case and are acquitted, you will then consider that that's no more than your due. If you're convicted, that's probably because of the unfriendliness of the judge and the incompetence of your advocate. The same applies in a civil case. A plaintiff who wins considers justice is done. A defendant who loses considers injustice is done. Thus within the whole nature of the legal process there is obvious scope for potential resentment. No one wants to be involved with the law anyway. No one wants to pay lawyers.

In saying this, I don't want to exonerate the lawyers entirely. Sometimes our profession has been seen as formal, as remote; sometimes as self-satisfied, sometimes even as pompous. Obviously a perception of that kind, in an area of life that people don't want to be involved with anyway, is not good for the reputation of lawyers. It may, of course, be a perception that is unjust to a majority of lawyers, but I grant that it undoubtedly exists. The fact that the profession is becoming more informal and more widely based socially is very important and ought to help its future development. Improved communications with clients, avoiding jargon and pedantic language, will also help.

The legal profession in recent years seems to have been in some turmoil, with one group trying to preserve its privileges, the other to trespass on them. It's difficult for outsiders to see which principles are involved.

The principle involved is essentially whether you want specialist advocacy, and if you do, what ought to be the rules that govern the work of advocates. The view taken by many at the Bar and by judges is that, to have good independent advocacy, there ought to be certain qualities an advocate accepts and strives towards. The first is that they dedicate

their whole work to advocacy or litigation so that they constantly keep their talents well honed. The second is independence: independence of large administrative burdens and independence of financial reliance on partners so that the essential pressure of the need to secure 'billable hours', which is a driving force of the corporate law firms, ought to be absent, and yet leave people the opportunity to make a reasonably good living. The third is that, in important cases, the solicitor prepares the case and the barrister presents it in court. This lessens any danger of the barrister being other than scrupulous in his presentation. He or she does not get close to the client, as they might do if they were involved with every aspect of the case. It is, moreover, extremely helpful and valuable to have skilled preparation done separately from the presentation. If the barrister is using the skills of an advocate as the principal skills, he should not be dissipating those skills by spending a great deal of time preparing cases.

I, for example, once had a United States lawyer come into my room, sit down in an armchair – he was the leading advocate for a particular case – and say, 'I've worked on nothing but this case for twelve years.' Now that is not good. He could not be gaining wide advocacy experience. Our principles involve acceptance on the part of the Bar of certain restrictions and obligations. First, as a self-denying ordinance, barristers don't have direct contact with lay clients. Secondly the Bar takes on cases popular and unpopular and should not refuse cases because they're legally aided.

The argument some solicitors have raised is that they should be entitled to take cases in court without subscribing to these principles. Clearly that would have major implications, because if solicitors were able to have all the advantages of following the profession of advocacy without accepting the rules by which advocates have been governed, then they would have an economic advantage. Let me illustrate in this way: if a barrister goes into chambers, he is briefed by a solicitor, so there is a filter of confidence he has to go through; but a solicitor who joins a firm could, if able to argue cases in the highest courts, simply argue for the clients of that firm without having to have his ability to do so vetted or proved by the solicitor instructing him. Those are some of the fears, and those are some of the concerns.

It is regrettable that there's been this argument. A legal profession should not be squabbling within itself. It has a duty to serve the public, and there are many more important issues. I think that part of the problem is in any event being solved, because more cases are now to be heard in the County Court, where any lawyer can argue cases. Hence the smaller cases are going that route, and there was in any event clearly a reasonable argument for widening the rights of audience of solicitors in the Crown Courts. But I feel it is regrettable that it's become a public

profile argument over a period of years, because the legal profession should be seeking to work together on the much more important problems that it has to tackle if it is to give a full service to society. Equally I don't know how far those solicitors who were pressing for rights of audience were representative of solicitors generally. In my experience, many solicitors were content with the existing structure, but the public undoubtedly saw it as an argument about who should be entitled to a particular slice of cake. It was a demarcation dispute and so seemed unattractive.

Would it bring costs down if solicitors were able to plead?

We shall discover. The answer is thought by many to be no. There was a Royal Commission report ten years ago which researched costs in detail. The government, incidentally, did not research costs at all before bringing in their current reforms. The research ten years ago showed that, in very small cases, the costs might come down, but in the majority of cases they wouldn't, and some might go up. If a large corporate law firm, for example, was both preparing a case and arguing it in court, as opposed to preparing a case and instructing barristers to argue it in court, I don't believe that costs would in any way go down. Equally, where you get a good provincial law firm instructing a barrister, the costs may be considerably below what they would be if you were having to go to one of the large corporate law firms to get a competent barrister. In other words, having a pool of independent advocates available to all solicitors is an important factor in ensuring that costs do not go up.

Isn't the argument that, because barristers are rather few, they can charge a lot, whereas if solicitors were allowed to plead, there would be more competition and costs would go down?

But, generally speaking, the Bar has expanded to meet demand. When I became a barrister in 1961, there were fewer than 2,000. At the last tally I think there were almost 6,000, and the numbers may now have gone even higher. Broadly speaking, the Bar has expanded to meet demand. There have been some areas where there's a shortage of specialists, but if the Bar were to erode or wither, there would probably be far fewer really competent advocates in particular fields, and they would all be tied to a particular large firm and not available to the bulk of solicitors. If the Bar were to be destroyed, then you would undoubtedly have less accessibility to good advocates. That, of course, would have implications not only in terms of price but also in terms of getting the representation you want in court; and the ability to get that representation is really a keystone of our system of justice.

Won't something have to be done eventually about legal costs? We seem to have reached a position where justice in a number of areas – libel, maladministration, even divorce – depends for all practical purposes on what money you have. You can't exactly buy justice in a free market yet, but many believe it can be denied to those who lack resources.

I don't believe you can buy justice by having money, but I think you can be denied justice by not having it. How do you deal with this? First, you must have a proper system of legal aid for the more disadvantaged. Within the past decade, the eligibility for legal aid has declined, and that is not healthy. Secondly, we must have simpler trial procedures. Thirdly, I don't think that contingency fees will necessarily help. If the contingency fee level is set high enough to be an incentive to the lawyer, it may be a source of abuse, and if it's not set high enough to be an incentive, then it will not make a substantial difference. Fourthly, I think we do have potential for development in the concept of legal expenses insurance. This exists, for example, in your household policy: you may be able to recover costs for a claim for negligence or nuisance arising in certain activities. It exists for trade unionists whose trade union dues give them legal insurance to enable them to pursue a proper claim if they're injured at work. But there's a whole area where legal expenses insurance has not been significantly developed in this country. I believe it's more developed in Western Germany, though I don't know too much about the details, but this may be one area in which our system can develop in regard to costs.

In your dispute with Lord Hailsham over increased legal aid for barristers, you fought the barristers' corner fiercely. You also decided to breach normal Bar practices and go public in the sense that you gave radio and TV interviews. Why did you do that?

I certainly took the view that, if a profession serves the public, the public is entitled to know what its practices and problems are. So it seemed logical that we should be willing to discuss any issue that anyone wanted to raise with us. I also thought that our case on legal aid fees was very good, and a case to get across to the public. We did get it across in a pretty good way. One large meeting was open to the press, and the press up to then had had an image of barristers as too élitist; withdrawn and too conscious of their supposed dignity to speak to the public. Now they were suddenly at a meeting where people were talking plain language about the problems of fees. I remember one member of the Bar saying, 'How do I keep myself in spite of legal aid fees? Answer: I work as a waiter in a Chinese restaurant in the evenings.' We had a number of these, and people from different ethnic groups and both

sexes, and the press realized there were a lot of human beings at the Bar in just the same way that there were outside.

What sort of legal aid sums would be appropriate in your view?

Figures change. The way I would look at it is that someone who is doing full-time legal aid work should be able to earn enough to be on a parallel with lawyers in government service or local authority service, but bearing in mind that barristers also have to pay their expenses and make their own pension contributions. It is a straight comparison between one area of public legal service and another.

But if I may pursue this a little further, large numbers of barristers are pretty well dependent on fees provided out of public funds for legal aid. How would you determine what level of remuneration is appropriate? Might the time come when there has to be a distinction between those depending on public funds and those who command private fees?

That distinction exists anyway. That's why it's so important for all those who command private fees to be willing to do some legal aid cases. I believe it's a very important factor in a responsible legal profession, but the level of remuneration must be such that qualified lawyers can say, 'This is a reasonable career.' If legal aid fees were to be significantly below what those lawyers could earn anywhere else, even in other areas of the public legal service, it would become more and more difficult to attract competent people to do the work. The same is, incidentally, just as true for solicitors who do legal aid work.

You described Lord Mackay's Green Paper on legal reform as 'superficial, unsupported by research, unaided by consultation'. Others, like Lord Hailsham, thought the independence of the judiciary itself was under threat. Was this not a bit of an over-reaction?

I don't believe so. May I take our Lord Chief Justice, Lord Lane, who, as someone very highly respected within the legal profession, reacted strongly against the document. Lord Rees-Mogg also described the failure of the government's arguments as total, and he is not a lawyer. It was, I thought, a serious mistake and an ill-informed document. May I take just a few examples from memory?

What the proposals suggested was that the way in which the rules for the profession were made should be brought under the control of the Lord Chancellor, this being a matter too important to be left by the government to the profession itself. Now, imagine if that statement had been made by the government of South Africa, namely, that the government should take control of the very profession whose duty it is

to represent the citizen against the government. Lord Hailsham and a lot of others found it virtually unbelievable that a government committed to democracy should feel able to introduce such a suggestion.

On advocacy, the suggestion was that advocates should be certificated by professional bodies but in accordance with rules laid down by the government. What would have been the criteria, and who was to determine the criteria? Again, it was to be the government. I don't believe that those who said that liberties are lost, not in one great stride, but by small and accumulating steps, were being over-dramatic. This was a very clear encroachment on the independence of the profession. It was seen that way throughout the Commonwealth, and seen that way in the United States.

One of the most remarkable features was that, four years beforehand, the government accepted the report of the Royal Commission chaired by Lord Benson. Yet the Green Paper never once referred to the existence of that report, never dealt with its arguments nor suggested why the government had suddenly decided to do a complete U-turn. The proposals as put forward would inevitably have benefited the large firms of corporate lawyers to the detriment of an independent Bar and to the detriment of the smaller firms of solicitors. We found it very surprising that there was no serious recognition of this danger. It is remarkable that the judges, who very rarely speak publicly, should have spoken out so strongly. It reflects a deep concern that the proposals were dangerous.

The question everyone wants to ask an advocate is do you need to believe your client? Would you defend a client you knew to be lying on the grounds that even such a client has a right to representation?

The basic position was explained beautifully years ago by Lord Birkett. If you believe your client to be guilty, but he is asserting he is not, then it is not for you but the Court to decide the issue. You are part of the process of leading to that judgement. If, however, the client told you he was guilty, then you would not be entitled to suggest he was innocent because, as opposed to simply having a shrewd idea, you would actually know he was guilty. If he said, 'I am guilty but I want to plead not guilty,' your duty would then be to say to him, 'I cannot represent you in that case, and if you wish to plead not guilty and have an advocate representing you, then you must not tell that advocate you are guilty.' It's essential to remember that the advocate's role is as a part of the administration of justice, and that the advocate is not the judge. The advocate's role is to present one side of the case to the best of his or her ability.

You are said to believe that advocacy is a pure science in that it can be applied with equal effectiveness to any case.

I don't know where that comes from. I'm not conscious of having said it, and I'm not conscious of believing it. I know there are some cases I can argue a great deal better than others. If, for example, I believed that my client was guilty and I had to put forward an explanation I thought was nonsense, I think I would feel uncomfortable because I would feel sure that someone would see through it. So I don't see advocacy as a science, but more as an art. I think there are very much advocates for particular cases. There are those who appeal beautifully to the emotions, those who are strong in cross-examination, those who are subtly probing. There are those who are brilliant at arguing a subtle civil suit who would be hopeless at arguing a criminal case and the other way round. So I actually think advocacy at its best is an art, a matter of flair rather than a matter of science.

What would you say was your strength as a QC?

It's very hard to judge your own strength. The starting point was that I liked to manage the case in the sense that, although the solicitor was involved in the preparation, I liked to be involved in considering the way forward from a very early stage. I believe that, in a complex case, good management before you ever get to the court is of the absolute essence – deciding which points should be argued, how strongly one can be pursued, whether one argument fits well with another or whether an argument might be so unattractive as to detract from another. In terms of personal strength, it's very hard to judge. I gained some experience of cross-examination when I went on circuit as a young advocate, doing criminal cases for four years, in court every day, cross-examining, thinking during the course of the case, adapting in the light of answers. I found that was of priceless value in my later civil work. I also, I suppose, tried to think what arguments would appeal to me if I was a judge, because I didn't much enjoy putting forward arguments that I did not personally find reasonably appealing. If I was cross-examining, I wrote out every question in advance, and sometimes, where there were two possible answers, I would write out at the next question: if yes, go one route; if no, go another. In the same way I made very full notes for written argument, even if I didn't use the argument in the order of those notes.

You did your homework well.

There's absolutely no substitute for it. When I was in silk, I felt it was right to delegate certain areas of research to good juniors, that being part of the teamwork; but in terms of the critical court work, there is no delegation to be done. I always went into court with a very full note indeed of the issues.

Some of your more celebrated cases seem to suggest that you did approach them in a scientific way. For example, in the GLC for fair fares, you were apparently defending the cause of socialism, but in representing the government in its ban on trades unions at GCHQ, some suggested you were defending the cause of authoritarianism against basic civil liberties.

The cases were about four years apart, so it wasn't brought quite into the focus you suggest. The way I saw the GLC case was that I actually felt that Ken Livingstone and the GLC had been elected and had, as part of their election policy, said they were going to attract people back to the Underground by a low-fares policy and subsidized fares. I felt deeply disappointed by the result of that case because, only a few years beforehand, in a case about education, the House of Lords had actually given weight to the fact that a Conservative local authority had been elected with a particular view on education and schooling, and this was a relevant factor in that authority deciding how it should exercise its discretion. I myself felt that the judgement in the GLC case was not the best judgement in the House of Lords in my lifetime. I still feel it should have been decided the other way. The GLC should have been allowed to implement their policy and see how it worked.

As for the GCHQ case, when it came to the House of Lords, which was when I became involved, it was an issue of whether the government should have engaged in consultation before banning trade union activities. The government said they feared that, if they engaged in consultation, there would have been trade union dislocation before they imposed the ban and the court accepted that evidence. It was my task to invite them to accept the government's view as part of the process of evaluating the rival arguments. It was not my task to form a political judgement. I think the legal judgment in that case was absolutely right. If I had to form a political judgment, I'm not convinced that the government went about it very sensitively. But can I emphasize that my views on the legal case have nothing to do with my political views. Each case has to do with legal rights and the limits upon power which are placed by administrative law. I didn't particularly agree with Ken Livingstone's policy, but I did take the view that he should be allowed to give it a crack, because they had been elected on that policy.

If I may press this a little farther, you said of the GCHQ case that you don't have to believe a point is right, you just have to believe it is reasonable. Isn't it better to believe something is reasonable and right at the same time.

If we carried that too far we'd get a situation where advocates only argued cases they thought were right. What would happen if there was a case that nobody thought was right? We are a cog in the machine of justice. The system of the administration of justice is a central element

in a democracy. Without a democracy you can't have an independent system of justice. Without an independent system of justice you can't have a democracy. The advocate is but one element in that system. His job is to ensure that a case is properly presented, which is a fundamental right. I have no sympathy with people who say they won't take a particular case because they're a Conservative and this seems a socialist cause. To adopt that approach is contrary to the duty of an advocate.

Did you ever take a case you considered absolutely hopeless?

Yes. In a career of twenty-eight years, one's bound to have had some hopeless cases. In hopeless cases I would generally advise my client to settle, to compromise, or not to fight particular issues. If, in the end, they didn't take that advice, that was their right. I didn't enjoy arguing hopeless cases, and I'm glad to say I don't think I argued too many of them, because clients were prepared in general to make the best of it in that situation either by settling a civil case or pleading guilty and mitigating sentence in a criminal case.

Were there ever any cases you wanted to win for their own sake, rather than for the sake of legal argument?

I can think of one example. It was in the late 1960s or early 1970s, at the height of what is now called the Permissive Society. A doctor had told the parents of a fifteen-year-old girl that the daughter had asked to be put on the Pill, and had been. He was the family doctor, liked the family and was gravely concerned about the situation, but it was suggested he had breached confidence by telling the parents. I represented him before the General Medical Council, and we established that the breach of confidence was not improper because, in all the circumstances, it was a reasonable judgment on his part that the parents should be told. I felt that was overall a very proper outcome.

There were other cases I was glad to win, such as the cricket case, brought by Kerry Packer and others against the Test and County Cricket Board. It wasn't because I approved of their particular brand of cricket, or disapproved of the MCC. I've loved cricket all my life, and I could see the disruption that action was bringing to cricket, but it produced a tremendous degree of unfair public revulsion against Packer. It sparked a tremendous degree of righteous indignation, when he was only doing something he was fully entitled to do – which was to set up a rival outfit. I cared very much about the result of that case, as a matter of basic fairness. In the same way, I thought Jeffrey Archer had been badly treated by the press over the allegation of paying money to a prostitute, and felt it would have been most unfair for him, and indeed for his family, had he not won. I was very glad and relieved when he did.

What is your view about the size of damages awarded in libel cases these days? Has the time come for some more rational system to be devised? For a man accused of dealing with a prostitute to be awarded many times more than a brain-damaged child hardly seems rational.

I believe that now a brain-damaged child would get more than Jeffrey Archer did in his libel action, if that is the example you have in mind. What we have to remember about that case was that the newspaper article cost him a position in life that he valued as much as any he had. Although he was a successful author, he had to resign his deputy chairmanship of the Conservative party, and Jeffrey Archer is passionately committed to politics. The paper did not apologize, and it put him through a severe trial which made the front page for a fortnight. Therefore it really sold its newspaper for a fortnight on the back of the trial. Now I don't believe, once you take all those facts together, that the award of damages of half a million pounds was unreasonable. The newspaper did not appeal either.

It's difficult to correlate awards for libel with awards for personal injury, but I would agree that in general there's obviously something haphazard about libel awards. It's very strange that they should be decided by a jury which does not have a figure mentioned to it and has probably never before sat on a libel case. I would say the provision the Lord Chancellor introduced into the Courts and Legal Services Bill, under which the Court of Appeal can review damages and substitute its own figure if it thinks the damages awarded by a jury too high, should perhaps be very helpful in enabling a more balanced and logical tariff to be presented.

In the famous Spycatcher *case, you had essentially to marshal the battered remains of a principle against the fact that anyone who actually wanted to know the substance of Wright's allegations could know them, and there was nothing anyone could do to stop it. Many onlookers found the absurdity of the government's position quite staggering, not to mention the vast cost to the public purse. Looking back, wasn't it all a bit of a nightmare?*

It wasn't a nightmare. The government was in a dilemma. The principle it wanted to enforce, that the secret service should keep confidence, was a good and sound principle. The difficulty lay in the fact that jurisdiction is territorial and therefore it couldn't enforce that principle in other countries. That meant, inevitably, that it couldn't prevent the book being circulated.

In fact, if Mrs Thatcher hadn't taken legal action against Spycatcher, *they would hardly have sold 5,000 copies.*

Absolutely right in the individual case. The action benefited Wright's

sales figures. But supposing the government hadn't taken action. Would it then have been said that anyone who wants to write a book about the security service can go abroad with impunity and write and publish it? She had a very difficult dilemma and there was no easy choice. Wright may have become a millionaire, but I don't think that necessarily makes the case a total disaster. It must have been made plain to others that the government would do its best to enforce confidentiality. The courts unequivocally endorsed the principle that the security service should keep quiet about its work. Equally, we're looking at the outcome with the priceless benefit of hindsight. It can't have been obvious to the government when it started that it would lose in the Australian courts. The judgment of the Australian High Court has not been highly regarded as a matter of law by many lawyers. It's easy to say now that the government lost and Wright became a millionaire. It wasn't necessarily so easy for people at the beginning to know that the government were going to lose before ever they'd argued their case.

Are there ever occasions when it may become necessary to flout the law? I have in mind what is sometimes called the tyranny of the majority: such areas as religious observances, or abortion, where people feel that the law clashes with moral necessity or natural justice.

I would in general draw the line between, on the one hand, peaceful and prominent public demonstrations and, on the other, defiance of the law. Any individual is entitled to defy the law, or certain laws, on grounds of conscience, and to go to prison for that cause. A journalist, for example, who decides he will go to prison rather than disclose his confidential sources, is, I think, fully entitled to take that view as a matter of conscience. But I don't believe that in general people should defy the law in a democracy. They should use all democratic means to get the law changed.

It's highly unusual for a barrister to step outside his profession, especially when a glittering career could presumably have led to an appointment to the bench. Why this change of direction?

It's hard to know the motivation in one's own life. I have an immensely high respect for judges and the judicial function. The results of the cases I've done all my life have depended on the quality of the judges and the way they conducted them. But I have never had an ambition to become a judge. It's hard to identify a single reason. I think the assumption that, because you are an advocate, you will necessarily enjoy becoming a judge, is not correct for everyone. I didn't feel I would enjoy the role nearly as much as I had enjoyed advocacy. So when I got opportunities to do other tasks that I thought equally valuable, I took them.

Shortly after being chairman of the Bar Council, I was approached to become part-time chairman of the Takeover Panel. The panel is a valuable institution because, where people are striving to win a battle, an organization that sets the rules and sees fairness for shareholders is vital. I got a lot of satisfaction from it, and I suppose it was because I'd had that partial involvement in the City that I was then approached to become chairman of NatWest. I hesitated over that for quite some time. To begin with, it involved severing my links with practice at the Bar, in contrast with the Takeover Panel. That job had been part-time and I'd continued practising. Secondly, I'd never had experience as a banker and was concerned about going into the unknown. I consulted a number of people who were encouraging enough to suggest I could do the job and emphasized that it was very important. Since I believe that large national banks are in a sense essential to the community and are national assets, I didn't in the end feel I should decline the challenge. I felt fortunate to be offered the opportunity to join in the work of the bank. I am really enjoying the work.

The profession of barrister has often been compared to that of actor, the court being like a stage where the performance is all and the adrenalin flows. Do you not miss that platform, that excitement?

No. I've never been sure how perfect the theatrical comparison was in civil cases. In criminal cases, yes. Gerald Gardiner, a wonderful advocate, had, of course, been an amateur actor and thought of going on the stage. I can see the element of acting, but in modern civil cases it's relatively small. But you're right that the adrenalin can flow, and that when the adrenalin flows and you do it really well, you get a feeling of elation. Obviously I will not get that particular feeling of elation again. On the other hand, advocacy is a very exacting, stressful process, a lonely process, both in the preparation and in arguing before the court. You and you alone are answering questions which may affect the outcome of an issue that is immensely important to your client, and so you are in a continuously exposed position.

Having been a part-time chairman of the Takeover Panel, do you think the law adequate in its present form to ensure that the merchant banks give sufficiently accurate information on behalf of clients to any legal entity or government department?

In general, yes, because of the responsibility placed on the merchant banks. The present position is that it is an offence to give false information during the course of a takeover and anyone who gives misleading information during that stage could be liable to prosecution. In addition, the merchant bank has a duty to the Takeover Panel to be responsible

for the accuracy of the statements it makes. If it fails in that, it is open to disciplinary action at the hands of its regulators. I therefore feel that the machinery exists for ensuring fair information is given to shareholders.

The official inquiry into sharerigging at NatWest in the County affair concluded that a highly unsatisfactory state of affairs had existed. Did this give you any reservations about joining the bank?

I joined them during the course of the inquiry and I was told of the problem. I had no reservations about joining because, although mistakes were made at that time, I was absolutely satisfied that NatWest is committed to the highest ethical standards and the mistakes made within the merchant bank were not typical of the organization. Dealing with that unfortunate incident was part of the challenge. That revelation affected everyone deeply. If you have, as NatWest has, a pride in your own ability and integrity, then you're much more affected by something going wrong than if you're a buccaneer who does not have that pride. It was inevitably wounding to a fine bank to have something like that happening.

Blue Arrow was a major setback to try to recover from. How did you approach the challenge?

We all approached it together. We appointed new management in County NatWest, which was given the task of ensuring that systems were in place to make certain that all dealings were conducted with total propriety in future. We had independent accountants advise us as to every area in which we needed proper controls. We submitted these to our City regulators, and they approved them. In addition, we have directors of high quality from the parent bank on the board of the investment bank. If you have a misfortune like this, you must learn lessons and make certain that you emerge stronger. Everyone is determined to do this.

I want to ask one last question about that. Your predecessor, Lord Boardman, a politician rather than a banker, was obviously unaware of what was going on at County NatWest and it was suggested at the time that his lack of sophistication in investment banking affairs was partly responsible for matters developing as they did. Isn't there danger in a chairman of a bank lacking banking expertise?

There must be a danger, but none of us can have all the expertise. I work closely with a very able chief executive, Tom Frost, who has been a banker all his life. I think our different backgrounds bring strengths to the partnership.

Now that you have been at the bank for some time, you must have a pronounced interest in whether Britain joins the EMS. Why is the present government so reluctant to do so when the rest of Europe thinks it such a good idea?

I don't believe that this country has ever been as involved in Europe as those countries which are part of continental Europe. Let me give one illustration from personal observation. Last year we were in France, which we love, at the time of the European elections. An election poster there had a photograph of President Mitterrand and Chancellor Kohl walking hand in hand into the future of Europe, but the interesting thing was that it was a back view of each of them. I don't believe that a back view of Chancellor Kohl would have been recognized by very many people in this country. Continental states have been more deeply involved with each other for a long time in a way that this country, with its island history, has been outside. It's no accident that the founding fathers of the European Community came from countries that had been the victims of invasion by each other and who recognized that the whole of the future lay in setting aside those aspects of nationalism which bred conflict.

Industry and business clearly recognize increasingly that we're part of a single market of 320 million people which will probably be expanded significantly by the addition of the EFTA countries and the people of East Germany. They see the opportunities. I think that our government, given our history, is understandably reluctant to surrender sovereignty and the freedom of independent action. I think that reluctance is made all the harder because, when we do subscribe to a European policy, we do implement it. Our government has a very good record of implementing directives, so it does tend to look at a commitment on the basis that it is a real and genuine commitment. That may explain why the government is being slow to surrender freedom of action – the freedom which has been part of our history – but it doesn't mean that we can stand apart from the process.

We are now part of Europe. It is absolutely critical that we should be involved in the shaping of the future of Europe, and we can't be involved unless we are, as a first stage, part of the exchange rate mechanism. Equally, our economic record does not suggest that there is any advantage in staying out. One of the depressing features is that after ten years of one of the strongest, most courageous and successful governments of my adult lifetime, we have double-digit interest rates, which look to be continuing for a long time, and we're close to double-digit inflation. The countries of continental Europe which have accepted the discipline of the exchange rate mechanism are now in a better position. France, for example, which began the 1980s worse off, is entering the 1990s considerably better off and with a higher GNP per head of population.

Italy, whom we once looked at with pity, has achieved considerable economic success in the past decade. The exchange rate mechanism is not a simple panacea for all ills. It will be uncomfortable when we join because it will put upon us the discipline of disinflation, but it's absolutely critical if we're to benefit from Europe.

Do you consider yourself a European?

Increasingly so. I don't consider myself equally at home in all the European capitals. I suspect that in another European country people will probably be able to look at me and my clothes and guess my nationality, but I feel very committed to the importance of Europe as a whole becoming a successful organization because it is important for all of us economically and politically and in terms of human tolerances.

So our future lies less with the United States and more with Europe?

Our future must lie with Europe, there's no doubt about it. It doesn't follow that there will not be a close and good relationship between the United States and Europe. It's important that there should be one, but the danger must be there that a United States somewhat weakened economically will turn in on itself. The Pax Americana has lasted a remarkably short time overall.

Yet many politicians in this country still believe that there is a special relationship between Great Britain and the United States.

There was clearly the great Churchill/Roosevelt combination in the war. Their exchange was one of the great co-operations in human history and must rank as an alliance without parallel. After the war there was the United States' involvement in Europe, then the nadir of Suez, which didn't do great credit to the government of this country and in some ways to certain members of the US government. Since then I think the special relationship was rather doubtful until it was re-created by Mrs Thatcher and President Reagan. It depended on the ability on the part of Mrs Thatcher, a brilliantly intelligent woman, to form a relationship with a man who had some good instincts and a genius for presentation but was not very clever or well informed. That was kept going for seven or eight years to the advantage of this country. Now I think that we're settling into a more professional administration of political relationships where the current administration in Washington recognizes that Germany is the focal point in Europe and, within that context, is anxious not to have too special a relationship with Britain. But, that said, the individual relationship between Britain and the United States, if not a so-called special one, will remain of some value.

How has it come about that Britain has exposed itself to legal proceedings in the European Parliament over its failure to comply with EEC regulations to protect the environment and establish, among other things, a healthy standard for drinking water. Should we not be in the forefront of nations giving a good example?

Yes, I believe that we should be active in seeking to achieve the standards. Sometimes you start from a position where you're somewhere behind and you need to play for time a little if you're to reach the appropriate standards. Equally, I don't think we should single out this country as one that doesn't comply with European directives. You can look at all the countries and see that they are having to take some time to adjust to European standards in particular areas. I don't believe we have a bad record in complying with directives of the European Commission, or indeed in complying with the European Convention on Human Rights. Water is clearly an issue, and the duty of the privatized water companies should be to improve standards, but as with so many areas, you can't always achieve your aim overnight. It's right that the issue should go on being highlighted.

I want to talk to you a bit about banking. What is the rationale behind banks lending vast sums of money to people who basically speculate on a particular market, whether it be land, property, commodities or even grandiose schemes that are extremely vulnerable to market conditions?

The banks have lending as a major aspect of their business. Their task is to lend to the creditworthy; to be a willing but responsible lender. They would not wish to be seen to be lending to those who will end up by not being able to repay, but they wouldn't generally wish to pass judgement on the commercial purpose of the regular customer who seeks to borrow money if that regular customer is willing and able to make repayments. So the banks have to evaluate proposals to form a judgement as to whether a loan makes some commercial sense.

Now, that's what takes me into my next question. My own banking experience leads me to believe that the honest individual, struggling to make it on his own, is given a hard time by the banks as far as collateral is concerned when he tries to borrow money. It seems that much stricter conditions apply to the small borrower. Is that true, and if so, why? When the property market collapsed, banks lost hundreds of millions of pounds. If they had applied the same rules they apply to a small borrower, it wouldn't have happened.

Banks do seek very substantial collateral, but when they lose money to that extent, it may indicate that the market has turned even more substantially than anyone thought possible. Because of the 1974–5

property crash, many banks are more cautious in lending money to the construction and property sector.

To the mind untrained in the complexities of banking, it seems inconceivable that banks should lose hundreds of millions of pounds in property transactions and in overseas lendings if they were to apply the same strict rationale as they do to the small borrower. Is it perhaps a case of waiving the rules to accommodate the mighty?

No, it's not a question of that. It may be that they make misjudgements because the sovereign countries or large companies appear to have the ability to repay. In terms of the sovereign lending to the Third World countries, it was certainly thought that the governments would not default. But there's no question of the bank saying consciously, we will accept a lesser risk because these people are 'mighty'. The one thing banks hate are bad debts. Commercial discipline applies equally when dealing with the large organizations as when dealing with the small borrower.

A previous barrister chairman of NatWest was Robin Leigh Pemberton, now governor of the Bank of England. Would you be pleased to follow in his footsteps one day?

I'm fully content to have undertaken an extremely large job with a very major bank, and in none of the jobs I have done have I ever given a thought to the future. I believe that Robin Leigh Pemberton has proved to be an extremely impressive governor in the way in which he has increasingly stated an independent line on the part of the bank. I believe that what he's doing to establish the bank as an effective spokesman in Europe for the appropriate policy for this country is very valuable indeed. The interest of the job of the governor of the Bank of England must be very much linked to the extent to which the bank is free to fulfil its essential role, which must be to secure sound money.

It surprises me that you have never been tempted into politics. Have you never been attracted?

Not enormously. In my late twenties or early thirties I thought it was something I might be attracted to a little later, but to make the commitment you have to make to the hours, to the loyalty to one political view, to the uncertainties of the future, and to some extent to the financial sacrifice, you have to have a certain dedication. I've obviously never had anything approaching that level of involvement or interest.

The economic policy of this government is to beat inflation at all costs. They

are doing this by maintaining a high interest rate which is itself inflationary. It discourages spending up to a point, but over a period it negates the very thing it aspires to achieve. High interest rates cripple small businesses, have an adverse effect on industrial expansion, make us less competitive in world markets, and above all divide the classes, since they widen the gap between rich and poor. What are your views?

High interest rates are obviously unattractive. But they would not now be necessary without rising inflation. High inflation has always operated in a way that presses down upon those who are disadvantaged, pensioners being an obvious example. So high inflation is obviously an evil. You then ask how you can reduce high inflation without high interest rates. Inflation was not initially made high by high interest rates. On the contrary, inflation grew again from 1988 in what might be described with hindsight as an over-lax monetary régime. The consequences were that the only way to bring it down was to raise interest rates. That way, as you say, has a degree of imperfection about it because it inevitably leads to distress in the personal business sector and to some distress for those who have taken on high mortgage commitments – and it clearly makes investment for industry more costly. No one welcomes high interest rates, but how would you seek to bring inflation down without high interest rates? What other mechanism could you bring to bear on it?

But we used to criticize the Labour government for having high interest rates, and now we have a Conservative government very much to the right and the highest interest rates ever.

I don't want to debate whether any one party's criticisms of another party's policy are right or wrong. I'd rather look at it in terms of what action has to be taken for the economy as a whole. In a sense it may be regrettable that one can't find a weapon other than high interest rates for bearing down on inflation, but I think it's generally accepted that it is, if not the only weapon you can use, a very important one in trying to reduce inflation.

The present government also pursues policies which basically encourage initiative through financial rewards. While there is nothing wrong with that, what I find disconcerting is the lack of compassion this government seems to project. Is that an inevitable result, do you think, of the prime minister's own character and personality – the Iron Lady image?

I don't believe it's an inevitable result of the prime minister's own character and personality. It is in very large part the prime minister's courage and clarity of thought that have achieved a considerable measure

of recovery for this country from the position it was in in 1979. I remember 1979 as a time when not only were prices controlled, when union pay claims bore no real relation to the productivity of the company they were involved with, when there was dereliction in the industrial North and Midlands, and when there was no serious hope that this country could achieve an economic recovery. It's perhaps easy in a time when we've reverted to some economic difficulty to forget the steps that have been taken during this decade. But I've recently seen, going to Midlands' towns such as Nottingham or Stoke-on-Trent, where I was born, the extent to which there has been a substantial increase in business or industrial activities and prosperity in those areas over that period. That hasn't come about by accident. It came from a very depressed base and a state of apparently irreversible decline.

Now it may be, and I can't really speculate about this, that the prime minister herself privately realizes that there is still an immense amount to be done to make her achievements permanent, and believes that if we relax too much we won't achieve it. It may be that this leads to a message being put across which does not sometimes appear to be a compassionate one. Undoubtedly there are administrative steps that have been taken, such as the alteration of the basis on which people sought social security benefits, which have not made life easy for the disadvantaged. The homelessness that's developed in the past decade is a reproach and concern to all of us, but I think it's difficult to be critical of the person who's been primarily responsible for what success we have achieved. Striking the balance is immensely hard. I suspect it will be struck in a different way in the 1990s, but that may be because of what was achieved in the early and mid 1980s.

How do you view the poll tax?

The poll tax at present is clearly socially divisive. There were many criticisms of the rates that were justified, but I don't think you can introduce a new tax which causes such dramatic increases in the tax burdens on some individuals and reduces the burden on others. Especially when the better off gain and the worse off lose. It clearly is too crude in its entire application. If it was to be introduced at all, it would have been desirable to have had it banded. You can't attempt to reduce taxation for the lower paid and then suddenly impose a high new tax upon them. But I do support the attempt to secure the proper accountability of local government.

Parliament has recently been considering legislation so that any remaining Nazi war criminals in the UK may still be brought to justice. In view of the time lapse since the war, would it not revive hatreds best forgotten and would it not

be extremely difficult to conduct proper justice when witnesses are perhaps too old to give accurate testimony?

The proposal is deplorable. When it was debated in the Lords, the majority was heavily against it. It will revive incidents which are historically as separate from today as the Napoleonic Wars from the battles in the Crimea, a fifty-year interlude. It creates a new offence in territorial terms – it makes past actions outside our jurisdiction into a crime in this country retrospectively. It calls for a near impossibility of accurate reflection and makes the presentation of a suitable defence almost impossible. It's a very retrograde step, and I hope very much that circumstances will never arise in which the Attorney-General gives his consent to a prosecution.

There are people who dedicate their lives to issues when they feel some injustice has been perpetrated on a minority or in some cases on a whole nation. Are there any issues for which you would fight on strictly moral and humanitarian grounds?

That's a very difficult question. There are many moral issues that inevitably involve one's time, commitment, and energies, and there are a number of issues that keenly engage one's sympathies. I'm involved in quite a number of them. I mentioned the problem of homelessness just now, and it is a slur that, in a capital city, people are sleeping on the streets. I also feel that there are certain central elements in our society that are very precious. We've spoken about the importance of democracy. I would say that anything that is an attack on democracy, which for all its imperfections is the best and fairest system of government you can have, would engage me strongly. Equally, I feel passionately about anything that attacks the fundamentals of the system of justice. You asked me earlier about my reaction and that of others to the government's Green Papers. I have not been able to think about some of the proposals in these Green Papers without deep concern, deep distaste and I wonder that a democratically elected government could have introduced them. If they had gone through as proposed, they would have put under government control the very profession which exists to represent the citizen against the government. And that explains the part that I and some others have sought to play in the debate. Although they have been amended, the original proposals were utterly deplorable.

Do you think religion is a force for good in our society. If so, does it have any drawbacks?

Religion is a force for good, a powerful impetus for human good, because it encourages imperfect human beings towards a better course

of conduct. I don't think it's necessary to be religious to seek to lead a good life or to be fully committed. The forces of humanism can be very strong in that particular area. Indeed there are clearly drawbacks and have been drawbacks to religion throughout history. It was the force of civilization, the force of education, but was also sometimes the supposed justification for wars of immense brutality. That has been the paradox of religion through the ages. But ultimately it enhances humanity.

What would you say are your greatest qualities, and what your vices?

I feel disqualified really to answer either question. I suppose I work reasonably hard at whatever I'm doing. I hope I'm reasonably sensitive to the views of others on the issues involved. I don't have limitless self-confidence, so a good result is something which I tend to need to sustain me. As to faults, there are plenty others could tell you about!

But human frailties.

Oh, human frailties . . . I can get cross, although it evaporates. I can very easily come to think I'm being overworked. I sometimes assume that my own contribution matters more than it does. Whether you call it vanity or what I don't know.

Isn't it always difficult to ignore public acclaim and remain unaffected?

I've always been somewhat surprised by any public acclaim. I was surprised that you wanted to do this interview. I think in terms of achievements that my own are reasonably modest. I've a long way to travel before I could say that I had made a real contribution to life. The Bar is a very critical profession that keeps you down to earth. All its members are proud of their own achievements, so no barrister will go into a room and be regarded as a star by all his colleagues.

What are the primary causes of marital breakdown in our society today, do you think?

It's very hard to generalize. I think it can be a combination of circumstances and issues. It also reflects the fact that society does not expect people to live together in situations which have become intolerable for them. In the past there were far fewer divorces, and people were in situations of considerable misery. The reasons are complex.

Lord Goodman said on television recently, that the absence of a wife added eight hours to his working day. Have you found that marriage adds to or relieves constraints on a working life?

I think that if anyone's unhappily married for a period, then they may take refuge from that in working even harder. If you're happily married, then you get a tug both ways. First, you can feel that your work can be very effective and therefore you want to do it, but on the other hand you can feel you want to spend more time away from the work with your partner.

If I could ask you to look into the future, what sort of country and indeed what sort of European continent do you foresee?

I believe that something more homogeneous will emerge. I hope that isn't just because I want to believe it, but I think it's extremely important. We come towards the end of this century with the developments in Eastern Europe bringing back a map of Europe that would not be dissimilar to the one that existed before the First World War, if it were not for the European Community. I believe that the forces of nationalism are not the purest of human forces. It's immensely important that we should try as a Community to transcend this and seek ever larger groupings of people to live in harmony and co-operation. I think and hope that the European Community provides the focus for those aspirations as far as Europe is concerned.

Have you any ambitions left?

Yes. On different levels. I took up tennis late. I'd like to be a better tennis player. I like history and am conscious of my ignorance – I'd like to be much more knowledgeable about English and European history. I would like to be a successful chairman of my bank in my very new occupation. I have no other really definite ambition except that I would like not to lose my links with the law. I'm glad to have become chairman of Justice, the all-party group of lawyers. I'm privileged to have the opportunity to take part in debate on law reform in the House of Lords. So I hope that, having moved into banking, I will still preserve in a very tangible way my links with the law and try to make a contribution to the development of the legal system and the substantive law. I am immensely fortunate in the range of activities in which I can take part.

Is it ever conceivable that you might return to the Bar?

I think not. I don't believe I would want to. I was a barrister for twenty-eight years. Barristers can go over the hill and fashions can change. I wouldn't like to go back to the Bar on a declining path.

The last question: If you were to live your life again, would you live it differently?

I would certainly go to the Bar, although I'm very conscious that the Bar is a demanding profession and would mean that, for twenty years probably, I would have to focus on it almost exclusively. The only thing I'm doubtful about is whether I focused too long on just arguing cases to the exclusion of other interests. The last six years, since I became chairman of the Bar and involved in public issues, have been the most interesting and personally satisfying of my life. So, looking back on it, I wish I'd got involved in certain aspects of public affairs and started to make a contribution there quite a lot earlier.

MICHAEL ASPEL

Michael Aspel was born in 1933 of working-class parents. He was evacuated to Somerset between 1940 and 1944. He first worked with the BBC as a radio actor before going on to be a disc-jockey and presenter of *Family Favourites*. His main television shows have included *Miss World, Crackerjack, Ask Aspel, Give Us A Clue, Child's Play, This Is Your Life* and *Aspel & Company*. He has had five sons and one daughter from his three marriages. His eldest son Greg died of cancer in 1989 and his nine-year-old son Patrick suffers from cerebral palsy. His charity work includes ITV *Telethon*, BLISS, ASBAH, World Family and many others.

I suppose the most important quality I retain from my original background is an inability to take myself too seriously. Mine was a very joky family and they realized early on that I had a kind of parrot facility for reproducing different accents and different types, which in the end was what got me into broadcasting.

My childhood was very mixed up because evacuation got into the middle of it. I don't know which are thought to be the most formative years, but I was sent away to Somerset when I was seven and came back when I was eleven, so I had already had other influences, or lack of influences, and become very independent. Evacuation is often used as a defence against all kinds of character defects, and I've never wanted to make excuses for bad behaviour. I just think that if I've behaved badly I should apologize. At that stage I was a mischievous child, always fighting, always leading people into scrapes, always rebelling – which surprises me because I turned into a very conformist sort of person.

Behind the experience of evacuation, though, was the awful yearning every kid feels about home: where is it, who are my parents? Four and a half years when you start at seven looks like most of your life. It wasn't something you could shrug off. But once that sort of toothache had gone into the background, we had a very good time. It was a great war, in fact. We romped around in fields and nobody ever wondered where we were. There was never any danger in being out on our own; we were in the fresh air; we made friends with the American troops. It was all very exciting. But at the back of it all there was a kind of lack of identity. We were with people who weren't blood relations, who weren't that interested in us. I remember that the GIs we got friendly with by running errands used to think us very sad characters. They always wanted to carry us off back to America and give us the good life. We couldn't quite see why they were so sorry for us, but if it meant they gave us chewing gum and a few bob, we were perfectly happy.

The fact that evacuation was a common experience at the time was not something you were aware of. You never thought of other people's circumstances, you didn't even have a mass feeling and other kids didn't count – it was only your own little circle. I don't think the common experience mitigated it at all. It was simply unremittingly difficult, and re-establishing relations afterwards was almost impossible. My mother, for example had an extraordinary war. One moment she'd had a husband and three children, and almost the next day her husband was in the army and her three children were evacuated. Once she was over the sadness of that, she also had a good war, with a job that was fun and a lot of friends. She was a young woman then and had a pretty good time. Once we were all home again, she had three children and, before long, a new baby to look after, and couldn't always handle it.

We had longed to see my father, this warrior coming back from the war, our Dad arriving home. We had stood at the end of the street, outside our flat in Wandsworth, to watch for his return, which duly happened, though the euphoria was short-lived. He seemed insensitive and unwilling to understand anything about us. From my present vantage point I can see the problems he faced and why he reacted the way he did. He was a fairly mature soldier by then, had been a sergeant and had other men to control, but found it difficult to readjust to children. Whenever we rebelled he resorted to violence; that we should have pretensions to anything artistic he thought in some way a betrayal of the working class.

My mother hadn't the strength, physical or otherwise, to sort it out, so it was an unhappy time, particularly for my younger brother who is now dead, but who was a very mixed-up child. He went away when he was four, stayed away longer than the rest of us, and came back when he was nine. He had been with quite well-off people, whereas I went to a very homely working-class family, the equivalent of my own, and never had that identity problem, never had to readjust socially in that sense. But he never knew who he was from that day on.

From about the age of twelve I was earning money doing a paper-round and helping with the family exchequer, so I became more of a contributor than the average child. I emerged from all of that as a malleable creature, ready for life to put some shape to. We didn't come out of our childhood with any fully formed views. It was all quite nebulous, and the only thing I suspected was that I wanted to be an entertainer.

My mother used to take us to the cinema, where we got in free in exchange for putting advertisements in the window of the flat. I was as entranced with it as any child could be, and wanted to be an actor. Later I wanted to be a cartoonist and a writer, but my main ambition was to

go to America where everything seemed desirable – everything unattainable here was there. That idea has stayed with me most of my life.

Being evacuated has made me over-protective with my own children. I used to think, my kids will never go through that, and then, by the greatest irony, I have become the father of three separate families. What that has meant is that I've become less and less sure of the right thing to do. Whereas my wife, whose two children are for her the first experience, has the innate wisdom to look after them and not to worry, I fuss and fret like an old hen. She says they will be all right, and I say they will not be all right. If they're out of my sight in our own garden, I'm afraid for them. I have become very neurotic about it. I'm sure that they are resilient, because they look at me with some disdain when I say, 'Where are you now?' and they say, 'Well, just at the top of this tree. What do you mean?'

On the other hand, I am pretty good with kids. I am patient with them, I let them trample on me, I explain things to them. I have a temper as well, and that's quite useful, because although I am the fool of the family, prancing around entertaining them with the cap and bells on, it is quite salutary when I do lose my temper, because they respond.

I suppose what I called my awareness of being working class when I joined the BBC was simply my lack of education. It was something one was very much aware of in those days, though of course it doesn't count any more. I was able to pretend, but I knew there was no substance to my pretence. The old-school thing was still very evident. When I divorced for the first time they said, 'It's the end of the career, old boy, you realize that.' It wasn't, as it happened, but it very nearly was. A few years earlier and it would have been. The BBC was such a closed shop. One had listened in the little flat in Wandsworth to Uncle Mac and all those hallowed voices, and the idea of ever being allowed to be a part of it seemed unthinkable. Even with my brash confidence when I was twenty or twenty-one, I still thought it wasn't for the likes of us. I wasn't made to feel it overtly, because people took me at face value, and since I appeared to be a freshly scrubbed middle-class lad, they thought that's what I was. But I knew I wasn't, and I was ready to be found out at any moment, and discovery would have meant banishment.

Of course I can still identify myself with the working class. All my relations are working class. There is a strange dichotomy, particularly in this country, about success. One is ashamed of having made it, or even having done reasonably well. One is constantly apologizing. I look after my mother, and I've helped relations out from time to time. I'm very happy to do so, and there's never any discomfort about it. I think my family still realize today that the public me is just a performance. I don't really feel that I have changed or that my relationship with the rest of them has changed. My mother knows that although I speak like

a BBC newsreader, I'm still her Mike and the rest doesn't matter. Our language is still the same, and even though the accents are different, the relationship doesn't alter.

The uncomfortable feeling I had at the BBC was wide and basic to start with, though it became slightly more specific towards the end – unless they were imagined slights; I don't know. I've never been one to look for offence or to fall out with people. I've always simply turned up, done the job, had a laugh and gone home. When I first applied, there was something in the rejection that was rather haughty, and one felt one was lucky not to be actually censured for having applied. The presence of Lord Reith still hovered over everything. Even today, I feel a weight on me when I go through Broadcasting House. A heaviness descends, and persists even though it's now 23,000 individuals who are much more individual than they ever were. In the early days, I was known by surname and had a staff number. It was a strange uncomfortable feeling. They didn't treat me badly as such, but they never exploited what one had to offer.

Everything is timing, of course; and if I had joined about ten years later, then it would have been easier. At that time, after you'd worked for them for nine months, they'd pat you on the head and say, 'Well done, here's something slightly more interesting,' but that was the extent of it. They wouldn't actually say, 'This boy is good, we must exploit him.' That happened with Terry Wogan, when they suddenly realized they had a talent on their hands and really should use him. I never felt I was working for an artistic organization or a showbiz set-up. It was just a lot of people. And going to the club at Broadcasting House was really like, I suppose, being in a common room at a university. There were simply people in tweed jackets, puffing on pipes and being terribly serious. You couldn't tell whether they were Light Programme or World Service; they were all BBC men and they had a uniformity about them.

The combination of qualities a television interviewer needs are doing your homework and being interested. You will be a good listener if you're interested and you realize that your subjects are rather more important than you in that context. Somebody once said that the ideal chat-show host is someone whom, at the end of the programme, you don't remember seeing or hearing. I can't go along with that entirely because you've got to have some status. If you're inviting people to be your guests, you must at least have the status of host, which entitles you to get involved in the conversation. Nevertheless it's their spot, their moment, and the better they are then the better the show is going to be and the more attractive to viewers. So sometimes you try to know

a little more about them than they know themselves. They're terribly flattered and pleased when you bring up something they've forgotten.

I always feel nervous before a show. The only time I went on feeling absolutely confident produced the worst show I've ever done. Complacency is the greatest enemy. If ever I feel myself in danger of feeling confident, I imagine hazards to put myself into a healthy state of fear. I may appear to be relaxed, but that's partly because I'm expecting something to go wrong, almost longing for it to. When things go too smoothly is when it all slides into a dangerous apathy or self-satisfaction. You should always be slightly on edge.

Adrenalin is a useful thing. It can lift you out of all kinds of depression and get rid of the most serious ailments. They simply don't exist when it's there. I have the strangest way of showing my nerves. I start to look as if I've been dead several months. When I'm in the dressing room, they sometimes get quite worried and ask, am I actually in a catatonic state, because I can't raise any energy at all. Then, about five minutes before I go on, I do a bit of shadow boxing, anything to get the blood flowing roughly in the direction of the brain. Once I'm on, nothing works better than that jolt of fear as somebody points the finger at me, which is the sign to start talking. The great thing about talk shows is that there are certain things you cannot prepare for, and it is rather exciting to know there's no point in rehearsing. If it's going to happen it will. At certain points you're going to open your mouth and hope the right thing comes out. Quite often it does. There was one producer who used to hit me on the back and say, 'Don't forget the one-liners,' as I slouched off towards the studio. A pointless instruction, because, of course, you cannot plan one-liners.

The worst thing is not when somebody is difficult or recalcitrant, but when they're apparently dead. There was one American actress to whom I made a light-hearted remark that was simply meant to settle her bottom on the seat. But she seized on it and launched into an endless story about nothing at all. Every attempt to move her on was greeted with, 'I'm not finished yet,' and I could feel myself sinking lower and lower. It went on for nine minutes. That can drag you down and rob you of any kind of life. Far better to have someone like Oliver Reed come on totally drunk. Then it's great. That's fine television, except that, of course, you can't ask a drunk why he drinks, but have to wait till he's sober; and can't be too tricky with him, because it's like kicking a cripple.

Another unproductive thing that can happen is when someone comes on who is very nervous and has either prepared an act they do on stage and assumed that's what you want, so you have to sit there listening to a string of gags and there's no conversation at all; or is so insecure that they have prepared a series of anecdotes they have told a thousand times

before. That, of course, is the same as an act, and it gets you no closer to them. Those are the things you wish to avoid. It's nicer to throw all of that out of the window and come at them obliquely about something they never suspected you even knew about, let alone wanted to talk about.

What you are after with your guest depends, interestingly enough, on the medium you're working in. I much prefer to interview on radio. I had a series on commercial radio for some years, and felt the conversations we had then were far better, far more productive than anything on television in terms of intimacy and revelation. A television chat show is really an entertainment, mainly looking for laughs. Not that there's any law against being serious, but I prefer to do it on radio. I would be given some homework by a researcher, I'd take it home, bone up, prepare the questions and thoughts, then go in and do it. You can pace it, you have commercial breaks, you have records. You can interview for forty minutes instead of the perfunctory nine that inevitably make for a glancing relationship. Sometimes after a TV chat show you think, well, that was fun, but we didn't learn anything and it had no value. I don't claim that what I do is important, but some of these radio things were quite revealing and intimate. It is something I miss.

You remind me that I once said of interviewing that it was a matter of sitting at other people's feet, which made for an unnatural relationship. It's an interesting point. The more successful your show, the less sitting at feet there is. When we have American guests, I know very well, of course, that England is not important to them. They're loath to come because the press is only going to chase them around. They don't know me or the show, so why make an effort? There's no need to come, but they do, and once you catch a few big names you build up a kind of pedigree. They watch the tapes we send them and arrive pre-warned. I found it rather embarrassing when, before I'd even started, an enthusiastic entertainer said, 'I've heard about this show and I know that you're so nice.' I thought, I wish she hadn't said that, I wish she'd discovered it for herself. On the whole there has been less of the sitting at feet in recent times.

The only people who put me in awe are writers. I have never felt in awe of the big stars. When I interviewed Elizabeth Taylor, some magazine reviewed the show as all right, but asked was it necessary to have such a fawning, crawling performance? My answer was that that was unfair; she was just pleased to see me. In fact it was a very relaxed encounter and I knew it would be all right because she had laughed in such a filthy way before she came on when the power pack for the radio mike fell from her inner thigh.

A few years ago I had the rare, almost unique privilege of seeing Margaret Thatcher frightened. She was obviously saying to her

daughter, 'Why did I ever agree to this?' It was an astonishing thing to witness, but within about thirty seconds of being on, she was totally herself and all was well. I certainly didn't cringe in her presence, because it was my show and I was entitled to ask the questions. Afterwards can be more of a problem. Standing in the hospitality room, you don't, of course, have the same status. You're just milling around. So then I keep well away. Without the safety of set and cameras, I don't push my luck.

With celebrities you do get a sense of unreality, almost like an actor interpreting a role, but it doesn't last long. There are those first few minutes of an encounter, and there's nothing more relaxing for an interviewer than to see fear in the eyes of his guest at the outset. To see an uncertainty is very, very relaxing, and I do see it from time to time. I realize why so many actors refuse to go on chat shows: they are afraid of exposing the real self. But the more extraordinary the screen persona, the more accessible they quite often are, because they're really quite vulnerable and you can sense a way you can use it, not cruelly but positively.

The criterion you apply to the use of any confidential information which comes up in the research is just innate good taste, I suppose. You can be bold in your questioning when you know it's partly a matter of public domain, but if I discovered, for example, that an actor had been arrested for some indecent act, I wouldn't think I'd bring it up. In the same way, with *This is Your Life*, many potential programmes have been abandoned when certain things have come to light, and there are a lot of people who leave instructions with their agents and families that, if anybody from the programme approaches them, they have their permission to kill. As if one might say, 'Remember when you were a prostitute, here is your first customer'; or 'When you were in prison your warder was . . .' Of course, I long to find something off beat, to discover that a great Shakespearian actor was once a lavatory attendant. That would be fine. That's what you look and hope for.

There might be certain people whom I would refuse to interview on grounds of personal dislike, but I won't say who they are. I would certainly demand to retain that right and would be very unhappy if anything was arranged without consultation. In fact, there's hardly anyone in the world whom that would apply to, but there have been a couple of occasions where I've used a veto. It would be too revealing to say why, but it would normally be something particularly vindictive which someone had done.

As for encountering hostility, I once had a very bad experience with an American actor who took himself so seriously that, although we spent a great deal of the programme talking about the worthy things he did in life, one hint of the more popular side drew threats of injunctions. We had shown a clip from his latest film, which was fairly boring,

and talked at length about his commitment to a certain country in the Far East and its people, his search for enlightenment and spiritual growth, and then I said, 'The mantle of sex symbol seems to sit heavily on your shoulders.' He left the building, saying he'd been betrayed. The next day he was issuing injunctions stating that if any hint of him being a sex symbol was allowed to remain in the edited version, the show was not to be broadcast. That seemed to me the ultimate in self-regard. When someone is so neurotic, there's little you can do but cut your losses.

I never feel that we have anything in particular to learn from American chat shows. The *Johnnie Carson Show*, for instance, is utterly different, and I think magnificent, the difference being that every American chat-show host is an entertainer. He could be a comedian or a singer, and is certainly a showbusiness figure. Our style is different, and people who have been on American shows are surprised to find themselves with somebody who is interested in them, who will allow them to speak and won't just give them twenty seconds before throwing them off for someone brighter. It's something they respond to, and we get a benefit from it. Judging by the reactions I receive in letters from around the world, people seem to think it works. In America it's a battle, a competition between host and guest to see who's going to come out as the most lively entertainer of the evening. I don't mind raising a laugh myself every now and then, but that's not the main reason I'm there.

Oh, yes, I've fallen in love several times when interviewing women. And marvellously once or twice, when it's been reciprocated – in the most glancing, perfunctory way, of course. It has happened when I have talked to somebody, usually on radio, quite intimately, quite intensely. Half an hour of concentrated conversation between two people can work wonders without being sycophantic. Sometimes there's been tremendous warmth, and it's been a joy to be told by the person who escorted her to the door what she said on the way out.

The physical attraction side of life I do regard as unequivocally important. It's also something that doesn't stop when you're thirty-seven and a half, with women or with men. I've met women of advanced age – very attractive – who respond to a little flattery. There's nothing grotesque about it. I don't mind flirting on the air. It's a game I enjoy playing, and it looks nice on television if people respond to each other and a little flicker occurs. I'm no Claire Rayner, it's not a therapeutic exercise, but it's fun.

I hosted the 'Miss World' competition about fourteen times, and I never really thought it offensive. If I had, even at that early stage when one would do almost anything because of the need to support a family and keep working, I would have said no. But the girls were not always

the mindless cuties that people accused them of being. They were often much better educated than the journalists who sneered at them. I never got too involved in the question of whether it was morally right or wrong, but they were happy to be there, and most of them regarded it as a harmless frolic. Although I enjoyed sending the whole thing up, I didn't really enjoy it. It was far too complicated, demanding and exhausting. I dreaded its approach and was glad when it was over. And far from it being a lustful riot, I didn't collapse exhausted through having gone to bed with fifty-seven different girls. In fact, in all the times I introduced the show I had only one relationship – during one of my unmarried periods, of course. So all it was was a merry romp, and it simply got out of date.

The occasional proposition does happen, and there have been embarrassing moments. There's nothing more difficult for a man than to reject unwanted advances. We're not equipped or trained to do it, and it doesn't happen often enough for one to become clever at it. You simply have to change the subject quickly or pretend to be so obtuse that you hope they'll go off you anyway. I remember being invited to a charity do in a pub somewhere in Middlesex. I went along as asked, to push over a pile of pennies, and was introduced to the president of the charity, a titled lady whom I had never met before but who seemed for some reason to be angry with me. 'You're terribly rude,' she said, 'and for that you must drive me home'; which I did. Then she said, 'You must have a drink to complete your apology'; and again I complied. Within thirty seconds I was being wrestled to the carpet. After about twenty minutes she said, 'You don't want me,' and I found I couldn't say, 'You're absolutely right, I don't.' I had to bleat about the girlfriend waiting for me and all that, then run for my life.

The lives of people I interview might influence me into reading something, say, but I have to accept that my character is pretty well set by this time. I can never read the Sunday supplements without becoming irritated. I pick them up with relish every Sunday morning, and within fifteen minutes I'm fed up, because they're full of very smart, beautiful, clever, accomplished people who live in the most wonderful homes. I sometimes envy the casual approach of the wealthy and privileged in that they may be twenty-five years younger than me and need never work again, while I shall have to work for the rest of my life. When I'm eighty, my youngest son will just about be in the full bloom of manhood, and I'm obsessed by the fact that I've got to get up there and keep at it. That's all. I don't envy them their lifestyle. I don't need it.

Describing me as having two lives – one make-believe with little substance and the other with substance but lacking the fairy-tale aspect – is a precise description. There is some spurious glamour professionally,

but my personal life couldn't be more ordinary. I insist on going down to the pub. I take the kids to the recce. I wear old clothes. My friends are not in the business, but are neighbours or local businessmen who may ask me about the shows that I'm doing if they feel like it, but equally well may not. They never treat me like those people who come up for autographs, and it's all very casual – 'Thought you looked a bit rough last night' – that kind of thing.

I get a great deal of satisfaction from work because it involves having some kind of a role in life. At home you don't always get the respect you want, your wife doesn't always listen to what you say, people don't answer your letters, workmen don't turn up. I find that infuriating, and when I start slouching around the house and getting depressed by the way my life is not succeeding privately – people not doing the things I would like them to do, however politely and patiently I ask them – I put on a suit, comb my hair and suddenly think, ah, this is more like it, I'm going to be a bit assertive now.

When I say I've never done anything of the slightest importance, then that is genuinely what I believe. How could I feel otherwise? There's nothing you could possibly list, apart from the charity things I've been asked to do, and perhaps the time I read the news, that is actually important. I'm not saying it's not worth while. If it gives pleasure, of course it's worth while in that sense, but if it ceased to exist at this moment, it would make no difference to anything or anybody, apart from a few old ladies – ten minutes of pleasure they would find somewhere else on television. No, it's dangerous to think you're important. I can write fluently enough if I'm asked to do 1,000 words here and there. I can make it entertaining, but not profound, not valuable. I don't worry about that. What I've been doing is something I never intended to do. I happen to be able to do it, but there's no great mystique about it.

If I do seem to display a certain lack of self-esteem, I can only say that, while I may not have been born with a sense of guilt, I certainly acquired one in my adult life, mainly because of being married three times. Nowadays, of course, that doesn't seem anything remarkable, but it was then, and it was largely the result of the fact that there were pressures put upon you to be a married person. If you reached the age of twenty-two and were not married, then you were some strange kind of creature. So I allowed myself to be drawn in. But it doesn't stop one feeling guilty and sad about what you've done, not only to the women you promised to live with and love, but to the children you had as well. I think being married three times is a terrible thing to have done.

So that is inescapable, and something I live with, although, thank God, I do see them all, and we have a good relationship. But it will always be a problem and I'm not over-endowed with self-regard.

My intellect won't allow me to finish reading books or learn about things properly. I pick up a paper and say to myself, by the end of this article, I will know about this and will have formed an opinion. But I read to the end and still haven't formed any opinion. I envy people who can be pedantic. I can't even be committed, let alone pedantic. These days people are far more politically aware than they used to be. I listen to my wife and to wives of local people talking about issues. I know the issues exist, I know what they are, but I find it difficult to articulate an opinion about them, and I don't know why that should be.

My own politics are that I'm a Conservative by instinct. I don't vote for what taxes I pay or for what will happen locally. I really vote for what I think is best for Britain. Mrs Thatcher may be intransigent, but she's extraordinary. Intransigence can work wonderfully well until things start going in the wrong direction, and then it's disaster. Mrs Thatcher wrote to me when my son was ill, before he died last year. It was kind of her, and I was touched, and it would be too cynical to believe it was simply a PR thing because she'd recently been on the show.

Where the equality of the sexes is concerned, I think the pendulum has swung too far and there is far too great an emphasis on women in broadcasting. Things reached the pitch when no male broadcaster seemed to exist any more. The only interest was in whoever was the latest woman in broadcasting, while there were certain female newscasters who possessed a basilisk eye and arch approach that I found profoundly irritating. My irritation was compounded by a focusing of press attention that negated the job they were there to do.

As for equality having a positive effect on family life, I don't know. My wife is an actress, and she's desperate to get back to it, and the kind of work she does takes her away from home far more than any woman who does a daily job. But I'm willing to support her in that, because she needs to do it and has a talent that needs expressing. If people commit themselves to a marriage and family life, they must remember that those things come first and anything else you want to do has to be worked out in the context. You can't simply abandon what you've taken on – says he who's abandoned it several times – but what I'm talking about is the way it *should* be done. Any play that my wife wants to do, any touring that comes into it, we have to work out very carefully, not only in terms of the organization involved, but whether it's right for her to be away so long. Families are being abandoned these days.

Yes, I can honestly say that I am as deeply supportive of my wife's career as she is of mine. Even more so, in a way, because I think she has a great deal to offer and I'm keen she should be able to offer it.

I really would and do say, 'Follow that up, do it, don't hesitate.' The only time I've hesitated is when it has coincided with a period when I was particularly busy, which meant that neither of us would be at home. But if a commitment fits in with her responsibilities and mine, then I want her to do it and will work extra hard to get away from work and be home early so she can take it on. I'm aware of her now – this talented woman who did West End shows – watching other people on the screen. She's not bitter or envious of anybody, but I know that she thinks she could and should be doing it.

I accept the pressures of my family responsibilities gladly. The advantages far outweigh any problems. I admit I sometimes get a bit wistful when friends say they're just off at a moment's notice to anywhere in the world. There's nothing like that for us. For example, *TV Times* has said to me, 'Wouldn't you like to take your family anywhere in the world for a holiday? We'll finance it and you just write a little article.' Well, that's lovely, but it has to be Disneyland. There's nowhere else you can take two boys aged nine and five, so that's the end of it. But I adore them so much that I don't mind being with them all the time. I work all the hours there are for them, but what they give me back is more than enough.

When you're a young father, then you've got to get out there and make a name for yourself or whatever it is you want to do, and other things take second place. Once you are a mature parent, all you want to do is go home. That is the time when you should be a parent; it's pointless taking on parenthood when you're still young and selfish. I can give my present kids the attention I regret I never could give my others, although, thank God, we're in constant touch and love each other. But they didn't get all they were entitled to.

I remember how angry I got with a priest who asked, when I was first getting married, 'Are you sure?' And the reason why I was so angry was that I wasn't sure. When you meet someone like Zsa Zsa Gabor, it seems that marriage is just a joke, but if you think of the words used, whether they're religious or secular, it's a tremendous promise and commitment. I doubt if such people even think about it or ever really commit themselves. And obviously neither did I, so there's nothing new about it, though I really did think at the time that I would stick with it.

I have, in occasional black moments, felt that there was some mysterious form of retribution at work in my life. In the same period when my brother was killed, my best friend died and my wife's brother died, all of them men in their early forties within eighteen months of each other. And my wife was losing children too – we had one that died at birth. I began at that time to look over my shoulder, but in the end I

couldn't accept there could be anything other than a series of rotten coincidences behind it all.

In coping with tragedy, I suppose I've had the inner resources to do it. I've never allowed myself to get into one of these 'why me?' frames of mind. I sometimes think sadly, what a list it is, but only when journalists remind me. The fact that my son has cerebral palsy has brought letters from people who have to deal with the same affliction, who say it's not a cause for gloom and despair but almost one for joy and inspiration. My son certainly has qualities that are strange and different which his able-bodied brothers don't have. And the son who died, well, that was a terrible loss. You can't say anything except I wish he hadn't died. But the manner of his death was something to be proud of. He was such an extraordinarily brave fellow, and such a fighter, that I'm very proud of him.

Certainly I have found that some good always comes out of misfortune. There were delights and consolations in most of these gloomy situations. The death of my son has drawn my attention to the work of the hospices, and I've appreciated that a lot more and been able to do something to help. Through Patrick's cerebral palsy, I've met a lot of people involved in that cause, as well as the children themselves, who are so admirable. It stops you being blinkered. I remember how, as a kid, if you saw somebody going round with what I now recognize to be the classic cerebral palsy symptom – the clawed hand – you'd just make fun of them.

I don't know that I'm very sensitive to criticism, but I suppose I do get irritated by people who never look beyond the obvious. For example, after we did the Telethon, I picked up my daily paper and found it described as twenty-seven hours of self-indulgent back-slapping. I felt it deserved more than a perfunctory dismissal.

It used to irritate me to be called bland. Cartoonists can't do anything with my face and *Spitting Image* can't make a model of me. They tell me it simply can't be done. 'Bland' seemed an offensive term. It's much better to be described as a pain in the arse. Yet I have come to accept that I am bland, and that for earning a living it is quite a useful thing to be, which is why I've turned it to advantage. If you're bland, you don't infuriate people enough for them not to want to employ you, and you can do a job well enough to be useful; and eventually people recognize that there are one or two qualities which are quite useful. I can't change the image. The dramatic things in my life don't show.

My present life and my working-class origins all seem like one continuous thing. I don't live in any splendour. Compared with what any American newscaster or weather forecaster earns, one is very much a backroom boy in terms of income, though it's good money. It's taken

me a long time. I've been married and sold houses and started again, and sold houses and started again, so I'm still establishing. But still feel completely at ease with all classes of people. I haven't left anything behind, and have just picked up a few things along the way, so I can talk to my old relations and old neighbours and people I meet in as comfortable a way as ever, while I'm less inhibited about talking to those whom I would once have felt shy to have spoken to. That's the great advantage. I'm still me, with a few embellishments.

I never worry about whether I shall continue in demand or favour, except in my role as provider. Broadcasting isn't something I dream of and live for; it's a means to an end, and my dependants are that end.

MARK BIRLEY

Mark Birley was born in Sussex in 1930, only son of Captain Sir Oswald Birley, the portrait painter. He went to prep school in Devon and then to Eton. He spent a year at Oxford and then did his National Service in the Intelligence Corps. After six years with an advertising agency he decided to go into the night-club business. In 1954 he married Annabel Vane-Tempest-Stewart, daughter of the eighth Marquis of Londonderry. They had three children but suffered the tragic loss of the eldest, Rupert, in Africa a few years ago. Mark Birley is the founder of Annabel's in Berkeley Square, named after his wife (who is now married to Sir James Goldsmith), Harry's Bar and Mark's Club. He has recently opened a health club, the Bath and Racquets Club.

Any question about my relationship with my mother is rather hard to answer. It must have had some kind of lasting effect. It wasn't so much a strained relationship, more the absence of any normal relationship. To her credit she was very keen on my taking an interest in everything artistic, including music and the ballet – she had been one of the original supporters of the Diaghilev ballet – but I was not musical. I think we got on better in her later years because there was nothing left to disagree or argue over. An absence of affection, that was the point. We were rather a divided family: my sister and I, my mother and my father. It was a pretty good mess.

I suppose the fact that my father was fifty when I was born must have made for some remoteness in the relationship there. I was extremely fond of him, but he was almost like a grandfather. We were sometimes rather united about Mama. The age gap was wide between them as well. I always got on pretty well with my father, but there were too many people pulling in too many different directions in the family: my mother saying one thing, my sister another and my father trying to get on with his work and painting and wanting a bit of peace and quiet occasionally. You can hardly blame him.

I never really thought of my nanny as being a kind of surrogate mother figure, but in a sense I suppose that is what she was. She's still alive today at ninety-six, and quite extraordinary. She's had every kind of stroke and should have gone but hasn't. She has moments of rather brief lucidity. I was devoted to her as a child. Frankly I was glad to leave that period of my childhood behind me, although I've wiped my mind pretty clear of all the bad things that happened. I expect it was Annabel who told you I detested Eton. I didn't detest it at all. I was relatively happy there, the thing about the place being that you had your own room and felt you were a bit grown-up as soon as you arrived.

I do admit to having many regrets about wastage of time. I certainly didn't work hard enough during my only year at Oxford. At that stage I lacked any sense of direction and didn't know what I was going to do afterwards. Not that many people do know, but I think I was more lacking in purpose and direction than most of my contemporaries. I had certain artistic ambitions at one point because I was born with a talent for drawing. Had I worked at it, I probably could have done something with it, but I grew bored. I didn't know what I wanted to be, but I knew I didn't want to be an artist, though that, in any case, was a time when artistic talents were being treated rather contemptuously. Had I been born in France, things would probably have been quite different.

The point where I first came into my own was, I think, when I opened a sort of advertising office, some years before Annabel's got going. At least the agency represented independence and I had it for quite a few years. Looking back, it was really great fun. Afterwards I had the Hermès shop in the corner of Piccadilly Arcade and Jermyn Street, but then I came to think that what I wanted was somewhere bigger and better, probably in Bond Street. Annabel's was just starting, however, and so I sold out, having decided I wasn't after all really interested in embarking on a larger shop which would only have taken up much more of my time.

Annabel's arose out of my friendship with John Aspinall. When gambling became legal, he was looking for suitable premises. I already had an idea for some kind of piano bar somewhere, something on a relatively modest scale. No. 44 Berkeley Square had then been empty for about twelve years, and after Aspinall saw it himself, he told me I ought to take a look. Of course, the basement to the house was very small, but we had the garden dug out and we connected up the whole building. I needed to persuade people to invest in it since I didn't have any money myself just then.

While Annabel's was being built, I was trying to gather a little team around me, and even then I realized that the key person was going to be the manager. I knew perfectly well that, unless I had the right person, I would be in every kind of trouble because I didn't really know how to do it myself. I remember calling at the Mirabelle and saying to Louis, the manager there, 'I'm looking for a manager. If you can think of anyone you think might be suitable, please let me know.' It simply didn't occur to me that he would want to come to me, but it was just at the time when the Mirabelle was being taken over and its staff were a bit unsettled. Louis said he thought he might be interested himself, and of course that was my lucky break, because he has been with me ever since and without Louis the story could have been very different. Then Mabel, whom I'd known at the old Wilton's, came to run the

ladies' room, and still does, and George Hobart, whom I'd known at Jules' Bar, was barman, though he has since died.

I know there are a lot of people who think I'm very difficult about a lot of things. Who's put you up to asking? I suppose it is true, yes, because I want to get people to think the same way as I'm thinking straightaway, and if I can do that, then everything's fine. With Louis, for example, we mesh well and we've hardly had a cross word in the last twenty-seven years. The fact that I insist on my staff always addressing me formally doesn't indicate a lack of friendliness or camaraderie or anything of that kind, its just that I feel that degree of formality should be maintained. When you're not working, it's a different matter altogether, but I don't really like the American system where everybody's Jim and Bob and goodness knows what, and everything's wonderful, except on Monday, when it's, 'Bob, you've done a great job but we need your desk.' That's all superficial.

I'm not good on committees. One of my failings is a lack of patience, and when I feel I'm right about something and that everyone else is wrong, then the whole process of listening to all the arguments makes me rather impatient. I'm used to taking my own decisions in my business without reference to anybody else, obviously within the constraints of what is possible. That rather autocratic way of running things has advantages and disadvantages, but one of the main advantages is that it makes for speed and makes your employees happier, I think. They like somebody who can say yes or no.

Speaking of management really does hit on one of the problems. I find that aspect very difficult. I suppose I've got about 200 staff now, and one of the difficulties occurs in part because my headquarters in Hays Mews is exactly the same as it was when I started twenty-eight years ago and I can't make it any bigger. Another office, in Charles Street, deals with the accounts side of the business, but the businesses are actually managed in quite an unorthodox way. It is still all a bit of a one-man band. The latest effort of building the Baths and Racquets Club has put a great strain on the office, because it took a great deal of time and effort. The new club's been open about a year now, and I still have endless problems with water leakages, builders and staffing. It needs a hell of a lot of everyday attention.

Management is the simple reason why I remain reluctant to take Annabel's across the Atlantic, though people keep suggesting I should do so. The usual concept behind this operation is to pick it up, put some paper round it, get on Concorde and dump it on a corner of Fifth Avenue. Yet I couldn't very well stay in America for a year or so and leave everything here in London to get on with itself. It would never work out.

I'll give you an example. Harry's Bar in Venice is owned by Arrigo

Cipriani, who inherited it from his father as a kind of licence to print money. He wasn't content with that and he had to go to America and get involved in a great shemozzle in New York, transporting all the key staff from Venice to New York. Of course, the bar in Venice started to go downhill. Who needs these headaches? He certainly didn't need the money, so what was the point? Nobody is content nowadays to do what they do and stick to it. It was the same with Geoffrey Bennison, who was very well known as a wonderful antique dealer before he became an interior decorator and did so much for Annabel's and Mark's Club. He also became a very great friend, and was a splendid raconteur as well as a bit of a snob. Well, whenever Concorde tickets arrived from all these very rich ladies in New York who said, 'Will you come and advise us on our cushions?' Geoffrey couldn't resist it, and off he had to go. It killed him, you know.

It's not so much perfectionism I'm after in the way I run Annabel's as the way I think things ought to be. That is not necessarily the same as perfection. I just want to get everything right in the way I think to be best. Of course, it is a matter of going on and on for years and staying interested enough to try to improve things.

In some funny way, Annabel's has managed to satisfy people's needs. It's a place they really like to be in. If you asked a selection of people to define their ideal night club, they would all answer with different specifications, but probably none of them would answer truthfully because they will all have little secrets which they're not going to disclose. But I think I happen to know what some of these secrets are, and Annabel's incorporates a few of them. Since I launched Annabel's, quite a number of other clubs have sprung up, and every time a new one comes along there's a fresh wave of excitement. I know perfectly well that a lot of people will go rushing off there, but equally I'm pretty certain that they'll be back. I strongly believe that, if you do your utmost to look after people properly, they will remain loyal.

Contrary to what one might suppose, there haven't been many appalling scenes in Annabel's. There really haven't been any big fights, though we've had lots of drunken behaviour. Geoffrey Keating, who used to be in charge of public relations at BP and who helped to promote Montgomery's reputation when he was on his staff during the war, used to sit there as if he owned the place. Whenever things got too much, after he'd insulted whole parties of Arabs and so on, we had a procedure for getting him out. One of the doormen used to walk him home through Berkeley Square, and as he passed the J. Walter Thomson building, he would stop, undo his flies and pee into the letterbox with great accuracy all over J. Walter Thompson's expensive stationery. After that he would be quite happy. He was like a lamb once he'd been led home. The stories of Geoffrey in Annabel's are absolutely legion. I used

to have frightful rows with him, but I adored him. He was one of my greatest friends, and was never frightened about the consequences of his behaviour, drunk or sober.

Perhaps I do have a slightly withdrawn personality, though it depends on the circumstances. I'm the opposite to extrovert, I suppose. I need to have people around me, but I don't need a lot of people. People think I'm a melancholic because I'm not for ever grinning at everybody. Nowadays everybody is expected to wear a permanent grin from ear to ear.

I find it perfectly easy to have close relationships, but I also find I've reached a point in life where I'm probably not going to make, or don't particularly wish to make, many more very close friends. Certainly there are a lot of people I love to see and who are going to be friends, but I'm not going to make any more very intimate friends. We all know hundreds and hundreds of people and it all becomes too much. The assumption of a lack of warmth on my part springs from an attitude of, oh my God, this restaurant owner really hasn't been to charm school, has he? I'm expected to remember everybody's name from either side of the Atlantic, and to say all those things people say when they're twenty-one. That's not my style. One of my strengths at Annabel's and the clubs is that, when I'm there, I think of myself as a kind of customer and so get a detached feeling about it. This is very helpful. If you allow yourself to grow too close to it all, you can only attend to detail and you can't see the thing whole.

If Louis says that I have a wonderful sense of humour, then all I can tell you is that Louis's idea of a good sense of humour is so awful and disgusting that the girls in the office have to be trained to listen to the stories he produces. As for being happy, I think it all depends. I don't know that you can exist in a permanent state of blissful happiness, though you go through periods of happiness. If you're too happy to much of the time, it seems to imply some kind of complacency that is rather unattractive. I realize I have a reputation for being a misery. I can become unhappy for all kinds of reasons, but to call me melancholic is to aim wide of the mark. If people say I find it difficult to show affection and to trust on an emotional level, there is maybe some truth in it. You've been doing quite a lot of research, I must say.

No, I wouldn't consider that the British have good taste. If we're talking about the post-war years, I would say most definitely not, and in fact they've been swayed in the opposite direction in hundreds of different ways. Architecture is the most obvious example. I'm one hundred per cent behind Prince Charles on that one. The wingeing of architects who feel they shouldn't be criticized by anybody unless it's by another architect seems quite extraordinary. It's such a pity we don't have a Lutyens around today.

My own passion for collecting is a sort of acquisitiveness, I suppose. I can get caught up in a new interest at the drop of a hat. If I had the time to go round all the salesrooms, there would be no end to the stuff I could get interested in. At Sotheby's recently they had the most beautiful old picnic baskets which I wanted to buy, but I didn't manage to go.

I once had the most frightful disaster, bidding for some drawings at Christie's. My secretary is very good at bidding – very quiet about it where I get over-excited. Here in the office that morning I told her I wanted her to bid for ten drawings and that when I wanted her to stop bidding then I would shake my head. Simple. The trouble was that we went separately to Christie's and I couldn't find her when I reached the saleroom. When the lots came up I though she'd disappeared off the face of the earth, so started bidding myself. Just as the items were being knocked down to me, the auctioneer said, 'Ah, a new bidder at the end of the room,' and on the bidding went again. When I got out of the saleroom, I found my secretary and asked, 'Where the hell have you been?' She replied, 'Well, I couldn't find you, but luckily I managed to buy one or two.' By bidding against me, she had managed to pay the world record price for one drawing.

I see quite a lot of Annabel, and yes, she is a most important person in my life. Getting married to her was the most important thing that happened to me, and Annabel, when all is said and done, probably shaped my life more than any other person, though without being particularly aware of what she was doing. The thing that you say she said to you, about me being the true love of her life, is reciprocated. Though if Jimmy Goldsmith walked into this room now, I'd be perfectly pleased to see him.

My God, do you have that typed out: 'Difficult to have as a lover, but, once the affair is over, the most wonderful friend?' I'm sure the first statement is absolutely true. I am not aware of being so difficult, but I suppose whoever told you must be right. I feel very comfortable in the company of women. By today's standards, I should think I probably discovered women pretty late. It was after I left school, I suppose, when I was up at Oxford. They have been important in my life, but none more so than Annabel, you know. But if I have never remarried, it's not because I consciously avoid long-term relationships. I've been with the same person now for quite a long time, and I don't know whether we'll get married or not. We probably will.

In respect of possessing patience, I probably made a very bad father. I should have gone to my children's schools more often, but I think they probably forgave me for not doing so. I remember one awful sports day, pouring with rain, when Rupert found a pavilion and said,

'Pup, don't you worry, you stay in here. I'll go and get you a glass of brandy.' All the other parents were busy doing something constructive around the place, talking to the masters or whatever, but I hated it. The children were certainly very much closer to their mother at the beginning and, to be truthful, probably are still, but we get on with each other well now.

When you look at your children, I think you look to see whether your own worst characteristics are emerging, but Robin, for example, is much more mature at thirty than I was at his age. He has a better aptitude for business; he's extremely hard working. He gets up very early in the morning, a thing that I have always found rather difficult to do. My daughter is the only one who has really inherited my artistic ability, and she now fully understands that talent needs to be combined with a lot of hard work to produce results. She is a good artist. I sense she's going to do great things. She is enormously talented and is working hard; she paints in oils, she draws. She has always drawn since she was a child, but now she has a very disciplined pencil. Her first exhibition was a great success and she's going to have another. John Ward, whose opinion I respect, thinks highly of her.

It is rather difficult to know whether one of my children will take over from me when I retire. I think Robin would eventually be quite interested, if for no other reason that that it could be a hell of a launching pad for something else. Rupert was far more literary. He would have liked to have been a writer. When I asked him what benefit he thought he had derived from Oxford, he said it was the ability to write. When he came down, he found it quite difficult to get a job. I'm all for people going to university, but I think that too many sons and daughters go up to Oxford or Cambridge and are promised by their tutors that the world is theirs if only they get a decent second in PPE – philosophy, politics and economics. It's not necessarily the case. I felt that Robin could have gone up to Oxford quite easily, but part of the strength of his position today is that he did not do so, but started work instead. Things have been difficult for Robin for various reason, mainly because of an accident he suffered in childhood, when he was only eleven. He was mauled by a tiger and the injuries were very serious. The lower part of his face was crushed in the tiger's jaws and he came within an inch of death. Luckily there was a hospital which dealt with motorway accidents and urgent cases only two or three miles away. They got him there very quickly, he was operated on and they managed to save his life.

The boys absolutely adored each other, though I would say that Rupert was the closer to me. I'm sure he could have become an accomplished writer, but unfortunately he wanted first to prove to all his contemporaries that he wasn't just some vague scribbler, that he

could actually make a success in business too. So he went to Togo. I don't know if you've ever been there. I hope you never have to go. All I can say about it is that it is a bloody miserable place. Even the American ambassador to Togo apologized to me for just being there. Rupert didn't exactly like it either, but he managed to make friends in a most extraordinary way. Everybody adored him. When I got out there after the accident, the warmth of feeling I found for him was quite extraordinary.

I did discuss with Rupert whether he would ever want to take over from me, but he was very sensitive and didn't want to be given anything on a plate which he felt he hadn't rightfully earned. He also felt that that would be unfair from Robin's point of view, so he was rather confused about what he should do. But quite certainly I think that he would have come into the business eventually.

On the subject of the tragedies in my life, I'll tell you something. I really hate people who wear their emotions on their sleeves. I simply don't want to show how I feel sometimes, and if I can manage to conceal it, so much the better. The spectacle of a man breaking down in front of people, in public, is always rather a sad thing to witness. I'd rather it wasn't me. In Rupert's case, at least there was something I could do. I was sitting out on my balcony having a cup of coffee before going to the office when my secretary rang and said she had someone from Togo on the line. I absolutely knew at that second that the news was bad. All they could tell me was that Rupert couldn't be found.

There was no reason at that point, or even after we got out there – Robin came with me – to assume he was dead. There was certainly no time to sit and mope. The question of abduction arose and we felt we had to get to the truth of the matter. I called in a firm of investigators, which deal mostly with kidnappings, and I must say they were very good, very thorough. At all events, we satisfied ourselves that there was no question of an abduction. Rupert used to go swimming at a particularly horrible beach where the currents were strong and you could easily be dragged out. There had been quite a number of other cases where people weren't recovered, and this is what almost certainly happened with Rupert. It was a very great shock to us all. Robin was absolutely marvellous. I had to have awful phone calls with Annabel, who used to sit by the telephone in London waiting for me to ring in the evening. I went back to that bloody god-forsaken place two or three times. I think Rupert was the only white man who ever went out there through choice. I miss him terribly.

I would describe myself as being more heart than head. I'm perhaps a little on the cynical side sometimes, but hard-headed, no. I'm vulnerable to failure or when I lose a friendship, and I daresay self-esteem

comes in there a little bit. But I'm hypersensitive, not thick-skinned at all, and I very easily get hurt.

We've all got regrets, mostly about things we didn't do rather than things we did. Timing is also important. I would like to have done everything a few years earlier. Probably we all feel like that. I expect I would live my life differently if I had the chance again. One often thinks, if only I was twenty-five years younger and knew what I know now. It would be like putting a bull who had already had one fight into the ring. I'd have been a much better student and everything else. In those days the dividend, if there was one, seemed far too remote to be worth bothering with. On top of that, schools were then very different. Boys nowadays look forward to going back to school after their holidays because they have much more fun. They have more freedom, they're more grown up and, of course, they travel. I was at school during the war years, and went abroad only in 1946 or 1947 for the first time, when I was seventeen. I know children nowadays who have been absolutely everywhere by the time they're twelve.

I'm not unduly apprehensive about the future. In general, I feel reasonably confident and optimistic. I'm not planning to take on a lot more work. I think I'd rather work a bit less fairly soon, though I don't see that I can retire. Anyway, what is it one would retire to? A kind of blank day.

WILLIAM F. BUCKLEY JR

William F. Buckley has been editor of the *National Review* for thirty-five years. He was born in New York City in 1925 into a staunch Roman Catholic family and was educated in Europe, Mexico and at Yale, where he took a BA in 1950. At the age of nineteen he joined the United States Army, leaving two years later with the rank of lieutenant. He married when he was twenty-five and the following year wrote his seminal work against the liberal establishment, *God and Man at Yale*. He is a syndicated columnist and since 1966 he has hosted the popular and influential weekly chat show *Firing Line*. In 1981 he received a Creative Leadership Award from New York University and his many books include *American Conservative Thought in the Twentieth Century* (1970) and his controversial novel about the queen of England, *Saving the Queen* (1976).

Who has been the primary influence on your life, apart from Edmund Burke?

My father, whom I found entirely admirable and in many senses unique. He was well educated but he was a self-made man. His father was a sheriff in Texas, which was a pretty high position after the Civil War. But there was no wealth in the South, none whatsoever, so he worked his way through university, and when his father died, put the entire family through university too. He went to Texas, started a business, married at the age of thirty-six, had ten children, educated them all, and we grew up a happy and well-informed family. He was an intellectual by inclination, a successful businessman, a wonderful father and husband. That's pretty unusual. The responsibility of ten children when you are in the oil business and knowing great fluctuations of fortune is something I've never had to go through, thank God.

What is it exactly that an American conservative seeks to conserve?

American conservatives are guided by the notion that there are some stable insights in the idea of America which are not subject to essential change. They might change in respect of modality, of emphasis, but not otherwise. In that sense we take the word conservative and use it a little bit differently from the way it might be used, say, in Russia, where they speak of the conservatives who want to restore Stalinism. What we want to retain is understandings having to do with the division of power politically, and other understandings having to do with the recognition of two cities – the city of God and the city of man – as coexisting in modern society and each commanding a loyalty.

Many might regard your conservatism as a natural consequence of being rich. Is there any reason why a poor man should be a conservative?

I should think so. The value of conservative arrangements to a rich man

is *pari passu* valuable also to a poor man. A poor man suffers much more than a rich man from inflation, for instance, and a poor man has a much greater chance to change his own status in a society with the upward mobility the conservatives emphasize. Nineteen per cent of the people in the lowest quintals in America moved to different quintals during the 1980s, which is a significant achievement. We're talking about a society in which, by current standards of poverty, 90 per cent of the American people were poor in 1900, a figure that has reduced to somewhere between 13 and 14 per cent. That shows a tremendous upward mobility, which obviously caused a broad prosperity to a lot of people who didn't have it. But just as you can go up, so you obviously have a chance to go down. Now, if you say that rich people are better off than poor people, I'd say that's so obvious it's hardly worth commenting on. But if I may say so, there seems to be more interest in genuine upward mobility in America than there is in Britain.

But do the rich become richer and the poor poorer?

No, it's not true. I had an interesting argument on this point with Kenneth Galbraith's son, who said that, in nineteenth-century England, the disparity between the most and the least rich was greater even than in America today. The answer to your question is that more people are getting richer, but there is a compensating elevation in the lowest quintal. What you really have is a structure to be compared with a mobile, a string to which various things attach. The whole string goes up. There is no other way to account for a reduction from 90 per cent to 13 per cent in the poor over a period of ninety years, and that 13 per cent reduces to 10 per cent when you take into account the market value of perquisites or necessities handed over by the state. The static analysis from which liberals tend to suffer is the assumption that, every time you earn one dollar, somebody else loses one dollar. It doesn't work that way. If you earn one dollar, it's likely that somebody else is also going to earn a dollar.

Milton Friedman says he's no longer willing to say that there's no such thing as a free lunch, this being the aphorism most associated with Miltonic economics. The reason he's not now willing to say it is that, if I give you a sweater in exchange for a shoe, we're both better off. Applying that dynamic analysis as distinct from the static analysis, you find a general elevation of standards. Obviously there are lacunae, but these don't affect the secular drifts.

You and Galbraith are friends, yet the public perception is that you are miles apart politically.

The common ground is civility, geniality. The public perception that

we're miles apart is exactly correct; he would be the first to emphasize it and I would be the next. If Kenneth's views had prevailed in American policy during the past forty-five years, first, we'd be broke, and secondly, we'd be a Soviet satellite. But he happens to be a wonderful writer, a wonderful friend, wonderfully genial, very gifted, and has a nice sense of humour, therefore I delight in his company.

It seems you have made only one attempt to enter active politics, when you stood for mayor of New York.

I stood for mayor only to make pedagogical points. I was never a candidate in any serious sense. In fact I predicted that my vote would be one per cent or less the day I announced my candidacy, but it was an opening to ventilate points of view that I had been ventilating for a number of years through other media. If, from time to time, through direct political exposure, you can get free access to the media to put forward points of view, it doesn't make sense to turn it down. It can't happen frequently. For that reason I ran, but I considered it then, and still do, to be an act of criticism rather than an act of political candidacy. In Britain someone can be simultaneously a critic and a politician, but not here. Here we have no safe seats.

Is the impression accurate that the very talented tend not to enter politics and that consequently our lives are ruled and shaped by the best of the mediocre?

I think it is, but I'm not entirely certain that this is upsetting. If one makes the general commitment to democracy that most of us are prepared to make, one has to recognize the virtue of temporizing. The intellectual and the very gifted man tends in the direction of hubris, total self-absorption and the conviction of his own correctness. For that reason he is probably a little less flexible than a democratic politician ought to be. I know that I always have to guard in *National Review* against judging a politician against the pragmatic measure, because the tendency is to insist that the paradigm is the correct way to judge him, and if you do that, you are engaged in the politics of evangelism, and that isn't very productive. You do get extraordinary figures that come in, but they tend to be extraordinary with reference to criteria other than those which singled out a Churchill or a Lincoln. Nixon is an extraordinary man. Reagan is an extraordinary man. Yet they are extraordinary in a strictly political context. They wouldn't be extraordinary in an academic context, or in most other secular contexts. So you do find among your so-called mediocrities remarkable men.

It sometimes seems that the politician able to give the best performance on television is the one who wins the day.

There is no question that a lack of success on television can be critical. One doesn't necessarily have to be telegenic, but if one repels on television, then that puts a quietus on a political career, even as it would in Hollywood. Most American voters get their news from television. You may have seen the recently published report that fifty per cent of voters did not know the name of the vice-presidential candidate on a Democratic ticket. Pretty disappointing. So the capacity of television to influence public opinion is a thousand times as high as any preceding competitor, and that works, I think, mostly against the common weal. Demagogy tends to attract more attention than statesmanship. Therefore I would guess that, given the rapidity with which the public can be influenced, it can more easily be influenced in a negative than a positive direction.

Has there been a degradation? The philosophical and political argument here tends to centre on the constitutional amendment that changed the composition of the Senate. After 1912, the responsibility devolved from the legislators to the people. Ken Galbraith is very insistent that the quality of the Senate is improved. I tend to resist that, making, however, a concession for the fifty years after the end of the Civil War when senators were very much the creatures of big-business bullies who were buying up legislators. But if I were to take the period between 1800 and 1850 and the period between 1900 and 1950, I would certainly prefer the quality of the first to the second. My reason is that the sense of security that came with being selected by the legislators – allowing you to have a name for yourself and be less dependent on whim – encouraged people of a certain character to think of themselves in the Roman sense as having a patriarchal responsibility to discharge. Remember that, in those days, people didn't think of politics as a full-time career. There were a few like Clay and Calhoun Webster who did, but it was a little bit *infra dig*. As a matter of fact, when Lincoln wondered whether he would go back to Congress, he actually consulted his friends about whether it would ruin his reputation to look so greedy as to want to go to Congress for a second term. A single term was considered about right, but certainly not three or four terms. Now it's a vocation.

In what important respects does American conservatism differ from the conservatism of the British Conservative government?

Conservatives in the British government are much more influenced by class than we are. In America we conservatives tend to welcome changes which would cause a little alarm in Britain. Here, if we find out, let's say, that sixty-five per cent of the upper quintal have arisen from the

third quintal or the second quintal in the past generation, we would feel that is terrific. No corresponding sense of pleasure communicates itself to me from reading the British press. That's one reason why Thatcher is not really all that popular with the old-time Conservatives in Great Britain, who think of themselves as guardians of a perpetual caste into which only a certain rash of newcomers is welcome.

How do you evaluate Mrs Thatcher?

I'm very much in favour of Mrs Thatcher. I was an early enthusiast. It's true of her, as it is of anybody who is around that long, that they develop, and what was once a rather amusing mannerism becomes a horrible affectation. So certain of her traits – and I'm talking now not only only about personality but about her traits as a leader – rasp in a sense that they didn't five years ago. But she has been a clear and positive leader, her priorities have been acceptable, and she has moved with uneven but general success in their direction. Inflation and unemployment are now going down a little bit, so I think history will think of her as somebody who did a lot to revitalize an economy that had lost a lot of faith in itself.

Many would say that the problem with Mrs Thatcher is that she doesn't appear to have compassion.

They're right. She doesn't. Interestingly enough, the same charge has been made against Ronald Reagan, even though he is an effective populist speaker in a way she is not. I have found it extremely difficult, in my personal experience, to know the extent to which somebody is compassionate generally from their public behaviour. I know men and women who seem icy cold but they are very philanthropic, but she doesn't give an impression of being one of those.

She had a very good working relationship with Reagan. The same chemistry doesn't seem to operate with Bush.

That's probably because Thatcher and Reagan thought of themselves as compelled by an ideological appetite to reorient their countries in a direction they thought correct. They were missionaries. George Bush is not a missionary, he is a consolidator. Thatcher and Reagan said that their countries had been going in the wrong direction for a number of years and they'd got to do something real fast to turn them around. That created an affinity of purpose compounded by what turned out to be a rather unexpected affinity of temperament, for they're very different people, she so precise and meticulous, he sort of sprawly and communicative almost by osmosis sometimes. Yet I know from conversations

that there was a genuine sense of I like her and I think she likes me. That was absolutely genuine. It was not put up for public display.

As to which of them was dominant, Reagan's a very subtle creature in that he tends to agree as a matter of manners but two weeks later will simply take his own course. The notion that Reagan was a creature of other people's thinking is historically incorrect. I'm not saying that he wasn't influenced in the general sense in which everybody's influenced, but he genuinely made up his own mind. Once, when he was briefing the congressional leaders at six o'clock while American parachutists were in the air, Mrs Thatcher came on the line and said, 'Ronald, I've done a lot of thinking about the situation in Granada, and we must do nothing for at least three months.' He said, 'You're quite right, Margaret,' but he was moved exclusively by the possibility that the Cubans were listening in to the conversation. He wasn't going to have American paratroopers shot down by Cuban fighter planes. Her feelings were hurt on that occasion. She was rumpled. However, that would be an example of his giving her the general impression that she was the dominant figure in any action, when in fact he was perfectly prepared to act.

Is the 'special relationship' fact or myth today?

I think it's a fragile fact. It's a fact that we speak the same language, that we haven't warred against each other for 150 years, and the slight geographical isolation of Great Britain, gives it just that little detachment from continental embroglios that makes for an affinity with our much more general geographical isolation. It is fragile in the sense that we are the great super-power and Britain is one no longer, yet Britain considers itself in almost every respect brighter than America: more stable, more mature, more at home with democratic institutions, and more at home with the stability of the caste or semi-caste system; which causes a certain amount of friction. Now the Brits are prepared to make certain broad concessions. For instance, in the new introduction to the OED they concede that all the important work of a lexicographical character is being carried on by Americans and recognize the great resources of America. But with that recognition goes a very considerable contempt for what are considered distinctively American manners, vulgarities, excesses, violence, so that the admiration that makes for the special relationship with America is a detached admiration and one that its really condescending. Still, it's useful and practicable and is to be encouraged. It occasionally figures very strongly, as, for instance, during the high point of the Macmillan-Kennedy association.

Is the British Conservative party right to resist the level of freedom of information you now have in America?

Yes, it is. I oppose the idea that an extension of democratic government presupposes instant familiarity with details of government which are not crucial to the general understanding. Your fifty-year rule strikes me as much more sensible than our overnight rule. Our overnight rule, of course, has limitations, but we have been permitted, for example, to read conversations by Richard Nixon which are useful to the Trollopes of this world but I wouldn't say were useful in enhancing a kind of alarmed and democratic society in which, while acknowledging that certain things go on, some measure of satisfaction should be taken in the fact that that knowledge is not documented every day. To read fifty or thirty years after Churchill's death about some of his unattractive vanities is, I think, a satisfaction to which I'm entitled as someone who is historically curious, but I do not feel that democracy functions better by having a freedom of information that could have told me about Churchill's private conversations while he was still living and contending for office. So privacy has a public usefulness which is, I would say, better guarded in your country than in mine.

The practice as opposed to the theory of conservative values in Britain seems to have entailed poverty at the level of living in cardboard boxes and beggars in the street. How is that to be avoided in a conservative scheme of things?

My information is different from yours. My information is that in Great Britain the thinking political class recognizes that England is subsidizing on a perpetual basis an indolent non-working class and chooses to do so rather than stoke up economic energy. We had that attitude here and there, towards Appalachia, for instance. I once wrote, thirty years ago, that John F. Kennedy went to West Virginia and guaranteed the coalminers that they could continue to not make coal for a living – which was what it amounted to. I see that happening on a much larger scale in Britain. It brings about a certain tranquillity: we'll have ten per cent unemployed and we'll just bear the burden. Now I may be completely misinformed, but if so, so are some of my English friends who have told me that this is pretty well the way it's going. I happen to think it's wrong for psychological reasons, and it's obviously wrong for economic reasons because somebody who is unproductive is not adding to the common pool. I tend to be enough of a puritan to believe that people really aren't satisfied unless they're producing something. It can be an intangible, like mother love, they're producing, but it has to be something. And the answer, of course, is that to get movement going in that direction, you've got to put the people on the assembly line towards productivity.

They've got to find this out in East Germany very soon, because that engine is going to be pushing right at them in a way it's not going to

push in Romania or Poland, which both have a more lackadaisical habit. In East Germany, with $125 billion invested in the equalization of the mark, people are going to find out that a working day is much closer to eight hours than three. *Mutatis mutandis.* Applying that to Great Britain, you would certainly simply not tolerate the perpetual dole without some effort to cause people to seek out work where work's available. By American standards the British are lazy. Not by Indian standards, or East European standards, but then even the Japanese are lazy by American standards.

Has your Catholicism had a significant effect on your political thinking?

I hope so. Catholicism, somebody once said, has everything to say about some things and something to say about everything. I don't think that's true. I don't think it has much to say about peanut butter. But I think that a believing Christian always has a second perspective. I'm going to write a book the year after next on why I'm still a Catholic, and by my standards, I will spend a fair amount of time on it. It's a faith that I have never attempted to conceal. I think it's simply incorrect to wed that faith to particularities of political positions. For instance, the notion that we should stand up under all circumstances against the Soviet Union is highly rooted in my belief in Christianity, and I quarrelled very openly with the bishops who argued against a nuclear deterrent, and quarrelled with the Pope on that silly speech he gave on capitalism in Mexico. But on the big issues – the incorrectness of a political society attempting to occupy the place of God – I think that's a very liberating concept.

Have I ever been disillusioned with Catholicism? I've often been disillusioned about what the Catholic Church has done or not done, but if you mean have I ever felt a weakening of faith, well, I lie down until I get over it. Christians call it grace. And grace is not earned, it's adventitious.

In your new introduction to God and Man at Yale, *you suggest that the interests of the state and those of civilization were sometimes at odds. What brought you to this conclusion?*

I think it was the indecision of prominent American universities to act in the way that Swiss universities had acted during the crisis of 1948 over Czechoslovakia, or as they did subsequently in Hungary. There were affirmations by the faculties denouncing this new act of Soviet oppression and servitude, whereas we were bound by the protocols of academic freedom against that kind of action. I remember the president of Yale never spoke to me again after that. He was a classicist, became a baseball commissioner, and died tragically of a heart attack a couple

of years ago. He declined to permit the Yale University Glee Club to sing in a one-hour ceremony celebrating the birthday of Solidarity, on the grounds that it would commit the university to a political cause. I thought that so flatulent and silly that I was provoked to write that book, which amusingly enough is referred to as my novel in the current *Spectator*. You can see how serious that interviewer's research was. The offence I took that provoked this book was a John Stuart Millsian notion that, as long as one believed in a position, one could not consider that position as having been fatally condemned. It would mean presumably that if one person believed the genocide against the Jews in Germany was excusable, one must consider that an open position. I thought that nihilistic.

The notion that a student going to Yale oughtn't to be helped in the direction of civilized thought but is told there is no distinction between the Declaration of Independence and the *Communist Manifesto* as to which is the more virtuous, the more enlightened instrument, I find more of a pose than a serious and thoughtful position. They took the view that any position taken by a faculty was not of anyone's concern. That may be true in graduate school, where you're hiring a researcher, but an undergraduate school should undertake to teach some of those values which were learned by a civilization after very hard work and to assume that a society doesn't have an interest in projecting what it has developed over two millennia is simply dereliction of duty.

How does one apply in the political arena principles derived from faith?

Well, you don't. It is not a simple exercise. If there are certain things you shouldn't do, you've got to ask yourself why should you not do them and who said not. Kant can plead his autonomous idea of ethics, but overwhelmingly we are taught these are religious prescriptions, whether under the Koran, the Talmud, the Old Testament or the New Testament. Certain kinds of behaviour are not tolerated. You have to refine the question a long way to decide whether you have crossed that line, but to be preoccupied with that exercise is the important thing.

What do you feel about the aftermath of Vatican II?

I think it was a terrible mistake. Having said that, I accept Vatican II as probably divinely instituted, but the lengths to which Vatican II has been taken are not the responsibility of Vatican II. For instance, there is nothing in Vatican II that says you should forsake the mass in Latin. There's quite a lot in Vatican II which says you ought not to forsake the mass in Latin. In fact it has been almost universally forsaken. That was the doing of bishops. There's nothing in Vatican II that says the suspension against eating meat on Friday shall end, but it did end. There

seemed to be no constitutional resistance built up in the clergy to these huge changes in the liturgy, and that surprised a great many people. Certainly the notion that the vernacularization of religious language would breed more Catholics is simply wrong – wrong judged against any criterion. The loss of vocations, the laicizations, the diminishing number of people in church stabilized at about sixty per cent of the level of 1963.

What is the chance of unification in the Christian Churches?

Slight, in part because faith has been highly diluted. Paradoxically, I think the unification of the Christian Churches is a development that would more likely come about after a maximization rather than a minimization of faith. To the extent that you become a fervent Methodist, you become a little bit more anti-Catholic than you were before. If you become more pro-Harvard, you become a little bit more anti-Yale. That's true through a certain stage, but if you then reach beyond that stage, your common concern is for the teaching of Christ more than for the denomination differences that divide. We certainly haven't reached that latter stage, and we're not far advanced into the second stage. There still are denominational enthusiasts. Southern baptists in America are one example. The Mormons would be another.

Does the new religious fundamentalism in America and what might be called the church of the extreme right worry you?

It doesn't worry me at all. In the first place, the so-called extreme-right fundamentalism was the workaday understanding of America throughout most of my life. I had the big deal in the moral majority on my programme, begging to find out what it is that I could be furious with him about. Did he believe in persecuting homosexuals? No; but he didn't believe a homosexual should teach in a situation in which peer pressure was an aspect. Well, I agree with that. Pretty soon I found myself thinking, what is it that these people want that Americans think of as extreme? It suddenly occurred to me. What they think of as extreme is what we totally accepted up until I was about forty-five or fifty years old – you know, people had a right to teach religion in schools, if it was acceptable to the community; pornography was not available at the local kiosk; commercial establishments were closed on Sunday. All that stuff considered absolutely preposterous was absolutely routine and acceptable right up until 1955, 1965, so I'm not in the least worried about it.

A lot of people regard sex as the motivating force in their lives, whereas the Catholic Church regards it as a means of procreation, not to be used for gratification.

What you say is not so in the Catholic Church. The Church has no ban against sexual congress during pregnancy. To say that procreation's a primary objective of the sexual act is no different from saying that the primary purpose of eating is to stay alive. It is, but that isn't mostly why you and I eat. We have to do that to stay alive, but that doesn't dictate in the least our appetite for cuisine. I would say it's rather healthy of the Church to the extent that it indirectly attempts to diminish the sex act as the principal Freudian compulsion in one's life. Individuals are often moved primarily by the sexual drive, but (a) it doesn't mean they ought to be, (b) it doesn't mean they can't be persuaded from being so. After all, there are celibate orders that are very successful, and it by no means suggests that subordinating the sexual drive is to deprive it of importance or that there isn't great joy and gratification to be got from it.

But isn't it a fact that the Church appears to begrudge sexual gratification?

On the surface it gives that impression, especially, for instance, in the *Humani Vitae* encyclical where it suggests that, if you're not willing to run the risk of pregnancy, you ought not to have sex. In that respect it certainly does. But it's simply not practised, even by Catholics who have no reluctance about going to communion.

At one point you were part of the CIA, which has had a bad press over the years in connection with such events as the murder of Allende in Chile.

Criticism of the CIA should restrict itself to things it didn't do well, but I don't think it ought to be criticized for anything it may have sought to do. In my judgement, the historical records are very clear that the assassination of Allende had nothing to do with the CIA. I've written nine novels about the CIA, and if I had to summarize in a sentence what I sought to say in them, it would be that, in an apocalyptic world, the nature and mandate of counter-intelligence is a moral need which can't be quantified. I mean by that that certain challenges arise which require and indicate the advisability of a certain action being taken which cannot discreetly be applauded. An assassination, for instance. Supposing you have Idi Amin, who's got hold of an atom bomb, and the CIA in the field finds out that at midnight he's going to dispatch a bomber with instructions to drop it over Jerusalem. The CIA man says he's got a man there with a sniper rifle. Does he pull the trigger and abort the mission? If I were the US president, I would tell him to go

ahead and do so, but under no circumstances would I, as a theorist, ask you to come up with a set of conditions under which it is OK to order a private assassination, because there are too many imponderables to make it possible to quantify such a thing satisfactorily. For that reason, I think counter-intelligence is an art form and has to be judged more pragmatically than aprioristically.

There are people all over the world who are astonished by an American government committed to democracy at home yet seemingly eager to league itself with the most repressive dictatorships.

There's absolutely no question that the containment policy of the United States invited abuse. There are even jokes about it: the president of Venezuela in 1956 is told that he doesn't qualify for more US aid than he is getting because he isn't enough of a communist problem, so he goes out and imports communists. At a more serious level, I've always found very liberating a distinction drawn by Senator Fulbright, and he was speaking from the other side of the political fence from my own when he said it. He said that the American government has no proper quarrel against the practices of any government in the world; however odious, unless it is a government trying to export its policies. I apply that, for instance, to the landing of the marines in the Dominican Republic in 1965 on the orders of Lyndon Johnson. Lyndon Johnson was convinced that Juan Bosch was going to make the Dominican Republic another Cuba. So the marines landed there, cleaned that situation up, but ignored entirely the western half of Hispaniola where Papa Doc was torturing people to death every night. We don't have the power to follow the Wilsonian mandate of making all the world safe for democracy. The logical distinction is to contain aggressive hideosities, such as the Soviet Union has been foremost in committing during the past forty years, and that seems a clean division on the relevant responsibilities of the state.

What about the moral dimension, especially where one is preaching morality in one's own country?

I'm glad you use the word preaching. The American people have very definite moral responsibility. John Quincey Adams said the American people are friends of liberty everywhere but custodians only of their own. He said that in 1828, so he was reminding us that we are for good people everywhere, but can't and don't have the power to take responsibility for them. For instance, I'm very sympathetic to the idea of any American who refuses to buy any product from South Africa. It may be mistaken as a matter of policy, but I'm sympathetic with the idea. I'm totally unsympathetic with the American government

attempting to boycott South Africa. There they are violating the Fulbright distinction in a way that is impractical and wrong. So the moral impulse to preach, inveigh and hector is and ought to be exactly that: a moral backed by whatever economic power an individual has, expressed usually through boycotts.

Yet it sometimes seems to the outside world that no degree of violence or repression is enough to cut off American aid.

It happens in part, I suppose, because of a notion that we recognize *de facto* power. If Perón is in charge of Argentina, we do business with Argentina. This is in part because that's the way nations work. It's also in part because there are mutual interests. We want to import certain Argentinian things; they want to import certain American things; so the question becomes, is the United States going to stand in the way of this exchange? In fact we're required under law to pass judgement once a year against individual countries as to whether they are or are not free. If a country is not free, the president must suspend all aid to that country unless, in the exercise of his judgement, it is strategically necessary to override this recommendation. They can go farther and have what they call state-specific prohibitions, which are levied against South Africa, against Vietnam, against Korea – countries with which even the president doesn't have the power to authorize trade. This strikes me as a not ill-considered way of doing things, as long as the president does retain the power in ambiguous cases to continue to do business. For instance, our handling of Pinochet's situation in Chile, however long his reign, was I think sensible. Chile regraduated into a democratic situation. There was damage done, but in historical terms, not huge. It was a comparable state to Franco's Spain. It would have been very wrong to have attempted to slow down the economic rejuvenation of Chile, which made its return to democracy likelier.

Have the lessons of Vietnam been adequately learned by America?

I don't think they have. I wrote a piece recently in which I said that President Bush, in going slowly on Lithuania, is probably correct in saying he is reflecting the will of the American people. I think he is making a mistake, strategic and moral, but he is undoubtedly influenced by Vietnam: that is, if the American people aren't a hundred per cent behind you, don't do it. The lesson of Vietnam is incompletely learned in part because it became so complicated along the line. The relevant school of thought was, if you want to win the war you can do it, but be tough. The second school of thought was that there was no way to win the war because it was a war that pitted you against indigenous forces. And the third was, it's a war you should never have gotten into

in the first place. A little bit of each of these lingers in the American mind. They haven't sorted it out, nor are they likely to, given the recent retrenchment of the communist empire.

At the time of Vietnam, I felt we should get on with it, and I felt it important for two reasons. No. 1, strategic, and no. 2, that our commitment to Vietnam, having been made by three presidents in such unmistakable accents, meant that the credibility of America's guarantees everywhere in the world was very much at risk. Every guarantee that we made in NATO could in the future be held to be of no account, given our failure to make good our guarantees to Vietnam. What we tried to do, in effect, was blame it on Vietnam: they were the ones that collapsed, we didn't desert them. In fact we did desert them.

Oh, yes, I do believe it was a war we could have won. And I believe it all the more now. It is increasingly documented that the war against Vietnam was against an invading force. The notion that it was a war against an indigenous force is simply incorrect. It became increasingly a war against an indigenous force as communist pressures against the peasants began to work. If you start executing everybody who doesn't co-operate with you, you get a lot of co-operation. There were a lot of Lidice operations that took place in South Vietnam, but the time to move would have been very early, in 1965, 1966. After that it became progressively difficult. But the great risk was China. We now know that China would have welcomed an American victory, but, of course, neither Lyndon Johnson nor Nixon was willing to bank on that, and therefore we exercised certain restraints we would not have exercised otherwise.

What led you to the imaginative work of writing fiction?

What led me specifically was an offer of a contract by a publisher. I had no reason whatsoever to suppose I could do it successfully, but I didn't want to do it on a gamble of which I was the only creditor. Therefore they gave me an advance on the following terms: I would send them the first 100 pages. If they liked what they read, they would guarantee the full advance. If they didn't, I'd keep one third. They did like it and it was a bestseller. That was *Saving the Queen*.

One reviewer spoke of Saving the Queen *as 'a hotchpotch of snobbery and twaddle'. Are you wounded by such criticism?*

Criticism like that would not wound me, because it's utterly incorrect. If it was subtle criticism and I thought it correct, that would very much arrest me. But I'm utterly unaffected by criticism that I think is motivated either by ignorance or malice. I pay no attention at all.

Your book Overdrive *was attacked by critics and readers, not on literary grounds but more for the personality that came across. Even friends like John Leonard called it a piece of self-indulgence. You seemed unaware of the offence such a book might cause. Was it a miscalculation? Did you regret it? Were you chastened by the experience?*

No to all of those. It was self-indulgent in the sense that it was easy to write in terms of research required, but it was bought by the *New Yorker*, where it was thought to be an interesting book. I had a tremendous amount of mail, all of which was very gratifying.

As one of the top journalists in the United States, your column is syndicated to over 300 publications. Journalists often see themselves as opinion makers, but can they form opinion in any real sense?

I don't think you can form opinion, but what you can do is open doors. I'll give you a recent example: how to handle drug policy. When I wrote *The Unmaking of a Mayor*, I was resolute that drugs should be proscribed. In the past eight to ten years I've come to the conclusion that it wouldn't work. Now, this is very different from coming to a position saying I had no right to proscribe them. I continue to reserve the right to proscribe, but empirically I'm instructed this doesn't work, so I have been talking in the last few years about examining the possibility of legalizing drugs under certain circumstances. What I have done is not so much form opinion as open a door to ventilate that alternative to people who might not otherwise examine it.

Have you reached a stage in life where, because people expect you to say something controversial, you do it for effect?

No, I haven't reached that stage, because I have a *Weltanschauung* and certainly won't spend any part of my life trying to make an awkward fit. If I take a position simply to be mischievous and am forever asked to integrate that opinion in that *Weltanschauung*, it would cause me much more pain than the momentary satisfaction I got from it the day before. So I just don't do it.

A lot of Jewish voters in the United States identify the right with anti-Semitism. Was that a factor when you ran for mayor of New York?

That's an interesting question. It's certainly a factor that, in 1965, the Jewish vote was very anti-conservative. I think three per cent of Jews voted for me – a very small percentage. I would guess that the automatic assumption in the Jewish community that the right was anti-Semitic had begun to attenuate around the late 1950s. We had something to do with that in *National Review*. By 1965, I don't think it was by any means

the universal conviction. In 1965 maybe a third or a half of the Jews thought there was a lurking anti-Semitism in the American right, but no more.

But was there an anti-Semitism in the American right?

I would say yes, among older people. You see, the cultural anti-Semitism, which was almost universal, was killed among middle-aged and younger people by Hitler, but persevered among those in their seventies. My father, for instance, was a cultural anti-Semite, and so, I hate to say, was just about everybody. But that, I think, was simply turned around by the experience of 1942–5 among people in whom it was not so deeply set.

Are you at all optimistic about peace in the Middle East?

I'm not an optimist. It seems to me that we aren't really any closer to a natural solution than we were three years ago, and the unsettled state of Israeli politics makes a movement there extremely problematical. I predict at least another four to five years of stalemate. After that I can see one of two things happening: either Israel, through a sheer sense of fatigue, attempts to come to a solution, or the Arab states in effect abandon the whole Palestinian cause on the grounds that it costs them too much time and effort, and the Palestinians become a nomadic people. The existing animosity is extremely expensive and time-consuming, and if there's no sense of progress, it might simply go in a different direction. Now obviously there are factors that are weighing in on the scene. The great Israeli nightmare has been that the Arabs would simply exceed them in population, which is the source of Rabbi Kahane's party. That seems to be temporarily relieved by the present prospect of 500,000 Jews coming in from the Soviet Union, which should greatly help redress that balance within Israel. But it's not going to bring about the kind of comity people want. A lot depends too on the attitude of the younger generation.

Are you sympathetic to the Palestinians' plight?

Totally. A people as well defined culturally, historically and ethnically as they are is entitled to a homeland. Israel is by no means uniquely to blame for them not having one. I think Hussein's most to blame for not having acted between 1948 and 1967. My impression is that most Jews agree with the Palestinians having a homeland, but they want to make absolutely certain that homeland doesn't become a threat to their own survival.

Your proposal in the New York Times *that, to stop the spread of Aids,*

victims should be tattooed on upper forearm and buttocks, produced a predictable outcry, but your biographer suggests you delighted in the resultant tempest.

Not at all. This is one of the thousand instances in which dear John Judis didn't exercise elementary perspective. In the first place, it came from an open conversation between me and Alan Dershowitz, a professor of law from Harvard. The question was how do you protect people who are uncontaminated from people who are contaminated and know they are? He said, well, the way, of course, was to prosecute them, make it a felony for anybody to have sex or exchange blood, exchange needles, share needles if they knew they were contaminated. I said that's hardly going to help the uncontaminated community because, by the time you prosecute, those people are going to be dead anyway. I went on to say that presumably you've got to have some way of warning the uncontaminated person that this other person has this communicable disease. In the old days there was a sort of smallpox mark that made it easy for nurses or doctors to know you had had a smallpox vaccination, so I suggested you might, for instance, have tiny tattoo marks. This was interpreted as wanting to tattoo people who had the disease for purposes of exhibitionism. My only motive was to give them a mark which could be inspected in private by somebody who might then be spared. But after I saw the fuss, I said, OK, I withdraw it, because people who can't distinguish between the use of barbed wire in Auschwitz and barbed wire to keep cows away from bulls can't distinguish between the use of a tattoo to damn somebody and the use of it to save somebody. I wonder how many people would be alive today who are now dead because my idea wasn't accepted.

In 1971 you pretended you had a further set of Pentagon papers. Why did you indulge in a game like that when in it was something you couldn't sustain for more than a few days?

It was to make a particular point. Reading the Pentagon papers we were convinced that there were other papers that were not exhibited, and the idea came to me, let's forge these papers, simply make them up. I couldn't have believed they would be so successful. I had six papers, for instance, ostensibly addressed or written to Admiral Radford, and when he read them he said, 'I don't remember these in particular, but I can't say they're not true.' In that sense it was almost dangerously successful. Whereas I had thought it would last about six hours, it lasted five days before I finally had a press conference. But I perhaps overproved my case, because attention turned to the scandal rather than to the pedogogical point we were attempting to make.

Were you shocked when the truth about Nixon became apparent?

By the time the truth became apparent I was not surprised at all. I thought the accumulation of evidence, showing he was implicated, had become overwhelming. I came out in favour of his resignation five months before the so-called burning tape. George Bush, then head of the Republican party, and I made a gentlemanly bet: George Bush said that Nixon would still be in office at the end of the year, I that he would not. Gerald Ford swore on my programme that Nixon was innocent nine days before he became president, so that was the part of the loyalist wing of the Republican party that, in my opinion, refused to see the evidence.

We spoke about your admiration for Ronald Reagan, but your biographer, John B. Judis, writes: 'Privately Buckley despaired over Reagan and the last years of his term', and goes on to suggest that you thought the Iran-Contra scandal 'incapacitated' Reagan. Was this a temporary crisis of faith or did your view of Reagan change radically?

I thought the Iran-Contra mess a terrible lapse in Reagan's own record. Irrespective of his not having had personal knowledge of the details, that it should have happened in his administration was definitely a blight on his record. But I don't remember ever saying that this caused a revision in my general attitude towards Reagan. I think he was incapacitated from November 1986 until the general pick-up in his popularity began about twelve months later. On account of that, 1987 was a lost year for Reagan.

You are regarded as an opponent of so-called women's liberation. Why?

The part of the feminist movement that upsets me is a part which urges an indiscrimination that is *extra natura*. To suggest that men and women are in every sense equal is in my judgement correct before the law and in terms of opportunity, but it's absolutely incorrect to suggest they are organically equal. Men and woman are just different. It has nothing to do with equality. Under the circumstances, a certain attitude towards women is logical and appropriate, and that includes a disposition to agree that certain occupations aren't appropriate to women. I don't think women in trenches is a civilized idea. And, as an aesthetic matter, I hate the approach towards genderless nouns such as 'chairperson'. The disappearance of the masculine as doing double gender duty is an aesthetic affront against literature.

Many American men, as compared with European men, seem dominated by their wives. What is the principal reason?

I think what you say is right if you compare it to Europe. I'm not sure it's all that right compared to England. At least, my impression is that there are henpecked men in England as there are here. American women tend to be more strident in marriage. Americans are more outspoken at every level, and there's no reason why that shouldn't be so among American women. But the nature of marriage imposes more natural commitments on the man than on the women. It's a very stupid man who doesn't take fully into account what his wife wants to do, but a marriage tends to be unsuccessful when the sense of authority is so disputed that there isn't a natural dominance by the woman over certain aspects of the marriage, or by the man over certain other aspects of the marriage.

Isn't the movement for the renewal of the idea of family unity doomed to fail in a modern context?

No. It's having a hard time, but marriage as an institution has been rediscovered in America. In the last two or three years, liaisons that would otherwise have tended to be simply that, have ended in marriage; so there continues to be in civil and religious marriage some sense of satisfaction that apparently couples don't get from cohabitation. There are a lot of civil accretions around cohabitation that may have something to do with influencing matters in one direction or the other, but by and large the idea of marriage continues to exercise a certain romance and a certain sense of security.

What do you see as the basic cultural differences between America and Europe?

The basic cultural difference is a completely different historical tradition. The memory of the European is much longer than the memory of the American. America is far more transient in its habits. I read somewhere that, on the anniversary of the liberation of France, somebody asked a farmer what life had been like under the Nazis. He said, 'Very bad, very bad,' then paused and added, 'but nothing like what it was under the Swedes in the seventeenth century. That was terrible.' That kind of thing is amusing to an American. We couldn't remember conditions fifty years ago, let alone three hundred years ago. The distillation of tradition in Europe is responsible for attitudes, loyalties and hostilities that tend to wash out more in America.

In 1984 you met Neil Kinnock, whose views on nuclear disarmament you found naïve. Have your own views changed in the light of Mr Gorbachev's initiative on disarmament?

Not at all. They've been reinforced. If Mr Kinnock had had his way

and other countries had imitated him, there's no reason at all to suppose that Gorbachev would have released Eastern Europe. He would have had every incitement to do the contrary and to renew the passionate goal to subjugate Europe. And Kinnock would not repeat today the arguments he used then, because he knows, among other things, that they lost him an election.

Might the trend towards disarmament in the Soviet Union reinforce the perception of those who see America as the greater threat to world peace?

It's so Orwellian in its stupidity to suppose that we are a threat to Europe that it's hard to answer on a rational level people who make the charge. God knows, a lot of them do. I simply have to believe there are Europeans – I've not met them – who think the United States has a dark design to subjugate Europe or start a war because wars are such fun. They must exist, but they can't occupy me intellectually because the idea is so perverse. When we called the Reagan administration's contemplation of an arms agreement with the Soviet Union a 'suicide pact', we were much concerned about getting talked into a situation in which a credible nuclear deterrent no longer existed. That threat has not disappeared. As Richard Perle has said, the Russians are angling to get a situation in Europe from this total *détente* which they haven't succeeded in getting in forty years: the absence of the nuclear deterrent commanded by NATO.

With the prospect of German unification, the collapse of the Iron Curtain and the emergence of Japan as an economic super-power, do you see American influence waning in the world?

Yes, I do. After the war we were consuming fifty per cent of international production. That's already cut in half. The *Economist* reminds us that we are still the most productive nation. It takes the American thirty-one minutes to make what it takes the Japanese an hour to make. So we've got a lot of resources, but it's true that we're very self-indulgent and the young generation is not being taught to work hard enough or to learn industriously. You can't be all that optimistic about the *per capita* competitive situation between a country whose schoolchildren work three hours a week on homework and a country whose schoolchildren work thirty hours a week.

You are said to have a long-running feud with Gore Vidal, who characterized you as 'the Marie Antoinette of politics'.

It's not really a long-running feud since I haven't mentioned his name in twenty years, nor he mine that I know of. The reference is to an

exchange we had on television in 1968, followed by a law suit. His case was thrown out of court; mine was sustained. I then accepted damages and an apology from *Esquire* magazine for publishing his piece, but I wrote a long essay on that whole episode, published it in 1969 and said I wouldn't speak any more about it.

I have seen it suggested that you are most disliked, not for your views, but for the figure you cut; for applying conservatism 'with the fastidious grace of a Regency man against a mantelpiece'.

I don't give much time to that because I am as I am. Judis talked to a lot of people who knew me when I was ten years old, and none of them charge that between ten and thirty I tried to ape anybody or anything. I had a cosmopolitan education, for which I had no responsibility. I too have read this business about me, as being a conservative, casting a sort of non-proletariat figure. I don't know how I capitalized on it, except by here and there writing autobiographical essays acknowledging how I live. If you drive round in a limousine, there's no way of disguising it.

Why do you so vigorously oppose the idea of Utopia as an ideal to strive towards?

The idea obviously is to live commendably in the eyes of the Lord. Utopia is not of this world, in my judgement, and I think that we are all going to be judged with some reference to how hard we tried and how honestly we behaved. Given the human predicament, none of us is going to do too well on that, but certainly the struggle ought to be to do as well as you reasonably can.

You've sailed the Atlantic, been down to the Titanic, *have even played the harpsichord in the concert hall. What drives you to do these extraordinary things?*

I've sailed the Atlantic twice and the Pacific once, and will sail it again in November. That's a combination of adventure plus something that I can write a book about. I've sailed all my life. Going down to the *Titanic* was an invitation few people have had, so I didn't think twice about it. Playing the harpsichord is a great strain, because I don't have the time or the natural talent to learn quickly and I'm struggling now with a chromatic fantasy, which is rough. I've played all my life, but only sort of episodically, yet the dream of playing something tolerably well in an exigent situation is a challenge.

Would I be right in thinking that underneath the polemical controversial exterior there is a less self-confident and more mellow William Buckley waiting to get out?

Well, I don't think those are contradictions. A lot of people have observed that my public persona is different from my private persona. All I can say is that, when I appear in public, I try hard not to be demagogic, and a failure to be demagogic may suggest that you don't care about what people think, though obviously I do care. That's why I'm in this business to begin with. Inevitably people are a little bit different in private from the way they are in public. All I can say is that this is not intentional.

Have you any regrets in your life?

No. I can't imagine having elected any other profession. Somebody once said, 'If you had worked in this other direction, might you not have become president of the United States?' The answer is that the chances of it happening are so infinitely small that I really can't take seriously people who plan to be president. That's simply a star falling in a particular direction. And I don't think I'm temperamentally suited to have been one. I'd like to have been one in the sense that I have confidence in my own judgement, so that would have been good. If you feel you know the correct approach, it gives you a lot of confidence. On the other hand, you might feel that in a democracy the correct approach would be politically unpalatable. In that event you'll be frustrated, so you go back to your little typewriter and think, at least I feel I want to be here.

SIR RAYMOND CARR

Raymond Carr was warden of St Antony's College, Oxford from 1968 to 1987. He was born in 1919 and educated at the local state secondary school in Hampshire from where he won a scholarship to Christ Church, Oxford. In 1940 he took a first in modern history and went to teach at Wellington. After the war he was elected to a fellowship of All Souls and in 1953 he became a fellow of New College. From 1964 until 1968 he was director of the Latin American Centre. His special interest in Spain was kindled by the Civil War when he had leanings towards the Republic. His publications include *Spain 1808–1939* (1960), *The Republic and the Civil War in Spain* (1971), and *The Civil War in Perspective* (1977). He married Sara Strickland in 1950 and has three sons and one daughter. He was knighted in 1987.

You were educated at a local state school, from where you got a scholarship to Oxford. How did this influence your views on state education as opposed to private schooling?

I came from a relatively humble background and wanted to escape it. People have a romanticism about working-class life, but the food is appalling, the conversation very limited, and I was determined to get away from it. Getting a scholarship to Oxford from the local state school transformed my life. The extraordinary feature of state education in the 1930s was the unbelievable poverty of resources. My school had no library, for example. I could never have gone to Oxford unless a professor at Southampton University had said I could use the university library. In the library of a state secondary school you had about two books on history. It represented an enormous waste of resources, because I was not the cleverest boy in the school by any means, and it's appalling to think back to people in the 1930s who were extremely clever and who never had a chance. I was the only person from my school ever to go to Oxford. I suppose that's being remedied now, but the intellectual poverty of the state system then, because of its lack of libraries, was incredible.

When I became a master in a public school, as I did after Oxford, the richness of the library struck me as extraordinary. The opportunities that were open to people in the private sector, partly because of the intelligence of the masters and partly because of the extraordinary resources, were what impressed me most. When you look at the library of a school like Eton, it's incomparably better than anywhere else.

You sent your own sons to Eton?

I suppose that was partly my wife's family tradition, partly because they would have better opportunities and partly out of crude snobbery

perhaps. I don't regret it. What Eton seems to have given my son Matthew, who was a rather nervous boy, is a sense of social assurance.

You must have arrived at Christ Church to find it awash with blue blood and privilege, yet by all accounts you took to it like a duck to water.

Christ Church, as you say, was awash with blue blood, but it was socially much more catholic than you would imagine. There was a posse of scholarship boys like myself, and there was the blue-blooded set who could on occasion behave rather badly, but I made a friend in that group very early on – a man now dead, called Simon Asquith – who influenced my life very much. I suppose I did in a way advance socially through him, and what I liked about these blue-bloods was their freedom from the inhibitions which had surrounded me in a puritan upbringing. My father was a low-churchman, and on Sundays I was allowed to read only two books, either *Pilgrim's Progress* or the Bible. He read aloud from the Bible every night. My mother was rather a pagan, and while my father was reading the Bible, she would have some cheap paper romance. She could tell by the tone of my father's voice when he was going to look up, and then she'd stuff her book under the table.

My father is probably more of an influence on me now than he was in his lifetime. We used to have terrible quarrels, mostly about whether or not India should become independent. He was an old-fashioned imperialist, a strong conservative. I had read Tawney's *Religion and the Rise of Capitalism* and become a critic of the capitalist system, as we all were in the 1930s, and this entailed quarrels with my father. In retrospect I've come to admire him, because he was a very upright man. By the late 1930s we had enough money to have a car, and when the war came the car was stored. After the war, some people came round to buy the car and offered him a very high price, but he refused to accept more than he had paid. That has led me, in retrospect, to admire my father's integrity.

My mother would mediate between us. My father and I were alike in having a violent temper and she tried to make us live peaceably together. She was a very simple woman: a post office clerk, later a milliner, and of absolutely straight working-class extraction. She was a Primitive Methodist while my father was an Anglican. My maternal grandfather was a great figure in the local Methodist Church and, as was usual in working-class or lower-middle-class families, he came to live with us. The combination of a Methodist and a Gladstonian Liberal on the one hand and an Anglican and a Conservative on the other made for constant tension in the house on both religious and political grounds, so that was another rather uncomfortable situation my mother had to smooth over, and she was very good at it.

What prompted you to become an historian?

The one bright spot in my secondary school was the history master. I think you'll find something of the kind in the background of most people in my circumstances. He was a very good teacher, a highly intelligent man, and as a result of his influence I took to history and got my scholarship to Oxford.

You graduated in 1940, then continued to teach during the war years. What kept you from joining up?

This also had a deep influence on my life. I was diagnosed as having an incurable heart disease, which made me grade 4, so the army wouldn't have me. At first, I must confess, I was rather relieved, but later one acquired a mixed sense of shame and envy. One felt one had missed out somehow. The reason why I engage in dangerous and semi-dangerous sports now may be because I didn't do what most of my generation did.

What are the main reasons for, or the lessons to be learned from, the professional study of history?

I suppose one can say that certain things can be learned: for example, that revolutions never accomplish what they set out to do, that all revolutions somehow or other go wrong. Take the Cuban revolution. I went to Cuba in the very early 1960s as an enthusiast for Castro's revolution, but after I got there I suddenly realized it was the sort of society where you couldn't say, yes, I support Castro, *but* . . . You had to support him absolutely or not at all. I was very put off by a great mass meeting of Castro's, and what I said about it made me highly unpopular with the left. I'd heard Hitler speak directly, and I couldn't help noticing certain similarities between Castro's oratorical style and Hitler's. With Hitler, for instance, you got these rather long, almost boring passages about steel production or something of the kind, then suddenly there came a terrific crescendo, a denunciation of the Jews. It was the same with Castro. Rather boring stuff about sugar production and then a vast outburst about America, imperialism and the like.

I also saw certain similarities to Franco. I used a phrase, 'the democracy of the *plaza*', which meant that you didn't have representative government but what you had instead was a huge gathering of the people in the square. I was present at Castro's Second Declaration of Havana in the Plaza de Revolución, and this direct contact with the people via the leader addressing the mass as a substitute for representative government struck me as totalitarian. I was the first person to write an article in the *Observer* criticizing Castro because, of course, most of the early coverage was wildly enthusiastic.

There are certain sorts of wide generalization like that – revolutions never succeeding in producing what they want, the French Revolution degenerating into the Terror and finally ending with an autocratic and military leader – but these lessons are so general that they can't, I think, help a statesman, because the circumstances each time put the whole thing in a totally different context. I'd be hard put to it to think of a statesman who's examined history and said he must act in such and such a way. I don't think a direct recipe can be deduced from history.

Can there be truth or objectivity in history?

Absolutely not. The historian, particularly the contemporary historian, is confronted by a vast mass of material. You have to have some selective criteria to bring order into this vast mass of facts, and inevitably your personal prejudices influence the facts you select. All you can do if you're writing as an historian is somehow or other make it clear what your criteria of selection are, so that people know more or less why you're saying the things you say. There isn't such a thing as objective history. Take the greatest historian, Gibbon. Clearly his prejudices are more or less against religion. He had the normal prejudices of a man of the Enlightenment and it is obvious in his writing. Take the way the seventeenth century is treated in English history. You have a clear division between what you might call the Hugh Trevor-Roper school and the Christopher Hill school, and they clearly hold very different views, Trevor-Roper ending up saying that whenever a radical appears you must beat him on the head. The historiography of the French Revolution is completely divided between people who see the revolution as the origin of all progress ever since and those who see it as a dark event which produced instability in France. I don't think there's anything called objective history other than a simple arrangement of facts and dates; beyond that nothing.

Yet if there aren't significant historical truths as distinct from interpretation, doesn't that seemingly reduce history to persuading people to think along this or that ideological line?

Marxism was a predominant influence on history in my generation, until Namier, who said that ideologies don't matter; that people are interested in patronage and power and there is no real ideological division between them. Namier came to be a great influence on my generation with his non-Marxist view of history, but so many historians in the 1930s were Marxist because Marxism offers a very simple way of examining history. Today, of course, nobody takes Marxism seriously and there's a certain empty philosophical space on the left which was, in the 1930s, entirely occupied by some kind of Marxism. Now

historians have no simple model they can plant on history and as a result there is a sort of neo-liberal interpretation.

If you take, for instance, Berlin's views on the Russian Revolution, he thinks there was a real chance of a sort of liberal or quasi-liberal scheme coming out of the revolution but it was ruined by Lenin. Berlin is prepared to say that, if a brick had dropped on Lenin's head, then the course of the Russian Revolution would have been completely different; and I have to admit that I, too, have come to believe much more in the influence of accidents and personality on history than I did when I was young. Take a simple example. The present King of Spain was educated by Franco and brought up by him as his heir and it was inconceivable to imagine that he wouldn't try to keep as much of the *ancien régime* as he could. Instead he became, in the famous phrase, 'the motor of change'. I don't argue that the King of Spain could have stopped the train of democracy, but he could have made its journey much more difficult and messy than it turned out, because after the departure of Franco he was the sole legal power in Spain. It couldn't have altered the course of history because, by the 1970s, Spain had become a consumer society and there's is a relationship perhaps between a consumer society economically and a consumer society politically. All the opinion surveys of late Francoism showed that what the majority of people wanted was what is vaguely called a Western type of democracy, so I don't think the king could have stopped the advance of democracy, but he could have hampered its progress.

Similarly with German history. Even A. J. P. Taylor seems at times to think there is some incurable defect in the German nation which is going to make them turn towards totalitarian solutions, whereas German historians would look on the Hitler régime as an aberration caused by one wicked man and say one can forget it all. Or take the French interpretation of the Second World War. According to certain French school textbooks I have read, the French explain that the war was won by the Americans and the Russians; they make no mention of the fact that, for quite a period, it was only England that was opposing Germany. Clearly a French person looks on the Second World War with totally different eyes from the way a Briton tends to look on it.

Do you see great actions or movements in history as having more significance than great human personalities?

They are very hard to separate. Take Islam. You can't separate the rise of Islam from the personality of Muhammad himself. Even more striking, in the history of Christianity it's very difficult to imagine its development without St Paul, because you can make quite a strong argument for saying it was St Paul who created or modified Christ's fundamentally

Jewish version of religion and created a universal Gentile Christianity. It's difficult to see a movement separate from the people who created it: to separate Calvinism from Calvin, Lutheranism from Luther. It's also perfectly possible to argue that there's nothing particularly original in Marx, that, going back to Aristotle, people have talked about the class struggle as the motor of history and so forth. Yet it's still Marx who somehow or other brings the whole thing together and makes it a creed.

In Eastern Europe now aren't we seeing the movement of the people as opposed to the individual?

That is an interesting example. It really does seem to be a people's revolution against a system which has ceased to work in every conceivable way, economically and ideologically. It is a genuine revolt against a system which has ceased to work, even as the French Revolution was, in a way.

If 1989 was an annus mirabilis, *don't the present political changes reflect not so much the decline of communism as a resurgence of nationalism that could become a threat to Europe's stability?*

I absolutely agree. That old Russian lead umbrella over Europe suppressed these nationalist conflicts, particularly in the Balkans. After all, the two world wars were produced fundamentally by nationalist conflict, and I do think there is a severe danger of minor irredentist problems, particularly in Eastern Europe. I welcome the removal of the Russian umbrella, though it did keep these nationalist conflicts under some sort of control.

Your interest in Spain was kindled by your emotional leaning towards the Republican side in the Civil War. How well do you now feel you understood the issues at the time?

I was on the left in politics then, and therefore considered Franco and the defeat of the Republic a tragedy. Like all my generation on the left, I put it down to Germany and Italy supplying arms to Franco. Of course, since then I've studied the Civil War, but I still consider the intervention to have been an important factor, even though at certain periods, say, from October to November 1936, the Soviet Union was supplying more arms to Spain than Germany and Italy were. Now I tend to blame the defeat more on the internal divisions of the Republican party whereas Franco had the sort of monolithic political and military structure you need for winning wars. The Republic never got a unified political and military command. One of the Republican commanders,

who became a great friend of mine, a great strategist of the Republican side called General Rojo, who went into exile then returned to Spain and lived very modestly, said in one of his books that Franco won the war politically. I think that's true, because he created a single political structure. Of course, one can argue that it was an authoritarian structure whereas the Republican structure was democratic, but the divisions between the communists and the anarchists and so forth undoubtedly weakened the Republican war effort.

Was there something peculiar to the Spain of that time that made democracy difficult to establish and maintain there?

In a sense there was. There had been various attempts to establish some sort of democratic régime in Spain from the Cortes of Cádiz in 1812 onwards. I would say the fundamental reason why the Second Republic failed was that society had become too polarized – the gap between the haves and the have-nots, to put it in crude terms, was too large. If societies are too polarized, democracy can't work. What democracy needs is the development of a large middle class to act as a sort of buffer zone to neutralize social conflict. In the 1930s, Spain did not have any such large middle class, and democracy is possible in Spain now because, paradoxically, of the enormous economic and social changes of Franco's régime itself. After all, the 1930s was a period of great ideological polarization in Europe as a whole. The Spanish Civil War was seen not as a domestic concern but as some cosmic almost theological battle between the forces of fascism and the forces of democracy. But if you think about the Civil War, it's really the result of divisions in Spanish society: the division between the periphery and the centre, between the Basque provinces and Catalonia wanting independent government. So there was a regional problem, and there was a religious problem.

The great mistake of the Second Republic was making a frontal onslaught on the Catholic Church. It was partly for historical reasons in that they thought, quite rightly, that the Church was on the right, but in making the onslaught they gave a rallying cry to the right: the Church in danger. This was a political mistake, and one which today's Spanish socialists have been careful to avoid. They've been tactful in their handling of the Church, because that is a lesson from history, and the present socialist government is determined not to give the right any such rallying cry. But, you see, democracy cannot really handle deep divisions in society. To use the language of the American social scientists, when the cleavages are very deep, that is something a democratic system finds very difficult to manage. And they were very deep in Spain in the 1930s.

Your book Images of the Spanish Civil War *shows pictures of Republicans*

displaying the skeletons of nuns and of Falangists shouting, 'Viva la muerte!' *Why did this savagery emerge in Spain at that time?*

There were two things. First, there was an outburst of anti-clericalism, church burning, digging up coffins and so on, which happened at an early stage and tended to die down as the war went on. Then most people became concerned with another issue on the Republican side, which was the suppression of the revolutionary euphoria described by Orwell in *Homage to Catalonia* in the example of the ruthlessness of the Communist party's elimination of rivals in the murder of the POUM leader, Andrés Nin. It caused great difficulties for me at the time, I remember, when, after May 1937, the communists embarked on their campaign against their political rivals on the left, because, curiously enough, the Communist party had become, as it were, a right-wing party by that stage: against the spontaneous revolution and in favour of order and so on. I think the communist policy was objectively correct: that you had to have political and military union. What was wrong with the communists was the horrible methods by which they implemented the policy.

In 1938 I went with Philip Toynbee to meet some people returning from the International Brigades, and through the Independent Labour party got some idea of the repressions by the communists in Catalonia in 1937. Philip Toynbee, on the platform, used that awful phrase to justify all this communist onslaught, that you couldn't make an omelette without breaking eggs. I asked, 'Well, Philip, but what about the alleged assassination of Andrés Nin?' and Philip said, 'Well, Raymond, you must learn to distinguish between a bourgeois assassination and proletarian justice.' This sort of double talk really doesn't do. Of course, Philip later left the Communist party.

Why did so many writers and intellectuals side with the Republic?

Evelyn Waugh and T. S. Eliot didn't – for ivory-tower reasons, that poets shouldn't be directly concerned with politics and so on. I would say it was quite natural for liberals to side with the Republic, and the whole thing was brilliantly engineered by the Communist party. When André Gide, who'd just come back from Russia, made some criticisms of what was going on there, he was howled down at a meeting. The intellectual support was genuine, but it was pretty carefully massaged and orchestrated by the Communist party.

Why is it that the Spanish Civil War has achieved such a legendary status among modern conflicts?

In the increasingly non-ideological general position that people assume

nowadays, they find a certain fascination in thinking of this as the last ideological war; as the last war between two conflicting political philosophies. I actually think they're quite wrong in this view. The Spanish Civil War was fundamentally a domestic concern, but it was, of course, encapsulated in the grand conflict between fascism and democracy. There were statements such as the resistance of Madrid being the tomb of fascism and so on, and public opinion was divided. Politics became incredibly bitter in Britain over the issue of non-intervention, so it retains a certain fascination as almost a last crusade. There was also the romanticism of the International Brigades – young men defending freedom, poets like Cornford going out. All of that is romantically attractive. Not in Spain, however. Spaniards aren't studying the Spanish Civil War. Most of the work on it is still being done by people outside Spain because the Spaniards find it too painful a historical experience to remember.

Had the Republicans won, might Spain have fared better?

One doesn't know what would have happened. Suppose the Republicans had triumphed. Would the Communist party have been the dominant force on the Republican side? If you read George Orwell's *Homage to Catalonia* – in my view the best book ever written on the Spanish Civil War – you'll see how Orwell was the last romantic. He thought he'd discovered an egalitarian society in Spain, but that was a bit of a romantic illusion. Historians ought to avoid hypothetical questions, but what Franco did was divide Spain into the victors and the vanquished, and the vanquished were to be excluded from public life. In the early days, they were persecuted and imprisoned. I suppose that if the Republic had won, you would have had the same division the other way round, but less illiberal perhaps.

Tell me something about the Spanish Right? The catch-all label 'fascism' seems to obscure our view of it.

Fascism is a sort of portmanteau word that was used in the 1930s to describe any right-wing movement, whether recognizably fascist or not. It's quite clear that Franco was perfectly willing to adopt fascist trimmings to please his German and Italian friends, but he was a traditional right-wing Catholic, and he never allowed the fascist party, the Falange, to acquire any real power in the Spanish state. Of course, we all used the word fascism to describe any conservative movement in the 1930s, but the Spanish right has never been and can never be fascist in any true sense, simply because it is fundamentally a Catholic conservative movement. That is precisely what Francoism was.

Spain has always been one of the bastions of the Catholic Church, but how does Catholicism stand in Spain today?

Is Spain really a bastion of the Catholic Church? This is the traditional image of Spain, but if one looks at opinion in Spain, I don't think one would describe it as such. The Church has been subject to increasing pressure since secularization and the onset of the ethos of the consumer society, which in many ways is much more frenetic there than here. Opinion surveys indicate that Catholicism is by no means the force that people imagine, but as always happens, if Catholicism were attacked by the government, then you would have a resurgence of Catholic sentiment. Too much of Spanish Catholicism has been shanghied by the right. Opus Dei, in particular, infuriated intellectuals in the 1950s and 1960s by trying to get every university appointee to sympathize with it, so I don't look on Spain as a particularly Catholic society. But I do think there is a residual feeling that somehow Catholicism is a specific Spanish characteristic. If attacked it would come to the surface, just as with the extraordinary Prayer Book controversy in England in the 1920s, when Parliament thought it ought to revise the Prayer Book and there was a terrific upsurge of outraged Anglicans who hadn't thought of the Prayer Book in years. Similarly, Spanish Catholicism could re-emerge under attack. Under Franco traditional Catholicism was much more important, and a much bigger bulwark and pillar of the régime, than any sort of extraneous fascist doctrine, so the left in general, though they don't attack the Catholic Church, see it as having sold itself to Franco.

You are well regarded in Spain and obviously enjoy the company of Spaniards. What is the basis of this empathy?

It's partly accidental, and that's why I tend to attribute importance to accident in history. As a young historian I was working in Sweden, then went to Spain for my honeymoon in 1950. We went to Torremolinos, which is now a disaster but in those days had only one hotel. Almost the worst crime of Francoism was the encouragement of the sort of speculative building which has ravaged the Mediterranean coast of Spain, but that is by the way. It was extraordinary to encounter this society, ingrained in poverty, isolated intellectually, isolated commercially even from the rest of Europe. So I began to think how it had come about.

I started to lecture on Spanish history in Oxford, and the Oxford University Press sent me to see Gerald Brenan to ask him to write the history of Spain in the nineteenth century. He was a rather prickly and awkward person, and he refused. I will never forget his words. He said, 'You know, Carr, you can't find the truth by writing history. You can

only find the truth in writing novels.' Now this is an extraordinary remark, and I brooded on it. What on earth did he mean? And I think what he meant was that the novelist can make the imaginative leap the historian can't make, because he's not constricted by the historian's footnotes and sources. The novelist can make the imaginative leap to get at the real essence of a society. The tragedy is, of course, that Brenan was a very good historian but not a very good novelist. Anyway, in the car going back to Oxford I thought, well, if Brenan won't do it, why don't I? That was the beginning. I devoted fifteen years to writing that book.

The book's no longer true, because Spanish society has altered so dramatically from what it was originally. The whole atmosphere was a contrast, embodying totally different values from the rest of Europe, so it had this terrific fascination, and once one gets involved in a country one is almost bound to say it's interesting. They are very sympathetic and very generous intellectually, the Spaniards – to me, at any rate. But really the original decision to study Spain was accidental, then became my life for fifteen years, and is even now.

I'm curious about the relationship between Spain and the Arab world, the Arabs having ruled Spain for three or four centuries.

Obviously politically Spain has imagined itself as a bridge country for better understanding between Europe and two civilizations, one the Arab, the other the Latin American. But the relationship with the Arab world is a terrific controversy in Spain. I think it's an ambivalent notion. The great controversy in Spanish history is between Américo Castro on the one hand and the extreme nationalist historians like Sanchez Albornoz on the other. Sanchez Albornoz regards the essence of Spain as its fight with the Arabs, in which it was the great paladin of Christian civilization that defeated the Arabs; whereas Américo Castro argues that Arab civilization immensely enriched this rather poor nation of shepherds and wheat-growers.

The tragedy, of course, came when, in the sixteenth century, they turned against the Arabs and expelled them from southern Spain. So it's an ambivalent relation, but certainly they have been very hostile to Israel and have only relatively recently re-established diplomatic relations with the Israelis. Remember that Spain was the first and only country to receive Yasser Arafat virtually as a head of state and was very much criticized as a consequence. It's difficult to say today what the Arab legacy to Spain is, other than a longer and more intense contact with Moorish civilization than any other nation in Europe.

Britain and Spain are both latecomers to the EEC and have both been rather separated from the rest of Europe, by the Channel and the Pyrenees respectively.

The Pyrenees are not quite the barrier the Channel is.

No, but do you think both nations will be able and willing to adapt to a much more closely integrated continent?

I think the Spaniards are doing it already. They have a terrific European euphoria. Again, they see it in terms of their past. What excluded them from the Common Market was not being a democracy, and now they are a democracy and think a corollary of this is being a member of the Common Market. You remember how, in the early negotiations, the Spaniards were outraged that Brussels put so many bureaucratic obstacles in the way. González is a very keen European, and of course the *on dit* in Spain is that he's fed up with being prime minister and sees his career in Europe. Spain's problems are exactly the same as ours: high inflation, very high unemployment. They're in a remarkably similar position to us, but having been excluded from Europe by the nature of their political régime in the past, they are now probably the most enthusiastic pro-European nation.

Mrs Thatcher, however, is a curious grass-roots democrat. She said a very interesting thing when she went to Spain: 'I don't understand it,' she said. 'González appears in the Cortes three times a year to make a state-of-the-nation speech, but I have to appear in the House of Commons every Tuesday, which is what democracy really is.' I think she feels that the sacred democratic tradition is represented by her appearing weekly in the House of Commons, and that this will be eroded by some impersonal bureaucracy. Her attitude is a mixture of old-fashioned nationalism and some sort of curious grass-roots democratic feeling, and she feels that Europe somehow isn't democratic.

You have been warden of St Antony's College, Oxford, founded as a graduate college in 1950. Do you see it as emerging with a comparable status to the more anciently based colleges?

It's doing different things. It has a peculiar relationship in the university because it is the one genuinely international college. When I left it, seventy per cent of the graduate students came from overseas. I suppose it is one of the few institutions where Arabs and Jews have to live together, and it has this idea of being an international community in a sense that an undergraduate college can't be by definition. We are concerned with international politics, particularly with Latin America, so it is extraordinarily fortunate that my successor is Dahrendorf, who was offered very good jobs in America but preferred to come to St Antony's, I assume because he was fascinated by its international status.

To what extent have the aims of the founder, Besse, been fulfilled?

He died, of course, and didn't see what the college would develop into. Besse admired the English public school system and thought that somehow or other it produced a peculiar race of honest entrepreneurs. I think he'd like the international flavour of the college. I think he probably thought of it as a reservoir for producing upright, honest, thrusting British businessmen. I never knew him, though I knew his widow very well.

Don't our universities tend to become havens which shelter people from the harsher outside realities?

Oh, yes. It's a curious result of the tenure system. If you take academic appointments, there is a five-year bar; you are appointed to your job, and after five years you are reconsidered for permanent tenure. Well, the bar is hardly effective, and to get rid of a post in academic life later on, particularly in Oxford, is fantastically difficult. Of course, the argument for this security is that it allows you to be independent of political action. Much of my life has been spent in Latin America, where any change in the political government of a country means that academics are sacked, and one can never convince British academics how lucky they are to be insulated in this way, at least from the effect of political change. It's very hard if your subject is, let us say, thirteenth-century Castile, to see what the connection is with unemployment or whatever it may be. Academics have been cocooned to a certain extent, and particularly in England, by virtual security of tenure.

Another thing that happens is that academics tend to import conflicts from the outside world into the very narrow world of academia, so that you have a certain amount of intrigue, jealousy, vanity and all the things that operate outside, except that they are played out on a very small stage.

I've heard it said that Oxbridge dons are impossible to dismiss except on grounds of moral impropriety.

Absolutely.

How far has your experience of academic life revealed the underbelly, as it were, of our ancient universities?

This, you know, becomes rather delicate, because anybody will be able to detect who is being talked about. I had two fellows, one of whom I thought was not doing any teaching and the other who was a hopeless drunk. I should have steeled myself and dismissed them, but the process of dismissing someone for incompetence, failure to teach or to research,

is enormously difficult at Oxford. You have to have a meeting of your governing body in which the fellow concerned has a lawyer defending him and the head of the college presides as an impartial judge. So unless someone does something really extraordinary, like setting fire to the Bodleian, which somebody did once, I believe, or is caught in bed with someone (though not even that now, of course), it's almost impossible to dismiss anybody in Oxford for failure, and above all for failure to teach, which is after all the main thing we're supposedly there to do.

But one hears from students that there's a lot of sexual harassment from dons.

This, of course, was an issue while I was warden, though it depends what you mean by sexual harassment. In the physical sense, I don't think it goes on much. Of course, it does with some. The difficulty would be when a tutor asked a pretty girl out to dinner and she'd say, 'I can't come Tuesday,' and he'd say, 'Well, can you come Wednesday?' or Thursday, Friday and so forth. Now, does this constitute sexual harassment? I don't know, but women have come to think it does. Of course there should be mechanisms to stop it, and obviously it does go on, but damn it all, in this respect it's not all that different from the business world, where there are constant complaints of employers using their influence and status to exact sexual favours from employees. Regrettably, I've had to deal with a few cases, so I know it happens, but I don't think it's very widespread. I suspect it's one or two old goats who can't keep their hands off a woman.

What view do you take of the current upheavals in the universities and the effects of government policies?

I think it's forcing them all into a massive reconsideration of aims. They should be much more connected with the outside world, funded if possible by the outside world, by business, with a direct interest in producing people who can go into business. Of course, the cuts have imposed not only a restriction on activities, but also an enormous workload on university professors and heads of departments in restructuring departments and so on. It's very odd, this advance of administration as against scholarship. When I think back to when I was at Christ Church and New College, for instance, a domestic bursar in my time did everything on the proverbial back of an envelope. Now there are endless forms to fill in. There is some justification in cutting, because there was an over-expansion in certain subjects in the 1960s, sociology being an example. It wanted thinning out, but it's like so much of Thatcherism: there was a case for rethinking, but it's been too radical a surgery.

But isn't it a function of government to look after our education as opposed to the private sector?

Yes, it is, but of course the present government believes that universities must become like American universities and find their own funds. When I became head of a college I thought that my task was to give some sort of intellectual leadership, create some sort of community. In fact the function of a head of a college is now fundamentally to raise funds and go round with a begging bowl. I became reasonably good at it, but I didn't like it.

Why is the present government so reluctant to see much value in higher education or artistic effort? We seem to be quite out of step with Europe. Why are we suddenly different?

I don't think it is sudden. The English have never had a mystique about culture in the way the French have had since 1870. Intellectuals have never played the role in English society that they play in continental societies. There is no parallel in England to, let us say, the generalized influence of Sartre in France. One might cite Bertrand Russell, but it's not the same. I don't think the English have ever been particularly conscious of a cultural mission. Nations tend to get interested in culture when their political dominance has been defeated. If you think of France, it was after the defeat of 1870 that the French started saying, 'Look, we may have been defeated by Germany but we are still the cultural capital of Europe.' I'm not sure that the present government is genuinely hostile to culture, though I suppose there is some truth in the idea that universities are no longer so much sources of civilization as factories for producing commendable entrepreneurs.

Do you yourself now have any political affiliations?

I suppose I am conservative. It's the usual progression. I was very far to the left in the 1930s, but not now.

So the political fervour and conviction of your youth has dimmed as you've grown older.

I suppose I'm in the intellectual's usual dilemma. When I was young I had simple political convictions. Now I tend to see right on both sides of every question. Remember what Hegel said about tragedy being the conflict not between right and wrong but between right and right. I do rather regret this. No, not regret exactly, but there's a great deal to be said for having simple political convictions that provide a sense of moral rectitude. The great thing about being on the left in the 1930s was that, not only did one feel one was politically in the right, but that one was

morally in the right; that the other people were evil. I suppose that, as an historian, what has happened to me is that I don't now see the excesses of the Spanish right as works of the devil. Perhaps that was why the left in the 1930s got into such a mess: they constantly saw their opponents as guilty of some moral turpitude or intellectual hypocrisy. They couldn't see that these people sincerely believed what were wrong beliefs, and I suppose that's how I've changed. I don't dismiss the right in Spain as hypocrites morally flawed, but see them as having misguided beliefs held quite sincerely. I think that is my main intellectual change. But in the 1930s one had this feeling that one had a certain moral superiority over the right. I still think, of course, that what we actually believed in was right, but I don't believe that those who believed in the opposite were imperfect human beings.

You've always been considered a colourful figure.

If you wanted to put it at its highest, most absurd level, take the title of one of Berlin's books, *Against the Current.* I've always been against the current. To be a supporter of Mrs Thatcher now is to be in some way against the current, just as it was in my home in the 1930s to be on the left. But I've never been in the limelight. I'm not an historian who appears regularly on controversial issues in the *Independent* or *The Times*. I'm not very famous intellectually.

Which writers or academics have most influenced your life?

Curiously enough, Berlin influenced me quite a lot, simply because he, too, is intellectually against the current. On the literary side, I'm a fanatic Proust fan, because although I didn't read Proust until I was about forty or even older, he opened a lot of insights into, for instance, the force of jealousy, the force of habit in life. I think one only admires writers who make one look at the world in a different way, and I suppose Proust made me do that. Who else? Among novelists, E. M. Forster, because again, to my generation, he was a sort of liberating figure. But then there came a terrible disillusion. I asked Forster to dinner with me in New College when I was a don, because he had some sort of relation with the college, and he came. You will remember that Forster's whole thing was that you mustn't worry about clothes, appearances and all that kind of thing. He arrived for dinner having had to change trains at Didcot and having left his dinner jacket on the Bath line. It turned out to worry him terribly.

You have also often been described as rather a Bohemian. Does the description please or irritate you?

I don't mind it, though perhaps my bohemianism has been a bit

exaggerated. As I say, I've always been against the current in a certain way. I didn't abuse my position as a tutor, let me make clear, but I was fond of women once and perhaps I made it rather apparent. I've always preferred the company of women to the company of men, so if this means bohemianism, then yes, I have been a Bohemian in my time.

Was bohemianism or a rather upper-class eccentricity something you ever tried to cultivate?

If you mean did I adopt bohemianism in my desire to climb the social ladder, I suppose I did. It depends, of course, what you mean by a Bohemian. I remember having discussions with David Cecil about bohemianism, and he always quoted Thackeray's *Vanity Fair*. There's a scene where Becky Sharp, in a hotel room eating a modest plate of ham, has a potential lover coming to see her. Before the lover arrives, she puts the plate of ham in the bed to hide it. But I don't call that bohemianism. Bohemianism is a revolt against current social mores. Now, I suppose, one can argue that, in the permissive society, a Bohemian is a rigid puritan. But one forgets how extremely inhibited sexual life was in the 1930s and 1940s when I was young. Then it was still accepted that you courted a girl and the end product would be marriage, which is something that doesn't occur to my children. The tortures one used to go through. Remember that scene in Stendhal's *Le Rouge et Le Noir* where Julien Sorel has to make an approach to a woman by the time the clock strikes twelve or he won't do it at all. A sexual advance towards a woman in the 1930s was an enormously serious affair. It needed a lot of courage or drink or something before one could contemplate it.

But you're renowned for your charm, which I'm told can be most disarming. What's the secret of it?

I don't know what you mean by charm. With women, so many men make the mistake of talking about themselves. I never talk about myself with a woman, ever, unless she asks a direct question. I'm much more interested in what makes them tick. Philip Toynbee and I used to have a competition. Philip believed in the direct physical approach and always said, 'Look, why not come down with me to the Isle of Wight for a weekend?' whereas I would spend my time talking to these women about whether they'd read Proust or what they thought of Maria Edgeworth or the Brontës. We kept a score, and on the whole I won. But that's all that one means by charm: taking an interest in what the other person's concerned with.

So would you say it's a powerful weapon of seduction?

No, no, wait a minute. You're getting me into difficult waters here.

Very few women want to be approached directly on the size of their bosoms or the thinness of their legs. They've had enough of that by the time they're eighteen or nineteen, so I've never made a direct sexual approach to a girl at the initial stages.

Why are Englishmen in general so uncomfortable in the presence of women?

It is both an upper-class and a lower-class phenomenon: an upper-class phenomenon in the way people enjoy things like their clubs, which they prefer to the company of women and which may be a relic of the English public school system. But it also occurs in the lower classes, because in a pub, for instance, you'll often see that the men start talking together about football or whatever and leave the women isolated in some other part of the establishment.

Why are the British so hypocritical about sex? The gutter press makes us seem, as a nation, obsessed with and titillated by sex scandals, yet we are illiberal on the subject almost to the point of prudery.

I can only agree with that. It's a persistent legacy of some puritan tradition and can only be explained in those terms. But it also happens to a certain extent in other countries. In Spain, for instance, there is a curious connection between money and sex. The Spaniards are obsessed by the sexual goings-on of very successful businessmen. There's a substantial pornographic press in Spain too, so I'm not sure it's totally an English phenomenon.

Do you hold what Mrs Thatcher calls Victorian family values in high regard?

Today I do. I am devoted to my family, and my family life means more to me than anything else. But I think Mrs Thatcher has got Victorian morality a bit wrong. Victorian society was extremely violent, one forgets how violent, apart from the extraordinary distortions and perversions Victorian values could produce. I suppose I'm a repentant rake.

Why a repentant rake? Wasn't it more exiting to be one?

It was more exciting, but in the end it involved somebody suffering. Irregular relationships ultimately end in somebody having to foot the bill, clear out or whatever, and exciting though they may be, they have painful consequences. The steady glow of married life is preferable to the brilliant flashes of the occasional attachment.

What do you feel about the resurgence of the idea of family unity, the need for families to work together and stay together to preserve the fabric of society?

In America it is pretty well restricted to the middle class. The problem of society is its marginated groups. They were always marginated but somehow or other they seem to have become more so. Perhaps it is an illusion. One forgets the extraordinary marginated groups of, say, Victorian England, but the difference is that the values of those groups were fundamentally the values of the non-marginated. Now the marginated groups have a set of values of their own, distinct from the values of society as a whole. I think that's what's happened. There is an underclass that modern society somehow or other hasn't managed to absorb into its own value structure.

Your son has married into the aristocracy, but how can we really justify the British class system in the modern world?

Clearly, either in an egalitarian or a meritocratic society, it sticks out like a sore thumb. But what exactly does one mean by aristocratic values? In a way what is meant is that you know who your father was, your grandfather and your great-grandfather, whereas I haven't the faintest idea who my grandfather was. I still think, in a strange sort of way, that aristocratic values have something to recommend them. I don't think they're entirely worthless.

You are a lover of fox-hunting and even wrote a book about it. Isn't it a rather unacademic pursuit, and one not in your blood, so to speak?

You say it's not in my blood, but it is in a funny way. My father was a man of extremely modest extraction, though a fanatic follower of fox-hounds on foot. Naturally I spent my youth criticizing fox-hunting as somehow or other upholding the Empire and all the things I disapproved of. Why did I take it up? Partly through my wife, who likes it very much. Partly because it is, though I wouldn't want to exaggerate this, a dangerous sport to a certain extent and I quite like the tiny element of danger involved. And partly because it gives you a certain privilege. You can ride over other people's land, and if you feel for the country at all – and I feel passionately – you want some connection with it more than just walking over it. When you're riding, you have to take the country seriously. You have to look at every stick, stone and tree. This sounds like romantic nonsense, but one gets into some direct relationship with the countryside that one doesn't have just wandering about.

Don't you sometimes feel beleaguered by the anti-blood-sports lobby?

Yes.

Given the elements of enthusiasm and excitement, isn't it actually quite a difficult

thing to defend? Many people find the whole idea of killing anything for fun repugnant.

One can't get round that argument, and I do find it extremely difficult. The argument you can make is not very strong or convincing – that killing foxes by hunting is a better way of controlling them than poisoning or shooting. I respect those who do feel that fox-hunting is cruel, full stop. What I don't respect is the people who attack fox-hunting because they imagine it to be upper class. They are the ones who, apart from the Animal Liberation Front, tend to be most radical about it. I find those arguments relatively easy to refute, but the argument about cruelty does cause me a great deal of moral doubt.

What might persuade you on the animal rights issue? Couldn't there be, for instance, a correlation between cruelty to animals and cruelty to human beings?

No, I don't think there is any correlation, though it depends what you mean by cruelty to animals. Direct cruelty, such as torturing badgers or deliberately looking on at animals' suffering, might involve some correlation, but I wouldn't say fox-hunting does. Very few people are interested, certainly none that I know, in the process of killing the fox, though of course that is the end of the thing. But the suffering of animals as a spectator sport clearly has a correlation with cruelty to human beings. I'm absolutely devoted to animals. I spend all my time with my dogs, my horses and so forth, and one establishes some sort of a division in the mind – some sort of disassociation between the actual cruelty involved in fox-hunting and the hunting itself. I don't believe that most fox-hunters would approve of Belsen or vivisection or whatever, but it's impossible to refute the argument that a certain amount of cruelty is involved.

I imagine riding with the hunt can make for strange bedfellows. Are you always at ease with the company you keep in those circumstances?

I wouldn't be happy with a smart pack in the Midlands. The clatter of upper-class voices would get on my nerves. My hunt is largely composed of local farmers, people of very modest extraction, though perhaps again I'm avoiding the issue. I choose to hunt with modest country hunts. I would not like the social hoohah surrounding a very smart pack. I certainly wouldn't. I wouldn't have anything in common with them.

In many ways you seem to enjoy a lifestyle associated with the old-fashioned country gentleman, but how far can one go before hedonism leads to decadence or even moral bankruptcy?

Are you accusing me of being morally bankrupt?

No, no.

In fact you might say that it's the opposite of decadence. Riding to hounds for ten hours a day may be morally reprehensible, but at least it's not physical decadence. I would say urban living is more conducive to moral collapse.

You don't like to drink now, I gather.

I enjoyed the effects. In a sense it's a liberating experience. One drops some of one's inborn inhibitions. But I've never been attracted either to drugs or gambling, two things I've always had an absolute horror of. I myself gave up drink for two reasons, the first purely pragmatic. I live in the country and my social life is dependent on driving long distances, so sooner or later one is going to get caught out if one drinks, and therefore one's social life will be destroyed. It's partly that, and partly that anybody of my generation has seen close friends destroyed by drink.

There are people who can drink and work. Physiologically I can't do it. If I drink I can't write, I can't even read properly. So it's not a moral decision but just adjusting to my peculiar physiological reaction to drink, which is very violent in the sense that it completely inhibits any productive work. My problem was not that I was an alcoholic but that I was quite nervous and if I went out to dinner I would drink more than I should. Philip Toynbee, who had a real problem with drink, always said that he had to drink to get going socially and then kept on until he went over the top. I think this is what tends to happen. It's been a social lubricant from the Greeks onwards.

When you were knighted in 1987, did it come as a surprise?

Yes, it did, though there's always a certain expectation that some heads of Oxford colleges will be knighted. My knighthood was designated by the prime minister, who knew how deeply I felt about her not being given an honorary degree. I'm not, for God's sake, saying that's why I got it.

You appear to have lived life to the full, academically, socially and physically, but you must in the course of such a rich life have encountered temptations.

I always had my eye to the main chance, I suppose, but I always knew how far one could go without disaster. That's what always saved me: some degree of essential meanness, essential pragmatism, instinct for

self-preservation or whatever you would call it. I've never really got into trouble.

If you were being self-critical, how would you criticize yourself?

A certain meanness, even in financial matters. I also criticize myself for not being totally honest about fox-hunting, for example, and for being a bit of a social climber. Going back to Christ Church, I was a boy from a miserable home who was suddenly confronted with these grand, free-spending, liberated people and acquired an almost Proustian admiration for their lifestyle and I suppose wanted to participate. But all this leisurely bohemian bravura was inevitable really, given my social origins.

What are your regrets?

Apart from the conventional things, like not having written better books, simply that at various times I've been inconsiderate towards my children and my wife. I've wanted to write a book that would combine the political and social history of Spain with its artistic production and its artistic life, but I don't seem able to do it. But I never had any political ambitions, and my academic life was more or less successful. I got more or less to the top of that particular tree. It's extraordinary, but I don't think I do have any regrets. I ought to have, oughtn't I?

MAURICE COWLING

Maurice Cowling was born in 1926 and was educated at Battersea Grammar School and Jesus College, Cambridge, of which he was a fellow between 1950 and 1953. After short periods in the Foreign Office and on the editorial staffs of *The Times* and the *Daily Express* he returned to Cambridge where he was a fellow of Jesus again between 1961 and 1963. Since then he has been a fellow of Peterhouse. He contested the constituency of Bassetlaw as a Conservative candidate in the 1959 general election. In 1970 he was literary editor of the *Spectator*. In 1989 he was visiting professor of religion at Columbia University. His works include *The Nature and Limits of Political Science, Mill and Liberalism, Disraeli, Gladstone and Revolution, The Impact of Labour, The Impact of Hitler* and *Religion and Public Doctrine in Modern England.*

Your early career was quite varied – Foreign Office, The Times, *the* Daily Express. *How did you come to move between these worlds and then into academic life?*

I moved not from them to academic life, but to them from academic life. The thing that motivated me from the start was falling in love with Cambridge when I got there in 1943, deciding that I wasn't ever going to leave. I was a research fellow in the early 1950s, but then I didn't get a permanent job. I was determined not to be a lecturer in Hull (or Reading), and that decided me. If I couldn't stay in Cambridge (or Oxford) I'd go to London. That's why I tried to become a journalist, then went to the Foreign Office. If I couldn't be in Cambridge or Oxford, I'd be in London, not Hull or Reading.

I've heard it said that you once felt a vocation and began to study for the priesthood.

It's not true. That was in the *Sunday Telegraph* recently. I was never studying for the priesthood at all. I read history as an undergraduate, and thought of being ordained, but decided before there was ever any question of going to theological college that I wouldn't.

The Cambridge I fell in love with was an ecclesiastical university, but by 1943, of course, Cambridge wasn't an ecclesiastical university. I was trying to find a role for myself and being a clergyman seemed to be one of the possibilities. If you ask me whether I was deeply Christian, the answer is that I went to college chapel and had a strong polemical Christianity. Maybe there was something there that could have been built on, but I'm profoundly grateful I wasn't ordained because the sort of social and intellectual reason that I had for being ordained is ultimately unsatisfactory; and I'm not sure of the depth or reality of my religious

conviction. It could well be that it was a polemical conviction against liberalism rather than a real conviction of the truth of Christianity.

What was it attracted you to the study of the nineteenth and twentieth centuries?

Because I was teaching it is one answer. The other answer is that what interested me were the relations between religion, politics and thought. I've always believed for as long as I can remember that something happened between 1800 and today which is important for understanding the present. Both things in fact operated to make me interested in that period.

What do you see as the main reasons for the professional study of history? Do people learn from the past in any real sense?

I'm an anti-professional don. I strongly disbelieve in and dislike the idea of an historical profession, which is a twentieth-century invention. Historians should be people who, like most of the great historians, are reflecting upon the nature of society in general, on religion, thought and politics. History happens to be the form their reflections are given. I don't think anyone learns from the past in the sense in which you use the expression, because what historians do is make up the past out of the material they have to hand. Any good historian's past is an embodiment of what he believes about the present. So it's not that you learn from the past, it's that you learn from the historian.

I place a very great emphasis on the inventiveness and creativity of historians in making the past up. We don't know the past; it's gone. The greater the historian, the wider the range and depth of consideration of the central problems of religion, politics, thought, economic activity; and also the greater the synthesizing capability. Therefore historians, just like philosophers or critics or novelists, have to be understood as contributing to general reflection about the present, though in their case they express themselves through the past. To think in terms of learning from the past is philosophically wrong. The difference between an historian worth attending to and one who isn't is the depth of his or her understanding of the nature of these questions.

Can there ever be objective truth in history?

The truth rhetoric is not one I like using at all. As I just said, what the historian does is take the material that is present and make the past that he wants to make and that he thinks plausible. Obviously truth comes into it in the sense that there can be a misrepresentation of the material, and other historians will tell you if you misrepresent it, but it seems to me that historical writing is a free activity; objectivity is not a useful

concept. All there is is the possibility of innumerable statements, made necessary to the historian by his perception of everything that comes under the central body of subjects I term public doctrine. Obviously historians are biased. There's no reason why they shouldn't be. Other people will correct them. It's a pluralistic activity.

I hope there isn't such a thing as a historian free from bias. Macaulay regarded Hallam as the most impartial historian he had ever read, but nobody now would agree. Hallam was a manifest Whig with a point of view – a point of view which gave great strength to his historical writing. Of course there are inaccurate historians, but the only sense in which you can usefully employ the rhetoric of truth is that a historian should succeed, without being inaccurate, in conveying to the reader a truth about the position he is holding. I do emphasize in this sense – far too much no doubt – the subjectivity of truth. All one can do when confronted by historical writing is to empathize with it and understand it, accept it or reject it according to whether or not the historian's general conception of the nature of social and human activity is congenial to you. I not only don't believe in the objectivity of historical truth, I don't believe there's any problem about it either.

You taught as visiting professor of religion at Columbia University. Do you yourself profess a particular religion?

I suppose on a census I would describe myself as a member of the Church of England. If you ask me, do I think I ought to be an Anglican, the answer is that I probably ought to be a Roman Catholic, but I don't see any prospect of that happening. It all depends on a rhythm in writing and thinking. Up to the time when I was in my late thirties I didn't know what I thought at all, about politics or, except for the early Anglican period, about religion. Writing *Mill and Liberalism, Disraeli, Gladstone and Revolution, The Impact of Labour, The Impact of Hitler* and *Religion and Public Doctrine* were ways of demonstrating to myself on paper how far I'd got. The position is that I haven't yet got to the point at which I know what I ought to conclude, and working it out on paper is a necessary process that isn't yet completed.

I'm not saying at all that I couldn't become a Roman Catholic. What I'm saying at the moment is that I feel quite a large part of the time that I ought to be a Roman Catholic. If you ask me whether it's likely that I'm going to become a Roman Catholic, that's a very different question – I have a very Protestant mind – and one for which I have no answer.

Is it possible to teach religion as an academic subject without seeming to try to

shift or undermine the actual faith that students may have as Moslems or Buddhists, say, if the lecturer is an Anglican or a Roman Catholic, for example?

It's very subtle matter, the relationship between teachers and pupils, whether it's lecturing, tutorial (in the Oxford sense) or supervision (in the Cambridge sense). I don't think it's necessary to assume that a teacher will best serve the interests of the pupil by proselytizing. There's a very subtle line between propaganda and critical exposition, but I'm sure it's possible to draw the line between the two. An Anglican or Roman Catholic, or indeed anyone else, may sometimes be teaching in a way which has nothing to do with his religion, that is to say, he may be teaching in the manner of the academic generation to which he belongs. What is more, every teacher exudes his or her own atmosphere, which isn't the same thing as instruction or indoctrination; it may just be a way of putting whatever it is that one's talking about, and may not necessarily issue in commitment or engagement to any particular religion or church or opinion. But there's obviously a problem.

England often seems to be regarded as the least religiously minded country in Europe. Given that religion so often seems to be a compensation for poverty, and therefore unlikely to flourish in an affluent society, could it ever be possible to revive real religious feelings here today? Christ thought it was very hard for the rich to enter the kingdom of heaven.

I thought the poor had difficulties as well. So do surburban nations, of which ours is one. The least religious in Europe? That's true in a sense, but it depends how you regard post-Christian sentiments, which are strongly and deeply entrenched in England, and especially liberal sentiments. If you regard them as part of a religion without creeds and without specific performance, then I would say that the English are, even now, fairly moralistic and are, in a secular sense, a religious nation. They are not now a religious nation in the sense of being ecclesiastical performers. The question really is whether these post-Christian sentiments and opinions, of which there are many in England as there are in all the nations of the modern world, are to be regarded as religion, or whether we are to regard their prevalence as evidence that the religious period of English history is over.

I tend on the whole to think that they are to be understood as a form of religion or substitute-religion. That's why I slightly take issue with you. They run very deep in the English mind, and in that sense England is certainly full of pieties and maybe you could even say full of religion.

My perception of the British Isles as a whole is that the Roman Catholic religion is very evident.

In its practices.

Is that because it's a minority, do you think?

Well, some of it is converted, and that is likely to be associated with observance. Some of it is Irish, and that is also to be associated with observance. It may be because it's a minority, but I don't really think that is the main reason.

Is it, then, because Roman Catholicism is a much more disciplined religion than the Anglican?

No. What needs to be explained is not particularly why Roman Catholics go to church, but why Protestants don't. Somehow the gut seems to have gone out of English Protestantism. It's turned into these post-Christian moralistic sentiments. It doesn't involve or insist on observance, but it may be that the body of sentiment is just as deep as ever it was when it did ask for observance.

But wouldn't you agree that in an affluent society there is likely to be less religion than in a poor society?

Empirically that's probably true. I don't really see *why* it should be so. This isn't exactly an affluent society; it's a suburban society we live in primarily, and I don't think any church has managed to address the problem of maintaining religion in a suburban society. Being affluent is part of it, but it's not only that, it's also the frame of mind. I can't really put a finger on it, but I'm sure the problem is that a suburban society has conventions and understandings which haven't really been resolved in terms of public religion.

But isn't temptation harder or stronger in an affluent society? If you're rich, you're tempted to do things that are not perhaps very Christian.

Oh, I don't think that's true. The temptation to abandon religion is not really correlatable to the opportunities for doing something else, but correlatable to the frame of mind in which everything that anybody can do is viewed. It's perfectly possible for the rich to be deeply ascetic. There are rich ascetics.

I admit that there is some sense in which affluence makes the observance of a difficult religion more difficult. But if you want to explain why there is less religion in affluent societies than in poor ones – if that indeed is true – then you have to look at the education being given in affluent societies as well as their affluence. It seems to me to relate to the education and development of the intellectual life of a society quite as much as to the affluence itself. If you're talking about English religion, the most affluent of English societies was Victorian society, and there was undoubtedly a deep and strong revival of religion in Victorian

England which was associated with affluence. There was almost an identity of timing between the affluence and the revival of religion, so that is not a good example.

You once stood as Conservative candidate in a safe Labour seat. What decided you not to persevere in trying to enter Parliament?

I enjoyed being a candidate, though it was very hard work and elections are like what I imagine having all your teeth out is like. It was simply that I decided in about 1960 or 1961 that I wanted to write a lot of books and at that time I hadn't written any. The main thing was to live in Cambridge, settle down and write, which I did. I didn't feel that I was going to get into Parliament, but I also half-thought that it would be better to write books. In any case, I'd always taught at least six hours a week in Cambridge – in supervision – ever since 1950, even when I was in London. That is what I wanted to do primarily, and all the rest – the Foreign Office, journalism, certainly standing for Parliament – was really a retreat because I hadn't got a permanent academic job. As soon as I got such a job in Cambridge, I had no desire to go on my travels again.

I'm still politically interested without being active in any party sense. I'm an intellectual Thatcherite, just as I was an intellectual Powellite, and I think it important that the Conservative party should be in good hands and that it should win elections.

But as an academic historian, don't you sometimes feel at least some ambivalence towards the present government, which on the face of it has shown an attitude bordering on contempt for non-vocational education?

I don't feel any ambivalence towards the present government, of which I am a warm supporter. The only thing I would say is that when Mrs Thatcher came in in 1979, then the government ought to have grasped the nettle and abolished half a dozen academic universities, or expanded the vocational side of universities and reduced the academic side. I believe the *academic* community is too big. I'm rather unusual in believing this, but I do. There is a great overlap between academic studies and vocational studies, even in academic universities, but basically the academic community is too big and the nettle ought to have been grasped. It's because it wasn't that we are in the mess we're in now. They really did not face the logic of their own belief.

What do you think 'the idea of a university' is, to use Cardinal Newman's phrase?

I think what dons should do in an academic university, or a college as

I prefer to call it, is a combination of maintaining scholarship and learning, teaching undergraduates as directly as possible, and writing. If you ask me what is the use of that, the answer is that it hasn't necessarily any immediate use, and that's why the institution shouldn't be very big – because it is a strange thing for young men and women to be subjected to, and not everybody is suited for it, and it's not good for everybody. So what I believe is that those who constitute an academic university have a duty to learning and scholarship, to teaching and writing. It's a self-regarding activity, and so it should be.

You'll notice that I say 'a college'. There are many universities in the world in which the only institution is the university and its faculties. In Cambridge and Oxford in my view the university is not the primary institution; the primary institution, except where it is the laboratory, is the college.

Why does so small a proportion of the British population go on to higher education as compared with France and Germany?

The reason is because the usefulness of higher education is not immediately apparent. Higher education ought to be directly vocational over a very wide area of its operation, and the more directly vocational it is, the more certainly it will attract those who might not engage in it. But they ought to engage in it; it's useful to them to do so.

A lot of people notice that, for an industrial or advanced country, Britain's management education is very behind that of Europe and Japan.

Yes, but that's because it's been assumed for a very long time in England that an academic education is superior. Now, I'm not saying it is superior; I am saying it's a very good thing in itself but not suited to everybody. It can be damaging to some people, and there ought to be higher esteem given to vocational education. The higher esteem that is given it, the more likely it is to be attractive to large numbers of people.

It has been something of a life's campaign for you to attack liberalism, which you see as inextricably linked with authoritarianism. Are you saying that liberalism is really a cloak for hypocrisy?

Yes. There's a phrase I quote from Sir Edwyn Hoskyns at the beginning of *Mill and Liberalism* about how 'the liberal is not only convinced that he is right, but is also convinced that other people secretly agree with him'. I've never had any desire to use liberal language. When I was a schoolboy, I read a lot of Carlyle and a lot of Belloc. I know that Belloc was a radical, but his language was not liberal language but a sort of reactionary Catholicism. And Carlyle, in religious terms, was a liberal,

but in political terms was obviously not. And that's just stuck with me. Liberal language has never attracted me and it assumes a higher rectitude in human conduct than I suppose to be normal. And since it assumes a higher level of human rectitude than normal, it's very misleading as an understanding of the way in which men behave socially, or indeed individually – but particularly socially and politically. I wouldn't mind if liberalism was just a cloak for hypocrisy. The problem is the people who believe it. They're much worse than the ones who don't. Hypocrisy seems to me to be a very minor evil and very necessary for the world. But very large numbers of people actually believe in liberal sentiment, liberal assumptions and liberal ways of thinking. It's not hypocrisy at all; it's self-deception.

Examples of those I regard as liberal would be Isaiah Berlin, for one, or David Astor. David Astor is actually the better example. When he was editor of the *Observer* there was an assumption that somehow all good men were men of good will; that there was a correlation between good intentions and good consequences; that the desire of all men and women to be in harmony with all other men and women and total self-development for everyone were somehow achievable without the difficulties which are inseparable from all political activity. Liberalism is essentially the belief that there can be a reconciliation of all difficulties and differences, and since there can't, it is a misleading way to approach politics.

The most important feature of political activity is precisely that interests and opinions are in conflict; that people do not mean the same thing when they say different things. Yet the liberal wishes to believe that, when people say different things or are pursuing divergent interests, they are somehow saying the same thing or pursuing the same interest. It isn't the case, and once you've recognized it isn't the case, then your politics are going to be more realistic than if you believe that it is the case. There you are. There's liberalism in a nutshell for you.

Your book on John Stuart Mill seems to postulate the idea that Mill wanted to substitute a 'secular' religion for orthodox Christianity. Why exactly would that be so objectionable? The story of orthodox Christianity has not always been a kindly or a happy one.

That book was published in 1963 and was really written out of the frame of mind I was in between 1944 and about 1950. To me then it was self-evident that the attempt to rid the world of orthodox Christianity was bad and wrong. I wrote the book in order to point out that, when you replace Christianity by what Mill would have replaced it with, you're not replacing something contentious by something self-evidently true, but replacing something contentious by something equally contentious. What I was drawing attention to in Mill was the

claim that liberalism was what all reasonable men would really believe if they were thinking reasonably. That is a highly contentious claim. Between Christianity and the post-Christian religion that Mill was propagating, there is an incompatibility and a conflict. It's not just a case of something self-evidently wrong being replaced by something self-evidently right.

In other words, what I was trying to say was, first, that liberalism is not as bland as it pretends to be, and secondly, that in relation to historic Christianity the founders of modern English liberalism – not only Mill but a lot of other thinkers as well – were not being bland and self-evident but contentious and controversial. Christians have, on the whole, been on the defensive over the last two hundred years – certainly in England for the last hundred years. What I simply wanted to do was to put liberalism on the defensive as well.

You speak at one point of that low-key respectability which is the real religion of the English people. Are you included in that?

No, I'm an amused observer of the English people. Like you.

Seriously.

There is a difficulty about this. What I believe in politically, I suppose, is a low-key hard line: respectable, faintly nasty edged, but also accommodating. In other words, Conservatism. That seems to me really to be what the Conservative party has usually stood for. There's been a change in the Conservative party during the past ten or fifteen years, but what I believe in is a bedrock of conservative feeling. I believe it's there in large numbers of Conservative voters, and used to be, and may still be, in large numbers of Labour voters. That seems to me to be a really good thing, and since you try to identify me with it, I'm happy to endorse the identification.

If you feel with Dr Norman and Enoch Powell that Christianity is not primarily a social doctrine, what value can it have at all beyond its use as a managerial weapon on the pie-in-the-sky principle?

Now you're giving me a real reductionism about religion, and I reject it. At the very least, in England and Europe Christianity has historically been a very important and independent part of public thinking, and isn't to be reduced to the class struggle at all. It's a matter of conviction, of opinion, of belief, and is not reducible to anything else.

Let me provoke you further. The unsympathetic will surely see your view of Christianity as a call to repentance and as a way of avoiding social responsibilities.

Three answers. First, the application of Christ's precepts is a complicated and long-term business, and it is not to be expected that they will be translatable into the easy formulae of policy or parliamentary or party exchange. Secondly, I'm not calling anybody to repentance. My books, except for *Mill and Liberalism*, which is a long time ago, are in no sense persuasions to any form of belief. What I had to say about Christianity there I wouldn't, indeed, say in that form now.

Thirdly, a point that arises from my first book, *The Nature and Limits of Political Science*, which came about six months before *Mill and Liberalism*. This was an attack on political science as it was in the 1960s when it had by and large a practical purpose – usually a liberal or socialist purpose. What *The Nature and Limits of Political Science* said was that academic subjects shouldn't have practical purposes, and that, when they did, they were demeaning to the academic function. In a way, I still half believe this, but I also believe that it is almost impossible in any humane study actually to detach engagement and commitment from explanation.

In fact the account of what an historian is doing which I gave you a little time ago is a complete reversal of *The Nature and Limits of Political Science*. In the conditions of the 1960s, when what we'll call in shorthand terms Liberalism or Lib-Labbism was in the ascendant in this country, it seemed a very good argument against Lib-Lab political science to say that it wasn't explanatory but was engaged or committed. But I have changed my view almost diametrically because I now really believe that engagement and commitment are unavoidable.

You have argued very persuasively for conservative values over the years, but the practice as opposed to the theory seems to involve poverty at the level of living in cardboard boxes and begging in the streets.

I wouldn't say I've argued for 'conservative values' over the years. Intellectually, I believe in a broad conservatism. Politically, I didn't have any connection with any political party until the mid 1950s. What you could therefore say of me is that, since the mid 1950s, in addition to having an intellectual opinion which is independent of my party-political opinions, I've also been a defender and proponent, in my own deviant way, of the Conservative party – which is not the same thing as conservative values. You notice I resist you when you use the phrase 'conservative values.'

As for living in cardboard boxes and all that, it happens under socialism as well as under a free market economy. But we haven't got a free market economy. We've still got a mixed economy. And though a good deal has been done since 1979 to desocialize the mixed economy, it is still a mixed economy. Obviously no one wants poverty or anyone

living in cardboard boxes, but the argument is – and it may turn out that they are discovering this in Eastern Europe – that a free market economy is better as a cure for poverty than a controlled socialist economy.

Do you see any dangers in the changes in society which are attributable to Mrs Thatcher and her form of government?

What are the attributable changes?

Hasn't Mrs Thatcher changed our society radically?

I don't think she has. Both Thatcherites and anti-Thatcherites wish to maintain that she has made fundamental changes. She has made some changes in government, in political policies, in the perception and the social constitution of the Conservative party. There is a slightly greater economic toughness in the public mind than there was when she arrived, but when you say she has transformed our society, I don't believe it.

Well, we used to pride ourselves in Europe, and particularly in this country, on the fact that although money was important to us, it wasn't everything in life. Now Mrs Thatcher has created what could be called the new spiv in our society, someone bereft of culture and motivated only by money and self-aggrandizement.

But everybody said the same about Macmillan. It's not a debating point I'm making, but a real point. It was even said about the 1951 government that they had given the opportunity to the spiv and estate developers. This will be said whenever there is a loosening of government economic control, but what you're saying about today just isn't true. Public schools, for example, are fuller than ever and more people want to go to them than ever before, and whatever public schools do turn out, it isn't spivvery that is being aimed at on the whole. The yuppy is really a function of the immense increase in property values in the south of England. There are very large numbers of people who feel much richer because of the inflation of house values as compared with the rest of inflation. It's a very complicated thing and is not all to do with Mrs Thatcher or the present government. All she has done is marginally to reverse the frame of mind which believes in the desirability of governmental involvement in the economy. If that has enabled a lot of people to make money, it seems to me entirely unobjectionable, and one can't tell what the effect will be. It seems to me just propaganda to identify that process or the decision to reduce the taxation of wealth with spivvery. It isn't the case that the alleviation of taxation has been a licence for spivvery.

But moral values in the City are not as high as they used to be.

I'm not an authority on moral values in the City. If what you're describing is the case, I don't think it's to be attributed mainly to Mrs Thatcher or to this or any government. Anyway, I'm not sure that what you say is happening is happening.

To many it must look as if what the new Conservatives really want is a mini America, but they do not seem to want to pay that part of the price which requires freedom of the press and access to government information.

I don't believe there are Conservatives who want an American economic system here. What this government has done since 1979 is comparatively limited when you consider the vast structure of governmental activity that is still operating. We still have a mixed economy, and although Mrs Thatcher as a rhetorician is a new market Conservative, she is also a responsible party leader. We aren't anywhere near an American economy and I don't believe it is a thing that needs to be considered as a matter of practice.

In any case, there's no reason why a free market economy should entail alterations in the Official Secrets Act. The two things are not connected. I don't know whether there is too much secrecy in government here or not. There is a long tradition of secrecy in the interests of national security, and no doubt it can be abused. I don't know whether it is being abused or not. But there is absolutely no connection between a market economy and the liberalization of the Official Secrets Act – none whatever.

Mrs Thatcher seems adamant that we should know less and less about what's going on in government.

I honestly don't believe that's true. I don't feel it as a citizen, so to speak.

They have a go every so often at the BBC.

The BBC has been one of the whipping boys of Conservative sentiment as long as I can remember, back to the 1940s and 1950s. There's nothing unusual in that, you know.

With regard to what you call 'a conservative moral order', you say that apart from the need for intellectual argument there is an equal need for what you call 'tone and posture'. Can this tone and posture ever be anything more than theatricality?

There is a low-key, hard-minded conservative posture which is of funda-

mental importance in English life, particularly in English politics. It embodies a real judgement of what is politically and morally possible, feasible and desirable. It's not full of large expectations. It's not Utopian in mind or intention. It assumes that the world is a difficult world and that there are some things which can be done and many things which can't; in other words, it operates with limited expectations. That seems to me to be entirely admirable and not theatrical at all. I think Mrs Thatcher is going through a bad patch, and I'm not saying that part of the Labour party aren't capable of embodying the same limited expectations. Certainly if Dennis Healey had ever been leader of the Labour party, that is exactly what Labour would have embodied. It's the expression of a very genuine and very deep mistrust of high-flown humbugging windbagging politics and morality. There's nothing wrong with that, is there?

In your preface to Conservative Essays, *you wrote that the Conservative party would have to promote a sense of history and cohesion among the people. Is that possible any longer, with so many conflicting ethnic and religious minorities?*

There is a difficulty about ethnic minorities, but in the same way that many Scots, Irish and Welshman have become assimilated to England within England, and Englishmen assimilated in Scotland, Wales and so on, so, I think, will a lot of ethnic immigrants be assimilated. Some will remain in ethnic communities and some will not, but there are various ways in which a nation can be governed, and immigration, once it has happened, doesn't seem to me to be fatal to a political system operating. As to the question of moral solidarity and cohesion, we'll need to see how things develop over fifty years, but obviously there is a difficulty.

One of the things that the Moslems, for example, are likely to lose if they assimilate is their religion. Assimilation can be the destruction of a religion, and that may happen, probably is happening, to some Moslems. I don't know whether it is good that it should. On the whole, I'm not keen on the idea of ethnic groups operating as ethnic groups, but I can see that if they don't, they will lose some of their features in a way which, if I were a Moslem, I would think undesirable.

You ask me whether I share Enoch Powell's view on immigration, and I have to say that that depends on what you mean by Enoch Powell's view. I regarded the substance of what he said in the 1960s – though not the rhetoric that he used – as being on the whole right. I've been surprised at the extent to which the situation hasn't turned out violently. In some places, of course, there has been a lot of violence. How long it will be before one can tell whether or not the level of immigration has been a bad thing is very difficult to say. It depends on what the

relations are between the immigrants themselves and the rest of the community over a span of twenty or thirty years, and it's not clear yet.

In your recent new preface to Mill and Liberalism, *you say that the contradictions produced by immigration were exemplified from a 'tolerable' point of view in the case of the Bradford headmaster, Ray Honeyford, but from an 'odious' one in the case of Salman Rushdie.*

I've read *The Satanic Verses* and I thought it a nasty, sneering, free-thinking book. I'm not in favour of Moslems executing death threats or using violence, and they have to observe the law when they're here, but I can understand why the book is offensive and it didn't seem to me to be anything but offensive when I read it. Some thinking Moslems take a view of the nature of religion, and the incompatability between Islam and liberalism, which runs parallel to what I'm saying in *Mill and Liberalism*, and that's why I mentioned Rushdie in that way.

Your way of interpreting history sometimes seems to arouse great antagonism among fellow historians. A reviewer recently wrote: 'The real subject is not the assault on Christianity, but Maurice Cowling's assaults on practically everybody', and accused you of anti-intellectualism, fuelled by a moral crusade. Do such accusations hurt you?

I couldn't stop laughing when I read that. I don't know what the animus is, but there must be some. All my critic was accusing me of was exactly what I was saying about ten minutes ago that historians are doing: spreading themselves on the past, as all historians always have done. I think he is a professor at the University of Minnesota, and I am deeply grateful to him.

I believe in answering attacks, but I do find it very difficult to be in any way emotionally injured by them. On the other hand, I do depend on having access to a correspondence column. You'll find there's a lot of stuff of mine littered about in correspondence columns over the years.

As for being on a moral crusade, no, no, no. I spent the first twenty years of my adult life knowing that I wanted to say something but not knowing what form to say it in, and really not knowing, as it were, which profession to say it through. In the end I found first the form of two polemical books, then three political books, and after that the religious books, which will go on a bit longer. The thing that has to be understood about me is that I'm really very insulated. I have contemporaries from whom I have learned a lot, and obviously older people from whom I've learned a lot, but there aren't many of them. Really I've been doing what I want to do now for twenty years, and I truthfully don't care about criticism, though I do like to answer back.

Who influenced you in your life?

There was the history master in my sixth form who had been sending people to Jesus College, Cambridge, for fifteen years, so it was perfectly natural to expect to go to Cambridge. I don't think the substance of his teaching was important. What was important was that he was an absolutely brilliant teacher. Then, in Cambridge, there was Charles Smyth, and when I came back after the army, there was Charles Wilson. He's important because he was an anti-Keynesian economic historian. Then there was Michael Oakeshott. For a time I wrote in Oakeshottian language but with an unOakeshottian crudeness. The thing about Oakeshott's writing was that it was subtle and mine wasn't subtle, but I borrowed the language. And then there was Herbert Butterfield. That's about it among seniors, and there are contemporaries, like John Vincent, for example.

I understand that Roger Scruton was influenced by you at one time. Are you happy to be allied with Scruton nowadays?

There was a time when I knew him very well when he was a fellow at Peterhouse. I liked him very much. When he became editor of the *Salisbury Review* and for a little while afterwards I thought there was something faintly wooden about his politics, but now I regard him as a very, very good thing. It's not only that he writes about politics, it's that he writes about everything else. He's written a very good book about architecture and aesthetics, a hugh great book about sex, a political book about conservatism, and very good books about Kant and Spinoza. He is a remarkably versatile and intelligent person. I used to have some reservations. I do not have any now. There are things I disagree about, and I have no wish to go to Czechoslovakia and meet all these dissidents. Now he's trying to found a Conservative party in Czechoslovakia. I've no wish to be involved in that.

You have been accused of cynicism, but a more recent suggestion is that you take the view that, in the face of the transcendence of God, no moral or political system has any authority.

I think one needs to put into that sentence 'no *ultimate* authority', because I obviously don't believe it to be the case that no moral or political system can have authority. One has, I think, to be very mindful of the limits and ignorance of even legitimate government. In Eastern Europe and the Soviet Union, for example, there has been a slow subterranean dissent from Marxism-Leninism which has now finally surfaced. It isn't surprising that the Soviet government had got out of touch and become rigid. It's taken at least thirty or forty years for this change to happen (it has obviously been going since the end of Stalin).

In a recent newspaper profile in the Sunday Telegraph *you were represented as saying that the last war was a catastrophic mistake. What possible alternative was there to going to war?*

I didn't actually describe it as a catastrophic mistake. I think that was the *Sunday Telegraph* profile writer. What I did say was that Churchill and Chamberlain were both imperialists who believed in the British Empire, and between them they got us into the war in September 1939. In that sense, they were responsible for the eventual destruction of the British Empire, and that was the point of my book, *The Impact of Hitler*.

It seemed to me singularly ill-contrived for the British government to be going to war with Hitler when Hitler might have been about to attack the Russians, and even more ill-contrived that, when Hitler did attack the Russians, he had already defeated the French army. What I'm saying is that the war shouldn't have been started in September 1939. Also, although, looking back, the war looks inevitable, there were in fact a number of alternatives. Historical thought has assumed that nothing is inevitable. On the question of whether Hitler was going to attack the Russians, the one thing that does seem clear is that he didn't know whether he wished to attack Britain but did know that he wished to attack Russia.

A third question I broached in an article in the *Sunday Telegraph* in August 1989, and also in *The Impact of Hitler*, was what would have happened if we'd allowed Hitler to attack the Russians and establish a predominance in east and south-eastern Europe? I simply asked the question, because I think it's impossible to come to a conclusion about whether a German-dominated Europe would have been better for Britain, whether it would have been better that there should have been no war between Britain and Hitler (assuming that the British Empire could have been preserved intact), and about whether one should welcome the Russian victory over Germany and Russian and American predominance in Europe. I simply asked these questions. I don't know the answer.

In the same article you suggest that our winning the war paved the way for what you call, 'priggery, puritanism and permissiveness'.

The point of the article was that after 1940 the student revolution of the 1930s, which was just like the student revolution of the 1960s only different in manner, got involved in the running of the war. Afterwards there was the appearance of Britain winning, and Britain in a sense did win, being on the side of the Russians and the Americans. But, from the point of view of Britain, the war was really not a good thing and I would regard it as, in effect, a defeat.

After the war the whole body of opinion which had been student

revolutionary in the 1930s became very respectable through having been involved in the war, and what was a form of defeat was presented as victory. It was a victory for liberal democracy, for anti-totalitarianism, for a sort of emasculated version of everything that the young had believed in the 1930s. I'm not drawing any particular conclusions from this, but simply saying that this frame of mind operated in all parts of the political spectrum, really until the late 1960s. That is what I mean by a wartime consensus which lasted politically right through Macmillan, he being a perfect embodiment of it, though I thought Macmillan a wonderful party-political leader.

It all went on until the late 1960s, when it was destroyed by a combination of student revolution, *Private Eye* – remember how *Private Eye* absolutely demolished the circulation of the *Spectator*, under Nigel Lawson, oddly enough – Powellism, and latterly Thatcherism. Between them, they made the whole of that consensus, which had lasted from 1940 to about the mid 1960s, look anachronistic and old-fashioned. I don't think it has ever quite recovered.

Why did you think the objection, widely shared, to using force in Suez in 1956 was 'so naïve as to be intellectually offensive'?

First, my objection in 1956 was to people who blew themselves up in indignation. There were prudential reasons for not invading Egypt, and it might have been better not to have done so; also the alliance with the Israelis, though it was secret, was probably a mistake. My objection to the objectors is that what they were really doing was what the anti-Vietnam war movement did in the United States. If they had only really used their arguments properly, they could have found prudential and political reasons for arguing against invasion. What was wrong was that that wasn't the mainspring of their argument, their mainspring being that force should never be used.

You ask about Christian ethics. I didn't want to make the point in a Christian ethical way, but if you do, then there is a long history of discussion of the sorts of occasion on which force is legitimate. And it would be very difficult to decide what degree of provocation was contained in Nasser's occupation of the Canal, whether or not that really was a ground for war. I can't see any reason of principle why it should not have been. It's not my business to pronounce on the application of the Christian ethical doctrine of a just war on the Suez campaign of 1956, but it's simply not the case that Eden's invasion of Egypt was an open-and-shut case of idiotic or angry aggression. It was the result of a very long series of incidents. The casuistry of the ethical doctrine would have to consider in great detail the relationship between Nasser's conduct

and Eden's reactions. The important point about it is that it is not an open-and-shut case; and a perfectly good case can be made either way.

Except that at the time Eden was in collusion with Israel and planning even before Nasser acted.

I thought the collusion with Israel was mistaken, not in terms of principle but in terms of prudence and policy. It doesn't seem to me that if, as Eden rightly or wrongly did, you took the view in 1956 that Nasser was an irreconcilable enemy of Britain's interests in the Middle East, then there is anything wrong in using the Israelis against him. But there is a lot of reason to think it was politically unwise.

What view did you take of the Falklands War at the time?

At the beginning I thought, oh dear, I hope there isn't going to be another Suez, i.e. a cock-up. Secondly, although it had to be conducted and had to be won, there was no British interest of any consequence involved. It was a far-away country of which, as Neville Chamberlain said, regrettably we know little. There may be some Antarctic interest involved, but that must be very minimal and probably would have been better got rid of before the war happened.

A reviewer of your Religion and Public Doctrine *called you illiberal and extreme. I don't expect you see yourself in this light, but can you understand why some people react like that?*

Oh, yes. I'm very happy to be able to tell you that I get under the skin of quite a lot of people. They think that I believe more reactionary things than I do because I like to use positions against them which I know will annoy them. Probably, if the truth be known, I'm a much broader and more central figure than even I'm aware of. That's a good answer to make.

It comes basically, fundamentally and originally from a desire, as I said earlier, to say something I knew I wanted to say before I found the vehicle through which to say it. Some part of what I wanted to say I knew would be antipathetic; it was meant to be antipathetic to the sort of people who regard me as – I don't know whether the word 'evil' isn't dignifying myself too much; but who regard what I'm saying as very wrong. Sometimes people think it's very wicked.

You have never married. Did your preoccupation with academic pursuits rule it out, or was there another reason?

Nothing to do with academic pursuits at all, and there isn't really any reason.

Your life as an academic suggests a certain stoicism, as if you were not prone to normal human frailties.

It's not an accurate impression at all. I have a well-regulated life which is not confined to Cambridge and which is, one might say, low-key and domestic and provides me with much happiness.

Some people are not interested in the pleasures of the flesh of any kind. Are you one of them?

Absolutely not.

So you're human like anybody else?

Oh, I should think so, yes.

Do you feel more comfortable in the presence of women or men?

There are a small number of women in whose company I am very happy. Peterhouse is still a mainly male college, but when I'm not in Cambridge, the company I keep is mainly female, and that is very good. As a fellow of a college, living in college during term but only during term, there is a sort of semi-domestic atmosphere which is predominantly male; but that is not how I live out of term when I'm not in Cambridge.

Are you, or would you call yourself, a bon viveur*?*

No. That implies a general inebriation, and a taste for wine and a discriminating taste for food which I don't have. I have simple tastes in food and I drink whisky or gin in large quantities, but only at certain times of the day. I don't really drink wine. That doesn't sound like a *bon viveur.*

Do you agree that religion and sex are the two strongest forces to effect our lives?

I think you're on the verge of another reductionism. The sexual drive is very strong in practice, but I'm not sure that it's as strong in thought. If you look at the content of European thought, it doesn't seem to me that thought about sex plays a very important part. It's a very strong and sometimes a sublimating drive in many thinkers, but it's not central. There is obviously a great deal of writing about sexual conduct in ethical discourse, in novels and in poetry, but it isn't the central feature of the thought of Western Europe. It doesn't play such a prominent part in the thought of Western Europe as religion does.

But mightn't its absence be detrimental to one's achievement, even intellectually?

I've never felt any frustration in work from that quarter. But perhaps that's because I lead a well-regulated, cheerful, happy life. I think there are a lot of people for whom sexuality is very strong, but there are also a lot of people, and I suspect particularly that there are a lot of English people, for whom it is not strong. I'm not in any way denying its importance. In the lives of some people it's primary, but not of English people on the whole, and I don't know any other nation well. For many English people, it is heavily operative when they're young, and then it becomes domesticated.

Why your obsession with religion?

I think because, when I arrived in Cambridge, that was the form in which intellectual power presented itself to me. One simply cannot tell what the effect of powerful teaching on a seventeen-year-old will be, but I'm quite sure that the effect of the teaching I had in 1943 is quite indelible and that's why there is this obsession with religion. If you want the autobiographical explanation, that's it, but as I said at the beginning, what every historian ought to be concerned about is this area of religion, politics, culture and economic activity. A lot of modern historians, it seems to me, are not concerned with religion, and ought to be.

As you've grown older, have you felt you've become more religious?

Neither yes nor no. The process is working itself out in writing the books, and I don't know what the outcome will be. I feel more convinced now than I was twenty years ago that religion is very central, whatever the form it takes. It should be very central to anyone's thinking life. But I'm certainly not more observant in religion than I was twenty years ago. In fact I'm less so, but you're right in a way in saying I have an obsession. But it's an intellectual obsession, part of the conception of what any thinker ought to be doing, and the fact that it takes historical form is accidental.

Have you an unfulfilled ambition?

Oh, I want to finish *Religion and Public Doctrine in Modern England*, that's what I want to do.

QUENTIN CREWE

Quentin Crewe is a writer, journalist, restaurateur and inveterate traveller. He was born in 1926 and educated at Eton and Trinity College, Cambridge. He joined the *Evening Standard* in 1953 and subsequently worked for *Queen*, *Vogue*, the *Daily Mail* and the *Sunday Mirror* before going freelance. His muscular dystrophy was diagnosed when he was six and he has been confined to a wheelchair for most of his life. Despite his disability he became the fourth westerner to cross the Empty Quarter of Saudi Arabia. He has also toured South America and made a 25,000-mile journey throughout the Sahara. He has been married three times: to Martha Sharp in 1956, to Angela Huth in 1961 and to Susan Cavendish in 1970. There are five children from the marriages. His books include *In Search of the Sahara*, *The Last Maharaja*, *In the Realms of Gold* and *Touch the Happy Isles*, which was shortlisted for the 1987 Thomas Cook Travel Book Award. Quentin Crewe now lives in France.

You had a conventional aristocratic upbringing, yet seem to have always wanted to break out of the mould: sacked from Eton, later sent down from Cambridge. What went wrong; why didn't you conform?

I don't know that things went wrong so much as that I just didn't get on with or fit in with my parents. They were very much older than usual in that my mother was forty-five when I was born, my father forty-six. By the time one is growing up, that makes a terrible gap. There isn't any memory left for the parents of what it's like to be a child. My upbringing wasn't altogether conventional in that my father was in the Consular Service, though in one sense it was a Victorian upbringing: one was brought down from the nursery at six o'clock and sent up again at seven. My mother was a very distant woman in a way hard to describe. My father was much more conventional. I grew up for the first five years in Sicily, until my father was moved to the South of France as consul-general for the Riviera. Then I went to live with my sister, and was brought up by her from the age of five. She was a much older half-sister, and had children older than me.

Again, funnily enough, I didn't fit in. It was a very hearty sort of background. My sister was married to a brewer who was keen on sports – shooting and hunting. But children are amazingly accepting of circumstances, whatever they may be. I accepted mine and I didn't necessarily feel unhappy. This is true of all human beings. If you go to Calcutta and you see how people live, you think they must be the most wretched and miserable people on earth. Not at all. They're laughing and joking, because that's what human beings do. Unhappiness is something you think of afterwards. I don't think I was unhappy in any day-to-day sense; it was more an overall feeling of not fitting in.

How did you manage to reconcile yourself to your disability?

That was very easy really, though one isn't ever reconciled in a sense. I was taken to a doctor when I was six at the insistence of my sister, who could see that I didn't walk or run properly, though my mother hadn't particularly noticed. The doctor said to my mother that I had muscular dystrophy and would die before I was sixteen, but to me he said I would be all right when I reached the age of sixteen. That was the last time the subject was mentioned with my parents until I was eighteen. I never went to another doctor in my childhood, and I was treated absolutely as if I were normal. I was expected to get on with it. No question of, oh, what shall we do about Quentin? Will he be able to manage? I was sent off to perfectly ordinary boarding schools, and that was fine, because it made me not think about it. My mother was generally unsympathetic, and annoyed by a suggestion that it had possibly come hereditarily from her. She wasn't having that, and said it must be my father. What they didn't realize in those days was that these things tend to happen more when the parents are so much older than usual. The imperfections in children from mothers over forty are now well known, and in fact my brother, just older than myself, had a cleft palate.

Quite early on I decided that I was not going to be sorry for myself. I remember overhearing an old cousin saying, he's so brave, and then he gave me a fiver, so in a way I'm grateful to my mother for her ruthlessness. My father used to make me walk across ploughed fields with a gun to shoot partridges. I used to fall down, and it was awful, but he made no concessions. I think an awful lot of my resourcefulness was, fortunately, born in me. I'm not subject to depressions, and I'm very bad at dealing with people who do have them.

I was, however, very lazy as a child, and always most dissatisfied with rules and conventions. I thought my prep school perfectly dreadful. I couldn't understand why the people there behaved as they did. The schoolmasters were bullying, the boys were bullying. All of this was foreign to me. Eton was much much better, but I was unlucky in being there during the war, when the younger masters had all gone off to fight. Our masters had all been hauled out of retirement and were a very eccentric lot. The absurdity of the rules was intolerable. If you wore an overcoat, you must never put the collar down. You had to carry your umbrella unrolled, so you carried the thing beside you, flapping like a dead bird. And so on. The sacking from Eton was for going up to London one day. I had a copy of the fire-door key made, and although I got back late, nobody knew I had been absent. But, of course, it was found out afterwards, and that was that.

I wanted to get into normal life, or what I thought was normal life, as early as possible. Although I found Cambridge very stimulating, it somehow didn't make me do any work. I studied law, but unfortunately

Roman law was what you had to start on, and that seemed to me both boring and idiotic. I didn't see why one needed to know about the manumission of slaves two thousand years ago. That aside, Cambridge was pure indolence. It was absolutely wonderful from the point of view of liberty and freedom, and suddenly I was into a whole new world and way of thinking. I was there at the end of the war, with great changes on the way, including a Labour government coming in, and that was all a great shock to my family, and so therefore to me; because one does in a way accept what one's parents tell one. Even so, Cambridge was an extraordinary release. There were so many things to unlearn in my life: all the things that had been dinned into me as a child. Anti-Semitism, for example, was a perfectly normal topic of everyday conversation; people would say, 'Oh, she's Jewish,' and that meant somehow that she was a little bit foreign. One had to unlearn all that.

How did the war years affect you?

Two of my three half-brothers were killed and the third was wounded, while my full brother was taken prisoner. In that sense it did impinge on me, and I was very aware of it. In another sense, some of it was fun. The bombs were nice and frightening, and there was something exciting about being frightened. I remember being in a swimming pool and watching a V–1 come over while I was swimming. It stopped in the way that they did, and I wondered where it was going to land, not minding because it was so exciting. But that sort of exhilaration had to be set against the distress of members of one's family being killed.

Did you go into journalism straight away after Cambridge?

No. I did lots of small jobs. My first was working in a bookshop called Sutherland's in Sackville Street. I loved it. It was very Dickensian and I well remember the comedy of getting one's £4 a week. The accountant was downstairs in the basement, and when it came to the Friday morning, you didn't go down and say, 'Where are my wages?' You went down and hovered about near the accountant's office until suddenly he'd look up and say,'Oh, Mr Crewe, there you are. Would you step this way a minute?' In you would go, and he'd give you an envelope, beautifully inscribed, your name in copperplate on the outside. It would have been very indelicate to open it there and then to see what was inside it, so you took it off to the loo, and there was your £4.

After that I went to work for something called the Art Exhibitions Bureau, an office that acted as secretary to various societies, such as the Royal Society of Portrait Painters. We used to hang exhibitions in various galleries, and it was interesting because it meant I met a lot of artists. But, again, it paid very badly, and I didn't really get on with

the owner, the organization was so fuddy-duddy. Then I worked a short time in a factory, then in a shipping line. The latter came about because I had a girlfriend who said she would leave me unless I got a job. I went out to an agency and picked up the first job going, which was as a ticket clerk in the French Line.

I was still able to walk a certain amount at that time, but was almost at the end of it, and was having a lot of trouble with falling over. In the end the doctors said I had better not keep struggling to work, and I was perfectly delighted to be told this, being, as I say, lazy by nature. So I stopped working and went to live in Italy, reading to a blind man – the scholar and historian, Percy Lubbock. I spent a year reading aloud to him for anything up to ten hours a day. It was good for my education and a pleasant place to live, and I also got to know Bernard Berenson and Harold Acton and all the people who lived in Florence in those days. Then I came home for a holiday, intending to go back and continue reading to Percy Lubbock, but a lunch with Lord Boothby intervened. John Junor was also present, having then, in 1953, just been made deputy editor of the *Evening Standard*. He offered me what then seemed the princely sum of £15 a week, and I couldn't resist it.

By all accounts, you got on well with Beaverbrook, though he was a notoriously difficult character.

Beaverbrook was able to enthuse people. You felt he was a man of action. At the time Burgess and Maclean disappeared, I said I would like to go to search for them. I had an idea of how to get into Czechoslovakia, which was where some people thought they'd run to. My editor refused me permission, but I went to Beaverbrook, who overruled the editor. It was his enthusiasm that was the attractive thing about him, and he had some very winning ways.

At a later stage I was doing some hard writing about art for the *Evening Standard* at the time when there was some unhappiness over how the Tate Gallery was being run by Sir John Robbins. Sir John did a great deal for the Tate, but he was also doing some rather funny things with funds that had been left to buy British pictures. He would actually buy something different and cook the labels on the pictures. I wrote rather a lot about this, and the deputy director of the Tate at that time, a South African called Larue Smith Larue, was sacked. Beaverbrook asked me if he ought to take him on as an adviser to help him buy pictures, and I said he should. Some nine months later, Beaverbrook called me to see him and said, 'You advised me to take on Larue Smith Larue. Now look at this picture. What sort of a picture do you think that is?' I told him it looked like a very nice Constable. 'That's what your friend Larue Smith Larue told me,' he said, 'and I paid £30,000

for that picture, which is worth only £30.' But what was rather touching was that he continued to regard the fake Constable as his favourite picture. In that way he could be very winning.

But he did do one thing to me which was inexcusable, and led to one of the acts I'm most ashamed of in my life. I was working at the *Evening Standard* late one evening when the telephone rang and Beaverbrook said, 'I've got a great story for you.' The story was that a man called Albert Crowther, who had been in gaol for receiving a stolen mantelpiece, had died there. The funeral had been that afternoon, and Beaverbrook wanted me to go and see Mrs Crowther and write a warm human story. I told him I couldn't possibly interview her the same day as she'd buried her husband. 'Oh,' he said, 'I thought you had a great future in journalism' – implying he was going to sack me, in that case. I'm ashamed to say that, instead of saying, 'All right, but I'm still not going to do the story,' I went to see Mrs Crowther, and it was awful. I waited for her until eleven o'clock that night when she came home with her family. I went up to one of the men escorting her and said, 'Look, I'm terribly sorry. I come from the *Evening Standard* and Lord Beaverbrook is particularly anxious that I should do a story. Could I just talk to Mrs Crowther for a minute or two?' He said he would ask her. Eventually he came out and said, 'Yes, she says she'll see you, but I think you're shit.'

I remember Harold Macmillan telling me how he was able once or twice to contradict Beaverbrook when he was minister of aircraft production at the beginning of the war. He did it by saying to Beaverbrook, 'If you do this, you will fry in hell.' Beaverbrook was terrified of hellfire. He was a son of the manse, his father a Presbyterian minister, so he was brought up in true Calvinist terror of God and could never really throw it off.

Weren't you romantically involved with Macmillan's daughter Sarah at one point? What did you make of Macmillan?

He was such a complex character. He was an extremely generous man, but had such a miserable family life that this coloured much of his nature and he spent a lot of time covering up his unhappiness. He was horrified by the betrayal of the people after the First World War; he genuinely minded it and wanted to fight for a better world. Perhaps he was a bit too world weary by the time he became prime minister, but I'm absolutely certain he would never have been party to brutality. If he could have avoided sending back the Cossacks, he would have avoided it. I'm certain it was not in any way a cynical act, and that he was not as deeply implicated as Tolstoy maintains; it simply wasn't in his character. He was extremely kind, and Sarah, incidentally, was not his daughter but

Boothby's daughter, and what he did for her was amazing. I remember when she was ill, and indeed had become an alcoholic, that he flew out quite anonymously to Switzerland where she was in a clinic. People recognized him at the airport and asked why he was there, and he replied that he was going to visit a friend. He took the trouble to go and see her, although she might have been regarded as an embarrassment to him. He was a good man in that sense.

Did Boothby care about her?

Boothby was more inclined to care about himself. He enjoyed the situation, enjoyed patronizing Sarah and giving her presents and so on, but he wasn't a proper father to her. He was a very shallow man, Boothby – clever but shallow. Macmillan occasionally gave an impression of shallowness, but that was part of his act.

During your time as 'Charles Greville' on the Daily Mail *gossip column, you proscribed stories about royalty, divorces and adultery. As a lover of gossip, why did you do that?*

The gossip columns had become so squalid at that point. One of the worst examples occurred when Selwyn Lloyd was getting divorced and a journalist pretended to be the godfather of Selwyn Lloyd's child. He went with a present to Carlton House and followed the nanny to find out where Mrs Selwyn Lloyd was. I considered that sort of behaviour intolerable. So far as royalty went, I didn't want a lot of royal family tittle-tattle in my column, and I certainly didn't want to have anybody's divorce or even anything about whether they were having babies. Of course, almost anything is legitimate gossip in ordinary conversation, unless somebody's told you something in strict privacy, but in the context of a newspaper, I don't think it necessarily is legitimate gossip. If the foreign secretary's getting divorced, then of course you write that the foreign secretary's getting divorced, but you don't hound his family.

As for the right to privacy and whether it's in the public interest to reveal indiscretions, I wouldn't say it matters if it's just somebody having an affair with someone else and it isn't going to affect anything. I know plenty of MPs who have affairs, and although journalists know about these affairs, they don't write about them. But I rather wonder when it comes to someone in Kennedy's position, for instance. It might be different if a man's judgement were affected by, shall we say, libertine behaviour or excessive womanizing. Kennedy was an example of a man who really did want to sleep with every woman he met. Whether this is a sign of immaturity, I'm not sure, but it might be relevant to whether or not a man should be running a country, particularly when it's the United States – rather a big country. On the other hand, this is such a

difficult area. You might also say there is something odd about a man who never sleeps with a woman.

You resigned from Queen *magazine because of a proposed supplement on South Africa. What are the liberal political causes you feel most strongly about?*

South Africa has always been top of the list, but about any tyranny, I think – and poverty. But how cynical we are in choosing places. For example, what is going on in Burma seems to me far worse than anything that is happening to Lithuania. What are we doing about Burma; what do we care about it? The Burmese are just left to rot. Nobody's standing up, shouting, screaming and saying the sort of things they're saying about the situation in Lithuania. We're terribly selective.

I do applaud the courage of people like Mary Benson who made the decision that what was going on in South Africa was wrong. Those people could lead perfectly comfortable lives in their own country, but chose to stand up for what they believed was right. It raises one of the big questions. Would one have joined the Hitler Youth Movement if one had been born a German child? Of course one would. Or supposing fascism had come to Britain, would one have stood up against it or would one have been as feeble as people were in Italy and in Germany? That's the kind of courage I most admire, and I just hope to God I would have had it, though I don't know if I would. To know that something is right is one thing. Whether you can live up to it is another.

The liberalism of your views on sexual codes is widely shared nowadays, but where would you draw the line about sex now?

Interfering with children. Anyone under sixteen. Otherwise I don't mind. Gross perversions are just very unhappy for the people who feel them necessary, but in general people make too much fuss about ordinary sex.

Don't you feel that the fundamental cement of society – the formalized partnership of man and woman – ought to be one of society's greatest priorities, even today?

When I was in Sri Lanka, I visited a man and his wife. His mother lived with them, and this was absolutely natural, a normal course of events. He expected to have his mother living there. And this is a terrible loss in our lives: the fact that we've cut down to these nuclear families of a husband, wife, children and maybe a granny flat. The whole thing is lost. I don't see that we're ever going to get it back. I don't see how we can or how we could make it a priority. You can't dictate to people how to live. You can't abolish the idea that women's lives have changed.

Yet I also think this is good in a way. I've always been a feminist in the sense that I can't bear it when women are just sat on and used.

You have a legendary reputation for seducing women in general and beautiful young women in particular. Most men who know you well are envious. What is your secret?

I've often wondered. I may tell you, it gets less easy, but I think they're intrigued by something different – that is to say, somebody in a wheelchair. The only explanation I can think of is that those women who have seduced me wanted to discover what it was like to go to bed with somebody disabled. Or there is always the other possibility, that one is less frightening to them, that one isn't a great beast who's going to leap on top of them and beat them. Whatever it is, I've been very lucky.

Extremely lucky.

Well, I don't think I'm able to shed any light on it.

Could it be because you are such a great raconteur?

I think, really, that what I said to you once about Lord Weidenfield is the answer: if you take a real interest in women, they respond amazingly. Concentrating on them at a dinner party, you talk just to one woman, exclusively to her, and brush everybody else aside. They find that very attractive.

So you don't have to work hard at it.

I don't work very hard at it.

It comes naturally?

I don't know, Naim. What difficult questions you ask. I think it's fading.

Your disability means that you need a male companion to help you, and some have been young, good looking and intelligent. Does the physical dependence ever develop into a physical attachment in the sense that you get a crush on someone?

Not necessarily. Young men can be attractive physically, but I don't think I get a crush. They've mostly been good healthy normal lads. I don't like ugly people. Of course, one has some ugly friends, but I find it much easier to like good-looking people.

You are also said to be a Professor Higgins type in that you become a mentor to your women or wives and thus able to exercise a power over them.

I don't think I've exercised power over them. I may have taught Angela a certain amount about writing, and I certainly introduced the others to various ideas that influenced their lives, but to call it power is going too far.

Is it a source of regret that your marital history has been so tempestuous?

Regrets are not very much a part of my life. Naturally I could wish that my marriages had turned out better, but on the other hand, for years they were a success. They were all good for a period.

What of the rumours that your first wife tried to kill you, your second left yet was willing to remarry you, and the third became so exasperated that she used to hit you? How did you come to generate such stormy emotional responses?

I really don't know. I'm nomadic, so that's perhaps one difficulty. Secondly, it's not at all easy to live with someone who's disabled. That's a particularly important point, and I certainly wouldn't ever reproach any of my wives for having found it difficult. It's better that a marriage came to an end than that they struggled on out of guilt, so maybe that had a lot to do with it. I always think I'm very calm, so perhaps I just picked tempestuous ladies.

One of your former wives said it was a great privilege to have been married to you. What is it about you that makes a former wife pay such a loyal tribute?

It must be partly her sweetness of character. Once she gives her devotion to somebody, it's for good. The fact that she didn't feel able to go on being married didn't interfere with the relationship, if you see what I mean. I don't think we ever at any point had any feelings of dislike for each other – just an inability to live together. I don't know whether the other two would say anything similar, but she is very nice.

Have you regretted any of your marriages?

This is too difficult an area to cover. The answer must be no. There was so much that was agreeable about all of them that they can't be considered disasters, and I have five wonderful children as a result. I don't think I would ever marry again. The point of getting married is if you're going to have children, and I'm not going to have any more.

How would you advise your own children about marriage and relationships?

It's something you can only learn by experience. I'd never advise anybody about marriage. The only time I've ever done it was with some-

body who then married the person I was advising them very strongly not to marry and who has had a perfectly happy married life ever since; so you can't predict. Look at the funny people who are married to one another and who get on, and then look at the seemingly compatible people who get married and don't stay together longer than ten minutes. It's all most peculiar. I don't think anybody can understand marriage at all till they've been married. It's very hard for young people nowadays because girls have changed and have become as independent as the boys used to be, and then they find it hard to give up that freedom.

Your daughter Candida called you great as a friend but hopeless as a father. How did you feel about that judgement?

It's probably true as far as my children are concerned. There's evidently something that I don't do that my children think I ought to do, because I don't seem able to get over to them my feelings for them. If one fails to convince them that one is a good father, one obviously isn't a good father.

You wrote in the Sunday Times *that you never felt responsible for your children. Many people might be shocked by such an idea.*

Of course I'm responsible for them in the sense that, if they're in trouble, I must get them out of it. But I don't feel responsible for their achievement and I don't think that, if one of them became a murderer, I would feel responsible for that either.

You also spoke with some derision about people who 'moulder on about what their parents have done to destroy or make them', but what greater influence can there be on a child than its parents?

Its own innate character. If you take twin babies in a cot, a few days old, their mother will tell you that there is something different about this one from that one. It's precisely that which I think is the interesting thing about human beings. Of course there are influences: school and environment, whether you're brought up in Yorkshire or Zimbabwe. But ultimately a child is itself, to my mind.

Do you think the fact that you have unavoidably spent so much time separated from your children may have coloured your view of parental influence?

No, I don't think so. I spent a great deal of time shaking off the parental influence that I had on me. Of course, bits go deep, but we can get rid of a lot of it.

Do you believe that children must fend for themselves to some extent?

Looking at my very rich friends who had given their children a lot of money early, it's nearly always been a disaster. Everybody in life needs to forge their way a bit. When things are too easy for them, it's corrupting. Strawberries from Kenya don't taste like good strawberries from the harsher climates. It's the same with wine. It's the northern wine that's best – Bordeaux and Champagne. The southern French wine is nothing like so good. The same thing applies to people. They've got to have some sort of struggle.

When explaining your unwillingness to instil any sort of sexual moral code, you said that doubtless you would have something to say if a daughter of yours became a 'courtesan'. Why choose that rather romantic word instead of 'prostitute'?

Well, to become a prostitute is unthinkable. I mean, none of them would become prostitutes. A courtesan is a possibility, I suppose. One could entertain the idea. But I would have something to say, merely because I think it would not make them very happy. There is a difference between the two words. A prostitute is somebody who's doing it straightforwardly for money, and a courtesan is probably sticking to one person at a time for a way of life rather than for straight cash. She might have a nice flat or house and a cash allowance, but not £200 for a night or whatever. But I'd never disown my children whatever they did. If they did something absolutely dreadful, I would feel very upset, but I would still think it was my duty to help them. It seems to me that love for somebody is complete, that it must encompass whatever their faults may be. You may get angry with them, you may get fed up with the child who's done something tiresome or annoying, but you can't ever abandon them. Love is constant, to my mind, and permanent. I don't feel for my daughters that they ought not to go to bed with somebody. That idea doesn't worry me.

People who were or still are close to you have mentioned the down side to your character, saying you can be hurtful, cruel and selfish, and can publicly humiliate those you love.

It's true except for the last bit. I suspect my children are putting forward this view. I am much too sharp-tongued, which comes from impatience with what I see as stupidity. As for being selfish, I don't know whether I'm more selfish than others. And I don't think I humiliate anyone. There's no malice in me.

Angela Huth told me that your daughter Candida has all your best qualities.

Obviously there has to be something in genetic influence. I'm not sure whether I'd set more store by environmental influence. In my own case, I was lucky to be brought up from the age of thirteen in a house full of books. There were 20,000 volumes at least, and marvellous paintings, beautiful furniture. All this had its influence too, but then there are lots of people who are brought up in circumstances of that sort who don't even notice there is a book or a painting there. We don't know the answer to this, and I don't think even psychiatrists do. As far as Candida is concerned, I would reverse the comment and say she has Angela's best qualities.

What did you mean exactly when you described your daughter Candida's books as done in good taste?

Her first romantic novel was done in an unvulgar way, but the second one wasn't quite so good. I regard a lot of romantic novels as being straightforwardly vulgar, and her first was not. But I felt the publishers then leant on her to put more sex into the second. She was hopelessly bad at writing about it, and it was obviously against her instincts. I daresay she could write about sex extremely well, but what she was trying to do was something somebody else was imposing on her, and it was hopeless.

You always give the impression of treating your disability lightly and inviting others to do the same, but beneath the composure must lie years of anguish, frustration and pain.

I didn't used to suffer much pain. Latterly I have, but if I started giving in to the idea of being unfortunate and allowed myself to think I'm unlucky, I would feel very depressed. It sounds trite, but one just has to count one's blessings. I sometimes ask myself if I would like to swop places with some very stupid athletic man, and the answer is that I wouldn't. I'd rather be me and I'd always rather be me.

Has your view of life changed with your disability?

Not really. I suppose I suppress the fact of it to some extent. In a way, I don't think of myself as disabled. It may sound stupid, but it's true: I think of myself as somebody who doesn't ski and who can't run, but then I look at someone else in a wheelchair and think, oh, poor them, they're in a wheelchair. It's bizarre, perhaps, but perhaps the only way of dealing with it.

Might you never have become such an intrepid traveller without the challenge of being confined to a wheelchair?

I often wonder that myself. Was I driven by some urge? I don't think so. I am by nature a nomad. I really want to wander. I'm never so happy as when I'm on the move. Bruce Chatwin was a friend of mine, and this was something we had in common.

What do you consider to be most important in your life?

Oh, my family, obviously. I think that is the thing everybody must consider of prime importance in life. I feel very strongly about my children, that I owe everything to them but they owe nothing to me. I don't think it's right to be proud of one's children. You can be pleased for them, but I don't consider that something my son does goes down to my credit. I mind passionately that my children should be thought of as being themselves. My daughter Candida writes extremely well, works unbelievably hard, but that's her, and it's nothing to do with me. Very little else matters to me desperately, except I think unkindness. I like good manners very much, though God knows I don't always write all the thank-you letters I should, but I do feel manners make the world so much easier to live in.

Looking back on a career embracing journalism, the restaurant business, travelling and writing, which has been most difficult and which has given you most satisfaction?

You missed out farming. Farming – which gave me enormous satisfaction, but was a total disaster. It's really writing that gives me more and more satisfaction as I find what I want to write, or, rather, how I want to write. I've enjoyed journalism, but my visit to South Africa was the only thing I would ever claim as something worth while, something that actually mattered. Writing has something else to it than journalism. I hate writing so far as the physical act of sitting there and trying to achieve something is concerned. That's absolute hell. But it does give one much more satisfaction in the end.

Have you ever been tempted to seek comfort in religion, or have your circumstances had the opposite effect?

They haven't had any effect on that at all. I certainly don't sit about swearing and asking why God inflicted this upon me, because I don't think He did. Religion does become more interesting to people as they get older, because they're nearing the end, but I'm not very frightened of death. I can't help but be impressed by the Eastern religions in countries like Sri Lanka, Thailand and so on, and of course in the Arab

countries. I find the everyday quality of Islam very impressive. When you're travelling in the desert, you see people praying five times a day, and it's absolutely natural to them. Religion ought to be an everyday affair. The Christian religion is much too shut away in its churches. It gives far too much power to bishops and priests. They are too dictatorial, whereas in Islam it's easily accessible, and in Buddhism there is the feeling that God is within you. I find that very attractive and possibly something which I will continue to read more and more about.

My research reveals your philosophy of life to be that nothing matters very much and very little matters at all. Is this anything more than a self-preserving maxim?

Of course not, and it's a joke to some extent. People make too much fuss about too many things, like all the food fads, for example. One of my complaints about the younger generation is that they're so self-absorbed; they think all the time about what's good for you and what's not. And all this health kick is really because they haven't got anything else to think about. I see no evidence that they are healthier as a result. People take themselves too seriously. We're all rather absurd in that way.

NIGEL DEMPSTER

Nigel Dempster was born in 1941 in India where he spent his first six years. He was educated at Sherborne and became a broker for Lloyd's of London. He entered journalism in 1960, first with the *Daily Express*, then in 1963 as a columnist on the *Daily Mail* where in 1973 he was appointed editorial executive and editor of 'Mail Diary'. Between 1969 and 1985 he was a columnist on *Private Eye* magazine ('Grovel'). His first marriage in 1971 to Emma de Bendern was dissolved in 1974. In 1978 he married Lady Camilla Osborne; they have one daughter. He broadcasts with ABC (USA) and CBC (Canada) and is under contract to TV-am. His books include *HRH The Princess Margaret – A Life Unfulfilled* and *Christina: The Last Onassis*.

You were born in India, but left when you were six. Do you remember anything of that life?

I remember everything because it's almost as if it were yesterday. There was sunshine and jungles and the sorts of things you can't believe a child had: elephants and tigers in the garden, pythons and boa constrictors. We literally lived in the jungle, 133 miles south-west of Calcutta. I know the distance, because when you buy a ticket in India it tells you exactly how long the train journey is. I've got a very clear memory from the age of two. I can say that because we had a dog that I remember dying when I was two. The whole joy of being born in India was that there were no guide-lines. You never felt that you had to do anything; you never felt you had to get up in the morning. I had no form of discipline. I learned Hindustani since that was the only language my *ayah* spoke, and it never occurred to me that there was any world outside. My *ayah* would sleep at the end of my bed, guarding me from the world. She was a wonderful person.

My father was managing director of the Indian Copper Corporation, and we lived where we did because the mine was near by – about the third largest copper mine in what used to be the Commonwealth. He employed something like 12,000 miners and was a tremendously hard-working man with no interests in life except mining. His whole joy was his work. He certainly had no interest in women or children, but would work seven days a week, fourteen hours a day, and all his people remembered him for that. When he married my mother he told her, 'All right, you can have children, but don't expect me to have anything to do with them.' A great treat for me was, he thought, to take me down the mine, so instead of being taken out to the zoo or to a film, as would have happened in England, my entertainment was to be taken down the mine. I can remember at the very early age of about four,

descending 4,000 feet into the bowels of the earth and seeing all the miners. It's an extraordinary memory I have of watching people knocking things out of rock deep underground.

My memory of India is one of total joy. We never wore shoes, we had a swimming pool, a tennis court and a staff of about fifteen. We even had what was called a sepoy, who, rather like the guards at Buckingham Palace, stood in a guard-box at the entrance to the house to make sure no one came in who shouldn't. There was no one who wanted to come in, so it was quite ridiculous. But it was an idyllic childhood, and so privileged, though everyone lived like that as far as I was concerned. I was born when the war was on, not that I knew about it. The only thing to occur to me as strange was having two airfields within about ten miles, one a US airbase and the other RAF. The officers used our swimming pool and tennis court, and I charged them gum in the case of the Americans and I can't remember what in the case of the British – whatever was going probably. It was a wonderful life, without responsibility, without care.

In later years, I went back several times. At thirteen it was difficult, because although I had only been away six years, everyone was speaking to me in Hindustani and I couldn't understand. I was there for the summer holidays for two months, and was glad to be back, but by then I'd become English, having been at an English boarding school in the meantime.

When the time came for me to leave for England in 1947, it never occurred to me that anything different was going to happen because my mother had explained that this was where I'd have to go to school, even though my father came from Australia. My father was forty-seven years older than me, and his father fifty-seven years older than him, so the Australian connection had vanished and my parents looked towards Britain as a place to educate their children. I saw nothing wrong with it, but what happened was a tremendous shock because I couldn't read or write and was coming up to my sixth birthday. The reason why I couldn't read or write was that I hadn't wanted to. In India I had spent most of my time in the servants' quarters, learning wonderful folklore and hearing stories of their lives.

The first thing that sticks in my mind about England was the cold from the beginning of the winter of 1947, which was the coldest winter until 1963. My clothes were totally inadequate. I'd never known such numbing, freezing cold, and in those days, of course, schools didn't have central heating. Also, I had never had to live in a disciplined society, but had always done exactly what I wanted. If I didn't want to eat, I didn't eat; if I didn't like the food I used to throw it about. The only discipline had been provided by my father, who sometimes used to beat the hell out of me with his belt, but that was fair enough.

The next thing about England was the austerity, because in India we had everything: milk, butter, animals we could kill. One of the great delights of my childhood in India was the cook's compound, where I watched him behead chickens. In England, where there was very little food, the fact came as a jolt, and certainly food has been something uppermost in my mind ever since. I wake up every day looking forward to meals, and I'm sure that's something to do with that period of my life. My prep school was very small. There were thirty boarders, and I was the youngest by far. It was an extraordinary life, and I almost forgot the previous life in India, because I realized that you had to adapt, and if you didn't adapt you were dead. You knew, if you didn't get on, awful things were going to happen to you – you would be put in Coventry, people wouldn't speak to you. You could literally not be spoken to because you had body odour. I remember boys at school and how awful calamitous things which they had nothing to do with haunted them for the rest of their lives.

But the first person who influenced my life was my English master there – a man called Michael Gardiner, who was a bachelor, I suspect an eternal bachelor. He was enormously interested in the English language and made me interested too. He was also a Catholic, and I remember our having a spirited discussion about Jimmy Goldsmith, of all people. I must have been twelve at the time, and the news was that Jimmy Goldsmith's wife, Isobel, had died in childbirth producing a daughter, also called Isobel. I started discussing this because the papers, which were rather blurred in those days, made it look as if Goldsmith had said, 'Save the daughter but let my wife die.' In fact, if you read up the story, you discover that what happened was that his wife had a brain haemorrhage that virtually killed her, then the child was born, and after that his wife died. Michael Gardiner told me that the Catholic ethic was that you save the child rather than the mother, and over that we had a tremendously spirited discussion. It's curious that it should have been about Jimmy Goldsmith, who now lives a couple of hundred yards from me.

After prep school I went on to public school.

Would you send a child of your own to Sherborne?

The extraordinary thing about Sherborne is that it's become a much better school than when I was there. The only reason why I went there was that my mother, who came from the Dartmoor area, remembered it as the best school in the West Country, the West Country starting, I suppose, somewhere near Salisbury and running through to Cornwall. When I went there in April 1955, it was a good, modest, second-rank public school. It goes back a thousand years, and Sherborne Abbey

apparently has the remains of Alfred the Great who was said to have been educated there. It's a beautiful part of the world, and my mother was entranced with its beauty. It's a much better school today; it's got tremendous endowments. If I had a son, which I never will, and he wanted to go to boarding school, I can't actually think of a better one. It's academically very sound, its sporting record is tremendous and it produces rather nice boys. Having said that, there are only about five of my contemporaries whom I still see out of, I suppose, a thousand boys I knew in my day.

Why do you say you'll never have a son?

Well, unless I marry again. Certainly my wife doesn't want to have another child. We had a daughter in 1979, and that seems to be it. I also feel that people have children for all the wrong reasons. We had a child for the right reason. We wanted a child and we got a daughter, whom I dote on, adore. I think people who go on having children till they have a son do it for all the wrong reasons. Many do it for reasons of inheritance, and it's a crazy motive. Why not just stop when you've got what you want; why buck fate? Anyone is lucky to have children that are normal, happy and healthy. One in ten children in Britain is born with some abnormality. I know enough people, like Jocelyn Stephens, who have suffered that way.

When you left school at sixteen, did you have any idea at all what you were going to do in life?

In those days, the whole public school careers system wanted to put you into the established trades, and in 1958, when I left, that meant the City, which meant stockbroking, Lloyd's of London, merchant not commercial banking, or chartered accountancy. There were other professions which you positively did not enter, journalism being one. You could just about go into advertising, which was a coming thing in those days, a fledgling industry. But everyone who left Sherborne went into either the industries, which people thought would give them a leg up into the future, or into the army, the navy or the air force.

I had absolutely no idea what I wanted to do, and leaving was a terrible shock to me, because I hadn't meant to leave so early. But I had been at boarding school ten years, and it was far too long. I had become rebellious and achieved a certain notoriety at the school. Everything that went wrong was blamed on me. I'd started people drinking, smoking, and talking to girls, which was not allowed. You actually used to get beaten at Sherborne if you talked to a girl. In the summer of 1958, I was booked to go to Davies's, a tutorial establishment in Addison Road, Holland Park, but the first thing I did when I came to London was to

get a job as a porter at the Westminster Hospital. The money was good – something like £8 or £9 a week – and if you worked the night shift you had to wheel bodies out and put them in the mortuary. I discovered more in those two months than I would ever have known otherwise. I saw bodies having their heads cut off at post mortems; I had to put stiffs into fridges at three in the morning. It was a quick growing-up process.

Then I did go to Davies's, the reason being that at Sherborne I was top of the class in English and history, for which I would win prizes, but bottom of the class in my other six subjects. The other people who were trying to get their exams were Etonians thrown out of Eton, Harrovians thrown out of Harrow. We all realized that the last thing we wanted to do was pass exams, so we'd go and have lunch in different places. Suddenly we learned that there was another life, and no one I met at Davies's ever achieved what they went there for. I realized I must have a new life, and one of the people at Davies's, whose father was a broker, said, 'Go and see my father', and so I got a job as a broker at Lloyd's, literally on my seventeenth birthday, and entered a new world. Suddenly in Lloyd's there were people from Eton, Winchester and Harrow, and I discovered the extraordinary life of débutante parties in the late 1950s, at the time when Harold Macmillan was telling us we'd never had it so good.

You could go about London and be wined and dined for nothing, though there wasn't much sex around in those days. In the late 1950s, perhaps 5 per cent of the girls went to bed with men; in the late 1960s, perhaps 5 per cent didn't. It never occurred to the people whose parties I went to that I was any different from those who introduced me. I got into that stream and stayed there simply by being amusing, charming and nice to the girls and their parents. There was an enormous amount of snobbishness. I'm sure you'll find hundreds of people out in the shires, thirty years on from the deb season of 1959, who will say, 'What a filthy little yob Nigel Dempster was. I always knew he was a parvenu. He gatecrashed my sister's party' – that sort of thing. So what? It doesn't worry me.

I don't think they gave a thought to me being Australian. They might even have thought it slightly romantic. All people really cared about in those days was that you didn't sleep with their daughter, and very few did. The deb parties were proliferating. In 1959, every day from the beginning of May till the end of July, there were at least two cocktail parties, and each weekend there were at least three dances. You could choose which county you wanted to go to dance in. All it required was a white tie and tails. My first weekly pay cheque was £6, plus 2s. 6d. (12½p) a day in luncheon vouchers. I also got an allowance of £200 a year from my father, and on that one could live very well. I shared a

flat in Lennox Gardens, which cost £2 10s. (£2.50) a week and was a good address. The rest was free, except for the cleaning of your clothes.

I don't think money made much difference. Girls liked men because they liked men. A girl who liked a man with a car was a girl who had a different view on life. But in those days we were all children. We fumbled each other occasionally; we made love if we were lucky. Very few girls were overtly after men with money, and I think it went on personality. I was still only seventeen, and it was amazing, because I was younger than the girls, and at seventeen or eighteen girls are much more mature than boys the same age. I simply don't know how I did it. It must have been with gritted teeth and perseverance, because I was very much a baby, though I had been seduced very young. In Devon, my home was with my grandparents, and about three miles up the road in Budleigh Salterton I had a friend with a large house who used to give parties in the basement. We'd fumble around with girls and, without knowing what we were doing, used to get laid. That would have been when I was fourteen or fifteen. It wasn't a satisfactory experience, but it wasn't terribly unsatisfactory either.

What sort of qualities do you need for work as a gossip writer?

First, a phenomenal memory. Secondly, an acquaintanceship with a wide section of society. No one could have invented a better gossip columnist than me because, by a quirk of fate – my upbringing – and luck I managed to meet an awful lot of people. I remember having dinner at No. 11 Downing Street, because Reggie Maudling's daughter was there and there you were, right in the midst of the government. From seventeen onwards I met all the children and grandchildren of the people who were Establishment Britain. That's why, to this day, they can say, 'God, that creep, that bastard,' but we knew each other, and because I had an innate interest in other people, I'm able to remember how, where and why I met them, what their ages were and who they were with. I have that sort of encyclopaedic memory and can recall things you can't get in cuttings. It's having a vast log-jam of past memories – that's the gossip columnist's art. By some fluke I managed to acquire it.

It never occurred to me that I'd become a journalist. In those years being a journalist was a very grubby profession; journalists were grammar school boys who wore dirty macs, behaved badly and worked in an appalling part of London called Fleet Street, which was somewhere you never went. Those of us in the City used to look west towards Fleet Street as if it was a sort of nuclear rubbish tip.

How do you check the information that comes your way? There must surely be lots of people who try to exploit your column for their own interests.

None whatsoever. If people were to ring up saying, 'Would you write about me?' you'd make them look so ridiculous. It's rather like a man asking a woman, 'Would you make love to me?' He fears rejection. Similarly, no first-person attempt to infiltrate is ever made because people fear being humiliated. My view has always been that if you don't want to get into a column then, like the Aga Khan, you surely will. I've been in gossip columns now for twenty-seven years, and I've never known anyone get a story beneficial to themselves into the columns I've worked on.

As for checking information, the information these days comes first hand. Part of the deal has to be that informants get paid for what they tell. Every part of the newspaper, from front page to back, is marked up every morning for payment. Sometimes we have seven or eight items a day. Sometimes our bill for payment to informants is as little as £50, sometimes as much as £500.

Everyone believes that gossip column stories are about marriage break-ups. It's absolutely untrue. The number of stories about marriage break-ups come to perhaps one every two or three weeks, and when they happen they are of historical importance. It needs to be noted that the Duke of X has left his wife because it's something to go into a book, a part of history. The idea of Fleet Street gossip columns being grubby little areas where we expose the seamy side of people's lives is wrong. Most of the stories are about money, privilege and power, and the other area is basically the historical aspect of Britain – births, marriages and deaths, with divorces obviously included.

A gossip column has got to be scandalous in terms of raising an eyebrow because you can't have a column which simply massages the back. There are two sides to every great person: the public side – the approbation of the masses – and the private side. That's life. If you get into some sort of dialogue with a journalist, as people in public life want to do, then the journalist enters into a pact with them. They get publicity for what they're doing, but as soon as things go wrong in their life, it would be foolish to have these rich, powerful and privileged people believing they can then pull the shutters down and say, 'Look, don't write about me any more.' They've incited the public's interest, and I'm afraid they've got to realize that once you're started on the treadmill, you keep going.

What sort of editorial freedom do you have?

When I went to the *Daily Mail* in August 1971, the paper had just merged with the *Daily Sketch* and something like 300 people had lost their jobs. Paul Callan and I were the first two signings to the new *Mail* to start columns, and I can honestly say that, from that day to this, I

have never suffered any form of interference from anyone. I can only assume that is a sign of great success, because you only interfere with something that's going wrong. I've never been asked by the editor or the proprietor to put in a story. I've never been asked to take one out. The measure of Lord Rothermere's urbanity is that, when I came back from the United States in 1973 and went to work on the Diary, my very first story on 8 October was that Lady Annabel Birley, who was married to Mark Birley and after whom Annabel's in Berkeley Square was named, was having another baby. She'd already had three, and this was her fourth, and the story went that Mark Birley was not the father but Jimmy Goldsmith was.

I rang up Jimmy, whom I knew even in those days, and said, 'There's a story that you're the father of the baby Lady Annabel Birley is expecting in January 1974,' and he laughed and joked but I wrote the story just the same. It appeared on the Monday, and on Monday evening Lord and Lady Rothermere went into Annabel's to be met by Mark Birley in a high fury. I think Lady Rothermere was allowed to stay, but Lord Rothermere was thrown out, and the measure of my esteem for Lord Rothermere was that I never heard a whisper about the story at the time. Five or six years later, someone asked did I know that after my very first column as Nigel Dempster on the Diary my proprietor was thrown out of Annabel's? My response came close to worship. Anyone else would have had me fired, but I never even heard about it.

If the trade of the gossip columnist is trivial, I think that all of life is trivial. Kierkegaard said all life will be gossip, and I suspect that my trade gives a far greater insight into the workings of those people who are above us in terms of power and privilege, position and money. People aren't that interested in the pronouncements from the pulpit or what's happening in the House of Commons, because the British are a very cynical race. No one cares what politicians say. We know they're all liars, cheats and fools. What we want to know is what's going on in their backgrounds, why they're saying whatever, why a certain minister does this, a politician that. The answer invariably lies in their personal life, and this is why the gossip columnist is as invaluable now as he was two hundred years ago, for the only way the British public knew King George III was mad was through gossip. The reason why the serfs, the ordinary working people of Britain, realized things were going wrong was through gossip, because there weren't any newspapers in their time.

What we do today is an advanced, streamlined version of village gossip, and we provide a fantastic service. People want to know if those who are rich, powerful and privileged are having a better life than they are. They're having a better life materially maybe, but things are going horrifically wrong for them too. Cecil Parkinson's daughter is a drug addict; the Duke of Marlborough's heir is a drug addict; the Marquis

of Bristol, with 4,000 acres and £20 million, is a drug addict who has been in prison. It gives people a sort of comfort.

Investigative journalism can be defended as part of a free society. If a minister, for example, has a liaison with a foreign embassy official, or shares a prostitute with one, it might well be in the public interest to reveal it. But if someone's husband or wife leaves, or takes to adultery, doesn't broadcasting it merely compound the misery?

Gossip columnists only print stories long after they've happened. Rarely do you write in the middle of a story. What you're doing is dotting the i's and crossing the t's. People go off with other people, people have hiccups in their marriages. By the time it gets into a gossip column, it's history. The people involved have explained it all to their children, they've moved out, moved into other houses, and it comes as something of a merciful release to see it written in a decent newspaper like the *Daily Mail* because then they don't need to answer any questions any more.

The profession can't be called intrusive because the people who are written about on the whole welcome journalistic attention. In this day and age, it's not enough to exist. You have to be seen to exist. People enjoy publicity and realize that if you are in the spotlight for whatever reason – birth or ancestry, accumulation of wealth, inheritance – it's a two-edged sword.

If you ask me whether we need a right to privacy in this country, I say absolutely not. The only reason anyone wants a right to privacy is if they've got to hide something. The privacy bill in France was introduced by a libidinous premier with a saucy wife. Pompidou didn't want the French papers writing about him or his saucy wife. Pompidou's personal life was a sorry mess, and so he passed an Invasion of Privacy Act, which means that in France you cannot write about any aspect of the private life of a public person. It also means that there are all known forms of chicanery going on. The French public have no idea whether their peers are murderers, rapists, finaglers, thieves or liars, and that's very sad.

Over the years there has been a call for a privacy bill here, but it's always come from members of parliament who have been exposed. In the 1970s, I exposed Maureen Colquhoun, who was Labour MP for Northampton and a lesbian. Many of the voters in Northampton may well not have known about her lesbian tendencies, but they certainly did when she and her girlfriend, Babs Todd, sent out change-of-address cards with a Sappho motif. I got hold of one of the cards and exposed her in the *Daily Mail* as a lesbian. All I was doing was bringing to a wider public what she herself had advertised, but all hell broke loose.

I was reported to the Press Council. I was this and that and all the rest of it. Meanwhile Maureen Colquhoun's leftist friends in Parliament – including one Arnold Latham, who was MP for Paddington, I think, and a particularly unattractive little man – tried to bring in a privacy bill.

Every time you hit the raw nerve of an MP – and the most recent is this one called John Browne, the MP for Winchester, who has caused his ex-wife great financial hardship – they start a rumble for a privacy bill. I never see the decent MPs who have their lives rent asunder, like Cecil Parkinson or Roy Hattersley, calling for privacy legislation, because they understand the rules of the game. And the rules are very simple: if you behave yourself, you won't be written about, and if you don't it's no good hiding behind a cloak of privacy.

I started off in this business with an enormous number of friends and ended up with very few, but the few I've ended up with are the same friends I've had for thirty years. All the people I've known for a long time understand that, if they do something horrible or heinous, it's going to end up in a column, and they'd rather have it in my column. They know it's a decent newspaper it's going into, and they know I'm not going to twist the quotes. The whole point about being British is that you realize that, if you've done wrong, you put your hands up and say, 'Got me!'

As far as outside pressures go, people realize that they'll get nowhere trying to put pressure on a journalist, at least one of my standing. Therefore the pressure comes in lesser ways, such as, 'What do you want to know? Can we do a deal? Could you perhaps say this rather than that?' People know that they can only put pressure on someone if they've got a lever, and no one has a lever on me. I don't need the money, I don't lead a salacious private life, so I can't be blackmailed on either count. No one can say, 'Look here, you've committed adultery with my sister, how dare you write that story.' I'm not saying I lead an unblemished life, but I am saying there are no areas of my life about which I can be pressured. The only pressure is internal pressure. If I write something, how is it going to affect my future?

I'm also helped by not leading a social life myself, which is a great joy. I belong to the most egalitarian club in the world, the RAC, which is full of very middle-class people, and our common delight is playing squash and running. I run marathons, the most egalitarian form of sport on earth. People who stop being friends with me I don't regard as friends anyway, because they can't expect a journalist to behave other than the way he does. You can't give a party at which something extraordinary happens and not expect a journalist who is there to write about it. Certainly people like Peregrine Worsthorne can't resist it. For example, we were all invited to a party at Jimmy Goldsmith's on what

happened to be a General Election night, and Jimmy had said to everyone that they could either come and not write about it or write about it but not come. So I said, all right, I'd come but wouldn't write about it. Then I was furious the next morning to find that Peregrine Worsthorne, who had been there, had gone and written about it.

The thing that makes me angry is that journalists should be viewed in this curious way. I don't know whether Jimmy will ever invite Worsthorne again, but the point for me was that I stood by my word. Nevertheless journalists are journalists and people must realize that occasionally they break every rule because the urge to tell overcomes the need for discretion.

Finding myself the occasional butt of other gossip columnists has, in fact, only reinforced my views about accuracy, because what I've discovered in ninety-nine per cent of items written about me is their inaccuracy – dates and places wrong, names and people wrong. All that has done is convince me to tighten guidelines to staff even further, so we check everything not once, not twice, but three times. We make the most ludicrous checks. Sometimes we spend two days ringing up to make sure 'Susie' is not spelt 'Suzy', because once you get one thing wrong, people doubt the veracity of the rest. I was brought up in the Fleet Street of the old days. I joined the *Daily Express* in 1953, when Lord Beaverbrook was at the helm and you used to get sacked if you spelt a name incorrectly or got someone's age wrong. Nowadays journalism is so sloppy. There's no form to it. I despair. The last redoubt of accurate journalism is in the gossip column.

Have you ever had information which you did not print for non-journalistic reasons?

I've always printed everything I've ever known, because, for a start, I work on the assumption that, if I don't print it, someone else will; and if someone else will print it, then I should have printed it in the first place. I must qualify that, on the other hand, by saying that I don't write homosexual stories. The *Daily Express* column has gone markedly downhill over the past eight or nine years, simply because of its preponderance of homosexual stories. They seem to find homosexuals intriguing. Why I don't know. Certainly the editors have never been homosexual. Homosexual stories have never been part of my diet, and the reason I wouldn't print them is simply because I find them tasteless and not because they impinge on my relationships with other people.

Once you said in defence of your profession: 'It is not the exposure of an indiscretion but rather the indiscretion itself that causes hurt.' Isn't that special pleading?

No. I know a lot of people who are privileged, who have ancient titles, a lot of people who have money and who are never written about. I could name you two or three dozen who live in houses filled with Reubens paintings and Chippendale furniture, Louis Seize this and Louis Quinze that, but these people are never written about because they've never done anything. They've led blameless lives, quiet, happy existences. Their children live likewise and the public and gossip columnists are unaware of their existence. If everyone lived that sort of life, then gossip columnists would obviously not have subjects for gossip.

You can very much lead your own life and avoid the press and public censure simply by leading a blameless, boring life. As soon as you start mixing it, you're going to be caught out, especially in this day and age. And once you're caught out, you've got to come to a decision. I don't lead a stainless life. I gamble, I drink a lot. But what I do doesn't affect my ability to write and comment. Once you lose that ability, then you've had it.

The kind of thing you're looking for in a gossip column has got to be financial or sexual or anything aberrant to the mind of the normal person who lives in Bootle or Chipping Norton, Budleigh Salterton or Bideford – people who lead Christian lives and have decent relations with their neighbours. Where I come into it is that I'm very much middle class, middle Britain. My background is not the rarified ionosphere of social life. I take a middle-class view, much like that of the *Daily Mail* itself. And I'm shocked by what people do and how they behave, and the stories that appear in my column are very much there because of my shock at what goes on. Richard Ingrams is the same, another middle-class moralist. We're helped by the fact that we lead fairly humdrum lives. I'm not an adulterer, not an alcoholic, not a thief, not a finagler, and anyone who is any of those things tends to jar on me, because I think this is not how one was brought up to behave. Basically the gossip column is a pulpit from which you're saying, 'You shouldn't be doing all this, but you've done it and now you're paying for it.' In the old days, they would have been put in the stocks and had eggs thrown at them.

I don't think we can ever be accused of causing hurt for the simple reason that any hurt and harm have already been occasioned by the people themselves. All we do is report what's happened. If you murder your wife, you end up in court and it's going to be written about. If you do something of an unworthy nature and you're a great, powerful or privileged person, one day it will come out. All we do is follow the age-old journalistic practice of producing for the public stories of interest about the people in positions of power and privilege. I don't incite people to leave their wives or to leave their husbands. I don't incite

them to become heroin addicts. I can't see how I can be blamed for the original act.

Which stories have you been most proud of?

I think there are very few stories in our world in the last twenty years that I haven't started. The best story of the last half century, the one story that got away, that I was never offered, was that madman Fagin sitting on the Queen's bed in Buckingham Palace. But apart from that, just about all the stories which have enlivened gossip life in the past twenty years have started in the *Daily Mail* diary. It's been a fantastic achievement, but one that was only realizable because it had at the heart of it the *Daily Mail*, a very good newspaper with a highly regarded patrician chairman, Lord Rothermere, and the best editor in the business, David English.

I have always had a very clear idea of my position. I work extremely hard six days a week. I'm the only journalist in the history of Fleet Street to have a column on both a daily newspaper and a Sunday newspaper, and on top of that I have various other outside interests. I'm contracted to TV-am to appear fifty-two times a year, to ABC in the States and so on. My reward for hard work is that I shouldn't be criticized. When I've been subjected to criticism in the past, I've always felt that if I'm going to be criticized, I'm not appreciated, and if I'm not appreciated, I'm going to leave. It's as simple as that. I'm awfully confident of my ability to find another role in the market place, and I've always felt that the best way of doing anything is to do it in public, which is what I exhort the people I write about to do. I've always had very public rows with editors and with my proprietor, and he with me. And it's always helped to clear the air. It's never been for financial gain, but entirely to preserve my professional integrity. The fact that I could run my column from Mars if I wanted, and no one would interfere, shows I've taken the right track.

You have regularly condemned the way some of the royal family are harassed by reporters and photographers, but where do you draw the line where they are concerned? Couldn't it be said that you simply want them to be harassed to the point that suits your own purposes.

By great fortune I've never needed to harass the royal family. Contrary to speculation, I rarely see the royal family. It just so happens that last night I went to a cocktail party which Prince Charles also attended, but that is another matter. What we have is confrontational journalism, a form of journalism usually exercised by photographers who harass not just the royal family but film stars and whoever – pushing up against them, knocking them to the pavement and then photographing them;

and there you have the story the next day – members of royal family or Robert Redford jostled to pavement, shouting and screaming, 'You fucking photographers!' That's not my thing. Our stories about the royal family are done at a remove. We don't get within miles of them. They never see us, we never see them. Our stories come from friends and, if I dare say so, even relations. I've never harassed any member of the royal family. I've never had a conversation with any of them, except at dinner. Our stories of the royal family are intimate stories about their personal lives, and I say personal rather than private because I don't think they have a private life. Obviously they do have personal lives, and the royal family, like anyone else, could have a private life simply by being private.

But weren't you once very critical of certain members of the royal family on a chat show in the United States, calling Princess Diana 'a fiend' and a 'little monster' and saying that Princess Margaret was 'obsessed with bisexuals'?

I never regretted that because all that I said was true. I told the American television show about Princess Diana's behaviour towards Charles, and it wasn't I who invented the words 'fiend and monster'. They came from a high-up member of the staff, not just a butler, valet or chauffeur. The Anthony Holden book on Charles and Diana totally vindicates what I said, which was that the marriage was going through a very bad period and she was behaving as she did because she was furious with Charles for neglecting her. A wife who is neglected behaves like a fiend and a monster, that is to say, she was being what Charles thought of as selfish. In fact I saw my remarks as a fine piece of journalism because they showed I was in the middle of a family row, and what better gossip can you have than that?

I was hardly the first person to draw attention to the fact that Princess Margaret liked bisexuals. In my own book on Princess Margaret, I pointed out that the man who became her escort for almost eight years, Roddy Llewellyn, had previously shared a double bed with Nicky Haslam, an interior decorator, and lived with him for at least six months. However, I never said what they did in that double bed. Every time I've been asked to go on television to explain something during the last sixteen or seventeen years, everything I've said has been borne out later in a book or a biography.

For the future, I cannot see the royal family lasting beyond the death of the Queen. The Queen is sixty-four this April, the Queen Mother ninety this August. The Queen, I would have thought, has a life expectancy of at least another twenty-five years, by which time Prince Charles will be sixty-six. I do not believe that the forces Mrs Thatcher has unleashed – the yobs, the lager louts, the young who don't really have

any feeling of history – will be royalists. You can only be a royalist if you have a knowledge of history, if you understand what the royal family's contribution to this country has been over the last thousand years. The lager louts of today are the parents of tomorrow, and I do not believe that their children will feel any empathy towards the royal family or think that Prince Charles is a good egg. The people who think Prince Charles a good egg are those around at the moment, and the only reason why the royal family is in favour is because Princess Diana is a pin-up, a jolly good pin-up too. In twenty-five years' time this country will have grown out of the idea of kings or queens, and when Charles ascends the throne, as he will as soon as the Queen dies, I think the gig is up. There will be a referendum at some stage after that, and the referendum will say, 'Thanks, but no thanks.'

It was an aristocrat who said to me that Dempster had done more than anyone to maintain class divisions in this country.

Others have said I'm a communist because, by constantly delving into the unsavoury elements of the aristocracy, like revealing that Lord Blandford, the Duke of Marlborough's heir, and Lord Bristol were drug addicts, I was undermining the class system. I think myself that, by writing about them in the way I have, by making it amusing and immediate, I have helped to keep the class system afloat. People want to belong to a class system which is admired, and we're never going to be without a class system in this country as long as there are titles and a royal family, and there are always going to be people who want to join.

Mrs Thatcher has changed British society during the past decade. Is that change for the better or for the worse?

She has changed it in such a way that she's made a new class of spiv. Now, whether the spiv would have risen without Mrs Thatcher I don't know, but she has given the green light to spivvery. All round Britain, but especially in London, you see illiterate yobs driving £60,000 cars and you're bloody sure they're not paying taxes. Mrs Thatcher has allowed these people to proliferate and profit, and it's the by-product of her greater design, the entrepreneurial society. Against that she has got to be praised for bringing down taxes. When I married my wife she was paying 98 per cent on unearned income, and I was paying something like 82 per cent on earned income. Those draconian measures to tax one out of existence were crazy, so that's the good part, but I deprecate what she has unleashed upon us.

What exactly happened to cause your rift with Private Eye*?*

There was only one reason. I went to work for *Private Eye* because I liked Richard Ingrams enormously and had known Auberon Waugh since my schooldays. I never got paid because I didn't want money and didn't ask for it. During their problems with Goldsmith I never took any salary, yet raised, I think, about £9,000 for their appeal, from among my friends. So I was working for *Private Eye* out of a sense of mischief and a sense of love for Richard and Auberon Waugh and Patrick Marnham. Clearly I was a very great selling point, and the acceptable face of *Private Eye* throughout all those struggles. People used to look on *Private Eye* as a rabble who poked fun at their betters, and tee-hee. I was the only person who had any position in society. 'Grovel' of *Private Eye* worked on a decent newspaper; his wife was a duke's daughter; he appeared on television and was a public person.

During the Goldsmith case, I was the centre-forward, very much taking on Goldsmith and his gang because I was on the same level as them, so to speak. That all passed, and in the early 1980s Ingrams was introduced to Ian Hislop, who I thought then, as I do now, was talented in the way of being able to write jokes, but no journalist. The fact that he was appallingly unattractive didn't help him. He was a runtish figure who looked like a sort of bat you see at London Zoo, and was always oiling up to Ingrams and no one else. I'm not saying he should have oiled up to me, for I wouldn't have given him the time of day. But then it became apparent that Ingrams was going to leave *Private Eye*, which, one must remember, was practically his only form of income. Although he did the occasional radio show, *Private Eye* was his whole life, whereas it was a very minor part of mine: maybe 5 per cent, and certainly less than 1 per cent of my income. I therefore became rather disquieted at Richard's absences and the fact that, during his absences, a totally unpredictable man was in charge of what I was doing.

I don't know that I ever spoke to Hislop at that time. I certainly can't remember having a conversation with him. I would go and do 'Grovel' and that would be the end of it. Then came what I most feared: a disgraceful act. I was playing squash in the RAC when Liz Elliott rang me up at about half-past eleven on the Friday and said, 'Look, we haven't got a "Grovel" column.' I said, 'Aah, I don't want to do one.' She said, 'You've got to do it, we're relying on it. We've got a blank page.' So I left the squash court, went to *Private Eye*, sat down at a typewriter and wrote the thing, the main item being that Sir Geoffrey Stirling, head of P & O, had had an illegitimate daughter. This was yet another *blah blah blah*, because he was one of Mrs Thatcher's blue-eyed boys and one of her unpaid political advisers. Underneath it I inserted

a story which was in the 'Grovel' folder about Cecil Parkinson and his new secretary and there were various other items.

I handed the 'Grovel' copy over, and for the first time in my life Hislop was there. I said, 'Look, these stories I can vouch for, but this one about Parkinson I know nothing about.' Now, what normally happened on a Friday or a Monday at *Private Eye* was that the lawyer would ring me and say, 'Look, this story . . .' and I'd say, 'Don't worry, it comes from a friend.' That Friday the lawyer didn't ring, on Monday he didn't ring, so I assumed Hislop had either had it passed by the lawyer or taken the story out. It was nothing to do with me any more. Then someone, in *Private Eye* perhaps, leaked the story to Parkinson. He issued an injunction for libel and had the issue scrapped. The first thing I read was that Ian Hislop, who was meant to be the editor of *Private Eye* in the absence of Richard Ingrams, had done what I feared, which was to tell the world that I wrote the story.

That was wrong on two counts. First, as an editor he should have protected his sources; secondly, I hadn't written the story in the first place. I walked in and screamed at Hislop, 'You know nothing about journalism. You're a little shit. I never want to have anything to do with you again. This has just gone to prove everything I've said to Ingrams about you. You have no knowledge of journalism whatsoever and I'm not going to put my reputation on the line for you.' And that was the end of it. My reward for having worked mostly without pay, certainly without any form of proper recompense, was that for the next three or four years I was written about, sometimes three or four times in the same issue, invariably in an unpleasant manner. They even said I was being paid by Peter Cadbury to write about him in a flattering way, or worse, being paid not to write about him. So I sued and won and got, I think, £8,000 plus costs. Cadbury also sued and won, so that vindictive little paragraph cost them about £25,000.

There were no other reasons for ending my *Private Eye* connection. I'm a professional Fleet Street journalist of some standing, and I helped out in what I believed to be a good cause, which *Private Eye* was originally. Then suddenly it became a commercial venture; they tried to make money. The reason I left was because I didn't see why I should have my career threatened by a man like Ian Hislop, who couldn't understand that the first thing an editor does is protect his sources. The reason why *Private Eye* has never had a decent story since dates from that time, because everyone in Fleet Street saw that Hislop didn't understand the basic tenets of journalistic behaviour.

I wouldn't say there's bitterness on my part, because that's a negative emotion. I just think *Private Eye* is now a rather pathetic magazine of very little interest. There is no information in it as there used to be in

the old days and you'd go golly or wow. Now I know more than they do, week in, week out.

I haven't spoken to Ingrams for a very long time. I've rung him once in the last two years. I feel that originally when Richard was involved in *Private Eye*, it was an excellent publication because it took on the Goliaths and, win or lose, went on taking them on. Then it became a tool for abuse. You don't use a publication to bash your enemies. You simply don't do it.

It is often noted that men with macho images are given a high profile in your column, suggesting you have a secret admiration for men who make a name for themselves by seducing women.

The only reason they get into the column is because, if you've got mistresses, you're an interesting person. Jimmy Goldsmith denies he ever said, after his marriage to Lady Annabel Birley, 'When you marry your mistress you create a job vacancy.' I told him he should stop denying it and go down in history as the author of one of the immortal remarks of our time. The point is that if you have a lot of women, then you are attractive and my readers find you attractive. The fact that you're a womanizer, like Dai Llewellyn, who was engaged to three attractive girls at the same time, is something readers enjoy, even though these people all come to grief in the end.

Jimmy Goldsmith hasn't come to grief yet.

He's come to grief emotionally. He's got problems ahead with the present mistress, I imagine. But I don't write about such people because I respect or admire their macho side. It's simply one of the crazy vagaries of life that people behave in this way – like sultans or potentates – and others love to read about it.

Lord Longford said of you, 'I like Nigel Dempster, but I can't bring myself to approve of him.' And the Mail *art critic, Paul Johnson, called your trade a loathsome business.*

I get on very well with Lord Longford and his wife, and I was a great friend of his late daughter Catherine. As for Paul Johnson, if he finds my business so loathsome, why is he collecting money by writing for my newspaper so frequently? I find him loathsome. I find him humbug. As someone once said about Paul Johnson in his leftie days, he eats more oysters than a duke. He is a terrible snob, the sort of person who'd be oiling up to my wife's father if he were alive. He'd have loved to have met the Duke of Leeds.

It has sometimes been said that you make an intransigent foe. Is this balanced, would you say, by your loyalty as a friend?

I don't think I've ever been intransigent and I don't think I've ever been a foe. I haven't got it in me to hate anyone. I don't hate Ian Hislop, for instance. I just think he's a twerp. People who are loyal to me are friends. We've always been friends and obviously I help them and they help me. I've never conducted a campaign against anyone, because if you were to do that as a gossip columnist, you'd lose your job. You're not employed to conduct personal campaigns but to write about the people out there who interest your public.

It doesn't happen that I walk into a parlour of my enemies and I'd be a damned fool to do so. I only go to places where I want to go. Anyway, who are these enemies? I've outgrown all my childhood enemies from when I was in my twenties to thirties. I'm bigger and better than they are. I work hard and I'm appreciated. The only people who are enemies now are those who have suffered by my exposing them, and I'm very happy to have such people as enemies because they should be exposed. There are a lot of unpleasant people around.

You married twice into the aristocracy. Is that a world where you feel entirely at home?

Ever since I went to deb dances in 1959, I've known a world which is populated by people who, if not aristocratic, are related to the aristocracy, simply because that is the tribe. When you mix at a certain level, it becomes almost impossible not to marry someone who isn't related to the aristocracy. It's just coincidence that, of the two women I've fallen in love with, one had a mother who was titled and the other had a title of her own.

You're not an Englishman, but most Englishmen, even those who are heterosexual, prefer the company of other men. What's your feeling about that?

If you've gone to an English public school and been brought up in a sporting ethic, you like to spend your leisure hours doing sporting things. You can't play squash with a woman, or golf with a woman, or tennis with a woman, because women are not very good at it. British men who have been to public schools tend to stick together because their pastimes are male-oriented. I take women out to lunch, not because I'm trying to have affairs but because whatever they do interests me, but the major part of your leisure hours must be spent with men.

Do you have ambitions outside the world of newspapers? For example, you breed horses.

I don't think I would be happy to leave that world, but obviously it's going to happen in the not too distant future. My whole life has been spent working ten to sixteen hours a day, six days a week. I wouldn't know what to do if I didn't work those sort of hours. My wife always says I'm the only person among my friends who works, but I wouldn't know what to do if I didn't. Breeding a horse is a two-minute job. In fact horses ejaculate so quickly it's about a thirty-second job. It just wouldn't be enough.

ANDRÉ DEUTSCH

André Deutsch was born in Hungary in 1917 and was educated in Budapest and Vienna. He came to England in 1939 and in 1941 was briefly interned on the Isle of Man. He learned about publishing at Nicolson & Watson where he spent three years before going independent in 1945 under the imprint of Allan Wingate. This was the start of his long association with Diana Athill who came with him when André Deutsch Ltd was founded in 1951. His authors have included John Updike, Jack Kerouac, Arthur M. Schlesinger Jr, John Kenneth Galbraith, Laurie Lee, V. S. Naipaul, Brian Moore and Jean Rhys. In 1962 he founded the African Universities Press in Nigeria, followed two years later by the East Africa Publishing House in Kenya. In 1984 Tom Rosenthal resigned his chairmanship of William Heinemann and Secker & Warburg and went into partnership with André Deutsch.

You're often referred to as a refugee, but aren't I correct in saying you came to England of your own free will and had already decided to do so before things became difficult politically in Hungary?

You're quite right. I came to England because of an uncle. My mother came from a large family, and one of her brothers, the most interesting, was an Anglophile. He was a businessman but also a translator who translated H. G. Wells into Hungarian. He had a daughter, and was frustrated in not having a son, so, with my parents' approval, took care of me in a way. When I was thirteen or fourteen he hammered it home that there was only one country where a gentleman with artistic, intellectual or literary leanings could live, and that was the United Kingdom. I remember having awful rows with my father, because he was a great admirer of Mussolini and thought it was really not necessary for me to leave. I left Hungary in March 1939, when things were still normal at home, and came out of my own free will without my parents' knowledge.

They stayed on in Hungary. My father was miraculously rescued by Wallenberg, the Swedish diplomat, when, as a dentist, he was working in a camp outside Budapest, his own place having been closed because he was Jewish. The news came one day that the following afternoon at three o'clock he would be on a train to somewhere in Germany or Poland. My mother rushed to Wallenberg, and they took him off the train at the last minute. Both my parents survived and came out in 1946, but hated doing so because by that time pre-communist Hungary was a reasonably comfortable place. When I visited my father, I was amazed at what you could buy. But when they arrived in England, there was rationing. My father said that England smelt of mutton. In Hungary people didn't eat mutton unless they were very poor.

The next year my parents went back and I nearly had a nervous

breakdown at feeling so guilty at not having looked after them properly. My father restarted his practice and then came out again when things got really bad in 1950. That second departure was immensely complicated, but more important was the fact that this time they fell in love with England and England seemed to love them in return. They never looked back.

At one point you were interned on the Isle of Man as an enemy alien. Did you feel resentful or just resigned?

Neither. Hungary came into the war the day after Pearl Harbour, which was 7 December 1941. Horthy, under enormous pressure from Hitler, declared war and joined the Axis. It was then that I was interned. We were shipped first to Manchester, where the zoo had been evacuated – they were afraid of bombs falling and the lions getting out and eating people – and the Hungarians were lodged in what had been the Parrot House. We were there two or three days and I met some very interesting people. Then we were shipped to the Isle of Man, where we spent six or seven weeks. I had good friends who went to the Home Office, and I was later released.

It is because of that internment that I became a publisher. I met a Hungarian called Francis Aldor in the camp. He was an impossible character who was a cousin of Arthur Koestler's and ran a publishing company. When my release papers came he asked me to work for him for £8 a week, which was a lot of money in those days. I didn't want to take the job, but the other Hungarians said, 'Look, for God's sake, Aldor is impossible, but it's an occupation.' So I accepted and worked for him for about three months. I knew nothing about publishing. I'd read many books and I was relatively literate, but I didn't know how a book was made. I learned quickly and left to take up a new job, working for John Roberts at Nicolson & Watson. Roberts is a nice man, a Welshman, still alive and about ninety.

Has being an exile been a significant factor in your life?

I never considered myself an exile. I thought that, as I lived here and spoke quite a bit of English, I actually was English, so I never had any complex about being a foreigner. And my friends, with very few exceptions, such as George Mikes, were all English.

You came to England out of a conviction that your liberal beliefs would be met with greater sympathy in London than in Budapest. Have you ever been disillusioned?

By and large, no, but there has to be give and take. Of course there are

lots of things about England that have disappointed me, but mostly I was glad I came here. In 1937 or thereabouts my father wanted me to go to America, which was the Hungarian dream. I even had a letter from the US Embassy in London to say that my application had gone through. But I didn't go, because by that time I already thought of myself as an Englishman somehow disguised as a Hungarian. When my parents finally met up with me after the war and heard the story, my father nearly fainted. He said, 'How could you have missed the land of golden opportunity? Think what you'd be now if you'd gone to America instead of staying here.'

At what point was your fierce resolve for independence as a publisher born?

I started Allan Wingate as an independent company virtually on my own, having been with Nicolson & Watson and learned a great deal about the surface of publishing. There was no depth, but I knew printing, invoicing, selling to W. H. Smith and reading manuscripts. My first great triumph at Nicolson & Watson happened when Mary McCarthy's *The Company She Keeps* came in and John Roberts, my boss, said, 'Laddie, you read this.' I read it and said, 'This is a great book,' and they published it. But afterwards there was a disagreement between Nicolson & Watson and myself. Through George Mikes I had come to know George Orwell, who was then very poor. He was the literary editor of *Tribune* and he asked me to write short reviews. If a review was not that short I got a guinea (£1.05); if it was really short I got 10s. 6d. (52.5p), and was allowed to keep the book to flog.

One day Orwell showed me a new manuscript of his that his regular publisher, Victor Gollancz, had turned down. It was *Animal Farm*. He gave it to me just before Whitsun, when I was going off with a girlfriend to a farm in Wales to get away from the bombs. I read the manuscript four times, ignored the girl, came back to London stomping with excitement, rushed into John Roberts and said, 'Mr Roberts, this is a masterpiece.' He said, 'All right, laddie, leave it here.' Weeks went by, and finally I went to Roberts, who said Orwell didn't know what he was talking about and had no idea of what went on in Russia. After I'd persuaded him to meet Orwell, Roberts and his wife and Orwell and I went out to the Players' Theatre. It was an unbelievably embarrassing session in which they were rude to Orwell, put him down and turned down his book. Orwell never told me that he had then offered it to Faber & Faber, where T. S. Eliot turned it down. I had suggested Jonathan Cape because they had just published *Darkness at Noon*. Having signed a contract with them and received an advance of, I think, £100, Orwell was surprised some six months later by their decision not to publish the book after all. I continued to see Orwell off and on, who

all his life was a timid, withdrawn and modest man with no intellectual arrogance whatsoever. I told him I hoped to start on my own one day, when I had the money, the courage and the experience. He said, 'Start now with my book. I don't want an advance.' But I wasn't mentally or financially ready. I wasn't experienced. And since Orwell had more integrity than anyone I'd ever known, I couldn't play the Hungarian rogue and pull a fast one on him. In the end *Animal Farm* was published by that marvellous publisher Fred Warburg.

Soon I became pregnant with the thought of publishing on my own, and I went to John Roberts who said, 'Laddie, you're young, you can work hard. You start a little publishing company with a few hundred pounds, and work there at night and stay with us and earn good money.' I was earning £4,000 a year, a small fortune, at the time. So I got a few friends to join me and I named it Allan Wingate.

Why Wingate?

I cannot pretend now and say this was a tribute to the great General Wingate. It was just a good English name. Diana Athill was working for the BBC at the time, and as Wingate was beginning to grow, I offered her a job, so that was the start of a long partnership.

Financial problems arose when we published *The Naked and the Dead.* A company can be in great financial difficulty if it has a big success on its hands, and cannot afford a substantial reprint. This was what happened with *The Naked and the Dead* by Norman Mailer. Seven publishers before me turned it down on the grounds it was dirty. You know what he used for the word 'fuck'? Fug – F-U-G. I was eighth on the list of the agent, Graham Watson at Curtis Brown. My first printing was 10,000 copies, and it was very difficult at that time to find a printer who had enough paper. A week before the book was published, the *Sunday Times*, then owned by Lord Kemsley, put a little box on the front page saying it shouldn't be published. Lady Kemsley was outraged and said, 'This is a book I wouldn't like my housekeeper to read, let alone children.' A great brouhaha started up. I had an inspector from Scotland Yard in my office three days running – a nice chap who took snuff, I remember. I was planning to go to America the next month, and so I asked him, 'Do you want my passport so I can't flee the country?' 'No, no, no,' he said. The attorney-general, Sir Hartley Shawcross, then pronounced it a very boring and harmless book that wouldn't corrupt the youth of England. So publication went ahead, and instead of 10,000 copies we needed 80,000. And I didn't have the money.

I was frantically looking round for partners, and the first to come forward was a man called Anthony Gibbs, dead long ago. He and others came in and Wingate began to do well, but by the summer of 1950

there was a major falling out between Gibbs and his friends and me. I had to go. Diana Athill, with whom I had become great friends, left too, and went into hiding so to speak. I was determined to start publishing all over again, and that is how André Deutsch Ltd came into being. Diana is still working there. She's my age, seventy-two, no longer a director but still doing brilliant editorial work.

We published her book, Instead of a Letter, *and I thought her charming.*

It's a little masterpiece. She's a wonderful person.

What was your last big book at Wingate?

It was a book called *Operation Cicero.*

They made a film.

They did. *Five Fingers*, with James Mason. The book was written by an Austrian, Ludwig Moyzisch, who during the war was the so-called commercial attaché at the German Embassy in Ankara in Turkey where the ambassador was Franz von Papen. Moyzisch was there because, as happened throughout the whole history of the Nazis, the hierarchy was divided, and Kaltenbrunner and the SD did not trust von Papen who was an old-fashioned *Junker* who knew how to ride a horse but did not behave like a good Nazi. The British ambassador, Sir Hughe Knatchbull-Hugessen, was an ass of a man and a keen amateur pianist, and he had an Albanian valet. The embassy piano in Ankara was out of tune, so Ankara radio station said, 'Sir Hughe, come and play your Chopin here,' and he went and played. Meanwhile Bosner, the valet, who hated the British because his father was accidentally shot in Albania by an English hunter, had made an impression of the key of the safe and bought a second-hand Leica camera. So while Sir Hughe Knatchbull-Hugessen was playing Chopin at the radio station, Bosner opened the safe, took out all the papers and started photographing them. Ankara in those days was a very important crossroads. The Allies wanted to keep Turkey out of the war whilst the Nazis were keen on the strategic advantage of a Turkish ally. The consequent political intrigue meant that the British ambassador was in possession of many secret documents. Bosner next rang the German Embassy and somehow got through to von Papen and, in whatever broken German he used, offered his services. It wasn't von Papen's style to deal with a spy, and he handed him over to Moyzisch, saying, 'You deal with this man.' That was my last big Wingate book.

What was your first big André Deutsch book?

The von Papen *Memoirs*. I'm coming to that. I was still suspicious of the *Operation Cicero* story and decided to go and see Moyzisch. He was living in the French zone. I had a friend who was then the *New Statesman* chess expert, a German Jew called Heinz Frankel. I asked Heinz to come with me and we travelled to Austria and sat with Moyzisch for about a week cross-questioning him. At the end I remember Moyzisch saying, 'Look, I've been at the Nuremburg trials, and what you fellows, particularly Mr Frankel, have done to me was a much tougher cross-questioning than anything I witnessed at Nuremberg. If you still don't believe me, go and talk to my late boss.'

Moving from one Allied zone to another could be done only with great difficulty, but Frankel and I got to a little place outside Hanover where von Papen, his wife and son were staying with his daughter and son-in-law. When we sat down and explained what it was all about, von Papen was absolutely marvellous. He was charming and confirmed everything. There was nothing we had to cross out as being untrue. It impressed me to such an extent that, as we were having our last session, I said, 'Herr von Papen, you ought to write your memoirs.' I was still Wingate then, remember, because this was before *Operation Cicero* was published. We started negotiating, and then came the break with Gibbs and company. There was a meeting with Anthony Gibbs and Charles Fry, who had come to Wingate from Batsford, and it was agreed that, for the next fourteen days, nobody would approach von Papen.

But before the week was out I had a telephone call and heard the anxious tearful voice of Franz von Papen saying, 'André, my dear boy, but you left Wingate and you are my friend.' He had been sent a letter by Sir Philip Gibbs, who was then still a great man in the land – a distinguished very right-wing *Daily Telegraph* leader writer – saying that his son wanted to publish his book and they had arranged to publish it jointly with Eyre & Spottiswoode. I rushed to Stanley Rubinstein, who said, 'Fly to Düsseldorf tomorrow and present your case to von Papen.' So I arrived, sat down with him and his son, Franz von Papen Jr, a lawyer, and explained everything, produced the contract, and von Papen signed it. The book was published late in 1952, and I sold serial rights to the *People* – a different paper then from what it is now – for £30,000. What would that be today?

Three hundred thousand?

Maybe. Deutsch was certainly under-capitalized because we were short on the investment target of £14,400, having reached only £6,700. Diana Athill and Nicolas Bentley, who had joined me by that stage, both supported me and said, 'We must go ahead, even if we go bust.' And now I had this treasure.

You always resisted being swallowed up by a conglomerate. Was that because you wanted to go on running your own show, or didn't you think the conglomerate appropriate to publishing?

There were no conglomerates in those days.

What I mean is that you were successful. You could easily have sold out to a conglomerate at some point.

Let me tell you what happened eventually. There was a lovely man in London called Raimund von Hofmannstahl, whose father was Hugo von Hofmannstahl, the greatest Austrian poet who wrote a lot of the librettos for Richard Strauss's operas. Raimund worked for Time-Life here as their 'Metternich', and Henry Luce had dreamt up a scheme suggesting that Time-Life, which was making so much money they didn't know what to do with it, should invest minority shares in distinguished European publishing houses and build up a family of publishers. Their first investment was Laffont in Paris, and the second was Rowohlt in Germany.

Raimund came to my office, introduced himself, and put forward the idea of investing in a minority holding, maximum 40 per cent, on condition that I, André Deutsch, retain the majority. I said I wasn't interested. I didn't like the notion. However, I discussed it with Arnold Goodman fully, and he pointed out that the company didn't need the money, and that a deal would only be successful if their dollars went to the shareholders. Anyway, to and fro it went, and Time-Life accepted his suggestion. Arnold asked me to breakfast and said, 'This is their final offer, and if you don't accept I'll have you certified.' I accepted, and they came in with 40 per cent, while I retained 56 per cent.

But later you bought their share back, didn't you?

I bought it back. Not long after the deal they called a meeting of the family in New York. At this meeting I met for the first time the then chairman of Time-Life, Andrew Heiskell, a splendid man. It was suggested that we meet at least twice a year at some nice place and talk about books, the first location to be Salzburg. I said, no, this was not the way; John Updike was not going to write a new novel quickly because he heard that all of us were sitting around a table in Austria. But next spring we met somewhere in southern Spain. We were not Time-Life guests, but paid our own expenses.

You had to pay for them yourself?

We had a few free dinners.

But you had to pay for the hotel?

Absolutely, everything. And we met in this ghastly clip joint in Spain. After that meeting I received all kinds of questionnaires from Time-Life asking me to give an account of my editorial policy for the next five years in relation not only to the list but in relation to our main competitors – the Collinses, the Weidenfelds, the Capes. I rang Arnold, who said, 'André, you don't have to answer. They have a minority share. There is nothing they can do. You don't have board meetings and you know where you stand. Next time you get a letter, don't open it, put it in the waste-paper basket.' I did that for weeks but one day curiosity got the better of me and I fished one out and read it. Its contents made me livid so I called Arnold and said, 'Look, you were a very good matchmaker, you got wonderful terms. Turn yourself into a divorce lawyer.'

That's when you parted company with Time-Life?

Yes. And because the money was not invested in the publishing company, there was no problem about paying it back.

Did you make any money out of the whole thing?

None of us did.

Would you call it a bad experience in a way?

It wasn't a bad experience. For two years I earned interest on whatever investments I made.

Your policy has been to publish only books you like, and you haven't touched anything that didn't appeal to you, even if financial success was guaranteed. Can such a policy survive in the increasingly commercial world of publishing?

The way you put it is very flattering, and by and large it's true. We once made a go for a commercial novel. Diana and I said it's rubbish, but my God, it will sell. And we fell on our faces; we just didn't know how to do it.

One of the big changes in publishing is that an author and his work are increasingly managed by computers rather than by readers and editors. In some ways it seems the fun has gone out of the game. Are you in any way attuned to this clinical progress?

I'm totally unattuned. If I were twenty years younger and a big conglomerate offered me a job because they heard I was successful and smart and Deutsch has been sold, I would be dead as a dodo. I wouldn't know

what to do. The extraordinary thing is how lucky we were, and I must emphasize how important luck is. In that period from 1951 to 1984 we carried out an old-fashioned sort of quality publishing and made some money.

Are you confident about the future of publishing? In the face of stiff competition from TV and films, will the reading public go on growing?

I think in the long run it will. In spite of the conglomerates and the new trends, if you take the reviews – look at your own *Literary Review* – quality books are published in vast numbers. How long that will continue, how long Mr Murdoch and his people at Collins will be tolerant of publishing good books, as they still do, I do not know. It was the Americans who hijacked publishing finance into the Hollywood bracket, but it's also happened in Germany. Backlist publishing has virtually disappeared.

Publishing nowadays is in my view virtually controlled by literary agents, who dictate prices and product. Is this state of affairs helpful or harmful?

Very harmful. The literary agents are ruling the day. Under strong American influence, they have kidnapped the publishing industry into a sort of crazy financial world. If I were running André Deutsch Ltd today I would have problems, just like Tom Rosenthal. Even Tom is now conceding defeat and is selling the company.

Tell me what happened with Tom Rosenthal after he went into partnership with you, because I was surprised when I heard about it. You've always been your own boss: he has ambitions. Weren't you bound to clash?

I wished you'd phoned me and told me not to go ahead. I had the notion when I was sixty-six, sixty-seven, when things were very different from what they are today, that André Deutsch Ltd, which Diana Athill, Nick Bentley and I built up, which had a reputation and made money, should continue as an independent quality publishing company. My first thought was that I would like to do what W. W. Norton did about fifty years ago when they created a system in which only employees had shares. When I was in New York I talked to a man called George Brockaway, who was the head of Norton, and asked him how this scheme worked. Then I talked to Lord Goodman and a few others, and they said, 'Admirable, but, dear boy, if you do that you will starve by the time you become seventy-five because you will have given it away.' Prior to Tom joining me my salary was £15,000. What can you save on £15,000 for your old age?

Nothing.

I had left the company pension scheme after the auditors had said, 'You are throwing money away because the business is by and large yours at 84 per cent. One day you'll sell and be comfortably rich for the rest of your life.' I was still anxious to secure the future independence of the firm and so discussed things with Paul Hamlyn, a very old friend. I first met Paul in, I think, 1945 at a booksellers' conference in Norfolk. At that time Paul was a small remainder merchant. We became good friends. The dialogue with Paul became quite serious, and our lawyers and accountants got together and a proposition emerged that was fair and reasonable. Then madness overtook me. I thought, my God, Paul spends more time on an aeroplane than I spend in bed. What if something happens to him? At that point I heard that Tom Rosenthal was retiring and went after him. The Paul Hamlyn negotiations came to an end, which Paul accepted elegantly.

But André, did you honestly believe that, at the end of the day, you could sit at the table with somebody who had equal power and think it was going to last?

I was besotted with the idea that I would be able to work with a man of Tom Rosenthal's reputation and experience. I thought that I'd be wise enough to accept that at the age of seventy-two I would hand over all the shares.

That was the agreement?

That was the agreement and we stuck to it, and that was my downfall, that was the mistake I made.

There was a honeymoon for a year or two?

Less than that.

Was it a personality clash?

Largely a personality clash. Also, Tom is a very expensive fellow. Entertainment, travelling. It's incredible. By the time I realized it was too late, there was nothing I could do about it. Last August, when I was approaching my seventy-second birthday, Tom said, 'I want to have a serious talk with you. Let's have dinner.' He took me out to the Jardin des Gourmets. Tom then said, 'André, according to our original agreement, on your seventy-second birthday you will cease to be joint chairman and joint managing director. You will have no shares in the business any more, you won't have any executive power, and we don't need you, but we do need your room. Could you by 15 November clear your room and go? You will become president.' I was shell-shocked. On the next day I asked Lord Goodman whether Tom had

the right to do that to me. He said he did. There were discussions to try and give me a limited amount of freedom to join another publisher, but I had to agree to give Tom £100,000. I thought it an obscene suggestion, and turned it down.

But where did Tom get all the money to buy you out?

There are all kinds of rumours. Tom – having been very successful at Thames & Hudson, and at Secker & Warburg – had a large sum of money at his disposal. I presume he borrowed the rest.

Was what he paid you adequate in terms of what the company's worth today?

Tom and I negotiated a deal similar to the one originally discussed between Paul Hamlyn and myself. In 1984 the financial world at large had not yet decided that publishing was a glamour industry, and what he paid then was a fair price.

Has what he paid you secured your future?

Yes. I can live in comfort.

When you signed the agreement with Tom Rosenthal, were you under the illusion that, come the day when you had to leave, he would be magnanimous and say, 'Stay and have the office?'

I believed that. Tom would say, 'Look how generous I was with David Farrar.'

So you had the impression that once you retired you would still participate.

Absolutely. He told me, whether he thought it or not, that my presence was going to be important to them, and I fell for it.

But why do you think he acted as he did? Were you so difficult that you made his life a misery?

You'll have to have an interview with Tom and listen to what he has to say. The original deal included a provision that the purchase price from Tom to Deutsch be reduced by £150,000, and for that £150,000 André Deutsch Ltd would buy a pension scheme for me, which meant that I would pay £75,000 and he would pay £75,000. I was told by all the experts that it would work with the tax authorities and we did it. The only difference was that I wanted to pass some of the £150,000 to Diana Athill, without whom we would never have succeeded the way we did. So we agreed that £35,000 be shifted to Diana. She was, of course, due to receive a pension under the company scheme.

I always looked on that as my thank-you to Diana Athill for her friendship and partnership all those years. It was a present from me, not from André Deutsch Ltd. Something that then made me very angry was when Tom, at a meeting in the office, said, 'This company has a heart. When André, Diana and Nick started the business in 1951, they were all young. Nick Bentley's dead, and because this company has a heart, we have to create something for the future of the people who work here, but we are paying an enormous amount of money in the process for this pension scheme.' He then mentioned as a part of all this Diana Athill's pension scheme. But that scheme was my homage, gift, debt, love – call it what you will – to Diana Athill, and nothing to do with the company. And this, in our second year of partnership, made me realize it was never ever going to work. Another thing Tom said to me fairly early on was, 'It's fun to work with you, but there are three problems about you, André. One, you were not born in this country. Two, you were not educated in this country. Three you were not in Her Majesty's Service.' Tom, you know, had served in Malta as a second-lieutenant, a gallant soldier.

What bearing does that have on anything?

I do not know. I was absolutely staggered. Tom's father, a distinguished, now very aged, scholar from Germany, was clever enough to leave Nazi Germany fairly early on. I think he came to this country in 1934, and Tom was born here.

Would you share the view that there is no love lost between individual publishing houses, and that gentlemanly behaviour, if it ever existed, is a thing of the past?

I think it existed to some extent in the past, but it doesn't any more. Absolutely not. And I wrongly thought that all the spiel I had had from Tom was true. There's another interesting thing which will prove to you again what a fool I am. At one point at the start of it all Lord Goodman said, 'Well, fellows, obviously this is going to be a marriage. What are you going to pay each other?' Before I could open my mouth, Tom said, 'I used to earn over £60,000, and I suggest I take £40,000, because I have a wife and two children.' I swallowed that without even thinking it through – Anne Rosenthal was a successful agent and the two sons were grown up. 'And you, André,' he continued, 'increase your salary from £15,000 to £20,000, because you have a very wealthy girlfriend.' I didn't see the insult in that sentence, that I was some sort of a kept fellow, and like a fool I accepted it. So a lot of what has happened that took the joy out of my life is my own bloody fault.

I'm lucky enough to be independent enough not to care especially, but I do find publishing the most disloyal of professions at the moment.

Perhaps you exaggerate. There are still decent people in the publishing world.

But it is no longer gentlemanly.

It's not a gentleman's profession. It is not. Mainly because big international finance has moved in.

I read somewhere that the highest advance you ever paid for a book was £40,000.

The biggest advance I ever paid was $25,000 in the 1960s, when it was a monstrous sum of money, and that was for Norman Mailer's *An American Dream.*

Did you recover your money?

We made money on the book, but the advance was never earned. But as you know, you can over-advance a book and make a profit, and you can get a book with no advance and lose your shirt.

Although large advances are not unusual in the United States, they are rarely given for works of non-fiction.

Yes, they are. I'm sure Arthur Schlesinger had a large advance.

But for Arthur Schlesinger you're talking about A Thousand Days, *the big popular book about Kennedy. Would you get a £600,000 advance on Bernard Shaw in America?*

I doubt it.

But increasingly in Britain huge advances are being given for non-fiction, despite the fact that the money cannot possibly be recovered by the publisher. Should we be subsidizing the rich and powerful in this way, or wouldn't the money be better employed backing struggling young new authors? Carmen Callil seems to have come up with a £600,000 advance for Michael Holroyd for the Bernard Shaw biography. Where is the industry going?

She wouldn't and couldn't have done it without being owned by the Newhouses. It's certainly not commendable, but it's a harsh capitalist world and there are a lot of crazy people who make these mistakes. You don't have to pay £600,000 for a brilliant first novel. If you pay £60,000, you're crazy enough, but this is the malaise of contemporary Anglo-American publishing.

Any fool can pay a huge sum provided his backers make the money available, but where is the flair, the expertise?

Doesn't exist. I'm with you absolutely. It's not true publishing at all. That's one reason why I wouldn't fit in to these organizations, because I'm too mean to recommend an advance of £600,000. It's totally unnecessary.

How does it help the arts?

It doesn't.

And where you have the same authors in the main commanding the big advances and getting all the publicity and reviews, where does that leave the Graham Greenes of the future?

I think the Graham Greenes of the future will surface, somehow, because ultimately the talent – and there we're talking of a very exceptional author – will survive.

You once said that publishers have been their own worst enemies by over-producing. Can you elaborate on that?

When I started Deutsch, I think this country produced around 12,000 books a year. Today we are publishing 58,000 titles a year. Everybody is chasing the goose that will lay the golden egg, and it is very difficult. One of the things that caused a falling out between Tom and myself was forcing the programme. When I was in charge I don't think we ever published more than about 90 titles a year.

What view do you take on the current issue of Salman Rushdie and The Satanic Verses? *It seems a very central problem for publishers, and, of course, for distributors. Do the protests really have substance?*

I can't answer that, because I can't put myself in the position of some militant Muslim. I think the protest itself is deplorable – the Ayatollah saying this man should be killed. I must tell you, though, that I have not been able to get into *The Satanic Verses*. I have a copy, but I haven't read it yet.

But even had you known of the offensive element, would you still have published it if you had wanted it?

I presume not, though I might have had the misguided philosophy to say, 'Here is a very fine writer's new book. I'll take it on.' But basically I am on the side of Penguin and Rushdie, and against those who

sentenced him to death, burned the book and so forth. There are books that one does publish even though you know it's going to upset people.

But shouldn't we have the self-discipline to censor ourselves?

You remember Hitler's architect, Albert Speer? We had his book offered to us and made the mistake of turning it down. But very important people advised me, 'You can't touch it,' and so somebody else published it in the end. Nicolas Bentley and Diana Athill were against it.

Have you ever been sued over something you published?

We had two libel cases, though one was a minor one about oil in the Sahara. That was a simple case. The big one was over the play by Rolf Hochhuth, *Soldiers*, about the death of Sikorski, the head of the Free Poles – possibly not my hero, but a brave man. It was known that Sikorski was a big problem to the British and American governments concerning Soviet Russia and the Poles, because Sikorski said it was the Russians who killed all those Polish officers in Khatyn forest, which turns out to be true. Sikorski was in the Middle East visiting his troops. On the way back to London he spent a night in Gibraltar. In the morning, when his plane, piloted by a Czech, was taking off, it crashed. The plot Hochhuth worked out was that Churchill and Roosevelt knowingly agreed to remove Sikorski. Young Winston Churchill discovered that the Czech pilot was alive in California. He shipped him over and helped him to start proceedings.

Ken Tynan had wanted Laurence Olivier to put the play on at the National Theatre, but Olivier was rightly advised that he shouldn't do it, because of Churchill's involvement. Tynan did manage to produce the play in the West End, but the libel action killed it. In the end we had to pay damages, and had to destroy all copies of the book.

What do you think of the libel laws as they stand at this moment in this country?

They have improved, but they're still not perfect. It's been said that British libel laws are really against the truth; that the more truthful a book is, the more danger there is of libel. I'm not sure I wear that, but they are very tricky. What great libel cases have we had in the last year or two?

Lord Aldington and Count Tolstoy?

Of course, terrible. And also the divorced wife of that mass-murderer. That was *Private Eye*.

Like myself, you're often criticized and parodied in Private Eye. *Do you mind much?*

André Deutsch and *Private Eye* became soul partners through Nicolas Bentley, because Nick illustrated Bron's diary in the early days. One day Nick said that *Private Eye* and us should sit down and see whether we could distribute their books, and they asked to use our imprint because they thought it would make the entrée into bookshops easier. The arrangement is now coming to an end. Then *Private Eye* started its series called 'Great Publishers of the World' or something of the kind. By that time I was friendly with Richard Ingrams and John Wells, his co-author on the 'Dear Bill' series. They did a piece that dealt with Deutsch.

It hurt me deeply. By that time Nick was dead, but I remember having a Saturday morning meeting in Diana Athill's flat with two other colleagues to discuss it. I also met Lord Goodman, and we were on the verge of suing when I withdrew. I am told that Richard Ingrams was surprised if not irritated that we did not respond and take up a fighting stance. Since then my relationship with the *Eye* and my personal relationship with Richard have improved immensely. They have been going for Tom Rosenthal, and Tom thinks I'm planting those stories, which is nonsense. I don't believe *Private Eye* is anti-Semitic. A lot of people say it is. I don't think they're philo-Semitic. But so what?

Does a satirical magazine like Private Eye *serve an important purpose as watchdog of political and social life, or is it just too scurrilous and irresponsible?*

It's been both. It's certainly been irresponsible, but you can't have it both ways. If *Private Eye* didn't go in the direction of exaggerating and getting out of step, it would be a different thing altogether. In fact I would say that *Private Eye* today is occasionally very mealy-mouthed.

Because of the large damages they've had to pay out?

Partly that. Partly change of editorship and age.

So has the sting gone out of it?

I don't think the sting's gone out of it, but it's milder and less offensive. They went for you time and again, and you employ Richard's lovely daughter.

I don't mind about that. You have had a rather ferocious reputation as an employer. I recall Ian Norrie writing that he would not have lasted with you and that few do. Have you asked too much from people who have worked for you?

In a way that is not untrue. But the records show that a lot of people have been with us for years and years. Of course there were rows,

misunderstandings and quarrels, but by and large nobody of quality or importance has left. When I was a lot younger I was much more difficult.

But tell me more about how you got along with Diana Athill. Did you and she ever clash seriously?

No.

Never?

We would argue about a book if she wanted to publish it and I didn't or vice versa. Diana is a very close friend. No, I never quarrelled with her, I never quarrelled with Nicolas Bentley. Lots of people enjoyed being my colleague, though some others couldn't stand me.

You mustn't mind me asking you these questions, but you have been called very mean. There is the legend about you switching off unnecessary lights and reusing old envelopes. Others say the salaries you paid were unrealistic and there was a joke that Diana Athill's salary was rumoured to be so low that she banked it once a year.

That was *Private Eye*.

What is the true position?

I would hate to admit that I am mean.

Careful then?

I was careful. I was parsimonious. And we paid ourselves very little. At the start of Wingate, Diana was paid £500 at the time. The question of reusing old envelopes – a routine long gone – was part of the pattern. Switching off lights was part of the pattern. Over all I think I am generous, but I admit there have been episodes when I exercised knowingly or unknowingly a degree of meanness, as I came to realize afterwards. Even now that I am financially comfortable, I hate wasting money.

Is it something ingrained?

I presume so, though my childhood wasn't based on any such pattern.

But you don't grudge yourself anything.

No, I don't.

Leaving Norman Mailer, your first bestseller, on one side, who are you most pleased to have published?

Now that I am practically out of publishing, I would say that the greatest pleasure in my life was the discovery of authors like Norman Mailer and John Updike.

What are your views on Mrs Thatcher?

Confused. Undoubtedly she has done some good work and shaken up this country, but she's gone too far. I don't like her manner and I wouldn't be at all surprised if, by the next election, she's out. After the war, I was a staunch member of the Labour party in Chelsea. When the SDP started I joined the party, largely because of Roy Jenkins. I sent him a telegram saying in effect, 'If you're serious about it, I will do anything, and I will join.' I have also known David Owen and his wife Debbie, who is a literary agent. I voted for Roy as leader, but Roy was soon out and then David became leader.

Why was Roy Jenkins pushed aside? It's never been clear to me.

I think he didn't give a strong enough single leadership. He's too much of an academic and an intellectual. I was sorry that Roy went, but then, at the beginning, David was very good, vigorous and young, and I remained a member and supported him to the end.

I know you are not one-hundred-per-cent Jewish and were not brought up to be orthodox, but do you feel part of the Jewish community?

In every important respect I consider myself a full Jew but I do not belong to a Jewish community, I am not religious. I don't go to the synagogue, for instance.

What do you feel about the over-sensitivity of the Jewish community? If for some reason I were to attack somebody who happened to be Jewish, you can bet your bottom dollar a lot of people would send up a cry of anti-Semitism. Why is it?

Well, look what happened to the Jews.

Yes, but lots of nationalities have suffered at the hands of others. The Armenians were butchered by the Turks, thrown into the Bosphorus in lime and so on.

I'm not saying I approve of the over-sensitiveness, but I do understand it.

So is it going to go on for ever?

If the Jews and the Arabs sort themselves out, I think eventually that it will disappear in two or three generations, or be much reduced. Isn't

the over-sensitivity there partly because anti-Semitism is still present practically everywhere?

To what extent? I rarely see a sign of it.

I'm certain and I know that anti-Semitism does exist, though I don't think personally I've come across it face to face.

But what prompts it?

Maybe a lot of people envy the success of the Jews. In Hungary today, which is trying to be more liberal and democratic than Britain, there is a great deal of anti-Semitism, and it will only be eradicated with time.

But isn't that the case everywhere: anti-Arab, anti-black, anti-German, anti-Jew? You're never going to eradicate those attitudes completely.

I doubt it. But I think if we have a liberal world ahead of us, it will be much reduced. Do you have Jews working for you?

In Quartet I had a salesman who, when he was working for me, went to New York and married a Jewish girl, and I was best man.

But if somebody applies to you for a job, you're not going to ask what his religion is?

Of course not.

Do you have Jewish friends?

A lot, certainly.

The one thing about Mrs Thatcher and the present government is that anti-Semitism is totally absent from their minds, as far as I can judge.

Recently there seems to have been an upsurge of anti-Semitism in Russia. It used to be said that it had religious origins, but the Russians have been promoting atheism for seventy years.

Anti-Semitism in Russia, going back to tsarist days, was so cruel, with the pogroms and so on, that it will take a long time to disappear. I'm quite sure that the present Russian leadership is not anti-Semitic. I can't imagine that Gorbachev is. I think there is still a very large Jewish population in Russia, and as you know, the Israelis are in a way worried about the number of Russians coming in, the Arabs are objecting, and there's been a lot of publicity. But give it another 200 years. Provided we don't have any more major wars, this will eventually disappear, as

the situation between the Catholics and Protestants in Northern Ireland will disappear in time.

Are you optimistic about the prospects of peace in the Middle East?

It's bound to happen. Were you not surprised and pleased when the Egyptians and the Jews decided they had to live alongside each other?

I was disappointed that the Israelis and the Egyptians signed a separate peace treaty without involving the Palestinians.

I totally agree but isn't it largely between all the Arabs and the Jews?

No, it is between the Palestinians and the Jews. But look what's happened in Eastern Europe. We were saying not so long ago that we wouldn't see it in our lifetime.

But neither with the Arabs and the Jews, nor with the Northern Irish Catholics and the Protestants, has there been the same subjugation of people as came about in Eastern Europe. Therefore the explosion in Eastern Europe cannot be repeated in the same manner in the Middle East and Northern Ireland. The pattern will be different, but I still firmly believe that we live in a better world today than the one we lived in only three years ago.

But it can equally be claimed that the Palestinians of the West Bank are heavily subjugated by the Israelis at this point in time.

I'm sure they are. The party in power in Israel and the prime minister are awful. I sympathize with the Israeli Labour party. I think they genuinely want a settlement, a proper, fair and lasting settlement. Have you been back at all?

When my father was still alive, just before I became a publisher. I took my wife and my little boy. It was a very emotional journey.

Your family were from Haifa?

Yes, and my grandmother from Nazareth. But let's get back to the questions I have for you. It's said that the second most important satisfaction in your life, after founding your own publishing house, has been membership of the Garrick Club. Why was it so long denied you?

It's important, but not that important. The truth is that I'm not a good clubman. I don't go in and lunch alone, or mingle in the bar and chatter, but I do love the club. I don't know why it was denied me so long, but as has happened with a good many other people, when I was first put

up for membership my backers were advised to withdraw my name, so it wasn't that I was blackballed. Then, years later, an author of ours, Lord Bethell, said to me innocently, 'I never see you at the Garrick. Why don't you come in more often?' I said, 'For a very good reason. I can only go if I'm invited.' He said, 'This is outrageous,' put me up, and I was in.

Why was it important? Because you felt it gave you the status you wanted?

No, no. It's just a marvellous club, full of interesting people, and I wanted to be part of it. Good heavens, I had no complex. I didn't wake up in the morning and say, my God, here I am, a reasonably successful publisher and I'm not a member of the Garrick. That never occurred to me.

Rumour has it that you don't enjoy the best relations with Lord Weidenfeld.

It's not true. My relationship with George has had its sunny periods and its dark periods. I've known him longer than anybody in the publishing world. I first met him when he was working at the BBC, and we became close friends. He was marvellous company, we were young, and we saw a great deal of each other. George was initially backed by the people who owned Nicolson & Watson. They gave him printing facilities and the money and paper. He had a magazine called *Contact*, and that was how he started. He then began in publishing, starting Weidenfeld & Nicolson proper about two or three years before I started André Deutsch Ltd, so in that sense his company is my senior.

George at that point was flirting with the idea of working for Israel and living there, and after a while he approached me with the suggestion that we merge. This must have been in 1952. We arranged to have a talk and I took Diana and Nick along, who were much in favour and thought George a brilliant man with excellent connections. But at the last minute I said to them and George, 'Right, let's merge, though we must have 51 per cent.' This wasn't because of any mistrust of George, but was based on my bitter experience of what had happened to me at Allan Wingate. Nevertheless George was deeply offended and the whole thing faded away, but George kept coming back to the idea of merging.

Years later George said, 'Look, I've tried to persuade you to merge, but you won't, and I accept it now. How about if I buy you?' I was amazed and put two questions to George: what with and what for? George said, 'What with is no problem because of the City and banks and my financial connections. As for what for, you have that building in Great Russell Street. We sell that, and we have space in Clapham, so we merge and the office moves down there.' But nothing came of it.

But you admire him?

I have enormous admiration, also some criticism.

You once said that women had been the greatest influence on your life.

I am more relaxed in women's company than in men's, though that is changing a bit as I get older, and I don't mean in any sexual sense. Diana Athill was a great influence in my life and involved in my career. I'm absolutely certain that, without the support of Diana and lots of other people in the office, André Deutsch could not have become what it turned out to be.

You're particularly fond of India. What attracted you?

Oh, the beauty of the country and the people. I discovered India rather late in life. However, my first exotic foreign involvement was the West Indies. Quite by chance, on a trip, I met lots of people and published many West Indian authors, including Eric Williams, a distinguished historian who happened to be prime minister of Trinidad. I also published Michael Manley, and there was a period from the late 1950s until the mid 1970s when we had a distinguished West Indian list. My next involvement was in Africa, where I started two publishing companies, one of which still exists. It's a political story, of course.

I was going down to South Africa, either on my first or second visit, and Billy Collins said, 'Don't just fly over Africa. Get out. Have a look at it.' So on the way down I stopped off in Nairobi, said hello to the press, the booksellers and so forth, and on the way back did the same in Lagos. Suddenly I got the idea that it would be nice to start a publishing company; not the old-fashioned colonial sort but something genuinely indigenous. With the help of the British High Commissioner, I met some very interesting people and started a firm called African Universities Press (AUP). It had 50 per cent Nigerian money and 50 per cent André Deutsch money, and was by and large educational publishing, of which I had no experience though I took on some excellent people to work there.

Did you lose money?

If you add everything in, yes, but at about the same time, I'd got to know Tom Mboya, and he became interested in what we were trying to do in Nigeria. At a Commonwealth conference in London he took me to meet Kenyatta, and they said, 'Once we have independence, why don't you do the same thing in Nairobi?' Eighteen months later I flew out to start the second genuine African publishing company, the East African Publishing House (EAPH). I was very unpopular in London.

Few people supported me or approved of what I was doing. One of the few who did was Mark Longman, another was Alan Hill.

Now you are semi-retired, what next?

I don't know.

But how do you spend your days?

If we were having this interview three years ago, I would be very different. More aggressive in my answers, more forthcoming. I'm not as sharp as I used to be.

Because of the circumstances?

Entirely. There has been a decline. Whether it's reversible, time will tell. I just made a major mistake when I decided to sell the firm.

If you could live your life again, what, if anything, would you do differently, apart from not selling the business.

By and large I presume the same pattern would develop, because I don't regret anything I've done, intellectually, morally or politically. I made lots of mistakes. I'm no genius.

Sometimes I say to my wife, there is only one thing I regret in life. I feel I should have started earlier when I see young men today achieving a great deal by an early age. The very wise answer she always gives me is, 'You were not ready.'

I think it's the other way round with me, because I achieved a lot when I was young. It was when I got older that I made the catastrophic mistake of selling the company.

But doesn't that tell you that money is not the source of happiness?

Of course it tells me. Not making a lot of money never bothered me. I now have more money than I need, but it's an ill-gotten gain. I got it because I sold the business. But I never attached much importance to money, otherwise I would have led a different sort of life.

DOMINICK DUNNE

Dominick Dunne was born in Connecticut in 1928, the second of six children of Irish Catholic parents. After graduating from Williams College he went to New York and studied under Sanford Meisner. He started as a stage manager and went on to produce a number of Hollywood films such as *Ash Wednesday* and *The Boys in the Band*. He is the author of *The Winners, The Two Mrs Grenvilles* (a *New York Times* bestseller in both hardback and paperback) and *People Like Us*. He is also a contributing editor to *Vanity Fair*. A former alcoholic, Dunne is separated from his wife and has two sons. His daughter was murdered by her boyfriend in 1983.

I'm not sure that I had a happy childhood. I was one of six children, and we were a large Catholic family in Hartford, Connecticut, a very WASP city. We were outsiders and I hated being an outsider as a child. It wasn't that we were discriminated against – I can't say that – but we were different from the others. It seemed, for example, that children's parties were always on a Friday, and in those days Catholics couldn't eat meat on Fridays. I used to turn scarlet every time I had to decline the chicken or whatever it was we were being given. I would be brought a poached egg, and I hated all that, but the discrimination, if that is what it was, was more on my side than on theirs, if that makes sense. Now, as an adult, I love feeling like an outsider, because I think that's what gives me the insights I have as a novelist and journalist. All those feelings I once hated I treasure, because that is what has helped me more than anything else as a writer.

One of the main influences of my childhood was my grandfather, after whom I am named. He was an extraordinary, brilliant man who had had very little formal education, yet was one of the most educated people I have ever known. He had an incredible love of literature and poetry. He made his money in the grocery business, but never forgot that he was born poor and had poor relations. He used to take care of the poor in the city of Hartford, and eventually he was knighted by the Pope for his charitable work. My brother and I would spend Saturday nights at my grandfather's house, where he read poetry to us after dinner. We hated it at the time, but it had an enormous influence. Then, on Sunday, he would take us down to the poor areas of the city. It was all an important part of our growing up.

I was close to my mother too, but I never got on with my father. I always felt I was a disappointment to him. I was not a good athlete. I was shy and had a stutter. I was very insecure. I was not a good student. Then, when I was eighteen, I went into the army. I was very scared,

drafted out of my fancy boarding school and finding myself with all these tough people. I had one friend, a boy from Yale who was a year older. They used to call us the gold-dust twins. During the Battle of the Bulge we were in combat for the first time and I was absolutely terrified. It was dark and raining, and we were retreating, losing the battle. Some men had been wounded, but although the lieutenant was told about the wounded men, he said we couldn't stop for them since his orders were to take us back. Something happened then that I have never been able to understand. My friend and I looked at each other, and some energy or something took over the two of us. We turned around and ran toward the enemy in the night, artillery shells flying over our heads in the pouring pissing rain.

God knows how, but we found two wounded soldiers in the pitch dark. My friend carried one and I carried the other to the nearest aid station, in the basement of a bombed-out house. The duty orderly said he couldn't do anything since his orders were to retreat, but we made him help. We turned on a generator to get some light and eventually got the guys into an ambulance. I was covered in blood, and never even knew the name of the one I'd carried. I never heard if he lived or died. But as I put him on the stretcher, he took hold of my fingers and squeezed them as if to say thanks.

My friend and I both got medals for that, and though I didn't realize it at the time, it was maybe the first indication that inside I had some kind of strength that I never understood. I felt I had the ability to do anything at that moment. It was almost like I was outside of myself watching. I didn't talk about it for years and years. Then, two winters ago, I had an amazing experience. There's a coffee shop near here, and sometimes, when I work late, I go over and have a sandwich at the counter. One day I looked up from my *New York Times* and saw a guy looking at me. It was the other gold-dust twin. We hadn't seen each other in over forty years. We both got up and each of us walked across and just hugged the other, and cried.

Hollywood is very unforgiving of failure. It will forgive, even overlook your forgeries, your embezzlements, and occasionally your murders, but it will not forgive failure.' I'm glad you picked that to quote at me from my latest novel. It's one of my favourite lines in the whole book. And it's true. If the guy's last four pictures are successful he will be forgiven anything. Take the famous forgery case out there a few years ago. The whole industry rallied behind the man that forged the cheque. He was the head of a studio, and they stood behind him. Again – this is dicey to talk about so I'm not naming names – a very famous man out there may or may not have ordered a killing; certainly it's been in all the papers that the possibility exists. No charges have been filed, but

the possibility remains. That man is not shunned. And God knows, there's one case after another of financial irregularities. During that famous forgery case, people whom I knew at the studio would say, 'It was only $10,000.'

Not all my days in Hollywood were unhappy. I had some great years there, until it turned bad for me and I began to hate it, but not every minute of my twenty-four years there was horrible. For more than half of that time it was wonderful. Even now, when I go back, I always have a funny feeling there, and I'm not just talking about my daughter's death. If my daughter hadn't been murdered I would still have this feeling. I grew so desperately lonely and unhappy there and I used to blame others for the destruction of my film career, but ultimately I came to realize that it was myself who brought it about. Maybe it was some sort of elaborate pattern in the grand plan of life to get me to go and write. None the less I didn't understand that at the time. I was drinking, I was taking drugs, I was doing all kinds of things, and my life became just awful.

In any case, I began to feel I might have some talent as a writer during my last years in Hollywood when my whole career as a film and television producer came apart. Having been very successful and then having started to be very unsuccessful, I was also experiencing this inner feeling that I should be writing. Of course, I was of an age when the whole idea of shifting career seemed just ludicrous, so I didn't act right away. Eventually, in about 1979, I moved from California to Oregon and started writing my first book. I had gone to my former wife's house, where I had things stored on the third floor. Among my belongings that I had long since forgotten were letters written to me during the Second World War when I was overseas, eighteen years old and a private soldier in combat. Those letters from years and years before were from my mother, father and sisters, and several times my father, who I thought didn't like me, said that my own letters home were so descriptive that I should really think about writing as a career. So I think it was always there; it was just dormant in me.

I'm happy now, because I have found contentment in my work. I love working for *Vanity Fair* and I love writing my books. I often get asked to go back to Hollywood to write or produce a movie again, but that's all gone, that's over. I seem to be bringing out a novel every two years, and in between times I write stories for *Vanity Fair* and travel a great deal. I have the kind of life where I don't have to answer to anyone. I go to Europe four or five times a year and to California just as often, and I love living like that. I actually don't need other people in my life. I've finally come to that conclusion. I love having friends, but I am basically a loner. I haven't even had a long relationship with a woman for quite a few years.

When *People Like Us* and Tom Wolfe's *Bonfire of the Vanities* get spoken of together, I am enormously flattered because Tom Wolfe is one of the really great writers of our time and I admired his book enormously. But our books are very different. He's much more of a satirist than I am, and I think I see more hope than he does. Everybody is ultimately bad in his book, there's nobody to root for, whereas I don't think things are that bad.

Three other writers I feel affinity with are Scott Fitzgerald, John P. Marquand and John O'Hara. All three have influenced me. As a kid I couldn't wait for J. P. Marquand's books to come out, and he had an enormous influence on me. I have a great affinity with John O'Hara in that he, too, was an Irish Catholic and moved in high social life, as I apparently do. I always identified with those two, and then, later, I read Fitzgerald, who's probably the best writer of the three.

When, in *People Like Us*, I described smart ladies in long ballgowns stepping over the down-and-outs in the street, it was an exaggerated image, but what eventually happens to New Yorkers, even the most wonderful people, is that the blinders go on and they stop looking. I have actually seen them coming out of a swell party and getting into a limousine, pulling minks around them and putting their jewels into their bags so they won't show while they're waiting for the chauffeur to close the door; and all this while homeless people are lying right there in the street.

When I said, 'The Reagans brought out the worst in many people,' it was what I really thought. I'm not a fan of the Reagans at all. From the very beginning of their administration, Mrs Reagan had this sense of opulence that went beyond the norm one expects from the First Lady. Everything had to do with possessions: she gave extraordinary emphasis to clothes, and there was the famous business of the china that cost so much money. I think that kind of set the pace for the rich. When the Reagans could have invited fascinating people to the White House, they chose the rich and fashionable instead, and sent a signal out to the country that flamboyance was OK.

Since you quote me my remark that the 1980s was the decade when the rich went public, I have to say that I can really only speak for New York, because that's where I lived during that whole decade. The rich were richer than they've ever been before, and it was truly disgusting how they flaunted their wealth. And the way they would invite the media into their lives used to fascinate me. All their houses were photographed. It was the era of instant art collections, instant antique collections, instant porcelain collections, instant jewellery collections. People just talked about money the whole time. You'd be sitting in somebody's house at dinner, and you'd know that the apartment you were sitting in was sold for $6,800,000, that the hostess's dress cost $22,000, that

the centrepieces from Marlow cost $600 and that the curtains from Sister Parish cost whatever. I couldn't get over it, this thing about money, money, money. It was really obscene. That was when I decided to write *People Like Us*. It's too early to define the 1990s yet, because I don't think a decade defines itself until about the fourth year. But the lives of these people have certainly gone into the closet again. And that's for the good, I think.

Critics always say this thing about writers, that they have a strong desire to belong to the world they write about, and I don't really know the answer to that question. I don't feel I want to be part of that world, because once you're a part of it you can't comment on it any more. As it is, I ride a very fine line between mixing in that world and writing about it. It's a very curious thing. I found that during the time I was writing *People Like Us*, which was about New York society and people involved in social advancement, I really did live the life of those people. I could never live like that again. I did it for several years, and I'm glad I did it, but I never have to do it again.

As for how, as a successful novelist, I can escape the fate of the rich as I describe it in my novels, I can tell you, in the first place, that my house is fairly sweet, very cosy, but also very small. I have no desire to move to a fifteen-room house. This is the way I'm going to live for the rest of my life. I'm really not interested in all the things that go with money, acquisitions and so on. I have been rich and successful earlier in my life, when I was in the movie business, and it did change me when I was young. I turned into somebody I never want to be again, so I've already had that experience. And it's not going to happen again. If people see a strong moralistic line in my novels, it is something which has evolved. What happened to me in my life has changed me for ever. I have been involved in drink and drug abuse, though that was years ago. I'm still a regular participant in AA, but even if I didn't go to AA, I would never drink or drug again.

Ask me about my writing. I don't like questions like that – about whether respect in the States is fundamentally linked to money. Answers always come out making me sound like an asshole – you know, giving great opinions. I'm just a writer.

Yes, when *Women's Wear Daily* somehow got hold of a very early draft of *People Like Us* – I never knew how – it was a very interesting experience for me, though I was scared at first. They likened me to Truman Capote, and said that, like him, I had bitten the hand that fed me. Truman Capote revealed confidences and secrets that people in society had told him, and I knew I hadn't done that. I therefore decided just to wait it out, and I almost enjoyed the experience of being shunned by those who had previously invited me. Some did call me up and ask

how I could have done such a thing, and a couple of people had their lawyers ring and threaten my publishing house. It was just fascinating, and I began to wonder, what do they think I know about them that I don't really know? Anyone who's read this book will see that it deals with the public life of these people. I don't know what their secrets are. Once the book was out, most people calmed down, but there are still a few who have never spoken to me since. I don't think, in fact, that I've ever betrayed a confidence. I always make sure that I combine three or four people into one character. Someone may recognize certain aspects of their own character, but never the whole.

In my interviews people tell me things they've never admitted to before. I truly don't know why, but all my life people have told me things. The simple answer, I suppose, is that I'm a good listener. A letter arrived today from a friend whom I had told of my experience the other night at a party in New York where a woman talked to me about the death of her son. This friend of mine writes: 'The image I have been unable to shake from my mind is the one you put there the other morning when we talked on the phone of your encounter with' – I'll make up a name – 'Mary. I'm dead certain that she hasn't had that conversation or even anything like it with another soul. What Mary told you may not strike the world as significantly historic, but I can tell you, even though I think you already know, that for her that was one fucking precious moment. I've played it over and over in my mind, the murmur of other conversations going on around you, the smell of the room, the rustling of dresses, getting up from the table and so on, until she came back into the room to kiss you good night. It all haunts me in a rather pleasant way and perhaps the reason why I can't shake it or don't want to is because practically everything else about her son's death haunts me in the most unpleasant way.' That letter perhaps shows that it just so happens that people tell me things.

The fact that public figures are no longer so protected from their indiscretions as they once were raises an interesting question. I'm in a dilemma about how to answer it. I don't think I would ever reveal something that was terribly private to a person's life. If I discovered that someone had committed murder I think I'd tell it, or if someone had stolen something – that's a different thing, if the person has harmed someone. But if it's about someone's sexuality, or someone's illegitimacy over which the person has no control, I wouldn't tell. I would say, though, that the investigative journalism we now have in the United States has gone too far. I've stopped reading *Spy* magazine. I used to be amused in the beginning, but it isn't funny any more. It's just cruel, and people are deeply deeply hurt by it.

If I say I have come to terms with tragedy in my life, it sounds so arch.

I believe in God, and I think that, no matter what happens, you go on, you don't give up. I believe very firmly in this. There are so many people who suffer a tragedy in their lives and never recover from it. I go out and talk a lot to groups or to people who have been through homicide experiences, and what I try to say is that your life can go on again, you can go out, go to movies again, laugh again, go to parties again. What has happened will always be part of you and will change you, but you have to go back to work, and if you've got other children, you have to focus on them rather than focusing on the tragedy that has occurred.

I was myself able to use the tragedy of my daughter's murder in a novel and in an article in *Vanity Fair*. Why shouldn't I? I was so enraged by the justice system that I could never have returned to my writing career if I had not written that article. My anger was at such a level that I was obsessed by what I had witnessed in the courtroom, and it was a release for me. I'm also very proud of that article. It's been used by district attorneys, by judges, and it's read in some law schools to show what can happen when a case goes wrong in court. The book did not deal with the tragedy; it dealt with the aftermath, with how you deal with feelings of revenge, of getting even with the person who has done this terrible thing to you. In *People Like Us* as I wrote it – I'm not talking about the movie of it, because the movie was a piece of shit where they changed the whole emphasis – the character of Gus Bailey was the seemingly passive person who worked as a journalist in New York, and none of the people with whom he interacted knew that he was planning a violent act, which was to kill the person who had caused him harm.

I know that in real life you have those feelings, and I know that in the groups of people I talk to they have those feelings of wanting to kill the person who has killed the member of their family. Now, I also know that you can't do it, nor would I do it, but that doesn't mean I didn't have the feelings, and as a novelist I could create a situation in which I could deal with those feelings, could act them out in a story in a way I couldn't act them out in life. Yet the fact is that when I got to the part where he shoots the killer, I couldn't make him shoot him, even in a book; so his hand moves as he shoots, and he wounds the guy but doesn't kill him. In life, however, I can never forgive.

If I could rewind the tape of the life I have lived, I would certainly have moved away from Hollywood sooner and started writing. But I also believe in the whole perfect pattern. Perhaps I'm better as a writer for having gone through so much, for having been broke for ten years, for having to worry about rent money, for having been successful, then unsuccessful, and having people whom I thought were my friends in

Hollywood no longer be my friends because I was no longer successful. I hated that while I was living it, but I got through it and now I wouldn't trade it. If it's all been just perfect for you all your life, you're going to have nothing to write about. You have to see both sides.

If I had it all again, what would I do? I would try to get to know my father better. I was afraid of my father, and I understand now that he was the kind of man who didn't have the ability to be gentle. It made me scared of strong men for most of my life. When I was in Hollywood I used to be terrified of heads of studios. Anybody who was in authority over me would frighten me. I no longer feel like that, but I'm a different person now. I used to hate being a Catholic in an Episcopalian city, but now, if I had to live it again, I would want it to be exactly the same. I used to think all life would be easier for me if only I was a Protestant instead of a Catholic, which is ludicrous. But I guess we never understand our lives until later.

I allowed my Catholicism to lapse for many years, but I have come back to it. I had a child who died, and after my child died I was in a state of despair. I was living in California then, and a man – a most unlikely person who had been a figure in the movie industry, been divorced I don't know how many times, been a great womanizer and everything else – came to see me and told me of a priest he thought I should go and see. I was so startled that this guy with his rogue life should have this idea, that I went to see the priest, and I don't know exactly what happened, but I started going back to my faith. I have stayed with it, and although I'm not the best Catholic in the world, I do practise my religion.

My broken marriage was a source of sadness to me. Still is. I was married to a wonderful woman. She's still my great friend. She has multiple sclerosis and is a total invalid. She lives in a wheelchair and cannot do a single thing without assistance. That all happened after we were divorced, although she was ill during our marriage and it was never diagnosed. I never wanted to get divorced, and neither of us ever married again. We went through a bad period, but the point of marriage should be that you weather out the bad patches. It's always upset me that my kids' lives were shaken up during that time. I wouldn't have gotten a divorce if I had it to do over again. She's probably still the most important person in my life. I think the failure of the marriage was my fault not hers. It would have been nice if things had turned out differently. For years and years I've missed the noise of a house, the children's sounds, dog sounds, maid sounds and so on. When I went to live alone, it took me years to get used to the silence. Now I'm used to being alone, and I kind of like it.

My chief regret has to be that I wasn't a better husband. That really took a toll. I hope I have been a good father. I know for a fact that my

children love me, and that's a nice feeling, but it's not to say it's all been perfect with the kids. Sometimes my sons can be really tough with me, but I suppose it is good that they feel secure enough to do so. One of my sons gave me hell the other day. A TV movie of one of my books came out, and it dealt with my daughter's death, something that was not in my book. It really bothered me too, but my son said it was my own fault, that if I had taken an interest and hadn't distanced myself from the movie so much and put it in other people's hands, this would never have happened. He got really mad at me, and I was hurt by it, but I realized also how much I had changed. There was a time in my life when, if he had spoken like that, I would simply have hung up the phone, but instead I understood his anger. Even though he was angry with me, he still loved me, and I knew that he knew that I loved him back.

JOHN KENNETH GALBRAITH

John Kenneth Galbraith is author of the classic work on the 1928 Wall Street crash, *The Great Crash* (1955). He was born in Ontario in 1908 and was educated at the University of Toronto, the University of California where he took his PhD, and later as a postgraduate at Cambridge University, England. He was a research fellow at California for three years until 1934 when he became a tutor at Harvard (1934–9) and then assistant professor of economics at Princeton (1939–42). He went on to be professor of economics at Harvard for over twenty-five years (1949–75), and from 1961 to 1963 he was the US ambassador to India. He has written many books including *American Capitalism* (1952), *The Affluent Society* (1958), *Ambassador's Journal* (1969) and *The Age of Uncertainty* (1977). He has been married for over fifty years and has three sons.

As a child, who influenced you most in your life?

I suppose I was most influenced by my father, who was a public figure of strong local importance in Ontario, and very much concerned with local well-being – an official of the township, official of the county, ran a co-operative insurance company, and considered himself responsible for everything that happened in the neighbourhood.

Did you ever consciously feel that you were going to make a great success of your life?

I took it one step at a time.

But you were always ambitious?

Many people think unfortunately so.

You are always referred to as a liberal. What does the term imply in American politics?

The word 'liberal' has a different meaning in the United States from that which it has in Britain or indeed Europe. There it has the connotation of the liberal preoccupation with free markets, freedom of speech and, to some extent, the limited role of the state. In the United States, the word 'liberal' recognizes the need for a large, compassionate and stabilizing role by government, protection of the individual from the hazards of life, including those of the work place, support to trade unions and a more generally supportive attitude towards those who suffer from personal misfortune. I suppose that the nearest counterpart in European terminology is 'social democratic', with a very large emphasis on the liberty of the citizen.

American political attitudes are often puzzling to Europeans, especially in relation to socialism. Does the word have very different connotations for Americans?

I think this is true. The word 'socialism' in Europe refers to the mixed economy, in which there is a substantial but by no means total rule by the state, and where the implication is benign. But out of long-established practice in the United States, socialism has been given a much more adverse connotation, so that some of my fellow liberals unquestionably back off from the risk of being called socialists.

I have the impression that you see yourself and your career as primarily one of economist and writer rather than of diplomat.

I regarded the diplomatic part of my life very much as a departure from the norm, and in some measure as an enjoyment. I had become interested, I think I can say fascinated, by India, as did so many others in the 1950s, and when John F. Kennedy asked me to go to India as his ambassador, I was greatly attracted by the idea of learning more of the culture and civilization, and of contributing something to better relations between the United States and India – taking that issue away from the professional Cold War warriors for a while. But I certainly never regarded diplomacy as more than a temporary career, or perhaps, as some people would prefer to have me say, a temporary aberration. Basically I consider myself a professional writer, yes.

When you were ambassador to India it was said of you by Krishna Menon that you behaved rather like a British resident during the Raj, guiding and influencing.

I think it fair to say that Krishna Menon's views on this, as on so many matters, are to be taken with a grain of salt. I certainly didn't see myself in the tradition of a British mandarin. There was nothing I tried more to avoid, but I did have sharp differences with Krishna Menon over his repeated attacks on the United States, and we came to a serious parting of the ways at the time of that quite useless war in the Himalayas when Krishna was defence minister. It was impossible for me to rally support in Washington as long as Krishna was defence minister, and I think he attributed his departure from that post in some measure to me, rightly or wrongly. So perhaps he had some reason to be a little prejudiced. I made it clear to the Indian government that his presence as defence minister was a formidable problem in our coming to India's assistance.

Since you ask, it was not part of my policy to have a high profile in India, but I think it fair to say that I have only a limited talent for anonymity and that at that time the United States was a source of very

large assistance to India. I was instructed by President Kennedy, to my delight, to spend a good deal of time out of New Delhi, making the acquaintance of Indian leaders and the Indian scene. I was a close political and personal friend of Jawaharlal Nehru, which served to keep me in the public eye. That was something, I have to tell you, I didn't entirely avoid. John F. Kennedy considered the relationship with India very important, and one must remember that India and Nehru were the voice of the so-called unaligned world; and I shared with Kennedy a desire to have the friendship and respect of those countries.

As for any influence that I may have had with Kennedy, I think everyone should avoid exaggerating such influence. President Truman once said of the great financier, Bernard Baruch, 'I don't see why he describes himself as an adviser to presidents. Doesn't he know that all presidents have more advice than they can use?' On the other hand, Kennedy made it clear that he enjoyed my letters and my telegrams and was pleased at the annoyance they caused some of the drearier and more orthodox members of his administration.

You advised Kennedy not to become involved militarily in Vietnam – advice he did not act on.

Well, I have to go back a bit. I have always thought that Kennedy had grave doubts about Vietnam, but he was under severe pressure at that time from the conservative establishment, the military and, I regret to say, some of my liberal friends, to show he was a man of muscle and vigour in the defence of what were conceived to be American interests. I talked to him about the problems we were going to face there – that we were replacing the French as another colonial power, that we were associated with remarkably unpopular and incompetent politicians – and right up until the time of his death I found him sympathetic and, on more than one occasion, anxious to have my views and also to urge my recommendations.

In asking whether the world might have been different had Kennedy not been assassinated, you are framing a question that invites speculation. On domestic matters, including civil rights and the war on poverty, which I greatly supported, I don't think Kennedy would have done more than, and perhaps not as much as, Lyndon Johnson. We should not for a moment minimize the important steps that Lyndon Johnson took to make the United States, and especially its race relations, more compassionate and civilized. So the question turns on what Kennedy would have done in Indo-China.

It is my feeling that, at the time of his death – and this is based on many conversations – Kennedy was resistant to the idea of any full military involvement there, although, needless to say, a great many

advisers had been sent. But one has to add that, if you had pressed Lyndon Johnson at the same time, he would have expressed the same reluctance. So the question is really one that cannot be answered: could Kennedy have stood against the forces that were pressing the domino theory and the notion we had to stand firm?

Why wouldn't Kennedy have fared as well as Johnson on the domestic front?

The difference was that Johnson, in his relations with Congress, always used slightly more power than he had, and while Kennedy's intentions were the same, he always used slightly less power than he had. It was partly the produce of personality, but also of Johnson's greater experience and authority on Capitol Hill.

But wasn't Johnson much more ruthless?

That's perhaps another way of putting it.

You have never suffered fools gladly, and seem to have taken a consistently abrasive line with the State Department. Did you feel this was how bureaucracies needed to be treated?

I did not believe that in pressing the case against the conventional Cold War warriors, and those who were oriented to military solutions, a conciliatory voice would have been very useful, and I think I would have to add that, on the whole, I enjoyed the power – the effect of what I saw as the harsh truth. People in a bureaucracy do not get annoyed by error. They get annoyed by what they don't want to hear. And one should never minimize the pleasure in causing that annoyance. I never thought it necessary to avoid controversy. On the whole I enjoyed it, especially if it was with people who needed to be corrected, and at that time I was in conflict with the leadership of the State Department over matters about which, I'm happy to say, history has been rather kinder to me than it has to them.

You once said: 'Politics is not the art of the possible. It consists in choosing between the disastrous and the unpalatable.'

That's what I really believe. If a public question is between what is obviously right and popular and what is obviously wrong and unpopular, no political problem is involved. A political problem only arises when you have a choice between a wrong course of action and a right course of action that is difficult and which provokes adverse comment and action.

In 1971 you said that only an intolerable level of unemployment could arrest the inflationary process. Twenty years on, do you still hold to that view?

No, I think not. I think we have now learned that we can have a substantially lower level of unemployment than was once imagined without inflation. I then felt that only a very high level of unemployment would arrest the interaction of wages and prices: trade union pressure pushing up wages with a compensating increase in prices and a self-generating cycle of that sort. The pressure of that cycle is much diminished for two reasons: the movement of some of our heavy manufacturing, where unions were strongest and where employee power was greatest, from the United States to Japan, Korea, Taiwan and other countries, and the general weakening of the trade union movement. In these last years, trade unions, more often than pressing for increased wages, have had to make concessions in order to keep their employers in business. This is a very great difference.

I still believe that one can come closer to full employment and a good and healthy rate of growth by having a prices and incomes policy in the central core of the economy, but I don't regard it now as being as absolutely essential as I once thought, for the reasons I mentioned. Prices are now much more restrained by international competition, and wage claims are much more restrained by the weakness of the employees in the traditionally highly organized industries. To be specific, the United Automobile workers recognize that in making wage claims there are limits to the pressure they can bring to bear on automobile manufacturers if the automobile manufacturers are not to suffer a loss of production to the Japanese.

I wouldn't describe the trade union movement as becoming more responsible but as becoming weaker, because of circumstances. A strong trade union movement requires strong corporations and strong employers. Employers have been weakened by the rise of external competition.

But we do now seem willing to live with levels of unemployment which, a decade ago, would have seemed impossible and scandalous. Have we become accustomed to indifference?

No. The question itself has to be revised. We have not had, these last years, high levels of unemployment in the United States. Our problem has rather been the movement of people from high-wage to low-wage employment. It is true that, in Britain and Western Europe, where there's greater rigidity in the employment structures, unemployment is more of a problem. But I still continue to think that it's a mark of a civilized society that anyone who wants a job with a good income should have it.

In the early 1970s, you were not among those who were anxious to see Britain

incorporated into the Common Market, but now, on the brink of 1992, full integration with Europe surely becomes impossible to oppose.

It's true that I never made a career out of advocating British membership of the Common Market, although, on balance, I would be in favour of it. But now, with the changes in Western and Eastern Europe and the reunification of Germany, I think there is an urgent need for European unity and the quieting of old nationalist attitudes. Having said that, I don't believe that 1992 is going to be quite as dramatic in the changes it brings as some of the talk makes out it will be. There will still be different budgets, different fiscal policies, different tax systems, all of that making European monetary unity questionable. National governments will still be stronger than the non-government in Brussels, so that people will look back after 1992 and think there was more talk and less change than might have been imagined.

Yet most leading Europeans, with the exception of Mrs Thatcher, want a strong federation.

That is right, but the emphasis will be on the federal character rather than on complete unity. It's possible in the long term, but I think that 1992 is only a step in that direction. One must always remember that economics and politics regularly substitute words for deeds, and this may well be true of 1992, especially in foreign trade matters. We are always talking about great changes in prospect, and when we look back we always find it very much less of a change than we expected. I have often noted that, while great importance is attached to the EEC, and rightly so, three countries that remained outside, namely Austria, Switzerland and Sweden, have been perhaps the most successful of the post-war economies. The reason for that is that we may exaggerate the rewards of reunification and minimize the rewards of wise and sensible administration by the individual country.

It is true that Spain is bubbling, but I wouldn't attribute all of that to Spain's membership of the EEC. Perhaps Spain was awaiting a renaissance.

A great many people in Europe look upon German unity as a mixed blessing, believing they have good reason to feel nervous about a newly powerful German state.

When one looks back over the history of German politics and economics in the past forty-five years, it has been very civilized, very successful, and a good manifestation of intelligent social democracy. I see no reason for recreating the fears of a half century ago. The steps toward the unification of Europe, in which I hope Eastern Europe will come to

play a part, make for certainty in this regard. Having said that, I hope that the Germans will treat with proper contempt, even alarm, those who talk, for example, about adjusting the eastern boundary with Poland.

Yet seven years after the Berlin Wall was built, you said that the Wall was a very good thing, and that at least it had preserved the peace.

I don't recall saying that. I will not take responsibility for casual comments of an earlier time. I was very glad to see the Wall go. It was, as are all such things, an insult to civilized manners.

Wouldn't a powerful economy from Britain to the Urals have serious repercussions for the United States?

That is a long-run prospect where speculation serves no useful purpose. I would like to see a strong federated economy going from Ireland to the Urals and beyond. I think that would be an assurance of peace and tranquillity and I can't think it would be bad for the United States.

But the United States has economic problems.

Oh, no question. There has been a strong tendency in Washington, and in the American economy and American economic practice generally, to substitute short-run comfort for long-run solutions. We have run a large deficit in our domestic budget when we could have had lower interest rates and more productive investment. After the war, our corporations developed a certain self-satisfaction and a bureaucratic sclerosis, and they have been further damaged by the merger and takeover mania which has substituted heavy burdens of debt for equity; and this too has been damaging to investments and new processes. All of these problems have been coupled with large and, in many respects, unnecessary military expenditure which has kept a very large part of our stock of capital and a very large proportion of our needed civilian talent in sterile war production. One of the great advantages that the Germans and the Japanese have had since the Second World War was in using their resources for the improvement of their civilian industry. We have learned that those who lose a war can win the peace.

I wouldn't blame the Japanese for a moment for their market dominance. We should blame ourselves. We have handicapped our industry by unwise fiscal policy, unwise interest policy, the damaging effects of financial manipulation, and the undue commitment of our resources to the Pentagon. Those are the matters which have given the Japanese their advantage. Admittedly, for cultural, linguistic and other reasons, the Japanese market is not easy to penetrate, but I would attribute less to

Japanese protection than I would to the lack of initiative of our own enterprises.

If you were suddenly given the reins of the US economy, how would you cure its ills?

The likelihood of my being given a free hand I think is distinctly questionable, but I would move strongly to reduce our military expenditure. I would use the proceeds from that to strengthen our internal educational system, improve our roads and, particularly, improve life in the central cities; and also to provide loans to ease the transition to democracy in Eastern Europe. And I wouldn't hesitate, if the proceeds from the reduction in military expenditure were insufficient for the purpose, to raise taxes. We live in a world of affluent and even frivolous private expenditure, but as regards public expenditure, there is a very great need.

The fear of raising taxes is a matter of political error. Power has passed to the people who are conservative and comfortable and who are able to do without the public services which are so important to those in our central cities and to the poor. This is one of the great misfortunes of our time. Maybe we're passing out of that stage, but it's slow progress. Meantime, when an urgent problem arises, our president, not wanting to spend money, makes another speech.

The populations of emergent nations and those of the former Eastern block naturally want the things that America and Western Europe already have, but is it actually possible to spread the same standard of living everywhere?

I would like to see greatly improved food, clothing and the basic pleasures of life in the Third World countries, and I think much can be done to that end. Some thirty years ago, I started the first teaching in economic development here at Harvard, which could have been among the first in the United States. There has been great disappointment for me as I've watched this problem since that time, the greatest disappointments being in Africa. But in some other parts of the world there has been great progress. So we mustn't be entirely without hope. I wouldn't say I'm optimistic about the future, because I feel very depressed about Africa, but, on the other hand, there is no question that India, Pakistan and also China, while so much remains to be done, are a more hopeful prospect than they were when I first knew those countries.

I wrote some thirty years ago in *The Affluent Society* that we must balance the consequences of consumption against its effects on the environment. And this is something that I still believe. On the other hand, I would like to see the rewards of higher consumption extended to the masses of people in the world who still don't have enough to eat

and wear and lack even the minimal enjoyments which we so appreciate. That is a very difficult problem. One only has to have experience in India and elsewhere in the Third World to realize what a difficult problem it is. But again some progress has been made. When I went to India, only large imports of grain from the United States kept that country from starvation. Since I left India, the population has doubled, yet India has more than the capacity to feed itself. So we mustn't be without hope.

Do you believe that we should be more dependent on government than on private enterprise?

Absolutely. One of the things that has weakened our standard of living in the United States in recent times has been the assumption that private enterprise is somehow the answer to all that can be done. This has been a way of evading responsibility and protecting the income of the affluent from taxes.

I remember you arguing that, if the market was really market led, there would be more houses and fewer television sets. I can see that up to a point, but is there not a sort of human inevitability about wanting, if you can't afford a house, a television set you can afford?

Oh, this is a very subjective matter. What I said was that capitalism provides television sets more easily than it provides houses, and that a homeless person in our time would find society much more compassionate and companionable if he had a house rather than a television set. The market economy does not meet the needs of people in that regard.

You once spoke of the way you thought Britain was 'living out the concern for some more leisurely relationship with industrial life'. Can that ever be possible for any nation in the future?

I would like to see an industrial, economic life where there was a more rational choice between work and leisure. We've moved some distance in that direction over the last fifty or seventy-five years, but I still think that universities, where leisure and academic freedom are considered to be interchangeable, are a model for economic life in general. Somebody that has to work on an assembly line should have a choice between the money he or she earns and the leisure he or she would like to have. Maybe we should have more opportunity for paid vacations, and paid sabbatical leave for people who have to do heavy manual labour. We consider both of those very desirable things for college professors.

What view do you take of Mrs Thatcher and the Britain she has created during the last ten years?

I am not a supporter of Mrs Thatcher. She has allied herself with the privileged community of her country, as did her friend, Ronald Reagan, in the United States, to the distinct disadvantage of the less fortunate and with damage to the social contract which had previously given the impression, at least, that everybody had an equal chance.

But in the United States she is considered to be the Iron Lady.

Not by me. I think Mrs Thatcher might now have even more difficulty in getting elected in the United States than at home. I cannot imagine that her poll-tax system would be peacefully accepted here in the city of Cambridge, Massachusetts.

Do you think Britain will come out of its economic problems?

We have built into the capitalist system a resilience that is greater than we sometimes imagine, so that while performance is not perfect, I have hopes, and indeed some conviction, that we will avoid the kind of disaster that we experienced in the 1930s or that Britain experienced in the 1920s.

You have long drawn the contrast between 'private affluence' and 'public squalor'. Do you see any evidence of the gulf narrowing?

No. I would say, for example in American cities, it's grown worse. We have a worsening disparity between the quality of our private existence and the quality and the needs of our public life. It's been related both in Britain and the United States to public policies that favour the affluent (including, in our case, the very rich) and penalize the services to the poor. If you're very rich, you can send your children to a private school, have your own library, and maybe your own policeman on the door. If you're middle class or poor, you need those services to be provided for you. We have had, in these last years in the United States, a preferential treatment for the very rich, including those who do not need the public services.

Liberal attitudes so often look like luxuries. Doesn't it become too easy to take the liberal view about racialism in, say, South Africa, provided one lives in Massachusetts?

No, I don't think so for a moment. I quite agree that it's easier to lecture people about their behaviour if they are at some distance, but any good liberal, and I think this is true of most of my liberal friends, is most concerned with problems that are close to home. And I would like to think that is so in my own case.

You have been an advocate of civilized politics, but what hope of civilized politics is there between, say, the Palestinians and the Israelis, or the Iranians and the Iraqis?

There's no question that religious and ethnic passion are the enemies of civilized coexistence, but I certainly don't think we should give up hope. Somebody coming to the United States fifty years ago would have been equally pessimistic about race relations here, and now, fifty years later, would agree that they have greatly improved. I'm certainly not going to give up hope of improved relations between the old cultures of the Middle East. I very much hope that we will have a new period when people of Sadat's stature will take the lead. If one predicts permanent conflict then one gives up hope of a solution.

You were writing about the problems of women's liberation and black emancipation in the 1970s. Do you feel satisfied with the progress that has been made in those areas since then?

No, certainly not. There has been progress, I don't doubt. Perhaps there's been more progress than I would have expected at that time, but we still have serious discrimination against women in industry, the academic community, many other places. We still have a sad difference between the economic prospects of a child who is white and one who is black. And there's no question that we must keep pressure, public and private, strong on both of those issues.

I have been much more fortunate than most people in regard to the support I receive in my work; I would not have been able to do the things I have done without a corps of assistants, most of whom have been women. But I still do not think that women have a chance for independence as long as they're confined to a household and family work. I make the same obeisance to the family as everyone else, but I do not doubt that the family can also be a disguise, an amiable disguise, for male dominance.

Some of your views sound old-fashioned, as, for example, when you said that fortunately there were all sorts of boarding schools 'so that children can be kept separate from their parents for a great part of the time'. Do you really think that is such a good idea?.

I've always felt that children take the good qualities of their parents for granted and the bad qualities as a licence for their own misbehaviour. There's much to be said, at a certain age, for children going off to school and seeing less of their parents. Old-fashioned or otherwise, I don't consider everything that's old-fashioned to be wrong.

You said at the same time that it was a huge loss when intelligent women stayed

at home. What exactly do you think is lost when intelligent women devote themselves to their families ?

I should think that a great deal is lost in the field of literature, music, economic achievement, much else. And I think that, so long as we confine women to the home and house and family in what I have called a crypto-servant role, we lose half of the intelligence and cultural resource of the community. I don't want to see any intellectually or artistically expressive woman confine her talents to her husband.

Unlike many people in public life, you have had a stable, fifty-year marriage.

I haven't any secret as far as the marriage is concerned. I simply picked out a highly intelligent, very beautiful woman. She accepted me and we lived happily ever after.

Will there ever be a time when the theories of economics are implemented fully?

Looking over some of the theories of economists of my time I have every hope that they will not be implemented. I regard economic policy as something to be governed by practical good sense and not by commitment to any corps of theoretical principles. I'm persuaded that both in the communist world and the capitalist world we have a great deal to fear from those who surrender thought to ideology.

You have made enemies as well as friends. Has that been a major source of regret?

I've taken it for granted but I've always had some impression that my friends outnumbered my enemies.

You once said that modesty is a vastly overrated virtue, but may it not help in the art of diplomacy to prevent unproductive confrontations between strong-willed people equally convinced they are right?

I think this is true. I wouldn't doubt it. But I also think there are occasions when one should have confidence in one's views and express them with considerable firmness.

Some of your critics have detected a certain arrogance in your attitudes, even to the extent of power mania. Do you plead guilty?

Unquestionably, yes. I wouldn't, of course, call it arrogance. I would call it commendable self-assurance.

The power side, though, has been a humbling thing in my life. In 1941 I was put in charge of all prices in the United States. You could lower prices without my permission, but you couldn't raise them. That

was an exercise of power which would satisfy almost any power-hungry individual, and I've often said that, in terms of the exercise of power, my life has been downhill ever since.

How conscious have you been of your own charm, and to what extent have you used it as a weapon?

That's a question I am forced to leave entirely to somebody else. I've contented myself with trying to write persuasively, and I've given a good deal of attention to that, but as to charm, that is something which is entirely for the judgement of others, and I advise them to be just a little bit suspicious.

Apparently the Baptist Church of your childhood provided you with what you called 'a thoroughgoing inoculation against churchgoing'. Was this ever a drawback in your public life?

Not particularly. I never made a point of it. I was fortunate to live in a community and in a country which is very tolerant in such matters. On the matter of making peace with God, I haven't yet given the matter serious attention. I'm reminded of what H. L. Mencken said when he was in his last years. He was told, as he grew older and when he was threatened with a stroke, that he should make preparations for the future. He thought about this for some time and said, 'Well, I tell you, if I have been wrong in my agnosticism, when I die I'll walk up to God in a manly way and say, Sir, I made an honest mistake.' I always thought that Mencken had a point.

Is there anything which you feel you still have to achieve?

I'm going to continue to do some writing and I would like, now that time has caught up with some of the books I've written, to do some correcting of my past errors.

Oh, yes, I have many regrets. No person who is at all thoughtful can look back on life and not see a great many lost opportunities. But I'm not going to list them. As for living my life differently if I had the chance, I'm not sure. I've had a reasonably adequate life. Life has been very good to me. Better perhaps than I deserve.

MONSIGNOR GILBEY

Born in 1901 of an English father and a Spanish mother, Alfred Newman Gilbey was educated at Beaumont and at Trinity College, Cambridge. He studied at the Beda College in Rome before being ordained a priest in 1929. He was chaplain to the Catholic undergraduates of Cambridge from 1932 to 1965 and in 1950 he was made a Monsignor. In 1964 he became a Pronotary Apostolic and in 1981 he was made an honorary canon of Brentwood Cathedral. He is the author of *We Believe* (1983) in which he expounds the moral and social teaching of the Catholic Church. He has lived in the Travellers' Club for the past twenty-five years.

First, about your vocation. How did you know God wanted you to be a priest?

A very difficult question to answer shortly. Plainly a vocation develops like any other living thing. I had a flying start through coming from a good Catholic home. My mother was a real Spanish Catholic, of the faith to the marrow of her bones. My father, on the other hand, came from a completely Protestant English background, but he was God's good Englishman and also a wine merchant like the rest of my family. He and two of his brothers went out to Spain and they all fell for Spanish brides; they were all – how should I say – converted at pistol point. I don't mean that literally, but there was really no alternative in those days. My Spanish grandfather, whom, alas, I never knew, was reputed to have said to my father, 'You are an entirely acceptable suitor, physically, financially, socially, but my daughter' – she was the eldest daughter and the apple of his eye – 'does not marry a man who is not a Catholic.' There was nothing to discuss, no argie-bargie. It was like the sun rising tomorrow. He undertook instruction for two years.

The fashion today is to dismiss people who become Catholic to marry a Catholic, but that is to undervalue that sort of conversion. Yet this is the beginning of an answer to your question: having a wonderful, very happy Catholic home. My parents started their married life in London, then moved to what was to be my beloved home in Essex, called Mark Hall – now entirely destroyed. It was in the English countryside, eight miles from the nearest church, and this was in the days of carriages nearly a hundred years ago in 1894. My father went to see Cardinal Vaughan, Archbishop of Westminster, and asked if we might have a private chapel in the house. Cardinal Vaughan said, 'You can certainly have a chapel but I can't give you a priest. You'll have to make your own arrangements if you can.' My mother then went to Farm Street to

ask if they could spare a priest, and every Saturday a Jesuit would arrive and stay until Sunday evening, having given us Mass in the morning.

In this way our background could not have been more favourable. We were five brothers, but I was the only one who, from the very beginning, felt called to the priesthood. We were brought up in an entirely Catholic atmosphere, and then we were all sent to school, again with the Jesuits, at Beaumont. The school in those happy days was run entirely by Jesuits, something that applies to very few Catholic schools now – there simply aren't enough Jesuits to go round.

Beaumont made a great impression on me, but however much I admired our teachers, I never felt at all attracted to the Jesuit way of life. It is one of their characteristics, a great source of their spirituality, to emphasize a detachment, but possibly because I was so wonderfully happy at home I felt drawn towards something slightly more rooted. It's always a matter of interest and admiration to me to find how wonderfully the Catholic Church uses all sorts of natural dispositions and temperaments. The Benedictines put immense emphasis on the stability of a place and vow permanent residence at a particular monastery. The Jesuits emphasize detachment, almost depersonalization, and that aspect didn't appeal to me.

A book that had a great influence on me was *Hugh*, A. C. Benson's memoir of his younger brother R. H. Benson. There were three brothers, the sons of the Archbishop of Canterbury at the beginning of the century, all of whom were prolific writers, though Hugh was the only one who became a Catholic and a priest. He was an immensely dynamic character, writing and preaching ceaselessly, a great convert maker, and it fell to me as a little boy at Beaumont to read what his brother had written about him. This presentation of a priest was so different from any I had known that I asked one of the Jesuits how it was that Hugh Benson was, as a priest, able to lead the life depicted. The Jesuit explained that he was a secular, and this was the first time I ever heard of the existence of the secular clergy. At about the same time one of the school's old boys, who had been called to the secular priesthood, came back from Rome, where he had been ordained and celebrated Mass at Beaumont with great jubilees.

Returning to my dear parents, however, those two strains – the Spanish and the English – gave me an immense love for England aligned with the strong Catholic tradition we had at home, and gave me a desire to be able to communicate the one with the other. As a keen fox-hunting family we were devoted to the countryside, and our friends and neighbours were nearly all rooted in that world. One was aware of how indescribably remote they were from what we Catholics considered to be the world and I was conscious of there being these two aspects of

the same civilization. I think that was the source of inspiration for me to want to be a secular priest.

I didn't wish to go straight in, as was customary in those days, but wanted, as it were, to appear in the world first. My first attempt, largely because of the Jesuit tradition and the geographical position of Beaumont on the Thames, was to try to get into Oxford in 1919. But the Jesuits sent so many priests to the war that Beaumont was at that time very short staffed. One of the great losses we suffered was having no Greek at all, and in those days Greek was an essential qualification for getting into Oxford. Therefore I turned to Trinity College, Cambridge. Looking back, it was one of the providential things in my life that I went there, and it has been the whole of my life since. I had four very idle but very enjoyable years there which, however idle, were immensely educative. I have no academic gifts; my academic history is abysmal. I scraped past a degree after three years' idleness, then went to Rome to study for the priesthood.

Were your family enthusiastic about your entering the Church?

My mother certainly was. They all had great awe and reverence for the priesthood, but my father hoped I wasn't becoming a priest out of bravado, meaning because I'd been saying it for so long. It would be wrong to call him enthusiastic, but he was certainly anxious that his sons should do what they felt to be their vocations, and when it became clear that mine was the priesthood, I think he took great pleasure in it.

Your family background was not a deprived one, so do you find any conflict of perspective between your vocation and your former life?

None at all. Our family situation was fortunate indeed; not rich as people think of riches today – we didn't have racehorses or a yacht – but a large family living comfortably. The question comes from that widespread idea of Catholics who don't understand the difference between the religious life and the life of the secular priest. So many people now talk as though a Christian ought to be a pacifist, ought to be a communist. I always refer them to that wonderful passage in the three synoptic gospels when a young man comes to our Blessed Lord and says, 'Master, what must I do to attain eternal life?' Ask nine people out of ten, including Catholics, and they concertina the conversation and in so doing miss the point by quoting Our Lord as saying, 'Sell all thou hast and follow me.' This was not at all what our Blessed Lord said. He said, 'Keep the commandments,' and the young man, expecting something much more dramatic, was disappointed and said, 'This I have done all the days of my life.' Then our Blessed Lord says, 'If thou wishest to be perfect, go sell all thou hast and follow me.'

He is making there a big distinction, which the Church has always observed, between those called to make the three vows of poverty, chastity and obedience and those not so called. People are slow to appreciate this distinction and don't understand that, to start with, a secular priest literally takes no vows. He takes no vow of poverty and if he has means of his own, he can keep them. He mustn't, of course, go into business – that would be incompatible with his priestly vocation – but if he has money, or money comes to him, then he may keep it. Celibacy, in the case of a secular priest, is not made by a vow but is imposed by law. It was only gradually imposed on the clergy over the years, and you find early on that many a bishop has a son who becomes a saint.

People always talk as though there were just two possibilities: that of the present practice of the Catholic Church, which has been imposed by law, and that which you find in all the Protestant denominations. This completely overlooks a great historic development which is neither. In all the Eastern Churches, in the Orthodox and also in the Uniates, a novitiate will, while still only a deacon, go and find a wife and then be ordained a priest. If he loses her, he is not allowed to remarry; which seems to us a rather arbitrary rule, but it is important to realize how wide and varied the practice is. I mention it as a necessary preface to poverty because if you are, for example, a married man with wife and children, then you are not free to give up all you have. You are bound, in justice as well as in charity, to do all you can to support them.

On the other hand, if you have once taken that vow of chastity, or accepted it as the secular clergy do, then you are free to ask whether Almighty God may not wish you to follow our Blessed Lord more closely by giving up all material things. For a married man to do that would be for him to commit a great sin of improvidence. Unless a vow of chastity is taken first, then you cannot ask yourself whether you're called to a vow of evangelical poverty. Nor, for similar reasons, can you turn the other cheek to the smiter, as I always emphasized when instructing young men at Cambridge. If you, as a man with no dependants, are going home one night in the dark, and an assailant leaps out of a doorway with the obvious intention of taking your life, then you do have an alternative. You make up your mind in that split second that either you knock him down and kill him if necessary to preserve your own life, or you say, 'I'll turn the other cheek to the smiter. He's a boor, a man not knowing what he is doing.' But if, as a married man, you come home to find your wife being beaten up and the children killed, then you're not justified in turning the other cheek to the smiter.

How has the ethos of the Church changed? Has there been in your time a palpable shift in the outlook and practices of the faithful?

Oh, yes, enormous, but always remember, it hasn't been sudden. People who know no history are simplistic in thinking that these vast changes are from a static to a turbulent Church. It is never one or the other. Every living thing grows and develops all the time, sometimes more painfully, sometimes less so. I talk to many young people and they will speak as if the Catholic Church they know didn't exist before the Second Vatican Council. The same applies equally in social and political matters, as though before the Welfare State was a period of terrible deprivation, injustice and tyranny. Both are long and complex issues with deep roots, and neither Church nor state remain the same for long. There are periods of greater and lesser change, and we have been advancing through an enormous one, yet there's all the difference in the world between how a Catholic and a non-Catholic sees these changes. A Catholic always starts with the absolute assurance that the Church cannot fail in her central purposes. Under 1,001 external changes, her identity continues as completely as it does with a human being.

Each human being has throughout life an identity no one else can simulate or take away. The Church is just like that: she is that same body, born on the first Pentecost and set to continue till the Second Coming. I am very conscious of the fact that, although the whole turn of my mind is singularly consistent, my understanding develops and clarifies all the time. Does that mean I change? Not at all. It's my self-understanding that changes: my expression of it increases in clarity, yet the identity runs through. So with the Church. She's that same identical body, and if she changes the language of her liturgy, that is immaterial. I have my own strong views that the change there was very ill-advised, especially in the way it was done, but that doesn't mean to say I think she has failed in any essential, central thing. She has not. She cannot.

The Catholic Church being radically hierarchical, will it be able to continue in a world that is increasingly liberal and democratic?

It can use, or try to adapt, the machinery of democratic thought and practice, but that will never be her natural way of thinking or doing. What you're talking about is egalitarianism. I think it is rather misleading to bring in the word 'democratic' since that is a form of government. Where does it come from? From a philosophy which is egalitarian, and egalitarianism is incompatible with two basic Christian concepts. It believes that men are born equal, but nothing could be less equal than the circumstances that attend the beginnings of all our lives. The egalitarian believes that if people are not born equal, then they must be made so. That is to fly completely in the face of Nature and the facts. Ultimately

it can't succeed because it isn't true; it has no foundation; it is a figment of the imagination of the rationalists of the eighteenth century that has now impinged on the Catholic Church. Many Catholics believe in egalitarianism and are shocked when you tell them it's nonsense. The idea eats into the belief that our relationship to Almighty God is an individual one. John Henry Newman says in the *Apologia* that he could never remember a time when there were not two, and only two, self-evident beings, his Creator and himself.

To say that everyone is equal in God's sight is absolute nonsense. Everyone is unique in God's sight, as every father of a family will understand. To say that a father loves all his children equally would not be according to human nature. He mustn't express the difference or show favouritism, but each child has a unique relationship to his father. The same applies to the whole of creation, not only to man. Not only does star differ from star, but God calls them by name; every pebble on the beach is unlike any other; every leaf on a tree is a unique creation; and manifest at the heart of creation is man, not merely plainly but absolutely unique, as we all are unique in our material circumstances.

We and the parents from whom we sprang were chosen out of all eternity by Almighty God. It is this that conditions the language, the culture, the timing, the colour. Equality doesn't exist. Each of us comes to the world with a box of tools containing advantages and disadvantages in our character, and that's the equipment, not anyone else's, with which we have to hammer out our sanctification. Mine is unique, yours is unique. No one has the same box of tools.

During your years at Cambridge, how did you come to see the function of the Catholic chaplain and did your views change over the course of time?

I'll answer the last question first. No. My job is absolutely clear because it was made clear by the history of the terms of my appointment. There was a long-running division of opinion in the Catholic Church as to whether, first of all, we should try to have a university of our own; an idea much derided today, but we forget that in the nineteenth-century revival of Catholicism several flourishing universities were founded in Europe. In this country we made three rather pathetic attempts to found a university with no possibility of success. The first was at Prior Park in the early years of the last century; the second was Cardinal Newman's attempt to found a university of Dublin; and the last was Cardinal Manning's effort to found a university in Kensington. All collapsed but all were part of a consistent policy. It came to nothing and most of us are very relieved – they would have become poor Catholic ghettoes.

That controversy was finally resolved by the pressure of the laity at the end of the last century. We were allowed to return to the ancient

universities of Cambridge and Oxford, but under various safeguards, most of them rather unrealistic. One was that there should be at each of the ancient universities a chaplain whose job it was – and this was quite clear – to safeguard the faith of Catholics who went there. So it was very much a protective pastoral charge, and those were the terms of my own appointment. Many people now think it should involve a more positive, outgoing approach, but when the office started, it was certainly seen entirely in those terms.

Your early days as chaplain seemed marked by disputes with the Cambridge University Catholic Association. Did they find you difficult?

Very. It stemmed from the early days, lasted all my time and continues still. By a great political error, the wonderfully devoted collection of Catholic dons who founded the Cambridge University Catholic Association were allowed to own the premises of the chaplaincy they had been responsible for acquiring. Having done the wonderful work of acquiring the premises, they were also allowed to become the trustees, thereby producing a sort of congregationalism unknown to the Catholic Church. Meanwhile the bishops, charged with the responsibility of safeguarding the faith of Catholic undergraduates, made no attempt to raise the funds necessary for the purpose. They were, of course, terribly handicapped by their own poverty and their difficulty in fulfilling or trying to fulfil the needs of Catholic education for the poorest classes. The whole of their efforts were, quite rightly, poured out to build Catholic schools, and they regarded going to Cambridge or Oxford as rather a rich man's luxury. It wasn't true then, and it's manifestly untrue today when every student is supported by the state, but the idea they wrongly had seventy years ago was that if rich men wanted their boys to go, then it was up to them to produce the means to support a chaplain and provide the premises. That was, and is, the position as trustees of that wonderfully devoted band of Catholic dons.

When, in your early days at Cambridge, you spent a lot of your own money on the library and furnishing the chaplaincy, was it done out of generosity or impatience with the trustees?

Neither. It was wanting to have things as I thought they should be, trying to make the chaplaincy a civilized centre. Since the bishops regarded the ancient universities as an indulgence allowed to rich parents, there was consequently a feeling, certainly on the part of successive chaplains, that a chaplaincy should be a place where they would themselves feel at home. Today, of course, the need becomes to provide a welcoming atmosphere in the chaplaincy.

By the early 1960s you were still having to meet the shortfall in the chaplaincy's budget out of your own pocket. How could that have been necessary?

The cry of poverty runs right through, doesn't it? Chaplains were generally appointed with an eye to their having some means of their own. I was there longer than anyone, so saw more of it, but the shortfall, as you call it, was something that affected every chaplain. They were sent there with a ludicrous sum. I can't remember what it was in my case, but it was grossly inadequate.

In the pre-war years you evidently took part in a number of evangelical events organized by undergraduates. Did you enjoy preaching in the streets of Saffron Walden or the fields of Wisbech?

Not in the least. I don't enjoy those things at all, but my policy was a simple one. I never tried to sell these ideas to the undergraduates as I felt strongly that a man should be able to come to Fisher House without having anything asked of him; that he ought not to be badgered to join this, that or the other activity. In those days, the Jesuit schools took up what used to be called the Catholic Evidence Guild rather strongly. It was a way of trying to get the boys to take an interest in our religion. They were encouraged to join the guild, to go in for quite stiff examinations to fit them for the purpose, and to stand on soap boxes in Egham or wherever, preaching to a rather unresponsive multitude. When some young men, mostly from my own school, Beaumont, came and said it would be a good thing if we, too, belonged to the guild, I said by all means, and I'll help you, but no one is going to be asked to do it by me.

As Catholic chaplain, did you feel under an obligation to aid in the conversion of non-Catholics who came into contact with you? Was there a conflict there between duty and social propriety?

First, it wasn't an obligation, it wasn't a part of my job. That was always, I emphasize, a preservative one. A fair number of undergraduates would certainly come to me, though, and say, 'I think I ought to become a Catholic.' I would always tell them, 'You must let your parents know what you are doing, and you must tell your tutor or the dean of your college. You are to come to instruction and you won't be able to become a Catholic for at least a year.' That was my practice. As a contrast, the most distinguished of all chaplains at Oxford was Monsignor Knox, a prominent convert who refused altogether to instruct people, and so he took a different line from me. At Oxford there were Jesuit and Dominican houses to whom he could send inquirers. I had nothing like that at Cambridge.

Is there anyone in particular you are especially proud to have converted?

No. It is always a wonderful privilege to believe one can bring anyone to a knowledge of the truth, but I would say I've never converted anybody. I've never set out to, I haven't the gift. I don't know how the Apostles did it. All those I've instructed have come on their own initiative and they've been a source of immense consolation and happiness. I absolutely love instructing people in belief. A number have found their own vocations to the priesthood, some to religious orders. I don't think many have made their mark in the world or the Church so that you would know their names. I can think of nothing more satisfying a priest can do than being able to tell people interested in the faith what is involved.

By the 1960s there seems to have been some resistance among Catholic undergraduates to traditional practices at the chaplaincy. Did that distress you?

Any move away from Catholic practices upsets me, but I don't allow myself to be distressed. I'm so profoundly confident, and when you have the gift of the faith, then you know that the Church can't fail in Her purpose. The Church teaches us the truth and gives us the sacraments, and we ought to offer thanks for what God has given, not for the folly of men's thoughts.

It was said of you by Peter Gregory Jones, author of The History of the Cambridge Chaplaincy, *that as a great preserver of inherited values you were a historian by temperament. What were the values you wished to preserve?*

That's an enormous question which takes us right back to the structure of society. Does one, or does one not, believe in the family? The traditional sociology of the Catholic Church is that it is the duty of parents to house, feed, shelter and (using the word as widely as possible) educate those they beget. That, of course, is a very unacceptable concept in the socialist world of today, which regards it as the duty of the state to care for housing, education, sickness and old age. Thus we have egalitarianism, the French Revolution factor, catching up with the Catholic Church.

Jones speaks of the sense in which you found egalitarianism after the war incompatible with your idea of man's relationship with God. Could you elaborate on this position?

The whole socialization of the world has been immensely accelerated by two world wars, but this is not just a post-war phenomenon. I never found egalitarianism an attractive concept. I always instinctively believed in a hierarchical society. Looking back over my life, I've been

extraordinarily consistent in what I believe, though I now formulate it much more fully. The family – the basis of society – is of its nature hierarchical. We come into families that are not of our own choosing and are not run by children. The first enormous impetus was the French Revolution. I always try to eschew the word 'democracy' because everyone uses it now as a term of undefined praise. They make their appeal to the democracy of the Greeks, of course, though there never was a more élitist society. The educated had a whole slave population to make their civilization possible. It was nothing to do with egalitarianism and that's why I would wish to use the word 'democracy' accurately.

It seems an odd distinction to refer, as you have done, to women as 'students' and to men as 'undergraduates'.

To begin with, women were not members of Cambridge University. Because the university did not admit women, Girton and Newnham started as women's colleges outside the university, and by stages, in one of those gradual processes of which I have seen so many, became incorporated. The first thing was to found women's colleges, then to allow them to come to lectures. First they didn't take examinations, then they could take examinations but couldn't be given degrees, only what was called the 'titles of degrees'. So there was a real distinction, not just one of my vocabulary. Women were *not* undergraduates, they were *not* members of the university.

You once explained your resignation from the chaplaincy as being over the principle of authority and its limits, but was that principle not focused on the opening of Fisher House to women?

If you like to say so, yes. As long as women were not members of the university, then there was a very strong case against allowing them in, and afterwards, because the position was constantly changing, the pressure increased. If the board, which was my authority, had ordered me to take in the women, I would have resigned anyway. They did not ask for my resignation, but passed a resolution that the chaplaincy should become mixed after I had gone. The real question became, should the nature of the chaplaincy be determined by the chaplain or by demand from below? At that point, I stood down on that principle.

If you ask why I opposed letting in women, it brings us back to fundamentals. Equality is a meaningless word and sex equality means absolutely nothing. The egalitarian believes that all people are the same. Men and women are not the same, they are complementary. A great friend of mine, Outram Evans, who was president of the Cambridge University Catholic Association for a long time, and my best ally, pointed out how immensely disparate the numbers were. There were

200 men and 20 women. You can't combine the sexes, other than on a complementary basis, without destroying the whole harmony of their relationship. I am totally opposed to the equality of the sexes.

In retrospect I have not modified my view at all. If it now seems eccentric, as you put it, then that is because of this wave of egalitarianism. What is so funny is how short people's memories are. I went up to Cambridge in 1920 when there were still these two women's colleges that were not part of the university and the women didn't enter the life one little bit. They used to come to our lectures and sit at a separate table, but I don't think I ever spoke to a woman student the four years I was there, neither did any of my friends. It was an entirely male society, a very close and happy one. That idea, I suppose, is much more common in northern rather than southern Europe. I know that some Latins seem unable to form the sorts of societies we have here, and clubs are the perfect example. I would move heaven and earth to make my club, where we are now, an entirely masculine one again. That would doubtless be considered eccentric, but from the moment of its foundation till twenty years ago, it was the law. It isn't my eccentricity at all; people just have no sense of history. Everything, even the Houses of Parliament, used to be entirely male.

My view is wholly compatible with the God-given design of women as complementary to men. They're different, yet people won't recognize the fact. The egalitarians have this absolute *idée fixe* that they're the same. They're not. Women don't like each other's company, don't form clubs. They don't like that to be said, of course, but the fact is plain to see. It's a wonder how nuns can live together, but they do. Whether we're talking about political life, the law, the Church of England, women are doing something they've never done before, and the fact is that it isn't working out equally – they're completely ignored. It's now fifty years since women have been in the House of Commons, and with the one staggering exception of Mrs Thatcher, have any of them come to anything? No. Women are different. I wonder why people can't see what is as clear as a pikestaff.

Would you discriminate against women?

There we have to define what we mean by discrimination. It's like all this talk of the underprivileged. Who has a right to a privilege? They talk of the children of poor parents being underprivileged, presupposing that someone has taken something from them. Words are used quite indiscriminately and the vocabulary is so meaningless that when you start trying to define what they are saying it becomes very difficult. Once you're an egalitarian, you have to believe that everyone has the same rights, so called. But who has and who has not, for example, the

right to vote? It's not man's right except by a convention in a particular civilization or country.

Through nineteen Christian centuries women have never enjoyed the same political standing as men, except accidentally; there was no idea of there being some universal right. Now everyone talks as if there were some self-evident reason whereby any country that doesn't have universal suffrage is out of court. It's arguable whether it's a good or a bad thing to have universal suffrage, but there is no intrinsic or fundamental reason why it should be so. We, particularly in the West, have been racing through two world wars to a universal principle, something unknown through all preceding centuries till a hundred years ago. All of that is a staggering assumption, and there is no foundation for it in history and none in reason.

It's quite another matter to discuss whether it's a good thing or not. I haven't a closed mind there. These things can be discussed, and you must discuss them and realize that what you are talking about is a relative not an absolute. It's the same with equal opportunity. Who has equal opportunity? How can I give someone in completely other circumstances than my own the opportunities I have and have had? Only one other force can even attempt it, and that is the state, and we are back to whose duty it is to educate. Is it a matter for the state or for the parents?

What is the real theological objection to the ordination of women? Is there scriptural warrant for it or is it primarily the authority of tradition?

It is a matter of the authority of the Church, which is one single thing supported by scripture and tradition and I don't like that separation of the two. The Protestant approach to Christian revelation is to confine it effectively to scripture, whereas I always regard the Church as teaching on Her own authority, which indeed arises from scripture and tradition. She is the authority. She's not getting it from anywhere else. Catholics always see the Church as being the authority in Herself. Of the Annuciation, for example, it was not only Mary, it was I who heard the angel voice.

I am against the ordination of women because it is not the Church's practice. I was dining some time ago in Trinity, my old college, and had next to me a very distinguished Anglican theologian who turned to me and said, 'Monsignor Gilbey, what would be your reaction if the Catholic Church started ordaining women?' I said, 'If the Catholic Church said it was all right, it would be all right by me. I follow what the Church says and does.'

For nineteen centuries the Church has not ordained women and I see no likelihood of Her doing so. Why? Because it's something basic to

Christian life and I cannot think She's got it wrong for nineteen centuries and will begin to put it right. It would be unprecedented against the whole background of the Church's history to think She might suddenly do a sort of *volte face*. The development of doctrine is a gradual unfolding of one thing. Catholics don't believe, for instance, that Our Blessed Lady became Immaculate in 1856 or that the Pope became infallible in 1870. It's a gradual developing of one truth and the ordination of women would be something quite otherwise.

Why is the Church 'She', not 'He'?

She is the Bride of Christ. She is always 'She', in all scripture and tradition. Forgive me for saying so, but I think you are always trying to get me back into what I call the Protestant position of having a view of my own about revelation.

With certain Protestant Churches already ordaining women, will any movement of an ecumenical sort be possible without some shift in the Catholic position?

I've never had any enthusiasm for ecumenism as the word is used and understood. When you talk of equality, it's a concept I don't understand, a concept that I think has no correspondence with reality and which denies two Christian concepts: first, the uniqueness of every single created being, made uniquely by Almighty God; and secondly, the fact that equality takes away the whole incentive of excellence, which, if properly understood, aspires to sanctity. Each of us should be trying to reach that height of holiness. Each man's vocation is unique. Look at the lives of the saints. They are not made to a common pattern. They include a lot of people in the world who are considered to be eccentrics.

We have remarked how the priests of the early Church married and Orthodox priests still do. Can you foresee a time when the Church will again permit marriage for priests?

That could happen, celibacy not having been imposed uniformly on Christian priests from the beginning. There has been a constant tendency that way, but as we know from the scriptures, Peter had a mother-in-law and presumably a wife, though she's never mentioned. In the early centuries, bishops and priests did marry, so there's nothing inherently improbable about married priests. Celibacy was a gradually, increasingly widely imposed discipline that could be altered without inconsistency. For many centuries, though, over more than a millennium now, it has been thought to be the ideal for the clergy.

Outsiders would say that for priests not to marry must inevitably cut them off

from a great deal of human experience. Would not a married clergy be better placed to understand and sympathize with its flock's daily problems?

I wonder. I'm not saying yes or no to it, but I do wonder whether you'd say the same about them earning their livings in work or business. Would you claim it as far better for priests not to be dedicated solely to their ministry or that they'd be better able to understand the cares and responsibilities of people living in the world if they shared them? It's perfectly arguable, but I view it all with great indifference. Of course, it was vigorously advocated in France between the wars – the idea of worker priests – but I think the authorities have now abandoned the concept altogether.

Would you have married if the Church had allowed it when you were ordained?

I don't think so, because tradition was still so very strong. I certainly wouldn't marry now, even if celibacy was lifted. I can't imagine it at any period of my life because celibacy in my day has been a requirement of priests and the position hasn't changed. If it ever should change, I would not oppose it if the Church said it was all right.

But would you be in favour of priests marrying?

I always dodge that question. It seems irrelevant, whether I would or not.

But you are an important member of the Church.

Not a bit. I couldn't be less important. I am wholly unimportant in the administrative world of the Catholic Church.

Yet if there were to be a referendum within the Church?

I'm not a democrat, you know. I would not reply. I would not return the ballot paper.

Are you saying you believe in autocracy?

That suggests there can only be autocracy or democracy. Heaven knows how many grades there are in a hierarchical society. If you ask me whether I believe in a hierarchical society, the answer is yes, with every fibre of my being, but that isn't necessarily autocracy. Hierarchical societies, of which there are many, starting with the family, all have a series of pyramids going up. Every army, every regiment, every corporation, every club, all have their power structures. I'm not, you see, remotely egalitarian.

You have loyally stated that if it's all right with Rome then it's all right with you.

It's not a question of loyalty, but a question of what I know because of what I believe about the Church. Loyalty is something you can give or withdraw.

Is it going to be possible for the Church to hold together in the future in the same way as it did in the past? In South America priests have defied the Pope's authority in the matter of holding political office; in the United States there has long been clear opposition to the Pope's stand on birth control: any number of Catholics are clearly using methods of contraception in direct conflict with the Pope's ruling.

The Church will hold together. Catholics of my generation – those who reached maturity before the Second Vatican Council – took it for granted that the tidiness of the Church at that period was the norm. People who have no historical sense find it hard to appreciate that what was taken for granted – the tidiness in theology, in administration, in running the Church – represented an exceptional period in contrast with the previous fifteen centuries. In the early Church, that of the Fathers, you find a much greater diversity of opinion and practice. The process of tidying has been a gradual one, dependent on all sorts of administrative reasons, communication and literacy.

The fact that people claim to be Catholics and part of the Catholic Church, and yet are out of step, is no new thing at all. You find it in the early centuries, the difference earlier on being that much more immediate and drastic action was taken against them. They may now have become too numerous; I don't know. I know nothing of what goes on in the directed mind of the Vatican, and very little of what is happening outside this country, so I can't say how far people in positions of authority in the Church have gone out of step. You tell me there are bishops in the United States who reject the Church's teaching. I should doubt it very much.

Have you ever disagreed with a pronouncement of the Church or felt at odds with any item in its teaching?

Not ever. I'd have to leave, walk out of the Church, if I didn't agree. As a Catholic, you simply have to believe what the Church teaches. It is a condition of membership. A Catholic cannot reject the doctrine of the Church yet remain a Catholic. What She teaches as right or wrong – those things are a *sine qua non* for a believing Catholic. That does not mean to say that a believing, practising Catholic has to accept the Church's policy on matters of administration and the like. It is possible

to be entirely out of sympathy with many of the things the Church is doing, as I regret the liturgical changes, for example. You can be critical of such things, out of sympathy with them, and even oppose them, but you can't withstand them. It might be better to drive on the right rather than on the left. You can advocate it all you like, but you can't just start doing it. So it is with things like liturgical changes. You may think it far better to be able to have one uniform language for the whole Western Church, and you may advocate it, but you can't in practice ignore, stand outside or oppose the existing legislation. We are committed not to policy but absolutely to dogma and morals.

Many present-day Christians would see the doctrine of Papal Infallibility as standing in the way of any sort of liberalization of the Church. Is the Church bound to adhere for ever to doctrines defined at a particular point in history?

The Church is committed to whatever She has defined. If you are suggesting that some past pronouncement imposing acceptance as grounds for becoming a Catholic might be changed in retrospect, then the answer's no. We must distinguish strongly between those things that can be altered and those that cannot. Policy can be altered; that can be done tomorrow. Definitions of doctrine, acceptance of which is necessary to being a Catholic, cannot be altered.

I would wish, however, to deplore as strongly as I can this approach to Papal Infallibility. What we believe in is the infallibility of the Church. First, the Church is a visible body here on earth, teaching infallibly what Christ has revealed to us in all sorts of ways. Secondly, that body cannot impose upon me error as a condition of belonging. Whenever She defines something, it must be accepted by every member and therefore must be true, otherwise She would be imposing acceptance of error. People talk about Papal Infallibility as if it were something never before heard of, but the infallibility of the Church is inherent from the very beginning.

When you say 'Church', do you differentiate between 'Pope' and 'Church'?

No. Quite the contrary. He is a part of it. Papal Infallibility is just one stated example of conditions for being a Catholic.

If faith is a gift of God, is it the duty of a Catholic to maintain a pious silence when it comes to a particular dogma in which he cannot compel himself to believe, even though he may wish to?

You can compel yourself to believe. If you have made the act of faith in Jesus Christ, and believe He is God, you will have to accept what He tells you. He came to open to us a whole cycle of knowledge

otherwise unattainable. A Catholic must believe the teaching of the Church in all aspects of faith and morals.

What would you say to those who find it impossible to subscribe to the dogmas of religion, who cannot, for example, understand how a good God can permit the innocent to suffer?

That's not dogma, it's a fact. We see suffering all about us and know in ourselves that we all suffer to various degrees. But we also know that God is infinitely good, infinitely kind, infinitely just, infinitely merciful, infinitely loving. It takes us back, of course, to something that *is* a dogma: the Fall of Man. There are two plains of knowledge concerning matters of religion. The first is the plain of natural reason. We can reach, and the majority of mankind have reached, a knowledge of the existence of the Supreme Being from which there follows man's free will, his consequent responsibility and his survival of death. That is what we call natural theology, and from there we go on to consider whether there has been a revelation, whether God has opened a whole cycle of knowledge to us that our native reason will bring us to accept only on faith. These are two completely different cycles of knowledge, the first requiring an act of reason, the second an act of faith. There was at the beginning of human history a complete dislocation of human nature that we call the Fall, made not by Almighty God but by the wickedness and sins of man.

Is the Church's stand against contraception to be defined as a dogma?

Yes, since it rises out of the whole concept of the purpose of sex. Sex is an inducement to continue the human race. People are so imprecise. The pleasure of sex cannot be put first. Unlike Protestants, there are many things we Catholics believe which are not found in the scripture. The Church has been left to continue Christ's Revelation.

It may seem to the outsider that the Catholic Church grudges man sexual pleasure.

We believe that the gift of sex is given to man primarily for the continuance of the human race. It provides the greatest physical pleasure known to man, precisely to give him the inducement to beget children. Who in their senses would go through the responsibilities of bringing children into this world, undertake the enormous expense of housing, feeding, educating them, bringing them up – all the annoyances and worries that lie in that – if there were not added to it the greatest of human pleasures? Many other consequences of exercising the sexual act exist – cementing affection between husband and wife, comfort, sustenance and so on –

but you can't rule out the purpose for which it is given in order to isolate the secondary consequences. A parallel is the pleasure of eating and drinking.

It's the puritan not the Catholic who thinks that the pleasure sex gives is wrong. Likewise it's the puritan who decries the pleasure of eating and drinking. That is very great too, though infinitely less so than the pleasure of sexual activity because the object is less important. The object of attaching pleasure to eating and drinking is really so that we may have an inducement to rebuild our bodily strength. You can't go for the secondary consequences and exclude the first, as the Romans did, when they had a vomitorium and, having eaten and drunk as much as they could, went out and made themselves sick so as to come back and eat and drink some more. That is to reject the purpose for which it is given to gain the lesser consequences. The use of sex for any reason excluding the main purpose is to do exactly the same.

Plainly, every sexual aberration or sin more or less excludes the main purpose. Solitary vice rules out the possibility of conception, as does unnatural sin between two people of the same sex. Fornications and adultery rule out the possibility of bringing up the children, and you cannot, always remember, separate procreation and education: bringing children into this world and bringing them up in the love and knowledge of Almighty God is a combined operation. In fornication you are plainly ruling out the very possibility of any children born to those parents being brought up within the framework of the family. Yet that is the first duty you owe them. Likewise, with adultery, you are side-stepping the whole function of the family by begetting children outside it.

So the Church itself does not discourage the pleasure of the flesh in general?

Of course not. To exclude it would be to negate God's purpose. God gave that gift, a most wonderful thing. It's impossible to exaggerate the sacredness of sex because, if you go back to the foundation of all we believe, God is the sole Creator yet man is empowered to co-operate with Almighty God in the specifically divine work of creation. We rightly say that God created you, created me. How did he choose to do it? Through the sexual activities of your parents and mine. He was the Creator, but men and women take part in that creative act, a supremely god-like thing. As soon as sex is used for lesser purposes, it's belittling the whole staggering gift, reducing it to an animal level.

Some clergy are homosexual, yet they remain clergy.

It depends on what you mean by homosexual. No one, whatever their status, is justified in committing the act of sodomy. It's as simple as that. But if by homosexual you mean people who find their own sex

more attractive and yet control their feelings, there's nothing wrong at all. It's no different from having a temptation to pride, or avarice, or anything. People always talk as though we can use sex as we like because it is a gift of Almighty God. Since the heterosexual can do as he likes, it's thought to be rather rough on homosexuals that they shouldn't commit sodomy. We are surrounded by a nine-tenths non-Christian population, and they all have the idea that any sort of sex is a perfectly normal thing. There's no need to marry, you can sleep with anyone you like, so it's thought to be unfair if homosexuals can't do the same.

But if a priest is a homosexual in the sense of committing homosexual acts, should he remain in the Church, should be be expelled?

I don't know whether he should or should not. That is a question of discipline. If you are practising sodomy then you are certainly in no fit state to celebrate the Eucharist each morning. But I must again emphasize the distinction between having a temptation and giving up the struggle. You're not a Christian at all if you give up the struggle.

Do you feel an intolerance of homosexuals or do you sympathize with their plight?

I sympathize with anyone who has committed sin, be what it may. As with a man who can't keep his hand out of the till, I have to go on telling him that he mustn't do it. We all commit sins, we must all try to avoid the sins to which we are most prone. If your sin happens to be to want to commit sodomy, then you must struggle against it very hard indeed. It can be done. People do get over their evil tendencies, by God's grace. The fatal thing is to say I'm very strongly tempted and I'm not going to resist it.

If reconciliation with the Eastern Churches is a foreseeable possibility, would the Papacy ever agree to the idea of the Pope as primus inter pares?

No, he can't step down from his position. I hope and pray that such a reconciliation will come about, and it seems to me a far less unlikely prospect than in the Protestant case. Protestantism is founded on a quite different belief, and every form of Protestantism, from extremist evangelical to extremist Anglo-Catholic, always comes back to private judgement. The concept of the East is quite distinct. It's an authoritative concept and this explains how it is that a bishop in the East could, in coming over, bring all his people with him. It couldn't happen in the West. If the Archbishop of Canterbury became Catholic tomorrow, he couldn't bring a single soul with him, not even his wife.

In the East, they are what are called autocephalus churches – that is

to say, the head of the Church is the head of the Church. Whatever he says goes. It's much closer to the Catholic concept. All the Protestant sects in the West, on the other hand, take a stand on private judgement and democracy is applied to religion. In the same way that democracy is the application of equality in politics, so is private judgement the application of equality to religious truth.

Can the Church respond effectively to the intransigence of Islamic fundamentalism without itself becoming intransigent?

The Church is intransigent. She can't change. The idea of the Church changing is as foreign to me as equality or democracy. The only thing we are interested in is the sanctity of an individual human soul. The only progress is the progress towards sanctity for the individual. It matters for all eternity what you or I do between our births and our deaths. Any progress outside that is a will-o'-the-wisp, an illusion. The great landslide was the Fall. From then on human beings have been struggling between birth and death to escape its consequence. The only moral improvement of any value is between conception and death.

The Catholic Church has placed an emphasis on private confession, but since God knows our minds and hearts, is there any theological reason why communal confession should not be equally effective in seeking forgiveness of sins?

It's necessary to distinguish between what Christ gave us through His redemption of us and the means He chose to communicate it. He has redeemed us by suffering and death and has chosen to communicate His gift through the sacraments, which we believe to operate infallibly. In the sacrament of penance, God's grace is given to us, brought into our souls, and so we have the covenanted means of our forgiveness. In the sacrament of the Eucharist, we receive our Blessed Lord, the Fount of Grace Himself, into our hearts. Almighty God is not tied to the sacraments, except, of course, that He's tied to honour them. His own omnipotence cannot, however, be tied by the gift He's made, though if you are asking whether God Almighty can work outside the sacraments, the answer is yes, of course He can. There is no limit to His power. If you are asking whether that exempts us from using the covenanted means He has given us, the answer is no, it does not. We would be very foolish to ignore them. Can He work outside them? Most certainly He can. Does He work outside them? We hope and pray that He does. But it's not our business. There's the short answer to your question.

There have been scandals in the Church over the centuries and the recent Banco

Ambrosiano affair suggests that its administrative and financial arms have become very secular. Are these things inevitable?

Yes – because of fallen human nature. You can't peg things. You may have the most wonderful and altruistic machinery for running the Church's affairs, but there's no guarantee it'll continue. We can make it a great deal better than it is, but we can also make it a great deal worse. The answer to all the events we deplore is fallen human nature. Only individuals can make any moral advance and therefore there are bound to be scandals. If you shall hear of wars, or rumours of wars, see that you be not troubled. And, perhaps, scandals, and rumours of scandals – see that you be not troubled. There are always scandals. None of us, God knows, fulfils his obligations perfectly. The degree of failure may vary enormously with the individual.

There was the book by John Cornwell on the death of John Paul I that suggested he was murdered.

Well, as I say, human nature is fallen. You find fallen human beings everywhere. I have no idea of the particular case, but there is nothing inherently improbable in a Pope being murdered, any more than with anyone else. There's no end to human villainy. The fact that a man is a priest, a bishop or a Pope doesn't exempt him, or those surrounding him, from the consequences of the Fall. If you are asking whether it is possible for a Pope to be murdered by his own entourage, then the answer is yes, it is possible – though I think it wildly improbable.

You are said to be a hunting enthusiast, but killing animals for entertainment, especially fox-hunting, has come to be regarded in a poor light by very many people. Is such enthusiasm really sustainable these days?

I don't like that notion of entertainment at all. It sounds like sadism. We must start at the very beginning. God gave man complete dominion over the whole of creation. Man is the apex of creation, and his use of it is conditioned by the good or bad it does to him, not by creation itself. People often talk as if animals had rights. Only rational beings can have rights, just as only rational beings can have duties. There are no rights involved in this at all. Consequently man has hunted from the beginning and deprived animals of their freedom – we call it domesticating them. He has made them breed and lead lives not natural to them. How can they possibly have freedom in the proper sense of the term? Freedom is the free exercise of will, and animals have no wills.

We take them into captivity, domesticate them, cause them to breed, prevent their breeding, castrate them, kill them for food, for clothing, and they have no rights to prevent it. The only question for man in his

dealings with animals is what moral harm may those dealings do to him? That is why I demur at the word 'entertainment'. It does man terrible moral harm to be a sadist. To enjoy and indulge in cruelty, to torture a cat, is sinful. To torture anything for the pleasure the act gives you is sinful.

So when you allow hounds to tear up a fox, isn't that sinful?

No. Of all the forms of sport, hunting arouses the most animosity, the strong, popular feeling against it being largely fuelled by social considerations. It's thought to be inegalitarian, aristocratic, but when you come to analyse it, it's the nearest to nature of all the forms of field sport. No one raises a voice against fishing, yet in terms of cruelty or pain inflicted, fishing may be the most callous sport of all. You can play a salmon for two or three hours with a hook in its mouth. I'm not saying that's wrong, I'm just pointing out how disproportionate the feeling is against hunting.

Hunting is the nearest to nature because you are perfecting what nature is doing all the time. At this very moment rabbits are being savaged by stoats, hens are having their heads bitten off by foxes. The whole of nature is, as Tennyson had it, red in tooth and claw. Whatever a hunter does is quite right for him to do, unless he is getting sadistic pleasure, and then he is certainly harming himself rather than the animals he kills. He is then making a beast of himself, doing himself moral harm. All Catholics will tell you the same. You can shoot birds, hunt foxes, fish completely freely, so long as you are not doing yourself moral harm.

Is it ever a worry to you that your lifestyle – living in a London club, giving dinner parties – might be misinterpreted by some members of the Church?

First of all, I think that worry is a sin. Worry means you don't really believe in divine providence. My favourite text in the Old Testament is, 'Be still and know that I am God.' Worry is unprofitable thinking about disagreeable things. With regard to my lifestyle, I'm not an egalitarian and I don't believe in a universally acceptable lifestyle. To return to the secular and the regular clergy, there are a lot of things that would be sinful in a member of an order who has abandoned the world and all personal money. He's housed, fed and clothed, and money is not his concern, so for him to throw a party might be considered a subject of criticism. But as I have said, a secular priest keeps what money he has, what money he comes by honestly. If he chooses to entertain friends, then he is doing absolutely nothing wrong. There's not any uniform lifestyle which it is wrong to step outside. To think there is egalitarianism is my *bête noire*.

Have you any regrets?

One has to distinguish between regrets and contrition. I suppose we all have regrets. Precious few in my case, I've been so lucky. But if you mean sorrow for sin – yes, that's a very good thing to have. I've committed many sins in my life and I am sorry for them at the present moment. One has to live in the present moment; it's all we have. One can't touch the past. It's the work of this moment to be sorry for the sins of one's whole life.

Are you looking forward to the next life?

I'm not, because I'm properly concerned for the private judgement. I hope I shall not have offended God Almighty gravely. I can't say I am certain of going to heaven. I keep hoping and praying that I shall die in the love and mercy of Almighty God and be forgiven all my sins, but that's His business. Mine is to do the best I can. My two great temptations are idleness and vanity. I'm very tempted to do nothing, and by vanity I mean liking to give and receive human affection. Thank God I have received a great deal and given a great deal, but that tempts one to think one is important, and one isn't, of course. So that's a general confession I will make at my last moment. If a priest comes when I am dying I shall say these have been the besetting sins of my eighty years of life and I shall ask for absolution for them and for many others.

How would you like to be remembered?

I don't expect to be remembered, frankly. I have made no mark on the world at all.

LORD GOODMAN

Arnold Goodman is senior partner in Goodman Derrick & Co., Solicitors. He was born in 1913 and was educated at University College, London. He served as a gunner in the Royal Artillery during the war and retired as major in 1945. Between 1965 and 1972 he was chairman of the Arts Council of Great Britain. He was chairman of British Lion Films from 1965–72 and master of University College, Oxford from 1976–86. He was director of the Royal Opera House, Covent Garden from 1972–83 and is currently deputy chairman of the British Council and a governor of the Royal Shakespeare Theatre. He is the only man in England to have received a peerage from a Labour prime minister (Harold Wilson) and to have been made a Companion of Honour by a Conservative prime minister (Edward Heath).

Your mother seems to have been the dominating influence in your childhood. Was your father a shadowy figure by comparison?

He wasn't a shadowy figure, but he was the less positive figure of the two. He was a very gentle, mild man, and I think he was a bit diffident about intruding, but we were as devoted to him as to my mother. My mother was enormously encouraging. She had all the pride of all the Jewish mothers put together. I don't think she had great ambition for us, but she was a woman with a good sense of values and she obviously wanted us to be happy and successful, because if you're not successful you're rarely happy. She was always there for us, and if ever we had any kind of problem or trouble, she solved it without fuss. She was a very remarkable woman. She had been a schoolteacher originally, and a competent pianist. She taught Mrs Gaitskell Hebrew. She saw me beginning to become successful. I hadn't been enobled and hadn't even become the chairman of the Arts Council before she died, but I had had modest success and it gave her great pleasure.

I don't look back on my childhood as the happiest time of my life, because I hadn't really found a balanced situation there. There were uncertainties about relationships with people, about the extent to which one promoted one's own activities and so forth. Anything that isn't positive causes doubt and doubt causes unhappiness. I certainly wasn't an unhappy child. I loved being a child; I enjoyed being at school. I was particularly fond of cricket, and I became an adept tennis player – I even got a tennis colour at University College London. I had a passion for reading, and I loved music. My father used to take us off to concerts on Sunday afternoons, and all of this conduced to happiness. Anyone looking at me would have said I was a happy boy.

I was educated at a grammar school established by one of the great trading companies, and it was a very good school. We had everything:

a good swimming bath, the river on which we could row, an excellent sports ground. It didn't ape the public schools, but it tried to extract what was best in them. I was particularly influenced by the English master because, for some reason, I was his favourite pupil. He played a great part in my life, and persuaded me of the glories of English literature.

If I had a son, I would not myself send him to a boarding school. I think that's a folly. It separates a boy from his family altogether and in a sense it antagonizes him, because a young child has to determine for himself why he's been exiled. I'm not at all in favour of boarding schools, but I would send a son to a good day school. There are several, like St Paul's, or University College School, or Mill Hill. Children require a certain amount of understanding, humane discipline, and a good school provides it.

My parents were always tight for money. My father was not a good businessman, but he contrived to get enough to give us a comfortable childhood. I didn't have a luxurious childhood, but I managed to travel a bit. I remember that I wanted to go to Paris, and when I spoke to my father he said, 'Well, what can you manage on?' So I replied rather optimistically, 'I could do a week on £5.' He produced a five-pound note and off I went. I found myself very strained for money after about four days, but it was very enjoyable. Then I wanted to go to Rome, because I've always had a particular interest in Roman affairs and Roman law and Latin, which was a language I had a great affection for. So when I said I wanted to go to Rome, he asked for how long, and I replied a fortnight. So he produced £10. I stayed at a little pension called the Pensione Bus, where I had a semi-pension rate, which meant that I got breakfast and dinner but not lunch. Without any great hardship, I dispensed with lunch for a fortnight, and then had a piece of good fortune when, wandering through the Coliseum on almost my last day, an elderly American gentleman, seeing me carrying an English guide book, approached me and asked if I spoke English. When I confirmed that I did, he asked if I would mind showing him round the city, and we struck up quite a friendship. He turned out to be an American ex-judge who had come over on the melancholy errand of bringing his wife's ashes, which he had promised to bury in Rome. He became very friendly indeed and took me out every day for another fortnight. I was therefore able to stay four weeks.

I always knew that I probably wanted to be a lawyer. There's a conventional range of occupations for middle-class Jewish boys: you become either a lawyer, a doctor or an accountant, and I certainly never wanted to have anything to do with figures and I didn't want to be a doctor. Therefore being a lawyer seemed a reasonable alternative, and I've always had a great affection for words.

You had a successful if comparatively modest career in the army. What were the values that emerged from this for you?

I'd been very spoilt as a boy. My parents' influence was protective to the point of mollycoddling, and the army was a revelation. It introduced me to the human race and showed me what excellent qualities existed there. I never met any unkindness. I was in the ranks for a while, then I was commissioned and went up to a command headquarters, where I got some modest promotion and that was that. But I enjoyed it very much. I learned how important it was to get on with your fellow men.

The idea I was living on borrowed time during the war would have been a philosophical meditation in which I didn't indulge. I never felt at all apprehensive, although I was a member of a very active anti-aircraft battery and we operated throughout the blitz on London, then in various other parts of the country, and were out during the bombing night after night. It never entered my head that I might be killed. I suppose, in a way, that I regarded myself as too precious a person for anyone to kill me. It was a form of vanity. I'm not heroic, but I don't think I'm particularly cowardly either, and although I had several quite narrow escapes when, on various occasions, bombs fell too close to be comfortable, I can't remember being worried.

You have been honoured by both Labour and Conservative governments, which seems a very unusual thing indeed.

If I had been a determined Marxist or a passionate Conservative, I don't think the other party would have employed me. I was evidently a neutral in these matters, and not really interested in politics. The reputation I had, for what it's worth, was that I was apolitical and that, on the whole, I didn't have violent prejudices one way or the other. My sympathy was towards liberal causes. For instance, I always took a strong line about South Africa and made several critical speeches. A liberal cause usually had only to heave into sight to find me supporting it, but not every liberal cause. I didn't believe in some of the more argumentative ones.

I don't feel that I have strong political convictions. I believe we should have a world where there is, on the whole, little interference with personal freedom. We should live in a world where everyone is entitled to be educated, in which everyone is entitled to be looked after health-wise. I do believe, to that extent, in what many people would call a socialist society, but not to the point of submerging other beliefs. It's true that I have a distaste for politicians, largely because I've met too many not to. I almost worshipped Jennie Lee, but she was an exception. And Nye Bevan was an extraordinary man, as was Hugh Gaitskell; and, in a strange sort of way, Ted Heath is extraordinary. These are all people who have qualities which rise above narrow political dogmas.

Where honesty in politicians is concerned, I don't think it's possible to be totally honest in any human context, but it's even more difficult if you're trying to persuade hundreds of thousands of people to adopt your views and vote for you. It would be imposing a tremendous moral strain never to exaggerate in the slightest degree, and exaggeration is a departure from honesty. Someone with a distaste for duplicity might well be as honest a politician, or indeed anything else, as you could hope to find. In fact, that might be a great encouragement to people to vote for him. This was certainly the basis of Mrs Thatcher's support at the start of her régime. People were persuaded that she was a change in the political scene, and that she was an honourable woman.

I have come to feel that our present democratic electoral system could be improved by ensuring that a greater number of people influence the elections. Certainly it could be improved by a system of proportional representation. One can be very dogmatic about this, because there are considerable dangers in a proportional representation which might, in the end, produce no government at all. But on the whole, I think we ought to have experimented with it. One of the things that can happen the way things are is that you can get such an overwhelming majority that no institution is safe, and that, of course, is a dangerous trend. We have seen the abolition of the Greater London Council, which clearly did very good work although it was open to objection because, in certain areas, people with extreme views got into power and did rather silly things. But they didn't do things silly enough to justify its demolition, and its destruction was a result of a system which allows one party to hold a majority of a size the Conservatives have today.

The cardinal point about Conservatism is that it binds the Conservatives together with one simple precept, which is a respect for property. And one reason why the Labour Party doesn't command that respect is because, by and large, it hasn't got the property. The respect that the Conservatives have for the initiative of the individual all turns on wealth, and there's no harm in that, but since it's a respect for a man who can amass wealth, it overrides any respect for intelligence, health or any other consideration. The Labour party is meanwhile a very disorganized, disunited group, but it seems to be getting better. They have been able to shed their more extreme element, and that gives them a better chance of recognition. I think they will come back into power, but when I don't know. It's not impossible it'll be at the next election.

At one point you undertook the task of trying to reconcile the difficulties in Rhodesia, and it looked as though you had managed to get an agreement.

I did get an agreement. What really happened was that the British government sent me out to negotiate with the Smith government, which

meant, in effect, Ian Smith himself. I negotiated with him and we were able to evolve a constitution acceptable to him, tolerably acceptable to the more powerful voices in his government and not wholly rejected by anyone. Then, when it came to it, one of the imperatives was that it should be acceptable to the entire population, black and white. Well, that was rather a silly requirement. There was no hope, when one came to think of it, of an agreement negotiated wholly between two white men being acceptable to the blacks. Smith was a wholly honest man, may I say. I never found him at all devious. He was obstinate, but the moment you had worn down his obstinacy and he agreed something, that was the end of it. He never went back on his word. The reason why the initiative failed was that the British government had defined a negotiation as something between two whites. They couldn't, in their wildest moments, have expected that that sort of negotiation was going to be either welcome or tolerable to the black population, which represented more than ten times the white population. When it came to it, Mr Smith assured us that it would be acceptable to the blacks, his reason for believing being, as he said, that his chiefs knew and respected him, would not betray him and would certainly vote in favour.

Now, Smith had lived in Rhodesia all his life and the Foreign Office had sent me out with a Rhodesian expert who had never before been to Rhodesia. As a result, no one warned me that the idea that the chiefs could control the tribes was completely wrong. The tribes controlled the chiefs. When the chiefs went back into the tribal lands, they were told to vote no, and to a man they did. The first mistake was to have employed someone, like me, who had never been to the country. My parents were born in South Africa, and I had been in South Africa many times, but never in Rhodesia. I knew nothing about the country. The second mistake was not to have sent me out with a genuine expert, because there were means of establishing that the proposed agreement was unacceptable to a great number of blacks.

The imposition of sanctions certainly worked in Rhodesia. That was a major reason for their seeking a settlement. When I arrived out there, people I'd never met before came up to me and tugged at my coat and said, 'Please, please, get an agreement.' The shops were almost empty of consumer goods. And sanctions are working in South Africa today. Very much so. I was in South Africa last October and the one thing perfectly clear was that they were obsessed with the fear of sanctions, and were producing literature and arguments, all specious and all designed to show that sanctions didn't work and ought to be dropped. It was clear evidence that sanctions were working.

I don't think Mrs Thatcher is right at all to ease sanctions. There has been no relative improvement at all, they've hardly changed anything. Apartheid is as intact as ever, with only a few minor changes. It would

be folly, having got this far, to cease the one thing that is having an obvious effect on them.

What is wrong with South Africa is that, in terms of demography, it's an idiocy. There are something like thirty million blacks being governed by three to four million whites. In demographic terms, it's an outrage, and the whites have used their power in the most disgraceful way. South Africa is a heartbreaking place. There are various housing estates, including one called Crossbow which houses three quarters of a million to a million blacks. It's thick with mud, and they live in the most improvised and rudimentary constructions made up principally of bits of iron, bits of tin, bits of cardboard. There is a water tap for every four houses, and no sanitation, just a bucket system. They manage somehow to keep these places relatively clean, but as conditions for human beings to live in, they are intolerable. The irony is that most people in Cape Town have never seen the place, even though you pass it on the way from the airport. There's a callous indifference to human suffering that makes the present régime an outrage and makes reform an urgent necessity.

If you were to argue that the one man, one vote principle cannot work because the blacks are not educated enough, then I don't know that one can say with complete confidence that there isn't a large percentage of the electorate in this country who are similarly unequipped to have a vote. The requirement to justify a vote is that a man would understand what is good for him. One saw it in Rhodesia. When they came to taking a vote on the proposed settlement, the blacks to a man turned it down. Their instinct told them that anything warmly approved by Mr Smith was not to their benefit.

As for making South Africa safe for democracy, who are you asking that it should be safe for – the three to four million or the thirty to forty million? I tend to think a secure solution is possible. Nigeria, for instance, is quite competently governed. You've got to remember that the difference is this: it is one thing to be governed by people of your own race, quite another to be governed by people of another race whom you have justifiably come to regard over the years as hostile. That is the basic consideration.

There is no reason to suppose that introducing democracy will stop the violence of black against black, but equally, there's a strong reason to think it won't stop unless democracy is introduced. My own feeling is that the black outrages against black are quite a different thing from white outrages against black, and that they won't cause the same resentment. The black population of South Africa is very large, and it has been kept in a depressed position by the whites. Years ago there was a minister of education who said something to the effect that they would

give them such education as they needed to carry out the simple humble functions they performed. That was a calculated insult.

Do you find that being the focal point of enormous pressure, as you were in Rhodesia, is something you are able to cope with easily?

I don't think I've ever felt under an intolerable pressure from other people's opinions. Perhaps I have an excessive and rather conceited faith in my own opinions, but I was never tortured by doubts. You couldn't achieve anything if you were tortured by doubt. On negotiation, I'm immensely patient. In personal relations, I'm not so sure, but negotiation should be a continuous process until you have reached a conclusion. You should listen very carefully to what the other side have to say, and make quite sure that they realize that you do understand their point of view and that, if you are rejecting it, it must be for valid reasons.

I would consider myself to be a good listener in negotiation, and in normal life I'm not an impatient listener. Of course, in this world one has to listen to a great deal of nonsense, but I'm very tolerant of nonsense because I'm tolerant of the fallibility of human beings. I wouldn't say that estimating your opponent is a very profitable activity. What you have to do is to estimate the strength of your case and the strength of a case which comes midway between the two cases, and ultimately it's your job to propound a tolerable solution acceptable to both sides, or all three sides. But you arrive there by instinct. It's not a calculated process.

The legal profession in England seems in turmoil at present, with one group trying to preserve its privileges and the other to trespass on them. Is it a matter of principle more than the scramble for money and power it appears to be?

It's not a scramble for money. I once said that the strange feature of the English legal system was that, although lawyers didn't enrich themselves, they could succeed in beggaring their clients, and this was an anomaly. I don't think it's a struggle for power either. It is really a struggle for prestige. It's as simple as that. The Bar have a built-in conviction that they have a superior status, but they fail to recognize, first of all, how numerically inferior they are. In actual practice, there are between 3,000 and 4,000 barristers – and that's probably an exaggeration – as against 60,000 solicitors, so it is obvious that if they are going to have a conviction of superiority then it must be a strong one because numerically they would be in difficulty. In fact the traditions of the Bar are really no longer appropriate for the twentieth-century situation, even less for the twenty-first. By this I mean their wigs and gowns, and their use of Latin, which very few of them understand or can construe. The whole edifice is built on a fraudulent tradition of

custom – a firm conviction that a custom that has retained privileges for them and has maintained them in a superior position in relation to the rest of the legal profession exists by order of the Almighty. To some extent it stems from the class system in this country, but the strange thing is that a great number of solicitors and a great number of barristers all come from the same class, the upper middle class. They've been educated at public or independent schools, and most of them have been to Oxford or Cambridge, so there isn't a great divergence of class. Nevertheless the Bar believe that their practices and traditions are better and finer. It's largely based on the Inns of Court, for which they have a sort of masonic affection.

Meanwhile there's very little doubt that our legal system is weighted against the poor man if he's engaged in a battle. We like to pretend that there's no advantage in retaining a better lawyer, but of course there is a great advantage, and I don't know how that is going to be changed. There will have to be a more expansive legal aid system, and the reform now taking place, whereby you will be able to use a single advocate, will greatly cheapen the matter. Although the Bar deny it, it's a matter of simple arithmetic. It is bound to be cheaper to employ one man rather than four.

But won't it be very difficult to make the people who have money less privileged than those who don't?

There are some things in which, by the decree of the Almighty, the rich are less privileged. They've no privileges in relation to fresh air; they've no privileges in relation to sea-bathing. Shortly they'll have to discover that they've no real privilege in relation to justice.

But if you're rich, you can go where there is fresh air. If you're poor, you're stuck where you are.

I'm not so sure. If you're born on the seashore, you get fresh air; however rich you may be, you won't be able to get more. I think that the extent to which money and justice are related is a bad thing, but it is much less so here than in the United States, although France is better than we are. They have something I have a special preference for, which is what is called a civilian system, that is to say, a Roman law system. I was trained as a Roman lawyer, and I lectured on Roman Dutch law at Cambridge. It is a system which doesn't depend on precedent. The English system means that you go back over every case decided since the year dot to see what cases have been decided in your favour. The Roman law system doesn't depend on precedent at all, but on principle, and if the principle is with you, then you win the case. This, of course, is much, much cheaper than a precedent system. I would say there is

quite a lot of reform that needs to be done in relation to the English legal system.

Why is our legal establishment so against introducing the American system of contingency fees in this country?

They're against it because they think it's *infra dig.* They consider it undignified for lawyers to work under circumstances where they're paid only if they win, but there are other objections that are raised. One is that it is unfair to the losing party because he can't get any costs. Once you start a litigation on a contingency basis, at the end of the day, if the assisted person wins the case, the defendant has no means of recovering the costs. It's well controlled in America, more so than you would think from the impression that is being conveyed here by the people opposed to it. For instance, there are strict rules that the lawyer may not take more than a percentage of the win – 15 or 20 per cent. And there is a rule in some states that the court must feel that there is a prima facie chance of success. A man cannot undertake a completely hopeless cause for the purpose of advertising himself, or perhaps forcing a settlement from someone who isn't very sure. It is, like every human institution, open to objections, but I would say that the objections fall down by the side of the alternative, which is that a poor man can't sue at all.

When you dismissed as 'poppycock' the Bar's fears for the independence of the judiciary under the Lord Chancellor, Lord Mackay's plans for reform, yours seemed almost a lone voice, and the general reaction was one of closing ranks.

It was only the Bar. The Bar, as I said, is a tiny profession of about 4,000 active members. There was no closing ranks among the 64,000 lawyers. What it came down to was the vehemence of the Bar's opposition and the pretensions they give to themselves, despite their small numbers. If you have an agreeable monopoly, it isn't difficult to evolve a highfalutin principle to enable you to maintain it. There is no principle that enables the Bar to maintain a position which is ruinous to every litigant.

Yet they maintain that the cost will not be reduced.

That is to maintain that Mount Everest isn't there. As I say, it's a question of arithmetic. It is manifestly cheaper to employ one person than to employ at least three and possibly four doing the same job. If the problem were approached with determination and integrity, it would become enormously cheaper. As for the notion that standards will go down, what standards? They have sold the myth that they are superlative advocates, but if you go to the Law Courts on any morning and pass

from court to court, the thing that will horrify you is the bumbling nature of the advocacy. There are half a dozen superlative advocates, Robert Alexander being one. There are a few others. Jeremy Hutchinson was a superlative. But the number can be counted on the fingers of one hand, and to keep to this pretence as the means of maintaining a disastrously expensive monopoly makes no sense.

Doesn't it remain iniquitous that most people will be deterred from sueing because of the horrendous costs?

That is not so much a reflection on the law of libel as a reflection on our legal system. I quite agree that the costs involved are prohibitive, but there are ameliorations now under consideration, a very important one being that the action could be brought in the County Court, where the case could be conducted by a solicitor alone. This could have a dramatic effect on reducing the costs.

I haven't myself represented many people in libel actions. I doubt if I've been involved in twenty libel actions that went to court in the whole of my career. I've always deterred people from becoming involved. A client is perfectly entitled to ignore my advice, of course, but if I thought the conduct of the action was in some way a persecution or an impropriety, I just wouldn't do it. There'd be no reason why I should. I've refused to act for a client very many times. I am under no obligation to do things I don't approve of.

When, in 1957, I undertook to represent Aneurin Bevan, Richard Crossman and Morgan Phillips after the *Spectator* accused them of being drunk on a British delegation to Venice, I agreed because the clients, and particularly Nye Bevan, who was quite a close friend, regarded it as very serious. He said, 'I was sent abroad to represent the Labour Party at an international conference, and now I am told that while I was there I conducted myself like a drunkard.' He took a very serious view of it, and he was entitled to.

Isn't it a mistake to pick twelve people from the public at random to decide in a technically complicated case, such as the Guinness one now?

You underrate them. First of all, if you have twelve people, statistically there are bound to be two or three of average, if not above average, intelligence. If they don't understand the case, it's because the counsel who are explaining it to them are inadequate. My own belief is there is almost no case that a jury, given proper advice and instruction, cannot deal with better than a judge alone. There is something about a jury that inspires confidence. They will arrive at perverse verdicts, but never at insane verdicts.

Oddly enough, a judge's going over the top in his summing up is

often the reason why a jury takes the other side, especially if they feel that the judge is loading the case too much. They are twelve people, not twelve fools.

Lawyers never seem very popular as a group.

I would say the general dislike is justified for the very simple reason that you go in search of a lawyer only when you're in trouble, and that is why lawyers are not loved. You won't find that doctors who specialize in cancer are the best-loved members of a community, and there's more reason for loving them than a lawyer who is going to try and extricate you from an unhealthy marital situation where your wife intends to take half your property. That's why they're not liked. It's not because they are rich. If you look at the 1,000 richest men in England, or even at the 10,000 richest, you won't find a lawyer among them. Lawyers do not make money. That is a simple fact. Certain barristers make huge incomes because they're in great demand, but that is a rarity. It's for the same reason that Placido Domingo gets higher fees than any other tenor. A highly accomplished barrister, like Robert Alexander, gets very large fees, which is only fair. On an average, lawyers are by no means extravagantly paid. I took three law degrees and obtained first-class honours in all of them, and I wouldn't say that the rewards that have come my way are even comparable with what I'd have got if I'd become a merchant banker. I never wanted them to be.

When Lord Mackay was disciplined recently by his Church in Scotland for having attended a requiem mass for a deceased colleague, did that make you wonder whether there was a case for saying that someone like Lord Mackay, who holds high office, should not belong to such a narrow, restrictive Church in the first place, that the latter is incompatible with the duties and requirements of the former?

The Church one belongs to must be a subjective consideration. No one can know what arguments propel me to remain Jewish. These are decisions that one makes for oneself, and they are decided inside you. I understand that Lord Mackay has now left that particular Church, and I must say I heard the news with great relief, but I wouldn't seek to impose my own view about what are the right religious precepts for a man of skill and judgement. In many ways, the fact that he remained a member of the Church of his fathers was a very creditable thing. It's true that it's a Church which appears to be redolent of prejudice, bias and rather absurd notions, but even so, you can't condemn the entire Moslem peoples for believing some of the idiocies they believe; you can't condemn all Jews for believing some of the idiocies we are supposed to believe. These are matters of personal opinion, and so long as he is

doing no damage to anyone else, no one has any right to interfere. You must remember that one of the great requirements of our present society is that people should have a faith, and I think that many of the difficulties and tragedies we encounter today are due to the absence of faith. Almost any faith is better than none. I wouldn't go so far as to say that, if you believe in cannibalism, that is a desirable thing, but whatever notions you may hold about religious precepts, to have some that are firmly held in your mind must be a good thing.

You are widely regarded as the best chairman the Arts Council ever had. Have its aims improved or declined since your time there?

As you know, at the moment there is a rumpus going on because it's proposed by the minister of the arts, who is not a very experienced person, that the Arts Council should have a very reduced function and that regional arts associations should take on the major task of subsidizing the majority of companies. I think this is wholly mistaken. To introduce local associations into the matter will be to introduce politics with both feet. I had quite a lot of experience in dealing with local authorities. Some were very good but a great many of them were awful, and the extent to which politics were brought in has, I'm afraid, had considerable support from this government. They view everything from a political viewpoint and don't think anyone should be promoted to any office of importance unless he is a member of their party. Things haven't improved; they've got worse.

A Labour government would have appointed a Tory to the Arts Council. Jennie Lee certainly would. You see, I've never been a member of the Labour party. When I said that what was wrong was the government policy of not countenancing non-Conservatives, someone remarked, 'Ah, but what about you? Is it not true that they appointed a person of liberal sentiments?' The answer to that was given by someone else, who said there was no party that wouldn't have appointed me.

On the subject of art for the people, especially opera, is there not a case for saying that most of the people who are contributing to the subsidies are providing an agreeable entertainment for a fortunate minority in London?

Well, that is an unavoidable consequence. If you were to say that no minority interest is to be subsidized because it isn't enjoyed by everyone in the country, then culture disappears. It is perfectly true, as I remarked many years ago, that one of the essential liberties of a free Englishman was freedom from culture, and if he doesn't want culture, he needn't have it. But that's no reason for depriving anyone else of it. The number of people who want to go to the opera is greatly exaggerated. A lot of people would like to go, and a lot do, very cheaply. You can get, if not

a seat, a position from where you can hear an opera for £2. At Covent Garden it's extremely uncomfortable, but if you're a young enthusiast, you don't have to pay £100.

My feeling is that, if you provide cultural material only on the footing that the whole world can afford it, there are innumerable things that won't be there. Education would disappear. You have to accept that a large part of desirable human activity is wanted only by a few special people. But those special people are very special. They dictate the shape and form of the country's culture and education, and I don't think there's any terrible injustice. The injustice is for the state not to provide the money. When you think of the cost of a single battleship or a nuclear weapon, it's absurd to say we couldn't afford a few hundred thousand or even a few million for cultural activities. Yet there is a bitter resistance to this, and it comes from very rich people. That is because most of them would rather go to gaol than sit through a performance of *The Ring*.

The boycotting of Wagner by many Jews after the war was, incidentally, an absurdity. It's ridiculous to regard music as untouchable because it was composed by a man who was an anti-Semite because he believed his illegitimate father was Jewish. The important thing to remember is that music has a quality and a standing of its own.

You once said: 'It is an article of faith with this government that anything remotely progressive in politics should be stamped out. It would have been too much to expect them to keep the Arts Council immune from this.' A great deal of anger seems to lie behind this statement.

It's something about which I do feel strongly. The Arts Council was founded on two principles, one being that, although it accepts money, it accepts no political direction or dictation as to how to use the money. The corresponding and comparable principle is that, in giving its money to its various beneficiaries, it imposes no degree of political control. In fact, it has subsidized many very left-wing adventures since there are not a great many right-wing adventures because intellectuals are rarely right wing. And what the Arts Council has to do is protect the integrity of intellectual and cultural thought, and if it proceeds to stamp on everything that it or Mrs Thatcher thinks has any appearance of culture, then it destroys an institution of international value. I do believe that, in the main, intellectuals veer towards left-wing opinions. By left-wing opinions one means opinions that are not maintained by anyone who has a bit of money.

One of the complaints made by the orthodox supporters of the arts on the right is that right-wing plays are never put on. The answer is simple. There aren't any right-wing plays. Go and search for them.

You might trace a tendency towards right-wing drama in, say, John Galsworthy, but he was essentially a liberal, and if you see one of his most famous plays, *The Silver Box*, it was a cry for the dispossessed.

As for working to persuade the unconvinced of the validity of the importance of art and artists, I don't know that I would persuade them. My father used to say that one of the principles of life is that a young donkey grows into an old donkey. I would make no effort. It's quite impossible to inculcate a belief by argument. You can only do it by providing culture that the young can absorb and come to love.

In the area of education and the mounting failure of the educational system, more money should be provided and less introduced. We could then be as well educated as the French, for example. We're a long way behind them at the moment. Happily we were never as badly educated as the Germans, because they were educated to tolerate enormities and outrages that would not be tolerated in England. There's a lot to be said for our system. It's one that encourages liberal ideas and makes it possible to live with liberal thoughts in a world where most people are illiberal. On that score, I'm a great admirer, and I can think of no other country in the world where I would wish to live, except perhaps one or two of the original British dominions, like Australia or Canada.

But what can be our grounds for optimism when we haven't enough teachers in the schools, university funds are constantly cut, students are saddled with debt before they even begin their careers, some of our fellow citizens live in cardboard boxes on the streets . . .

I think that is an exaggerated statement of certain outrages that are very limited in number. You see, the number of people living in cardboard boxes is tiny, and they are nearly always drug dependent, and it is impossible to eradicate the drug desire. They are people who find it impossible to organize a sane life and provide themselves with a roof, but I don't think that is a prevailing mood in any substantial number of people. England is more humane, more civilized than almost anywhere else. I won't say that the Jews are universally popular, but they are not persecuted, and the only man who tried to mount a campaign of anti-Semitism was brought to a sharp halt.

Did you ever encounter anti-Semitism yourself?

As a Jew I've had rich rewards, and I don't believe that being a Jew has interfered with them in any way. I've had appointments, I've had honours, and I can regard myself as being very fortunate indeed. I can't attribute any misfortune of mine to anti-Semitism. It's impossible to say that there weren't people who, when they came to review the

situation, didn't feel they'd rather appoint a Roman Catholic or a Presbyterian than a Jew, but I've not encountered it.

We seem a lot more restrictive than the Americans on accessibility to information. Do you think freedom is divisible in some way?

Freedom is indivisible. I think the rules should be applied with common sense. If a man divulges the time at which he takes tea and that he takes three cups and he's given two pieces of sugar, that is not a secret. On the other hand, if he proceeds to divulge the reasons why a particular civil servant wasn't promoted and things of that sort, then that can be very injurious to someone's career and is something in which there can be no public interest – or shouldn't be, unless there's some scandal associated with it.

The government's latest piece of legislation does not provide public interest as a ground for defence. I think this is very difficult, because any civil servant who feels that there is a profit in divulging the secret would be able to present a case that it's in the public interest. I'm not at all sure that you should be able to betray your trust because you believe there's a public interest. It is for the government to determine what is the public interest, not an individual civil servant. It can't be determined by anyone else. The trouble is there's a great deal of hypocrisy about these claims, especially by the press. The claim to freedom is really the claim by the newspapers to publish titillating information that will sell more copies. That's what the claim for freedom derives from, not from any lofty motivation. I think one has to have that in mind when considering the strength and nature of the claim.

You have known many national leaders of different political persuasions and all sorts of people in positions of authority and influence. Is that a world you find attractive?

I don't find people of influence more attractive because they have influence. It is usually that they have attained influence because there is some rather arresting quality about them, and, of course, that is bound to be an important consideration in assessing your interest in them.

I have not admired very much people who are evidently self-seeking, but it would be wrong for me to indicate who such people are. I admired Hugh Gaitskell very much. I also had a considerable admiration for Ted Heath, although of recent years he has been much influenced by a sense of pique. The politician I admired most was Lloyd George. He was a man who made his own way from the most humble background by employing quite exceptional persuasive and oratorical talent. He was one of the great orators of the day. And it's a source of great satisfaction to me that he was a solicitor.

To ask if he was a womanizer has nothing to do with anything. You might as well ask did he like curry? That a man likes women is so idiosyncratic a matter that it doesn't bear examination. I don't think he did his career any harm, because the investigatory journalism of our day didn't then exist. Had it existed, Lloyd George would have been ruined within hours.

No, I don't think the British are more hypocritical about sex than other nations. I don't think they're more hypocritical than the Americans, and the Europeans are also hypocritical in the sense that they have decided to conceal their feelings about it. The French are liberal to the extent that it would be unlikely that a Frenchman would be ruined because he had a mistress, but it would now be equally unlikely that an Englishman would be ruined for the same reason. There's a general loosening of moral standards that is very welcome.

You knew Harold Wilson.

Yes, as well as anyone could.

He now appears to be a rather discredited politician, with the whole political establishment seeming to have deserted him.

I think that's because he was an unsuccessful politician in the sense that he lost the ultimate election, and he is not the easiest man to support. He was an extremely kindly man, but he also had some massive faults, and one of those was that, before he did anything, he got into the habit of looking over his shoulder to see what the effect might be before he decided. That is a very grave defect in a politician, who should go boldly ahead and do what he thinks right. I liked him very much. He was very kind to me, and I'm not sure that he's wholly discredited.

If he now seems not to be respected, that is because the organs of respectability are Tory organs. *The Times*, the *Daily Telegraph*, the *Daily Mail* are all Tory papers, the assessment of these people is a Tory assessment, and Harold Wilson was the most hated one of all because he was the one who provided the greatest risk to their beliefs and policies. I would say that has a lot to do with his present assessment.

Any desertion by his own party was on purely pragmatic grounds, because the public wouldn't support him. I'm not even sure that his own party have deserted him. It's easily said, but if Harold Wilson returned to leadership, he'd have a much greater chance of success at winning the election than Mr Kinnock. Harold Wilson was absolutely hated by the Tory press. The Conservative party has one inflexible principle which distinguishes it from the Labour party. Whereas the Labour party has all sorts of notions which add up to a policy or don't,

the Conservative party has one notion only, which is to preserve private property. They saw in Harold Wilson a really dangerous threat to their well-being.

What view did you take of the alleged MI5 plot to oust Wilson?

It wasn't an MI5 plot, but it was a plot by a few cowboys in MI5, and it certainly took place. My own offices were raided twice and I hadn't any notion why until much later, when I discovered that they had been searching for documents that might in some way incriminate Harold Wilson. We had no such documents. I don't think any such documents existed. But there certainly was this disgraceful activity on the part of a few hot-headed fanatics, who saw in Harold Wilson a danger to their whole scheme of life. Of course, we didn't know of this until long afterwards.

What advice would you have given, had you been asked, on Harold Wilson's so-called 'Lavender List' of honours?

I did in fact offer some advice, I won't say to whom. It was an extremely unwise and reckless list, and my advice would have been not to go ahead with it. It couldn't have mattered twopence to Harold Wilson whether some unworthy businessman was going to get a knighthood or a peerage, so he had no great personal advantage to get out of it. He had a certain weakness towards particular influences, and he didn't have the strength of character to resist them. I think the 'Lavender List' did him great harm, but I'm equally sure that there was no element of corruption in it and that he was doing it because he thought he was obliging someone or other. He should have had a stiffer resistance to obliging people.

Ted Heath, too, is not highly thought of at present.

If Ted Heath is not highly thought of at the moment, it's because he has attacked the existing Conservative front. I've known Ted Heath since he was a schoolboy, and I met him in a rather unusual situation. I was a very junior partner in a firm in which my senior partner had a passion for rose-growing. His ambition in life was to become the president of the National Rose Society, now the Royal National Rose Society – everything being royal these days. He achieved his ambition in the last year of his life, but before that, while I was still in partnership with him, he used to go regularly down to Broadstairs where he had a patch of ground where he grew his roses. Being rather a thrifty man, he said to me one day, 'You know, it's too expensive to keep coming down here. I'm going to build a little cottage.' He got his plot of ground and

he had the cottage built by Mr William Heath, Ted's father, and that's how I got to know him, and we've been, I won't say close friends, but very good friends ever since. My impression of Ted was that you didn't have to know him long to know what was in him. He's not a complicated character. He's good natured, honourable, sympathetic and kindly. Obviously he has the usual vanity of a man who has been prime minister and wants to be prime minister again, and he has a number of massive faults, but they're more than counteracted by a great number of massive virtues.

Aneurin Bevan was a great hero of mine when I was a student. Do you think that, had he lived, he might have mellowed and perhaps even risen to be prime minister?

One of the great tragedies of the post-war story was the deaths of the two people who would have made a significant impression on the Labour party. The first was Hugh Gaitskell, the second Nye Bevan. Had Nye lived, he might easily have become the leader.

Gaitskell was a man of moderate comment but absolutely rigid principle, and he compares very favourably with the rest of the Labour party leadership. In my view, he was an outstanding figure. First of all, he was an extremely nice man, secondly he was very articulate, and thirdly he was a man of firm purpose but moderate speech. He would have made a very good prime minister.

Michael Foot, though a great admirer of your powers, once spoke of what he regarded as your 'stunning political naïvety'. Do you think of yourself as politically naïve?.

I think of myself as politically disinterested. That may amount to naïvety. Michael Foot himself is a man of great naïvety, and his greatest naïvety was to believe that he could possibly become the leader of the Labour party. He is a scholar and a man of great integrity, but he was mildly corrupted politically by a feeling that a great prize was within his grasp.

You describe yourself as a subscribing Jew, comfortable with the Jewish faith and race, but not formally practising. Do you ever feel uncomfortable about Israel or the Israeli position vis-à-vis *the Palestinians.*

Mine is one of the loudest voices of protest. I paid various visits to Israel recently and sought every opportunity to tell the government how wrong I thought their policy was in relation to young Arabs. And I do feel extremely uncomfortable about it. I think it is very wrong that a community and a race, if you like, that claims to be fully civilized has

been shooting young Arabs by the hundreds. I have no doubts at all that the policy of the Shamirs and Sharons is a reactionary policy that should have no support from liberal Jews.

As a former soldier, did you feel indignant when the Jewish underground, in their fight against the British Mandate, killed British soldiers in Palestine immediately after the war?

No, I didn't feel indignant. It was one of the unhappy inevitabilities. One very much wished that it hadn't happened, and particularly the episode of the sergeant. All of that was very horrible to a British Jew.

Would you say that the Middle East problem is just too intractable to find a solution?

Oh, it's easy to identify intractable problems. You'll find one in Cyprus, one in Northern Ireland, one in Nigeria. There are intractable problems, and one just has to wait and do the best one can to oil the machinery. There is perhaps more likelihood of a solution in the Middle East than elsewhere, because the Arab world is quite practical. What they have never been able to recognize is the enormous benefits that a civilized Israel would bring to the Middle East, but I think that is the sort of recognition which one can hope will come about.

The Israelis, however, have now adopted a policy which I think is thoroughly unfortunate, and that is apparently to accept that they have an empire-building function. The worst position you can have between two conflicting nations is when one of them believes that they have God's support for empire building.

You said in a recent interview that you have always had a sense of being an onlooker, which sounds strange, coming from someone who has been so thoroughly engaged in so many things.

I've always had a sense that I'm not as seriously committed to any course of conduct as other people. I know in my own mind that I'm ready to find a solution that isn't necessarily the orthodox one. In that way I regard myself as being more of an onlooker than many other people.

As for my reaction to emotional upheaval, I would be very ashamed of panic or loss of control. There are a great many things that induce irritation in me, and I think they're the orthodox things. I have a deep sense of justice and thorough intolerance of injustice, especially when it is to the weak and in particular in relation to children. This is a catalogue of rather obvious virtues, but I don't think I'm given to the more sensational emotions. I don't boil with fury and go out and attack people

with axes. I'd require a lot of provocation before I attacked anyone with an axe.

I'm certainly not intolerant of mediocrity, since you ask, or one would have to be intolerant of ninety-nine per cent of the human race. Nor would I arrogate to myself the right to judge everyone. I'm intolerant of inadequacy where someone is doing a job that requires a special talent which he hasn't got, and then, like most people, I get a little irritated, but I certainly wouldn't arrogate to myself the right to determine whether someone is mediocre or not.

Do you ever feel loneliness?

I don't need people all the time. I'm perfectly happy to spend the afternoon reading a book, or watching a television programme, or going to the cinema or to the theatre. Last night I heard a wonderful performance of Verdi's *Requiem.* That gives me delight. I don't need other people there holding my hand. But that is one of the great advantages of the arts: they are a consolation for loneliness.

Do you ever regret not having married?

I can't say I regret not having married, because I could have married. I had some interesting opportunities. There have been women who have been influential in my life. I don't intend to particularize them, but certainly I can think of three. It would be impossible for me to mention them. That would be breaching their privacy, not mine. I do regret not having children. I have a great affection for children, and would have enjoyed very much playing some part in bringing them up, but you can't have everything in this world.

On a television interview you said you did not want to reveal to a million viewers your reasons for not marrying. Isn't this creating a needless mystery?

It's not a needless mystery. It is a belief that, in certain aspects of one's life, one is entitled to privacy. I do not owe the world an explanation of my personal and private life, and I don't intend to give it one. If it's a mystery, it's quite a healthy mystery, and scholars can investigate it for the next hundred years. I certainly don't intend to elaborate on it. It's not a sinister mystery, I assure you.

Have you felt more drawn to religion with advancing years?

No, I haven't. I regard most religions as superstitions, and I certainly haven't been drawn towards any particularly active superstition as I get older.

You have led an exemplary life, have defended and championed the underdog, yet you must have been, like everyone else, exposed to all kinds of temptations. Did you ever succumb?

Succumbed to temptation? I don't think consciously. If a temptation rose up in front of me, I would walk round it. I'm sure there are many areas of my behaviour which I now regret, and many decisions I've made that I think were wrong. It would be a very strange human being who didn't believe that, but I don't think I've consciously succumbed to temptation. I don't think I had many wild oats to sow. Some people sow enough wild oats to make it an agricultural problem, but I had no great interest. I wasn't addicted to drink or drugs. I smoked heavily at one time, but gave that up. I'm probably beginning to sound altogether too virtuous. I had encounters with women which gave me great comfort and pleasure, but that's all I can say about it. I've not been devoid of human feelings.

There are certainly things that I've regretted, but not burning issues, not things that wake me in the middle of the night, shrieking in my bed. I have a high degree of complacency. On the whole, I think I'm reasonably satisfied with myself. That is not a virtuous thing to be, but it does make life easier.

DEREK HILL

Derek Hill was born in Hampshire in 1916. He was educated at Marlborough and left school in 1933 to study stage design in Munich. In 1935 he travelled to Paris and Vienna where he designed sets for *Agamemnon*. The following year he studied theatre design in Moscow, Leningrad and Kiev before returning to London in 1937 to do sets and costumes for Frederick Ashton's ballet *The Lord of Burleigh*. He went to Paris in 1938 and, encouraged by Edward Molyneux, began to paint. He had his first one-man show in 1943 and since then has had several exhibitions in London, Dublin and New York. His portrait commissions have included Sir John Betjeman, Isaiah Berlin, Osbert Lancaster, Kenneth Clark, Prince Charles, Laurens van der Post and many others. Since 1954 he has lived in Donegal.

My father was quite well off. I don't mean that he was a rich man, but my great-grandfather was the first person to have a steamship which took coal from Newcastle to Southampton. The first time I remember painting – drawing, I should say – was at Sunday school. We were asked to draw the wheel of life with virtue at the top and vice at the bottom. Instead I drew a picture of the clergyman. I was smacked and sent home, but never had to go to Sunday school again.

I did, of course, paint at Marlborough. We had an art class run by a likeable old man called Colonel Hughes, who executed charming etchings and engravings. From the very beginning I wanted to be an artist and in this I was helped greatly by my elder brother John. He had been made to go into a cloth works at Lille in France, because my father owned Laverton & Tucker's at Trowbridge, Somerset, where they made marvellous West of England cloth, and wanted him to follow in his footsteps. John was most unhappy and finally persuaded my father to let him leave, and after that my father took whatever he said seriously. So when John said, 'Derek wants to paint,' my father said, 'Then for God's sake let him.' I must say my father was wonderful about that.

He and I were absolutely the antithesis of each other. He adored fishing, adored shooting. As a child, whenever there was a pheasant shoot, I used to have to carry off those poor wretched birds, still kicking and shaking. Having to do that was something I loathed, and is the reason why I have always hated shooting. My father was also a cricketer who used to play with W. G. Grace, was a great friend of Ranjitsinhji, the Indian cricketer, and captained Hampshire for fifteen years. He wanted me to love cricket as he did, but the game bored me to tears through being made to go out and practice it every evening of my life. In the end my father let me get away with it.

My time at Marlborough wasn't bad at all. I was reasonably well treated. I was regarded as an aesthete because of my interest in the arts

and writing, but I also happened to have an extremely nice housemaster of whom I was fond and whom I appreciated. It is true that there was appalling bullying at Marlborough in those days, but I managed to escape the worst. On the Sunday of the 'new boys' concert', I happened to be taken out by my parents, which was a piece of luck since the ritual was to make you crawl along a very hot radiator on your knees while singing some such song as 'Clementine'. When you reached the end you were tipped into a wastepaper basket with your behind up in the air and beaten by all the prefects. It was known as the 'new boys' initiation'.

Once my father understood that I wanted to paint, he said, 'Well, if you are going to be a painter you must be a painter that makes money.' I thought theatre design would be the option which most interested me and became, at first, a sort of apprentice to Oliver Messel, who did the sets for *Helen* and *The Miracle* and all those great Cochrane productions of my youth. Then some friends of the family suggested that Munich would be a good place to learn theatre design, and so it was, and I went there when I was just seventeen. We learned a great deal about contrasts – hot and cold, rough and smooth, high and low – and spent hours making contrasts on bits of paper. We'd have a bit of cotton wool, a bit of sacking, a bit of cotton, and then a bit of velvet, perhaps. It was part of the Bauhaus, of course.

I arrived in Germany in the same year that the Nazis came to power, but unlike young people today, we were still children at seventeen. We didn't realize what Hitler signified any more than a lot of other people back in England. I never liked it because I hated the noise in the streets, the marching. I hated army things and was always a pacifist. What made me so was seeing the film of *All Quiet on the Western Front* when I was a boy. It so appalled me that I talked a lot about it with my uncle, who was a general, and later on, when I had my tribunal as a conscientious objector, he attended and vouched for me, and said that I had always had those feelings, that they weren't just brought out because of the war.

I did once see Hitler in a teashop. It was May 1934 and my mother and an old aunt from Scotland were visiting me. They were less political than anyone you ever met, less even than I was then, but they both said how they'd like to see this famous man they'd heard so much about. Every Monday afternoon Hitler was known to stop for tea at the Carlton Teeraum in Munich on his way from Berchtesgaden to Berlin, and so I took them there. At about a quarter past five he duly appeared. I said, 'I must telephone Unity Mitford and tell her.' I'd known Unity before she went to Germany; her sister Pam lived near Marlborough, and I used to go out to see her when I was at school. Along came Unity in a taxi and said rather pathetically, 'Derek, I shall never forget you after this. It's the greatest thing that ever happened to me.' Until then she

had only seen him in the distance, never close to. But apart from bringing Unity closer to Hitler, the most extraordinary thing about the occasion was my mother and aunt walking out of the teashop, giving the Nazi salute as they went. I was horrified. I never particularly liked moustaches on people and I merely thought Hitler a dull-looking little man. Yet almost until the war my mother still believed in him as a bulwark against communism, against vice in Europe and everything undesirable.

After Munich I went to Paris to learn stage design with Paul Colin, then the great *affiche* painter in France. He had a school to which Louis Jouvet used to come every week and talk to us about the theatre. I did drawings and in the mornings went occasionally to a school where Marie Laurencin taught. She was an adorable old creature, charming. I don't think she taught me much, but I loved her and her personality.

Since I did want to draw really well, I went next to the Kunstgewerbe in Vienna. There we were trained by a wonderful method. You were given sheets of blank newsprint, brush and ink, and a model posed for five minutes only. You then had to do your drawing of the figure within the five minutes. The first hundred you just tore up as useless, but gradually your eye became trained because, as soon as you put ink on newsprint, it sinks in and you can never alter it. The method really did teach me how to draw and I've been grateful to it the whole of my life.

My professor in Vienna was the great Joseph Gregor, who wrote a book on Russian theatre and was famous in those days. He was one of the last librettists for Richard Strauss. Gregor was asked through the Burg Theatre for someone to design a production of the *Agamemnon*, and under his aegis I took on the commission. He oversaw everything I did, since I was still only eighteen or nineteen, but then the Nazis marched into Austria and the whole project collapsed. I never could understand why they objected to it. I did all the designs and still have a few of them.

When I was in Vienna I never thought of becoming a painter. After Vienna, when I went across Siberia, I drew and sketched, and later, when I was in Bali, I painted quite a lot of the dancers. But again, that was all concerned with theatre and dancing, and it was not until just before the war that I took to actual painting and went back to art school. The business of becoming an artist is the business of looking and seeing – seeing what one thinks is beautiful, whether it's a personal reaction to a landscape or whatever.

It does now seem rather extraordinary how, at the age of nineteen, after experiencing Hitler's Germany, I went on to live in Stalin's Russia. I found the Soviet Union incredibly restricted, of course. Gregor sent

me, saying, 'I've nothing more to teach you. Go to Russia and I'll give you a letter of introduction to Tairov,' Tairov then being, with Meyerhold, one of the great men of Russian theatre. I stayed in what was called a hard-class hotel and for about six months attended rehearsals and performances. Tairov got me into anything I wanted to see in the theatre and I think I went to sixty productions. But, outside the theatre world, you never met anyone. George F. Kennan, later a leading authority in the West on Russia, was a secretary at the American Embassy, and he and his wife once gave a dinner for me to which they invited theatre people. Out of about twenty who were invited, ten answered, five accepted and one came. The one who came was Bulgakov, whose great play, *The Days of the Turbins*, was originally written in 1926 and later banned, but then had its ban lifted on Stalin's intervention when Bulgakov wanted to emigrate. If you read the Shostakovich autobiography you'll see that he and Bulgakov were almost the only people who could do no wrong, though they maybe had their knuckles rapped from time to time. It was astonishing how Bulgakov remained in favour, because within a year of my being in Moscow, nearly all those I had met there were banished, sent to the Gulags or murdered.

Again, I can't say that I felt the tension of the dictatorship. Obviously people were not going to talk about their secrets to a young English student who hardly spoke a word of Russian, but today, of course, we know that what went on was dreadful. Meyerhold's wife was murdered in the most horrible way, and he was then sent to Siberia and disappeared. He had been the greatest producer of them all.

In Russia I just caught the last scene of what was really the most fantastic array of theatre – the gipsy theatre, the children's theatre, the Vakhtangov theatre, the realist theatre, the Kamerny Jewish theatre, the Tairov theatre, the Stanislavsky theatre, and so on – the whole thing collapsing within a year. There were endless theatres with performances every night. You couldn't say that every production was a success, but each one had a startlingly good idea behind its staging. Ballet and opera, on the other hand, were done in a very traditional way indeed. I saw Ulanova dance in her prime. She had been away ill for over a year, and this was the night of her come-back. It was unforgettable. She took about twenty curtain calls with Stalin sitting there in his box.

Travel was extremely difficult. I ran into formidable opposition when I insisted on going to Novgorod. First they said there was no train, and when I discovered that there was one, they told me I couldn't get on it unless I had a certain ticket. When I said, 'All right, I'll go by car,' they said I couldn't because it was too expensive. In the end I went to the station and bought my own ticket, and they said at once that they were delighted for me to go so long as I took a guide with me. Naturally I said yes. Being very interested in Byzantine architecture, I saw all the

churches and the wonderful mosaics, the marvellous frescoes. I became fascinated by early Russian art and the icons of artists like Rublëv. It was all very formal, very unbaroque, very unsensational in a way. Someone like Rublëv transcended the formality and got such a marvellous sense of feeling into even those Russian icon faces. Nobody's ever done it as well since. But it also appealed to me because you must remember, it was the period of Art Deco in Europe and Art Deco is a very formal style.

When I went on to Peking, the journeys to the country, to the Ming tombs, were wonderful. I rode out on a pony across a plain with nothing, not even a path, and there was the marvellous avenue of animals and stone gods that you went through. Now it's just a highway. I would never want to go back. Peking was perfection then, an old Asian city. Now, I'm told, the walls have been pulled down and there are high-rise buildings.

Everything has changed so much. When I was first in Bali, I stayed in a little single-storey hotel – practically the only hotel in Bali. Now there's a Hilton and an Intercontinental. The beach I used to bathe on had one bungalow in which an American painter and his wife lived. Now there's a row of high-rise hotels. I also went to live with a Balinese family in the mountains, a wonderful experience, but you couldn't do it today. Similarly, I worked on a boat from Shanghai to Saigon as a steward, but that would be impossible now because of the unions. I never want to see those places again. Why should I?

I have often thought of writing a memoir of those times when I travelled across the whole of Russia and on to Burma, China, Japan, just before that entire world ended. The late Hamish Hamilton was constantly asking to do an autobiography. I sent him a few chapters, and he wrote back saying yes, it was getting on, but what they wanted was scandal. I said, 'If that's what you want, may I use your letter as an Introduction?' That rather ended it.

I was a conscientious objector during the Second World War, though if you ask me what I would have done if we had got the same sort of totalitarian régime in Britain as I had seen in Germany in the 1930s, I would have to tell you that I don't know. That was the question at my tribunal: if you saw your mother being attacked, would you be willing to defend her? My answer, of course, was yes, certainly, but I didn't think it correct for a government to tell me to take the life of someone I'd never met or who might have been one of my Munich friends, or an Austrian friend from Vienna. I felt very strongly about it. To be sent out willy-nilly by a government was something I just could not agree to, though I was determined to do something to help. Three or four nights a week I sat up on anti-aircraft watch in an old millhouse, but I

felt that farming was much more my thing because of my love of the country. When I had my tribunal they said, 'You must continue farming,' so I farmed in Wiltshire, literally for the duration from the war's first week. I loathed the idea of war. Was I right? Look at the outcome. Who are the richest countries in the world today? The vanquished.

I love the theatre, and still do, but I'm not a theatrical person. I'm very bad at coping with temperament on first nights. There was a lot of temperament on the first night of the *Trovatore* I did at Covent Garden, though that was not until after the war, in about 1949. My father had begged me not to do it. 'Derek,' he said, 'you're still too young for such an enormous proposition.' There were three hundred or so costumes and six or seven sets and it all had to be finished within about four weeks. 'Don't,' my father said, 'you'll be given another chance,' but I didn't take his advice and went ahead. It was a failure, as I realized.

Before the war, in 1937, I had designed the sets and costumes for a ballet for Freddie Ashton at Sadler's Wells. That was charming and quite a success. It was called *The Lord of Burleigh* and was done in a sort of Pre-Raphaelite way with music by Mendelssohn. Ashton was one of the wittiest, most human, lively and endearing of characters. His imitations, which he did even in the theatre, were marvellous, though I could never claim to have known him extremely well because I wasn't all that involved with the ballet world.

I also designed a play that had been an enormous success in Vienna. It was called *The Melody That Got Lost*, and in England it was certainly lost before it began. I never did anything else for the theatre. The seeds of my turning to painting and away from stage design were sown at an extraordinary meeting when I was in Paris. At an art school in London there had been a black model whom I once painted with a white towel over his shoulders. Lady Scarsdale happened to buy this painting, and it was seen by Edward Molyneux, who liked it so much that he asked whose work it was. Lady Scarsdale said, 'Oh, it's by a young English painter living in Paris.' One day in Paris my studio doorbell rang and a man stood there who said, 'You must wonder who I am. I'm Edward Molyneux, and I think you can paint. You must give up stage designing and take to painting. There are very few people who can do it, but you can. Every day my car takes me to the rue Royale to my business. Once it's taken me, it will take you wherever you like in Paris and you can go there to paint for the day. Whenever a picture's finished you can bring it to me, and I won't criticize it, but you can compare it with my collection.' I knew Molyneux's name because it was a name in Paris, like Schiaparelli or Chanel, and I'd worked for Schiaparelli; I even made masks for her in her shop.

Molyneux's collection included Renoirs, Cézannes, Corots, Manets.

It was one of the most beautifully chosen collections of Impressionist paintings ever. Much later he sold it to Paul Mellon's sister, and now there's an entire room in the National Gallery in Washington devoted to her collection. When I went to see it I nearly cried, because every picture was one that had taught me how to paint.

Both my mother and father died at the time when I was staying with Bernard Berenson at the Villa Tatti, and Berenson and Nicky Mariano became almost my substitute parents. I loved them both. Nicky was one of the most remarkable human beings I've ever met, one of the three great women in my life. Berenson himself I always found compassionate and generous. After all, I lived there more or less for five years, simply because he admired my painting and for no other reason. I stayed at his villa in the garden, for which I paid no rent. Naturally I paid the old couple who looked after me, and I paid my electricity and so on, but I was virtually his guest, and then Yehudi Menuhin followed after me. I only knew BB when, I suppose, he was eighty-four, and he died about ten years later at ninety-four. So he was at the end of his life and I can't speak of him in his earlier years.

I certainly never detected any untruthfulness in him, even if he wasn't always correct in his judgements. I'm absolutely convinced, though, that he would never have made an attribution falsely for the sake of gain. The whole story of his row with Duveen was because he refused to recognize the Allendale 'Adoration of the Shepherds' as a Giorgioni. If he had done, Duveen could have clinched a deal with Mellon, who was anxious to possess a Giorgioni. The deal fell through, much to Duveen's chagrin. Berenson had integrity, and while he did make a good bit out of attributions and opinions, hardly anyone before him had given such opinions on paintings. He created the list of pictures for a whole important period, and some attributions were right and some were wrong. If he sold a great picture to Mrs Gardner in Boston, say, then maybe she did slip him something privately for getting it for her. Maybe Duveen or whoever the dealer was did slip him something for putting business their way so that he made two commissions. But when all is said and done, look at how he used his gains. He formed one of the greatest art libraries in the world, used his money to buy great works of art and left Tatti and all it contained to Harvard University.

At the end of his life it became very touching because the thing he really loved was gazing at the Roman pines or the cypresses against the sunset. When we walked in his little garden, he would build a miniature dam across the stream before all at once letting out the water and saying, 'Think how Leonardo would love to have been with us now.' It wasn't done as an affectation; it was quite genuine. His bitter complaint about other art historians was that of course they wished to date the birth of someone like Giovanni di Rimini or some other obscure painter, but

none of them would ever want to pick up a piece of wood or stone simply because they enjoyed the feel of it or liked its shape.

The reason why I went to live in Ireland thirty years ago was that it simply happened that I saw the house in County Wexford and said, 'That's the house I'd like to live in.' I like remote places, especially islands. Every year I still go to my little hut, ten feet by nine on the top of a cliff on Tory Island off the coast of Donegal – no electricity, no water, only a small gas ring. I have to carry every drop of water about half a mile in buckets every two days from the lighthouse.

I love solitude, and when I'm on Tory Island I can get up and paint when the sun gets up at about half-past five or even earlier. In the middle of the day I read, write, rest or go back to sleep for a bit, then paint again in the evenings. I'm totally happy there. I try to make it a rule to be alone several hours every day wherever I am. Certainly there are periods in the year when I want to be alone, as when I go to Tory Island or do one of my pilgrimages to Mount Athos. Essentially I am a loner, which is why I'm so seldom in London, but I am also gregarious in the sense that when I do come to London I like meeting my many friends to whom I'm devoted.

I see no end to the difficulties in Ireland at the moment. The whole agony is based on a myth that Southern Ireland wants Northern Ireland. If any politician in the Republic was given the North tomorrow, he'd put his head in a gas oven, because they haven't the resources to govern it, pay for the National Health and all those things. The idea of Ireland for the Irish is perfectly understandable, especially if you're a young man in the South with no job. You can be paid to be in the Provisional IRA and it provides a moment of glory and adventure. I understand it, but it has no practicality. I've never suffered personally. The Irish have been incredibly nice to me, and touch wood, I've never met any nastiness at all.

I knew Mountbatten in Ireland, but my links with him went right back to my childhood when I was about eight and my parents bought the Dower House at Romsey. Above it stood Broadlands, built by the first Lord Palmerston, and we could see its towers – very early Gothic revival – from our house in the valley. We lived there all the time I was growing up, and Mountbatten was always kind and friendly to me. Later on he helped with and came to my exhibitions. Once he decided he was going to help you, then the whole of that fantastic Mountbatten machinery would be turned on on your behalf.

I painted him later in Ireland, and it's a picture I'm devoted to. I told him, 'I'm not going to depict you as the great leader, I'm going to show you in a fisherman's jersey, which is how I see you now in Donegal. If you want medals, you can get them and pin them on the picture

yourself, because I won't paint them. I'm going to paint you as a human being.'

Mountbatten was a very moving person, I found. He told me once that he had only had two great friends in his life, that they were both dead and there was only his family left. I think that was true. He was a lonely figure in a way, but proud of being part of the royal family, and that seemed to cover up a sort of inner anxiety he always felt which had started with his father, in the First World War, being attacked as a German. That affected him terribly. It was a motivating force behind his personality – to overcome that feeling of inferiority at the beginning of his life. Perhaps it was what made him the opposite later on, but I always found him human. He wasn't someone who was interested in small talk, but he was in personalities. If he inspired hate as well as love, that was because he was such a success. I'm afraid it's rather an English thing that when people get on top there's a great wish to pull them down again.

Prince Charles I've painted twice, and he sometimes asks advice about his own paintings. I've painted with him twice as well, I think. He does watercolours while I do oils. I can't do watercolours and I don't think he would be so good at oils, but he is very good at watercolours. He gets the feeling of the place, and it gives him enormous pleasure, which is the chief thing. Obviously I don't like every building that he likes or dislike everything he dislikes, but the great thing about him is that he cares about what he says and thinks. He minds terribly, and if one day he's king, then he won't be able to say these things any more.

When I first painted him he was nineteen. He came in one morning looking very cross and I asked, 'Sir, what is it?' He said, 'I've just learned this morning that the people who make damask linen have destroyed the wooden blocks used to make it with.' For a boy of nineteen in his world really to mind about such a thing was, I thought, extraordinary. I've never forgotten it. He doesn't seem to fit into the normal pattern of royalty, and at the same time he has this extramural sense of caring and minding. He really does mind about forests in Brazil being burned, and you can often see his worried look and concern. That's what I admire. Some may call it eccentric, but it wouldn't be eccentric in anyone else. He just happens to be royal. He has also enjoyed himself in lots of ways, and now has become interested in the opinions of elderly people, like Laurens van der Post, whose portrait I painted for him.

A lot of people say I'm a society portrait painter, but nothing could be farther from the truth. I could never be that because I could never flatter. I'm sometimes asked why I do more men than women, and the main reason is because they're heads of colleges, heads of businesses,

clergymen or whatever. I've painted three prime ministers, a lot of bishops and maybe nine or ten OMs, all of them men. A portrait of a beautiful woman is much more likely to be intended to go over the fireplace in the drawing room, and that is something I'm less attuned to than painting men from the business world.

I've no idea how to flatter. I can paint charm in a woman, but there is almost always one problem in particular with women aged between forty and sixty. They don't like having wrinkles, they want to be made to look absolutely their best as if they were ten or twenty years younger, and I don't know how to do it. In America I was once asked to paint a lady of about sixty who was a much-loved grandmother. She had blue hair and was very good looking, but naturally she had wrinkles. I thought, I must put her against the light, then we won't get so many wrinkles. Therefore I placed her in her conservatory with a green background and the light behind her. After about two days I asked her if she would like to look and see how it was beginning. She said, 'Derek, I think it's just the saddest thing I ever saw.' So I asked her, 'What would you like it to look like?' and she showed me a photograph of a friend sitting on some sort of sofa and got up like the Queen of Sheba waiting for Solomon in a pink-satin evening dress, covered in diamonds, bracelets and necklaces. I said, 'If you gave me two million dollars I couldn't do that. Let's call it a day. I've done this sketch of you and there we are.' I took it away and the cousin of the lady, with whom I was staying, kept it. Now it's above the fireplace in the son's house, and they absolutely adore it.

Freddie Ashton didn't like the portrait he asked me to do of him, but later in life he said, 'Oh, Derek, if only I'd bought that picture.' Portraits can, of course, be so disliked that they get destroyed, but such acts seem to be motivated more often by vanity than spite. The Sutherland Churchill portrait was disapproved of, I thought, only by Lady Churchill, but apparently he didn't like it either and that was why she had it done away with.

One portrait I did of a famous person, thought to have been destroyed because the sitter didn't like it, was given to an art student so the frame shouldn't be wasted. Obviously one does mind when something like that happens. On another occasion, Nancy Mitford helped in the process when she suggested that a head I did of an old lady in Paris ought to be burned, it was so unflattering. And burned it was. It was put into the fire one Christmas Day. I minded that very much because it was one of the strongest oil sketches of a figure – like a Goya – that I'd ever achieved. Nancy herself didn't do the burning, but she treated the incident as a joke and couldn't see I'd be hurt. She sent me a Christmas card with a match inside and 'Love from Savonarola' written in it.

There was, by contrast, the young Italian labourer whose mother cut

up my portrait of him to patch his trousers because I'd used such good linen. I was riveted and fascinated by that story, completely bowled over by the total openness and honesty behind it. When I told old Berenson, he was flabbergasted and said, 'Derek, it's incredible to think, after what you've told me, that any pictures ever survived from the past.'

Properly helpful criticism can happen in the most unexpected ways. Someone who you think knows nothing about painting may look at a picture and say, 'Yes, but shouldn't the shadow go across that road? It would join up the two sides of the picture.' It may be a thing you'd never notice yourself, but then you see it as absolutely right and alter it. Every picture worth its salt has an abstract base, the abstract quality being like the bones of a human body. On the bones you put the flesh; on the flesh you put the clothes; over the clothes you put the make-up. The fundamental bones at the bottom of a picture are what make it a success. I've recently done a big landscape from drawings of Mount Athos, and I still go on painting it because there are little things that I come to realize. The process can go on for ages. Very often I want to alter portraits years after I finished them.

I think of myself as equally a landscapist and a portraitist. I am interested in people, but as a bit of a loner I also love landscape and being in the country, though again, I do love the contrast between town and country. It's like my Bauhaus education in Munich. What I mean is that if I went to a place like Deauville, which probably I wouldn't, I'd like to stay in a very good hotel, but if I go to somewhere in the middle of Turkey to look at a mosque, I don't mind if the sheets haven't been changed since last season.

I see my work as a portrait painter as quick and immediate, hoping to catch the fleeting moment, though a reciprocal feeling with the sitter is just as important. With the fleeting moment, though, you have in a way to take in the norm as well. It's like painting a cloud in a landscape. By the time you've painted the cloud, it's no longer there. It's the same with a mouth. The mouth gives expression to the face. Seamus Heaney, whom I painted recently, was very amused when I told him, 'Your mouth isn't a physical feature, it's an expression.' He wrote a little poem about it, which was charming of him. But the mouth is the thing that moves. You may protest, 'But the eyes move too.' Not to the same extent. The eyes, the nose, the chin are all more or less physical features, but the mouth is an expression. Therefore whenever someone says there's something not quite right about the mouth, it's because that person may never before have seen that particular fleeting second of an expression.

Every now and then you do get a block when you come to paint a

particular individual and find you can't, but I've sometimes managed to get over it. When I painted Christopher Hill, the Oxford historian and Master of Balliol, I went through torments for about three or four days. I felt I hadn't got him, or into him, or anything. Suddenly it worked one day, and he said to me, smiling, 'Oh, Derek, I'm so sorry because I loved the look of agony on your face.'

I never make a sitter talk. It's the sitters who usually want to talk to me. I don't instigate what they say, but I like them to talk and prefer them not to sit like dumb images. For that reason, I don't approve of painting portraits from photographs. It's too easy. I might take a photograph to get the way of their shoulders if they're leaning against a certain piece of furniture, but I would never do a face or head from a photograph because, in my view, it takes two to make a portrait. When I painted you, I felt there was a fundamental attachment between us, as people and as human beings. That is something I have to feel with my sitters, the talking being a part of it.

Talking never diverts my concentration in the slightest. In Ireland I quite often give, not paid lessons in portrait painting, but lectures in Londonderry, that unhappy city; I feel I owe them something for the horrors they've been through. I speak to fifty or sixty people and paint a portrait of one of them, talking away the entire time as I demonstrate what I'm doing and why.

I've only once painted the portrait of an entirely silent figure: a character who was a sad young boy, a grandson of friends. He later, alas, committed suicide, and I won't say who he was because it is still a torture for his family. But he was told to sit, he sat, and there was absolutely no reflection between us of any description. I thought the picture showed it, yet it is a portrait the family love and see as a part of him.

As for the distinction between painted portraits and photographs, it always seems to me that some of today's photographers are great artists and I never know why people always want paintings rather than photographs. Photographs are, as such, often just as good. Even so – perhaps I'm very lucky – I feel that I do get closer to the subject in a painted portrait than most photographs would. I also think that the earliest photographs have perhaps never been bettered: those of Octavius Hill and others of his period. In the Scottish National Portrait Gallery in Edinburgh there are folios of Octavius Hill portrait photographs, and they are like the most marvellous monotypes, etchings or drawings – exquisitely beautiful works of art.

Of course, one of the problems for a portrait painter today is that people have less time to give to sit. For a member of the royal family, for instance, you are allowed about four sittings, and then the rest does have to be done from photographs. William Coldstream, a painter I

much admire, sometimes used to hold sixty sittings before a sitter was even permitted to look at the portrait.

How indeed do you price a painting, with all these variables coming into play? You've hit on something very difficult. Normally I hardly ever sell my paintings. I even buy back my landscapes when they come up at Sotheby's or Christie's. When I do pictures of business people or heads of colleges, I charge what I think is a correct price, though if they're great friends, I charge very little. I don't think of it as a commercial proposition in any sense. I make enough, certainly, but I never accept a commission until a portrait's finished. Afterwards, if it's liked, it can be bought like any other picture. I never feel it's fair that someone should commission a painting and then, if they don't like it, have to pay the full price for it. That is wrong. If you go into a shop and don't like something, you can change it. It wouldn't please me to know that someone who had a portrait by me had put it in the loo, saying, 'We can't bear it but we had to buy it, it's by Derek Hill.'

I would say that every picture by another artist that I've collected tells me something as a painter. I've collected things from Landseer oils to Picasso etchings – Picasso paintings, of course, I couldn't afford. But for the first Landseer I bought I paid £20 or £25. One of my Landseer's was a picture of a dead pheasant that I have since given to Ireland. There's nothing I hate more than a dead pheasant in life, for reasons I have told you, but the quality of this Landseer was so extraordinary that it gave me something as quality of paint.

I've never collected anything because I thought it was fashionable. Nothing was less fashionable than Landseer when I bought mine. I also bought a little Henry Moore statue for £25 in the early 1940s, when he was hardly known. I happened to like it; it said something to me. Every picture I've bought has had to say something to me as a painter. There has to be something in the quality of the painting which perhaps touches my own work and is the reason I like it.

Brushwork is to me, as a painter, of the utmost importance – the actual quality of the paint. As in Frans Hals. The 'handwriting' of his brushwork on a piece of material, whether it's a ruff, a sleeve or a shawl, is miraculous, as is the quality of his hands. Even the great Velázquez, whom I admire enormously, was inclined to hide hands with a fan or a piece of material, perhaps because he didn't much relish painting them. But the hands of some painters – Signorelli's certainly, and those of Frans Hals – are triumphs one never forgets.

The painters whose work I've most admired have been Piero della Francesca and Masaccio from the early years of painting, Rembrandt, and then, more recently, Corot, Cézanne and Manet. Seurat I admire enormously for the underlying abstract qualities in his work, and today

I admire a lot of Picasso. In every period he produced one or more masterpieces. Perhaps a lot of water flowed in between, but he was a very great painter. Even old Berenson used to say Picasso was probably the greatest draughtsman since Raphael.

There can also be a certain clumsiness in painting which is often extremely attractive. For instance, Roger Hilton, a painter whom Gray Gowrie so much admires, has a mass of clumsiness in his painting, yet Gray thinks he's one of the greatest painters in England this century. I am not so sure, but I see what he means. When painters are too correct in everything, they can lose a lot of their mysterious technical quality.

I think of myself as a classical more than a romantic painter. I admired Cubist painting enormously, and that is very classical painting. The severity of the classical in art is something very important to me as a painter, whereas Claude – and this is not to decry Claude – means less to me. Among modern Italians I particularly admired Morandi, who had a sense of static beauty in his pictures. You may protest that he was a bore, that all he painted was bottles, but just look at those bottles. When I used to go and see him he would say, 'Derek, these bottles are like a ballet. I make them dance and suddenly I say stop and then I paint them.'

I first heard about him because someone I knew during the war occasionally used to take out paints to him in Italy. Then, when I went to Berenson's, I visited him in Bologna and we became friends. He was an enchanting man, like a monk, with a row of frightfully bad teeth. He had a charming smile and grin, and he led one of the most unworldly lives I've ever met with in a human being. His studio lay through his two sisters' bedroom, and he hardly ever moved away from Bologna. I'm not sure that he ever had been abroad, and he couldn't have cared less about money. He let his dealer have his pictures for almost nothing, knowing full well that the dealer would make millions out of them eventually.

You ask me how I assess Francis Bacon. I think that Bacon does, sadly, epitomize what we go through in the world today. No other painter shows the underlying horror and haunted feeling of what goes on with drugs and crime. His early paintings were marvellous technically – the actual paint quality, the construction. I feel, though, that he has brilliant ideas for a picture, puts it on canvas rapidly – slashes it on – I don't mean in a bad sense – but then very often doesn't compose the rest of the picture so well.

Lucian Freud is another painter who is very able indeed, a great painter really. I especially like his early ones, done in a very Germanic, very precise style. Some of his more recent pictures are also frightfully good and have a truth to them. Truth in painting means a sort of fleeting moment of poetry, if that doesn't sound pretentious. '*Versuchen die*

Wahrheit,' as they say in Germany. Truth is always being looked for in a way. No, unfortunately I wouldn't consider that the truth you see in a Francis Bacon painting is any sort of exaggeration. Anything you see in a Bacon happens every day in every capital of the world.

Love can inspire an artist, yes, but if you are an artist you find beauty in anything – in any human being, male or female, in an animal, whatever. So far as lust as a driving force goes, Caravaggio, for instance, was notorious for his loose behaviour. I don't terribly like the man or his period, but he was one of the truly great artists of his day. I don't myself fit into the carousing category. I've never liked drinking, I don't enjoy debauchery, and now I'm too old for it anyway. When I was in Munich I used to enjoy going out occasionally, and I suppose I have enjoyed sowing a certain amount of wild oats, but it never impinged on my painting, which is the chief thing in my life. Perhaps it impinged too little and I don't get nearly enough passion into my pictures. Perhaps they are too static. I've probably missed out on something. Perhaps I'm a frigid character and that's why I like this abstraction at the base of my paintings.

The reason why men in general so often prefer to be with other men is probably an extension of the public school thing. It's not necessarily in the slightest bit sexual. The public schools are in a way forerunners of men's clubs. I use a man's club – the club I belong to in Ireland – simply to get away. It's like a sort of banishment for a bit, but personally I love the company of women. I find them extremely attractive – I'm not talking here of pretty scatter-brained blondes – and I'm fond of them and feel that I'm very often stimulated by them. Many of my greatest friends have been women. The three great women in my life have been Nicky Mariano, who was like a second mother to me, Kathleen Ferrier, the singer, and above all Evie Hone, the stained-glass artist. I was also devoted to the writers Elizabeth Bowen and Rosamund Lehmann and others.

The fact that I never married was not a conscious decision at all. It simply never happened. When my much-loved old aunt was dying and I went to see her, she said, 'Derek, will you promise me one thing?' I said, 'Yes. What?' She said, 'That you'll never marry.' When I asked her, 'Why, why?' she replied, 'Because you'd be such hell to live with.'

There were three people I would love to have married, two of whom are still alive. One I wanted to marry, but I don't think she wanted to marry me. She married one of my best friends, who wrote and asked would I mind if he married her. Naturally I couldn't say, 'Yes, I would mind,' because that would have been horrid. Another was a great friend, but she would have been impossible to marry because she loathed

anything to do with the house or housework. She was an artist and a very remarkable one. The third, I'm afraid, I simply missed.

It's probably true to say that, if I had really ever been down and out and had needed to earn my living as an artist purely, then I might have been a much better painter. On the other hand, perhaps it's selfish of me, but I do think that a painter must paint for himself before he paints for anyone else, for the public or whoever. It has been a privilege for me to be able to do that, but privilege is for me a very interesting subject.

When I was seventeen or eighteen I attended one of the great operatic productions in the whole of this century: Toscanini's *Falstaff*, in Salzburg. I realized then that it was a privilege to be there, and that privilege isn't to do with class, grandeur or snobbishness. Privilege is something like hearing Backhaus play a Beethoven concerto or Callas sing in *Traviata*, or being allowed to spend the night, as I once was, in the Taj Mahal, and to see that incredible building at sunset, during the night with the moon, and at sunrise in the morning. I have had a very privileged life from that point of view. Not in a worldly sense at all, but just having the incredible luck to have seen and heard so many extraordinary moments, like Pavlova dancing or Melba singing, as I did when I was a child. That is what I call privilege.

As I get older I feel that I get less religious in the sense that the external things of religion matter less to me, whereas the internal things, which have nothing to do with such forms of outward show as going to church, matter more. Emily Dickinson once wrote a very beautiful thing: a letter to a friend who had lost both her sons. Never forget, she said, that we below can never be alone again with the thronged heaven above us. I always thought that such a beautiful remark, and it has something in it. I feel that the people I've lost whom I loved in life are there, looking after me in an odd sort of way. I can't explain it. How can one explain these things?

If I were ever to be banished to Siberia, and they said I could take just one of the world's great paintings with me, I think it would probably be Piero della Francesca's *Resurrection*. It shows a figure of great majesty, rising out of a tomb into another world – a vision of ethereal sensitivity.

PROFESSOR STANLEY HOFFMANN

Stanley Hoffmann is a political scientist and has been professor of government at Harvard since 1963. He was born in Vienna in 1928 but lived in France and graduated from the Institut d'Études Politiques. He received his doctorate from the Paris Law School in 1959 and two years later he emigrated to the United States where he was naturalized in 1960. He has written several books including *The State of War* (1965), *Gulliver's Troubles* (1958), *Primacy or World Order* (1978), *Janus and Minerva* (1986) and *The Mitterrand Experiment* (co-author, 1986). Since 1969 he has been chairman of the American Center for European Studies.

You lived in France as a child and your education was French. Did you, do you feel French?

Yes. Less than I did ten or twenty years ago, because time passes and I don't have that much leisure to go back. And in recent years my work has been much more in international relations, largely because international relations is a full-time job these days and frankly many more students are interested in international politics than in those of France. I'm not a historian, but a political scientist, and in political science the number of people interested in France is very limited in America for the time being. Basically I still feel at home in France and have most of my friends there, but French politics and intellectual life have known more exciting periods than the present. I was much more *engagé* in the 1960s than I've been in the 1980s.

What effect did barely knowing your father have on you as a boy and later in life?

I don't know. It is extremely difficult to talk about a negative. Undoubtedly it had a profound effect, but I can't really say how profound since I don't know what I missed. I wasn't aware of missing my father. I didn't have many friends when I was a child, and the few I had either had no fathers or else my impression was that relations between their parents were pretty awful.

How did you manage to avoid the attention of the Gestapo and the Milice during the war period?

It was complicated because my mother and I were not Jews. She had converted, and I was baptized a Protestant, so most people had no idea of whether we were Jews or not. What people did know was that we

were foreigners, and that was just as bad. If you were Austrian in 1940–3 it meant that, at the time of the Anschluss, you had refused to become a German citizen. The danger was always much more from xenophobia than from anti-Semitism because nobody could have proved we were Jews. The answer is really that we were in Nice, and Nice was first Vichy, then Italian, and the Nazis didn't come until September 1943 after the Italians dropped out of the war. We stayed for three more months, and I had wanted to stay because I was in the last year of high school. But my best friend was arrested and never came back, and after three months of hearing of so-and-so being arrested and so on, my nerves just gave in. We spent the last nine months or so of the occupation in a small village we knew near Montpellier. What we didn't know until after we got there was that there were by then as many German soldiers of my age as there were French peasants and shopkeepers. But the soldiers turned out to be perfectly harmless, and there was no Gestapo. In a sense it seems amusing to have felt secure among a thousand German soldiers, but one certainly felt more secure than in Nice, because there was no police.

You have said that you owe to the period between 1938 and 1944 'all my convictions about human nature, the fragility of the political order and the resilience of societies'.

Watching something like the collapse of the Third Republic, then the collapse of Vichy and the descent into quasi civil war in France at the end, was quite an education. Also, all of my mother's relatives who had lived in Vienna till the Anschluss came through Paris on their way out in 1938, 1939, and that taught one a lot about the fragility of political régimes. And society! What I thought was extraordinary was the way in which, despite all those shocks, people and public services just went on. French society managed to survive the switches from the Third Republic to Vichy to a fascist period to the very effervescent turmoil of the liberation, and in fact got rejuvenated as a result.

That has always made me sceptical, and I may have had that in mind when I wrote what you quote. Americans in particular tend to overestimate the success of totalitarian régimes in changing societies fundamentally. They can cow them, intimidate them, repress them, oblige people to live a sort of double bookkeeping and lies, but the idea that totalitarianism reduces people to atoms and destroys all social institutions strikes me as a bad guide for understanding what actually goes on. It seems to me that somehow society, compressed and repressed, goes on living. It's not entirely reassuring, by the way. It's reassuring if you think of the limits of totalitarianism, but it also means

that societies are extraordinarily plastic and can follow one leader one day, another the next, with amazing and sometimes frightening speed.

In the same article, of the Nazi–Soviet pact of 1939 you wrote that, when the news broke, 'Britain and France could no longer weasel out.' It is a phrase that might offend a European, especially as it comes from someone born in Austria who later became an American citizen. Why did you use it?

Because I'm not in agreement with appeasement and am very much annoyed at the whole trend of historical literature, mainly British, which is now rehabilitating appeasement. Paul Kennedy is one example. I'm struck by all the volumes that have come out, essentially explaining that the poor British really had no choice and Munich wasn't so bad a calculation after all; that Britain was in decline and over-committed, so what else could she do? The French, after all, had an alliance with Czechoslovakia and were much worse off after Czechoslovakia was destroyed than they were before, so it seems to me, as I've written elsewhere, that the Americans and the Soviets were just as guilty of appeasement as the British and French. There's enough blame to distribute all around. But in the particular instance of Poland, Britain and France were on the first line. They were the ones who had to decide whether to go to war or not.

You have said it was the Ionesco play Rhinoceros *that best encapsulated for you the way so many people were transformed into monsters. Why were so many transformed in this way?*

It wasn't so much the transformation into monsters that I had in mind as a refusal to recognize what was going on in the beginning at the start of the play, when people find there's nothing special about seeing a rhinoceros in the street, and all they argue about is whether it's an Asian or an African rhinoceros. It's called the shock of non-recognition, and the British, I think, were particularly good at it. The French knew more or less what they were dealing with, but they were afraid, and that's a different problem. The British refusal to see that the Hitler phenomenon in the 1930s was something radically different from anything they had dealt with in the past continues to strike me as amazing.

I recently read the memoirs of Felix Gilbert, the historian, and he has some interesting pages about how he went as a refugee to England in the late 1930s and found it unbearable. He would explain what was happening in Germany and people would be very nice, very empathetic, then essentially behave as if it couldn't be quite as bad as that. That is what I had in mind: the refusal to see that there was something quite new which might shake everybody up, and therefore that any attempt at dealing with it by such traditional methods as compromise, bargaining

and appealing to the man's good feelings was doomed. I don't think everybody turned into a monster, thank goodness, but many had too much understanding for the monster and started explaining: 'What else could he do? He has good reasons. And look how awful our régime is.' There was not so much identification with the aggressor as too much willingness to give him the benefit of the doubt.

But what could *the British have done? Neither they nor the French were prepared militarily.*

In the early 1930s, neither was Germany. Up to Munich the German army was not in very good shape. At the time of Munich, the German military commanders were very unwilling to risk war. They didn't think they could win. It seems to me that, at the time of the Rhineland, Hitler could still have been stopped without very much damage to anyone. I think 1936 was really the turning point.

You have said that Catholics probably made up the biggest part of the resistance, along with the communists, and that it took people with faith to flight against the Nazi faith. Did you have faith yourself?

No – in the sense that I was neither a Catholic nor a communist. I've never been much of an ideologue, and I'm certainly not a religious person. Yes – in the sense that if I asked myself whether I ever believed this would end badly, I always thought, to use the famous cliché, that there was light at the end of the tunnel. I don't think I ever thought otherwise, probably because I was a child. Children have blind faith that everything will be all right: the Allies would win the war and things could not but go up. The darkest moments were immediately after the Japanese entered the war, when they started conquering Singapore. But I don't think I ever doubted for a minute that we would survive and the Allies would win. Though maybe if you had asked me whether I thought so in those couple of weeks before we left Nice in the dark in December 1943, after that friend of mine had been arrested, I'm not so sure. I was worried more about personal survival than the outcome, but by then it was clear that the Germans had lost.

Why exactly did you leave France?

I left France in 1955 out of choice. Frankly I did it only for career reasons. I will try to spare you the complications of French Law, but I had planned, like all my classmates and friends, to become a civil servant. But the French have a law that says that, if you are a naturalized citizen, you cannot become a civil servant for five years, and the minute you enter the *école d'administration* by *concours* – by competitive exams – you

are a civil servant. So, after graduating, I had to wait five years, and during those years I got myself a doctorate in law, came here as a visiting graduate student for a year, and thought, for academic reasons, not for others, that this was wonderful. When I got back to France I was all set to take the competitive exam to the *école d'administration*, but then discovered they had changed the deadline for applications. They had advanced it. I would have had to wait another year.

In a sense it came as a blessing. During my year in America I had really concluded that I didn't want to be a civil servant but wanted to teach. Then the question became what and where. In France, my doctorate being in law, I would have had to become a law professor, again by competitive exam. And it so happened that I wasn't interested in law, or not, at least, in most aspects of law, and that the milieu of the competition for law exams was absolutely dismal. They were the dullest people I've ever had anything to do with. So when Harvard had the good idea of asking me to come back and teach, I came.

Do you feel fully assimilated into American life?

No. After all, I don't live in America. I live in Cambridge, Massachusetts. I'm saying not that Cambridge isn't America but that it is a small corner of America which is very cosmopolitan and, in some ways, closer to Europe and untypical. I was in southern California last week, and my impression is that there is a bigger cultural difference between there and here than there is between here and Paris. It has something to do with distance, with space, with people's concerns. The biggest cultural difference is probably the lack of historical baggage. I am sure there is some, but people don't carry it the way the Europeans carry history.

I don't feel terribly American, and if you ask my American friends or colleagues whether they look on me as an American, they'll probably say no. It's not tangible. I can only answer with impressions and anecdotes. I have a very brilliant colleague, now a dean, who to me is the quintessence of America: immensely bright, unbelievably hardworking, full of energy, a specialist in European politics. He was chairman of my department for several years and was always deeply uncomfortable with me, even though he knew I was supportive and helpful and so on. I think it's because there was something wonderfully, humourlessly straight about him, and I'm rather on the sardonic side. I like making fun of things and don't obey the rules in meetings. I interrupt or deflate people, or make jokes because most meetings are so deadly that, if nobody's there to crack jokes, who would survive them? But you don't do that with Americans. It's a matter of cultural style, and my style is French, there's no doubt about it.

You've sometimes seemed to suggest that much is to be learned from both

individual and national psychology. Do whole nations really have psychological stances of a sort on which policies and decisions can be based?

I'm not a great believer in national character, but I do think that there are styles, combinations of beliefs and ways of doing things that differ from one country to another and which one has to note. The French don't look at the world in foreign policy the way Americans do. The two countries are fascinating because you are dealing with two melting pots. Both have a sense of mission, yet neither understands the other. So I do think there are differences. The word character is not the one I would use; I would say style and beliefs. Character is profoundly individual and you find individuals of every possible character in every nation. But there are national ways of doing things which then shape expectations and behaviour. The French civil service and the American civil service have very little in common, for instance. American ideology has to do with democracy, liberalism, progress, but you don't really find the same consensus in France because the French are always divided on all sorts of things. There is very little division in America, except at traumatic moments like Vietnam, and afterwards it disappears again.

You obviously admire America and its institutions.

Not all of them. I'm not an admirer of American society. I admire some of the institutions. The universities, for example, I think are extraordinary. I admire the American enthusiasm for learning and the really extraordinary capacity for assimilation which continues. That is why I'm not terribly worried about the hispanization of America, since I'm sure these people will be absorbed the way the Irish, the Poles and the Italians have been. But I do not admire the callousness and the complacency that most Americans have about things like poverty, misery, social security issues. The indifference to homelessness is appalling, quite extraordinary.

I don't admire American politics very much either. Americans have a profound hostility to the idea that there are some problems only the state can solve. They still have this belief that everything can be solved by what Mr Bush calls a thousand points of light, by voluntary co-operation. That's just not true. It's very striking to Europeans who come here: the neglect of so many problems that are simply swept under the rug on the assumption that a dose of economic growth will take care of them all. No, I'm not an unmitigated admirer of American society.

How do American universities compare with French ones?

French universities are a disaster. Thousands and thousands of students are parked and weeded at the end of the first year by anonymous exams

which throw half of them out. It was a system built for a very small number of higher-education students that has not been well adapted to the age of mass education. They're underadministered, underpaid, underorganized; the libraries are in dreadful condition; and as long as they continue to have a separation between other institutions and the *grandes écoles*, which are indeed very good but deal with something like two per cent of the higher-education population and are highly vocational, it will remain the same. They're a little bit like Harvard Law School or Medical School. They train élites for élite positions while ninety-eight per cent are in these enormous parking lots known as universities. As long as you have that separation, you're not going to get a good system, and there is still an enormous resistance to change, to making them more competitive with one another, giving them more autonomy or, above all, giving them more money, because basically people don't trust them.

Americans perhaps measure success more in terms of material wealth than any other nation. Isn't there a danger in this of cultural, spiritual and even moral standards being sacrificed?

I wish I were convinced it was a uniquely American phenomenon these days. My impression is that it has become rather widespread too in the prosperous Europe which has emerged since the 1960s. On the other hand, one tends to exaggerate the degree to which intellectual achievements are not respected in America. American intellectuals are not paid, that's for sure, but they have concocted a myth that they are victims compared with European intellectuals, and I don't think it's true. There are different definitions of intellectuals. Certainly the French have a whole tradition of intellectuals as the conscience of the nation, but while the Americans would never take a Sartre seriously as a political guru, they would take him seriously as a philosopher. The notion that Americans dislike, distrust or don't take their intellectuals seriously is wrong. They don't pay them, but, you know, my French colleagues are no better paid than I am.

American business allows a greater degree of flexibility than the European when it comes to fast practices. As a common example within existing law, a man can bankrupt himself, cause misery to small investors and re-emerge six months later without loss of stature. Can that be justified?

I don't think it can be justified, but what I'm not sure of is whether it couldn't be true in Europe too. American business practices are often quite scandalous, but there is a reaction. How successful it will be remains to be seen. Americans may sound very naïve, but they plan to introduce and teach ethics in business schools, and that is new. For

instance, somebody left a huge sum of money to the Harvard Business School – $30 million, I think – so the future leaders of American business will know something about ethics. The interesting thing about this country is that, whenever you have a great excess in any direction, there will be a reaction. The reaction may not be equal to the excess, but you can always count on self-examination and on some people doing something about it.

That's certainly one of the biggest differences from France, where people rely on the state. Sometimes that's fine where only the state can do something, for people couldn't voluntarily organize something like the French social security system. On the other hand, one shouldn't expect people in France to get together and take big initiatives to solve anything, because they don't do it. Even when they do, the funny thing is that they expect a subsidy from the state. But in America you can expect people to get together and say, 'We must do something about this.' It isn't always successful, but they do it. There's a habit of collective self-reliance, which is quite different, and that is one of the good aspects of America.

The American dream comes true in so far as any individual, irrespective of birth or origin, can attain greater heights than anywhere else in the world, but has that dream on the whole brought happiness?

Depends on what you mean by happiness. Happiness is certainly in part a product of one's social success or standing, but it's also a problem of individual character and individual life; and many people are miserable for reasons to do with private life. I was struck, again when I was in southern California, by the degree of middle-class opulence. But New York at this point is a pretty depressing place, as are parts of Boston. Everything in America pertaining to blacks, and relations between blacks and whites, is a very depressing story. In that respect the legacy and the weight of slavery and of discrimination are enormous. My field of study is not American society, but it is very clear that in many parts of the country black society has completely broken down. Those blacks who would like to do what the Jews and now the Asians are doing, are seen by their fellow blacks as traitors. It reminds me, in some way, of the European working class at the end of the nineteenth century, in the sense that individual success is betrayal and the successful feel guilty if they leave their class behind and become middle class. Asians do not feel this at all, because there the ethos is individual success.

Is it true to say that American women have, in taking over more leading roles, tended to emulate men at the expense of their own gender and lost much of their identity?

No. It is very difficult to generalize about anything American. It may be true of some, but it isn't true of others. There are lots of women in America who are indeed feminists, who have achieved positions they didn't have before, whether in universities, which were not very open to women at the teaching level, or in politics, or in business, and who seem to me not to have given up anything. They have now acceded to positions that men used to have, but they haven't been defeminized in the process.

Have the feminists achieved their goal? First of all, I'm not sure they were united about their goal. As far as I can see, there is a big split in the American feminist movement. But it is true that this was a very male society in which lots of positions were closed to women and they have certainly, slowly, achieved something. If you take a university like Harvard, the proportion of women on the faculty remains very small, and it's not through lack of talent. Discrimination takes complicated forms in academia, as you may imagine. No academic will ever recognize that he is sexist or a discriminator. The tendency is to apply to women standards which are harder than those one applies to men. Unconsciously, not deliberately. Plus the tendency to like only certain kinds of women: those who are very feminine, those who play the old game of being charming and friendly and who smile. If a woman is tough, aggressive and too intelligent, there will be quite a reaction.

Hasn't the law reached a stage in America where it almost favours women?

I wouldn't say that. Both in respect to minorities and to women, what the law says is that you must make an extra effort; that there are intelligent people out there and you must make more of an effort to find them. I think that is entirely right. The law does not say you must adopt different standards, however.

Where divorce is concerned, women have actually found that ease of divorce often is a boomerang, that they're much worse off than before and it's not always been to their advantage. They're beginning to have second thoughts about the way in which the law works in a society which is riddled with lawyers to an unbelievable degree. That's one of the big differences with Europe. In this society, law is essentially a horizontal affair of contracts and relations between people. In France, the law is essentially a command that comes from above and is applied to groups, but with very little relationship between groups. Here you can't make a move without consulting a lawyer. That's very good for the legal profession, but it entangles people in much too much conflict. I see this even in the university. You cannot adopt a resolution on anything without consulting a battery of lawyers because of the risk that you will be sued. The price is a heavy one – except for the lawyers.

Europeans look on with incredulity as American governments preach freedom and democracy while propping up vicious dictatorships in Central and South America in an apparently cynical form of vested interest.

I'm not sure that's the wrong view. After all, nobody is consistent, and people live with a remarkable amount of contradiction in their beliefs and lives. The American faith in democracy coexists with a deep and unconscious sense of superiority over Latin Americans. There is a hidden national contempt: we know better. Basically that's how Americans see Central and Latin Americans. I'm struck by a complete lack of empathy, a real mutual dislike, though Latin Americans are much more outspoken about it. Americans don't like to admit they think some people better than others. That's not part of the ethos. But it's there, and then, of course, you start justifying all those interventions in terms of exporting democracy, though most people know it's nonsense.

What do you think will be the result of German reunification? Has the German psyche changed?

Nobody's very comfortable. Interestingly enough, the Germans aren't either, and when one talks to young Germans they are very ambivalent. They see themselves as West Europeans and are not sure that the cousins they are suddenly absorbing deserve to be absorbed. They are almost more frightened than anyone, because they know a lot about their own past. All the French I meet take more or less the same line, which is the Pascal wager: we must bet on their being good because, *sotto voce*, we have no alternative. The Americans, who are farther away, are quite open about their reservations. Basically they are very dubious. On the other hand, I wouldn't talk about psyche, because many nations go through phases of madness. The French nineteenth-century view of Germany was that it was a nation of romantic dreamers, and then came Bismarck and Hitler and everything in between. Psyches change. The French went through episodes of great brutality.

William Shearer recalls that after the First World War the Germans had a liberal democracy, the Weimar Republic, but couldn't work it, and the result was Hitler. Can history repeat itself?

I'm always reminded of a quote from my ex-colleague and ex-friend, Henry Kissinger, who was asked apropos of Vietnam whether Nixon's administration would repeat the mistakes of the previous one. He said, 'No, we are not going to repeat their mistakes, we are going to make our own.' I don't think that history repeats itself. For all the flaws, the Germans have gone through much more soul-searching than, for instance, the Japanese have about the Second World War and about a

fascist past. I always have a great deal of trouble dealing with Germans of my age and older, but I have enormous sympathy for the younger ones whom I've seen over the years, who strike me as very decent, who have learned a lot and have thought a lot about what went on, so I'm not too worried. I'm more worried about pure power factors: the fact that, in a sense, it is not good in Europe for any one country to be much more powerful than the others. That's never good. It induces fear in the others and a certain amount of hubris in the one who is too strong; and in that respect a sort of disequilibrium is created. But I don't think that is necessarily going to lead to another Kaiser or another Hitler. The times are not the same.

The safety of Europe perhaps depends on Russia feeling safe, but after all that's happened, how can the Russians possibly have any confidence in the Warsaw Pact?

I don't think there's a Warsaw Pact left. What is likely to make them insecure is not threats coming from the West but their own internal conditions, and that is a huge worry. Frankly, whatever scenario one can imagine for the immediate future of that enormous country, I don't see them becoming a threat to their neighbours in Europe. For a very long time they will be so busy dealing with one another. There are perhaps three scenarios. One that somehow Gorbachev makes it and reform continues. Another that there's disintegration and civil war, which is what many of the visiting Russians now talk about. And a third, that there is some sort of Bonapartist nationalist Russian reaction, restoring law and order in a country which is certainly not used to disorder. In all three cases, it seems to me, they're going to have their hands full with their own problems.

I really don't know what the chances are of Gorbachev surviving. I'm not a Soviet expert, and in any case, Soviet experts are divided. Until a few months ago I thought his chances rather good. I'm not sure any more. His greatest strength comes from the fact that there isn't any visible alternative, but that may not last for ever. If you really do have a period of ethnic unrest and economic decline, the demand for somebody with muscle could become irresistible, especially if the army then joins in; though I think one exaggerates the degree of autonomy of the Soviet army. So I don't know. Probably poor Gorbachev himself doesn't know.

As for the way the Soviets view the prospect of a united Germany and its relationship to NATO, I wouldn't feel that deep down they want a Germany that could play one side against the other and be a huge untied giant in the middle of Europe. They don't have many cards left, and the only card they have is a boomerang, which is the presence

of their troops in East Germany. Now, of course, those troops are not going to be too popular there, and if the Germans finally recognize the Polish border, then the Poles will undoubtedly ask their Soviet troops to go home. The next thing is that you have 300,000 Soviet soldiers isolated in a united Germany, and if I were a Soviet general I wouldn't like that very much. My guess is that, in exchange for accepting the inevitable, they will ask for various limitations on the size of German forces, for no nuclear or chemical weapons in Germany, and for lots of economic aid. I don't see what else they can do. From talking to American officials who deal with this point, the interesting thing is that their impression is that the Soviets haven't had time to define their bottom line. Things have moved so fast, and they've been so preoccupied with their internal problems, that they haven't yet had time to think that through. Sooner or later they will have to.

Many of the Russians one sees here, those who come from Soviet institutes, make a very strong case for a Germany in NATO, the reason being that they're afraid of the Germans and think that a Germany contained by Europe and the United States is much better than an uncontained Germany. They make a strong case sometimes for the maintenance of lots of American troops in Europe because they don't look at the United States as an enemy any more but are worried about the Germans.

On the American side, the American public is deep down still very distrustful of the Soviets, but the government less so. After years of dealing with Gorbachev and his people, the government seems to have come to the conclusion that they are no longer the enemy. But America is an ideological nation – probably the last among the advanced countries – and there is a long residue of deep public dislike of the Soviet régime. If tomorrow Russia becomes a democracy with a constitutional system like America's and lets all of its nationalities go, then there would be a change of opinion, but I don't see a profound friendship developing between the United States and the Soviets as long as the régime in the Soviet Union is what it is; as long as you still have a command economy and an apparently all-powerful president and so on.

Is the Russian president less powerful than the US president?

Probably much less, but the impression remains that he has all the emergency powers and can use them to take over the government of Lithuania, or to block demonstrations in Moscow. The American president couldn't do that. The Russian president may be much weaker deep down, because the strength of the opposition is much greater, but formally he has powers that no America president has, so there are still lots of people who suspect he's a new tsar in the making.

Where did the communist revolution go so wrong? Must all revolutions end in bloodshed and tyranny because, in effect, they are civil wars?

They don't end in bloodshed and tyranny because they are civil wars, but because they set up ideals and expectations that cannot be met except by tyranny. It was the same with the French Revolution. No revolution that I know of has ever been able to achieve liberty, equality and fraternity all at the same time. Certainly the Soviets' attempt at simultaneously achieving massive economic development, liberation from exploitation and the reform of human nature could not have been made without resort to the state, which is the one thing Marx left pretty vague. Once you have to reform people by state decree, you are on the path to the guillotine or the purges and the gulags, and that is not the best way of reforming human nature. The problem is not so much civil war as demanding too much of people. I'm basically a reformist, not a revolutionary. You can demand too much.

To what extent is the political stability of Eastern Europe going to depend on the provision of capital?

That's a great deal of the problem. You're dealing with countries most of which have no democratic structures or traditions. Whether they'll be able to create some will depend very largely on whether the stores are empty or well stocked. Turning bankrupt communist economies into successful market economies is very chancy. On the other hand, even if you had more successful economies, it wouldn't necessarily solve all problems. What I worry about is the lack of democratic traditions and the resurgence of all kinds of ethnic problems that will always provide scapegoats when something doesn't work properly. The sudden enthusiasm for the market as the answer to everything worries me, because it isn't. What happens when they discover that the totally free market isn't necessarily any better socially than a command economy, that it creates inequalities that go way beyond what people can tolerate?

How far is it the cost of nuclear weapons that has driven the Soviet Union into perestroika*? Has the West in effect won an undeclared economic war by forcing Russia to spend more than it can afford?*

I don't think it's that, though certainly they spent a hell of a lot there, and it has a great deal to do with the fact that, as many critics of the Soviet system point out, they never really succeeded in developing a civilian economy in the first place. The one thing they did know how to do was run a war economy. That was the only part of the system which went reasonably efficiently. But the basic failure was the failure to know how to run a consumer economy in an age in which people's

expectations could not really be contained much longer. Even if they had diminished their military budget by a third or a half, it would have remained the problem. I would say it's a victory of one economic system over another, but I'm not sure if that can be put down to the fact that we broke their backs on military spending. One has to remember that we practically broke ours as well. There is remarkably little gloating, except on the far right, the reason being that Americans realize that, though they won the Cold War, they're not in good shape either. They're the biggest debtor, they have a huge deficit, they have a backlog of unresolved social problems that is enormous. And while they're in comparably better shape than the Soviets, they're not, God knows, in good shape.

Writing about Gorbachev's initiative on arms reduction you said: 'If only this country, America, had a wise and bold president engaged in new thinking of his own.' What did you mean by that exactly?

It seemed to me, in arms control in particular, that the long-time American tendency to haggle about insignificant details was slowing down the process enormously. In fact America's hand was forced by the Soviets once the Soviets started conceding things which absolutely nobody thought they would. The whole nuclear field has bred a group of people who have turned what is essentially guesswork about deterrents, which is based on common sense – 'I shall not take excessive risks because I can't know what will happen if I do' – into a science in which every weapons system has to be here or there. I always thought that utter nonsense. It didn't make any difference whether we had 15,000 warheads to their 12,000 or they had 15,000 to our 12,000, yet people have invested their whole careers in the question, and for a long time, particularly in the 1970s and early 1980s, American policy was hostage to those people. Then, amazingly, the Soviets started climbing away from all that, which obliged the Americans to follow. I would not have predicted it.

How was it that all the experts were taken by surprise by the recent changes in Russia and Eastern Europe?

Because we have taken the totalitarian model too seriously. There's been too much kremlinology, too much of a belief that, if you understand what goes in the Kremlin, you don't have to find out what goes on in the Soviet Union, because, after all, there was no such thing as Soviet civil society. Nobody realized the degree of anarchic discontent among nationalities, among consumers, among workers. Nobody really understood what was going on. Nor did anybody pay enough attention to the generational phenomenon. Gorbachev expresses a generation of

apparatchiki who came to the conclusion that the system was bankrupt. He was not alone. This was really a whole group of people who said we cannot go on like this; a little bit like the whole generation of French politicians and civil servants in the 1980s who came to the conclusion that Europe was the only way in which France could resolve its problems. Different scales, but the same sort of phenomenon.

The possession of nuclear weapons by the super-powers does not seem to have prevented wars anywhere except in Europe and America, so what now stops us from supposing that they are irrelevant to warfare?

Because I'm not at all convinced that smaller powers will use the same reasoning. I'm worried about the little ones, so to speak. I'm worried about powers which, unlike the Soviet Union and the United States, are locked in a real life-and-death situation. It was never a life-and-death conflict between the super-powers, never the Soviet Union *versus* the United States, but always a conflict about somebody else – about Vietnam, about Western Europe. Nor did either one really, it seems to me, ever want war. The United States is basically a peaceful country with hotheads, and the Pope's reasoning about the Soviets, that they would willingly sacrifice as many people as they lost in the Second World War to gain world hegemony, has always struck me, if you will pardon the nastiness, as something only a Pole could say; and a Pole who hates Russians, not Soviets. On the other hand, India, Pakistan, Libya and what have you, especially Israel's Arab neighbours, are the countries that worry me. I don't buy the notion that somehow the possession of nuclear weapons brings wisdom. The reasons why no war ever broke out among the five powers that officially have nuclear weapons are not reasons that one can expect to be reproduced mechanically all over the world.

There is much less sympathy among Europeans than among Americans for Israel. Do you see any long-term solution to the Arab-Israeli question?

Of course, we can all dream and speculate. It seems to me that, if Israel managed to change its electoral system, it would be a first step. The present system is like Weimar, doomed to paralysis. I'm a great opponent of proportional representation because I think it makes government impossible. On the other hand, I'm not even sure that a system like the British, the American or the French would necessarily lead to a victory of those people in Israel who want peace through compromise and acceptance of a Palestinian state. They are still a minority, and I'm very pessimistic. I have been there often, I have written a lot about it. I have almost given up writing about it, because I find it so gloomy a topic that one can only repeat oneself. Yet there is increasing questioning

of Israel in American society, much more than there used to be. I think there are three factors. First, for a long time there was a very powerful argument, which sold extremely well, that Israel was the best bastion of democracy and anti-communism in the middle East; so that was a Cold War aspect. Secondly, there is an enormous amount of guilt in American society about the way they treated the Jewish problem in the 1930s: how the United States could have helped more, but didn't. And thirdly, you have deep American dislike of the Arabs. I don't know why, but it's there.

To many people in Europe the methods and ideology that now serve Israel bear a disturbing resemblance to those from which the Jews themselves suffered.

I couldn't agree more.

What makes the once oppressed turn oppressor?

I wish I had an answer. I used to think it was essentially the weight of the past: having been victimized so long, you have a desire for absolute security, which, as Kissinger used to say, makes everybody else insecure. That is maybe part of the story. I am told by Japanese experts that many Japanese still see Japan as a small vulnerable society which cannot open its borders – cannot do this, cannot do that – because in the past they have been very vulnerable.

I find Israel such a painful subject. It is so difficult to argue about. Some of my best friends are Israeli, and many, of course, are in the peace movement and find it equally difficult to justify. I don't know. Maybe it's that everybody is capable of acting like a master and a victimizer when his turn comes, especially if he has suffered a lot. Alas, it seems to be part of human nature. I am convinced that if you could only play a sort of mental experiment and have the Palestinians and the Israelis living more or less peacefully side by side for a couple of years, then each would realize that the other is not only not an enemy but extraordinarily similar in many respects. The problem is getting to that point. I do not see it happening. That's what worries me.

Can common ground ever truly exist for the application of ethics in international relations? With South Africa, for example, it seems easy to advocate sanctions from the comfort of New York or London when someone else pays the price.

I'm struck by the fact that, if you take the particular issue of sanctions, it was the black organizations themselves that supported the idea, knowing full well that the argument made against sanctions, that it would hit the blacks first, had a large amount of truth in it. I'm more struck in this whole area of ethics in international affairs by the differences in

ethical systems: the clash between self-interest – 'I must get what I want' – and ethics, which almost inevitably goes beyond self-interest. That strikes me more than the differences between, let's say, an Islamic and a Christian view of the world, or an American and a communist view. Those differences seem to me a minor problem. Deep down there are not that many ethical clashes. We need to look at the clash between ethics and non-ethics rather than any clash of different ethical ways of looking at the world.

But aren't we facing two rather different concerns that could make everything else seem quite insignificant? With the destruction of the environment and ever-multiplying numbers of people, mightn't the human urge to reproduce turn out to be the greatest enemy of all?

Yes, but both questions have something to do with the whole issue of development. It is reasonably clear that, in countries that do develop, the population increase slows down. It is also clear that the destruction of the environment is something many countries consider indispensable to their own development. Even when you talk about conflicts which are not between states or nations but against nature, they have a way of turning into conflicts among nations. For instance, environment could easily turn into a conflict between developing nations saying, 'Look, we are simply doing what you did in the nineteenth century, so who are you to preach abstinence to us?' and the advanced countries. The same with population. Clearly many nations say, 'Why should we accept lower numbers? We are fewer and poorer than you.' So I think the potential for conflict of a traditional sort among nations is very high over those issues. The notion of everybody forming a common front to save the environment or limit population is something that is, if I may say so, a view only scientists could hold.

You've said that the world has become disenchanted with ideologies, but can any society last long without at least notional ideals? Unless they have some generalized sense that the future will be better, aren't they bound to generate a new conservatism manipulated in the interests of the most powerful sectors of society?

You're right. On the other hand, there's a big gap between having a programme and not degenerating into complacency or cynicism or conservatism, and having a messianic ideology which one thinks will produce a new man and can be exported to others. I hope that will come to an end, because it's very dangerous. Yet I think there is a possibility lying somewhere between conservatism and cynicism and the great ideological utopias that were essentially products of the eighteenth century.

I have read that you thought it likely that, had you gone into politics, you would have been 'obnoxious and a failure'. Why should you think that?

I don't have any patience. If, let's say, I ever became an adviser to a president, as so many of my colleagues seem to want to do, I would find the atmosphere in Washington not much to my liking. I have many colleagues who have done it, and it requires an enormous patience. It also requires bureaucratic skills, which means manipulation, buttering people up, intrigue, telephone calls and meetings. All of this – for what? The attraction is usually the attraction of power or influence, but it's not what interests me most. I just don't have the talent for it. I like speaking my mind, whether it's politic or not.

Some people just love power. I'm not saying that I don't like a measure of it. Any academic likes to have some little margin of power, at least over the conditions in which he lives, and I like being head of this centre and so on. But that's in order to have an interesting life, not to govern people, tell them what to do and have the sense I am shaping history. Whether or not writers about politics have any effect on the real world is a question I've often asked myself. It's like throwing a bottle into the sea. You never know. I never thought it was measurable.

From time to time I'm told by American foreign service types that my books have influenced them. Since I know perfectly well that American foreign service types have very little influence themselves, I take it with a grain of salt. Basically I don't know, and I don't care. The influence one has as an academic is on one's students. If they take seriously what one writes and then use what they've learned in later life, one has some influence. But who knows? Certainly I write because I hope it will be read and that people will think about it. Basically I write because there is a puzzle that I want to solve.

You once said that a lack of historical reflection breeds the illusion of quick remedies, citing Germany's reinforcing authority in the face of terrorism. What alternative is there if terrorist gangs are using machine guns in public places, as the Baader-Meinhof gang were doing? Wasn't your observation the sort of thing to make the public at large wary of intellectuals?

What I meant was that it is perfectly possible to fight terrorism without limiting public liberties. I don't think there is a clear-cut choice here or that the only way you can do it is by suspending constitutional guarantees. It seems to me that, on the whole, both Germans and Italians handled it reasonably well. I did not sympathize with the lawyers who screamed bloody murder the minute their clients were in gaol, but neither did it seem to me there was any need for emergency legislation suspending this or that constitutional provision. I feel that's a mistake. For instance, to take a recent example, I think the Bill that the French

Parliament just passed against racism is a mistake. It's a Bill which isn't going to be applied, because if you applied it you would have to institute censorship. It seems to me that there are ways of dealing with this other than by regulating speech. You have to regulate acts. Certain acts are not tolerable, period. On the other hand, you don't have to condone emergency police powers, or endlessly lengthen the period in which people can be detained without a warrant or things of that sort.

In what sense does history matter? Many schoolchildren today in Britain and America seem ignorant of basic facts of their national or recent history. How worrying is this?

Ignorance is always regrettable. On the other hand, there are lots of people who do know some history, and you are usually going to find them in leading circles – in politics, in academia, in the intellectual world. Therefore what these people know or don't know of history becomes quite important. They will probably have to deal with people who remember only too much history, and will be at a great disadvantage if they don't.

History is a matter of interpretation, and there are two aspects. One is ignorance *versus* non-ignorance, and the other, among people who are not totally ignorant, is difference of interpretation. There's not much you can do about that. In fact, what makes history interesting, certainly to a non-historian like myself, is that you do have endless battles and re-examinations and different ways of looking at the past. But I am more worried by the fact that so many people don't know any of it at all, including lots in high places, and not only in America. I teach in France from time to time, and have a sense that, largely because of a number of curricular changes in the past thirty years, the amount of historical grounding that French students have is on the way down. History has been replaced by mathematics.

There has been a lot of talk about a 'United States of Europe', but this seems to ignore very simple facts – a dozen separate histories and a dozen separate languages.

I don't see a United States of Europe comparable to the US of America. The countries are too different. But there is such a thing in politics as creation and innovation, and it is perfectly possible to find a half-way house between sovereign national states, on the one hand, and a federal system on the other; and I hope it will be found. I think they are marching toward it, partly because it is very much in their interest. The British too – certainly after Mrs Thatcher disappears from the scene – will come to the conclusion that national objectives cannot be reached by national means. All one has to do is to listen to visiting French

politicians who come over here. They remain as French as can be, but realize that the national objectives can't be achieved simply by unilateral means; that it is in their interests to make those national objectives compatible with those of their neighbours because nothing will be gained by fighting.

You have cited Mrs Thatcher as an obstacle to European unity. Can this obstacle be overcome, and how long will it take before a Europe emerges that is not fragmented by what you call 'mentalities' – different sets of assumptions and attitudes?

I believe it's beginning. To put it unkindly, Mrs Thatcher is probably a transitional phenomenon, if a respectable one. Britain, after all, has been a great power, and it does take a long time for a great power to accept seeing itself as essentially one no longer. She is probably the only person in Britain who still believes in the special relationship with the United States. Certainly nobody here believes in it, and my impression from talking to British civil servants, of whom there have been quite a number here over the years, is that they do not share Mrs Thatcher's views of the world. My guess is that she will be exactly as de Gaulle was for France: somebody whose role in history is essentially to restore national self-esteem, and after that it becomes much easier to accept sacrifices of sovereignty. You can't do it otherwise, and in that respect I have a certain sympathy with her, though not with her social policies.

'Being a permanent denouncer of recurrent mistakes is after a while no fun,' you said a few years ago. Have you resigned yourself to a life of no fun?

No, no, no. It often is fun. I was thinking there of my writings on American foreign policy. As somebody who is not in the government and has no intention or desire to go into it, I can only be a critic, but it seems to me that in much else of what I've been doing, especially in my work on France, I'm not just a critic. I'm trying to offer interpretations and analyses which are something more than criticizing other people's mistakes.

You spoke in an essay of dualities between your private and public personae. How can they be at odds?

I probably give people the impression that I'm much more on top of things and sure of myself than I am. Let's put it this way. The private self is much less on top of things than the public one.

You've achieved a great deal academically. Do you have any secret ambitions in other directions?

In another life I would have just loved to take some time off to sing. I have a good voice, I've never done anything with it, and I adore classical music and *lieder* in particular. Secondly, I would have loved to have become a movie reviewer. I'm a great movie fan, but nobody has ever taken me seriously. I've been condemned to being a political scientist.

RICHARD INGRAMS

Richard Ingrams was born in 1937. He spent the war years with his mother in Scotland before being sent to board at prep school. He went to Shrewsbury School in 1950 and from there to University College, Oxford, after serving as a sergeant in the Education Corps for his term of National Service. He joined *Private Eye* in 1962 and succeeded Christopher Booker as editor the following year. During his twenty-three years at *Private Eye* he defended many libel suits, most notably against Sir James Goldsmith and Robert Maxwell. He married in 1962 and had three children, one of whom died at the age of seven. He continues to work for *Private Eye* and writes a weekly column for the *Observer*.

I was born in 1937 and brought up in Scotland during the war, until 1945 when I went to boarding school. My recollection of my parents is that they weren't together much of the time. My father was a merchant banker who went abroad a lot and then, during the war, was working in the Ministry of Economic Warfare in London with all kinds of secret operations that I still know nothing about. Not even my mother knows what he was really up to. I was therefore brought up largely by my mother before I went to school – my mother and grandmother, actually. We lived in my grandmother's house.

My mother, who is now eighty-one, takes her religion seriously. She was a Catholic convert whereas my father was very anti-Catholic. He wouldn't, for instance, allow any priest into the house, except for Ronald Knox, who had taught him at school when he was little. His attitude to religion was negative. That was why he insisted that two of us boys must be Protestant, though the rest could be Roman Catholic. As far as religion is concerned, my mother has been a major influence in that direction and I do regard myself as religious. What I didn't know until recently is that I am a baptized Catholic, my mother having secretly baptized her two non-Catholic children, feeling she had a duty.

I considered converting at Oxford and still feel inclined towards Catholicism, partly because, where the Church of England is concerned nowadays, it's become exceedingly difficult for someone like me to feel any loyalty, though I have felt it in the past. Now, with the kind of things under discussion in the Church of England – women priests, gay priests and the whole secularization of the Church, all developments towards which I feel unsympathetic – it's become impossible to hold it in the kind of romantic affection that someone like John Betjeman stood for. It doesn't exist any longer, though it was once a powerful pull. Very possibly I might convert to Roman Catholicism in old age.

I can truly say I hardly knew my father, who died when I was about

fifteen. I wasn't close to him, but I regarded him with a certain awe, partly because he was never around. If you were sent to boarding school it meant that after a certain age you barely knew your parents. You started to live a separate life from early on and never spoke to your parents about what you did at school or about your parents to the boys at school. You were almost ashamed and didn't own up to having parents, or sisters either – not that I had sisters.

A story in the press that I had a Nazi father arose, funnily enough, when a book on Philby was published. Kim Philby at one time belonged to an organization called the Anglo-German Fellowship – a group of British who were sympathetic towards Hitler and Germany before the war. One of the illustrations in the book showed Philby sitting at a big dinner in London, and there were my parents in the foreground. My father was quite possibly sympathetic towards Germany, even to Hitler at that stage, but since he was also working for British Intelligence I do not know how far he became involved for Intelligence reasons. Certainly if you look at Hitler's blacklist of key people whom he considered dangerous and who were to be bumped off, you will find my father's name.

If my father was secretive, it must have been partly because of his job. Recently I read in the diaries of Bruce Lockhart, the political head of operations during the war, that he sent my father before the Nuremberg trials to speak to Göring and all the big Nazi war criminals on behalf of the Foreign Office. Well, I had no knowledge whatever of that. When I was a little boy, I would have been highly impressed by the idea of my father meeting all those evil men, but I never remember him mentioning it.

As to whether I was myself a good father, you would need to ask my children. I would say that I was keen my children shouldn't have the same relationship with me as I had with my own parents. When they went to boarding school, we therefore chose schools close to home so I wouldn't lose touch, and it made a tremendous difference. My relationship with them is far more intimate than my relationship ever was with my parents. I was also working at *Private Eye*, so was at home more than most fathers, and I liked being a father. I particularly liked reading to my children – partly for my own pleasure, of course.

When my son Arthur died, he was seven, and his death was a time of great stress, especially for my wife. As far as I was concerned, it was far worse than the deaths of my two brothers since I and they were never particularly close – again, partly because of the public school attitude. They were a different age from me and you could only have friends who were the same generation. My brother Rupert was in any case killed at about the same time as my son Fred was born, so I was involved in the birth of my own child while the death of my brother

was something – well, I don't say that it passed me by, but it didn't have a tremendous effect.

But the whole business of having a brain-damaged son imposed a great strain, more so on my wife because – and this is often difficult to grasp – a mother can love her child regardless of its physical condition while a father probably doesn't quite share that attitude. I felt affectionate towards Arthur, but because he couldn't speak or do anything apart from smiling like a baby, I couldn't feel towards him as Mary did. When Arthur died I think I inevitably felt a sense of relief, partly because of his own distress and pain. He was medicated much of the time, so I felt a great sense of relief – release, I should perhaps say.

Shrewsbury when I was there was still very, very old-fashioned. I recently read the memoirs of Maurice Bowra, in which he describes his school as it was before the First World War, though I thought it could have been a description of Shrewsbury as it was in the early 1950s. He describes particularly well the emphasis on classics, and even in the sixth form in my day we were still taught classics to the exclusion of almost everything else. The only concession was divinity, and that consisted of reading the New Testament in Greek.

My recollection of the people who gave speeches on prize-giving day is of how they would tell us we were to be the leaders of the future. 'You are very privileged to have had this education,' they said. 'You have a duty to your country to be a leader.' It actually made a great impression on me, and when I went into the army and failed to become an officer I was most upset. Why did I fail? I think they saw a bolshevik.

The propaganda of being told, 'You are leaders,' led you to assume automatically that if you went into the army you'd be an officer, that you wouldn't have to mix for too long with all those other people. That was how I assumed it would be, and I was very shocked when it wasn't. The point about the terrible public school system is that it's very strict in that way: either you conform or you become rebellious. I became a rebel, not in a courageous but in a cowardly way, but rebellious nevertheless. I found in the army the same kind of class structure, only more so, with three orders, officers, non-commissioned officers and other ranks, all clearly marked out, and realized that the officers weren't really fit to be in charge and that it was the non-commissioned officers who knew how to run things. The discovery made me even more of a bolshevik.

At Oxford I read Greats because I hadn't learned anything apart from classics. I still know virtually nothing about history, and my knowledge of literature hasn't been gained from school. I know a little French, but no other language, and I know nothing about science. I am therefore very ignorant and have meanwhile completely forgotten all the classics.

So if you gave me Greek to read today I wouldn't be able to follow a word. The one thing I did benefit from was having to do philosophy, though I couldn't understand it or see what Ayer and all those people were on about, or that it mattered, though it was somehow of benefit. Wasn't it MacNeice who said that if you read philosophy at Oxford then you never believe anything that anyone says to you ever again? If it's done well, it trains you to think about the meaning of what people say and analyse what they're really saying – something people don't do normally. Since most people talk balls all the time, it is a useful training.

I remember Ayer being on television with Muggeridge when they were all talking about God. As Ayer's turn came to speak, he said, 'Well, I think we ought to define what we mean by God.' Malcolm said, 'Oh, Freddie, don't be silly. What a stupid thing to say. How could you be a professor of logic?' and he stamped on him. Ayer was so offended that he never spoke to Malcolm again, but of course Ayer was right: they should first have decided what they meant when they used certain expressions.

As a student I enjoyed being involved in plays and reviews, though I never did great acting. I remember in particular putting on shows at the Edinburgh Festival, and I enjoyed it all, but wasn't much good at it. I would have liked the company we started at Oxford to succeed, but it was something you could only do with a grant, and when we tried to get grants from various sources, we failed because we were just two or three young people whom nobody knew.

My only other experience of the stage has been acting in Keith Waterhouse's play *Mrs Wilson's Diary* with Joan Littlewood directing. Again I enjoyed being involved, because of Joan, she was such a brilliant person, and it was great fun to do. Now I don't hanker after the stage at all; I don't even go to the theatre. I'm not interested in it and I don't even find actors interesting. They're boring, terribly boring. I listened to Charles Dance when he did *Desert Island Discs*, and he'd nothing to say, and the music he chose was hopeless. Actors shouldn't be allowed to speak, not even when they're Olivier. Olivier did what he did and, like a lot of people, didn't really understand how, so when he talked about it he was almost incoherent.

Lasting friendships? John Wells was someone I met at university, and then there were Andrew Osmond and various others. Peter Jay was a great friend in those days, though I've fallen out with him since. He worked for Robert Maxwell at one time and I find that hard to stomach. I feel we haven't much in common any more.

But I did enjoy my time at Oxford and remember thinking, when I left, that I would never be able to bear to go back because, having been so happy there, I would be overwhelmed with nostalgia. Of course I did go back and never felt a thing – partly because all the people there

whom I had known had also left. But I remember clearly that original feeling of happiness. It was the first place you went to after all the silly time in school and in the army where you were free to do whatever you liked. Also there were lots of girls, and I'd never had the company of girls, what with boarding school and the army.

I do enjoy the company of women, and now I'm very old and grey I like the company of young girls – my daughter and her friends, for instance. I love being with them and I suppose they make me feel younger. But I'm not one of those who can't live without women. I'm quite happy living on my own and wouldn't mind being a hermit. There are very few people I like to be with, and if you don't drink, as I don't, you've no wish to be with anyone you don't know; you don't want to be among bores.

Is there something inside me that wants to break out? If you mean by that having affairs with lots of women, I wouldn't want to. Men who behave promiscuously get into all kinds of difficulties that are better avoided. The idea that it's pleasurable to live that kind of life is quite mistaken, and anyway, if you genuinely like women, you don't want to make them unhappy. Did I ever err in that regard? My lips are sealed.

Where journalism is concerned, I don't take it seriously. I agree with Ron Orr when he said that once a journalist thinks he's something more important to do than fill up tomorrow's newspaper, he should pack it in and do something else. I always firmly believed that journalists who take themselves seriously or believe they have influence are bad journalists. The person who has exemplified that for me is Harold Evans. He started off as probably quite a good journalist, but developed into someone who thought he was highly influential. Look at him now: editor of some travel magazine in New York which nobody reads. He's completely forgotten, whereas someone like Bron is still there. It's very important for a journalist not to have high-flown ideas about what he or she is doing, and not to think it's important.

One of the curious things about *Private Eye* is that people seem, on the whole, to have stayed on indefinitely, perhaps for too long. Even when they leave they seem to be drawn back. You ask if I was being trivial when I said Christopher Booker was removed from the editorship because of the length of his holiday. The fact was that he somehow seized control of *Private Eye* and both Willie Rushton and I thought that Booker was no good at being editor. He was so indecisive: he could never finish an article or anything and we would all sit around till late at night trying to get the magazine to press. I felt that *Private Eye* could only survive if he ceased to be editor and I became editor, but it was perfectly true that he went away on a long holiday. Naturally he was

upset at the time as he hadn't expected anything of the kind to happen, and there was then an estrangement for a couple of years when he had nothing to do with me. But he came back and has been there ever since, and now we are good friends.

When Bron left I was still editor and his departure upset me. It wasn't that alone, though, which prompted me to give up, since he didn't come in all that often and would keep himself very much apart from the rest. On the other hand, perhaps I felt that him and Dempster leaving represented the departure of two key figures who were very much a part of the 1970s *Private Eye*. Maybe I thought, well, it's time to go, since journalism is always changing and it's no use thinking you can go on doing the same thing week after week. Coming up with something different can be quite a strain – constantly providing novelty.

As an editor, you need to be a despot to a certain extent, and where *Private Eye* is concerned it is essential to have a fairly clear idea of what you want. There isn't time for too much democracy in meetings, and in the end a lot comes down to personal decisions. Since I am rather obstinate I find it hard to change my mind and admit I've been wrong. I was criticized a lot, for instance, over Goldsmith, and was accused of getting an obsession about him. Perhaps I did.

The Goldsmith period brought us all very close because *Private Eye* was under threat and there was the camaraderie of wartime. Dempster and Gilliard and Patrick Marnham and Paul Foot and I used to meet and plot how we were going to deal with the enemy. Nigel Dempster I shall always associate with those times, but he's very temperamental and the trouble with journalists is that they become torn between being journalists, which means being critical, attacking and making nuisances of themselves, and being nice to people – writing flattering things about them, having lunch with them, going to stay on their yachts. Even in my own column on the *Observer* I sometimes feel a temptation to get involved with influential people, to be able to ring up cabinet ministers and say, 'Could we not have lunch?' They'd certainly agree, and before you knew where you were you'd find yourself caught up in the PR side and your edge would be gone.

The most upsetting aspect of what has happened to Dempster has been to see what he has written in his column about Goldsmith and Aspinall, the people who were once our enemies, and to read about how Sir James has bought a new house and so forth. It certainly is not the Dempster of old. I sense he would like to come back, but I don't think Ian Hislop would have him, though it's not for me to say. In any case, Hislop is not so interested in the Dempster type of journalism as I was, and Nigel is not so interested in that style of journalism as he used to be. He seems to have lost that scurrilous edge.

I think Bron was, from his own point of view, right to leave when

he did as he probably had shot his bolt. And after that, of course, I left myself, feeling I'd had enough. Once I'd done it too I felt more sympathetic towards Bron and realized how he must have felt. For a long time I had been concerned that there were no young people on *Private Eye*, that it seemed we would all go on till we dropped dead. When Ian Hislop turned up, it was absolutely wonderful as I had been hoping someone might come along who could take over. Nevertheless it was a difficult thing to expect of anyone because the job involves two quite distinct halves: the jokes written by particular people and the story side. That makes for two camps, and the editor has to have a foot in each. The people who come into *Private Eye* are on the whole interested in one or the other, the joke people tending to look down on the journalists and the journalists tending to look down on the joke people. Ian never had that attitude, but liked both sides, and in fact had done some very good stories as well as jokes for the *Eye* before taking over.

I'm most impressed by Ian, seeing how young he is. He understands the point of *Private Eye* very well and knows how it works. The Sutcliffe libel action has been the most serious thing ever to happen to us because it threatened to involve such a huge sum of money, while the danger remains that something like it could happen again. To begin with I thought it was maybe the end of the magazine, but the fact that it's kept going has been very much to Ian Hislop's credit. I've been through these libel actions, and the fund-raising, before, and couldn't do it all over again.

Do I continue to exert a tremendous influence? If that's in any way true, it's partly because Ian Hislop and I get on well and tend to see eye to eye, though I do try not to interfere and wasn't, for example, involved in the Sutcliffe business. I didn't even attend the court hearings. I used to feel, partly because there was a lot of difficulty when I gave up the editorship, that I should continue to stick around and see things were all right. Now I feel I could slip away tomorrow and *Private Eye* would carry on and I wouldn't be missed. I might miss *Private Eye* a bit, but if it came to the point where I felt I was bored, that it didn't mean anything much to me any more, I would give it up and try something else.

I have always been impressed by something Chesterton said, which was that it is easy to be solemn, hard to be frivolous; that if, as a journalist, you have the choice between writing a leader in *The Times* and a whole page of jokes for *Punch*, then you pick writing the leader because it will be much easier to do. That is very true, and Chesterton is an example of a man who was brilliant and serious but who regarded it as his duty to be amusing, to make people laugh. It sounds as though I'm comparing myself with him, which I wouldn't wish to do, but as a journalist I do

think one should try to be funny and tell a few jokes. I also think that being serious carries a great danger of coming out with terrible clichés and points that are perfectly obvious. Most people grow serious when they are drunk at about half-past eleven at night and start to tell you things which they think are highly important, though they never are.

The written word has very little effect on the way people behave. People read something – I'm guilty of this myself – and the next day can't remember what it was. I often say to someone, I really enjoyed your article, what was it about? I can't remember. It's hard to say what influence any of these things really has. If you take Mrs Thatcher, who has been ridiculed *ad nauseam*, not just in *Private Eye* and the press but on television as in *Spitting Image* and so on, does it have any influence? I would say not much, not much.

I certainly don't believe in the power of the pen. You should engage in journalism for personal reasons. Wasn't it Larkin who said that he wrote in order to have something to read? I always felt that about *Private Eye*: that I was bored with reading those other newspapers so wrote *Private Eye* for something to read. Does that make sense? I still get this impulse to snatch up and read the latest *Private Eye*, even though I know what's in it. A lot of it is to do with boredom with journalism, and *Private Eye* has been a way of amusing myself.

Yet if journalism as a whole never changes things, I've often thought that publishing a good cartoon is probably more effective than, say, a leader in *The Times*. If you want to influence how people think about Mrs Thatcher, a good cartoon is more effective than a long piece because it is, first of all, a picture and no one has to make an effort. People don't often remember things, but they may remember a particular cover of *Private Eye* more than an article they've read inside. If people like satire, perhaps it does some good.

I agree that satire is bound to trivialize in a way. It's like the cartoon again: a simplifying of the issue. One of the cartoons I've felt very proud of in *Private Eye* was done by John Kent and appeared during the Falklands War. It showed a war memorial with a bust of Mrs Thatcher on top and underneath the names of those who had died, the inscription reading: 'They Died to Save Her Face'. I was much criticized for it, but was proud of it because it seemed to me to be what the Falklands War was all about. It was a simplification and there was more to it than that, but then I also thought the description by Borges of the Falklands War being about two bald men fighting over a comb was brilliant. When you say such a thing, it says it all, and there's no need for a history of the Falklands War. Two bald men fighting over a comb is, of course, simplifying the issue, but it is also the truth and the truth is always simple.

Bron once said that politicians are social and emotional cripples. I

thought that was good. It's important for people not to hold a high opinion of politicians, and one of the strengths of the British is that they don't on the whole. Even Mrs Thatcher, the most successful politician of our time, who has done more than anyone, is not liked very much in her own country, and that's a good attitude. The danger begins when people start admiring politicians. Then you have Hitler, Mussolini and the Ayatollah; all these people who are thought to be wonderful. The right attitude to have is Bron's: quite untrue but the right way to think: to assume that such people are somehow sick and have something the matter with them. So long as people think like that, then the country will be all right.

But if satirists are ever only venting private spleen, then it's wrong. You should never get a kick out of being indignant. Malcolm Muggeridge, who influenced me greatly, is someone with a satirical outlook, and maybe Bron is too to some extent. With both of them I have the feeling of their being apart from society and viewing it from a distance. In Malcolm's case, there is a sense of great disgust at all the things he sees going on, a sense that the society we live in is corrupt and heading for some form of totalitarianism. I don't have such a feeling myself, but in a way wish I could. Journalists like Bron or Malcolm have a much clearer vision of what is happening than more conventional commentators, even when, as in Bron's case, there is a view of people which appears to be farcical – the Swiftian kind of idea about people eating their children. Take television personalities. I'm sure it is very rare for them to have what I would call a satirical attitude, a vivid feeling of disgust. I don't have it because I'm too normal, and you need to be slightly abnormal to think like a true satirist.

Malcolm was to me a kind of father figure who greatly influenced the way I see politics and other matters. I first met him in about 1963 with Claud Cockburn, who was another old man who influenced me. I have come to believe that we have many old people who are ignored because the whole of society tends to focus on the young. There are still a lot of old buffers who are pretty active, and people have forgotten about them just because they are old. To some extent I am interested in old people because I have been involved in biography, where you naturally tend to be writing about people older than yourself. But now I'm getting to be one of the old men too, so feel my father figures are all gone.

The secret of life, as Dr Johnson said, is that you must always try to do better than you did in the past. I would like to write more books, but don't have any good ideas. I'm always dining with publishers who invite me to write, but I've only ever written if I've felt a great compulsion. It's never been something that some publisher has suggested over lunch. What I ought to do is write the life of Muggeridge, and since

I've done most of the work already, I think I could finish it quite quickly.

There have been politicians I liked and admired. Jo Grimond is one, but he didn't get on. On the whole, the people one admires in politics lack the ruthless ambition that makes more successful politicians unpleasant. I often think there are plenty of nice people on the back benches of the House of Commons who are simply ordinary MPs you never hear about. The same is true in the Church: there are admirable men but they're not bishops. It is always thought that you should admire those who reach the top, but the good people usually don't. Apart from politics, those I admire are some of the old men I've mentioned, like Muggeridge; and Betjeman, whom I knew quite well and was very fond of. I never knew Larkin, but I admire his writing; and then there is Graham Greene. In the musical field, a great hero of mine was Casals, the cellist, a wonderful, a great man. I sometimes feel there aren't any great men any more.

As for those I positively don't admire, when I was a television critic I tended to get highly irritated by certain people, more so than nowadays. There was something about television personalities. I felt animosity towards, for instance, Esther Rantzen, even Michael Parkinson. I recently saw again the film where Rod Hull's Emu attacks Parkinson, and it was such a wonderful moment, something you'd longed to happen – the best thing ever on TV.

Television aside, people like Goldsmith and Robert Maxwell appear to me to be in the roles of almost Dickensian villains since both are devoted to the making of money and are total materialists, though perhaps that is being unkind to Maxwell as he does do work for charity. On the other hand, I cannot help suspecting that Goldsmith would on occasion find it hard to write out a cheque unless he was getting something back. You and others tell me that I have an obsession with him, but I don't like the idea of him exerting influence. He is politically ambitious and has a dictatorial streak which reminds me of Oswald Mosley. I met Mosley a few times and found him a difficult man to like: he was obsessed with power and talked about what needed doing in the country, when what he really meant was that he wanted to do these various things himself and there was no question of anyone else being consulted. He had a real thirst for power.

Mary and I had dinner with Mosley once and I was most impressed. His political charisma was clearly defined. At a certain point the conversation stopped and he began to speak about what was going on in the country and what ought to be done. Then he started to wave his arms and it all became slightly hypnotic and quite frightening.

A lot of those who saw Goldsmith when he was interviewed on

television thought he came over well, which was an indication of how he could sway people. I found it awful because he knew that, since it was going out live, it couldn't be edited, and so he did not seem to me to answer the questions directly. I've seen him do the same thing in court, but people were still impressed.

The Sutcliffe damages have been more immediately worrying than any government secrecy measures. Ways will always be found around official secrecy since, in the end, these things come out and no attempt by government can suppress them, as Peter Wright has shown. The greatest threat to *Private Eye* is suddenly to have huge damages awarded against it which, unless something is done, could mean the end. The problem is more of a threat to those with least resources, because if Rupert Murdoch has to pay a million pounds to Elton John, he can write a cheque and it won't have too much effect on his bank balance.

The English libel laws are far less liberal than those in the United States. The whole idea of the United States was founded on the idea of the people being able to get away from repressive laws and being free to speak out. By contrast, the law in England is weighted against the defendant in a libel action and the advantage all with the plaintiff. Then these juries give arbitrary awards, as for some reason the judge can't tell them what they should do; he can't even give an indication. It's a simple point which everyone has been making for years, but they've never got round to changing it, and on top of that you have the horrendous costs of litigation, including barristers' and solicitors' fees. Moreover, it was always my experience in a libel action that the one thing you thought needed saying was never admissible. I remember trying to say that Robert Maxwell was a man whom the Board of Trade had alleged, in 1971, was unfit to run a public company, and they said, oh no, we know what you're trying to say, Mr Ingrams, but you can't refer to it. It seemed to me that it was an important point, but I wasn't allowed to make it in the witness box.

How do you resolve the problem of printing what is known to be true but for which no evidence can be produced? That has always been a problem for *Private Eye* and is partly why we have our record of libel actions. I don't see any way round it. If you never printed anything you couldn't prove in court, you'd never print anything at all. We are never deliberately inaccurate over a big issue, though we might print people's names wrong to annoy or tease them, or embroider a gossip story – that I wouldn't deny. But we never set out to be deliberately inaccurate. I got into trouble in the Maxwell case when I tried to impress on the jury that, so far as I knew, I had never put anything in *Private Eye* which I knew to be false, apart from the apologies, which I knew to be

insincere. The judge was most annoyed. He couldn't understand how I could say such a thing.

It would be very hard to discuss in the abstract the question of whether we've ever gone too far or caused hurt to someone's life. If you tell me I have caused the ruin of a particular individual, then I can talk about that and maybe be made to feel remorseful, but looking back I can't think of a case where *Private Eye* ruined people undeservedly, though the circumstances vary so much. Obviously many crooks have been exposed by *Private Eye*, and while some of them haven't been affected at all, others clearly did suffer. If I look through back numbers, as I sometimes do, I feel on the whole that our targets were justified. Even Dempster had a good instinct for going after the right people and knowing who the baddies were, and that's what's required.

There is one regret I have from a long way back. After the Conservative MP Commander Courtney was photographed in bed with a woman in Moscow, the KGB circulated the pictures to various newspapers like the *News of the World*. The fact that this had happened was mentioned in *Private Eye* and as a result he was dropped by his constituency and his political career brought to an end. That was a clear case where we were wrong to do as we did since we were really playing the KGB game.

I certainly wouldn't feel that any love of punishing people came into the Parkinson case, and I don't feel an urge to punish people for their sexual misdemeanours. At least I hope not. You have to remember that a good journalist with a piece of information has an irresistible urge to get it into print, no matter where. In that respect *Private Eye* sometimes benefits as a last resort, for the people who work on it are not gentlemen – not all of them. One of the world's gripes against journalists is that they behave in an ungentlemanly manner, but that's the way it is. If I am in conversation with anyone, I naturally think in terms of whether they are telling me a good story, and whenever people say, you mustn't use this in your magazine, I always think they mean they want it to go in, and so take no notice.

Am I hurt by disloyalty? My staff is grotesquely disloyal and I'm watched carefully in all that I do. I don't really mind because this is how I expect journalists to behave. If ever there is a crisis, then people are always loyal.

On the question of anti-Semitism and anti-Zionism, I read a well documented article by Christopher Hitchins that brought home to me clearly how the Zionist movement is basically anti-Semitic. People such as Balfour, who were responsible for the State of Israel coming into being, were quite anti-Semitic and believed that creating a Jewish state would

be a good way to get the Jews out of their own countries. It's always seemed to me that the Gentiles most keen on Israel are anti-Semitic.

I wouldn't agree that *Private Eye* was ever anti-Semitic, but I don't consider that the State of Israel has been a success. People won't face it, and now it's growing worse. Israel is only kept going with American money, yet the Americans, and to a lesser extent the British, keep up the pretence that the country is something good that deserves our support. Personally I can't feel any great involvement in what is going on in the Middle East. People in this country seem too much concerned with the question of Israel and the Palestinians, which after all has nothing really much to do with us, and I don't see what the British government can be expected to do about it.

Naturally I feel sympathy with the Palestinians when I see what is going on on the West Bank, and that is why I was particularly interested in the Hitchins article, because what is happening there is a sort of racism. The Jews are saying to the Palestinians, we don't want you people; this is our country; we must keep our race pure. But because there are so many powerful Jewish lobbies, particularly in the United States, you're made to feel guilty, or you're attacked for anti-Semitism, if you mention the fact of racism in Israel.

I used to admire Mrs Thatcher quite a lot and I think she has done many good things. As a journalist, one is aware of how the printing unions have been crushed by her, and they undoubtedly were a restriction on the press. For example, you could never have started a paper like the *Independent* in the old days. There is no doubt, on the other hand, that she has been in power too long and has grown to be power mad. It happens to all those people. In my experience, women (this is a sexist remark) are unable to cope with power, not only in politics, but also in publishing, journalism, or wherever. Women in positions of authority can't do it as a rule, or else they manage for a time, but after a while they crack up.

People say there should be more women in politics, but one of the good things about women is that on the whole they don't want to go into that world. They are not in general ambitious, they don't want power; or if they do want it they want to exercise it over individual men, not over men or men and women generally. The reason why there aren't more women MPs is not because men are prejudiced against them but because there are so few women who actually want to do it. Men and women have totally different urges, most men being ruled by women within marriage, for instance. Dr Johnson was absolutely correct in saying that the law has wisely given women little power because Nature has given them so much.

I wouldn't wish to attack individual feminists, but I do feel it's

dangerous for women to think they are better off without men or vice versa. It seems to me that we both need each other, yet the whole women's movement is geared to the idea that women should dispense with these dirty, nasty men. It's the same the other way round: men can't get by without women. It's natural for women to want to have children, and encouraging them to think that somehow they're better off pursuing a career seems to me a wicked thing to do. It asks women to turn their backs on their natural instincts and produces much unhappiness.

I feel sure that feminism is in part responsible for our huge number of divorces, because women are encouraged to think that, if they are unhappy in their marriages, they have no reason to stay enslaved to a man; that if they don't like it they should just give up. That's wrong, and it is just as wrong for a man to make the same assumption. Women have a natural urge to kick over the traces, as I've constantly found with those I've employed on *Private Eye*. Every so often they think, sod this, I'm off to do something else. If you apply that urge to a marriage, then it can't be a good thing.

My own view is that once you're married, you're married come what may. The whole thing may go wrong, and obviously does from time to time, but to go to the extent of divorcing I find a very objectionable idea. Obviously I can't make predictions for myself. Maybe in ten years' time I shall be divorced, but I hope not. You've been told I once didn't speak to my wife for six or eight months? Well, I thought it was the other way around, but I managed to survive the silence because I can get by on these things. Like my mother, I'm very self-sufficient and don't mind being on my own; and if I'm not getting on with my wife, then I've always my children to talk to. I also feel that whatever difficulties one may get into, whatever rows there are, if you have been married to someone for a long time then the relationship is very difficult to destroy. It contains something that defies any kind of disagreement. Inevitably a relationship will impose strains, because I suppose one likes a quiet life, but you never do get a quiet life, particularly if you want one.

Is there a wide puritan streak in me? Some people use puritanical in the sense of being against promiscuous sex and divorce, abortion and so on. If that is the meaning of being puritanical, then I am, but if it means being against people enjoying themselves, then I'm not. I'm all for people having a good time, and all for them drinking and smoking, though I don't do either myself. There are a great many puritans around who conduct campaigns against things like smoking, even against dogs, and there are strong puritanical influences in society which I'm much against. People tend to think I disapprove of drinking, but I don't. If I

seem to it's only because I have a weakness. If I could drink one glass of wine with my lunch it would be all right, but only one glass is no good to me. I'd rather have no wine than just a single glass.

I've never dared to engage in drug-taking because I'm scared I could easily become addicted. The same applies to the occult – séances, spiritualism or anything of that sort. I deliberately keep away from it all because, I suppose, it has an attraction. Addiction to women? That's quite different. Where sex is concerned, you can only become addicted to perversion, which raises a point that people don't usually realize about homosexuals: that they are like addicts. This is why so many people have been infected with Aids, because homosexuals are in the grip of an addiction they cannot stop. You could never become addicted to women in that sense, though you could grow addicted to beating women or strapping them up or whatever.

My antipathy to homosexuality is directed against homosexual campaigners rather than individual homosexuals. If I'm sitting side by side with a homosexual at lunch, I'm not going to get up and spit in his face since I don't feel that individual repugnance. I don't feel repelled by homosexuals if I meet them. I do object, on the other hand, to the politicizing of homosexuality and the propaganda and promotion of the idea, because I don't believe in the notion being peddled that people are born that way and there is nothing to be done about it. It may well be true of some homosexuals, but the vast majority of those I know seem to me to be quite capable of heterosexual activity and to have a choice. Promoting the idea that they ought to make a choice in favour of the homosexual way of life therefore seems to me a great mistake.

I was impressed to hear Rabbi Blue say on the radio that, although he is a homosexual, he never uses the word 'gay' since there is nothing gay about being a homosexual: it is all very difficult and complicated and not particularly nice. I think that is true of the homosexuals one knows, whose lives on the whole are neither happy nor gay. So to encourage anyone to be like that rather than be married and have children – which is, after all, the main thing in life for most people – is to impose a terrible penalty.

I've never had any ambitions for either of my children. Neither Mary nor I ever pushed them academically, and neither of them did very well at school. I could never get worked up about A-levels or O-levels because I never thought these things mattered. Consequently I never bullied them into working hard. I'm disappointed about their schools, not from their point of view but because I think the schools themselves were bad. I don't know of a good school. I'm very fond of my children, get on well with them and am very proud of them. We're a close family.

I should think my children would have a healthier attitude towards

society as a result of *Private Eye*, that they would be automatically suspicious of all kinds of public figures or television personalities and much better able to assess people than I was at their age. Both my children have good judgement and would not be taken in by charlatans, of whom there are so many around.

As you say, my daughter Jubby has earned a reputation for being something of a free spirit, but I couldn't claim I felt indignant about that incident when she was discovered in the gents at the Reform Club. I'm sorry it resulted in a ban on the *Literary Review*, but it caused me no great hardship or agony. A moment of annoyance maybe, but that doesn't really mean a thing. On the other hand, I was pleased to see that *Naked London*, the book showing her and Fred in the nude, sank without a trace, because I was slightly annoyed about that one. Fortunately no one paid it the slightest attention.

My great hero is William Cobbett, author of *Rural Rides*, who was the sort of character who spent his life attacking politicians. He was forever being put into prison for libel and other offences, yet even so went on and on. He wasn't a revolutionary like Paine, who, though I admire him, was head-in-the-clouds. Cobbett was different: a sensible man who felt a strong antipathy to the Establishment and consensus thinking. I am very much aware of there being a consensus view on certain subjects. If you take someone like Mrs Whitehouse, the consensus view is that here is a lunatic Mrs Grundy waving her umbrella, a ridiculous figure to be laughed at and ridiculed. I therefore tend to identify with Mrs Whitehouse, my instinct being that where you have a consensus it must be wrong.

The moment everybody agrees how terrible everything is in South Africa, then I feel there must be something good about the place. Kierkegaard said something along these lines: that 5,000 people shouting the same thing can only be wrong, even if what they say is true. The same principle applies to much of modern-day journalism. Child abuse, for example, has become a major issue on television, and a kind of hysteria has been worked up because it is something on which everyone can agree. No one, except possibly Bron, will get up and speak for the child abuser, but all will agree he is terrible. In the same way, it is very easy for a vicar to make awful statements about South Africa in a sermon since no one will contradict him. All the time people try to get on these bandwagons of consensus issues.

All my instincts are radical, a radical instinct being one that automatically sides with the underdog, the dispossessed, or the poor – the Palestinians, the Catholics in Northern Ireland, those who are in a minority. It is a basic instinct I hold, coupled with a mistrust of the rich and powerful, and I have come to the conclusion that it is quite rare. Most

people are fundamentally obsequious, including journalists. I think it is very sad. I think and hope my own instincts are too powerful to be seduced, for it is always right to be suspicious of the powerful and wealthy. My other great hero, Dr Johnson, said that the insolence of wealth will creep out, and I like that very much. It distressed me to see how someone like my friend Peter Jay seemed before my eyes to relish the power and wealth that his association with Maxwell brought him.

Since I am suspicious of, and distrustful of, the powerful, and these tend to be right-wing, conservative, fascist people, that makes me, as their enemy, left wing. On the other hand, I don't particularly identify with the Labour Party because there are many aspects of it I don't like, such as militant feminism. I would be more comfortable in the old-fashioned Labour Party. The whole idea of Marxism is abhorrent to me, the great mystery of our time being how many clever people have managed to give their allegiance to Russia, a terrible society in which there is not even enough bread to eat. They can shut their eyes to that and all the outrageous things done in the name of Marx. I used to like to think a lot about who would be in the Resistance if Britain were occupied by a foreign power, and I often assess people in that way.

Left-wing intellectuals also tend to be atheists, so I have an antipathy to them on those grounds. Malcolm Lowry, who wrote that marvellous novel *Under the Volcano*, said he was a conservative Christian anarchist, and I always thought that was what I have been and what Muggeridge has been. I consider people like Germaine Greer and Bron to be conservative Christian anarchists too. I would call us a little party of our own.

LORD LAMBTON

Lord Lambton was born the son of the fifth Earl of Durham in 1922. He first stood for Parliament when he was twenty-two years old and six years later he won Berwick-upon-Tweed for the Conservatives. He disclaimed his peerage but was allowed to sit in Parliament using a courtesy title. He served from 1951 until 1973 when he applied for the Chiltern Hundreds. From 1970 he had been Parliamentary Under-Secretary of State for Defence. In 1942 he married Belinda Blew-Jones and they have six children. He lives in Siena and is the author of several books including *Snow and Other Stories* (1983), *Elizabeth and Alexandra* (1985), *The Abbey in the Wood* (1986) and *The Mountbattens* (1989).

You come from a family with ancient roots. Did the legend of the Lambton Worm figure prominently in your childhood?

No. It was always a sort of fairy story and I don't think anyone took it very seriously. Two books on it have been published, and there was an opera which played in Oxfordshire. But it is a classic story about how the first Lambton broke his word. The witch who told him how to kill the Worm insisted that afterwards he must kill the first living thing he saw, so he told his father to let the dog go the moment the Worm was dead. His father was so excited, however, that he forgot to let go of the dog and instead came running up himself. Lambton failed to kill his father, and although he killed the dog afterwards, the family was still cursed. No Lambton was to die in his bed for nine generations.

The last one had the worst time of it. For eight generations the heads of the family did die in their beds, but when the ninth was ill and his servants thought he was going to depart, they kept trying to throw him on to the floor so he wouldn't die in his bed. Then one day he got better, went for a drive in the park and died on the bridge. So it did turn out to be true in a way, but before that he was so nervous he used to keep pistols by the bed to stop his servants throwing him on to the floor whenever they thought he was dying. It was always rather a comic story.

The family history is certainly interesting. There was a major setback in the seventeenth century when one of the Lambtons was a Cavalier. In reprisal for him being on the King's side all the coal mines, which we always depended on for money, were flooded. But worse than that – or more expensive – was the fact that he had two wives, and by the time he died at the age of fifty-six there were twenty-seven children, and that was ruinous. He had needed to extend the house and educate all twenty-seven, a considerable undertaking even in those days.

What really changed the family was marrying into the Villiers family – a very remarkable one which had a great impact on English history. The Villiers connection produced my family's greatest member, a governor-general of Canada and the man who created the Reform Bill. He was much more a Villiers than a Lambton. Most Lambtons were rather staid and uninteresting I should think from their portraits.

Does being born into the aristocracy give a special viewpoint on the rest of society and the contemporary world?

People who are well born and brought up, go to public schools and are surrounded by people who look after them, do have a sense of security. That's partly due to the fact that you mix with all classes from an early age. The keepers, the groom, people like that. One always got to know them, so there was never any feeling of class antagonism, which is what makes for uncertainty. One realized they were just as good as oneself, if not better, so there was no sense of superiority, which is the sort of bogus thing a lot of *nouveaux riches* try and achieve. When you are fortunate enough to be born and brought up with members of all classes, you don't have that sense, and you think and know everyone is the same as you are and treat them accordingly.

Being born into the aristocracy certainly gives one confidence. I was brought up to think that you always said what you thought. My family always did that. I suppose the classic example of that came about when my first cousin, Alec Douglas-Home, was made prime minister. When his mother was asked what she thought of it, she said well, quite frankly, she'd have preferred Mr Butler – which was straight speaking. For the most part people were delighted, but she was really rather disappointed, and his brothers only said he was a good shot or something of the kind.

As an aristocrat you have a certain position in society which is not shaken much by what you do, and that is the great strength. So many people are terrified they will be dropped by society if they open their mouths and tell the truth. In my political life I always tried to be quite straightforward. I couldn't stand Harold Macmillan when he was prime minister and was always speaking out against him. I was criticized a lot for it at the time, but now the wheel has come full circle and I think that a lot of things I said would happen have happened. Macmillan didn't know the meaning of truth. He was an actor, moved by emotion, and that is a bad thing for a prime minister to be.

Was Macmillan an eccentric? I think he was a conscious eccentric. At the end of his life he tried to accentuate his eccentricity and started telling stories about himself which others had told but which had never occurred. For instance, the book about him by Alistair Horne has a farcical bit where Macmillan was talking to Kennedy who supposedly

said, 'I don't know about you, Harold, but I get a headache if I don't go to bed with a woman for three days.' It was just a story, but Macmillan began to believe it, as he did with a number of others told about him. He started retelling them himself as though they were the gospel truth.

As for eccentrics generally, there are certainly nothing like the ones about that there used to be – in the countryside, anyway. When I was a boy, parsons were often eccentric because the countryside was so cut off from towns that people there were able to develop their own little kingdoms, in the Church, in the law, or as landlords. They became little kings on their own and did and said what they wanted, and so they became noted figures, almost caricatures of themselves.

There have recently been disadvantages attached to being an aristocrat because, after the war, the upper classes were rather looked down on. They were blamed for the war and were thought to have been behind the pre-war governments, and many of them were in those governments. I think the return of the gossip column has given them a new lease of life as glamorous figures. The man more responsible than anyone for that is, I suppose, Nigel Dempster – a remarkable columnist in his way, though he's said some very unpleasant things about me. He's a remarkably readable writer and he's made the whole class much more interesting than they were before he started on it.

The often rather bad publicity in the past has sometimes made it hard for people from an aristocratic background to get into the House of Commons. Before the war, if you had a name, you could get into the House of Commons, and a lot of very unsuitable people got in just because of their title. That doesn't happen now. Those who do succeed in being elected do extraordinarily well, and today we have the example of William Waldegrave, who is an aristocrat, and I think young people like him are surmounting the prejudice. One of Mrs Thatcher's chief assets is that she regards merit as the criterion, and if you have merit, it doesn't matter who you are. If you don't have merit, it doesn't matter who you are either. She looks for merit in any level of society she can find it.

Speaking of the charm of the aristocracy, don't make any mistake about it, a great number of the British aristocracy are not charming. Some of them are absolutely minus charm. Charm is quite distinct from breeding. The Irish peasant has enormous charm, but you wouldn't call him an aristocrat. There is hardly an Irishman who can't charm the birds off a tree, the old blarney, as they call it. In fact, the Irish lower classes are probably more charming than the upper. Charm is found in every stratum of society, and it can be quite a dangerous thing because it influences people and makes them like whoever has it. Even villains can be charming.

Yes, I did know Sir Oswald Mosley, and he had charm without any doubt. He also had a gift of mesmerism, which was the strength of his political standing. I liked him very much, actually. He was fascinating to talk to, had an extraordinarily clear mind and knew exactly what he wanted. He proposed a scheme in the early 1930s which, had the Labour or Conservative party accepted it, would probably have done away with unemployment years before it happened. But he was turned down. He had left the Conservative party because he found them so old-fashioned, and tried the Labour party but found they were in their way just as conservative. So he was driven out by his own talents.

It was a pity. He was a most remarkable speaker. I went to hear him after the war, and you could see people listening to him, really drinking in what he said. Of course, what he was saying by then sounded so old-fashioned that he was out of tune with the generation of Gaitskell and Butlerism. It was a hopeless uphill battle, though he did foresee the survival of Germany, the revival of Germany, and the reunification which is likely to come now as well as the necessity for a strong Europe to balance it. In fact, he foresaw many of the situations which now exist.

People are inclined to dismiss Mosley as a fascist. He wasn't a fascist in many senses of the word. He was basically a radical, though of course he did go too far towards Hitler. I think he would have made a radical leader of the country, but he was too gifted not to be in a hurry. Had he waited his time, he would probably have been prime minister in the 1930s, but one of the troubles with people who are given to a belief in their own leadership is that they are seldom prepared to wait. Therefore they make mistakes.

The classic example of a man born with all the gifts of leadership in his generation is Sir James Goldsmith. He is a man who can talk to people and mesmerize them into believing what he believes, because he believes it so strongly. He is the most Napoleonic figure of this generation. Goldsmith has built up a stupendous fortune out of bravado and a belief in himself, and has the power of leadership, but whether that power is dangerous is another matter. It's a great pity that he wasn't made a member of the House of Lords, and although he might have been in too much of a hurry to achieve a great deal himself, the very fact of him being in the House would have meant there was a constant flow of ideas and impressions. He is the most iconoclastic person I have ever met. He makes one understand great men in the past who overcame extraordinary obstacles by sheer force of personality.

How in a democratic state can we justify having an unelected house of peers as part of the governmental system?

I think the House of Lords really works rather well now, because when you say unelected house of peers, that is true in some sense, but in another, now that the government can make life peers, you are getting a good number of people brought in from outside. I wouldn't say the hereditary peers were showing up very well at the moment. A large number of the efficient ones are the life peers, especially in the Labour and Liberal parties. The hereditary House of Lords is a fairly harmless anachronism, but the more life peers of the right sort you get into it – and by that I don't mean the sort Wilson elected – the better it will be.

You always have to reward your supporters, but I think Mrs Thatcher has made one or two bad appointments to the House of Lords. On the other hand, the most extreme, the most violent of her supporters, who chanted a song about Heath after he had been defeated, was never rewarded at all. So she hasn't rewarded all of her followers, not the most extreme ones, and she's always had a lot of so-called 'Wets' in her government. She still has. Whitelaw was for years one of her stand-bys, and he was certainly not as right wing as she was, but he always supported her in the long run. To return to Wilson's honours list, I think it was very strange and rather regrettable because they kept going to prison. A very funny lot.

Was your own entry into politics the fulfilment of an early ambition?

I always wanted to be in politics and I fought the 1945 election when I was twenty-two. I think I was the youngest candidate in England. Of course, I was overwhelmingly beaten. Then I fought the 1950 election from bed – I had pneumonia. But I got in for Berwick in 1951 when I was just twenty-nine. I have to say that although I did regard political life as a ruling passion, when it came to it I minded being out of it much less than I had expected. To begin with, I don't think I really ever had good enough health to be a politician. One of the great requisites, certainly for the modern politician, is health. I had incipient jaundice for years which made me feel very ill nearly all the time I was in politics. I really don't miss anything about politics very much, though I'm still quite interested. I always read the political articles in the papers and make up my own mind about a subject.

You ask, concerning my own experience, whether there should be restrictions on the private lives of public figures. Well, I don't see how you can have them, but there are dangers attached to the rather quaint state of affairs that exists at the moment. Before the war, politicians knew exactly what private life they wanted, and everybody knew about it. Dozens of members of parliament of all parties went to bed with their secretaries, had love affairs and indulged what are called sexual foibles, but it was never in the papers. Everybody knew, but it was

always considered a joke. Suddenly every little thing is in the papers and these things become public property because the American system of reporting, which didn't exist here before the war, now does exist and goes after exposing people. In the United States, before the war, a large number of very decent people would not go into politics for fear of being exposed as this or that. The same thing is happening here today.

The reason comes out of both public hypocrisy and the press emphasis on circulation figures. The papers do it because they know it sells copies, but they also do it because they know people like it. Morality always has been a red rag to a bull. I remember Macaulay's famous statement that nothing was so ridiculous as the British public in one of its fits of morality. There always was a terrific degree of hypocrisy about it all.

It is rather a curious contradiction that just when the greater part of the people of this country are far more immoral than ever before, these same people want to impose morality on others. Sexual drive very often goes with political drive. If you look at Lloyd George, he was almost manic in his pursuit of women. I once had a secretary who was said to be Lloyd George's illegitimate daughter. She told me how her father would advertise in the papers for so-called assistants, women who used to come from abroad. He would try to seduce them, and very often succeed. This daughter told me how his wife became so desperate at his peccadilloes that she eventually hired from Ireland a one-armed woman with a squint, and even then Lloyd George seduced her after a week. None of it ever came out in the papers. I think you do constrict talent if you suddenly constrict morals.

I'm not sure it's really in any way that the British public want their politicians to behave like saints. They do enjoy the scandals enormously, they love reading about them, but I don't think it matters to them. I don't want to talk about myself here, but I recall that when Profumo resigned in 1960, there was a poll taken in his constituency and an overwhelming number of his constituents said they would vote for him again. If Profumo had not resigned, he could have been re-elected with a very large majority in Stratford-upon-Avon and have stayed on in Parliament. He could have said, 'I told a lie. That was the mistake I made, though I don't think it is a resigning matter.' His resignation arose out of trying to contain the thing so that other people would not be dragged into the imbroglio. The great majority of my constituents said they would support me, too, but I had also resigned by then. There was really no alternative the way things are. I received a great number of letters of sympathy and one of the papers had a poll of three or four hundred people, and they said what had happened had nothing to do with my politics.

As for the so-called security aspects, when Profumo left I made a speech in the House of Commons saying it would have been much

more dangerous if he had not been to bed with Miss Keeler. By going to bed with her it was made perfectly plain what he was doing with her, and nobody should have minded because he was probably only doing what 80 per cent of the members of the House of Commons had done. If he had not gone to bed with her, he would have been talking about God knows what and it would have been very suspicious. But everything was turned upside down, and the fact he had been to bed with her was made the reason for his resignation.

Morally speaking, I haven't changed my view that most men would expect their wives to be tolerant about what are essentially unimportant episodes. If every wife left her husband because he had been unfaithful to her, there would be very few marriages going. When I said at my resignation that there's a world of difference between doing something and being found out, I think it was just the truth. It always has been the truth. A lot of leading Conservatives were having wild love affairs, had long-standing mistresses, so long as it didn't become too public. Look at Kennedy. Everybody knew roughly what he was up to and nothing about it ever came out. The American press was so much quieter then than it is now, and he was a hero to the press as well as to the public, especially to the rather left-wing press, so everything was covered up.

Interviewed by Robin Day in 1975, you said you had sometimes, when abroad, taken such drugs as hashish and opium on the basis of autres pays, autres moeurs. *Where should legislation stand in combating the serious drug problem today?*

I think it's a terrible problem now. There's all the difference between things like opium and cannabis and the hard drugs. Heroin really is a killer, as is cocaine, but the terrifying fact we have to remember is that alcohol was also a huge killer in the 1930s in the United States after Prohibition. I don't know what the answer is. Nobody seems to have any difficulty getting drugs. People who want to have them have them, and if they don't get them they seem to murder or steal to get them.

It would certainly be quite interesting if some country did try the legalization of drugs to see what the effect would be, but here you come up against practical politics. The fact is that if any party in Britain tried to legalize drugs, all the inborn hypocrisy of the English character would cry out against it, and legitimately in some ways, because the risk might be considerable. I don't think it's a risk that any politician will ever be able to take because the opposition party would climb on a moral bandwagon.

We once had a generation of giants in politics – giants in rhetoric and personality.

Now the species seems quite extinct, the level of debate reduced to slanging and point scoring.

One of the reasons is that the right people aren't going into politics. It is now a hell of a life. I don't know quite what the divorce rate for politicians is today, but it is enormously high. You have this terrifically intense constituency life these days, where you have to go every weekend and make speeches and think not about the state of the country but about the state of your constituents. When constituents demand more and more attention, it's not good for politicians. Constituents ought to elect a man and then leave him alone, not insist on his coming to tea once a week or once a month.

Rhetoric aside, I think Mrs Thatcher will be remembered as a very remarkable prime minister who achieved more than Churchill did in his peacetime days, though she certainly wouldn't have been as good a war prime minister as he was. Churchill was too old once the war was over. After he had a stroke the country was ruled in reality, though nobody knew it, by three men, Sir Jock Colville, Sir Burke Trend and Christopher Soames. They really kept the front up. For many months Churchill wasn't fit to be prime minister. I don't think the men of that generation were always quite the giants they were made out to be. Butler may have been a giant, but he had clay feet. And Macmillan's achievement in this country was to leave it in the most appalling state for Wilson or anyone who succeeded him.

I certainly would have been a Thatcherite today. I find the present demeaning of Mrs Thatcher rather low-spirited because she has achieved really extraordinary things for this country. The fact is that when she came in the trade unions had defeated Callaghan and were ready to take over. Her battle with Scargill was a historic battle and very few people would have been able to go into it with the strength she showed or to have succeeded as she did. That was really crossing the Rubicon for this country. If we hadn't been led across, I don't know how we would have managed, because the country was getting into a worse and worse economic mess and she has created a sort of economic miracle. We're having a bad hiccup at the moment, but fundamentally our economic position is still strong despite the so-called crisis.

Wilson is said to be discredited now, but I think it's a little hard on him because he's not very well. The trouble with Wilson was that he was too good-natured and he found it very difficult to sack anybody. Then, of course, he thought the way to placate the unions was to feed them, get them to Downing Street, give them drinks, lay on parties for them, and in that way he bribed them to follow him. And, of course, they just took more and more and ratted on the Labour Party. It was Wilson who created the third estate: the trade unionists who were really

directing the government. Once they had defeated Callaghan in 1978, they then tried to defeat Mrs Thatcher. Callaghan was a much more considerable man than he's made out to be, but he never had a chance as prime minister and it was actually Mrs Thatcher who took the bull by the horns and pulled the country out of a sort of bog where restrictive practices were bringing everything to a standstill.

In The Times *of 20 January 1975, you said that not only were Sir Keith Joseph and Mrs Thatcher discredited as contenders for the party leadership, they were also discredited as leading Conservatives . . .*

What I meant then was that those who were called the 'Wets' regarded Mrs Thatcher and Sir Keith Joseph as dangerous lunatics, and when it looked as though she was putting herself forward as a candidate, there was a tremendous movement to discredit her. It didn't succeed because of the strength of her personality and the very shrewd campaign carried out by Airey Neave on her behalf in the House of Commons. She beat Heath to the amazement of everybody. The Tory Party couldn't believe what had happened; it seemed impossible. I did not know her very well and had no idea she had all these qualities underneath her slightly genteel surface.

I can understand Heath's lasting bitterness. He is a remarkable man with great talents, but he does find it difficult to communicate and he has been his own worst enemy. He is a shy man, a very shy man, who has lived for himself and for politics, putting politics before private life most markedly. He is basically a kind man, who has good instincts, but he doesn't quite understand how to deal with people. One of the jobs of the prime minister is to see the chairman of the 1922 Committee every week to get the feeling of the back benches, and I remember, shortly after Heath became prime minister, that Vere Harvey, the then chairman, went to see him. Now, Vere Harvey had been in the RAF and was a man who liked a drink, one who would settle down with a whisky and soda and talk twice as well if he had one. Heath didn't understand this at all, and Harvey wasn't offered a drink of any kind. The next time Harvey went in to see Heath, he asked for a drink, and Heath rang the bell and said, 'Bring a cup of tea for Air Commodore Harvey.'

This incident showed a misunderstanding caused by Heath's total concentration on the mechanics of politics to the exclusion of the human beings who ran them. That was his fault: he lived for politics, and when he became prime minister it was his dream come true. He thought he would transform Britain, but then he was hit by two very unfortunate things. The first was the price of oil suddenly going up from \$3 to \$15 a barrel, which totally upset the whole British economy and made

everything he had planned impossible. The second was the miners' strike, which led to him being very badly advised, in my view, about the date for the election. Who was responsible, I do not know, but I do know Lord Carrington was against the date for which the election was called. It should either have been for two weeks earlier or two weeks later, and to have called it just after giving in to the trade unions was a disaster.

Heath minded what happened terribly, and I think he considered it was fortune and not his own mistakes that was responsible for him no longer being prime minister. He saw, as he thought, success being dashed from his lips just when he had the answer, for he passionately believed in himself as a conciliator, someone who could draw all Britain together. He was always a member of the one-nation group, as I had been years before, and that made him mind dreadfully about his failure. But he minded especially because it was a woman who unseated him; he felt that made him look stupid. I wouldn't say it did at all, but it was all a great pity because the country needed Heath and, had he held his ground and been able to overcome his bitterness, he could certainly have served Mrs Thatcher and built up a power base in the party which might have made her style of government much more difficult.

Whether it was all for good or ill, I don't know, but Heath minded beyond how a prime minister should mind, the reason being that he was so totally engrossed with politics that he didn't have anything except his music – which is a minor consolation – to fall back on. He wasn't married, he didn't have children, he didn't have a family life at all. It was a tragedy – really very sad. One only wishes he could take a new lease of life because he is still a man of remarkable quality.

In 1976 you said you were afraid that if the Conservatives lost the election there would be few conservative beliefs left to conserve after another five years of socialism. After ten years of Thatcherism, many would claim we see the yuppies reigning supreme and ruthlessness and single-mindedness dominant at the expense of compassion. What is your view?

You have to be brash to make money, and so there is bound to be a lot of attention concentrated on the yuppies, but I don't think they're any worse than people who made money in the Victorian age, who talked about brass, who built hideous houses and churches. The money we're spending on the National Health Service has never been greater, and it's never been a more inefficient service. Meanwhile nobody knows exactly how to tackle the problem. You could say that Mrs Thatcher has tackled it in quite the wrong way. It should be tackled by concentrating the public's attention on the number of people in the NHS who are actually nurses or doctors, or assistants to doctors or contributors to

medicine. These numbers should then be published alongside what I would call the number of fellow travellers who hang about hospitals filling in forms, wasting time, red tapers and so on.

What I don't think you can say is that someone who spends the money she spends on the NHS can be without compassion. It seems to me that she cares passionately about things. She wants to get a country which is self-supporting as far as possible, where people can work hard and make money if they can. The NHS should be efficiently run with nurses doing the job and not this enormous wastage of money on those who are not actually employed in nursing. I cannot understand why the arguments have been so badly presented, and I think there is still time before the next general election to look at the whole matter of presentation and the refiguring of the structures of those engaged directly in medicine and those who are red-tape hangers-on.

Another question on which Mrs Thatcher has played it all wrong concerns the sort of federation we are to have in a United Europe. The majority of countries want, as much as she does, not a tight but a loose federation. They want to be able to continue making their laws in their own way. Mrs Thatcher, by leading with her chin, has made it possible for other countries to hide behind her and not come out with their opinions, and therefore she has miscalculated her tactics. Had she played it more skilfully and kept more in the background, others would have done what she has done and she need never have been labelled a bad European.

Whether Mrs Thatcher would win an election tomorrow is almost impossible to tell. When an election comes, it's like Dr Johnson said: When a man is going to be hung tomorrow it concentrates his mind wonderfully. When you're going to elect a government tomorrow, it concentrates your mind in the same way. I don't consider Kinnock is a very impressive personality, and I'm sure the Labour party would be a house of Babel if it were in power again, because there are left-wingers and right-wingers and there are ambitionists. I don't think they quite know what they would do.

Are they really going to renationalize? If so, where's the money coming from? Who's going to pay for it? Whether Mrs Thatcher can be unseated would depend on whether the economy was right by the time the election was fought. People vote for their own pockets as much as for anything. And if things are good, they're not going to risk it by having the Labour party back again and a lot of meaningless policies and unknown expenditure.

Do I find Mrs Thatcher colourful or attractive? No, I don't find her colourful and I don't find her a very attractive woman. I don't think she has many womanly graces, but I do think she has courage and convictions. Basically what she wants is to create a prosperous country

which can pay for itself, pay for its health and social services of all kinds, and not go bankrupt in the process. She has made great steps in that direction despite this momentary hiccup.

A lot of young journalists claim to find her sexually attractive.

Is that so? Well, some years ago there was an association of prostitutes in Italy who were known as the Grandmothers of Milan, and I think the youngest was seventy and the eldest bedridden and eighty-seven, and they did roaring trade with very young people. So perhaps she does have this peculiar fascination for the young.

Journalists have sometimes commented to me – especially if they come from the Daily Telegraph *– that they take exception to having to address you as Lord Lambton when you have in fact relinquished your peerage. Can you clarify this?*

I don't think there has really been any confusion. What I had was a courtesy title which is borne by the eldest son of a peer. It is not a lawful title but a courtesy title. I sat in the House of Commons when my father was still alive as Antony Claud Frederick Lambton, Esquire, commonly called Lord Lambton, and that is really all there is to it. In the Peerage Bill it is absolutely stressed that courtesy titles do not exist in law. I continued to sit in the House of Commons after my father died. No change was made in the register of the House of Commons because it wasn't a legal name.

What is your attitude to the monarchy as it exists today?

I see it as a very sensible institution. Franco brought back the monarchy in Spain, and when he was asked why, he said for the simple reason that it saved so much time. If you haven't got a king you have to spend a terrible lot of time at receptions and such-like events. You either have to have a president or you have to have a king. The Queen is immensely popular and she has really done a rather wonderful job. She's been queen for thirty-eight years and she has never made a really serious mistake in all that time. Now that is a remarkable thing. You don't want a very brilliant, dynamic queen, or a queen who interferes in affairs of state. She hasn't interfered and the whole royal family continues to be a source of enormous interest to people.

The only danger I see about Prince Charles is that he might start interfering in politics and it's something a king can't do. Neither Edward VII nor George V nor George VI nor the Queen have done so. But I think that when Prince Charles does become king he will find that he has so much to do, such varied responsibilities, that he will probably not branch out into opinions too much. It really wouldn't be his function.

I know he has said some things that made people think him eccentric, about talking to flowers and bushes, for instance, but for hundreds of years people have been talking to flowers, to bees and trees; all countrymen do it. And Prince Charles is much more of a countryman than people realize. There is no reason why he shouldn't make a good king so long as he doesn't mix himself up with the politics of the country. He's obviously got charm, ability and a love of art, which no member of the Hanoverian family has had since the Prince Regent. And he can express himself quite well. But it's an impossible position, being Prince of Wales. It must be immensely frustrating. I think one has to forgive anyone who is Prince of Wales a great deal. He must be bursting all the time to express his own real opinion.

When you wrote your recent controversial book about Mountbatten, was it simply to put the record straight or were there other factors?

I wrote a novel some years ago, published by you, called *Elizabeth and Alexandra*, about the last Tsarina and her sister. They were Mountbatten's aunts, and I had to go through a lot of the Mountbatten papers to research the book. To my extreme annoyance I found that practically everything he said was lies. He was a myth-maker – he lived in the land of myth. I don't know what the things were that I brought out that anyone is said to have objected to, because the most damaging thing had already come out in Zeigler's book: the business of his trying to get the name of the royal family changed to Mountbatten-Windsor. It does seem rather ridiculous that Mountbatten, who was pure German, was trying to foist a German name on to the British royal family. He didn't succeed, of course.

No doubt my book wasn't welcomed in royal circles, but a lot of the royal family aren't great readers, and if they had been they would have found all the same undesirable things coming to light in Zeigler or Mountbatten's own books. He said the most extraordinary things, and when I quoted them I was said to be wrong, though when Mountbatten himself said them, they were supposedly all right. He could not tell the truth; he simply couldn't. He didn't know how to.

Mountbatten, you see, had an agonizing youth as a German boy among four or five hundred English boys. He was mercilessly bullied and in my view retreated into mythland for ever afterwards. But my book, you know, hardly dealt with Mountbatten himself; it really dealt with his family. He was as untruthful about that as he was about himself. For example, he always claimed to be royal. He wasn't royal in any way. His father was known to be the illegitimate son of a German baron, his mother the daughter of an impecunious Pole whose father had a very strange career which I could have brought out but didn't. In

fact, I wasn't nearly as unpleasant as I might have been about the Mountbattens.

His books about his family are absolutely packed with imagination. He had this curious love of grandeur that he couldn't get away from, and in his memoirs one is shown how he was never wrong, never made a mistake in his life, and so on and so forth. I don't know how one would feel about him if one had been one of the people sent by him on the disaster of the Dieppe raid, but he was a very interesting man because of his remarkable personality. He was a remarkable leader of men, with the charisma to make those who served under him adore him and minimize his faults. If you met him, and he wanted you to like him, you would, but although he had the great qualities of leadership, he wasn't a considerable man otherwise. He wasn't a clever man, he was almost illiterate, and the books he advised his daughters to read you might suggest to a ten-year-old boy. But although I wrote political journalism for about thirty years, I never once attacked him. What finally really annoyed me was discovering a man gradually creating a whole school of history which was an absolute myth, all to glorify his own family.

I didn't really go into the rumours about his sexuality, though a lot of people sent me some of the most grotesque things relating to him. One was a picture of a man with a fox and hounds tattooed on his back, the fox going up his behind. I asked two of his friends who had known him very well and often seen him bathing, and they said such a tattoo simply didn't exist. But I wasn't looking for any evidence of that sort because, to begin with, his children are still alive, and secondly, it is quite wrong to go into a person's sexual habits unless they have had a profound influence on his life. Whatever habits Mountbatten may have had, they didn't change his character one iota. He was a man entirely devoted to ambition and to righting the wrong he thought had been done to his father by becoming First Sea Lord. His sexual life wasn't really sex. It was just exercise, that was all. Going to bed with a woman was no more important to him than going for a mile run.

I know nothing whatever about the Queen's feelings over any influence he may have had on Prince Charles, but he was probably very kind and Prince Charles is known to have been very fond of him. He was kind because he was in love with royalty, longed to be royal himself, always used the royal door at Knights of the Garter meetings when he had no real right to. He adored royalty, and his diaries after 1920 reveal how incredibly ingratiating and obsequious he was to the then Prince of Wales, Edward VIII, as a young man. Prince Edward had been best man at Mountbatten's wedding and afterwards stuck by him. Mountbatten always did everything he could with him, would travel to India with him, use him in every sense he possibly could, and

then, after the abdication had happened, he didn't even go to his wedding but gave the excuse that he hadn't been asked.

Well, he usually went to everything without being asked, anyhow, and the former Prince of Wales was very upset indeed. Afterwards Mountbatten did try to go and see the Windsors and get things out of them, but there was such antagonism that the butler or footman was eventually asked to stay in any room where he was in case he put something in his pocket. He behaved in a very odd way to the Windsors, though when one says he liked Prince Charles, I'm sure he did. Whether he would have gone on liking Prince Charles if Prince Charles had stepped down as heir to the throne is hard to say. He certainly didn't like the Duke of Windsor after he abdicated – until he died, when he was his best friend again.

About your literary career: what are you working on at the moment?

I'm writing six short stories about the Holocaust. I wanted to write fiction again because it seems to me that one of the troubles with making people realize about the evil of the German reaction is that so many books about the Holocaust are presented as statistics. It is quite impossible to comprehend a book that says 350 were taken and gassed in Auschwitz, next day 400 went to Belsen and had nothing to eat. What I'm trying to do is to fictionalize and put flesh on some of the things that actually happened and make them happen to real people, and to show that those who carried out many of the atrocities were not necessarily extreme Nazis but quite ordinary people who were sucked into the Nazi machine. I think the Germans have a habit, a national habit, of needing orders, wanting to obey orders. I don't know what the position is today, but as long ago as about 1800 Goethe said the trouble with Germany was that Germans prefer order to justice. I think that is quite true, and it is alarming what is happening now with the deaths of so many millions being reduced to statistics.

One of the tragic things in the world today is that Israel has begun to behave in a manner in some ways not dissimilar to how the Germans behaved in the war. You have virtually a state of war in Israel, and they are treating the Arabs like enemies. Remember the pictures on television of Israeli soldiers breaking bones. Power degenerates into cruelty. I've always sympathized with the retention of Israel as a state, but I very much doubt the Israelis will be able to hold world opinion if they go on as they are at the moment. I think they will have to withdraw from the territories, certainly from a large portion of the territories, because they can't continue to rule people who don't want to be ruled without using methods reminiscent of what happened in the war.

But to get back to fiction, what I'm interested in is telling a story,

because the whole of life is a story. I was rather annoyed when I wrote a book called *Snow and Other Stories* and a critic said it was a fault that the stories were open-ended. An open-ended story is much better. All Chekhov's stories were open-ended, such stories being just glimpses of someone's life in which the author tries to portray what they were like. Story-telling is the same sort of art as painting. Berenson, the noted art critic, used the word 'tactility', which he said was one of the great virtues of painting. You had to feel that the person in a portrait was so real you could touch him. Well, I think fiction wants to be the same, wants to create real people whom you feel you know and could touch.

I remember that the late Duff Cooper – the First Lord of the Admiralty during the war, probably forgotten by the younger generation – once told me how, when he was at school, one of the masters read them a Sherlock Holmes story and said, 'Now I've read you this story I want you to remember one thing – Sherlock Holmes is a far more living personality than I am or any of you, or probably than anyone you'll ever meet.' And I believe that is the aim of all short-story and fiction writers. If you look at the Russians, again and again there are so many people you feel you know, who might come into the room. Anna Karenina and Natasha in *War and Peace* are two of the greatest characters I suppose anyone has ever known. What I am trying to do in this Holocaust series is bring to reality events which have been lost in detail. Make something real.

Certainly fiction does have an effect on the way people think and behave. You only need to look back at Goethe's *Young Werther*. The book completely transformed a whole generation of upper and middle class young Germans. Literally hundreds of them killed themselves as a result of trying to be this tragic German figure. You see, the Germans haven't much sensibility, and as soon as they were suddenly told they did have sensibility, they persuaded themselves they could love, and when they found they couldn't they simply killed themselves, which was an extraordinary syndrome. Salinger was someone else who affected a whole generation. With *The Catcher in the Rye* he made a whole generation of American boyhood comprehensible.

Do I approve of censorship? Not really. I don't think it does any good. However, in a way censorship very often helps an author. The Victorian novelists, for example, were greatly helped by not being able to write about sex. It's always said that Thackeray in *Vanity Fair* could not portray Becky Sharp as the little prostitute she was, and that that caused a novel to be written which describes her absolutely perfectly. It means you have to dwell on the details which bring the person to life. Curiously enough, the sexiest book I've ever read is probably *The Mill on the Floss. Adam Bede* and *The Mill on the Floss* are books of the sort of intense female frustration that could never possibly have been

conveyed when there weren't morals to be kept, laws to be kept, and restraint on authors. It did pose an author great problems, but when these were overcome the result has been masterly. People's thoughts are far more interesting than the physical jerking which pervades modern literature.

Yes, I was quite waspish in my review of John Mortimer's book on Tuscany. John Mortimer's a very good writer, but I think rather a contemptible man. He believes it's absolutely fine for him to be a left-wing socialist and to drink champagne at night. When a writer descends to the level of his book about Tuscany, full of the most embarrassing things and written at the lowest common denominator tourist level, I think one wants to be as waspish as possible. I wish I had been hornettish.

Baroness Falkender made a comment to me about your great charisma.

I don't think I've got very much charisma.

Do you hold any religious convictions?

Not very strong ones. I have a vague sort of hope that there may be an after-life, but I see no logic to prove it and every sort of logic to disprove it. There lingers something in me, however, from beliefs imbued in my subconscious in the past, the idea of there being some world beyond to which people one loved have gone and where one can meet them, though where it can be and how it can be set up is something quite beyond me. I only wish I had the faith of a good Catholic.

I find it very difficult to believe in God. It's quite easy to believe in the Devil. If there is a God, what has He been doing in the world? Why has He created one and a half billion Chinese mostly living in starvation? There are millions of people being born and dying in India. Every day the dead are pitchforked into carts by men going round the streets and throwing them in like bundles of hay. Why is God doing all this? Is he punishing mankind as he did in the Old Testament?

You have to have the grace of belief, yes, but you have to believe a lot of damn silly things as well, especially if you're an old-fashioned Roman Catholic. Then, of course, one of the main reasons why religion is dying is nobody believes in Hell any more. Hell was a very salutary weapon in the hands of governments and priests. It kept a lot of people under control. In Italy, where I spend much of my time, the priests used to rule with a rod of iron and the wretched people believed that, if they sinned, they would go to Hell and it would be everlasting. Practically every church had a picture of Hell, flames, devils pulling people away from Heaven by the legs and sticking things inside them, killing them.

I can't understand what God is doing. I mean, if you look at the world now, what has Aids to do with the Africans – with poor people? Then you get that old arse Runcie whom I can't understand at all. He seems one of the most inadequate Archbishops of Canterbury there ever has been, a rather pathetic old man who doesn't want to upset anybody, but only wants to please everybody, yet doesn't know how to. He seems a disaster for the Church of England because he appoints people who deny a number of its tenets, like the Bishop of Durham.

I don't know what's happened to Christianity. People no longer believe in God, really, but in some sort of instinct. I myself have never been able to understand what form He takes. As for the Trinity, what's the point of the Trinity when One will do? Why should God want to shelve off his responsibilities on to the Holy Ghost and the Son, and why put his wretched Son on the Cross? Why portray it for the rest of the world to gloat at in every church in Christendom? The Christian religion is the only one I know which portrays cruelty as its symbol. The Moslems are nothing like so cruel.

But everyone has an inherent cowardliness, and as you grow older you either consciously or unconsciously try to persuade yourself there is an after-life, because the idea of leaving everybody you know and all your family behind is not appealing. You just have to face the fact that that's it, really. I feel so sorry for old people who live thinking that the reward of life is going to be in Heaven. When you're nearly dead it gives you a compensation to think that there's someone who's going to look after you just beyond the nursing-home bed, that there's a beneficent man who's going to take you up to Heaven. It gives you a certain satisfaction as you lie there, whereas if you think you're going to be stubbed out like a cigarette end thrown out of a window, then it depresses you. So naturally you try and see pleasant alternatives. One does it all through life.

Looking back, do you ever wonder how you might have fared if you had stayed in politics?

I always thought after I left politics that the most important thing was to make another life. The most pointless thing in life is regret. It's the biggest waste of time in the world. One's life is a train on a one-way journey, and once you've passed a particular point, there's no way you're going to get back. The only thing is to go on and enjoy the other places where the train arrives. I wouldn't say I'm a very happy person, but I don't think I'm very unhappy either. I'm not bitter and I'm very interested in people. There's no such thing as a happy life. I always rather despise those who complain of an unhappy childhood, especially once they have reached the age of twenty-five. Everybody

has difficulties as a child at one stage or another. In fact, children who are too happy often lead disastrous lives because they're not prepared for the buffets and blows of fate.

As to my marriage, I have been married for over forty years and my wife and I live apart for most of the time. It is an arrangement that of course has its difficulties, though it is probably the best compromise there is. The whole of life is a compromise. Nothing is black, nothing is white. No, I don't really believe in divorce, though that, I should think, is probably a result of convention. As a child I never knew anyone who had been divorced. Childish impressions have an unpleasant way of fixing themselves in your mind.

For friendship, my greatest friends have nearly all been women. I find women more sympathetic than men. I also find them more logical. Men are so illogical because ambition is always distorting their logic. They're channelled and much more selfish. Women are watchers of life, observers in life, manipulators behind the scenes in life. I find their views much more interesting than those of men, who are always walking down their own road, not looking this way or that, just talking about the things they meet on the road – usually very boring.

Have you an unfulfilled ambition?

No. At my age – I'm sixty-seven – you can't really hope to do anything immense. One of the consolations of age is that you see the pettiness of material success, how it doesn't very often bring happiness. Also, when you're young, you mind whether people like you, you mind if you've said something stupid, you mind if you're not asked to some occasion or other, but when you get older you look on these matters with slightly detached eyes. You mind much less and things are much simpler. I don't think I could bear to be young again.

SIR YEHUDI MENUHIN

Yehudi Menuhin was born in New York in 1911 of Russian Jewish parents. He and his musically gifted sisters were educated by private tutors. He made his début in San Francisco at the age of seven, in Paris aged ten, in New York aged eleven and in Berlin aged thirteen. Since then he has played with most of the world's orchestras and conductors and received numerous awards and honours, including peace prizes. During the war he played nearly 500 benefit concerts for the Red Cross. His first marriage was dissolved in 1938 and two years after the war he married Diana Gould. In 1963 he founded the Menuhin School of Music in Surrey. In 1965 he became a KBE and in 1985 he adopted British nationality, two years before he received the Order of Merit.

Albert Einstein said when he heard you play as a young boy, 'Now I know there is a God in heaven.' Were you aware of the extraordinary nature of your talent?

I'm still not aware of it, and I become less and less aware of it as I listen to very remarkable talented children who play beautifully, and then hear of others who rob banks at the age of eleven, others who tap into computers at the age of twelve and learn the secrets of the Pentagon, and others who storm into Tiananmen Square and are ready to be immolated for their peaceful purposes. I feel more and more that I'm one of a great many people, almost one of a great many young people, and at the age of seventy-three that is probably a permissible illusion. When I was a child I felt absolutely normal and resented any allusion to *Wunderkinder* and prodigies. I hated it and I think I was right then and am right now. No doubt I played beautifully and had deep feeling, but Einstein was a man who was very impulsive, very emotional, and he could have said the same thing about his own remarkable intuitive discovery of the oneness of the universe. Anyone who looks on an insect or a flower could say there is a God within us and we are a part of that God.

I am indebted to the quality of my parents and my teachers, and their high-mindedness. There was never any talk of money in the house, no vulgarity; always high purpose, good literature and poetry and a great deal of fun. I was spared all the preoccupations with violence, or with sex, or with the unhealthy worries and frustrations that many people have to live under; the bad air, the sidewalks they have to walk on, the ugliness they are surrounded by. I feel therefore fortunate and grateful. I believe firmly that children bring a great deal into the world that they then forget. Learning is a process of forgetting. It sounds a paradox, but none the less, as we learn to live in the world, we forget that

intangible quality we brought with us when we were born. People are conditioned by their prenatal stage.

I know that my mother was looking forward to having me and was very happy, and very much in love with my father, during the time she carried me. I was therefore surrounded by love, appreciation, warmth, health and trust, as well as encouragement to follow in the good ideals of unity. I remember, as a child, being disturbed when I saw the exhaust coming out of cars, because I knew instinctively that there was a unity in the world, that whatever came had to go, that whatever was burnt was transformed into something else. All these philosophical questions preoccupied me. One of my earliest dreams was to bring peace to the world; I imagined that if I played well enough it would happen. I will probably play in the Sistine Chapel next year some time, but it won't bring peace to the world.

The real demands that were made on me in my childhood were qualitative and organized. My mother impressed upon me that, if I were serious about the violin, I would have to work a certain number of hours each day. I worked early so that I could go out in the late-morning sun and walk, run and play tennis. After lunch and a sleep, I worked again. The public did not see the demands. What they saw were the fruits of the demands, which were the joy of making progress and playing, of expressing oneself. There is nothing like music to give a person overall co-ordination. It asks everything from the mind and from the co-ordination of the body from the fingers to the eyes. Everything is involved, and when you use everything, everything falls into place. It's when you use only a part of yourself, like sitting in the office and concentrating on one thing, that you have to compensate with other activities, but playing an instrument or conducting is, in fact, as near a complete activity – physical, mental, emotional and spiritual – as you can have, and in that respect it keeps one in good condition, unless one abuses it.

I was also lucky since children who pursue a career very often leave the parental nest early and have to fend for themselves, but I don't think any child in the world can have seen more of both parents than my sisters and I did. Of course, they had their frictions because they were totally different characters. My father was very emotional and deeply moral and felt for the whole of humanity. My mother was very maternal and felt for her own children first, then for others. She was highly disciplined and a remarkably strong character. So they had their differences from time to time, which resulted in sadness, for you always want your parents to be happy together – as they mostly were.

When we went to France in 1927, my father took leave of absence from his school and had to decide, after three months, whether or not he'd go back. It was a major decision: either he cut himself off from

any further income, and could be with the family, or he abandoned his wife and three children in Paris and went back to earning his $300 a month. He took the right decision, which was to remain with the family. On our return to San Francisco we were self-supporting. In those days there was no income tax in America and prices were reasonable, and when we returned I gave a concert at the Civic Auditorium that earned enough to keep us all for a year and a half.

There are, it follows, always penalties to pay. The sort of life I have been describing has its own inbuilt penalty, which is that the children don't have experience of the outer world. We travelled so much that of course the outer world did penetrate quite a lot, but it was always kept at a certain distance from the family, which meanwhile maintained its routine. When we were seven, eight and nine years old or thereabouts, we would go every day at eleven o'clock to the park in San Francisco. Later on, when we were in Sydney or Melbourne for a month, we would go to the Botanical Gardens every day at the same time and feed the swans and walk or run around. But that was when I was nineteen, so the routine had gone on unbroken for twelve to fourteen years.

The concerts were always in the evening, so they didn't interrupt the day. Any tribute or adulation from the public was also kept at arm's length, although I would be aware that the concerts were sold out. My father looked after the business interests and the rest of the family life on tour. Later it took me a long time to get accustomed to dealing independently with people on a one-to-one basis, for we had never been to school to receive a formal education, though my mother saw to it that we had wonderful tutors. And when you spend your life with Mozart and Beethoven, Bach and Schumann and Brahms, you are living with great minds. It is a privilege given to very few people, for the greater composers are those whose works convince the interpreter of the great and good truths, eternal and immutable, recognized in the proportion and structure of their works.

When you hear your first recording of the Elgar Violin Concerto, conducted by the composer himself, do you see it as the definitive performance?

No, I don't. Rarely, if ever, do I consider any musical performance a definitive one. It can be nearer or farther from the absolute truth, but music is a live substance, and even today performances in the recording studio can still be 'live' if you play the whole work, or a whole movement, through, for even today retouching is not always feasible in many cases. When I listen to that recording of the Elgar, I enjoy it, and I have listened to it perhaps twice or three times since I made it. I always feel it is a beautiful recording. It has the ardour of youth; it has deep feeling; it has the authority of the composer himself; and it has the historical

uniqueness of the fact it was done with the composer. Therefore I am very moved by it. Naturally I can imagine certain things I could do better or differently. But it doesn't matter; it's beautiful.

It is true that, when I came to my early thirties, I had to rebuild consciously the techniques which up till then had been unconscious. It happens with everybody. For instance, you can speak a language that you know well without thinking of the grammar, and you grow up speaking it well depending on who you've heard speak it. It's what Suzuki, the Japanese violin teacher, calls the 'mother-tongue method': imitation and repetition, by ear and by sight. Then, as soon as your mind is awake, you fall from grace, you leave the Garden of Eden, you begin to be responsible for your own actions. What you first knew you later have to understand, and you must find the path to natural knowing, and it may take years. I've traversed every minute section of that path. I could play beautifully as a child, then I had to learn what it was I was doing, and sometimes, at certain periods of my life, I lost some of that original spontaneity. Now I have it absolutely, because I just feel a piece of music. I know it, can judge it, can seize it much more quickly, and one of the great things is that I can teach, which I maybe wouldn't have been able to do had I gone on as an instinctive violinist.

It often seems difficult to relate music to moral, social or even symbolic values.

It depends on the music. There are as many different kinds of music as there are kinds of literature. You can have moral music. For instance, I have just done the Brahms *Requiem* in Hamburg where it has been done every year for ninety-two years in the church where Brahms was baptized. It was a real service and one of the most moving things. No applause. People know the words, know the music and are cleansed after it. It is like an emotional purge.

Then you have music which is entertaining, music which is brilliant, music which is music to dance to or eat to, and music which is more intellectual. Certain of the last works of Beethoven are very intellectual. All the different types of music each speak of the life of a people, or of a period. Through music we can relive the very same feelings and thoughts that the composer had wherever he was living, and we can know his society. We know the courtesies of the court in Mozart's days from his music, and we can feel with him how even tragic things were presented in a way that wouldn't shock the perfection of the elegance and so on. Music is remarkable in that respect because it's an art of time, and during the time it takes to play, it's like a life. You live through it.

There has never been a people, a society, without music. Music is the organization of vibrations, palpable, oral, audible vibrations. As such it

keeps us in touch with the universe. It allows us to express ourselves. The other night one of the friends of the Menuhin School decided he'd try to get us some support, which of course we need very badly. The government pays for the tuition, but not for repairs, or for scholarships for our overseas students. This man invited ten very important Japanese businessmen, and I produced three charming Japanese girls from my school. One played the violin and two played the piano. They played beautifully and the evening was a great success. The Japanese woman, as we know, has never been liberated, but our music gives the Japanese woman a chance to become totally liberated. What these little girls expressed in their music were some of the most touching feelings you could imagine. Who would have thought seventy years ago that Japanese women would be liberated by Western music? But it was the fact. They played with such emotion and such beauty and sensitivity, it was overwhelming.

Why does Britain show such general reluctance to support the arts by comparison with America and Europe?

It's a different background. In Germany, the state supports music and is a very great source of security to musicians. There are literally hundreds of opera houses in Germany. In America, support has come traditionally from the private pocket. In Britain there has been traditionally relatively little support, although it has grown enormously compared to what it used to be. It's a matter of collective tradition. England can't imitate others. It can only grow in its own way. I have to say that I have always loved and felt at home in England and London, so that when the British government offered me British citizenship, I accepted with joy, though on the understanding that I did not lose my American nationality.

Which contemporary violinist do you most admire?

Gidon Kremer, a wonderful violinist and interpreter.

What prompted you to record with musicians outside your own sphere, like Ravi Shankar and Stéphane Grappelli?

There are no boundaries where such superb musicians are concerned. They are simply the masters of their art, and enlarge one's mind.

What is your assessment of Furtwängler, whom many have criticized for remaining in Germany under the Nazis?

A very great conductor and an absolutely clean man, no question of that. He stood up for Hindemith, he protected a great many Jews,

helped many out of Germany, and himself had to escape towards the end of the war. He happened to conduct the orchestra when some of the German leaders were there, but we can't expect everyone to behave in the same way. Sometimes it takes more courage to remain in your country than to leave it. Those who stayed suffered a pretty bad fate, and those who came out, after all, escaped. Yet there was this feeling of superiority among those who escaped, thinking that they showed great determination in leaving it behind. I would say, Jew or Gentile, you can't blame those who stayed, you can't blame those who escaped. It's just the way things went. But Furtwängler himself was a man of integrity.

The anti-Semitism I have seen in my own lifetime has had a psychological impact on me only to the extent that I know it is important to maintain the dignity of the Jew and to avoid a kind of behaviour that might prompt a response. The caricature of the Jew is the businessman with the big cigar, who does exist sometimes. They can be charming and interesting people. What bothers me sometimes is that they are a little bit like the desert flowers. When they have only a drop of water they blossom. They make the most of the opportunity, as they did in Germany before the Nazi days, when they occupied extremely powerful positions. That must have created a certain amount of resentment. Of course, it gives no excuse for anti-Semitism, but you can understand it. The Jew does not stand out in Italy or in Greece, nor would he in China, since the Chinese are far cleverer at business than the Jew. There are so many different types of Jew, but traditionally people have fastened on the Jew who is obviously different from them. But there are so many who are in no way different. It's like the problem of the black in the United States. There are almost a majority of blacks that are nearly white, and no one bothers about them.

It is true that the Jews are far too sensitive, though they have perhaps been sensitized by history. They are too ready to imagine an insult; they are not prepared to give enough leeway, even to allow for a certain misbehaviour; they do carry a chip on their shoulders. They have to compensate, and it is part of the psychology. One can understand that too, and one must understand it. They have to compensate for certain established assumptions. If it's not one thing it's another. If it's not religion, it's jealousy or it's race. Yet it's none of these things actually. It's simply that people are nasty and want to condemn anything if they can find a little difference; can say that hair is frizzed instead of straight or there's a detectable accent. Then they pounce on it.

Unfortunately, the Jews have come to Israel with the narrow aim of making themselves an independent nation, to a large extent disregarding the environment and the rest of the world. They didn't come to establish a nation with the Palestinians and a wonderful federation (though now

they realize that perhaps they should have done). They came instead with the pure desire to establish a Jewish state to the exclusion of everything else. They did it very successfully, but they did it ruthlessly, and probably the sense of fear is equal on both sides. I feel that the only solution lies in a federation, totally equal, as in Switzerland. If both have an equal title to the land, what else can you do? Meanwhile there is something cruel about all of us. We are capable of the most horrid things, especially if we have suffered them ourselves.

Why have so many leading musicians been Jewish? I think it's ascribable simply to the fact that there were so many Jews who emigrated from Russia to the United States. The Jew in Russia, having been oppressed, found expression through the violin, because he was living in the same world where gipsy music was prevalent – in the Ukraine and the south of Russia. The violin was simply a Jewish instrument. A rabbi in New York told me that he was in Palestine, as it then was, in the early 1900s when the Russian pogroms were going on, and that hardly a Jewish refugee family arrived without a violin case. And I don't think that, in those days, the violin cases were filled with watches and stockings; they held genuine violins. The Russian Jews arriving in New York brought with them a tremendous intensity of music making, much like the Negro in the United States whose first step to emancipation was singing the spiritual or playing the piano. There have been a great many musical traditions, only one of which was that of the Russian Jews, and today the Russian schools are producing as many non-Jewish violinists.

Your former marriage to Nola Nicholas apparently provoked a lot of adverse criticism from the Jewish press at the time.

I wasn't aware of it. If they had criticized me for other reasons, I would have accepted that certainly, and as it turned out, it was not a successful marriage. That was as much my fault as hers, but I didn't realize there was that criticism. Any number of Jews marry out of their religion, and I wouldn't either applaud it or condemn it. It is just one of the things that happens or doesn't happen.

Has the adulation you have received ever tempted you to abuse the rewards of fame?

No, because I had to play the violin. The violin is relentless, and all the adulation in the world won't enable you to play in tune unless you play in tune. When you measure yourself not by trivial adulation but by the work you have to do, then your measure is quite different. You can't be spoilt. Besides, I have a marvellous wife, and she is so wonderfully loving and loyal and, at the same time, very critical. That's the most

wonderful kind of marriage. Marriages where the two flatter each other and reinforce each other are very dangerous in a way, especially if they have no children. People must have other people to criticize them.

Your wife has called you long on vision and short on imagination – a deficiency, she says, which makes you infuriatingly impractical.

Diana has a marvellous capacity to visualize things as they actually are. For instance, she will see an empty room and be able to imagine it decorated long before it is. I see the goal, but I don't necessarily anticipate the details, although I'm willing to put up with the process as long as the goal is kept in mind. Women are possessed by the process and men see the goal. They're both essential. Sometimes the goal proves more short-sighted than the process, and sometimes the process proves more long-sighted than the goal. We balance each other that way.

I am only too aware of Diana abandoning her own talents in our marriage, and I have often felt guilty about her self-denial. I have tried to compensate and have worked very hard to persuade her to do things she wants to do. But it takes a lot of persuasion. Even when she is here alone for a week or two, she will never lift the telephone to ask a friend round. It's this feeling that she can't indulge herself – a kind of extreme Protestant sense of not giving yourself pleasure. As soon as anything can be turned into an obligation or a duty, she'll do it right away. It's very curious. It is a kind of self-denial, yet no one shines in company more than she does.

Whereas your father rejoiced in your public performances, your mother longed for you to belong more to yourself, as she put it. Did their contrasting attitudes create an ambivalence for you?

You can call it ambivalence. You can also call it balance. I love my privacy and studying my score, but I also love meeting people and going out. I love playing the violin and I love conducting – two totally different occupations, one private, the other public; one dealing with one voice, the other dealing with many voices. I can make the best of different situations. If you put me with political people, I am quite at home and interested, or if you put me with people on the street, I am fascinated by their mentality and way of life. I must say, however, that there is a great deal today that revolts me in the vulgarity and noise and the lack of depth all around.

As a young man you wrote: 'Our ancestors were more honourable in that they did not trouble to conceal their feelings, they simply fought it out. In this sense the greatest hypocrisy goes hand in hand with the highest civilization.' You

seemed to think then that hypocrisy was not an acceptable price to pay for civilized values. What do you think now?

I would now be a little hesitant about using the word hypocrisy because there can be various ways of clothing one's thoughts and emotions, some of them extremely good. For instance, is it hypocrisy to walk around clothed in warm weather when we could go naked? It's a form of hypocrisy, but it's a very useful and acceptable form, though many people who go to nude beaches show that there is a longing to be without clothes. In the same way, we clothe our thoughts, depending on the person we are with. That is a form of courtesy, not necessarily hypocritical but sincere in itself. If I know a person has lost a dear friend, I am not going to speak myself about a loss I may have had, because it wouldn't be right, even as the Chinese feign gaiety in these circumstances in order to make you feel happy and not to burden you with their sorrow.

I think I am more aware today of everything that goes to create good in the world, and therefore I am more concerned with the building-blocks of good than I am with the abstract idea. The abstract idea is important, but after a while you realize that it is more important to do things. It is very important to have goals, otherwise you don't know what you're working for. In a way, I had a naughty sense of delight when the politicians were taken completely by surprise by the events that Gorbachev encouraged in Eastern Europe. All they could say was that it was going too fast. This was because they were comfortable in knowing where the enemy was, where the guns were – their mind didn't have to exercise itself; they knew what to expect. But as soon as the barriers were broken, they didn't know where they were, and they still don't. Nor do they know where they're going. But I know where they're going. I know what's happening in Europe.

I have a feeling that the next great struggle of the twenty-first century will be that of the federated principle – the principle of interdependence – against the backlog of the old nationalist thing. We'll still have to fight that, but the new road is the interdependence of peoples and cultures, and that is the road we must travel. Anyone who stands against it is in the rearguard, and that's why the creation of all these new nations since the Second World War is such an anomaly. It is out of step with the end of the twentieth century. Meanwhile it is still too early to pronounce factually on the vast changes the liberation of Eastern Europe has wrought, but it is obvious that it will enrich all the arts – music, literature, painting and sculpture.

On the question of where my own musical talent came from, I would say that heredity plays a big part in talent, but so does environment. That is one of those questions that goes on for ever in the sense that

you can't have only environment and no heredity, because you might be a dog, a cat, a human being or a fish; and you can't have only heredity and no environment, because then you might be a plant that withers in the wrong kind of earth or in the sun without any water. You have to have both, and I had both. I have no doubt that I'm strong and, although I couldn't live the life of the businessman or commuter, in my own way, for my own purposes, I have plenty of vitality and a natural sense of what I need to feel well in terms of exercise and diet. I am not one-hundred-per-cent vegetarian, nor would I care to proselytize, but I have simply found that I dislike being carnivorous and that my instinct has proved right for me.

I have a very keen sense of the use of time, and I begrudge time spent that is not invested, just as some people feel about money. They don't want to give money away, they'd rather see it grow. I'm not quite like that with time, because I always have time for people whom I feel I can be of some use to and I generally find time for young musicians who call. But what I always like to do is to set a score, or give a concert, for a particular purpose. Everything I am doing now fits more and more into the scheme of things. Whereas previously I would go on tour for three months just to earn money, today I try to make each concert and each tour a contribution to and a step towards a future, whether mine or somebody else's. I only wish that there were forty-eight hours in each day, in that life has presented me with so many more interests than I have had time to follow and so many crafts I would have liked to learn.

I have been very fortunate. I have no axe to grind, I haven't suffered humiliation. I haven't ever suffered the unnatural death of any close friend. When I speak, I always speak with the thought in mind that I am perhaps speaking to people who haven't had that blessed sort of good luck or privilege. My fulfilment lies in interpreting the works of composers, because even interpretation holds a certain measure of creation. I only do what I love and feel I need to do, and if this does amount to a great deal, it comes from an independent choice.

I don't have any right to a feeling of superiority or to pass judgement. On the contrary, I feel that I have been spared by a kind destiny. My life is a constant sense of repayment for what I have had and a desire to protect the future. It goes without saying that there are still things I would wish to achieve in life. There is no horizon.

LORD REES-MOGG

William Rees-Mogg was born in Somerset in 1928. He was educated at Charterhouse and Balliol College, Oxford, where he was president of the union and the university Conservative Association. After graduation he did two years' National Service in the RAF before joining the *Financial Times* and eight years later the *Sunday Times* where he became deputy editor. In 1967, aged only thirty-nine, he became editor of *The Times*, which he remained until 1981. Between 1981 and 1986 he was vice-chairman of the Board of Governors of the BBC. He was chairman of the Arts Council from 1982–89 and now runs the Broadcasting Standards Council. He married in 1962 and has two sons and three daughters. He was made a life peer in 1988.

What sort of a childhood did you have?

An extremely happy childhood, though rather a lonely one. We lived in a fairly large house in the Somerset country, about ten miles from Bristol, and there I lived what was, I think, a very old-fashioned childhood. It probably hadn't changed much in broad style since the nineteenth century. Until I went away to school when I was nine, I didn't have many friends. My two sisters were older, and I was very close to the nearer sister, who was still at home, my elder sister having gone away to school. I was educated very much by my father. He taught me Latin, Greek and French. I also had an excellent relationship with my mother. She had been a Shakespearian actress in the United States and acted with Sarah Bernhardt on Broadway. She had strong literary interests and we read *Macbeth* when I was in the nursery. She would read out the lines of Lady Macbeth and I would repeat them after her, because that was before I could read. She was the strongest influence on me. She herself had had a very interesting and happy childhood, living in West Chester County in the 1890s, and she made that vivid to us. She brought me up with the American set of ideas: not quite that every son can become president, but that everybody has a duty to make the most of themselves in life. She did this with a strong literary and imaginative feeling.

Was it at Oxford that your conservative beliefs and ideas were principally forged?

No. I think I arrived at Oxford with a set of ideas and beliefs already somewhat modified by my generation and the mood of the times. I was very interested in political history as a schoolboy. I had read with great fascination, as I think a lot of schoolboys do, about Disraeli. He had enormous appeal for me when I was fifteen and sixteen, and I thought

his kind of imaginative conservatism was extremely attractive. So I suppose I went up to Oxford with a set of political ideas pretty fully formed. I had a very interesting time at Oxford because it was a period when a lot of extremely interesting people were there. We were a mix of people who had just left school, with others coming back to finish off a course they'd started before the war. My contemporaries included, among the politicians, Margaret Thatcher and Shirley Williams, Edward Boyle, Tony Crosland, Tony Benn and Jeremy Thorpe; and then there was Robin Day of the people who've become famous in related fields. It was a very strong mix.

You have described yourself as fearfully pompous in those days. Would you try to be different, given another chance?

I don't know. One would probably go about things in exactly the same way, because it emerges out of temperament. I invented the idea of being a young fogey even before the young fogeys existed. I had a strange feeling, when I was a little child, that life belonged to maturity, and I remember lying under the nursery table and thinking, it's going to be extremely nice when you're in your forties, when you've got something of a stomach and a gold watch chain spread across it. I thought that the point in life which would be really enjoyable. I was pompous. I had the idea at school that one should form oneself, and that one's personality should be what one believed in. I read about Aristotle's magnificent man and thought that must be the right kind of person to be. One of the characteristics of Aristotle's magnificent man was that he never ran, never betrayed haste. I remember walking from my classroom to my house, being caught in a shower and deciding, well, I'm going to be Aristotle's magnificent man; then walking slowly through the shower to demonstrate that I could adopt this character. That, in a teenager, does lean towards pomposity.

You stood twice as a Conservative candidate but failed to be elected. Were you set upon a political career?

I expected to have a political career when I went up to Oxford, and I spent most of my time there in politics. I became a journalist unexpectedly. I was offered a job on the *Financial Times* and took it because I thought it would be interesting, then found that journalism suited me. For my first eight years as a journalist, on the *Financial Times*, I thought I was going to have journalism as a sort of occupation which would make it possible for me to be a politician. Then, in 1960, I went to the *Sunday Times* when it was at its period of maximum expansion. It was moving ahead extremely fast, and the opportunities in a professional sense were good. I came immediately into contact with Roy Thomson,

whom I greatly admired and enjoyed working with, and I thought, well, if you've got a first-class newspaper proprietor whom you get on with extremely well, and you're in your early thirties, you'd be absolutely crazy to give that up for something you're not certain would work out. Then came 1963, when the Conservative party seemed to me to be turning its back on the twentieth century when they chose Alec Douglas-Home as leader. I felt alienated by that, so at that point decided finally that journalism was going to be something I would enjoy and which would probably be more useful as well.

But I never felt completely sure that politics wouldn't come back to me in some form or another. I always was basically a political journalist, forming political judgements, and then in 1967 I became editor of *The Times* and that required a detachment from politics. I gave up belonging to the Carlton Club and so on in order to create that detachment.

On the question of whether I'd have been a successful politician, I've seen people who made successful politicians who seemed to me to have roughly the sort of mix of qualities I had. But they didn't make the most successful politicians. I would say that I had a mix of qualities not dissimilar from those of Keith Joseph: more interested in ideas than anything else, able to argue most cases plausibly once convinced of them. In the early days, I sat on a Conservative committee with Keith Joseph, and we were, I suppose, two young intellectuals that the Conservative party thought well of. He'd just got into the House. I was trying to get a seat. Perhaps I'd have had a career not dissimilar from his.

But in the end many considered him rather mad.

Oh, I think if I had been a politician a lot of people would have ended up thinking me rather mad. I might not have made some of the mistakes that Keith has made, but equally I wouldn't have done some of the good things he has done.

Your career in journalism is a success story culminating in becoming editor of The Times *at the age of thirty-nine. What did you hope would be distinctive about* The Times *under your editorship?*

What we were trying to do was combine a very strong sense of the quality and the traditional virtues of *The Times* with modernization. We hoped to get circulation up beyond the half-million point, which we didn't succeed in. That now has been tried three times this century. Northcliffe tried it; we tried it under Roy Thomson and with his support; Rupert Murdoch has tried it. It's failed each time, and there must be very good reasons why it doesn't succeed. Eventually we said, all right, we haven't managed to get it above 500,000, so we ought to

concentrate simply on quality and excellence and see who wants to buy it, try and make it break even, be willing to charge a relatively high price for it and accept the circulation that results from that policy. I found that more congenial, and I'm probably better at the aspect of journalism which concentrates on really trying to understand the world as it is rather than on the aspect which concentrates on the audience.

Something we found with the *Sunday Times* was that it was quite difficult to straddle two audiences, that there was an audience of perhaps 750,000 that wanted a quite serious quality Sunday paper with a lot of information in it, and beyond that you had to find an audience which, if it wasn't going to read you, was going to read the *Sunday Express*. You had to find ways, as Denis Hamilton was extremely skilful in doing, of keeping both audiences happy. With *The Times* the equation is different. The basic audience in my time was somewhere between 300,000 and 350,000, and to get beyond that you had to make the paper more exciting to an audience which was, in some ways, less demanding, or less willing to absorb difficult and complicated material. You can only produce a paper of real quality if you don't need to be afraid of boring people, because a lot of important information isn't desperately exciting, and, if presented in a very exciting way, is being misrepresented.

Not everyone was happy with the sweeping changes you introduced to try to boost circulation.

I'm sure we didn't do it perfectly, but *The Times* as an institution, like every other institution, needs fairly radical change every generation, and you can't make the necessary minimum of change without upsetting quite a few people. It wasn't me who actually put news on the front page, but only six months before I arrived, *The Times* still had classified ads on the front. So the changes had to be fairly rapid, because we were dealing with a paper more appropriate to the 1930s, perhaps more appropriate to 1910, but in the conditions of the late 1960s. The changes had taken place much too slowly in the previous history of *The Times*.

You once described the readership of The Times *as 'limited but important'. That seems a rather exclusive idea, as if readers of other newspapers are of lesser importance.*

The Times had a very high proportion of readers who were prepared to inform themselves thoroughly because they needed to for their work. These are naturally people who occupy the most important positions. There will always be a place for newspapers which primarily serve that purpose, but they must always expect to have a fairly moderate circulation. If you don't need to know what the real composition of the

American Senate is and are only going to enjoy jokes about Vice President Quayle, then you want a completely different kind of coverage of American political affairs from the one *The Times* ought to be offering.

When The Times *was in difficulties, you wrote that you would not seek investment unless you could promise a sound return. I see the commercial honesty of that position, but why shouldn't subsidy play a part in a worthwhile enterprise?*

Newspapers are very subject to pressure from people who have invested in them. You can't expect people to believe in the integrity of a subsidized newspaper unless it is being subsidized with the ultimate commercial view of restoring it to commercial balance. They will think that people are putting money in because they want to get some benefit in terms of the coverage given to their own interests or their own views, and they will usually be right. Even if it's not true, there will still be an element of distrust.

But isn't that so with a proprietor as well? What about Lonrho and the Observer?

Yes, but readers are shrewd. They know what Tiny Rowland is interested in and they have a shrewd suspicion of what he is not interested in, and they see that large parts of the *Observer* bear no trace of his hand while other parts seem to show considerable trace. The proprietor has to satisfy the readership that he's not using the paper for his own ends.

You also spoke about no longer believing in a proprietorship which did not include employees in its shareholding.

I think that the system which the *Independent* has got – I'm not a shareholder of the *Independent* though I write for it – is the right one. There are widespread shareholdings among the staff, and there are also fairly widespread, purely commercial shareholdings outside the staff. Hence nobody has anything remotely approaching a controlling interest and there is therefore no proprietor as such. That's the model I was hoping to establish for *The Times*, had the Thomsons been willing to break up the papers, but we were only bidding for *The Times* and they wanted to sell *The Times* and *Sunday Times* together. That's what we would have tried to establish, and it was a model that could have worked. The *Independent* has shown it does.

How independent in reality from the proprietors are editors of national newspapers?

It depends entirely on the editor and the proprietor. I only really had experience of the proprietors of the *Financial Times*, who gave us complete freedom, and the Thomson family, proprietors of the *Sunday Times* and *The Times*. The Thomson family were so good from that point of view. Roy Thomson was once asked on television why he didn't have a general political line running through his newspapers, like Beaverbrook, and his reply was, 'I'm a very rich man and, like most very rich men, I hold very right-wing political views. I own two hundred newspapers, and it would be absolutely ridiculous if all my newspapers held my views.' That was how he worked. He didn't actually hold terribly right-wing views; he held the views natural to a man who had a strong sense of the small communities of Canada in which he had spent his early working life, and who believed in what I would call community politics. The only thing he ever said to me was that he expected the editors of his newspapers to represent the interests of the communities they were serving. That seemed to me to be a very sound, broad principle. I certainly wouldn't call that very right wing.

I never fell out with a proprietor. I had great luck with them. My first proprietor was Brendan Bracken, who was something of a genius. He was a remarkable man who had played a most important role in the success on the domestic front of the Churchill coalition government during the war. He was warm and supportive in his old age to the people who worked for him. I couldn't have had a better proprietor. During the Suez Crisis, at a point when I genuinely didn't know what to do, I rang him up, not because I wished to consult my proprietor but because I wished to consult somebody who might have some idea about what on earth was going on. He quite correctly refused to give me advice of any kind. 'You've got to work it out for yourself,' he said, and that was the only occasion on which I ever consulted him upon a policy issue.

With Roy Thomson I had a relationship in which he too was totally supportive. He had a very congenial personality and no desire at all to impose his views on the editorial side of the operation. The same was true of his son Ken. In the end, Ken got fed up with the British print trade unions, but that was a different matter.

But since you left the industry, we've a new set of proprietors, and a lot of them are very powerful in the sense that they do interfere editorially.

Naturally, as a journalist and an editor, I don't like it. I would only be prepared to edit a paper on the basis of the editor being the person who made the decisions. However, a proprietor obviously always has

considerable influence through whom he chooses to be editor anyway. It's probably reasonable to say that proprietors don't have to be as non-interventionist as the Thomsons were. It is perfectly legitimate for a proprietor to engage in the debate, and I don't see why he should be expected to be totally reserved. On the other hand, he ought to leave the last word in the editor's hands, because the editor is the only person who has real access to the staff, and it's the staff of a newspaper who are employed to find out what's going on, who know what's going on and put the editor in a position to form his judgement on the basis of full information.

When Rupert Murdoch moved from Fleet Street to Wapping, was it primarily to relocate the newspaper or principally to destroy union dominance?

I think it was to destroy the dominance of the unions. The unions had become entirely impossible from the point of view of running a newspaper in any reasonable way. They were charging an enormous amount for delivering an extremely poor service, and I regard the success of the Wapping move as a real charter of liberation for the British press. In fact, I think there was no alternative. The Thomson Organization was extremely patient, extremely reasonable, highly professional in talking to unions and so on, yet had totally failed to get the unions to agree to the introduction of new technology on any reasonable terms. There had been a little progress made, but far too little. This was similarly the experience of the other responsible Fleet Street managements, and even of very good managements whom the unions had every reason to trust. Rupert Murdoch had to win, and he wasn't going to find it easy. He was facing unscrupulous and, in many cases, quite ruthless opposition. I admire what he did.

Do newspapers have an obligation to tell the truth under all circumstances, or can there be a counter-obligation to suppress items in the national or, indeed, in a sectional interest?

It gets more difficult the bigger the issue. I was relatively willing as an editor to suppress stories which seemed to me to be of no importance, but which were going to be very distressing to individuals: the sort of case in which somebody's child has committed suicide and the family are deeply distressed and don't wish it to be known. I would always listen to arguments about that because, if the person concerned was not a significant figure, I didn't see any reason to cause pain and suffering where no real news value existed. So, on the small scale, I obviously had a prejudice of a strong kind in favour of publication, but was prepared to overrule that principle in cases where there seemed to be great hardship likely to flow from it. If you take the other end of the

scale, the great event, I think that almost always more harm comes from not telling what one knows. On the other hand, you run into a difficulty. Suppose, for instance, that a newspaper knows there is going to be or may be a devaluation. If they report it, they make the devaluation quite unavoidable and in a sense take over the prerogative of government.

What principle can be invoked to limit press freedom without destroying the very concept of freedom?

There are two views about press freedom. One is the American view – the First Amendment view – which makes it an absolute. The other is the British view, which makes it one of several principles that contend with each other. The obvious example is the contempt-of-court questions that arise over the reporting of trials, and particularly the reporting of evidence before a trial takes place. I believe, though this is not the view of most journalists, that the British principle is the right one. Is it more important that people have a fair trial or that newspapers be free to publish anything they feel like publishing? My own view is that it is more important that people have a fair trial, that civilization depends on that rather than on the other. So I think one should see press freedom as something that has to fight its own corner against other principles, the security of the state clearly being one, the right to fair trial another, the right for the citizen not to be injured in his reputation (the old libel question) a third. The libel laws are plainly very unsatisfactory at present, but that there ought to be libel laws I have no doubt. And I think that the American situation, in which press freedom is absolute and all other principles subordinate to it, is less satisfactory than ours.

Was Mrs Thatcher right to try to suppress Spycatcher*?*

No, that was just silly. It was going to be totally ineffective. It's part of the cult of the secret service, which is all a lot of nonsense. In my experience, people who go into these secret organizations rapidly lose touch with reality because the organizations have lost touch with reality. *Spycatcher* rather showed that up. The truths that it told – and there were some – and the confusions in Peter Wright's own mind, were examples of the deformation of the intellect that secret Intelligence work causes.

What are your views on the Salman Rushdie affair?

Complex. There are a lot of principles involved. One is the principle of the freedom of speech, and I believe that we must maintain in our society the right to publish any novel which is inside the law. The law requires that a novel should not incite to racial hatred, and I think that's

a wise law. It requires that it should not incite to specific crimes, and that's an obvious thing. And so one ought to start off by upholding Salman Rushdie's right to publish, but then comes the question of the sensitivities of the Islamic community.

It seems very understandable that a minority community in a country which predominately does not share their religious views should be highly sensitive to anything they regard as a mockery of those views, and that the anger in the Islamic community is a natural response to a book they found offensive. I don't know whether they should have found it offensive or not, because I didn't find that section of the novel very easy to follow and don't know enough about Islam to judge how offensive it was. Clearly it was offensive, and so we have the question of what form their reaction should take. Obviously it's totally unacceptable that there should be any threat to Salman Rushdie's life, and I regret the fact that those who did seem clearly to threaten his life have not been prosecuted in the ordinary course of the law, because upholding the law is another important principle.

Salman Rushdie has to take responsibility for what he has published, and I think he should have known that this was going to be very offensive, that it would be deeply disturbing and provocative to a rather vulnerable community in this country. He says that the novel was written out of the great spiritual torment he had gone through, and was an expression of quite profound experiences that he believed could be helpful in the dialogue which ought to be taking place inside Islam about the contrast between the old beliefs and the modern world. That seems to me to be a perfectly reasonable answer to those criticisms, but at the same time the criticisms themselves are legitimate. There's a perfectly reasonable dialogue which could take place along those lines, and in the end Rushdie has to take responsibility for what he's written. There's a certain naïvety in the Rushdie position. People have got to recognize that they're dealing with different audiences, and something which might be perfectly acceptable to one audience can be entirely unacceptable to another.

As a Roman Catholic, do you find the Roman Catholic religion gives you a kind of discipline that other Christian religions might not?

Well, the Church of England is plainly going through a difficult period in which both English culture and the Church of England's culture have lost a measure of confidence. The two things probably go together. The important thing about the Roman Catholic Church is that it is obviously still alive, that it's unquestionably able to give Roman Catholics a feeling of a living religion on which they can base their faith. Unfortunately,

many members of the Church of England feel that the life has gone out of it.

In the course of your lifetime there have been some very radical changes in the organization and the liturgy of the Roman Catholic Church. Did you approve of the changes introduced by Vatican II?

Basically. I approved of everything except the changes in the liturgy. The general movement towards a more liberal doctrine of the Church was, in my view, entirely right. Having in my childhood felt stifled by the rigidity of the structure, I found the personality of Pope John XXIII an inspiration. The greatest religious inspiration I've had in my life came from his personality. The only aspect that went seriously wrong – the rest had to happen – was that we lost the Tridentine Mass, which was a thing of enormous religious power and beauty. We should have retained much more frequent use of the great Latin prayers, even though a vernacular Mass was in itself desirable, since it was better that children should be brought up to understand what it was that the Mass was saying. So I thought there was great loss in the liturgy, and I hope this will eventually be reversed and that the Tridentine Mass will be reintroduced as a perfectly normal, though not invariable, form.

As for the future of Church unity, I think that ecumenism is something which will happen in God's time rather than ours. People have a very great attachment to the forms of their Church practice, and the present division and problems in the Church of England and the difficulty over women priests mean that unity between the Roman Catholic Church and the Church of England is not going to happen at all rapidly.

I take the view that the one certain reality is the reality of God; that all religions, let alone all Churches, are aspects of an understanding of that reality; that human culture means that different nations and different people can get the best understanding for them through different formulations. I wouldn't be a Roman Catholic if I didn't believe that that was the highest available formulation, but there clearly is something in human nature which has created this variety in the formulations and in the worship and understanding of God.

The question of the ordination of women is meanwhile a cultural question. The difficulty for the Catholic Church, as I see it, is that it is a world Church whereas the Church of England, in real terms, is not; it's a European Church. In North America and Western Europe, a major cultural change has taken place in the relations between women and men and in the role of women. It has therefore become perfectly natural in these areas for women to be ordained. I don't any longer think that, even if I were a member of the Church of England, I would necessarily be opposed to it. The Catholic Church, on the other hand, is a Church

which has its largest membership in Latin America and a very large membership in Africa and other parts of the world where this cultural change simply has not taken place and where the attitude towards the role of woman is still what it was in Europe in, say, 1910. The Catholic Church has no option but to respect the totality of the cultures of its members. I suppose it's likely, as Europe has given the lead to so many other cultural changes, that if one takes a long-term view – a period measured at least in generations – then this change will become more or less universalized. If it does, then I can see no absolute theological bar to the ordination of women. I think it will happen, but it probably won't happen so long as it could mean a great division between the Catholic Church as it is in Europe and the Catholic Church as it is everywhere else in the world.

Oddly enough, I'm less sympathetic to the idea of Catholic priests marrying than I am to the ordination of women. I'm worried by the idea that you can't have celibacy among the clergy, because it seems to me that we live in an age where we have made sex an idol. The view that nobody can lead a happy life unless it is centred on sexual activity seems to me palpably false. The view that there is no value in a man or a woman deciding to give up their sexual activity in order to devote their life to some greater cause, or to God, seems to me also wrong. Therefore I feel that, to give up the celibacy of the clergy at this particular moment, would be to be making a sacrifice to the idolization of sex which is one of the characteristic defects of our age.

So do you consider sex negative?

Not at all. Sex is a good thing, just as food is a good thing, though gluttony isn't. Sex is a matter of enormous importance because it perpetuates the species. It's the deepest emotional experience that many, perhaps most, people ever feel. It's God-given and it's also a natural animal passion which, like other natural animal passions, gives enormous happiness and satisfaction. All these things are true, but what I think it isn't is the Holy Grail. If people say life is nothing except sexual fulfilment, that being the be-all and end-all and more important than any other aspect of the development of the human mind or spirit, then it's taking something very good in itself and making it the only good, so downgrading all the other goods which people might want to follow. It becomes a falsehood.

Christianity, of course, has always been bothered with puritanism, and there's quite a bit of puritanism in St Paul, though I really don't see any evidence of it in the life of Christ himself. It seems to me that Christ did not have the fundamentally puritanical attitudes that St Paul had, and although I regard St Paul as a very great man, I have, with

some reluctance, to criticize him in this respect. Because of this flaw in his make-up, people are inclined to reject the extraordinarily rich variety of understandings that St Paul gives us. It was he who started Christianity off, and so you have in the Early Church unbalanced views about the nature of sex, which is a pity and has done harm.

Throughout the history of the Church, these unbalanced puritan views have fought with a more naturalist, broad and wholesome view, and I'm on the side of the naturalist, broad and wholesome view. Even so, I think the Church has got a certain number of things right which the twentieth century gets wrong. The Church has been right to distrust the separation of sex from procreation as something that leads to a misunderstanding of the nature of sex. Sex is serious in that sense. Again, I share deep fears about turning man from being a free animal to an engineered animal. There is all too great a likelihood that we shall have an engineered race of human beings within a few decades. The Church's consistent opposition to mechanizing sex, though it may have looked obscurantist in the light of the science of the mid-twentieth century, will, I believe, look remarkably far-sighted in the light of the science of the twenty-first century.

But isn't it also somehow true that the Church would wish us to derive our essential pleasure from things spiritual? Is this realistic?

A lot of the Church's teaching and the teaching of the Gospel is an urge to perfection. This is what human beings at their highest would be, and I'm much more conscious of the gap between the ordinary daily life of business and perfection than I am of that between the problem of sex and perfection. Yet the problem is essentially the same. To become in the highest degree the spiritual being man is capable of being, and which I believe all men are capable of being (I have never thought there to be only a few people capable of becoming saints), we would have to sacrifice everything. We would have to give up attaching superior value to any of God's gifts and would certainly not be bothering ourselves about the profit-and-loss accounts of our businesses. We would certainly not be bothering ourselves about the pleasures of sexual activity or the pleasures of the table. In so far as we were acting in the world, we would be devoting ourselves to care and concern for other people, and we would expend, I suppose, a good part of our time in contemplation of the divine.

This would be a completely different life from the life which all but a very few people actually lead. The life of the contemplative monk has been designed to allow a few people in cloistered circumstances to lead such a life, which I think Christianity believes is the highest. I've no doubt that Christianity in this sense is right: that it is the highest form

of life. At the same time, it has to be reconciled with the ordinary existence of ordinary people, and so Christianity will always be preaching things which are simultaneously true but not going to be followed by the great majority of people.

The present government is often perceived as radically different from previous Conservative administrations. Is the public perception of its radicalism misplaced?

Mrs Thatcher has an extremely powerful and determined personality, and after ten years as prime minister she has a great deal of confidence in her own judgement. So I think one is, indeed, dealing with somebody who has an exceptionally strong will and who is proceeding by way of trying to determine policy and then trying to push it through rather than by the more cautious route of consensus. This is bound to achieve objectives which couldn't be achieved in any other way besides being upsetting to people. Sometimes it can lead to error. It's a different way of doing things.

I don't see this government as radically different from previous Conservative governments. The situation in 1979 was that the post-war settlement, which had been a socialist settlement imposed by the Attlee government and had certain characteristics, had reached the end of its useful life. The characteristics were a very strong predominance of the trade unions in economic and industrial affairs; extremely high marginal tax rates, going up to 98 per cent on unearned income and to 88 per cent or whatever it was on earned income; tight financial regulation, exchange controls and all the consequences; and a very substantial state-owned sector of industry. What the Thatcher government did was to say what all Conservatives thought – and anybody who didn't think this wasn't a Conservative – that these four aspects of the Attlee settlement were damaging the national interest and it was right to demolish all of them. And Mrs Thatcher has demolished all of them. The trade union dominance has been destroyed by successive Acts and the defeat of the miners' strike.

These measures have been absolutely a precondition for any substantial and continued recovery of the British economy. Taxes have been brought down to a level comparable with that of the rest of the world. We've moved away from the Swedish model and gone towards a model which is comparable to that of, say, the United States. I've no doubt at all that, in terms of the health of the economy, it is immensely to the advantage of the country and not just to the advantage of the rich, as is shown by the fact that the tax actually paid by the highest tax payers has risen rather than fallen. It's therefore led to a real increase in the revenue of the state as well as, obviously, to a substantial increase in

the revenue of the people concerned. I don't say that every privatization has been ideally carried out. I would rather have seen some splitting up. But I've no doubt at all that privatization has led to a great improvement in the efficiency of the industries concerned. One can take an example such as British Airways: a thoroughly overmanned, undermanaged affair in its state form and now one of the most efficient airlines in the world.

Again, the ending of the strict financial regulations has, I believe, contributed substantially to the efficiency of the economy and has certainly allowed an enormous overseas investment that makes us the second largest overseas capital owners in the world after Japan. Therefore the decision to cut down the four pillars of the Attlee legacy has been absolutely right. It required a great deal of courage and determination, but it was entirely in line with Conservative philosophy, with what previous Conservative governments would have liked to have done, even if, given the historic circumstance they were in, they didn't feel they could.

But hasn't Mrs Thatcher changed the very fabric of British society in the sense that there's now so much emphasis on money as to make us comparable with the United States?

Being half American, perhaps I'm not the best judge. I have always been unsympathetic with the British distaste for thinking about money. In my childhood people still talked about trade as though it was something not quite socially respectable. I certainly thought in that way when I was at university, and I'm disappointed to say that I found the same with my children at university. The universities' view, perhaps understandably, is that being a don is the highest thing anyone can aspire to in this life, the next best thing being to be a civil servant, a bureaucrat of some kind, and the lowest thing of all to make society's living for it. That seemed to me a distortion of any reasonable values, so I feel that if there has been a change – and I'm not sure there's actually been as much change as is said – it's a change for the better.

My own view is that the health of our society depends upon entrepreneurs, not primarily on civil servants or even on business managers. It depends on people who actually change things by taking decisions which involve a risk to either their capital or their careers, or to both. These are the agents of change in an economy, and these are the people who deserve to be given a reasonable status in society. I don't mean an exclusive status. I don't admire people for being multi-millionaires any more than I admire people for being Nobel Prize winners. Obviously not. I admire both.

I certainly wouldn't feel that government concerns with prudential financial management crowd out all other human values. The greatest

evil I've seen in my lifetime in economic terms is inflation. This has done far more damage to human values than any degree of prudence on the part of government. Loose government finance leads inevitably and necessarily to an increase in inflation, and prudence is absolutely a necessary safeguard against inflation, which causes far more social suffering than prudence.

How do you assess Mrs Thatcher's strengths and weaknesses?

Her first strength is, as I say, an indomitable will. She is a person formidably determined to get her own way. Secondly, she has a deep root into English attitudes – though not, I think, into Scottish or Welsh attitudes – which she has developed among what one could call the Conservative working and lower middle classes. It's a strength of support that no previous Conservative leader has been able to command. She has developed it because she understands those people, indeed comes from them. It's been a very great strength, and she has a powerful if rather legalistic mind. She enjoys the kind of debating that's concerned with winning the argument rather than with establishing fine shades of distinction. She has, however, the weakness of the rifle against the shotgun, in that she has pinned down her targets one by one, has hit those targets but hasn't got breadth and scatter. She is not good at keeping the whole situation in mind at once. She was the right person for the situation in 1979, which needed a series of substantial radical changes, but now her qualities limit her ability to deal with a complex world in which the tasks are less obvious.

So can she be seen as the right person for the next decade?

It doesn't look at the moment as though she's going to be the person for the next decade. The relationship between her and the public has obviously soured. I'm perfectly sure, though, that her place in history is assured. She's a great prime minister, and probably her permanent achievements – because I don't think there's any intention in the Labour party, even if they do get into power, to reverse the major achievements – are comparable to the permanent achievements of the Liberal government in 1906 and the Attlee government of 1945. That is to say, Thatcherism will be the dominant structure of the country for half a century. No doubt other major changes will happen, but I wouldn't exclude the possibility that she will fight through this very difficult period when mistakes have certainly been made. It may be that the country will come to see her again in a more favourable light.

How easy do intellectuals find it to deal with her? She seems on a different wavelength.

Intellectuals in this country are so ignorant. The trouble with this country is that it has a very strong intellectual group which is extremely parochial, and in this respect, at least, Mrs Thatcher is rather less parochial than they are. She is after all dealing in fundamental matters of social organization and philosophy with an intellectual community which has consistently rejected Popper and failed to take in the major economic theories of the Austrian school. I'm not saying that Popper should have been regarded as correct on every issue, though he is a genius and an extremely important figure. But the whole of the argument for the open society and the consumer-led market economy, as made consistently by Keith Joseph in the second half of his political career, is one with which the intellectuals have failed to engage at all.

Are you sympathetic to those labelled the Wets?

I find them personally more sympathetic than the Drys, but intellectually less sympathetic. Most of the people who had the sort of education that I did, the sort of opportunities I enjoyed and have had the sort of life I lead, are Wets. I would say, on the whole, that the Wets have failed to think things through and that the intellectual positions they have come to occupy are not sustainable. But my sympathies are with their set of values and moral attitudes.

Is the Conservative party today in any real sense the same party that you supported all those years ago in Oxford?

It's a much more democratic party than it was. The old Conservative party had a balance of power that favoured what could be called the upper class. By that I mean an upper class consisting basically of three groups: the old landowning class, including the aristocracy but also including the landowners in general; the upper professional class; and the upper business class. When I was young, those three dominated the Conservative party. Their attitude towards social problems was essentially that they wanted to feel comfortable in their consciences, which was a perfectly genuine altruistic feeling, and that they wanted peace in their time and were prepared to use public funds to buy off trouble. The modern Conservative party is not dominated by those classes. It's got a centre of gravity which is somewhere in the middle of the middle class, with characteristically lower middle class conservative attitudes becoming much more important.

Can 'Thatcherite economics' be applied to the arts? Can you ever define whether a sculpture or a poem is cost-effective?

You can't. The public subsidy of the arts ought, in my view, to concen-

trate to a very large extent on public subsidy of the audience. I'm not quite sure what the central principle of Thatcherite economics would be thought to be. I only know that the central principle of my economic views is that of consumer sovereignty. Consumer sovereignty leads you, in political terms, to democracy, because the consumer is sovereign through the vote. It leads you, in economic terms, to the market economy, because the consumer is sovereign through the choice of his own personal expenditures. This means that you get a society which is determined by the sum of the wills of the people in it and the sum of the choices those people make. If you apply a principle of consumer sovereignty to the arts, you can say that it is reasonable to subsidize the consumer, but you should avoid as far as possible giving the subsidy straight to the producer.

Obviously this is a difficult principle to apply, and I don't even think that it should be applied rigorously. There are cases when producer subsidy is justified, but when I was at the Arts Council I found myself having much greater intellectual conviction about the desirability of improving access to the performing arts – making it possible for people to get to concerts, opera or theatre at prices they could afford – than trying to identify individual artists and saying, 'You ought to have a grant but you can't have one.' I could never see that we had any way of determining which of the applicants was an artist who ought to be supported, whereas if you leave it to the consumer but help the consumer to buy the product, then the consumer makes that choice. By and large, he or she is the person who ought to make it.

It is said that, as a nation, we spend very little on the arts as compared, for instance, with France.

As chairman of the Arts Council, I discussed this at considerable length with the French, and their high expenditure is largely because the French have allowed their arts to become bureaucratized. Much of it doesn't benefit the arts. For instance, the French have an inspectorate of music like our inspectorate of schools, whose job is to go round seeing that subsidized orchestras are playing in tune. This inspectorate alone employs more bureaucrats than the whole Arts Council of Great Britain. Plainly they are on the arts budget in France, but equally plainly there is a zero benefit to the arts.

There are certain things which France does better than Britain. I'm sure, for instance, that what you could call the quality of French intellectual life is higher than that of Britain. More books of a genuine intellectual quality are published. There is more intellectual debate. Reading *Le Monde* is an intellectual experience of a different kind from reading any British newspaper. Oddly enough, that is something which emerges

entirely from the unsubsidized private sector. If you look at French music, opera, theatre and the principal performing arts, theatre is unquestionably better and better provided for in Britain than in France, and British music is at least as good. Compared to the quality of orchestras in Germany and Austria, France and Britain are second-class nations, but it is not at all clear that France is a better second-class nation than Britain. So it seems to me that there is really no evidence that the French are getting value out of their arts expenditure.

As Arts Council chairman, you must have had to deal with Mrs Thatcher from time to time. Did you find her sympathetic to the arts?

I only went to her in the last resort, so I didn't see her at all often. When I had a real difficulty, as over the question of the replacement of the funding which the metropolitan counties had been doing, I found her consistently helpful. Her view of the arts is, again, rather characteristic. She believes that the arts are a part of being a civilized nation. The phrase that she rather likes, about putting the Great back into Britain, she sees, in artistic terms, as meaning that Britain ought to be a great artistic power. She is particularly interested in high-profile arts companies.

On the other hand, I was able to pursue a strongly regional policy, and I suppose that the support we were able to give Simon Rattle and the Birmingham Symphony Orchestra was the symbol of what I was trying to achieve in my period at the Arts Council. I explained to her why I was doing it and how I thought that we ought not to accept that excellence in the arts was purely metropolitan in character. She supported that view, and I found no difficulty with her in pursuing a policy which wasn't exactly in line with the rather national concept she had.

Is it true to say that independence in the arts only exists to the extent that the government wishes it to be preserved?

Anything that the government funds depends ultimately on the government for its continued independence. The government can pursue the arm's-length principle, which, in my time at the Arts Council, they consistently did. But if they wish to destroy it, then the government can destroy it. In my own case, the policy we pursued was basically a regional policy which caused the government some discomfort because the London companies obviously would have preferred a higher proportion of the money to be spent on them. They resented the regional policy and lobbied against it. The regional policy meanwhile had the support of the Labour controlled local authorities in the regions and, broadly speaking, the sympathy of the Labour party itself. Thus we were pursuing a policy that was, at the very least, bi-partisan in political

terms, and actually wasn't particularly characteristic of the rather centralizing aspects of Conservative government during the 1980s.

Do you think that further sponsorship from the private sector is really the best way forward?

I think that mixed funding is the way forward. Arts companies cannot rely on any single source of funds. They can't even rely on the box office. Perhaps the Americans don't turn up, or they have a bad run. They can't rely on central or local government because either of these may become short of funds or there may be a political change. And they can't rely solely on industry and sponsorship. Therefore my own view is that they should, in that situation, try and maximize the support they can get from each source and maintain as good relations as they can with both.

Do you find any conflict of interests between your religious beliefs and your present chairmanship of the Broadcasting Standards Council? It must surely be very difficult for you to make disinterested decisions.

If I were the only member of the council, that might be true, but the council is a mix of people. We've a bishop on the council, for example, and obviously I know what his religious views are; and we have a Scottish clergyman. I don't know what the other members' religious views are, and I wouldn't inquire. In practice, the combined view of the council, which is what matters, comes out fairly liberal and broad minded – certainly not significantly different from the view I would expect, say, the governors of the BBC to take, who would have a different religious mix. I don't find that I am consistently on one wing or the other of the council. I suppose the most one could say about the influence of Catholicism is that it's given me a very strong interest in the sort of questions we address, sufficient, at any rate, to make me willing to take any sort of issue on, even if it can only make one unpopular.

You are in a position to monitor, even censor, what is to be shown on television. Why do you think there is a need for censorship? People have switches on their TV sets, after all.

Well, not really to censor. Censor implies the right to preview something and stop it being published, which we don't have and don't seek. We're an after-the-event body. The reason why television is different from the print media, which can simply be set standards on pornography by statute, is that it's both intrusive and impermanent. Because it's impermanent, you don't automatically generate evidence which can be

checked against legal standards in the way you do with print. And because it's intrusive, people feel far more strongly about it than they do about newspapers, which, if they don't like, they don't buy and therefore don't see.

The main aim, to my mind – and this corresponds with the aim of the European legislation of the Council of Europe Convention and the European Community directive – is the protection of children. This is the chief point which needs to be kept in mind. People ask, 'Well, but shouldn't parents decide what their children view?' In fact, parents aren't very well able to decide what their children are watching. A majority of families nowadays have a second television, very often in the children's bedroom, so that children in practice view what is being generally shown. If you expose children, particularly at a formative stage, to a great deal of very violent or pornographic material, there is ample evidence that it's likely to do them harm. There's also widespread agreement among the public and television people that one needs to have codes of conduct to avoid that.

But isn't it true that there is as yet no reliable evidence that the type of programmes people see on TV affects the way they behave?

It's extremely difficult to prove any psychological connection, whatever subject one is talking about, because of the multiple causation of most human conduct. While it is perfectly true to say that all studies of psychological motivation have great difficulty in determining the relative weight to be given to different factors, the common-sense, generally held view, and the view which I think would need to be disproved rather than proved, is that if beer advertising sells beer, then violence advertising sells violence; that there is a connection between repeated exposures in any form of communication and a tendency for people to be influenced by those exposures. There are real difficulties in getting scientific standards of proof, but that is common to all psychological experimentation.

Every country actually finds that there has to be censorship of television in some form or another. The Dutch, for instance, who have, like the Americans, a constitutional provision that they shall have no censorship of any kind, turn out, when you press them, to have a number of rules which are either observed by the broadcasters, because the broadcasters accept that they have to be observed, or else would be enforced at law because Dutch law also has provisions. For instance, the Dutch take a very broad-minded view of pornography, but if you introduce either a child or an animal into a pornographic scene, it becomes illegal in the Netherlands. The question is therefore not whether they should be censoring but at what point they censor. The

Dutch also have great concern over the right to privacy, and therefore, during the course of a trial, Dutch television will not name the defendant, which goes well beyond any provisions of a similar kind that we have in Britain.

Every culture reaches a point at which it says no. The point is different in each country and different in each generation, so you need to be sensitive to interpretation and public opinion. But broadcasters do need to have regard to the culture in which they live, and the cultures are, to my mind, entitled to make these sort of distinctions, and will in practice make them in somewhat different places, though there are large areas which are identical in virtually every culture.

Broadcasting has always been subject to regulation. We're moving from a highly regulated system to one that is much less regulated. We're moving from a four-channel situation to a twenty-channel situation, and the Broadcasting Standards Council is a body which is therefore exercising a far lesser degree of control. It exercises perhaps an important advisory role in place of bodies that formerly exercised a very tight degree of control. The consideration of the welfare of children justifies at least this amount of control over television, as does the fact that there are matters which the public is not prepared to accept on television because of the medium's domestic nature.

Nevertheless doesn't any attempt to introduce or reintroduce moral values by way of censorship or legislation unavoidably involve a paternalism that seems inappropriate to the late twentieth century?

It's a very common view, as I recognize, and if I were particularly worried about it I should obviously find myself disturbed by it. In fact it's a view based on a lack of understanding of the problems. When one sees the sort of material which, say, the British Board of Film Classification won't allow to be shown, one is aware that there is a considerable amount of material which, I'm sure, has no place on television nor in the cinema; material which appeals to very dangerous perversions, is principally sadistic and anti-women and, in some cases, destructive of children. This material, at any rate, you have to find a way to eliminate. People say, but isn't pornography fairly harmless? Isn't it a choice that people ought to be free to make for themselves? Real pornography is anything but harmless and is invariably concerned with destruction. It's not a matter of a simple celebration of the erotic or anything of that kind. It's usually profoundly hostile to women, sado-masochistic in character and often paedophile.

You get combinations of paedophile and sado-masochistic elements which are, to my mind, by their nature very dangerous. They're appealing, fortunately, to rather rare perversions, but to very horrible ones.

This material, at any rate, we have to find a way of dealing with in a satisfactory way, it seems to me. I don't think one can say, don't do anything and this won't happen. There is evidence that it does happen, and there is also evidence that, if you allow pornography, the shock effect soon wears off and the pornographers have to seek ever more extreme forms to achieve the effects they were achieving earlier. So where you have both sex and violence coming together, we have to find a way of keeping it off the screens.

An Observer *profile described you somewhat unkindly as 'a classic Victorian bourgeois who rails against private immorality while condoning public amorality'. How would you defend yourself against such a criticism?*

That's false in every respect, as far as I know. I don't spend any time railing against private immorality. I hold a different view about what constitutes public morality from the *Observer*'s: I think mine is better based, they think theirs is better based, and that's all there is in it. The fundamental cultural influences in the development of my thinking belong much more to the seventeenth and eighteenth centuries than to the nineteenth. I don't feel any particular sympathy with the Victorian bourgeoisie, whom I see as stifling, limited, aesthetically weak, over-paternalistic, over-authoritarian and not genuinely liberal. I don't feel sympathy with either them or their period. The Victorians I sympathize with most were not those who are most identified with the period.

The people I feel most at home with are the late seventeenth-century group, including Boyle, of which Locke and Newton are the greatest; that group who changed the whole world of thought at the end of the seventeenth century and in the early eighteenth century: the Scottish Enlightenment on the one hand and the English literary tradition on the other. I don't recognize myself as being a nineteenth-century bourgeois figure.

But have your views on morality changed over the years?

Everybody's views on morality must change to a certain extent over the years. I've become less censorious because I've seen more of human nature. One probably starts out with a fairly rigid moral grid that one then finds doesn't relate to the extraordinary inconsistency of all human beings. In human life there is a series of pulses of energy rather than something which can be formalized into a completely rigid structure, and you have to allow for the fact that people will combine in themselves the highest moral standards with patterns of conduct which seem inconsistent with them. That's something one learns from experience. One is educated by one's children to a very large extent. They educate you because they are other personalities in whom you have complete

confidence, and hence their experiences, thoughts and so on enter in in a way that other external thoughts and experiences do not.

Do the Mary Whitehouses of this world have a useful role in our society?

Yes. It was very desirable that the case Mary Whitehouse wanted to put should have been put. I don't think it did any harm that broadcasters, who have a position of quite extraordinary social power, should be faced with criticism of their actions and a need to consider whether they can justify their editorial decisions. She was right in saying that children should be protected, that there should be a great deal of concern about the welfare of children in terms of what television is put out, particularly during the period when the younger children are watching. The importance that the watershed now plays in British television programming is significantly the result of her work. I would therefore say that she has done a lot of good work without saying I agree with everything she has said, which I don't. Some of the emphasis that Mary Whitehouse had from the beginning did represent, I think, a failure of imagination.

The Observer *profile also suggested that you came to distrust Keynesianism through a dislike of Keynes's homosexuality. Is there any truth in that? Are you intolerant of homosexuality?*

Not at all. It's one of the subjects which, in my experience, you can't use a perfectly rational argument about without immediately being substantially misinterpreted. What I did once write, and I think it is probably true, was that Keynes came to adopt a philosophy of life that said in effect that there were no rules of morality, but that there were certain aspects of good consciousness which were the highest goal people could seek. I think he came to adopt this because he was homosexual and was therefore unable to reconcile his own personal life to any morality or set of rules in the sexual area. The attraction of this set of ideas was quite largely that they gave him a consistent philosophy of life that allowed him to be a homosexual without any limit on his sexual activity. You get much the same thing in E. M. Forster, who holds much the same views.

I went on to argue that Keynes's fundamental philosophy of life had a very important influence on his approach to economics, that Keynesian economics attacked the rules of classical economics and that, in the end, Keynesian economics become an almost rule-free pragmatism. Now this still seems to me to be perfectly true, and a rather similar view was later taken by Skidelsky in his biography of Keynes. It was a matter I discussed before Skidelsky, but I was interested to find that Skidelsky, reviewing the whole of the evidence and going into it in great depth, came to much the same conclusions about the development of Keynes's

underlying thought. Simplifying it, you get a direct relationship between Keynes as an adolescent, deciding that the taboo on homosexuality must be rejected, and Keynes as a mature economist, deciding that the taboo on convertibility into gold must be rejected. This seems to me a completely prejudice-free argument. It isn't based on any dislike of or feeling of hostility to homosexuality. It's simply a tracking of a rather important element in Keynes's development. But I found the moment I said it that people misrepresented it as anti-homosexual, and the *Observer* repeated the charge.

You once described your 'impotent guilt' on a walk from the Royal Opera House to the Savoy Hotel for supper. That seems to suggest an awareness of the majority who lead more ordinary lives, and a consciousness that there is an unbridgeable gulf between you and them.

My impotent guilt was about people who were sleeping in cardboard boxes, not about the majority. I don't feel any impotent guilt about my relationship with the majority. We are now in a society very different from the society of my youth, where the majority lead lives which, in economic terms at any rate, are reasonably satisfying. We have changed from being a society where 20 per cent were comfortably off and 80 per cent were poor to one in which 60 per cent are comfortably off and 40 per cent are poor and 20 per cent, or half of the poor, are very poor. My feeling of impotent guilt applied to the people who were sleeping in corners, homeless, leading lives which were obviously extremely difficult and miserable; and the fact that I could think of nothing useful I could do about it, other than support charities and occasionally give them money if they ask me.

It is obviously a great social evil. I do give support to charities which try to deal with it, and I think that's the right thing to do, but I can't pretend that I think it effective or sufficient, and I don't know what to do about it otherwise. It's a long-standing problem, and it was the start of much of the work of General Booth and the foundation of the Salvation Army. Perhaps that's the best approach yet developed towards it.

The novelist Simon Raven has created a character widely regarded as a caricature of yourself. Do you find that disturbing?

I don't find it at all disturbing. It appeals to my vanity to have characters based on myself. In the case of Simon Raven, the character is an extremely unpleasant one, and it's a kind of extrapolation of what I think is a rather accurately observed potential of the dark side of my character. If I had gone on from what I was like as a schoolboy, and developed in the nastiest possible direction, I could have been not unlike

that. We all have a dark side. It never completely disappears. Indeed, we wouldn't be balanced personalities if it did. I would say it's a rather interesting portrait, if a very unpleasant one.

It is going to seem to many that you have led a model and puritanical kind of life. Has that in fact been the case or were you, like most people, subject to the waywardness of youth?

I was very romantic in my youth and led a rather model and puritanical life because I tended, in a rather Victorian way, to be in love with unattainable young women. I didn't sow many wild oats, but more because I was going round like one of Tennyson's Knights of the Round Table than for any other reason. Everybody's tempted, of course, but what I had was a tremendously strong sense of the incredible attraction of the feminine principle. I think, when I was in my early twenties, that I felt that very much more strongly than natural earthy lust. The companionship of attractive and beautiful girls gave me an enormous delight, and I was very much in love with them, but in those days – and we're talking about the early 1950s – we lived in a more puritanical age under more puritanical presuppositions. I suspect I was always rather mooning around the place.

I continue to enjoy women's company very much. I wouldn't say that I feel more comfortable in the presence of men than of women since I enjoy each about equally. I certainly like male occasions and believe there is a role for all-male clubs just as there is a role for all-female occasions. There are certain aspects of what might be called the natural psychology of each sex when they want to be with their own sex. But I wouldn't want to be in a men's club all my life, or to lead that sort of a life.

The English culture is one of restraint. I don't know why it should have become so. It wasn't always. When Erasmus came to Britain he was amazed at the way the English spent their time kissing each other. From a continental perspective, it all seemed very odd. The English have now become a non-touch culture, and neither Englishmen nor, in my experience, Englishwomen actually like being embraced by a stranger. There are, of course, people who throw their arms round everybody, but on the whole Englishmen and Englishwomen find that equally embarrassing. I don't think Englishwomen are more physical, in this sense, than Englishmen. Kissing at parties has become much more normal nowadays, but I don't notice women walking the streets with their arms round each other in the way it might happen in a really physical culture.

Women have been important in my life. My marriage has been extremely important and one of the strongest influences. My mother

was a very strong influence, as were the women I was in love with in my twenties. My daughters, and the way they see the world, have been strong influences too. So, in all my closest personal relationships, women have played an absolutely vital part. My marriage is beyond friendship. It seems to me that the difference between marriage and other relationships is it's total quality; that it comes to be a part of the whole of one's life in a way that, in the end, no other relationship is, except that between the mother and the small child perhaps.

What was your attitude towards your own children and what advice have you given them as young adults?

I always believed that they would pay no attention to anything I said, that they would only pay attention to how life seemed to be lived, and therefore that preaching to them would be useless. I tried to teach but not preach, and I encouraged them to read things that had interested me, talked about things that had interested me and so forth. I don't believe that direct preaching works. The only way parents can influence their children is by conduct. Preaching without conduct is hopeless.

Do you relish the cut and thrust of controversy?

Oh, enormously. I'm a professional controversialist. I know how to do it, and I enjoy doing it. I try not to be too savage about it, but my favourite poet, saving Shakespeare, is Alexander Pope. If anybody is silly enough to write an article contradicting me or saying I'm a fool, a scoundrel or a rogue, then that is enormous fun, because it provides a splendid opportunity for counter-attack. I'm a professional duellist, fighting with paper bullets.

Which post has given you the most satisfaction so far?

Undoubtedly editing *The Times*. It's the most important and difficult job I've done, and therefore the most satisfying. It was also the one for which I had to make the greatest sacrifices. Otherwise I've always tended to do jobs which left me with spare energy for thinking and doing things outside that one single channel, and I'm not really temperamentally well suited to the single-job life. I feel I'm much more relaxed, much happier in my present position, where I'm doing half a dozen different jobs, turning from one to the other and having sufficient energy to enjoy my leisure, than I was in doing the wholly absorbing single job. So I wouldn't be sure that *The Times* was the job I enjoyed most, but it was the one which gave me the greatest satisfaction.

Do you feel, with Malcolm Muggeridge, that as one grows older one becomes more religious?

At some periods in my life I've felt more strongly religious than at others. The intensity comes and goes in a strange way that I can't account for. It doesn't have a progression. If you start off with the faith of a child, you then discover that you've got to think it through and emerge with an adult faith. But I don't think anybody can or should go without experiencing doubts and trying to think them through. I can't say I have any doubts now, but on the other hand I have a total sense of mystery. I remember, when I had doubts, that the phrase in the Athanasian Creed about the Trinity – not one Incomprehensible but three Incomprehensibles – seemed to me absolute rubbish, because how could one possibly believe in a doctrine which required one to believe not in one incomprehensible thing but in three incomprehensible things at once? It now seems to me to be the simplest, plainest statement of the truth that could possibly bc made, and therefore my present frame of mind is that I combine a feeling of total confidence of the existence of a reality, and therefore in that sense an unquestioning faith, with a complete intellectual conviction of the inability of human beings to comprehend that reality in any defined way. I don't think I'm likely to change.

Do you have any one deep regret in life?

I suppose I shall always regret not having had a time in the House of Commons. It was a very important part of what I thought my ambition was when I was a young man, and I would like to have seen whether I would have been able to make out in that environment. That's a regret, but it's not a regret in the sense that I would have preferred it to what actually happened. I prefer what actually happened, but if one could have two lives, it's the alternative I would chose.

I've been immensely lucky. I've had an extraordinarily happy life. I had only two periods which I would regard as times of trouble. Adolescence is a bit difficult for everybody, but I was also rather ill at the time and found it quite a difficult period. Again, there was the time when *The Times* shut down for a year, which immediately followed a period in which my mother had died, and life went through one of those phases, as it does for everybody, of difficulties coming together at the same moment. Otherwise I've had an extraordinarily fortunate life, and anyone who has seen five children growing up, all of them reasonably happy and well, must feel profoundly thankful for it; and for a marriage that has worked for twenty-eight years, and to have had a varied and interesting career. It seems to me that I've had an extremely happy life, and I have on the whole a relatively happy temperament. I tend to feel mildly happy rather than mildly depressed more than fifty per cent of the time, which is all one can ask for.

WILLIE RUSHTON

Willie Rushton is an actor, author, cartoonist and broadcaster. He was born in 1937 and educated at Shrewsbury School where he met Richard Ingrams. He founded *Private Eye* in 1961, the year of his stage début in *The Bed-Sitting Room* by Spike Milligan. His television career includes *That Was The Week That Was* and he is the author of many humorous books including *Pigsticking: A Joy for Life* (1977), *The Filth Amendment* (1981) and *The Alternative Gardener* (1986).

Do you retain happy memories of your childhood?

Actually I have a very early first memory. I may be one of the very few people you interview who can remember being in his pram, which must have been in about 1938. I was born in 1937, so from a year old I have a picture in my head. It is of the pram handle – the pushing bit – and a boy climbing through a broken fence to collect his cricket ball, which he'd hit from his garden into ours. I checked up afterwards when I lived in the house again after the war. The hole in the fence was there. I can still see the bar with which the pram was pushed in the foreground, and bits of blanket and the rest of it. So I do have a very early childhood memory. I imagine I was happy then.

When the war started, I suppose this had some bearing on childhood. Father went off to it. He was in Bomber Command, so vanished off to East Anglia, while I went down to Newport in Monmouthshire. That was a slight muddle. It was an English county but had a Welsh church and Welsh licensing laws, though neither of those things bothered me at the time. At about the age of nine I had a perfect Welsh accent.

Part of the reason for being happy as a child was possibly that I had a very good basic education pounded into me. When I was about three I was sent to a very strange little school, a kindergarten run by two very fine old women – wonderful old ladies who had, I think, done the same for my mother, and her mother before her. They just gave you the three R's. Absolutely whacked them into you. I still have to go nine threes are twenty-seven, nine fours are thirty-six. By the age of five I could read and write, do addition, subtraction, multiplication and division. I often wonder if that isn't the way to do it: grab this little bit of flesh and just insert all those things into it very early before the child even knows it's hit him. My own son's education was a much more

slower process. In fact my wife and I had virtually to teach him to read at the age of about ten.

Although times were quite rough since the war was on, we seemed to get around rationing. A farmer called Hodges used to come in with illicit sacks of potatoes and other things when nobody else could get any. I ate too much, which is probably why I've been very fat for most of my life. When I was about nine I was sent off to a prep school in Buckinghamshire. It was very similar to the one in Evelyn Waugh's *Decline and Fall*, where Captain Grimes appears. It was run by an ex-artillery major who had hit on this brilliant idea of starting a prep school, and was full of old men who called themselves colonel, captain or major. All of them were fairly ignorant, but they somehow got me through common entrance. I rather enjoyed not being at home. I never remember being homesick. Perhaps that's in my nature. I liked my family, especially my father. Mother went on a bit, but if I was on the psychiatrist's couch I don't think I could actually level too many things at her. I just got on better with Father.

Then I went to Shrewsbury, and arrived on the same day as Richard Ingrams. All my reports used to say, 'Could try harder', but when anyone wrote things like that, my father used to send a sharp note to the teacher saying, 'This is your fault. If the child doesn't pay attention to a teacher, then there must be something radically wrong with the teaching.' Which I always thought was very good. You don't often get that response from a parent. I think he was right. He was particularly annoyed by history and English masters, but he didn't much care about mathematics, because he couldn't do that either and could perfectly well understand why I wasn't interested in it, or indeed about foreign languages, although I learned a sort of terrible French. But English and history were, he felt, the two things I should concentrate on properly, and were of the greatest interest. He could never understand how those could be taught boringly. There had to be something very wrong with the teaching if you could make history dull. I have this theory that nowadays they probably make sex education dull as well.

I quite enjoyed Shrewsbury, besides which I got to know Richard Ingrams, Paul Foot and Christopher Booker there, which eventually prompted *Private Eye*. I never had the faintest desire to send my own son there, (a) because my wife is Australian and thought the English public school was quite the worst thing that could happen to any young Englishman, and (b) because I vaguely agreed with her. Shrewsbury was definitely a damper on several fronts, although I'm aware that I quite enjoyed going through the system and felt that coming out at the end was a sort of mild success, rather like national service. But things like the sudden introduction of women into my life came as an enormous shock, the only women I had met previously having been fat jolly girls

with acne who brought the vegetables over at mealtimes or swept up around you, or rather serious hatchet-faced women with stiff white aprons who would force the most unmentionable things between your lips.

I don't think I was much engaged in homosexual activities at school. I never really fancied my fellow man even then, and anyway, the bicycle sheds and the pavilion were an enormously long way away. The other thing missing at Shrewsbury, apart from women, from whom you were protected, was any awareness that there was anything else except the *Daily Telegraph* and the Tories. It wasn't a particularly Tory education, but Shrewsbury just persuaded you that you were middle class. You didn't wear a stiff collar, just a semi-stiff collar, and it was all reasonably liberal. Shropshire countryside, pleasant and quiet, buzzing bees, P. G. Wodehouse, and Lord Emsworth living down the road with his pig. A nice place to be raised, but always this vague suspicion that most people in the world were middle class, and those were the people you'd meet and get on with.

It was the army that changed that when I suddenly discovered the *Daily Mirror* and my fellow man. I found the friends I made were more the thuggish Glaswegians and the hairy-chested Liverpudlians than my public-school contemporaries. They were also a useful sort of bodyguard. In Germany there were many German youths eager to conduct World War Three. With the score two nil against them, I think they felt they should. They used to set on us in bars, and suddenly my companions would become bodyguards, knowing that I'd be totally useless in any fracas involving broken bottles or boots. These very burly Glaswegians would say, 'All right, Will, under the table,' and they'd beat the hell out of the German youths while I hid with a glass of beer and the remnants of a veal chop.

Do you regret not going to university? I don't necessarily mean in an academic sense, but university often provides an environment without pressure in which to experiment and test ideas without immediate consequences. Do you feel you missed out on all that?

The reason I didn't get there was my appalling lack of mathematics. I took O-level mathematics seven times, and in my last year they told me I was never going to get it, but that if I did biology, that would do instead. So I did biology for my last year, and when it came to the exam – this was one of the great watersheds in my life – there on the table in front of me was something in a bottle. The first question was, 'What is this?' I just wrote down, 'Disgusting', and walked out. The decision had been reached. I was not to go to university. But by going into the army I sometimes think I had the best of university educations

in a way: all the chances to experiment and the extra-mural activities without any of the bothers. Most people thought I was at Oxford. The fact that they didn't see me at lectures didn't surprise them. People still say to me, 'You were at university, weren't you?' Since I realize it means something to them, I say, 'Yes, I was,' and then I'm in the happy position of being able to say, 'Well, I got a first in Greats at University College, Oxford,' or, 'I was at John's, Cambridge,' depending on my mood and whim. I certainly got a lot of the advantages of university as the result of going up to see people at weekends. At the same time I was actually learning a few tricks of how to live in London, which was quite useful to the others when they came down.

At one point, I believe, you decided on the law as a career.

I didn't decide. What happened was that not going to university suddenly became a major family crisis. My father had died while I was in the army, and I got a compassionate posting back from Germany and saw out my military career as a clerk with the Westminster Dragoons. During all that time there was a certain maternal and grandparental panic, and a general panic of old friends of Father's, and I didn't know what I wanted to do. I hadn't the faintest idea what I wanted to do. I could do half *The Times* crossword, I'd had a public school education. I knew a lot of hymns. I could draw a bit, I could definitely make jokes, and I could write a bit. My qualifications were definitely vague and I thought, not knowing anything about anything, that advertising was probably it. But a friend of Father's told me I should get a qualification and recommended I become a solicitor. It was going to take seven years, which seemed rather good to me, being then about twenty. I went to this office as an articled clerk, and it was a very funny year. Everybody should have to do a year in an office. It's been very useful in my life; it persuaded me never to go back into one. I also discovered how easy it was to be a solicitor, which has stood me in good stead. I can almost buy and sell my own house. It's very easy. That they can take so long over buying or selling a house is one of the great cons of history. It was therefore good experience, but I realized that it wasn't for me. Exams began to loom. I was going to have to go off to law school for six months. I thought, I can't go through all that bloody education again, so decided then and there to become a freelance cartoonist. Big decision. Broken-hearted mother, broken-hearted friend of father. Everybody bursting into tears. The end of the world.

The 1960s is not a fashionable period now. Looking back it sometimes seem

to have been so brittle and trivializing, as if everything was theatrical and nothing had substance. Do you think it really was like that?

The sixties weren't actually a revolution. In revolutions people tend to get hung from lamp-posts, or to vanish, or at least stop carrying on their work. In fact all that the sixties did was to widen the options. Suddenly Carnaby Street was invented, which did no harm to Hardy Amies or Norman Hartnell, or Pontings or Barkers, or Derry & Toms. *Private Eye* did no harm to *Punch*, which was our only rival really. What I've always liked about the sixties was that they were very amiable. There was a certain daftness. But there was also an intelligence abroad, and bags of opportunities. There was the vague sense that everybody thought: we'll change the world.

Then there were wonderful things such as the Profumo crisis, which helped *Private Eye* a great deal, and the end of the Tories and the arrival of Harold Wilson – the thought that the world actually was changing. It was certainly the decade I was happiest in.

Was there a kind of shift in society at the beginning of the 1960s which made room for a new degree of irreverence?

I'm sure of it. A whole load of people who had lived as children through the war and been teenagers in the forties and fifties, suddenly found everything was just right. And the public was ready for something exciting to happen. I remember when sweet rationing ended, I went out and had twelve Mars Bars almost immediately and was sick as a cat. I think this happened generally, and perhaps there was a sort of feeling that rationing was over at last. When Harold Macmillan said, 'You've never had it so good,' it was actually true. There was still a great deal of poverty, but there were more people who could afford things they hadn't been able to before.

That Was the Week That Was, *otherwise known as* TW3, *was really the first of the professional satire shows. How was all the material assembled?*

It was nearly all commissioned. Ned Sherrin was the genius behind it. He used to sit reading the papers in one of those extraordinary little houses that the BBC had bought at Lime Grove, and would suddenly think, that's a good idea for Waterhouse and Hall to write a piece for Roy Kinnear about. So he would farm things out, though ideas were welcome from anybody. There were people who had one great idea in their life, and sent it in and we did it, but in the main it was commissioned.

I don't think there was a line drawn on the material we used. Ned Sherrin to all intents and purposes ruled untroubled. We were lucky in

that it was done by Talks as opposed to Light Entertainment. Light Entertainment hated *TW3* because it wasn't theirs. There were three reasons for the show being good: Donald Baverstock and Alasdair Milne, who were both good toughies in those days, and above them the distinguished and wonderful woman Grace Wyndham Goldie. The only item that was ever cut on the grounds of taste was a song that I wrote for David Kernan called *Euro-opportunities for English Gigolos*. It was censored on the grounds that it got quite dirty half-way through. It started like this with a spoken verse:

From the Roman spring of Mrs Stone
Through a wearying summer till October,
I bring a touch of Latin
To the matrons of Manhatten.
And wealthy widows,
As they watch their figure go,
Say, 'Let's get down to Napoli
'And grab ourselves a gigolo.'

Then it launched into the song itself:

Fornicatione is Italian for love,
Copulatione is sent from heaven above,
Frustratione flutters in their withered loins,
I bring *sensatione* for a fountain full of coins.

And when the summer's over
And I'm sick of the fleshpots,
And I know that a fresh lot's
Not due till the spring,
Hibernatione – I kiss them all goodbye.
Their one *ambitione* is see Napoli and lie.

And when the winter's over
And it's back to the grindstone,
To the mink and rhinestone
And those sleepless *nottes*,
Better take *precautione*,
She may not be past her prime.
A-a-a-abortione
Cost a million a time.

Love should be free,
But in Napoli

It's a *professione*
Without a *pensione*
And they'll call me 'Stony Tony'
If they ever turn to
Artificiale inseminatione.

Such a lot of TW3 *was political. Were you subjected to pressure from political interests?*

The balance was done for us in a funny way. The most famous thing I ever did probably was the Macmillan, so while he was prime minister I had a wonderful time. Then he retired with his prostate and I had a wonderful last night, singing *The Party's Over* to full orchestral backing, which left not a dry eye in the house. Lance Percival then took over as Lord Home briefly, and after that, of course, in came Harold Wilson, and Roy Kinnear was designed by nature to play him. I always feel mildly responsible for the twelve years of Tory misrule. I remember how, at *Private Eye*, we began to wonder, is this the end? We had a wonderful time attacking the Tories, with Profumo, Macmillan and so on, and we were terribly worried. Basically we rather liked Wilson and George Brown and all those people. We did hope that they were going to make things better and that life would improve, but what then was going to happen to poor old satire? Would there be a role for us in the new golden age?

I can't remember any pressures being put on us until we were taken off, though questions had been asked in the House. They concerned the famous case when the thirteen MPs who had never spoken in the House of Commons were named. Some of them had been there quite a long time and had never actually got round to making a maiden speech. It caused a furore that these names should be revealed, but it was a perfectly reasonable thing to do, particularly for their constituents.

The only major furore wasn't political but religious. We did a *Which* consumer's guide to religions, which was actually quite funny. Jews rang up quite happily and said, 'Look, we don't mind what you say about us, but weren't you a bit rough on the Roman Catholics?' The Roman Catholics rang and said, 'Look, we're as tolerant as the next man, but surely Islam got a bit of a whacking there.' What had seemed to us all rather a gentle piece caused an outcry.

Was everyone aware of the serious edge to the material in TW3*? Was there a sense of outraging the establishment?*

No, funnily enough. Basically we were picked for our acting abilities, not for our political know-how. In the main, we just thought of ourselves as the front men, not as deeply committed leftie thinkers. Ned

Sherrin himself is a Tory of the old school, not your bearded leftie in sandals, which I think a number of people thought he must have been to have come up with the show.

Some have suggested that the success of the show was to do with the final loss of empire and all the old British certainties being eroded.

It happened in America as well. I think it was world-widish – more that events suddenly were right. Profumo couldn't have happened at a better time. I'm very sorry for him, but it was a wonderful thing to have happened when it did. It was somehow a perfect end to the Tories, whom we'd had for ten or twelve years or whatever. People were ready for a really good laugh, a gossip and a bit of scandal – a perfect atmosphere for satire to flourish. We all thought that another golden age was about to dawn, that things were going to be wonderful. And they were, briefly. Camelot was viewed in the distance, but then the cloud cover came down again.

You stood for Parliament in Kinross and West Perthshire against Alec Douglas-Home. It seems to have been just a publicity exercise – a lost deposit for a lot of press coverage. But didn't you feel a little humiliated, even under those circumstances, when you got only forty-five votes?

The way that came about was that the *Private Eye* lot were sitting around in the Coach and Horses, discussing the business of the Tory for Kinross and West Perthshire having given away his seat so that Lord Home could step down from the Upper House and take his position as prime minister in the Lower in the by-election. We felt something should be done about it. Screaming Lord Sutch had done it, without much success either, but he had begun to inject a little jollity into what I was to discover was a deeply boring and beastly exercise. Having broached the matter, we were all going quietly to forget it, but got back to the office to find that walls do have ears. Clearly we were bugged. Immediately the *Evening Standard* was on the phone asking if I was standing in Kinross and West Perthshire. I said, 'Yes,' though I swear to God I meant to say no. From then on it became a sort of procession event, and it all started rather well. John Calder, the publisher, a cheerful little Scot, told me I could have the use of his house and butler in Kinross. Another man, an Ulsterman, rang and said he would be only too happy to provide the names of the ten constituents I required in order to stand. He said, 'We will support you and back you. We're deeply upset about this man being foisted upon us.' So it all smelt rather good as we trooped north.

With Paul Foot on the *Daily Record*, we thought we were going to get pretty good coverage. Ingrams came up too, and Bernard Levin

actually wrote my manifesto. I remember driving through Kinross on the way to the Calder home, seeing all those television aerials and thinking, we're going to do all right, it's going to be fine. Not so hot when it came to the very first public meeting and we met the Ulsterman for the first time – a man of enormous drunkenness, as indeed were his other ten. I was rather nervous, being younger then, but thought I'd done rather well since I'd drawn a packed hall, and the speech itself went rather well too. (The attendances were terrific. We always pulled more than anybody else, even Home.) I remember there being half a pint of water in a nice big tumbler in front of me. I downed this glass of water, which I discovered, as the last drop passed my larynx, to be neat malt whisky. A nice old lady got up to ask a question and as I began to answer there were cries of, 'Stand up when you're answering a question!' Suddenly I realized that I couldn't. The legs had completely gone. The question time did slightly undo the force of the speech itself, but although I was pissed, I was no way as bad as my senior representative, the Ulsterman. We then went back to his place and the most appalling scenes occurred. One day I shall record it in a novel.

After the first few days, Ingrams and Co. had to head back south to do the next *Private Eye* and suddenly I was alone. I will admit to a certain desperation as I realized the election was not swinging our way. I met Home once, in a place called Crieff. He was going to speak to the Women's Institute at the bottom of a hill, and I remember setting off down this same hill, to all intents unable to stop. I came face to face with him and asked if he was going to live in the constituency – a very fair question. He answered with what George Gale, who was then writing for the *Daily Express*, described as words of intense wisdom. 'Wait and see,' he said. I was savaged in the Tory press next day for my absurd questioning of the prime minister, while he was congratulated on his brilliantly diplomatic and skilful reply.

The Liberal was actually doing quite well, though he did make one error of judgement. He was the only person who was a local in the whole thing, but he kept turning up late and apologizing for getting lost. In the end I told everyone who had thought of voting for me that they might as well vote for the Liberal, for in that way they could possibly beat Home. I like to think that it justified my forty-five votes. The Liberal did come second, and I said it showed how many of my massive following actually took my advice and voted Liberal instead of for me. I didn't go up for the election. I watched it on television and was very glad I wasn't there. Some of the joy had gone out of it. It had become quite ugly by the second week.

So were you left with any serious political ambitions?

No, it wiped them out for ever. It cured me of active participation in politics for the rest of my life. But I do feel quite pleased when I meet deeply dedicated political figures and can actually turn to them and ask, 'Ever stood for Parliament? I have.' That's the one good thing to have come out of that appalling fortnight in Kinross and West Perthshire.

The successor to TW3, Not So Much a Programme, More a Way of Life, *was a bit of a disaster. The critics hated it. What went wrong?*

It didn't work. It was a bit like Alun Ayckbourn writing a musical. I think the critics were waiting for something to go wrong, and Ned probably overdid it. An empire was being created. He'd taken over the weekend, having cleared pubs on Saturday nights. All these things have a sell-by date and maybe people expected more from satire. *Not So Much a Programme* was much more a chat show and much more relaxed than *TW3*, and it never really settled. I wasn't on it for long and I certainly didn't fit into it very well. I went off and toured *That Was the Week* in America, which was wonderful. One-night stands in strange American colleges and universities, across Canada and down the other side.

As one of the founders of Private Eye, *can you tell me why so little care seems to be taken over checking stories for libel?*

When it actually becomes a libel case, the source quite often vanishes into the mists of time. A man who has said he will stand by you, that the story is as solid as a rock and he swears, on the body of his dead grandmother, that every word he has told you is true, often disappears when it comes to the crunch. They vanish. The stories were better to start with, I think. Many of the ones that have been true have worked extremely well. I never really went for the personal gossip, and when *Private Eye* started, we didn't want to do it. But where it is a matter of Parkinson and his secretary or something of the kind – where he's representing a government that swears by the Victorian way of life, that thinks family is sacred, that children should really be going up chimneys by the age of eight – and it's a case of hypocrisy, I think you can reveal some of these sexual activities. In many cases it's hurtful and unnecessary, and only when it's a bishop or a cabinet minister, or somebody who does not practise what he preaches, is it perfectly acceptable. But in the main, if it's just a very quiet affair on a dredger somewhere in the North Sea – ships that pass in the night – then I think it's best to avoid featuring it.

In *Private Eye*'s case, those who sue for libel are mainly journalists, who are sensitive souls when it comes to being attacked themselves.

But why they do it, I don't know. I've been libelled a few times in my life and never felt the faintest urge to do anything about it. I think it's madness to sue somebody for libel. The case doesn't come up for about four years and then it goes through the entire thing all over again. The Andrew Neil business was totally stupid. I hadn't read the story. The first I heard about it was when it actually appeared in the courts, when I admit I enjoyed it enormously. It's never occurred to me to use the courts. I might ring up whoever it is and say, 'You've got that wrong,' and they send you a bunch of flowers and a box of chocolates. What would probably be fair would be if the apology had to be the same size as the original attack. Normally the apologies are tucked away at the bottom of some tiny corner, but if you're libelled on the front page, then the apology should be on the front page.

Do you think satire is ever effective in the sense of changing people's habits or perceptions? It has always seemed to me dependent on the very attitudes it draws attention to.

In the old days in the Establishment, one of the complaints was that the audience were actually the very people whom the Establishment had set out to attack. They would sit there rocking with laughter and refusing to believe that it was about them at all. 'That's damned funny about old Bertie,' they would say. 'How lucky I'm not like him.' I think satire is a marvellous way of making a serious comment without appearing pompous. If I wanted to make some point, I would much rather *Private Eye* did it in a humorous manner than Peregrine Worsthorne in a leader in the *Sunday Telegraph. Private Eye* has a lot of serious things to say, but it doesn't have a column with a black border round it saying, 'But seriously, folks . . .' To return to your question about libel, some people think they're so important that everybody has read this libel and cares about whether or not they've done whatever they're said to have done. Other people in the main don't. They usually forget about it, which is what I've discovered on the few occasions I've been done over: that very few people had read about it and I was the only person sitting there saying, 'The bastards!'

Some reviews can be quite vicious, and you have had your fair share. Are you sensitive to criticism?

Not very. Some reviewers get their facts wrong, but that's all right. Television critics in the main don't know much about television. I'm a good target. A lot of people have a go at me because of something *Private Eye* may have said about them twenty years ago. I always tried very hard when I was working with the BBC and *Private Eye* to separate the two. I don't think I've ever split on anyone, except Denis Thatcher.

And even then he emerged from it with some credit. He'd just been seventy and gave an interview to his daughter in which, when asked the secret of his having lasted to the age of seventy, he said, 'I put it all down to gin and cigarettes.' I then found myself standing beside him at a rugby match, and wasn't quite sure what to say to him, so made a comment about how I thought he should bring out a T-shirt saying 'Gin and cigarettes'. He said, 'I missed out two other things. Sleeping and fucking.' I thought such a wonderful remark should be passed on. It was a nice rounded little story, and I thought it would suit *Private Eye* very well.

Philip Larkin, in his poem 'Churchgoing', says something to the effect that, although people hide behind ironies and jokes, underneath there is an urge to be serious of which they are half ashamed. Were you ever conscious of such a feeling?

No. All my life I've done the jokes. My responses to most things have been humorous. As the great Kurt Vonnegut Jr said, there are only two reactions to any human event. One is tears and one is laughter. He'd always preferred laughter because there was less clearing up to be done afterwards. There's a certain truth there.

No, I don't think satire trivializes, though it sometimes makes too much of trivia. All headlines are the same size, and it's very silly to see a headline about some unimportant event, which just happens to be the most important event that day, printed the same size as if it had been something monstrous happening in China. If we had an honest world, the newsreader could come on and say, 'We're terribly sorry, but very little of interest has happened, so we'll play you some light music instead.'

All comedians are traditionally supposed to want to play serious parts in the theatre. Do you share that ambition?

They're easier to do. Comedians in need of a rest think how wonderful it would be to do a bit of drama, when you don't have to worry about getting a laugh, don't have to time things right. I've only done one in my life, and that was *The Colditz Story*, in which I appeared as a commando major. I thought it absolutely wonderful. You just rehearse, then do it. Whether I would feel the same about *Hamlet* I'm not sure. If I played Hamlet I would probably get more laughs than most Hamlets.

Professional comedians are often said to be melancholy underneath. Do you fall in that category?

No, no. If I ever do get into any sort of depression I laugh myself out

of it in no time. There have been moments in my life, as in everybody's, when I've sat staring at the walls, but it's never lasted long.

Are you moody?

Oh, yes. Especially on the mornings when the brown envelopes are thick upon the mat. My moods are now regulated to some extent by my diabetes, which I developed about four years ago. Part of the illness is that it produces appalling changes of mood, but I find I'm terribly bland all the time now. I haven't got much of a temper, and it's usually trivial things that get me to explode, like unnecessary bureacracy or people who won't budge.

Will future trends in comedy be towards the more kindly and domestic or the more anarchic and violent?

I don't know. Anarchic and violent smacks very much of alternative comedy, which I always thought meant that there must be something rather more amusing on another channel. How quickly they've gone benign. All those alternative comedians are now working for the BBC and doing terribly proper things – like Ben Elton doing the *Wogan Show*. American alternative comedians are far better than ours. There are some wonderful jokesmiths in America, very odd stand-up acts that really do take risks. They do jokes that are very daring and ultimately very funny, but they're not based on old joke forms. Humour could take quite an interesting bend shortly.

Have women been important in your life?

I worked for women at an earlier stage, probably, than most at the BBC. I suppose that's the moment one should have discovered whether one was sexually strong or not. I always thought in the main I wasn't. The fact that men and women are different is absolutely clear to me. The basic difference is that women tend to over-react and men tend to under-react. I've always liked women, but then I don't dislike anybody. If they're pleasant, it doesn't matter about sex, class, colour, creed or religion. If they're pleasant, I've always enjoyed long talks with women. I think that once you get sex out of the window you can have a very good relationship with a woman. Sex is the mess in the middle, isn't it? Nobody nowadays quite knows, when he is working for a woman with vast padded shoulders, whether he should pinch her bottom or call her sir. It's a very muddy area. I find now that if you open a door for a woman at Harrods you should have a solicitor standing by. You may be rewarded with an enormous thank you or you may be given a look as though you'd just farted loudly in a cathedral.

Sex is basically a mess. Luckily, with diabetes, your libido is absolutely wiped out, so I now find myself in a very restful relaxed state, like St Augustine. St Augustine and I are the only people I know who, to all intents and purposes, have given it up. The hassle ain't there any longer. I'm back to the warm handshake on the doorstep. It's very 1950s. I can disappear into the night without any feeling of, oh, I should have pressed a little harder. I feel quite serene at the moment, even though it has been brought on by illness. In any case, I think I was going off before that. The English are a mess, really. They are either in violent pursuit or they're lying in front of the fire with their feet up. This is probably true of almost every activity we do. I mean, they're either pelting over the hedges in hunting pink, blasting trumpets on a horse, or absolutely comatose in a club with a newspaper over their heads. There seem to be no half-measures.

I'm sorry for women who have anything to do with Englishmen. An Englishman feels it's his right not to do anything, that lying there on a sofa with a newspaper, a glass of beer and the television on is his divine right. I think women are much better than men, and much nicer. They're very bright, they see things very clearly. They're stimulating, invigorating – bloody annoying sometimes, but that's perfectly reasonable. You just have to try and think your way into their sex and grasp at the bits of female about you. Feminism, though, has a lot to answer for. It may have achieved certain goals, but it is deeply confusing when you have a woman prime minister who isn't a feminist. Her impersonations over the years have been of male Tory ministers, their rather brutish moods and tempers. And now she's become what she thinks is feminine, and it's even more confusing.

The introduction to one of your books describes you as a part-time single parent. Has professional commitment, with you and your wife spending long periods apart, put particular strains on the family?

No, I think it cheered it up a lot. The reason our marriage has held together over the years is the fact that we have spent long periods apart. My wife pops off to Australia quite a lot. She has children there from a previous marriage and she's been running families in two hemispheres for as long as I've known her.

Would you describe yourself as a good father?

I don't know. You would have to ask my son. It all depends on what you expect from a father. I haven't tried to whack him with my principles. I think I've done most of the things for him that I should have done. I made certain he had a reasonable education, the best available at the time, and whereas I think all education should be free, I paid for his.

That was because I didn't want him looking me in the eye at the age of eighteen and complaining that I sent him to the local comprehensive and he had a rotten education just because that made me feel rather more left wing and pleased with myself.

Like all well-known figures, you must constantly be recognized in the street and in restaurants. How do you deal with it?

I was lucky, in a way, that I was recognizable from about twenty-two on because of *TW3*, and I made a decision then that it wasn't going to affect my life in any way. If I wanted to go round to the pub in my dressing gown, I would continue to. Some people are amazingly rude, though I don't think they mean to be. It's just that they say the first thing that leaps into their mind. 'You've put on weight,' they'll say, and there are those who circle you and prod you. Because of television, they think you're not real. They walk around you and say, 'He's a lot fatter, he's taller, isn't he?' It's a very peculiar sensation, particularly when you realize half-way through their perambulation and prodding that they actually think you're Ronnie Barker.

I imagine another drain on your time and privacy is a stream of invitations to open fêtes and so on. Do you undertake much charity work?

Basically I'm a Lord's Taverner. I like them a lot. They're forty years old this year, and they're cricket orientated, which is what I like. They're my no. 1 charity, and the money goes in good directions, basically for buses for handicapped children and sporting facilities for the fit ones. I feel that's a good area to be in. What I refuse to do is answer letters asking for money. I don't charge expenses, and I give time, but I don't give money. So begging letters get absolutely nowhere.

When your Twelve Great Moments in History *was accepted by the V&A, the curator said your work was in the Beerbohm tradition. Did that make you wonder whether you should have been a caricaturist first and foremost?*

I've never known quite which way my career would go. My career is based on very rarely saying no. I don't often start anything. I tend to wait to be asked. I think I've been lucky. I've always had something to do. I've usually got a book to illustrate, or, if I'm not acting, then I'm cartooning, and if I haven't been asked to illustrate anything for a while, I've still got some regular jobs like the *Independent* and *Private Eye*. If I'd really tried, I could have become a political cartoonist. I was approached years ago by the *Sunday Telegraph*, but I didn't want to be tied down. Now I'm actually starting regular work. I'm signing a contract to do three pictures a week for the *Daily Telegraph*. It's the first

time in my career I've signed a contract for anything that was going to last longer than about a week. That may show that I'm slowing down as the years go by. Perhaps this is my mid-life crisis.

I was thinking the other day how extraordinary was the speed with which I suddenly hummed upwards, with all the luck in the world, by being in the right place at the right time. By the age of about twenty-three I'd done two things which, in the main, should have been ambitions to achieve by the time I retired: a big television show and starting *Private Eye*. That is quite enough for any gravestone, in my view.

Most of my friends were outside showbiz and became junior executives. At the time when they were usually getting £650 a year and a car, I was earning forty, fifty, sixty quid a week. Of course, all these blokes catch you up. Now all my contemporaries have vast Tudor homes in Woking, three or four cars and wives, and children at Eton. That makes you wonder. I had a very jolly time in the sixties and seventies, but now I should be earning about three times as much as I am. The other day I met a man walking along the Cromwell Road. He came up to me and said that we'd been at school together, that he'd been three or four years after me, and that he'd just bought my mother's house – the massive house where I was raised, today worth about three quarters of a million. I couldn't afford it. I wandered home, gnashing teeth, saying, something's going radically wrong here, why am I not chairman of some vast enterprise? Then I thought, no, no, it's all right.

Do you have any religious feelings or affiliations?

No, I never have, really. My father was an agnostic. I was baptized, and was always taken to church by the grandparents in Wales, but I've rarely been to church since, and it doesn't mean a lot to me. I've never felt the need for the comfort of it. I do pray occasionally, but I'm not absolutely certain who to. They're very small-scale prayers, as when there are four hundred fertilizer salesmen waiting for a laugh and I just say very quietly, get me through the next bit, please. Or, let her be in a good mood. That sort of thing. They're not good ideas for global development or anything like that.

A lot of people get more religious as they get older, but that's a major cheat – people who are suddenly born again just so they think they'll get through the pearly gates, if there are any. It's covering all your exits. What happened to Muggeridge was terrible. Conversion on the Reigate bypass, a sudden flash of light. It never happened to my hero Claud Cockburn. They were both good old lefties of the old school before the war. Muggeridge went one way and now he lives on muesli; Claud's dead, but he never shifted, and I always admired him the more for it.

Somebody's got to do an awful lot of heavy persuasion to make me believe that either the Archbishop of Canterbury or the Pope or the Ayatollah or any other great religious leader has the answer. It's faith. It's persuading yourself that one of those gentlemen has got it right. Whatever it is, if there is anything, cannot be so simple that the Archbishop of Canterbury can have any grasp of it.

If you suddenly discovered that you didn't have long to live, how would you employ your time?

The basic priority, which shows I'm decent, is to see the family all right, but I would keep smoking to the grave. I can't think of any one thing I would do. If you've set out on a line and you've stuck to it, sometimes against the odds, it would be unfair suddenly to switch direction simply because you were about to drop off the twig. I would probably just work on a theory that medical science is such that they're probably wrong anyway. If some man looked me in the eye and said I'd got a year to live, I would immediately take that as a clear suggestion I was going to live for another thirty. I'm too much of an optimist.

ARTHUR SCHLESINGER JR

Arthur Schlesinger Jr has been Schweitzer Professor of Humanities at the City University in New York since 1966. He was born in Ohio in 1917 and graduated *summa cum laude* from Harvard in 1938. He has held academic appointments at Harvard and Princeton and between 1961 and 1964 he was special assistant to John F. Kennedy. He is author of many books including *The Politics of Upheaval* (1960), *The Politics of Hope* (1963), *Robert Kennedy and His Times* (1978) and *A Thousand Days* (1965), his account of the Kennedy administration, for which he won the Pulitzer Prize.

At Harvard you were once reported to have said, 'I love teaching but I hate students.'

I don't recall ever saying anything like that, nor is it what I feel. On the whole I like students more than I like teaching. I don't mind teaching and I work hard at it and believe I have done it reasonably well, but there are some people for whom teaching is an organic part of life and for whom deprivation would be equivalent to amputation. I regard teaching as better than ditch digging as a way to support oneself, and I find students quite agreeable, but I'm essentially a writer, and if I could have figured out a way of life that would have removed the necessity for teaching, I would have done it. At present I can't retire, because if I were to bring home the books that I have in my office to a house already overflowing with books, my wife would throw me or the books or both into the street.

As a celebrated American historian, you have been special adviser to a president of the United States. How did you reconcile the two disciplines: that of distinguished politician and that of political aide?

It's only in recent times that the two professions have become distinct. For a long time the two were fused in the same person without any sense of incompatibility. After all, Thucydides was an Athenian general and Julius Caesar was a far from dispassionate observer. Gibbon wrote in his memoirs, about his military experience, that the captain of the Hampshire Grenadiers was not useless to the historian of the Roman Empire. I think the opportunity to see how worldly decisions are made is as likely to enrich the historian as much as to corrupt him.

In my own case, in the United States, my mother was collaterally descended from George Bancroft, the first great American historian, who wrote a history of the United States in many volumes. George

Bancroft was also Jackson's and Van Buren's political man in Massachusetts. He was Polk's secretary of the navy, minister to England and to Germany, and was also a very productive historian.

You have to avoid turning history into political partisanship. Another historian once said of Bancroft that all his volumes voted for Andrew Jackson. One must guard against that. But even in libraries historians are not devoid of prejudice. The problem is that the historian can never escape the egocentric predicament, but he must continue to seek an objectivity he can never attain. At least he should take care to declare his interests.

Advisers to presidents are not elected representatives and some might not consider such appointments to be proper in a democracy. Does that not bring special problems and difficulties to the job?

It need not. A president can't do everything himself. From the beginning of the republic, presidents have had people to help them. Andrew Jackson formed what was called his 'kitchen cabinet' – advisers who were not members of the regular Cabinet but with whom he would discuss politics and choices – and that aroused a certain amount of newspaper and partisan protest, but, as Jackson recognized, criticism was really aimed at him, not at them.

The present White House staff was established in 1939 when FDR secured the passage of the Government Reorganization Act. That created the position of special assistant to the president, and he was given half a dozen of them. Up to that time, presidents had *de facto* special assistants, but they were mostly on payrolls of other agencies and were coopted. The new special assistants were supposed by Roosevelt to be endowed, in the phrase he borrowed from Tom Jones, the friend of Lloyd George, with a passion for anonymity. That passion for anonymity has waned in recent years.

In Britain we recently witnessed the resignation of the Chancellor of the Exchequer over the issue of Mrs Thatcher's personal economic adviser. What was your reading of the situation?

I guess Nigel Lawson had reached the point where he couldn't take Mrs Thatcher any more. Mrs Thatcher was getting economic advice both from the Chancellor and from her personal economic adviser, Alan Walters, and Lawson found the situation intolerable. I suppose he would have found it tolerable if his advice had been taken more often. I assume it was the culmination of various frustrations. Working with Mrs Thatcher, I would judge, is not always the easiest thing in the world.

We have a similar situation structurally in the United States. The president has a department of the Treasury, but he also has a Council

of Economic Advisers, both established by statute. The chairman of the Council of Economic Advisers and the Secretary of the Treasury often bring in conflicting advice. There is a third figure, the chairman of the Federal Reserve Board, which is an independent agency. Appointments to the Federal Reserve are made by the president with the consent of the Senate, but the agency itself is not accountable to the president. So you have a triad arguing over the economy.

Since economics is far from an exact science, I don't think it does any harm for the president to hear two or three positions. In the end the president makes the decisions. The American cabinet does not enjoy the authority that, theoretically, a British cabinet enjoys. The president has the monopoly over decision, whereas theoretically, if not always practically, decisions in British government are collegial; all members of the cabinet are implicated. A quarter of a century or more ago, Dick Crossman pointed out that cabinet government was giving way to prime ministerial government; in effect to presidential government. Mrs Thatcher has certainly illustrated the point.

In the present administration under Bush, or the previous administration under Reagan, did the advisers have autonomy, or was the president involved in everything?

In Reagan's case, he was indifferent to most of the business of government and he let people move off on their own, so long as they conformed to his set of *laissez-faire* principles. Bush is very much interested in foreign policy and probably follows that quite closely. Roosevelt had great intellectual curiosity; so did Kennedy. But Reagan was quite passive. He had no intellectual curiosity.

Who among all the presidents of recent years was the most autocratic?

All presidents are ultimately the boss in the executive branch. The most autocratic by temperament clearly was Nixon, but that was because he was insecure. He feared Congress, hated political opposition. Nixon would like to have been an elective dictator. He did not understand that debate and opposition are the essence of democracy; so he regarded opponents of the administration as disloyal to the country and put them on his enemies list. I am proud to say I was on it. Nixon was certainly the most autocratic by disposition. Roosevelt tended to give people a loose leash, but then to rein them in rather abruptly, and cut them off if he felt they did not justify his confidence. Eisenhower was interested in what he was interested in and indifferent to what he was indifferent to. He was actually a rather tense man within, but there were a lot of things he just didn't care about.

There's been a historical revisionism about Eisenhower, and now

counter-revisionism is setting in. For a time there was a theory that Eisenhower, underneath his grin and his apparent indifference and his fractured syntax, was really a very strong president. And it is evident that he played much more of a role in foreign affairs than we understood at the time. Eisenhower was a crafty man, a good politician, a selfish man. He used Dulles in what we call a good cop/bad cop routine. Dulles would do the unpleasant things and Eisenhower would be the man of peace. On the other hand, Eisenhower's instincts were good. For example, he was very sceptical about the missile gap. Having been a general, he didn't take the Pentagon very seriously. He was constantly saying – in private – that we were building too many nuclear weapons. In his farewell address, he talked about the dangers of the military–industrial complex.

Yet he did very little about these things. He complained about over-targetting by the Pentagon, but would not stop it. The military–industrial complex was really created during his presidency. One of the worst things he did was to use the CIA as the president's private army. He was sceptical about the regular army, so he never used it, and instead started the bad presidental habit of using covert action and clandestine means to achieve ends which, in a democracy, ought to be approved by the legislature, by public opinion.

Kennedy tended to get more involved in the processes of decision making than most presidents. He did not hesitate to call the man at the desk in the State Department or the Agriculture Department and so on if he wanted to find out what the situation really was. He would bypass the Cabinet minister in charge, which irritated cabinet ministers but exhilarated the people at the desk who received the presidential calls. Kennedy was very accessible. We could get him quite quickly by telephone, and late in the afternoon, if the door between his office and the office of his secretary was open, it meant that his special assistants could stick their heads in. He'd be reading or talking on the phone and would say, 'Come on in.' Sometimes he would just like to chat.

I find it hard to recognize the swollen White House staffs of the present time. During the Depression, Roosevelt had a smaller staff than the wife of the president has today, and he fought the Second World War with a smaller staff than the vice-president has today. Our White House staffs now are bloated. Many presidental assistants rarely see the president and have to make appointments days or weeks in advance. The great inflation of the White House staff came with Nixon, and every president since has carried it on. They all begin by saying they are going to reduce the size of the White House staff, but they never do.

As special assistant to Kennedy, your responsibilities ranged from speech writing

to general advice on major issues. To what extent was it a position of real power and influence?

It was not a position of real power at all. But for an historian it was a fascinating experience to be around when decisions were made. I don't think my presence made any difference to anything, except to me, but it was very enjoyable. Working with Kennedy was exhilarating. I learned a great deal, and perhaps I was able to play a marginal role on some matters.

Did he take your advice?

I was opposed to the Bay of Pigs. I was part of the group involved in planning it, and I thought it a bad idea. I talked to Kennedy about it, and he wasn't very enthusiastic himself, but it was an expedition he had inherited from the previous administration. He was trapped because, here he was, a naval lieutenant from the Second World War, and if he were to disband a project that the great General Eisenhower had approved, people would have been critical of him, and the word would have gone around that Eisenhower had been prepared to overthrow Castro and that Kennedy refused to follow through. Then there was what Alan Dulles of the CIA called the disposal problem: what to do with 1,200 Cuban exiles who had been trained in Guatemala. Kennedy couldn't quite see how to disband them without disturbing political consequences; so rather reluctantly he let the expedition go ahead.

He was a man of great intellectual curiosity and high intelligence. He liked to hear varying viewpoints. I suppose I was one base he liked to touch, probably just to see what a professional liberal, so to speak, would think about this or that issue. One thing on which I may have helped was the question of the centre left in Italy. The Eisenhower administration had said that the United States would not countenance the entry of the Partito Socialista Italiano (PSI) into an Italian government. The US veto struck all of us as outrageous, and at a very early point I talked to Kennedy about it. I went to Italy and, when I came back, strongly recommended that he indicate we would have no objection to the socialists entering the government, which he did when Fanfani made his visit in 1961. The State Department continued to try to preserve the Eisenhower veto, but the PSI had long since abandoned its fellow-travelling inclinations of a decade earlier. Still it wasn't really until Averell Harriman became under-secretary for political affairs that we were able to turn the State Department around. Eventually the socialists entered the government, and nothing much changed one way or t'other.

You have often been called an American liberal. Is that with a capital L?

'Liberal' means something very different in Europe. In Italy the Liberal party is a rather conservative party, and through most of the Continent liberal is understood to mean Manchester *laissez-faire* nineteenth-century liberalism with an admixture of anticlericalism. In Britain the Liberal party has come to mean the party of good-hearted, somewhat eccentric people. American liberalism is really the liberalism which Lloyd George and Churchill embraced before the First World War and it could, I suppose, be called social liberalism rather than classic liberalism.

What it means essentially is the intervention of the government to enlarge opportunity for those who are poor or handicapped one way or another in life. It means the interventionist state, provision of basic levels of welfare and so on. It does not mean the command economy, or centralized planning. It's Keynesian liberalism, the market working according to rules of the game with sufficient regulation in the public interest to prevent greed from undermining and subverting the system.

Reagan represented the reaction against all that, and greed took over in the United States in the 1980s. Greed brings out the worst impulses of capitalism. The solution in my view is to do what Roosevelt did: to rescue capitalism from the capitalists. If you're going to have individual freedom, you have to have mixed ownership. Private property is essential for freedom of speech, freedom of the press, freedom of political opposition and the like. But capitalists don't understand the virtues of their own system. If they have the money, they don't have to have political power too. I believe those capitalist states are best that are run by people who are not over-impressed by the wisdom of the business community.

In 1959, you said that the biggest issue between Democrats and Republicans was the allocation of resources between the public and private sectors. What do you see as the biggest issue today?

The biggest issue is the role of government. The view of the Reagan administration was that government is not the solution; government is the problem; if only we could get government 'off our backs', then our problems would solve themselves; or the processes of the market would solve them.

I would say that is manifestly not the case. Getting government off our backs means putting business on our backs. Deregulation has largely been a disaster. One reason I was a little late for our interview is that I've been calling the telephone company to get the phone fixed. We used to have a regulated monopoly. If the phone didn't work, they would send someone to fix it. Now the monopoly is broken up in the interests of deregulation, so you call one place and they say, 'Well, we're not responsible for that,' and you have to call another place, a separate

company, and so it goes on. The idea of deregulation was to bring competition into, say, the airlines. But competition did not last long. Where is Freddie Laker now? Where is People's Airline in the United States now? Competition has resulted in much more consolidation than existed under regulation.

Deregulation produced the leveraged buy-out scandals, the savings and loans scandals, the housing scandals. Regulation in the public interest is a requirement in any advanced industrial society. So is a measure of government intervention to help the poor and the disadvantaged. Democrats stand for affirmative government as against the Republican faith in negative government.

It sometimes seems that the politician who is able to give the best performance on television wins the day. Is that a cynical view, or has the stature of presidents and politicians diminished?

Television has had considerable impact on politics, but more on the party structure than on the character of politicians. In the United States the theory was that, once television became dominant, all successful politicians would have to meet standards of histrionic skill and personal pulchritude. Ronald Reagan came along in apparent vindication of this view. But actually Ronald Reagan succeeded because the country was entering a conservative phase in the political cycle. He would have been as effective in the age of radio, as was Roosevelt, or in the age of newsreels, as was Warren G. Harding, or in the age of the penny press, as was Franklin Pierce. I don't think he was a unique creation of television.

Indeed, he's almost alone in meeting those anticipated standards. If you look at the rest of the people who have run for president in the television age since Kennedy, none has been any good on television. Lyndon Johnson was a disaster. So was Barry Goldwater in 1964. In 1968, Hubert Humphrey and Richard Nixon were both disasters. George McGovern and Nixon; Jimmy Carter and Gerald Ford; Carter again against Reagan; Mondale, Dukakis and Bush – none has been any good, except for Kennedy and Reagan. The television age, in short, has produced few politicians conspicuously good at television. I think that effect has been much overrated. Indeed, consider two people who were very effective on television, handsome, telegenic, well-spoken, and possessed in addition of substantial political records. One was John Lindsay, who used to be mayor of New York, the other was John Connolly of Texas. Both tried for the presidency, and in spite of the fact that they were much better on television than their opponents, they did very badly.

Where television has had a potent effect, however, is in weakening,

enfeebling and perhaps eventually destroying the political parties. Television and the public opinion polls have deprived the political party of two of its most vital functions. In the old days, politics was a three-tiered operation. You had the politician, and you had the voter, and in between you had the party. The party would interpret the voters to the politician and the politician to the voter. The party was the great mediatorial agency. When the politician wanted to find out what public opinion was like in his constituency, he would ask the head of the local party organization. When the voter wanted to know how to vote, he'd listen to the head of the party organization.

The electronic era has ended all that. When the politician wants to know what public opinion is, he no longer calls up the political leader; he takes a poll. When the voter wants to find out who to vote for, he doesn't listen to the local political leader; he watches the tiny screen and makes his own judgement on what he sees. The parties are left to wither on the vine. During elections there used to be bumper stickers, buttons, torchlight processions, parades, volunteers. None of that any more. It's all done on television. I think the weakening of the party structure is a much more potent effect of television than any change in the character of candidates.

Many have the impression that people of great talent tend not to enter politics and that consequently our lives are ruled and shaped by, some would say, the best of the mediocre.

That assumption would certainly seem verified by the experience of the United States in the last eight or ten years, but it's a chronic, not a permanent, condition. It's a condition we've been through before, and I think that people who are turned off politics by the fact that it's too rough or too inquisitive or too political probably wouldn't be much good in government anyway. In a democracy, to be effective in governing you have to be effective in persuading. Democracy is government by consent, and I'm always sceptical when people say so-and-so would make a great president, but he won't submit himself to the rough and tumble. Unless he submits himself to the rough and tumble, he's not going to make a great president.

It's not a new complaint. You can find it in Bryce's *The American Commonwealth*, which was written a century ago. Bryce said that he kept hearing in America how a reckless and abusive press kept 'the best people' out of parties, but, 'I could not learn the name of any able and high-minded man of whom it could be truly said that through this cause his gifts and virtues had been reserved for private life.' It's a recurrent theme, and perhaps it's more an alibi than the real cause of abstention.

I've argued elsewhere that there's cyclical rhythm in our politics. We

alternate between periods of liberalism and periods of conservatism. The conservative periods generally tend to attract rather mediocre people. In this century, for example, the Reagan years, the 1980s, were a re-enactment of the Eisenhower 1950s, which were a re-enactment of the Harding/Coolidge/Hoover 1920s. In conservative periods personal gain is the dominant impulse. Similarly, at thirty-year intervals, you get periods when public purpose dominated: Theodore Roosevelt, ushering in the Progressive Era of 1901; thirty years after that, Franklin Roosevelt, the New Deal; thirty years after that, Kennedy and the New Frontier. If the rhythm holds, the 1990s should be much more like the Progressive Era and the New Deal and the Kennedy/Johnson years than like the 1980s.

There's nothing mystical about the thirty-year periodicity. Thirty years is the span of a generation. People tend to be formed politically by the ideals that prevail when they come of age politically. Those who grew up during the Progressive Era – young people like Franklin and Eleanor Roosevelt and Harry Truman – carried forward thirty years later the ideas they absorbed when young. Similarly, young people who grew up when Roosevelt was setting the nation's course – people like John Kennedy, Lyndon Johnson, Hubert Humphrey, Robert Kennedy – carried forward those ideals when this generation's turn came thirty years later. In the same way, Kennedy touched and formed a generation. If the rhythm holds, the Kennedy generation's time will come in the 1990s. Government is attractive when it's innovative, when it tries to meet problems, when it's idealistic. Then good people rush to join. When it's run by a Warren G. Harding or a Reagan, you get crooks and hustlers.

Talking of Truman, was he a strong president?

Yes, he was a strong president, a man of good instincts – emphatic, more decisive probably in appearance than he was internally. He was a very attractive man, a lower-case democrat in the strongest sense. He had absolutely no front, no pretence, no pomposity. He could work with a large variety of people. He came out of the Middle West, had a limited education and so on, but from the start he was an avid reader, and he knew quite a lot of American history. He made some mistakes, but he was a good man and a good president.

Was he right to remove General MacArthur when he did?

He was absolutely right. He should have done it some weeks earlier. I believe he was right, too, in the decision to drop the atomic bomb, terrible as that decision was. I believe he was wrong, however, to enter

the Korean War without the Congressional authorization he could have gotten.

But as a liberal would you, in his shoes, have dropped the atomic bomb?

Yes. I was in the army at that period. I was in Europe, facing redeployment to the Far East. Naturally I was grateful for the end of the war. But there are deeper reasons to accept Truman's decision as a tragic necessity. Even after the second atomic bomb was dropped, opposition to Japan's leaving the war was so intense that there was an attempted *coup* against the emperor. A group of Japanese historians wrote a book a few years ago called *The Longest Day* describing the events of the day after the dropping of the bomb on Nagasaki. The emperor managed to get on radio and succeeded in quietening things down. There was always the prospect of fanatical resistance that would have resulted in the deaths of many Americans and many Japanese. God knows what would have happened to the poor British prisoners of war. I was in England once when the decision to drop the bomb was under attack, and the letter columns of *The Times* and *Telegraph* were filled with letters from men who had been in POW camps. They said that if the war hadn't come to an end, they would have certainly died. It was a tragic decision to drop the bomb, but the Japanese should have thought more carefully before they bombed Pearl Harbor.

Theodore Roosevelt once said that America should speak quietly and carry a big stick. Did Kennedy subscribe to the idea of America as global policeman?

I wouldn't say that Theodore Roosevelt implied that America should be a global policeman. He just said that in foreign policy you should be prepared for any contingency but shouldn't go around provoking trouble. Roosevelt did occasionally employ the big stick, as when, for example, he fomented a revolt in Panama in order to build the canal. But although he played an active role in the taking of the Philippines, he later regretted it and felt that in that case the United States was getting involved beyond its own vital interests. He wasn't a globalist. But he was perfectly willing to use American power where he thought American vital interests were concerned.

Kennedy was definitely not a globalist. He had a very acute sense of the limitations of American power. In 1961 he said, 'We must face the fact that the United States is neither omnipotent nor omniscient – that we are only 6 per cent of the world's population – that we cannot impose our will upon the other 94 per cent of mankind – that we cannot right every wrong or reverse each adversity – and that therefore there cannot be an American solution to every world problem.' Wilson had said we must make the world safe for democracy, and in a deliberate

modification of that line, Kennedy in his American University speech in 1963 said we must make the world safe for diversity. That was his abiding view. He had no illusions about a *pax Americana*.

Kennedy's great triumph was surely the Cuban Missile Crisis and there must have been tremendous pressure on him at the time. Was he surrounded by advisers, or did he really have to think it out for himself?

He listened carefully to conflicting advice. It was essentially an argument between those, on the one side, like Dean Atcheson and the Joint Chiefs of Staff, who believed that the missile bases should be taken out by surprise attack, and those on the other, like his brother Robert Kennedy, McNamara, the secretary of defence, and George Ball in the State Department, who felt that the missiles should be negotiated out. There's no question in my mind where Kennedy stood from the beginning, and that was that they should be negotiated out. In effect, that was what we did. We traded. It was not known at the time, but a deal was made by which we removed the Jupiter missiles from Turkey and the Russians removed their missiles from Cuba.

To those on the outside it looked as if we were close to a third world war. How close were we?

Well, we all thought we were close at the time. In retrospect, I wouldn't say we were. The United States had a vast superiority in nuclear striking power, and also vast local superiority in the Caribbean. Khrushchev, I think, was a gambler, but he wasn't bent on suicide, and he had no intention of pushing the issue to the point of military conflict. The great danger, as Kennedy felt most keenly, was not that Khrushchev would go to war through deliberate decision, but that something would go badly wrong down the line – something, somebody, somewhere, some crazy general on one side or the other, an accident which the other side would misinterpret. That's why he was so insistent throughout the crisis on maintaining very tight control of every ship in the blockade of Cuba and of every plane near the Soviet Union. One of the crises came when an American U–2 suddenly strayed over Soviet soil. That was completely wrong, and Kennedy was every much concerned that the Russians might misinterpret it. The fear of war was not a fear of a deliberate decision but a fear of an accident spinning events out of control.

Might Kennedy have actually ordered troops into Cuba if the Russians hadn't backed down?

In the end he might have done. There were two messages that arrived

from Khrushchev, one rather reasonable, the other much tougher. The first was far more personal, and it was Robert Kennedy's suggestion that they ignore the second and respond to the first, which was what they did. Following that, Robert Kennedy was sent to see Dobrynin, the Soviet ambassador, and it was then that the question of the Turkish missiles was raised. Robert Kennedy said in effect, they will be out in six months, you have my private assurance, but this is a totally separate issue. If you ever publicly say a deal was made, we will repudiate it. The reason for that was that Turkey was in NATO, and certain people, including Harold Macmillan, were very concerned that a decision involving the security of a NATO country might be taken without consultation. The deal was not known for fifteen years. I found out about it in Robert Kennedy's papers and wrote the first account in my book on him.

We now know further that Kennedy called in Dean Rusk and asked him, if this didn't work, to prepare an appeal to U Thant asking the UN to take a more active role, which U Thant was prepared to do. Dean Rusk produced the document last year. Kennedy wanted to avoid military action except as a last resort. Had there been no other way to get rid of the missiles, Kennedy would have sent the troops in, but he was prepared to exhaust every other avenue.

Was Kennedy in any significant way different from presidents before him? Others had faced crises, but Kennedy had literally the prospect of Armageddon if he made too grave a mistake. Did he grow into that sort of authority or was it native to him?

He certainly grew in the presidency. On the other hand, I would say that among my contemporaries he was already the best qualified, the best equipped of those I knew, to be president. He had a combination of natural authority and natural detachment. He saw issues and saw himself with considerable objectivity, which is quite rare in politics. He felt very strongly the weight of responsibility created by the invention of nuclear weapons. After the Cuban Missile Crisis, when both Kennedy and Khrushchev had looked down into the nuclear abyss, Kennedy came out absolutely determined to move as fast as he could toward some restraint in the nuclear arms race. His first objective was a test-ban treaty, and in this he was enormously encouraged by David Harlech, David Ormsby-Gore, the British ambassador in Washington, and by Harold Macmillan. Macmillan was very good on the dangers of the nuclear arms race, and Ormsby-Gore had been UK representative at the UN on disarmament commissions. He was very hot on that subject and with Macmillan he fortified Kennedy's determination to do something about it. Had Kennedy lived, I think he and Khrushchev would have

proceeded beyond the test-ban treaty much further down the road to *détente*.

How do you think the world would have been different had Kennedy not been assassinated?

Kennedy and Khrushchev would have pursued *détente*, and I think, too, that Khrushchev might have lasted longer. Castro thinks Kennedy helped to save Khrushchev after the Cuban Missile Crisis. Certainly if Khrushchev had been able to show some results in the international realm, then it might have helped him a bit. However, Kennedy's intention in his second term was to concentrate much more on domestic affairs. He felt he had to spend too much time on international matters where, as he said, there was a new crisis every week. I think he felt he hadn't paid enough attention at home. He was much concerned about racial justice, about the war on poverty, about economic growth without inflation. The Great Society programme that Kennedy prepared and Johnson brought to enactment would have been the centrepiece of his second term.

Would you agree that President Kennedy was more popular abroad than he was in the United States?

No, he was popular in the United States, but I think probably there was less opposition to him abroad. A lot of people in the United States disliked him, as they had disliked Franklin Roosevelt. Conservatives, people in the business community, felt he was not their friend. Then his strong stance on civil rights and racial justice in 1963 turned a lot of people against him, especially in the South. But even at the nadir of his popularity, after the civil rights fight in the summer of 1963, he was only down to something like 60 per cent in the polls, which wasn't bad.

After his death, it became fairly common knowledge that Kennedy had been something of a womanizer. Would it have affected his political status had it been known at the time?

I don't know. I may say that, working in the White House, I was not aware of anything undue going on. If you went to the Kennedys' for dinner, there were always pretty girls, but I'm all in favour of that. So, I understand, are you. But it wasn't a conspicuous feature of the Kennedy administration. I think it is much exaggerated. No doubt things happened, but in that Kennedy was like Lloyd George, Martin Luther King, and other eminent political leaders. It seems to me we've got the whole thing out of proportion. Martin Luther King was indeed an incurable womanizer and notoriously unfaithful to his wife, yet he was also a fine

man who did great things for his race, and great things for his nation. Pol Pot of Cambodia, on the other hand, was splendidly faithful to his wife, never looked at another woman, and all he did was to murder a million of his countrymen. I'm not sure that the adultery test is particularly relevant to statesmanship.

In Kennedy's case, you say it was all common knowledge, but I don't know how common common knowledge was. There had always been a lot of gossip about Kennedy, before the presidency, but during the presidency I don't think there was so much. As for those around him shielding him, I didn't see much to shield. He worked very hard at the presidency.

There must surely have been a lot of nervousness about Jackie Kennedy. What would she have done had she known?

I've absolutely no idea.

In contrast with his brother, Robert Kennedy inspired perhaps as much hate as love. Why did he produce those extreme reactions?

John Kennedy was a man of reason, Robert Kennedy a man of passion. John Kennedy looked at something, such as the treatment of the black minority, and he thought it was irrational for a society to act that way. Robert Kennedy thought it intolerable. They couldn't have been closer, but they were quite different in this regard. John Kennedy was a realist disguised as a romantic, Robert Kennedy a romantic disguised as a realist. Robert Kennedy did the tough, the unpleasant things. During political campaigns, he would be his brother's son of a bitch, tell people off, fire them and that sort of stuff, but he was in a way a far more vulnerable figure than his brother. John Kennedy gave a sense of invulnerability. He was a reserved man, always in control, always poised, always filled with imperturbable self-possession. You felt he was equal to any circumstance. John Kennedy liked his friends, but Robert Kennedy *needed* his friends. This vulnerability was one reason that so many people – in the press, for example – found him so attractive; that and his humour. He was very influential with his brother, but not infallibly so. Sometimes John would listen to Robert, and disagree and not do what Robert Kennedy thought he should.

At least one reviewer of your biography of Robert Kennedy – I think it was Anthony Howard in the Observer *– talked of your transparent romanticism in your view of your subject.*

It's impossible to write with complete objectivity about anything. That's why I made clear in the Foreword how I felt about Robert Kennedy,

but subjectivity need not disqualify a biographer. You don't have to hate the subject of your biography to write it.

Robert Kennedy became attorney general of the United States without ever having appeared in a state or federal court. Shouldn't an attorney general have had more experience?

Many people felt that. The *New York Times* wrote a leader strongly criticizing the appointment, as did many other newspapers. Alexander Bickel, who was a distinguished professor of law at Yale, attacked the appointment. It was a risky appointment to have made. In fact it turned out very well, and by 1968 Bickel was a strong supporter of Robert Kennedy for president. Robert Kennedy knew the problems. He surrounded himself with first-class people in the Department of Justice and is generally agreed to have been the best attorney general we've had since Francis Biddle in the Roosevelt administration. But there was great criticism at the start, and understandably so.

It is said that, had Robert Kennedy ever become president, he would have been a disaster because he was to tough, using very strong tactics and so on. Would you agree?

No. I think he would have been a very successful president. He combined the qualities of an idealist with those of a realist. In other words, he had that capacity which his brother had, which Roosevelt had, which Wilson had: to tap the latent idealism of the American people; and he did it very successfully. At the same time, he was an astute and practical politician, so that he could mobilize the means to attain his objectives. The liberal tide of the 1960s was still running strong and in 1968 Nixon was elected president almost accidentally. He got barely 40 per cent of the vote. Had Robert Kennedy lived, he would have been the Democratic candidate and I think he would have been elected. There was a third candidate in George Wallace, who got about 12 per cent of the vote. Many of those who voted for Wallace were white working-class people who probably would have voted for Robert Kennedy. As I say, the liberal tide was still running strong, so that many things such as the Environmental Protection Administration, the Occupational Safety and Health Act and so on were produced by Congress even in the Nixon years. That tide would have enabled Robert Kennedy to move much farther along the path of reform. And by 1968, though a lot of people hated him, he was predominantly a very popular man. I think he would have become a very effective president.

You were a bitter critic of America's policy of escalation in Vietnam and what

you saw as America's obsession with political victory. Do you believe the lessons have been adequately learned?

No, I do not think so. I cite the American enthusiasm for our glorious victories in Grenada and Panama as examples. Panama would seem to me to raise three issues. I do not believe that the United States should undertake unilateral military intervention in Latin America except in cases of extreme emergency. I do not believe that an American president should go to war without congressional consent, except in cases of extreme emergency. And I do not believe that super-powers should launch sneak attacks on small countries, except in cases of extreme emergency. Noriega was a thug and a squalid, vicious fellow, but he was not a threat to the national security of the United States and his régime did not create an extreme emergency. I regret that kind of intervention, even as I felt that the invasion of Grenada was unjustified. I believe that the long-term interests of the United States lie in the world of law – movement toward a world of law – and not in the United States imitating the old Soviet Union by becoming a law unto itself. What we did in Panama violates everything from the Rio Treaty to the Montevideo Convention and the UN Charter.

In one sense, though, we may have learned a lesson from Vietnam. We are no longer attacking people our own size. We attack countries like Grenada with no army, navy or air force. When Japan attacked the United States at Pearl Harbor, FDR called it a date that will live in infamy. Why? Because it was a sneak attack. But at least the Japanese were picking on someone their own size. We launch sneak attacks against Grenada and Panama and Libya, and most Americans seem to be proud of it. I would say there's been something of a decline in American moral sensibility in recent years. Robert Kennedy opposed the sneak attack on Cuba during the missile crisis on the ground that it would be a Pearl Harbor in reverse. For 175 years, he said, we have not been that kind of nation. We seem to have become one in recent years, and I regret it.

Is America still trying to punish Vietnam?

No. I think it would be quite popular in the United States if we restored diplomatic relations with Vietnam. American Vietnam veterans have gone to Vietnam and had amiable meetings with their Vietnamese counterparts. Just as it turned out to be popular to restore relations with China, so it would turn out to be mildly popular to restore relations with Vietnam. I don't understand – well, I do understand – why we're not doing so. The reason is that the Chinese wouldn't like it, and George Bush feels it very important not to alienate the Chinese. That is why he and previous administrations, beginning with Carter, have continued

to give the Pol Pot government, the most vicious government of modern times, the Cambodian seat in the United Nations; why, to this day, we are seeming to support the inclusion of the Khmer Rouge in the new Cambodian government, whereas the sensible thing would be to make a deal with prime minister Hun Sen and promote a government around him. But the Chinese are opposed to that because of their traditional hatred of Vietnam. That, I believe, is why we have not restored relations with Vietnam, rather than any desire to punish.

One of the things that puzzles and depresses Europeans about American foreign policy is the treatment of Central and South America. No degree of violence or repression seems enough to cut off American aid. Priests are killed, nuns are raped and still money pours in. Or so it seems to the outside world.

Well, it puzzles many Americans too, I can say. At no point, according to the polls, did a majority of Americans favour aid to the Contras in Nicaragua. The majority has always been opposed to such aid. Nicaragua became a personal obsession for Reagan, and an inherited concern for Bush.

Why, if most Americans did not demand aggressive policies in Central America, were presidents able to pursue such policies? Bush's obsession was Noriega of Panama. Presidents have power with Congress when they request something they claim as essential to the security of the United States. Congressmen, even though they may disagree with the request, often feel under pressure to vote affirmatively, on the ground that otherwise their opponents at the next election will call them soft on Communism, soft on the Sandinistas. Legislators permit themselves to be intimidated into going along with something of which they really disapprove.

The case of Noriega was more complicated because Noriega was a thug and involved in the drug trade. Even people like Senator Dodd of Connecticut, who has been very restrained on Central America and was himself in the Peace Corps there, knows the area and speaks excellent Spanish, supported the invasion of Panama. But why this obsession with tinhorn dictators like Noriega and Ortega? The population of Nicaragua is under three million, less than the population of Brooklyn. The notion that this country is a threat to the security of the United States is ridiculous. The Noriega intervention was very popular in Panama, but not elsewhere in Latin America, and I think Bush is going to have mend fences. Bush is a moderate man, and I hope he will take it easy in Latin America for a while.

Will it ever be possible to control the import of drugs into the United States, bearing in mind the trouble over quite a small-scale gangster like Noriega?

Getting rid of Noriega will have no effect on the drug problem in the United States. The drug problem is essentially a demand rather than a supply problem. As long as the demand exists, it will be supplied one way or another. If we were to cut off all the import of drugs, then laboratories would spring up all over the United States to manufacture the drugs to meet demand.

Is the 'special relationship' that has been said to exist between Britain and the United States a fact or a myth today?

It's a cultural fact, and it's become a political myth, but the cultural reality remains. The common heritage means that Americans are going to feel closer to Britain than they are to anyone else. The Bush administration appears more inclined to regard Germany as its ally, and I take it that the Bush relationship with Mrs Thatcher isn't as chummy as the Reagan-Thatcher relationship. Actually the European statesman whom Bush seems to get along best with personally is Mitterrand.

As for myself, my ties with Britain are long and strong. I first went to England in 1934 when my father was giving a series of lectures at the University of London and I was sixteen years old. Then, in 1938–9 I spent a year at Peterhouse in Cambridge, where I met many people who remained close through the years, like Charles Wintour and Noel Annan, Eric Hobsbawm and Aubrey Eban. Then I was in London in the spring of '44 and was there until November when I went on to France. There I got to know Nye Bevan well. He was an enchanting man. After the war I met a lot of people among the young socialists in that period, so my political associations were mostly on the left. I got to know Hugh Gaitskell, and in the 1950s, of course, we became firm friends. Roy Jenkins, Dick Crossman, Tony Crosland – I knew all that generation of Labour people. In the 1960s my dear friend Pamela Berry exposed me to many Tories.

What about Macmillan? Historians now tend to say he was devious, a great actor who did nothing for Britain but who ruined the economy and so on.

I would have thought that Alistair Horne's two fine volumes would have done something to restore Macmillan's reputation. I liked Macmillan very much. He was a great performer. The last time I saw him was when he came to New York, I think in 1981, shortly after Reagan became president. Jacqueline Onassis gave a small dinner for him and I said to him, making conversation before dinner, 'Very odd, isn't it, to have an actor, Ronald Reagan, as president of the United States?' I was trying to think whether there had been many others in high political office who were once actors. I said, 'After all, Madame Mao Tse-tung was an actress, but I can't think of any other actors.' Macmillan looked

at me and said: 'Actors? Actors? Politicians are all actors. We're all of us actors and Roosevelt and Churchill were the best actors of the lot.' I liked him, I thought he was great fun. His instincts on several things were very good – on nuclear weapons, on colonial matters, on monetary questions. He was a monetary heretic. He believed in evolving some kind of international monetary system. And he was a Wet. I mean, he was no Thatcherite.

Mrs Thatcher has dominated the political scene in Britain for more than a decade now. How would you evaluate her?

I suppose she did do something to shake up the British economy, though it's now in trouble again. I suppose her approach may have improved British competitiveness in world markets. She liberated the newspapers from the printers' unions, which was a good thing. She appreciated Gorbachov quickly and she deserves credit for that, as does Reagan. A lot of the alleged Soviet experts and wiseacres were warning against Gorbachov, saying he was just trying to get the West to relax its guard. Mrs Thatcher said early on that he was somebody the West could do business with, and she was right. I consider that she's made Britain a colder, crueller nation and that it's time for someone to come in and stand, to use George Bush's phrase, for a kinder, gentler Britain. But the worst things she has done have been in the realm of freedom of information. The rewriting of the Official Secrets Act was a travesty.

Take one single example. It now appears that a group within MI5 tried to drive Harold Wilson and his government, duly elected by the British people, out of power. David Leigh has written a book about the Wilson affair that makes the most serious charges you can make in a democracy: that a group of people in the Intelligence services tried to defeat and subvert the democratic process. If something like that had happened in the United States – if charges were made that a group within the FBI or the CIA had tried to overthrow an elected president – all hell would have broken loose. There would have been congressional investigations to see whether the charges were valid or not and so on. Roy Jenkins did try to get a parliamentary inquiry, but Mrs Thatcher quashed any hope of such an inquiry. Since you don't enjoy the benefits of separation of power in Britain, Parliament could do nothing. Worse than that, the press showed little curiosity.

It seemed to me that you'd want to know in Britain whether an MI5 group had in fact done these things. Are these charges fantasy, or did they really do what David Leigh and the *Spycatcher* man – Peter Wright – said they did? I would think people would be interested in establishing the facts and, if those were the facts, to make sure nothing like it could ever happen again. But the British Parliament and press seemed to

regard it all with total indifference. Mrs Thatcher succeeded in hushing the whole thing up, as she would have hushed up Watergate.

Under your system, you can hush up any kind of political scandal. She has fortified the British tendency to sweep everything under the rug and to make information hard to get. Obviously some things have to be kept secret, but, on the whole, most official secrets could be made public with no harm to anybody. You have to fight against a tendency to classify everything as secret, and if Mrs Thatcher has her way, no one, including Parliament, will know what the hell is going on in British government. That seems the most troubling aspect of her stewardship.

Not only from Mrs Thatcher but from politicians on both sides of the Atlantic we have heard a good deal about the need to restore the ideal of family unity as something essential to preserving the social fabric. Can such a movement succeed in modern times?

First, as an historian, I wonder whether the family was always as great an institution as it's cracked up to be. People look back to the golden age of the unitary family of the nineteenth century when divorce was very difficult. But then you read about those families and the suffocating effects on the children, the paternal tyranny, the child abuse, even in a family as noted as that of Leslie Stephen. My impression is that the family has always been an ambiguous thing. It can be a source of strength; it can also be very crippling. Moreover, the family is bound to change in a society in which divorce is easy, birth control is easy, abortion is easy. Bonds are not going to be maintained as long, and in some cases that's bad. Other times maintaining bonds may artificially prolong a marriage that is dead, maybe crippling everyone involved. So it's important not to sentimentalize or romanticize the historical family.

Still, the total collapse of the family is obviously a source of great trouble for society. We have it in the underclass in this country: families where there is no father and no stability. But, on the whole, restoring the ideal of family unity seems to me partly an exercise in fantasy because I don't think the family ever played that marvellous stabilizing role which some think it once did.

From our side of the Atlantic, if often seems that American governments are excessively vulnerable to pressure groups like the gun lobby or the pro-Israeli faction. Do pressures change with presidents or are they simply pressured relentlessly?

They're pressured relentlessly, but they may or may not bend to the pressure. The National Rifle Association has had no effect on Democratic presidents, but it's very powerful with Republican presidents. It has some effect on Democratic legislators, particularly in districts where a

lot of hunting goes on. The Zionist lobby has impact on both parties, and it's only recently that people have become willing even to describe the operations and pressures brought by the Zionist lobby. Pressure groups can distort our policies, as in the case of Israel. Support by the United States for Likud policies was disastrous for Israel and a disaster all around. Jewish Americans have, of course, been very generous contributors to political campaigns. It should be added that, as far as I can see, the Jewish community in this country is not monolithic, and many Jewish Americans are very much opposed to blank-cheque support of right-wing governments in Israel.

There is nothing new about foreign pressure groups. The Irish lobby had great impact before the establishment of the Irish Free State, and resolutions for Irish independence were constantly being introduced and so on. We're a polyglot nation – a nation of nations, as Walt Whitman said. That means that the Poles, the Jews, the Irish, the Italians and so on all constitute pressure groups of one sort or another. Black Americans, having long ignored Africa, have suddenly constituted themselves a pressure group for black Africa.

Pressure groups are a pain in the neck for a lot of presidents. But they have to deal with them one way or another.

If you were an adviser now in the Bush administration, what advice would you give the president with regard to the Arab-Israeli conflict?

I'm not an expert on the Middle East. We don't have much influence with either side, as far as I can see, and I'm not a great believer in meddling in the affairs of other countries. I don't think we do it very well, I don't think we have enough knowledge. We tend to become prisoners of our clients, as we did in Vietnam, and they manipulate us more than we manipulate them. Where our vital interests are involved, I'm all in favour of action to defend them, by force if necessary; but where our vital interests are not involved, I'd say let other countries solve their own problems.

America has had quite an unexpected and overwhelming triumph in the way Eastern Europe has begun to embrace democracy. What should happen next?

Once the exhilaration is over, these new governments in East Europe are going to face a lot of tough problems. It's up to the Western governments to do everything they can to help them meet them. Mitterrand's proposal of a development bank for Eastern Europe will take a couple of years before it can get started, and meantime the World Bank should be playing a more active role. I might add that policies should come just as much from Europe as from the United States. While I think that the United States is poverty-stricken in ideas, I'm somewhat

dismayed that, except for the Mitterrand proposal, more good ideas haven't come out of West European governments as to how to help Eastern Europe. The model of the Marshall Plan might well be used, and that, as you will recall, called upon the governments of Western Europe to get together and make their own proposals for economic development and the allocation of funds. Just as the governments of Western Europe met in Paris in the spring of 1948 to respond to the Marshall offer, so the governments of Eastern Europe might get together and present joint proposals for their own economic reconstruction.

By and large, I'm hopeful about Eastern Europe but troubled about the Soviet Union. It's very important that Gorbachov survive. I suppose his strength lies in the fact that the people to his right are afraid that, if he goes, the whole thing will swing farther to the left, while the people on his left are afraid that it will swing farther to the right. Therefore neither has a strong interest in overthrowing him at this point. But events may overthrow him. I'm not sure that the changes he's made are totally irreversible. Look what happened in China. I can see the army feeling it has to restore order, and then people coming to power who feel that Russia needs a heavy hand. A lot of the freedom of the press, the freedom of the theatre, the freedom of the movies, could easily be reversed.

With the prospect of German unification, the disappearance of the Iron Curtain and the emergence of Japan as an economic super-power, do you see American influence in the world as waning?

One certainly begins to wonder who won the last war. Japan is well on its way to attaining its Second World War objective of a Greater East Asian Prosperity Sphere. A united Germany is poised to dominate Europe. All these things are troubling. I wouldn't be surprised if, by the year 2000, a united Germany were demanding revision of its eastern frontiers, an *Anschluss* with Austria, concessions to German-speaking minorities in neighbouring countries. The Allies may retain the legal capacity to impose a treaty, but I doubt that a united Germany, the most dynamic economy and most populous state west of Russia in Europe, is going to respect any limitations we try to impose regarding the inviolability of frontiers or rearmament or nuclear weapons.

I don't suppose Germany or Japan will ever again become a military threat, because in the age of missiles they're simply too vulnerable. But they do have dynamic economies, and they have extremely ominous, portentous, mystical, humourless, chauvinistic, nationalistic traditions. Both countries have new generations coming to power that feel no sense of responsibility for or guilt about the Second World War, and may well nurse a desire for vindication, even perhaps for revenge. Germany

at least has had forty years of democratic experience and has produced democratic statesmen like Helmut Schmidt and Willy Brandt and Richard von Weizsäcker and even, in his own way, Adenauer. Japan hasn't produced anyone comparable. It's been a one-party state, and a crooked and authoritarian one-party state at that.

German historians are beginning to say Hitler wasn't so bad, that he was only imitating Stalin. Japanese historians are even worse. School text books so gloss over Japanese aggression and atrocity in the Second World War that they've provoked official protest from China. Japanese historians who try to write the truth are subject to official persecution. Both countries are filled with a kind of hyper-nationalism and the prospects are troubling.

Is the United States in decline? Not irrevocably. After all, remember that both Japan and Germany suffered from what Paul Kennedy called imperial over-stretch – that is to say, from taking on burdens beyond the capacity of the economy to discharge – and in addition suffered devastating military defeat. Yet they've come back. If the United States can pull itself together, it can come back too.

Might the trend towards disarmament in the Soviet Union mean that America could be perceived by some cynics as much the greater threat to world peace in the near future?

I doubt it. I mean, some people may like to say it, but I don't think the United States will be seriously regarded as a threat to world peace.

You once said that there is no such thing as a correct perspective in history. What then do you see as the historical biographer's primary function?

Tell the truth as best you can, as best you see it. The historian is constrained by facts, he has to respect facts, and then he arranges the facts. The mere act of selection involves interpretation, so you can't escape interpretation, and interpretation cannot escape subjectivity. You try to do the best you can and make discounts for your own predilections. For the historian, the important thing is to reconstruct the past as much as possible in its own terms rather than in terms of the present. But you can't escape the present, and that's why every generation finds new issues in the past. American historians, for example, discover new pasts as a result of new concerns about racial justice or sexual equality. That's why Benedetto Croce said all history is contemporary history, why Oscar Wilde said the one duty we owe to history is to rewrite it.

In your successful and varied career, which period do you feel you enjoyed most?

My career may be varied, but I don't think of it as particularly successful.

I regard it as a study in frustration. I always envied Malcolm Muggeridge's title for his memoirs, *Chronicles of Wasted Time*. The part I enjoyed particularly, I suppose, was working with Kennedy, but I'm an historian and a writer, and my great frustration is that I've spent so little time doing that which I do best, and there's been so much time wasted in various virtuous or entertaining projects. Sometimes I feel that my life has been nibbled away by good causes. What I want to do is finish *The Age of Roosevelt*. I'd also like to write a novel. I suppose I'd best like to be remembered for my historical writing. I've enjoyed politics, politics is a great sport, but essentially I'm an historian.

COLONEL TOWNEND

Henry Stuart Townend was born the son of a clergyman in 1909. His father died when he was nine and he was sent to St Edmund's, Canterbury, a school for orphaned sons of the clergy. He became captain of games and at fourteen won the open mile in five minutes. He graduated with an MA from Brasenose College, Oxford, where as captain of athletics he had won a full blue for both the half-mile and the mile. During the war he served with the Royal Artillery and was seriously wounded. He was awarded the OBE in 1948 for his work during the Olympic Games of that year. Since 1951 he has been headmaster of Hill House School which he founded with his wife. Hill House was attended by Prince Charles.

You attended a school in Canterbury for the orphan sons of clergymen. Was that school a major formative influence in your life?

Everything I've achieved in life I owe to that school. My father and my grandfather were clergymen, so I was brought up well, but there was no money. After my father died in the First World War, my mother had four children to look after, and the school took me from the age of nine until nineteen, educated me free, clothed me and made me completely. There was a wonderful master there called Powers who found out my talent for games, particularly for athletics, and he trained me. In those days we were all thin and food was rationed. In the mid-morning break I'd go up to his room and he'd have a great cup of hot Ovaltine ready for me to drink. Ever since then I've lived on Ovaltine. I drink it during the night and all day long. But it was he who discovered my talent, and as a result I became captain of games, captain of the school and captain of my house; and because I won the athletic championships for all the public schools, the only time a single boy has done it, I managed to get to Oxford. I wasn't too bad at mathematics, but the money to educate me came from scholarships and grants because I could run.

The school was without doubt the greatest influence in my life. My mother was very good and she worked hard. From about the age of seven I used to get up and light the coal fires in the house and do things to help her. But my great urge to achieve reached me after I went to school. That's where I was given the chance to compete, race against other children, get into the team, be head of the house, head of the school. My mother didn't influence me in that way, she wasn't the sort.

I don't remember much from before the time I went to public school at nine. It was wartime, a hard life. After I had gone away to school, I didn't miss having my family around because I didn't know what that

would be like. You only miss things when something is cut off. My father had died when I was five. If he'd died when I was fifteen, I probably would have missed him, but as it is, the most I can remember – and I'm sure this has been put into my head by others – is that he used to cut my hair, because one couldn't afford to go to a hairdresser.

Are you religious?

I've never been religious. I'm the odd one out. I loved my army life but I'm not religious. Sometimes when I look up at the sky on a clear night and see all those stars, I wonder what on earth are they doing there? There's nothing on them. We haven't found a single one inhabited. What a waste of time. But who is making them go round? I know why we don't fall off the earth, but who's got it to spin, what started it, where does it come from? It's astounding.

Religion goes absolutely wrong though, doesn't it, when it comes to the Virgin Birth and so on? But I don't believe that bishops should discredit what it is their job to preach. The Bishop of Durham should not say that we mustn't believe what's in the Bible. It is his job to preach it. I don't believe in it, it's mythical like the good old Greek things we learned at school, but it doesn't harm anybody to believe. I'm all for letting everybody go their own way. We all know that you can't have a virgin birth, but it doesn't harm you to believe that one did happen.

You should therefore respect other people's beliefs. I'm all against downing others because they're not the same as you, and that is the whole object of this school. All nationalities have a right to believe, so you don't say they're wrong, but you do say, 'That's yours and this is mine. That's your cup of tea, this is my cup of tea.' I believe in joining people together, and the time to join them is at the age when they're forming their ideas. It doesn't matter who you are, you can be white, black, rich, poor, any religion, any country, great big America, little El Salvador, they're equal. They're all friendly, they don't want to fight each other. They're not going to tell each other what to do.

I'm all for Britain being in Europe, because we gain more than we lose. What's the point of having enemies all around you? Why not have friends? The only way to make friends is by joining them. Otherwise we sit here in isolation and nobody wants to know us. It's like being in London and not talking to your neighbours. I like people of other countries. That's why I love Switzerland. They're international in their outlook. I like the French and I have nothing against the Germans. Of course, I shall never get over the harm Germany did in the war, but it was not the people who are running Germany today who did it. You don't punish the children for the sins of their fathers. I accept all

religions. I like going to other churches and seeing the different things they do. I find nothing wrong in it. We're too self centred in England. We think we're God Almighty, but there are marvellous things in the rest of the world.

You distinguished yourself in sports at Oxford and gained a Blue. Was that an outstandingly happy period of your life?

I loved every minute. I had a marvellous time. Oxford between the wars was a great place and games was a big thing in those days, and I was at the great games college. I was an international and played for the University and got my Blue in the first year. I was a hero among the people of Oxford, which meant life was wonderful and I went around everywhere and travelled the world. Even though I had no money, I led a wonderful social life. Everybody wanted to meet me as the president of the athletics tour, so I was invited out to all the college dinners. But I also worked and got my degree.

Did you sow wild oats at Oxford?

I've always been keen on women. I think all athletes are. An athlete is a man who believes in physical fitness, who spends an awful lot of time with practically no clothes on, doing exercises, showing himself off. Girls like him because they see this fellow winning races, so I always had plenty of girls coming around. I think women are exciting things. At school we never saw girls, of course, and when I was at school the teaching staff were not allowed to be married. The only women we saw were those who worked in the kitchen, and we call them 'skivvies'. We used to meet them after dark underneath the double tree by the cricket pitch, but at the time when I left school I knew practically nothing about women. It was only when I got to Oxford that I started to learn about them, and today I'm happier in the company of women than of men. I also like mixed company, but I'm not what I would call a club man who wants to shut himself away in a London club where no women are allowed. Here, in my school, for example, there are plenty of women teachers who are better than men teachers, and I feel they bring colour and excitement into life.

I've always admired physical fitness in both women and men. I'm a great believer in physical fitness because, when you're old like me, money doesn't mean anything to you, but physical fitness does. I climb mountains, I run up and down stairs, I can get anywhere, because all through my life I've believed in keeping fit. I like a woman who wants to keep fit. I don't necessarily want to turn to a woman who is very beautiful to look at.

A woman must be able to make a happy home. She must be a good

hostess, she ought to be able to cook because one expects a woman to cook. The best profession for a woman is a nurse. My wife was a nurse. It's a wonderful profession, and you don't want to be nursed by a man, you want to be nursed by a woman. This is where the kindness comes out. They're firm, and they are full of intelligence and can talk about everything, but they're also kind, and one expects kindness. I don't like a soft man, but I like a soft woman. Even to touch. I like the softness of a woman, and I wouldn't like a soft flabby man. I very often feel that it's rather pleasant if a woman expects you to knock the nail in the wall, climb the ladder. The man has to be a strong personality, the one who leads, and the other, the woman, is a kind creature who puts you wise, tells you you're a stupid fool when you say something you shouldn't say, makes you comfortable, sits you down and makes you relax.

I like a woman who keeps herself clean and tidy, not all dolled up like a film star. I can't stand a dirty woman. I'm still very attracted to some women when I see them, but I'm very discreet with them because they don't want me at my age, and I'm not at the moment interested in being married again because I doubt whether I should get anybody as perfect as my wife. We fitted together absolutely unbelievably. She was brought up hard, but she was a quite outstanding nurse. She had the same problems in her youth as I did, had to fight her way up, and she was tidy like me, and the whole thing was absolutely perfect.

Now that she's gone, do you feel a great void?

Oh yes. The idea that you get over it is bunkum. It's like losing an arm. You live with it, but something has gone that you can't replace and you're lonely, lonely at night, when you've always slept together in the same bed, a double bed, and there you are, suddenly alone. I must say I think it is much easier for a man than for a woman. I think if one in a marriage is going to die, then let the woman die first, because a lonely woman can't do a thing. A man can go on.

After Oxford, you joined the army and fought in the Second World War.

After Oxford I went to a Swiss university for two years, but only to play games. I always intended going in the army. Everybody else in my family went into the Church, but there was one uncle who had been in the army, so I decided to follow his example. I was a gunner and I loved it. The army ingrained into me the business of loyalty and duty. If you were told to do this, you did it, you didn't question, so when the war came I quite naturally said, here is my profession, I'm ready for it. I was doing staff jobs in college until we had Germany's invasion

of our European neighbours. I wasn't in the fighting up to Dunkirk, though afterwards I protected the coast with my guns.

The actual physical fighting I did after D-Day. Then, as a major commanding a battery, I was always in the front line. I had been a colonel on the staff, but went down a rank because I wanted to command a fighting unit in action. An artillery major is always in the very front line, observing the shells and sending the messages back to the guns. He's not back at the guns, he's always at the sharp end, and to say one isn't frightened would be absolutely stupid. Of course one is, but it's one's duty. The more of the enemy you kill, the better. That is the object of the game, and you have also got to advance. There's no question of saying, 'I'm not going there.' One just goes, it becomes ingrained.

I think it comes from playing games. If it is a fairly tough game, your duty is to go for the ball and be damned to what happens to you. I got wounded. We had been going through a forest, which took us about six days, and when we reached the far end the Germans counter-attacked. I was shaving at the time and was determined not to stop. I always used to shave against a tree. The mortar bombs were bursting all around and I was hit in the head and the eyes and they said I'd never see again, though in fact I see very well. They bandaged me up and back I went, right back to base hospital, and they took pieces of shell out of me. I still have some bits of metal in my head. Then I got up and dressed and said to hell with this, and lorry-hopped back because with my rank I could do that. I got back to the front line just as my replacement was about to take over the battery.

I'll tell you one strange thing about having been through the war. Nothing worries you afterwards, nothing at all. I'm sorry for the people who just missed it. If you missed it completely, as my son did, then it's history, but I would have hated to have been just too young to go through it. I went through it, but having gone through it, so terrible are one's experiences, that nothing worries you again. However much trouble comes along, you've seen something worse.

What did you make of the Falklands War?

The Falklands War was a very difficult operation. It was not a proper military operation because of the lines of communication. We relied on two aircraft carriers, and if the other side had sunk one, where would we have been? Yet we got away with it. It was a gamble, and the bravery and the discipline of the fighting forces was excellent, particularly that of the Royal Navy. It was all very professional, but if they had been up against certain other armies in the world, they wouldn't have stood a hope in hell.

Mind you, it was a damned stupid thing to have done for a bit of barren land and some sheep. I don't know how many casualties there were, but think of the families of those who were killed unnecessarily for the sake of a few damned sheep. And, let's face it, the Argentines are there, a great big country, and we go on holding on to this little island which almost touches the coast, like the Isle of Wight. Why can't we give it to them, and buy their meat as we used to? There's nothing wrong with the Argentinian people. They made a mistake, but we all make mistakes, like not paying our taxes or whatever. Gibraltar is the same. We should be above it and admit that things have changed. In the old days, we sent an army and smashed things up, conquered, and painted the maps red. Now it's time to give them back.

What do you make of Mrs Thatcher?

She's odd, she's unique. We've not another woman like her. I myself don't think that politics is a very good profession for women, just as I don't want to see men nursing. Women are better teachers than men, but men are streets ahead of women when it comes to politics. They're used to saying, 'You stupid little idiot, sit down you fool.' Women are touched by it and they haven't got this masculine *bang, bang, bang*. And if they're normal women, they've got a soft voice. But Mrs Thatcher is not a normal woman. She bangs on at people and won't bend or take advice.

When you are in a team, you have got to work as a team. It doesn't matter if it's an athletics team, a football team or a government, you've got to make people work together. You must listen to them, and then you must either persuade them to come your way or else you have to move their way. The mess she made with the Chancellor of the Exchequer in 1989 was childishly stupid. Lawson may be an obstinate man, but he is also very able, and people don't just walk out like that unless something is very wrong. She doesn't seem to have this power of bringing everybody together. She has done an amazing lot for the country, but on the other hand she has set a lot of people against each other. I think it would be a very good thing if we had a change now.

The brains of men and women may be the same, but they have different qualities, and because of that I don't think a woman is a very good person to lead. When she is in charge, she's apt to become very bossy. Women headmistresses are notoriously bossy. It's difficult to find a woman headmistress who is kind and who is ready to look at another view. She rather says, 'This is what we're doing, we've always done it this way,' whereas a man will be more flexible.

Aren't you very bossy as a headmaster?

Well, the *News of the World* did nickname me 'Colonel Bossyboots'. That was because I issued a circular telling parents that the teaching staff were not allowed to be ill, the reason being that if they are ill, who looks after the children? You can't say to the children, 'Right, I'm very sorry, I'm not coming in today, don't come to school, but tomorrow we'll work to midnight.' Everyone has to be physically fit, and to make sure they're never ill we take £30 a day off their bonus pay if they're away. Therefore they keep themselves fit. The *News of the World* got hold of this circular and called me 'Colonel Bossyboots' as a result, but I didn't mind because I don't give orders unless I know people can carry them out. That doesn't make me bossy, it makes me someone who gives orders.

I'm never ill myself, never away, never at all. I don't miss even one hour. Others are the same here in school. They all turn up. They keep themselves fit. They don't go beating it up at night. What happens sometimes in other schools is that staff are up to three in the morning with a boyfriend or girlfriend and, instead of going to work the next day, they say, 'Oh, I do feel ill.' They're not actually ill, they're just tired. But if you fine them, by Jove, they turn up. It's most effective. Here they get their pay as a bonus four times a year at the end of each quarter, and the lowest bonus is £200 a quarter. When you've been here two years, you get £800 a quarter, and if you're a bit special, you get £1,200 four times a year. So if you're ill, it comes off the bonus. It doesn't matter what you're away for, unless it's a funeral. But if you go to someone's wedding, or a royal garden party, or Ascot, you'll be fined out of your bonus, because it's not fair on the others otherwise.

How did you come to start the school?

What happened was that after the war I left the army because there was no future in it at that time. I then helped to organize the Olympic Games in 1948, and because I was so used to giving orders which did not always go down too well, someone said, 'Why don't you start a school?' I said, 'Don't be silly, I'm not a nanny.' But we rented a house in Switzerland and took children from public schools for the summer holidays, and afterwards, in London, we got this house at auction for £250. I was told I was mad because I only had £150. We had sold our car and some of my wife's jewellery, and we managed to get the money together. I went to the auction, very nervous, and paid for the house. Then we had nothing. We lived in one room downstairs and cooked in the fireplace. We only had one table, one chair and a tennis ball, nothing else. But we did have a little leaflet printed, and we pushed it through doors all round the place, and waited and hoped.

Finally, along came Mallalieu, the member of parliament, with his

little boy of five. That was in 1951. He asked where the rest were, and I said, 'Well, they're late,' though in fact they didn't exist. We eventually got to nine with a Countess Devine who brought her little boy. She said to me, 'If I give you this sixpence, will you see that my little boy is potted before lunch. I said, 'Yes, for this sixpence I will most certainly see that he's potted before lunch,' because sixpence was most valuable to me in those days. We had no money, did everything ourselves, and went on like that for the first year. Why anybody was so mad as to send their children to a school with just ourselves, no equipment, no experience, nothing at all, I shall never know. It was an absolute miracle.

In 1950 you stood as Liberal candidate for Torquay. Have you maintained an interest in politics?

I'm not terribly biased one way or the other. I am not 100 per cent Conservative, though I did sit on the London County Council as a Conservative member for Chelsea. And I'm not really a socialist, because I've not been brought up in great poverty. In the vicarage there was no money, but it was a decent home, so I'm in the middle. I'm a great believer in individuals, in individual enterprise and the self-employed. I'm really a Liberal. I thought after the war that there could have been a Liberal revival, because people were tired of left and right. Churchill had won the war, but he was not all that much of a conservative, he was really in the middle of the lot.

I was so conceited when I fought the election that I put in my diary the day I thought I'd be taking my seat in Parliament. I got the shock of my life when I wasn't elected. My meetings had been wonderfully attended in Torquay. We had torchlight processions at night. It was a marvellous time. I loved jumping up on the stage and making speeches, and when they didn't elect me, oh, what a bang down it was – one of the biggest disappointments of my life.

The glamour of Parliament seemed rather like what I'd experienced in athletics: everybody cheering and clapping whenever you gave speeches. I thought I made a great candidate. I thought, 'I'm going to be an MP, I shall be prime minister,' and all the rest of it, just like winning a race. It got into my blood and I would have loved to have been in Parliament. Once again I would have fought my way up. But I picked the wrong party. I should have realized that it didn't matter what I thought, I wasn't going to get in unless I picked one of the other two parties, and of those two I would have picked the Conservatives and would have been on the Conservative left wing.

Today, in my view, teaching is the top profession because it's bringing up youth. The whole future of any country depends on the young people who are growing up, and the better they are educated, then the

more successful that country is going to be. Education is vital. It is the Minister of Education who should be No. 2 in the government, not the Chancellor of the Exchequer. Any damned banker can get the books right. Here we have a private system, the best in the world. They not only teach you how to read and write and do your maths and Latin, but they teach you how to live with other people, how to lead, how to achieve things. The state system should now be brought up to be its equal. We need someone in charge of education who realizes how vital it is to do this and who will give people their head. Instead we have all these civil servants shooting out bits of paper which I throw away. I'm proud of what I'm doing, for if you're successful, then you're proud of being a success. There's not much point in anyone saying this school isn't successful, because it's gone from nothing to being the largest of its kind in the world, and I own it all, and our exam results are unique.

I understand your wife was very much the moving spirit behind the founding of the school.

I would say it was 50–50. I used to do the games, and she was more important on the teaching and looking after the welfare side. She did all the cooking and she chose the uniform, which I couldn't have done. I'd have stuck to the awful dull grey that other schools had, but she said, 'If you put children in grey uniforms, they'll have grey minds, so let's give them some colour.' And first she chose one beautiful colour, not brown but cinnamon, and then we chose the second colour, not yellow but gold – a wonderful rich colour. the pupils as a consequence are colourful, alive. She was also better than I was at making them happy, and on discipline and principles.

The first principle is always the safety of the child. You can't put a price on its head, a child is the mother's most precious possession. The second principle is happiness. It's a wicked thing to make children unhappy. They're only unhappy if adults put unhappiness into them, otherwise lives are naturally happy. You don't want children to hate coming to school, so we never made it like a normal school with desks so they thought they were going to the dentist. You can't really expect children to like going to the dentist if it's painful, but there should be nothing painful about school. You haven't got to tell the children they'll be punished if they do this or don't do that. In my day you were beaten, but there's no need for it. You lead from the front, and everybody wants to be at the top. Children love being first, they love competition. So first you ensure safety for the child, then you ensure happiness, and after that comes good manners and discipline.

You can hear a pin drop in this school. We teach them that if they are in an underground train or a bus, and are sitting down and a woman

gets on, then if that woman looks as old as or older than their mother, they give up their seat. In the case of a man, then the man has to look as old as or older than their grandfather. We give them that rule and we say that is courtesy. If they don't do it, we tear the uniform off them, since it's a disgrace to the school.

If a lady comes into or goes out of a room, I always stand up because I was brought up to do it. The teaching staff at the round table in Switzerland all stand up when I come to take my place – which is old-fashioned and I wouldn't insist on it today, but it is very pleasant when you see it done. Safety, however, is the most important principle. When I say it is more important that children should learn to swim than to read and write, that's because if the child drowns, the parents can never get over it. We don't consider any child to be safe anywhere until they can jump in the deep end and swim a hundred metres.

Do you think there is a case for some sort of governmental control in private education? Even child-minders have to be registered, after all.

In general, the parents who pay the fees will see if the school is right or wrong, will look at how it is being run. But picking a school is a gamble. We know of some quite wicked people running schools. You can either do a lot of good, or you can do immense damage. Of course, I could equally have started a milk bar or a vegetable stall. Whether it would have turned out to be successful, one cannot know. You do in fact have to be registered as a school once you pass about six pupils. People come from the Ministry of Education, but the whole thing is very lax so far as the private system is concerned. They believe that if people pay high fees, then they're damned stupid unless the school has a good reputation. What you need to do is study the people who run it at the top. Are their views right or are their views wrong? I personally feel that parents will do this job in a much better way than any body of inspectors, who will do most of it on paper and spend very little time finding out how the school is really run. The parents see it, and they tell other people. We have never, except for the very first year, advertised for boys or girls. Everybody comes here by word of mouth, through existing parents.

I don't think that if I were minister of education I would insist on any increased supervision. I would say that people at the head of a school should prove their worth, that they should have a paper qualification, a university degree or training college diploma, to prove that their own education has reached a certain standard. After that I think it is up to them to establish their school and see whether people will go to it. You don't want to start by having a lot of entrance exams, because then you will get nobody.

It's actually a very hard life, running a school. It's day and night non-stop. People always think their child is brilliant, however dull he may be. Their child could never commit a crime, could never steal. And then they want to come and talk to you all day long, and it's all your fault if he doesn't pass his exams. There are not many people who can stand running a school for many years. If you worry at all, you can't do it.

I told quite a few parents this morning to go and boil themselves. They wanted to talk to me. but I said I couldn't. I'm sick of talking to people, and I laugh at them, which is something I can do only because I own the school. I'm in a very, very strong position. I say take it or leave it. Every Wednesday I talk publicly, put over what I believe in and say, 'Don't come here if you don't like what I believe in. If you want them to do nothing else but sit and work, go somewhere else.'

Your son will presumably take over from you eventually. Is the school likely to change its emphasis then?

Oh, I'm sure it will. His wife is a trained teacher and I think it's possible it will become more like a normal prep school, which it's not at the moment. There's nothing I can do about it, but I'm going to go on running the school until I drop dead or until I can't move around on my feet. Retirement is a fatal thing. Once you retire, you go absolutely to pieces and nobody wants you. You're as dull as ditchwater, living always in the past.

There's no real clash between my son and myself, and that is perhaps for a rather strange reason: we are so different. He has been brought up easy, I suppose, and I was brought up hard, but, like me, he works day and night. He's very keen on music and he wants to achieve in that area. I don't talk to him about music, and he doesn't talk to me about games. On the other hand, if he had been a games player, he would be furious not to have been as good as me.

The thing is that he has achieved greatness in music and we have music scholarships everywhere. I've got to the top in games, he's got to the top in music. He's no use at games, I'm no use at music. He gets on with his side, I get on with mine. His wife collects the fees, because I'm terribly bad at that, but there's not the slightest doubt who's in charge. I believe in one person running a thing. The boss takes the responsibility, gives the orders. That's the army way. You'll attack at eight o'clock in the morning, you'll all turn right. Everybody knows you ought to turn left, but the boss says turn right, so everyone turns right.

Prince Charles was the first heir to the throne to attend a private school when he came to Hillhouse. Why do you think the royal family sent him here?

I don't know the real reason. I think they wanted some small school, as we were in those days, here in the centre of London. My wife had, as a nurse, worked a lot with Sir John Weir, the Queen Mother's doctor, so there was that connection. The Queen may also have talked to her prime minister, Macmillan, because all his grandsons were here. One day the Queen's secretary asked if I would go and have tea with the Queen, so I went and had tea, quite alone with Her Majesty, nobody else present in the room. She asked me whether I would take her son at the school, and if I didn't jump at it, that was because it's not a very easy thing to decide on. You see, we have children in this school at the moment whose fathers are rulers in the world, like the Sultan of Brunei, but that doesn't cause us any trouble. The problem with the English royal family is that everybody else always wants to know what they're up to. It's not they who are the problem; the boy himself was no problem at all. It's the fact of the press being forever out there with cameras, watching us walking through the streets and giving us no privacy whatever.

Our British royalty are oddly situated. They're unique in the world at the moment, so far as I can see. They hold a special place from birth, and in principle they have no idea what the outside world does. They haven't seen it. wherever they go, everything is cleaned up. And here we were for the first time with a Prince of Wales who had to try to lead a normal life alongside the other children. It's something that's very difficult for a school. Everybody wants to know what he's doing, how he is. Is he clever; is he dull? Is it true that he's fallen down and broken his teeth? What's he been eating for lunch?

We used to let the press in, but only after school hours. Even so, it all got to be very trying. We said at the outset we'd treat him normally, and the Queen was always known as 'Charles's mother'. He walked through the streets to games, down to the Duke of York's every day, but my wife had to walk beside him. There was no private detective, we did it all ourselves. I taught him to swim, I taught him football; and I taught him Latin, believe it or not. He used to come up to this room on a Friday afternoon and sit on a stool and have tea with my wife, waiting for the Queen to pick him up as she was going off to Windsor.

Prince Charles was happy here – he's always said that – and as far as one can gather this was the one school where he was completely happy. One reads that he was not happy at Cheam, not happy at Gordonstoun, though quite happy at Timbertops in Australia. We had no real problems with him, because we treated him normally. He wanted to do things, he loved physical fighting, and games and football. I hope that I put into all the children here the same object: fight for it, don't sit back, get to the top, work hard. No one achieves anything without working. Make a mark, make yourself be somebody. Don't just be one of the

mob. Be odd, stand out, even if you've got a flashing thing on your head or whatever.

Do the old boys of the school ever come back to visit you? Does Prince Charles?

The others have; everyone else comes in all the time. I don't think Prince Charles goes back anywhere. I don't know. He has sent messages from time to time through other people.

So you've never seen him since.

No. Doesn't go to Cheam, doesn't go to Gordonstoun; you never hear of him visiting one of his old schools at all. That is rather unfortunate, I think, rather unfortunate.

There must be quite a large number of people who would regard schools like yours as primarily a way of maintaining social dominance for the rich.

I suppose they always will think that, because we hope we produce leaders, and the minute you're a leader, then your social position goes up. Even if you lead a trade union, your social position rises. Scargill can go anywhere because he's a leader. My view is that if you're given a good education, then you're capable of leading, if you have it in you. I'm a great believer in leadership and it's a marvellous life to be a leader. It's like winning a race, a marvellous satisfaction. But there are both rich and poor children here without the slightest doubt. Anyone who works in this school, anyone who drives a bus, for example, is allowed to send his children and grandchildren for just £10 a term. All our bus drivers have children here. I think it would be quite unfair to work in this building in any capacity and see what other children get and not get it for your own because you couldn't afford it. They can't afford my fees, so they get the bill in the normal way, but just send me £10. In that way, no one can say they don't pay school fees.

So far as admissions policy goes, we don't test academic achievements at all. I choose the mothers, because if I feel that a mother believes in our principles of good behaviour, good manners and discipline, then the work be damned. If I feel that the mother is not like that, then I turn the child down. Every school has its own system of choosing, particularly in London where the pressure is so great. We get more than a hundred applications a week. But the character of the child comes from the mother, and if I like the mother, oh, I'll take that child, and if I don't like the mother, I don't want the child around.

We don't ask them their religion, like other schools. We take all religions. We never ask a parent's profession. On the other hand, we are a school to help people coming in and out of London, so if people

suddenly arrive here, we take their children, because we set ourselves up as a school to help them. Every week a child leaves, but we ask for payment only up to the last day and no longer. We don't ask for any warning, because the parent may be ordered away in their job at short notice. We like this floating population. We cater for it, we're professional at it. Other schools can't handle it, it's too difficult for them.

But some people must think that children in schools like yours are set apart in the sense of being detached from all other social strata.

I can talk to the Queen or the dustman. But other people, born in well-off homes, can't talk to the dustman, they don't understand that sort of life, they haven't had to do it, particularly those who say, 'I can't make my bed, my servant makes the bed.' I say to them, 'You damned well make your own bed here.' We've got a class system in England, but I don't believe in it. I believe in the Swiss system, where everyone is socially equal. The road sweeper is proud of his job, and so is the President of Switzerland, but they're dead equal. That's how I treat our children here: everyone's equal.

The man who washes our pavements, whose name is Simpson, I always call 'Mr Simpson', never just 'Simpson', in the English way. I say he is as important as anyone else. He keeps all the dog dirt away. Every night he washes the pavements so we have none around here. He's just as important as Mr Williams who teaches Latin. Two different jobs, but both equally important and socially equal. One may have more pay than the other because of his qualifications, nothing wrong with that, but you don't look down on the other. Not on your life.

I try and drill it into them here that they cannot buy anything extra, that they can't give the school one penny. Normal schools put out an appeal to parents if they want to buy something new. As soon as you do that, you have to press their child to pass all its exams. So nobody's been allowed to give me one penny, because everybody here is absolutely equal in status. We're about the only private school I know of that won't accept any subscriptions from parents. I don't like hereditary peerages. I don't mind Mrs Thatcher being called whatever you like once she's done her job, but why should children who have done nothing get a title? It's all wrong, and it makes people feel very superior. I don't like snobbery at all. I believe only in the snobbery of personal success.

Everything we do is done out of school fees. The school fees are not high, and there's no waste. There's no office, no secretary, no typewriters, no bursars. I do it all myself: all the taxes, pay the staff, pay the bills, the whole lot. All the kitchens are run by teachers. They do all the cooking, so there are no overheads whatsoever. In most schools

money is absolutely wasted. We have very little paper work. We don't even have any stamps. The parents come and collect their bills and so on. We've cut it all out, and everything has been built from the fees, including the house in Switzerland.

Whenever we take boys to Switzerland, I pay. It is included in the fees. They don't contribute one penny. We provide all their clothes, all skis, climbing boots, air fares, spending money. The parents don't even have to give them pocket money. They stay out there for five or six weeks. I take them, and then I go out each week. Four teachers from here go, and we have one based out there. The boys have full lessons, except at weekends, when I take them mountain climbing or skiing. We do difficult, dangerous, high climbs, and I point out the dangers. No one ever passes me. I go ahead, I don't talk. I'm watching all the time. I turn back the minute it's too dangerous for them, and point it out to them. You have no right to endanger the life of someone else's child. We have no right to take a risk, so we never take one. That's why they never go in the mountains without me. I always lead them, always take the responsibility and always get them back.

The one great difference between this school and other schools is that they are owned by trusts and the headmaster is appointed by the trustees and is an employee. My school has grown from nothing, and I own it all, and I want to make it the best in the world. The other thing about it is that it is a school for all-rounders, a school that joins rich and poor together and makes them equal. As a matter of clear printed policy, half are English boys and half are non-English; and half the teachers are English and half are non-English; and we stick to it. Half the teachers come from New Zealand, Australia, South Africa and – about fourteen of them – from France; and half are from the United Kingdom. But the non-English are English speaking by birth. This gives us a strong international flavour, and I'm a great believer in one world. I don't believe in this attitude of be damned to what happens across the Channel. That's not going to help us at all.

Have you ever had to expel a pupil?

I did once, but always regretted it. I felt we had failed. It's our job to put a bad child right, and so it's a failure if you haven't put them right. Expulsion is something so final. Education is so vital, and if you chuck them out, where are they going to go? It's like publicly executing them: an awful thing to do. In the past they expelled children just for breaking some sort of law, or jumping into bed with some other boy, and what a stupid way of dealing with it that was. If they don't want them jumping into bed with another boy, why not say you shouldn't do it? But you don't expel them.

I feel we should teach children what's wrong, that we should go out of our way to put children right. You should lead from the front. Punishments for young people need to be very carefully thought out. It's a wicked thing for an adult to strike a child. Adults are being sadistic when they hit children, and a lot of teachers in the past were sadistic and enjoyed seeing a child being hurt. I never allow it here. Anybody who did it would be sacked. In fact I'm being taken to court at the moment by a teacher because I sacked her. She's admitted in court that she used to hit the boys, but, just the same, she has gone to the court of appeal for wrongful dismissal.

Would you say that, by and large, you have a committed staff?

Oh, yes. I don't think you'd be happy in this sort of school unless you were committed to teaching. The teachers are gifted, they believe in what they're doing. You wouldn't get on in the army unless you believed in military discipline, in marching around and being smart. It's the same with school – you must believe in what you are doing.

They are a wonderful staff, and I'll give you an example. I was eighty in April, and one of the teachers said, 'I hope you are going to be at the school tonight.' When I arrived, all the teaching staff were assembled. They'd got a great cake with eighty candles on it, and gave me a beautiful present. I was so moved that I got up on a stool and said, 'All your salaries will be put up by £1,000 a year as from today.' That cost me £150,000 extra a year, and the bank manager had to run an overdraft because I couldn't recoup it until I could put my fees up. But imagine the effect on the staff's morale. I'm a great believer in patting people on the back, as you do in the army. I don't have to consult anybody. In a normal school I would have had to consult the governors. I'd have had to ask, 'Do you mind if I put all the salaries up by £1,000?' They'd have said, 'Don't be so damned stupid. That'll cost £150,000 and you've got to wait until September when the fees go up to balance it.' The bank manager told me I was mad, but he laughed his head off.

A recent TV programme about Hillside showed the younger boys being instructed in the use of firearms by a former South African soldier. Some might find the idea of that a little disturbing.

We do shooting because it is very good discipline and we have a beautiful indoor range. Now, you can't teach anyone to shoot unless you've done it yourself. Most people, particularly today in this country, have never done military service, but the South Africans have. Occasionally we have a New Zealander as instructor, but we like the South Africans. They're very well trained, the ones that come here, and the fact that

you don't like the policy of their government doesn't mean everybody in the country is wrong.

I've toured their country and the South Africans are marvellous people, and why should we criticize them? The people who come from there into this country come because they want to follow English rules, English habits. You mustn't down a South African in the same way as you shouldn't think all Germans are bad. How you solve the South African mess, I don't know. If you haven't the problem yourself, it's too easy to tell other people what to do, and if you do have the problems, it's not so easy to solve it.

In the same TV documentary there was some talk among the boys of children in comprehensive schools being 'bullies and cockneys', as if they were somehow the same thing and the inevitable product of state education.

That came from a bit of a snooty boy. He shouldn't have said those things. I'm sorry they put it in, and we told him so afterwards. These are things which you don't say about other children. Just because you're lucky, and they're not so lucky, you don't do it. It was a horribly superior thing to say, and the BBC shouldn't have put that bit in, for it did us no good. Maybe they wanted to balance the programme.

Is there not a danger that a thirst for leadership may sometimes undermine democracy?

Yes. It can produce someone like Hitler, for example. I met Hitler at the 1936 Olympic Games. I could speak German fluently, having spent two years in Switzerland after Oxford learning the language. None of the others in the English delegation could speak German, and somebody had to go up into his box, so I was the one who was told to go. I was then a serving officer in the army, but I was swept off my feet by the magnetism of the man. It was comparable with Churchill's magnetism and leadership. He had brought the German nation up from absolutely nothing and bankruptcy after the war, and had given it a pride in itself. But at that time the evil side of his leadership wasn't known about. When I liberated Buchenwald at end of the war, and stood on the gibbets, I saw all the horrors he had done.

There are great leaders and there are evil leaders. The good ones are those who have it in their blood. It probably started at their schools when they were captains of teams, and they feel it is a duty to lead and to get to the top. If you've got the quality of leadership, then you're lucky, because it is a very rewarding thing. I enjoy every minute of it. I feel like God Almighty. I'm in charge, I've got control of everyone in this place. I tell everybody what to do, I organize it.

The Olympic Games seem to have changed in character since your time. Does much remain of the true Olympic spirit?

The 1948 Olympic Games were extremely happy. Everybody was equal and a spirit of friendship was most marked all the way through. We had an exceptionally difficult time organizing them, because after the war we only had eighteen months as opposed to six years to do it in. All the food needed to be imported, I had to build all the camps for the competitors, and I had to fight officials to allow the athletes to come into the country, because after the war nobody was wanted. Yet we managed to get everyone together and the games were an immense success and very efficiently run. Today there is so much money in it. The athletes have got to win, because it means millions to them. The opening ceremony has become such a spectacle that very often the host city goes broke. In 1948 we made a profit.

The Olympic Games should be purely for athletes. That was the original idea in Greece, and that's what they should remain. I don't mind bringing in a few extra things like wrestling, rowing and fencing, but as soon as you have everything under the sun, then it turns into a mess.

Do you ever feel, as you grow older, that you become more entrenched in your ideas?

I hope I'm flexible. If I were not flexible I'd still have a rolled umbrella and a bowler hat. I've got them but I don't sport them. If you have achieved things, then you're always looking for something more to achieve. I've finished with athletics, I've finished with what I've done in the army. Subsequently I built up this school, which is recognized as one of the top schools in the world, so now I want something new. I've recently found a fresh challenge in television. I come over very well on TV, it appears. I've got all the recordings and the letters still keep pouring in from all over the world. I haven't yet read every one of them. When you're dealing with young people, it's very difficult not to be aware of the future. They're always talking about it and they think you're an idiot if you don't.

I can't speak about my experiences in the last war to anybody unless they were there too. I can't even talk to my son about it. It's just history to him, over and gone. I like being alone; I look after myself. I wash my own underclothes and socks. I clean my room. I make my own bed always. I love being in the mountains, but I love having the children there behind me. I wouldn't be a monk, for example, or go and live on a desert island. I quite enjoy a crowded city.

When I finish, I'm going to drop off a mountain. I don't like people asking me how I am. My job is to look fit, even if I feel like death. One day I shall just drop. I hope I do. But I won't retire, because then you are useless and all you do is moan about taxes and young people. You might as well be dead.

JOHN UPDIKE

John Updike was born in 1932 in Shillington, Pennsylvania. He graduated from Harvard in 1954 and spent a year as a Knox Fellow at the Ruskin School of Drawing and Fine Art in England. From 1955 to 1957 he was a staff member of the *New Yorker*, to which he has contributed short stories, poems and book reviews. He is the author of thirteen novels (including *Couples* and the *Rabbit* series) and seventeen other books which include five collections of verse. He has four children by his first marriage and since 1957 he has lived in Massachusetts.

Your distaste for the idea of someone writing your biography led you to write your autobiography. Why should the idea of someone else writing about your life be so disturbing?

I'm still trying to inhabit my life, and there's not room for two people there; I'd rather be alone. Also I'm still using my material and my memories, still coming to grips with my own life. The biographies I've seen of living people are either libellous, in an attempt to make the life sensational and interesting, or very dull, and since I have a limited amount of energy I would rather put none of it into dealing with a biographer. I have four living children, an ex-wife and a present wife, all of whom deserve some privacy even if I don't. When I am as old as Graham Greene, and if I am as distinguished, perhaps I will invite a young man like Norman Sherry in, but I'm nowhere near that stage of eminence.

I admit an outsider might be more truthful in a way, but in my autobiography I tried to put down some of the things only I could know. The things anyone can find out I will leave for somebody else to deal with. A life is a very strange thing. My mother died last fall, and I've been reading letters I wrote to her in the 1970s, which isn't so long ago, but how much I've forgotten of the day-to-day routine! I suppose a biographer goes through all that: finds the letters, tells what was happening all those years before. I don't want to face that now. I'd rather try to be a creative writer while I still can.

It is flattering to think that a lot of people might find me interesting to read about, but I honestly don't know how many there are who want to know all about me. Perhaps six; ten at most. We begin life usually with our mothers being very interested in everything we do. They record every word we say and every bowel movement we manage, and maybe that's enough of that kind of attention. I would rather have my

works interest people, but have them come out of a slightly mysterious centre. It's very hard in this day and age to maintain any privacy or any personal mystery at all, since people are interested in the real lowdown, as we say in this country. We do pick up a lot of books expecting to learn what the writer has been doing lately, which almost brings it down to a level of gossip, though maybe it's a healthy kind of interest. We read the books of Erica Jong or even Philip Roth in part out of curiosity about them as the authors of their previous books. But one would like to think that writers do more than just divulge their recent histories, and that there is some capacity to imagine lives other than their own, or some capacity to draw larger lessons from their own lives. Without being as reclusive as Thomas Pynchon or J. D. Salinger, I have tried to stay out of at least some of the gossip columns and to avoid some of the many interviews I'm invited to give.

You become less effective as an artist the more interested you become in yourself as a person; and the more you encourage an interest in yourself as a person, the more you're in danger of becoming a fat-headed, lazy artist. Better to wear your hairshirt and hide in a cave than come out and try to be a beautiful person. There are so many beautiful people in the world now – so many in the New York nightclubs and the London clubs – that I don't think a writer should attempt to swell that particular throng. It's one thing to wish your books to be elegant, another to wish to be elegant yourself. I'm all for elegance in the right places, and my concern is to try to be elegant in the books. But I'm not sure that elegance is the supreme human quality we should aspire to. It seems to be like a pear. It goes rotten very quickly. Maybe we need some sturdier virtue, something more like a potato that will keep for months and even a year in the cellar.

Did you always want to write?

Not really, but my mother was a frustrated writer. She would send off manuscripts and get them back, and was trying to write through much of my childhood, so the notion it was a worthy thing to try to do dawned upon me. But my first artistic itch was to draw. I did a lot of drawing as a child, and continued certainly through college. I was on a magazine at Harvard and did cartoons and covers, but by the time I got out of Harvard, the writing side of me had become the stronger and seemed the more saleable, the more useful side. I had some early acceptances, and by the time I was about twenty-three was committed to being a writer. And I'm lucky, because you can draw in writing – in a way, incorporate the visual art into the writing – but you can't really write in drawing. Writing is quite a broad activity in which you can

use almost anything you know at some point, and I would say that my drawing skill has been useful to me.

I draw very rarely today. Occasionally an amusing birthday card to a child. The *New Yorker* have sometimes asked me for illustrations, so I have had three drawings published there, always attached to an article. It's strange how, when you sit down after years of not drawing, the art picks up right where you left it. Basically I still draw the way I did at twenty-two. I'm no better, but I'm not much worse. It's fun to try, but I really don't have the time to draw for pleasure. When I had small children I occasionally drew them as babies. Then I bought a camera and stopped drawing.

Do you find writing easy?

Some days are easier than others, and it's never totally easy. There's always a little jump into it, like into a swimming pool. I tend to postpone and make a cup of tea, and circle the desk and answer some letters. But by and large I've been pretty good about sitting down to it finally and doing a certain amount each day. I would not class myself as one of those people who really sweat out each day's work. I think I write fairly easily as writing goes, maybe too easily, yet there's always some effort to it, and some serendipity, some surprise. You always find things you didn't know you were going to say, and that is the adventure of writing: that you can't plan it entirely but need to have faith each day that you launch yourself at this blank piece of paper, knowing in a general way what you're going to try to cover but not knowing exactly. You hope for things to happen that you can't foresee, and the life of the prose is in these unforeseeable harmonies, these characters who do something other than was planned. All those little surprises are what make it such an entertaining profession. People who can make a living writing are very lucky because not only is the day short and the labour not too difficult, but you have a kind of self-therapy. You're always, in a way, expressing yourself, which they tell us is healthy if you do it to a psychiatrist. You're constantly finding out what you know and feel which you didn't know you knew or felt before.

You're right that it is lonely. One of the reasons I was happy to come and meet you was that I must vary the loneliness somewhat. Now that my children are grown up and my wife works, I'm alone in the house for much of the day. All day, from seven to six. But then I was an only child, and maybe my tolerance for being alone is greater than that of many. I can take several days of not talking to anyone without too much discomfort. After a while, of course, the need to make contact becomes very pressing, but on the whole I like it and I guess I talk to myself and I'm my own company. I have telephone contact with various

editorial people. The mail is of great interest to me, probably more than for a painter, say, or a musician. There are these various ways of relieving the loneliness. But there's no doubt ever that you must be alone at the moment of actual work. You must face yourself to that degree, and many don't want to do that. Most people enjoy the constant company of others. It's like having the radio going in the elevator – something to chase away the silence, this awful silence at the background of our lives that we're trying to shut out. The writer in some ways tries to face the silence, at least for the three or four hours a day that he works.

Nobody can be entirely self-sufficient. I'm very dependent upon the fact of getting published. My enjoyment of writing is not so keen that I would do it if there were no rewards. Proust and Kafka would both seem to have had fairly low expectations, though both had some publication. Proust paid for his first book to be published, and Kafka fought to be published, but even writers as hermetic and exquisite as these at some point welcome the actual experience of getting published. And for me, who's been published quite early, it would be very sad if my publishing house and the *New Yorker* magazine were to stop publishing me. I need that kind of stimulus. I seem to need a fair amount of attention, in fact, or I wouldn't publish so many books.

Some American authors go years without publishing. Thomas Pynchon just now published a novel after seventeen years of silence. I don't think I could ever go so long. For all of my tolerance of solitude, I do like that annual fuss that surrounds the book. And like many children in this country, especially of my generation, I have a sort of love affair with New York City. I was a small-town boy – in fact I was a farm boy for a while – and I thought that where I was going to find happiness was in New York, presented to my generation as Fred Astaire and *Top Hat*, penthouses and beautiful women in lovely long white gowns. So I always thought I'd live in New York. When I got there I found there were some of the things I had expected, but there was also a great deal of hassle and no place to raise a family. My wife had no natural social life there, and was lonely. I was working, so was not so lonely, but we didn't stay long. Yet I've been able to keep a hold of New York with the writing. I talk to it often. I have friends there. When I go I feel at home. I've tried to be a New Yorker without paying the very real price of living there.

Can you tell me something of the relationship between the life and the fiction?

I suppose I am somewhat more autobiographical than other writers appear to be, though when you look into a writer like Tolstoy, who seems almost a god-like omniscient above it all, it turns out there is a

surprisingly high degree of autobiographical material. We all need some kind of personal stimulus, some moment that we want to expose or tell about, and writers can be variously clever over how they're going to package it. But these two elements – a personal sharing and a kind of packaging – I think are true of everybody. In my case, the package sometimes may seem very thin, a little cellophane around the nugget of life, but it is in my mind always a package. Even if I tell the events of one afternoon in my life, I'm not telling every afternoon, so there has been an act of selection and a sense of shaping.

Some of my work may look more autobiographical than it is. I prefer to think it doesn't really matter. I'm alive now, and having a life of a kind, and while I'm alive I must share what seems to me momentous about it. To be too discreet or too cunning would be self-defeating. But always I sec it as a change, a metamorphosis. There's no such thing as offering the reader your life. What you offer is a set of packaged moments that in some way you have witnessed, maybe out of the dead middle of your experience or maybe in the sense of imagining. I don't think the distinction matters terribly much. In some way you must make your life interesting, must give it a kind of relevance, an application beyond that of just telling what happened today. As long as you do that and make the ideal reader care, you've fulfilled your responsibility. Meanwhile you live your life the best you can.

People talk about being put into a book as though they can be actually lifted out of life and inserted, but we know that the two orders of existence are really very different. There are the flesh-and-blood people who have all kinds of qualities and fully occupy space and time, and there are fictional characters, who are really just a few words tossed on to a page. It's such an enormous difference between the world, on the one hand, and a book on the other, that I've felt fairly free about writing sometimes about my life fairly directly. Take one example. *Couples* was a long novel that was certainly about a kind of milieu that I felt, and I made the observation that we were all set up as couples and expected to be very happy yet weren't. Having decided that here was the sociological condition worth telling about, I felt obliged to disguise all of my friends heavily so there was almost nobody in there who could say, 'That's me,' though they could all recognize the general feeling.

There's a little novel of mine called *Of the Farm*, which is autobiographical in tone. It's first person and is about a woman very like my mother, set on a farm exactly like hers, but the situation is false. The hero has a second wife. I did not have a second wife at the time, and didn't acquire one for another ten or more years. So more often than not we write not out of what happened but out of what might have happened. We write out of tendency as much as of the fact.

Are fictional characters more interesting than real ones?

I think not. A real person has endless depths. Just the anatomical qualities of a real person are fascinating: what makes the molecules click, what makes the psyche and the mass of memories each person carries around. A real person is overwhelmingly large in terms of potential data that could be expressed. Fictional characters are therefore interesting in part because we can stand them. They don't overwhelm us, they're often very simple. If you look at even complex-seeming characters in fiction, they're really quite simple: basically dolls with maybe three or four moving parts so our minds can encompass them. They're interesting because they're involved in a story, and a story is a suspense of some kind which makes us care about what'll happen next. We read it in the faith that it's going to have an end, that all of our immediate questions will be answered one way or another.

So we are excited by stories, whereas life doesn't seem quite to have a story, but is many stories all interwoven. Perhaps we read fiction in part as a relief from the enormous factualness of life that seems to have no clear point. A fiction writer has assumed a certain obligation. He will somehow resolve the fate of his characters. Even fairly *avant-garde* works do this in a way. When we put down *Ulysses* or *Remembrance of Things Past*, we feel it's come to an end and that the author has said everything he wants to say. In *Ulysses* Molly Bloom gives a kind of blessing to life itself, and in Proust the author arrives at the revelation that time can be made to reverse itself, or does reverse itself, and it's this which justifies a life. We always come to some point of satisfaction in fiction, and we consent to be interested in the faith that all of the anxieties and questions aroused within the microcosm of the novel will be answered and placated; that, unlike life, there is no tomorrow with its own set of questions. When the book ends, there is no tomorrow.

A fictional world must have both lightness and weight, the lightness coming from the fact that, when one mind is processing it, it will somehow add up and be entertaining and, unlike life, won't contain long dull stretches. But it must also have some weight. There must be an illusion that this is enough like life so that the processes we observe in the work of art can be applied to the life we then lead. This feeling of actual instruction as to how to live is very much one of the reasons why we read a fiction, in so far as we do – and most people don't. Not only do most uneducated people not read books, but a lot of intelligent people, especially men, abandon fiction. Therefore fiction has rather a small audience, but those of us who do read it and try to write it hope for some revelation about life; that we somehow emerge from the book slightly more humane and able to cope with real-life situations.

In the past twenty or thirty years fiction has become much more

sexually explicit and realistic, and this has been deplored in many quarters. But for me it often has the great moral virtue of attempting to tell us how the other sex feels about sexual transactions and, in demonstrating the sexual adventures of the characters, making us more knowing and perhaps gentler and less deluded; less egocentric in our own romantic behaviour. I often read female novels just to be illuminated as to how women think, though clearly not all women think alike. Nevertheless it is interesting for me to read about romance from a female point of view: what the expectation is and where the disappointments lie. All of that is information, and we do read for information. A slight embarrassment is that, given two novels of equal virtue, we would rather be in one about Saudi Arabia, say, than one about the city we live in. We're interested in strange places, in other lives. We travel in a way through fiction, since we can't travel entirely by ourselves, and all this fairly humble curiosity gives the writer an opportunity to expand the consciousness of his readers, to give them experiences they won't otherwise have since life is so short.

Do you subscribe to the idea that sex is the lifeblood of our existence?

In a word, I do. You might broaden sex to something like love or Eros, and if what goes on between the mother and the infant is sex, then certainly sex would cover the whole field. A lot of what we do is apparently unsexual, but I think Freud is correct: everything really has a sexual goal. In other words, the hard-working Wall Street expert in financial mergers works all day so he will cut an impressive figure, perhaps so he can buy seductive clothes. He will certainly try to enhance his own maleness, his own plumage, as it were. The job, the work, the factory, all these are male plumage. I think a lot of what we do for the pay-off comes in erotic terms. And we're far from truly knowing how our emotional life as children blends into the erotic life of the mature adult, though surely it is a continuum in that we are at every point of our lives seeking for confirmation and approval from someone else. At a very humble level, we want our bodies approved of and accepted in the various physical ways that sex allows. Beyond that, we want in some way to be confirmed in our immaterial being as well. I suppose this to be an erotic search which can be carried on via many partners or one partner, or via a stamp collection.

There seem to me to be a lot of people who really should not be enlisted in the sexual armies, as it were. There are people who have honourable reasons for just not caring, many who in the older societies would become monks or priests or eccentric bachelors – formerly a very honourable thing to be. We're in danger now, in the late twentieth century, of forcing everyone to become a sexual hero, a sexual superstar

when there are probably a number of alternative ways of working out the basic erotic patterns of your life. But when all is said and done, novels are almost invariably about love. It's as if we were saying that we are most alive when we're in love.

A writer's experience must include other people's books. Is there a distinction between what comes from experience of the real and what comes from books?

You certainly shouldn't write out of other books. I've not taught much writing, but I have done a little, and the students by and large haven't really learned to see, to have the language for their own lives. They don't see what they're living, and all they know is what they've read in books, and so they have to process their reality through what other writers have done. It's quite rare for a young man or woman to come into their own voice, their own material, much before the age of twenty-three or twenty-four, because the books we've read control what we see and screen out so much of what is real about us. We are all creatures of literary tradition, and it is the ability to be excited enough by the world of print to wish to enlarge it, to take a piece of your perception and experience, turn it into print and make it join on to this big antarctica of things in print, which is the basic impulse. In other words, to take your life out of being something impermanent and trivial and purely personal and make it something that can in some way enlarge the experience of people you don't even know. It's a great act of transformation, and if you can do it, it's a great privilege to expand that world of print.

It's true there are too many books, and most are junk, but to a young person it's a sacred world and a world he is totally locked out of. To find the way into it and be on the other side of that wall, to be one of the producers of the books is, even at the age of fifty-eight, still exciting. As to influence, I think you do somehow close down and that the major reading experiences of your life occur before you are twenty-five or thirty. That is to say, the writers who really give you your voice are apt to have been encountered by that age. The more of a voice you get, the less you can start to change it and the less you are struck by other people's, but the writers whom you really value and love are the ones you think have shown you the way to what you know. In my case there is the English writer, Henry Green, who in some way opened me up to what prose could do. And there's the American writer, J. D. Salinger, whose short stories seem to belong to my world. I thought I could write stories like that, whereas I couldn't write stories like John O'Hara or Hemingway. In some way, you need those few spirits who release you, show you the way to speak yourself.

When you're in college you tend to read what they tell you, and

having a lot of catching up to do, I read mostly English classics – *Beowulf*, Chaucer, Shakespeare. But for all the admirable writers you read in college, in some way you're reading them to fill in your sense of history and prepare for examinations. Once I got out of college, I read a lot of Proust, in English, because I didn't have enough French to take him in French, and that year I spent at Oxford I read Henry Green and some more Salinger, as well as a lot of Kierkegaard for personal reasons. But I think Kierkegaard did something for me as a writer. There's a tremendous energy and rhetorical skill in him, and he's not afraid to do something thoroughly. The gift of being able to write novels came in part, I'm sure, from Kierkegaard and Proust. I also read Kafka, but I'm not a very Kafkaesque writer. I found him exhilarating because he faces those depressing things, our entrapment and our impotence, and there's a kind of relief in just voicing them. Of course, you tend to feel somewhat superior to Kafka as you read him. You think, well, I'm not that sick, not that neurotic, so in some way you can lick the sugar off the pill and not swallow it.

That's one thing we always do in reading, of course: take what we want out of a book, and there's always more we don't take. Unlike the motion picture, which gives you itself and all of itself in a big bang, a book will only give you as much as you're ready to hear or to see. It's amazing to reread a book you read ten years ago. You realize you didn't read it at all. It's almost like a brand-new book. One of the marvellous things about books is the layeredness and the way, all the time, they have secrets to give.

To come back to the novel as the product of expert imitation, is it more convincing when experience like marriage or parenthood can be taken direct from life?

You can fake quite a lot, and the level of realism we demand from the novel isn't extraordinarily high. Our wish to be entertained and instructed is so strong that we will forgive quite a lot of fakery, but there comes a point at which fakery invalidates a novel, and we put the book down, realizing we are learning nothing. Flaubert, though unmarried, wrote well enough about marriage, and there's an American writer, Ann Beardey, who has no children but has just written a book about the problems of child rearing. So it is possible. There's also many a sex change where a male writer has more or less plausibly become a woman and vice versa. Nevertheless, what we really have to share is stuff we've experienced.

As soon as I was married my writing almost immediately became better, I think because I was somehow a step up the ladder of life. Marriage is something that most writers should not seek to avoid. I

wouldn't have missed having children for anything, and when I had them around me I certainly wrote better about children than I would have if I'd never known any – better, in fact, than I can do now. In my most recent novel, which has a ten-year-old and a four-year-old, I found I knew what they were like, having had four children of my own and lived with three stepsons, but also that I had grown a little out of touch with how children of that age act and think. In general I would say use your imagination, but there are limits to what imagination can do.

It's very possible to draw upon a personal encounter so early that you don't yourself know what you're using. Some of Henry James's later novels have this quality. He was drawing from very youthful memories without quite knowing it, but in the end a character is a person, and we have to have some general knowledge of people before we can begin to write novels. I don't think that even a very superior mentality from another planet, with all kinds of statistical information about human beings, could write a novel. In a novel, we are recycling people we have met, and we may be using the nose of one or the arm of another, or it may be a nose we saw in the movies, but there's certainly some human input that has to happen before there can be any output in the form of character creation.

I don't think the craft can do these things by itself. There is craft, and more of it than the romantic conception of the artist allows, but the ability is to make a thing coherent. It's like making a bird house. You imagine it in your head, and then do the little fitting that needs to be done. A great deal of what you might call carpentry goes into making a satisfying book, but in making a bird house you still need to have the bird inside it, and the bird flies out of your experience and your own passion about your experience. For example, I went to Harvard, not far from where we sit now – an admirable institution, but I've never been moved to write very much about it; enough people have already done so.

I've met hundreds and hundreds of people in my life, but perhaps only a dozen have really gotten through to me in a way that prompts me to want to make them characters. I use the same people again and again, because only they somehow have got to me. Therefore things have to get to you, and not all of your life will; but when you sit down to make a book or a short story or a poem, you have to have something that you want to package, something you want to present to people in some form. The craft can do the form to a degree, but an awful lot of what we call writerly craft is nothing more than authenticity. It's not putting down phoney words; it's trying to have a voice that speaks; it's really wishing to communicate. That is what makes a great deal of the style, and no amount of rules is going to give you that voice.

What sets 'literature' apart from other fiction?

In part a willingness to forget or sacrifice readers, to push forward. You can still be quite a popular artist and do this. It's a feeling of adventure and a willingness to take risks which makes the real writer distinguishable from the unreal one. It often takes a century, of course, to discover who was real and who was not. It's not always apparent at the time, and there are many creditable writers now who probably won't matter much in a hundred years. You could even call literature a higher degree of playfulness, in that the literary writer is willing to play with the thing and not just trying to construct an engine to process a reader's emotional patterns.

I don't read much cheap fiction, I just don't have the time, but when you watch television, you sense these machines instructed to run you through a set of emotional manoeuvres. You're supposed to care about the guy, you're supposed to want him to sleep with the girl, you're supposed to get excited when they're in a car being chased. There's a kind of mechanical working over, a little like a massage. Some kind of massage accompanies a literary masterpiece too, but somehow it's more than a massage. The writer, as he or she goes along, makes discoveries perhaps, and in some way is open to interventions from outside the mechanical pattern. I suppose you can also merely say that literary writers are brighter than the others; that their vocabularies are bigger, their willingness to play with language and their intuitive knowledge about the world greater. The quality of their writing has an adventurous experimental freedom. The great artist is more free: freer to see more and to eliminate more; to do without certain kinds of obligatory performance.

Your autobiography is often provided with footnotes on the use you made in fiction of some incident or person.

That's a rather arbitrary set of footnotes. Just what occurred to me as I was writing. Several times I've given female characters experiences based on my own. I turned a pulled tooth into an abortion for a female character, and also reversed a churchgoing situation. It doesn't much matter, you know. As the structuralists say, the opposite is often virtually the same thing, and what's important is the structure. To put it on to a woman or to make it upside down is no great trick. I thought it would make the book in general more fun to read if, in some places, I acknowledged, yes, you have seen this before, or this may ring a bell for those who are devoted Updike readers. It was fun to do. It added a little dimension.

I am interested myself when writers talk about books, especially if they're admirable books. It's interesting to read Graham Greene on the

period of his life when he was writing the early novels, *The Power and the Glory* and so on, because even though he doesn't say much, it's all helpful, and in a way it humanizes the books. A book in the end has to float free of the man's life, but while he's alive it's fun to see these strings and to realize how much he made of something that was little; to see the imagination in operation and realize how little it needs sometimes to take off in a big way.

You wanted your autobiography to be in some sense 'representative in its odd uniqueness of all the oddly unique lives in the world', but is it not inevitable that some lives are more interesting than others?

I suppose some are more interesting than others. What I think is irreversibly interesting, and true of all of us, is that we're trapped inside a certain body and a certain set of circumstances, even a certain moment in time. Although I suppose this could be dismissed as a metaphysical riddle saying that you had to be somebody, so why not you, my childhood perception, as I began to grapple with being alive, was the extraordinary strangeness of being me instead of somebody else. And so the philosophical emotion behind the autobiography was the feeling of being self-conscious, of being conscious of being this self instead of another self. Then you stay self-conscious, and it's probably not a good thing. The memories which are most affecting are gathered by and large when you were least self-conscious, when you were either young or intensely engaged in some life experience. I'm aware of myself as a writer now, as a man who is recognized on the street, as a man who has the costume of a writer. In a way it's like a little static in the head all the time, which I try to tune out, but there's no doubt that I am somewhat self-conscious.

But no two lives are alike and we would rather live some than others. Most lives on this planet are miserable, and one of the tragedies surely involved in the human race right now is that so many lives are wasted before they've begun, largely because of poverty. I've been very fortunate. Anybody who's fairly healthy, and was born into the United States when I was, is in a tiny minority of blessed people, living in an area that is more or less disease free. Even compared to my grandparents, how relatively little pain I've had. Think of the toothaches that people in the nineteenth century put up with, the infectious diseases that would lift away a whole set of children, the powerlessness of all that. To be alive in an era when so much of that particular kind of powerlessness is gone is a great privilege.

Anyway, I wasn't writing about how lucky I was to be me, but more how strange it was to be me. It's a little like Heidegger trying to write about being, being as an entity: in a sense it's absurd and doesn't get

you anywhere, but on the other hand it is something to face. There is a kind of miracle involved in anything existing, and a kind of miracle involved in being you. So I hoped that some of that sense of the miraculous would express a gratitude, a glad-to-be-here kind of feeling.

You wrote about Christmas and the way the idea of a snowy Christmas was more real to you than the bleak brown ones you actually knew. Was it that imaginative vividness that prompted you to become a novelist?

Certainly a susceptibility to that kind of imagery was what prompted me. All those snowy Christmas illustrations that appeared in children's books and old-fashioned magazines like the *Saturday Evening Post* were very real to me, more real than the muddied brown world around me. Had I not responded so strongly to those little pretend worlds, had I not wanted to enter in and get on that hearth and rug with Santa Claus in the sleigh, no doubt I would never have chosen to live by my imagination the way I have done. From early on I loved these images of another world: comic strips, illustrations, Christmas especially. The stylization of Christmas was so far advanced in American commercial art. Artists knew how to draw it, how to make those little windows with the frost in. There was a kind of vocabulary of Christmas that had descended through generations, so it was intense as a totally imaginary experience that had nothing to do with the real Christmases I experienced. All that excited me, and it seemed a good way out of the world I was in.

The experiences that gave you such pleasure as a child, like being out of the rain, but only just out of it, you explained as pleasurable because 'the experiencer is irresponsible, safe . . . there is nothing he can do or ought to do.' This sounds very like an analogy for the art of the novelist, who is also 'morally detached, safe and witnessing'.

That's very good, and entirely your invention. I hadn't thought of it like that, but now that you mention it, writing a novel is rather like being out of the rain that you're creating there on the page, but just out, so you can smell it, feel it and hear it. Being in a little shelter out of the rain still affords me pleasure. The house I live in now has a kind of open garage, and it still gives me a thrill to stand there with the rain falling all around but not quite on me. I guess that novelists are often people who are fascinated by the rain but don't want to get wet. It's a good point.

Edmund White once said it was the particular curse of adolescence that events were never adequate to the feelings they inspired. Do you feel something similar?

It's true that when you write about them you have to be careful some-

how to make them seem in proportion to the response. It's possible to be very superior to adolescent experience. On the other hand, it is a human experience. We are as alive at thirteen as at thirty-three, and it deserves to be put into print. I think we have to try to rid ourselves of our own myths about adolescence and write about it. What is awkward from the standpoint of a novelist is that adolescents don't really have their grip on the handles of the world yet. They can't make decisions, they can't decide they will marry, they can't decide they will sell the company. They aren't quite grown up. All they can do is feel and thrash around, so in that way they're unsatisfactory. I found I could write about adolescents quite easily in short stories, but that they won't carry me through a novel. You need adults who can do grown-up things to get you through a novel.

You wrote in your memoirs that you were conscious of wanting to 'show them in Shillington', to revenge your father for the slights you and he felt had been put upon him. Did you come to feel at last that you had done so?

I wrote that when my mother was alive, and I suppose, had she been dead, I would have included her, because in a way I was trying to work some kind of revenge for her as well. It was she who felt that Shillington was a hard place. To me it seemed enchanting. It was kind to me and I love it, but I was aware that somehow there was a level of respectability that my parents didn't quite get into. Among my motives has been a wish to show Shillington that we weren't intimidated. It was a typical small town full of people, none very rich, none very poor. Somehow I have a wish to show Shillington people that we can make more money than the factory workers from the hosiery mills. What sticks in my mind as a social insult was that my father, though he had the prestige, such as it was, of a schoolteacher, made less than the full-fashioned knitters, and there was a funny feeling about being, not exactly at the very bottom of the social scale, but certainly at the lower end. If I'd stayed in Shillington I'd probably be at the lower end of the social scale myself. I had to get out to show it.

You describe yourself in your memoirs as malicious, greedy for a quota of life's pleasures, an obnoxious show-off, rapacious and sneaky. That is certainly not how you are perceived publicly.

I think that anybody who knows me would agree with all those adjectives. I was an only child who never had to compete with a sibling, and my parents were both, in their way, very loving and indulgent. Just the fact that I had the presumption to become an artist is rather ridiculous, isn't it, with no qualifications except that I felt treasured as a child. When my mother died, among her things in the attic was a scrapbook

containing many of my drawings done when I was three and four. Not every child gets that kind of attention. The good side of it is I have a certain confidence, and by and large I've acted confidently in my life and had good results. The bad side is that I like to be at the centre of attention.

As to being malicious, I think I am more than unusually malicious. That joy, that *Schadenfreude* we take in other people's misfortunes, is well developed in me, though I try to suppress it. I detect within myself a certain sadism, a certain pleasure in the misfortunes of others. I don't know whether I'm average in this or whether it's exceptional, but I'm interested to a degree in the question of sadism. People who are sadistic are very sensitive to pain, and it's a way of exorcizing the demon of pain.

I'm so aware of my enviousness that I try not to review books by contemporary Americans. I'm not sure that I would really give an honest opinion, and that's sneaky. People who are cowardly and don't especially enjoy confrontation or battle tend to be sneaky. In this unflattering self-characterization, though, I was no doubt just doing my Christian duty of confessing sins. Human nature is mightily mixed, but surely all these malicious and cruel aspects are there along with everything else.

One reviewer, talking about Couples, *called you 'the pornographer of marriage'. Did you resent the tag?*

Not too much. I wasn't trying to be pornographic. I was trying to describe sexual behaviour among people, and the effect was probably the opposite of pornographic. Pornography creates a world without consequences, where women don't get pregnant, nobody gets venereal disease and no one gets tired. In *Couples* I was trying, to the limits of my own knowledge, to describe actual sexual situations and show them with consequences. Without resenting that phrase, I don't think it describes very well what I was trying to do.

One is always sensitive to criticism to a degree. If they tell you you're the best thing since Shakespeare, you want to know what's so great about Shakespeare. I remember especially some reviews I got early. When I began to write, the big figures on the scene were Jewish, by and large: Malamud, Bellow, young Roth and so on. The literary world was Jewish, and up comes this little WASP out of the country, writing in a style influenced by Proust. I think I irritated some people, because I did receive a number of harsh reviews of books that were in their way quite innocent and well meant. I was told I had nothing to say, was told it repeatedly, so some of those darts stuck in my skin and I still remember them. On the other hand, it's part of the game. Every profession has its hazards and harsh reviews.

At least I mattered enough to get bad reviews. I was enough of a presence to deserve to be debunked, and I should have taken some comfort from that. I've never consciously tried to adjust my writing to please critics. It would be a mistake, because you're never going to please many of them. Some of the things said were no doubt fair, as I see now, but when you're a practising artist you can't afford to be too much into the critics' skin. You have to push, to keep going with your own vision and your own sense of reality, and let others make the judgements. On the other hand, I was always protected from adverse judgements by the fact that I had the *New Yorker* magazine in my corner. They liked me and took most of my things, which meant that my livelihood and my ego gratification came from the same source. I could always hide behind the fact that I was a *New Yorker* writer and the people who weren't were just jealous.

I think *Couples* was certainly of its time, just in the fact that it spans very specific years and refers to a lot of historical events. In a funny way, the book is about the Kennedy assassination. It's also about the introduction of the contraceptive pill, the fact that the danger of getting pregnant was almost entirely removed and that a certain amount of promiscuity resulted directly from this technology. It also turns out that it was the pre-Aids, pre-herpes paradise, so it was a moment that's gone, a moment of liberation which broke not upon a bunch of San Francisco hippies and young people, but upon middle-aged couples, yet was a revolution of a kind. It is very much of its historic moment. Those wives did not work, but now, in that same economic group, the wives would have jobs, or half-jobs. But these were people who married in the 1950s and thought family life was going to solve all their problems, then discovered it didn't.

I hope it's not too dated. I haven't read it since I checked the last proof. No doubt some of the writing I would improve if I could get my hands on the text again, but I don't think it's dated more than any book that has some roots in a historic moment. All novels belong to a certain time, to two times in fact – the time in which they're located and the time in which they're written. That book was written a few years farther on from the moment it describes, so in a way the characters are innocent Kennedy characters, whereas I wrote it in the era of Johnson when the Vietnam commitment had deepened and widened under us and people were beginning to burn flags. In a way I was already looking back on an innocent little paradise.

In a novel like Couples, *aren't you concerning yourself with what is really an American middle class?*

I think our middle classes are pretty distinct, and because we don't admit

we have a class structure, the other classes are less accessible in a way than they perhaps are in a very class-conscious society like Britain. Somehow to know that there are upper and lower classes, and even some of the traits that determine them, seems to make it easier for writers like Graham Greene or Henry Green or Evelyn Waugh to cross those lines and put before us convincing thugs and servants and what not. Whereas, in this allegedly classless society, we are timid. On the other hand, American experience places you in proximity with quite a range of class. I have no first-hand experience of city ghetto life, but I do remember what it's like to be shabby small-town and shabby country, and I've been able now to get a peek into the moneyed classes, so in a way I have a sufficient social range. But the English do seem to create multi-class novels more easily.

With an acceptance of more sexually explicit writing, much of the so-called literature of concealment has disappeared. Have more relaxed attitudes always been good for literature?

Any strategy of concealment can benefit the work of art, because it imposes certain demands. Rhyme in poetry, for example, had the advantage of forcing people to recast lines and a certain ingenuity came in. Often they were driven to find words they wouldn't ordinarily have found. And so it was with sexual concealment. In a way, you closed the bedroom door, you conveyed something was going on, and everyone knew what. It seemed important to me in the early 1960s to write about sex explicitly, because it was a little frontier. Some had crossed it already, but always in banned books. Henry Miller crossed it, and *Lady Chatterley's Lover* had crossed it, but Joyce was the best model in this because, unlike Henry Miller or D. H. Lawrence, you can't say Joyce is sex obsessed. *Ulysses* is not about sex but about life, yet sexual words and references occur and it feels right in the sense that, on a spring day in Dublin, this is how people's energies would be flowing. With that in mind, it seemed to be important to be as realistic as I could. I don't feel the need exists in the 1990s. Now people are more or less free to write what they want. I do it less because it does seem not to be an artistic frontier at all, though I would like to think that the freedom still exists for those who want to exercise it – even freedom to be pornographic if pornography is taken to be exciting. I don't see why a piece of writing can't be sexually exciting. Certainly writing excites us romantically, after all. Why not try to excite us sexually?

You have sometimes been accused of sentimentalizing your women characters.

I'd have to know the characters in question. I have tried to grow in my depiction of women without abandoning my own sense of women and

my own wisdom and experience of them, but I suppose I've tried to give them more credit for being something in addition to being interesting to men as sexual opposites. The women in *Couples* might be sentimental. I'm not sure. I'd have to read the book again. But as women have become increasingly vocal about their feelings, their long-held anger and their long resentment of male views about them, so any male writer to some extent has to look into his heart and try to make his portrayal of women as honest and fair as his portrayal of men. I wouldn't want to treat them better than I treat my men.

Women have been important in my life, from my mother on, in ways I don't even know as well as a lot of ways I do. I married young, and my first wife was exceedingly helpful, shaping not only my work but my whole outlook. My second wife too. If I had to be condemned to one sex, I would rather spend my time with women than with men.

You parted from your first wife. Are modern divorce rates prompted by modern conditions, or is it that divorce has become less difficult and more affordable?

The alternative activities to marriage that society has provided have, I think, diminished. It was quite possible to be very unhappily married in Victorian America and not exactly know it. You were off at the office; you then went to the club. The wife had her own circle and sets of entertainments. In a way, once you were past the child-making phase, your contacts could be fairly few and formal, and expectations of marriage were perhaps not quite so high. The post-war world in the West has put many of its eggs, as far as personal happiness goes, in the marriage basket. The demands on marriage have upped, which increases the stress. Also, of course, this is a Protestant country without the Catholic restraints on marriage, so that many a marriage that people would, in the old world, have lumped with the help of lovers, or doing without, or the Church, or any number of other things, now has no convenient way out except divorce.

Having been through one with children who, if not exactly babies, were a little too young to have their parents break up, I'd say it's something to be avoided if possible, but it's not maybe the worst thing to happen in many circumstances and the fact that it happens to so many children now has to some extent lessened the burden on each of them. You're no longer the pariah or odd-ball if you have a split family, since at least half your friends do too. It's not that we are indifferent to marriage; it's expecting so much of it that makes people become dissatisfied.

Do you write better under stress?

I have written under stress, but I wouldn't recommend it as a steady thing. As Wordsworth said, emotion recollected in tranquillity is the

optimum, so by and large I try and arrange a tranquil life around myself, and I write best in it. Of course, you have to have something to write about and that often does involve undertaking or going through some stress. I'm a compulsive writer who doesn't wait for the perfect day before he writes, so I've written on some poor days and written when I was in considerable discomfort. The one thing to be said for writing when you're unhappy is that at least you're having an experience of unhappiness. In a funny way, if you're always tranquil, always satisfied, always the orderly writer who goes and does his job, words are in danger of becoming too cheap. You write too easily. Some of my best writing has been done under stressful circumstances. Nevertheless, a simple bourgeois monotony is to be desired for a steady productive life.

Dr Johnson said that a man not married was only half a man, but Cyril Connolly added to the dictum by saying that a man who was very married was only half a writer.

It raises a ticklish issue. It's true that people are always only partially married, and that a writer writes to some extent with the unmarried, the lonely, the solitary adventuring self. My own temperament has led me twice toward marriage, maybe because I don't have Cyril Connolly's needs. He was a bit of a gadabout, I gather, as many writers have been. I have the feeling that, like many Englishmen, he needed a generous amount of bachelor freedom to feel a hundred per cent a man. Trying to think about notable twentieth-century writers who seemed thoroughly married and none the worse for it, I come across two immediately: Thomas Mann and James Joyce. I've seen too many American writers suffer in a way from not being married or being stable enough. You can easily fritter away your talent in drink, wasted energy and exhausting skirt chasing; or, indeed, in pants chasing – why leave the women out of it? In marriage the mind is unmarried enough. The mind is a kind of a bachelor, in any case. It's maybe a good mix to have the body very married.

You spoke of your memories of growing up as being 'used up and wished away in the self-serving corruptions of fiction'. Do you feel that somehow you are intruding upon the reality of those who live in memory?

I suppose so. I feel also that you are selling your life in a strange way, including the people who were standing around while you were living it, which brings something a little shabby into the transaction. When I was a little boy, I was much impressed by a fairy story about a wishing hide hanging on the wall. Every time you make a wish, a little piece flies off. Eventually there's no hide left. I think I have that same feeling about writing. Each time I turn something into a story or a novel,

another piece of the hide is flying off. Fiction is self-serving in so far as the writer is ultimately in control and anything too embarrassing will be suppressed. The general trend of the distortions is therefore in his own favour, so in that way it's corruption. Nevertheless it's what I do for a living, so I can't be too apologetic about it. But there's something consuming about it and a typical writerly fear is that you've used up everything you want to say. In fact you never do. Somehow, with a little patience, there's always more. But you write very close to what feels like exhaustion, to what feels like the end of your story.

In what sense do you live *your novels as you write?*

Things sharpen as you write. On the other hand, you have to have some notion of the little scene. I saw a lot of movies as a young man, and I still go to the movies. There is some degree to which our imaginations are all cinematic. I think of the novels as scenes, but I often don't know exactly what's going to happen. Sometimes the characters say less than I had hoped, sometimes more, but in general they hold within certain bounds of what can occur. A novel is unlike a play in that there is a weave of the verbal action with the background: the room, the scenery, the kind of day has somehow to come into it. The human mind wanders constantly, picks up little bits of the past and so on. All of that has to be written too, as well as the voices. It all gets sharper, and you hope it gets sharper again when you see proofs. Sharp seems a good way to think of it; clear. There should be a kind of clarity and a certain clash of edges; little jumps whereby the reader knows we're going forward. Each sentence should be a slight shock. I once saw that as a description of style, and I've tried to remember it: that good style is a succession of small surprises. I don't think it was Cyril Connolly, but it could well have been an Englishman. And so, yes, there are the surprises which are surprising to the writer, and then to the reader.

Do you feel at your peak as a writer now?

It's hard to know if I'm getting worse or if my critical sense is getting better. Just looking at the life curve of most writers, in America especially, you tend to peak young when your memories are fresh and youthful. It's a rare writer in this country who gets better after thirty, and many have blown up by the time they're in their forties. So at my age you're working against the trend, but in some ways I know more than ever. I'm less naïve, and it's only a question of energy. Writing is in part an athletic feat. It's all in the head, but it's a matter of images and words, of making it all have a kind of spring and a tension.

You have written only one play, Buchanan Dying*. Was that just a matter of seeing if you could do it?*

I'd tried to write that book as a novel first and found that the historical novel posed problems in terms of fakery and bluff that I couldn't meet. I might be able to do it now when maybe I'm not so inhibited about faking, but writing it all as a play was a way of unloading the considerable amount of material I had accumulated. It was bliss to write a play, bliss to try and picture the stage and to know you were making an artificial thing and could do away with all of that scenery that the prose writer is constantly creating. If the play had been produced on Broadway and been a great success, no doubt I would have tried to write others, but since it was too long and produced only in a few truncated college versions, I received no encouragement to become a playwright. Evidently I don't feel strongly enough about the form to do it on my own. I've never much enjoyed other people's plays, frankly, and I'm not a great theatregoer, so a number of things have combined to prevent me from trying another, though some day I might. I don't know the theatre very well, and I'm scared of getting involved with all those other people: the director, the actors, the agents.

You once described living in modern America as like skating on thin ice.

I don't remember saying that, but a lot of being alive is a little like thin ice. There's a sense that you must keep in motion or you'll fall through, that there's never a settled place. You look at European societies, let alone Asian societies, and there seem to be moments of rest, certain roles that people achieve whereby they are honoured by the societies. Think of how a fifty-five-year-old Italian man looks, with his grey hair and wonderfully trim suit – everything just so, everything exactly right on him. He is happy, filling his skin totally. Englishwomen of a certain social class have that same air of filling their skin. Their role, their expectations and their abilities are in exact accord, and there is a satisfaction. Here I don't think we are provided with these niches of final achievement. You always need a little more, are always running, always in motion, always having to prove something. That is I guess what I mean by skating on thin ice.

I believe Americans more than Englishmen have a sense of a void underneath, maybe because we came to a wilderness and there's so much of the land that's still wild and raw: the sense that nature is not a tame collection of fields and villages, not a man-made thing; that we are strangers on the planet and the void is all around us. That's an American idea, a part of the blackness Melville talks about: the American sense of reality that makes one anxious.

Do you feel pressure as a writer to reflect the times you live in?

At thirty I was on the crest of cultural developments: the songs being sung were the ones I was singing and so on. Now I'm fifty-eight, I'm aware of there having been several cultural waves since me. But in general I feel we all reflect the times we are alive in, are products of a certain set of decades and might as well admit it. Although not all of my books have specific years and dates, many of them do. We are all so calendar conscious in this day and age. The fashion designers change fashions, the news media keep producing new stories. It would be silly to try to write a timeless book about a century that is so very time conscious. Just by beginning to particularize, you're going to get into a certain time-specific feeling, no matter whether you want to. I always admired Ivy Compton-Burnett, who always wrote about families who were having their discussions around 1900, and she made it work. We're not too interested in what fifty-eight-year-olds do any more; the interesting age for us as novel readers is the mating age, people, more or less, up to the thirties. It used to be that people or characters were all twenty, surprisingly young in fact.

The English novelist and critic Malcolm Bradbury wrote of you: 'His books are uneasy celebrations of American life, troubled interplays between bright domestic interiors and dark history . . . which sense like the couple themselves that Grace has gone but might be restored with aesthetic care and attention.' Do you believe that Grace has largely disappeared from the American way of life, and are you in the business of restoring it?

I've read that description and it seems just. Maybe it's typically American, however. I was reading another English critic the other day, and she makes the point, about American writing in general, that it's all against a background of utopian expectation. The Puritans came here expecting to create a utopia, so we Americans tend to be very hard on our own society, because it isn't perfect. No society is, but perhaps only this one expects to be perfect. My life has taken me from the Depression, of which I have selected memories, to the Second World War, which I remember quite well, from an adolescent's point of view, as a time when we and the British and some few others were fighting what seemed to be the forces of utter darkness. We emerged triumphant as well as very powerful, so obviously from the high plateau of 1945 there could only be a slide down.

I've been a witness to that long slide, but on a political level I'm probably more pro-American than most American writers, and more willing to give the government the benefit of the doubt. Nevertheless, in the texture of life around me, in the way people behave toward each other, the way the cities look, the amount of garbage of all kinds –

garbage in the trash masher, garbage on the television sets – there's a lot to complain about. I suppose I have registered this in my novels, but basically I try to describe the human condition as I happen to have seen it as an American. If I had been born in England or France, I would be writing about Englishmen or Frenchmen, but I happen to have been handed this subject and love the idea behind America and the natural landscape we were handed – or rather that we grabbed. But there's a lot wrong with the country when you compare it with the ideal we're trying to live by.

With so much talk of censorship in the air at the moment, would you say people's lives are particularly changed or affected by the fictions they read?

Well, mine has been. It's not the only thing that's affected my life, but certainly I've been affected by the books I've read, especially by a book like *Madame Bovary*. One is encouraged to fall in love by reading about people falling in love. In some sense our erotic expectations are shaped by what we read, as our notions of our responsibilities to society are also, I'd say, somewhat shaped. I'm trying to distinguish between my reactions as a citizen, as it were, and my reactions as a writer, because clearly, as a professional writer, I'm especially open to being affected by books. I'm always trying to learn how to do things or always willing to be surprised. But one very good American novel, *The Adventures of Augie March* by Saul Bellow, not only really told me about Chicago, which I'm happy to know, but also excited me and made me feel better about being American.

I think that censors are correct that books, even in this day and age, can be quite important. They're very important in societies where they're censored, and where, of course, it has a reverse effect. The Soviet Union was until recently a country where writers mattered enormously because they were almost the only people who would even begin to tell the truth. They couldn't tell all of the truth, and they often got kicked out and had their books censored, but nevertheless, in both the Soviet Union and Tsarist Russia, they were caretakers of the truth. That will probably change as the pressure on them becomes less and less, and they'll eventually achieve the status of writers in the West, where what they say doesn't seem to matter much. But it does matter to a degree. Our notions of how to be human are to a considerable extent affected by what we read, and even if we don't read we go to the movies, we watch television shows prepared by people who have read, so in a way there's a trickle-down effect of significant writers in that it permeates pop culture and affects the way people act.

If my own books were censored, I'd quite mind it. I'm not used to it, of course. As an American I was raised on the Bill of Rights and so

regard all attempts at censorship, even fairly mild ones, as a great affront. George Steiner kept telling us in his columns that Eastern European writers were better writers than Americans because they had to cope with censorship. This may be, but it's still not a price I want to pay. I don't like the revival of puritanical school boards and library staffs. The pernicious effects aren't so much at the front line, because there are lawyers to fight these suits and the censors often lose, but at a remove, when the publishers start to pull in their horns; they would rather not go to the trouble of seeing a controversial or too sexy text into print. So even when they apparently lose in the courts, the censors win in the publishing houses. I can't think of too many cases where I'd be for a book being censored. In wartime I might consider the right of the government to censor a book that gave away military secrets, but I certainly don't think there's anything sexual that should not be put into print now. I find censorship offensive, and every artist has an obligation to resist it.

What, indeed, about television? I would say that is a real issue. Without wanting to sound too pontifical, the United States has a fairly puritanical past. We were founded by Puritans, we participated in the great Victorian prudery, and in pop culture we have always lagged behind France and Britain with what could be shown. Bare breasts on television, for example, are highly uncommon here, not that I think that seeing the human body will harm children. Presumably they have experience in their own little lives of naked adult bodies. I would say the violence is more alarming than the sex.

I just wouldn't know where to draw the line, though neither would I trust the censors to know what's good and what's bad for us. No sooner had we suppressed violence in television that it might turn out that, psychologically, it was saving lives to have all this surrogate violence. Bruno Bettelheim wrote a very nice book about the violence in fairy stories and how they should not be bowdlerized, should not be made less violent, the violence being the point. It helps the child to exorcize its very real fears. So although I wouldn't say there never can be any censorship, in general I don't trust the people who would administer it and I'd rather take my chances in a censor-free society.

Well-intentioned liberalism, some would claim, breeds ironies, such as that there have been more deaths in abortion clinics than in the whole of the Second World War. How do you, as a writer, cope with such ironies?

As a citizen you take certain stands, like everybody else. You vote for certain candidates, have certain feelings, some strong and some weak, about positions. But almost all things worth discussing have two sides, so there is always more to be said about the paradox of liberalism. I

was struck, during all the Vietnam protests, by the eagerness of American liberals to wish upon the South Vietnamese a kind of government they wouldn't want for themselves. That, to me, seemed paradoxical, but no doubt there's much to be said on the other side. As a writer of fiction, you can certainly enjoy having two opinions or more about everything, and give them each a voice. A novel is a good arena, not to vote, but to express your knowledge of the contradictions.

In writing fiction, I'm not compelled to express a view, but I am allowed to be as alert as possible to the paradox and the tension involved in all these instances. To be human, after all, is to live in a state of tension between opposites, making decisions that are the best of a series of bad choices. So many of our choices have a bad side. It's one of the things in which the Christian doctrine of original sin makes a kind of sense. We're in a position as humans where we cannot but do something wrong, no matter what we try.

At the time of the American involvement in Vietnam, you were misinterpreted and castigated as a 'hawk' and government supporter, but wouldn't a policy of non-interference have matched your sympathies most closely?

I just don't think that the United States, at least in the mid 1960s, could avoid interfering. The Vietnam involvement went back to Truman and Eisenhower, and Johnson was in a way just picking up the overdrawn cheques that other administrations had written. I suppose an all-wise government would intervene only where it could win, and stay out where it would lose, but I don't think there is any government that wise. I could understand perfectly well how we got into it. I could have wished we could get out, but I did differ from many of my dovish confrères in understanding how we got there. It wasn't so different from Korea. We were trying to prevent the southern half of a country from being taken over by the northern half. I admired Truman for looking at China back in 1947 and saying we're not going to get involved with that. We didn't, and it's still running its course. I suppose an all-wise president would have looked at Vietnam and come to the same conclusion, but I did feel sorry for the administration and for the Americans trying to make sense of this muddle, and I was shocked by the amount of hatred for our own government that seemed to be present in the young and the old in this society.

It seemed to me wrong to be enjoying the benefits of being an American and to pretend we could enjoy those benefits while always having clean hands. I don't think you can. Obviously the great power is great in part because it's willing to use force, but all peace, including our personal peace and our right to walk down the street, is based upon a threat of violence somewhere behind us. So I was happy when we got

out of Vietnam and sorry we were there so long, but it seemed to me a more honourable attempt than was alleged by many.

Famous novelists are often called on to sign public petitions for good causes. Do you have any feelings about that sort of pressure being morally intrusive?

It is morally intrusive. On the other hand, if it's a cause I believe in I'm happy to sign. I've signed a number of petitions, but they may not be as common here as in England. I get a lot of requests from Britain, strange to say, to sign things, or to contribute to this and that. I have no quarrel with most liberal causes and I once signed a petition saying that Cassius Clay – Mohammed Ali – should be allowed to be heavyweight champion even though he had resisted going into the army. I got some theatre tickets for doing it, so I remember that particular cause with pleasure.

May I quote you something you wrote that reminded me of Blake: 'The essential self is innocent and when it tastes its own innocence, it knows that it lives for ever'? Can you elaborate on that?

That's one of those feelings you don't have all the time, but there are moments when you seem to be tasting your essential self and the kind of bliss that goes with it. There's a moment near the end of *The White Hotel* by D. M. Thomas in which he describes this moment, a sense of revelation and of everlastingness that I think is a real human sensation for whatever reason. If we ever try in our imagination to delve beneath our circumstances toward our actual selfhood, as in the course of my memoir I did, I think we come upon something that tastes good rather than bad, that tastes delicious. Our basic feeling about cosmic matters is that somehow life is good, and that it is good to be alive and be a witness to the world in its processes. I suppose that's another way of talking about this essential innocence: a certain goodness at the root of things that we feel but can't prove.

You have had to contend with psoriasis, stuttering, claustrophobia, asthma. Have such problems tended to isolate you and turn you into an observer, hence a novelist?

The psoriasis was isolating to a degree where I felt insecure and didn't feel I had hundred-per-cent credentials for being human. I was embarrassed and in some way ashamed, and entered more timidly into the standard human adventures than I would have otherwise. On the other hand, psoriasis is not to be classed with having a real disease or bad eyesight or one arm. I want to keep it in proportion, but it certainly did have an isolating effect and made me feel that I was somehow

singled out; and this feeling of being singled out also helped me in choosing a solitary profession. I think I'm less claustrophobic now than many people. I seem able to fly in aeroplanes and go through tunnels without much of a quiver, whereas some people really can't, so I'm not as claustrophobic, it turns out, as I thought. I've had a pretty successful life by and large, so that's eased me out of some of my neurotic feelings. Asthma was not good, but it seems to have been cat related and did go away. I still think of myself as a basically healthy person.

But you actually say that nothing, not even love and sexual contentment, has reconciled you to your psoriasis.

Certainly the psoriasis has made me doubt my humanity in the ideal way, and that kind of doubt isn't easily erased. The personality you acquire as a youthful psoriasis sufferer will stay with you all of your life. I'm really beyond being made to feel wonderful. My skin insists on having psoriasis. We've tried everything against it, with immediate success, and then a slow leakage back into failure. That's happening now, and now it's returning I realize that with it returns this sense of being unclean and unfit, which I suppose has the effect of channelling me into myself as a writer: the books don't have psoriasis, the books are clean. I've had a lot of love compared to many, but no amount of love would ease away the self-distrust that comes from having had psoriasis at such an early age as I did. I notice that my daughter, who has a little bit of it – it came on in her twenties – doesn't seem to have this really bad feeling. She just accepts it as normal. It's not her fault and doesn't much matter, whereas I feel it is my fault and does matter greatly.

Would you now see the early reviewer, who said of you that you wrote very well but had nothing to say, as having passed an unintended compliment? Auden, whom you admire, once said that art cannot be a midwife to reality, so perhaps writing well is exactly what a novelist should do, and there is no real reason why he should be more right about life than anyone else, is there?

It was a kind of a compliment, and Auden is to a degree right, though he is perhaps more right about poets than prose writers. The basic itch has to be the verbal itch, the wish to play with words; and content follows upon the fascination with words. It is felt of a prose writer in this country that he ought to have something to say, and it is true that you write best when you feel you have something to say and your subject is sufficiently strong to give an energy and thrust to the writing. Therefore I was hurt to think I had nothing to say. It seemed to me I did have things to say, and that they weren't the things that had been said already. The trouble with that kind of critic is that he thinks

everybody is going to write like Dreiser or James Jones, but I had my own message and my own particular slant, and I believe the fundamental desire, without which you do not have a writer, is the wish to make books and to find something to say. So I suppose it wasn't such a bad thing to have said about me, in a way.

Talking about the way a writer's work is reproduced endlessly, you called it 'a mode of self-assertion that leaves the cowardly perpetrator hidden and out of harm's way', but isn't the opposite true too – once something is in print there is no going back and you are subject to all the vagaries of taste and opinion?

On the one hand you are out of the rain, as we were saying earlier, but on the other you're getting all wet constantly because you've extended yourself, you've thrown this hostage out there. It's not you, it's cut off from you. It's like a baby, only even more remote than a baby. Once the publication has occurred, your mind is on other things and you don't really see the effects it's having on any but a few people. You read a few reviews, you get a few letters, you see the sales reports. Otherwise the book just fades away and you don't have to harvest the results. It's not like a personal act where you must be there to reap the grain, so it's an extension of you, but a relatively painless one. I've always had a distinct feeling that I am myself John Updike and have a certain history and birth date and a certain body, but that what my books say is quite detached from that, is in a way the real me. I try to be honest, to describe what it's like to be a person, an American male, but it's not really me and I don't feel endangered by the books as they make their own way in the world.

You asserted that: 'My assets as a novelist I take to be my taste for American life acquired in Shillington.' What is it that is really characteristic of American life?

Having written that, I wonder if it is true. Maybe I've had enough American life. We are certainly becoming more European as we become more civilized and the wilderness recedes. Yet Europe has learned many lessons from America in the past forty-five years, but the difference, I suppose, is that this country was based upon the notion of equality. It was there at the very start in the Puritan settlements, was reinforced by the Constitution and the Bill of Rights, and the notion we are all equal and must prove ourselves is still there. So we are not hopelessly handicapped by any conditions of class, even of race, though certainly to be black in this country isn't an easy row to hoe. Then there's the fact that so much of our culture is in the way of being lowest-common-denominator culture. On the one hand, it's vulgar and simple minded, on the other there's a kind of energy. Think of the Hollywood movies

of the 1930s and 1940s, which were mass culture with a vengeance, yet they now seem works of art in their style. We're able to see that in fact this was an art form and that it can't be done now. I like the levelling that happened in America and the fact that any structure is going to be put up from scratch. You can begin again, and every generation begins again. That's what I would say the difference is between America and Europe.

In view of some of the rather unsavoury aspects of Christianity through the centuries, what now remains of Christianity in your view that seems worth clinging to?

Well, it says: 'Fear not.' It tries to assuage our basic dread, to placate our fear that comes from being a death-foreseeing animal. The New Testament also holds out the idea of people being equal in the sight of God, and that is as useful a way to try to form society as any. It obviously holds up a number of other ideals, not all of which it has always lived up to, but I like the need, the empowering yes of it. In my own life I've taken courage from a sense that I was doing something useful and relatively harmless, but to some extent the energy has all been generated by faith, and by unreasonable faith, because it's a long way from Shillington to the Ritz Carlton. And so, having lived by faith, I intend to be more indulgent of faith.

I'd say my Christianity is a way of coping with life. It regularizes my week, puts something in it that is entirely voluntary. I get to see a lot of other people who've also gotten up on a Sunday morning and put on their good clothes, and it holds up a set of standards that aren't strictly worldly. It says there are other standards, and it's healthy for a writer to realize that what matters so much maybe isn't the results we get but the spirit in which we do something. Sometimes the best success comes to people who don't try too hard, and Christianity has enabled me maybe not to try too hard but to try enough.

I wouldn't say I've found that I become more religious as I get older. I was most religious when I was in my twenties and most scared. The older I get the less scared I seem to be, and in a sense the less needy. Yet I'm still a churchgoing Protestant, though it's been many years since I read theology with any real passion. I used to read a fair amount of it. I was so desperate to find some place where I could stand. Now I seem to think I'm standing on a place, but the rug could be pulled out from under me at any moment.

I don't think a society should enforce religion. In this country there's a lot of constitutional language saying it should not, though America does seem a little too pious. All the presidents talk about God, for example, as though he's right next door, even though some of them

have not been very religious, or at least very faithful churchgoers. It seems very bad when a country professes an official religion, and I would resist that here, and resist even the tendencies toward it. Government of the society presided over should be minimal. It should be the least number of laws that can create order, and everything else should be left up to human initiative and human emotion, even human whim. A society that tries to create goodness is in danger of becoming a tyranny. This constitution, as I understand it, doesn't expect people to be good but allows for them to be bad up to a certain point and then says the rest must step in. This seems a more realistic approach than the kind of total package the ayatollahs of Iran, say, would like to enforce, or which you find, for that matter, in Mao's China, where a total lifestyle, a total set of directives is offered you by the state.

For the last ten years or so you have displayed signs of anxiety at growing old. Are you fearful for your art, or is it more to do with mortality?

One doesn't like being mortal, and one certainly doesn't like feeling one's body stiffen and age under one. I'm not in bad shape at fifty-eight, but there are things I used to be able to do that I can't. I used to be able to hold a broomstick in my two hands and jump up in the air and over it while still holding on. This is not a great accomplishment, but it was something I could do, and at a party in the late hours I would sometimes do it and astound the other party-goers. When I was little I used to wonder how these big people around me could stand being so close to death, and still walk around, smiling, being silly and cheerful, reading the newspaper. How could they hack it? Now I'm in that position, I see that you hack it in part because you have no choice.

I don't think I'm abnormally aware of being old. My wife has a healthy and brisk attitude towards the ageing process. She doesn't deny it, but she thinks life is there to be lived and our duty, as long as we're alive, is to enjoy it in some way. A lot of writers are dead at my age, and certainly many are dead as writers, so some of that may be a pep talk to myself, saying don't give up, don't stop trying, don't get complacent, keep trying to learn. You have fewer grey cells, but maybe you can make better use of the ones you have. There are advantages to being fifty-eight. A lot of decisions have been made already, a lot is behind you. Your child-raising years are over, you've made your career choices. In a way your mind is clearer to concentrate on meaningful things. I'm aware that I tend to make my men older than myself. I put a lot of them in their sixties, for some reason. My present novel is all about getting old and useless, though I myself still feel in pretty good shape.

Do you still feel you have an unfulfilled task?

I haven't many regrets, things I'd go back and change. I've certainly behaved badly on occasions and foolishly on others, but the basic decisions of my life were the choice of profession, where to live, which women to marry, which college to go to. I've been lucky in those decisions. I think they've been the right ones, and the world has tended to confirm me in that thought.

I have hopes of writing books better than the ones I've written. I do feel I have something still to say, and to locate that thing and say it seems possible and worth doing. I'm in a position in which what I write will get published, will get some attention, so I'm well located and should try to measure up to the opportunity I still have.

I'd like to think I'm pretty adventurous still. A certain safety enshrouds me now. I can't escape safety to a degree, especially since American writers, as we've said, burn out so notoriously that if I do nothing it'll be no great disgrace; I'll merely be behaving like most of my predecessors. If I look back on my novels, they've all had an element of self-challenge. They're all stunts in a way, they all had some trick at their heart. I don't know if that's good or bad, but I was able to write them because the trick amused me.

Fiction is potentially frivolous, and since I came from a line of practical people, doing something so impractical and making a living at it makes me feel guilty in a way. My initial ambition was aimed a little under where I've actually landed. I wanted merely to be a cartoonist or a magazine writer and to make a living at it. Instead I've found myself catapulted into trying to write literature, really trying to write lasting and significant stuff. I suppose the kind of language I use is a way of protecting myself from the true awesomeness of trying to write really well. It doesn't mean I don't try to write well, but I have to frame it in some way a little lightheartedly or bashfully to make it possible to be productive, because it's quite possible to get overawed by writing. The only final response to the awesomeness of what you're trying to do is silence, and I don't want to become silent.

SIR FRED WARNER

Frederick Archibald Warner was born in 1919 and educated at the Royal Naval College, Dartmouth, and Magdalen College, Oxford. He was a Royal Navy midshipman and served as a lieutenant-commander during the war. In 1946 he joined the British Foreign Office where he worked as a private secretary until his promotion to first secretary (Moscow) in 1958. He has been head of chancery, Burma (1956–8), Greece (1958–60), ambassador to Laos (1965–7), ambassador to the UN (1969–72) and ambassador to Japan (1972–5). He was a Euro MP from 1979–84 and since then has worked in the business world (Guinness Peat Group, Chloride Group Ltd and General Reinsurance Co. Ltd). He married Simone de Ferranti in 1971 and has two sons and a step-daughter.

You were a posthumous child and consequently never knew your father. How did that affect you?

It affected me very much. It meant that, for the first six years of my life, I was alone with my mother, enormously attached to her and very jealous of anybody who came near. There were just the two of us. When I eventually got a stepfather, I think it was too late to feel the full influence of a father. Although he was an extraordinarily kind and sensitive man who was very nice to me, he could never really replace a true father. You don't notice at the time, because you're yourself and you don't know what you're missing. It is only much later that I've realized how important it is to have a father to help make certain essential patterns in your life when you're still very young. I often, when I was in my twenties, thirties and forties, turned to the photograph of my father when I was in a difficult situation and said, 'You were never there to help me. Can you help me now?'

But I can't remember ever being unhappy as a child. I think you remember the good things and it is difficult to remember the bad. I do remember, however, being very worried in the early years after my mother remarried that she and my stepfather would want to get rid of me, that I no longer had a place in the nest and they would want to kick me out or send me away somewhere, or even smother me with a pillow. It was a feeling that I was no longer really needed. The fears were completely unjustified. They couldn't have been nicer to me.

I couldn't say I remained close to my mother, because I think we all tend to grow away from our mothers; and if you then lead a life full of travel and adventure, as I did, and move into completely new worlds, you do move away from your mother. But I always went on seeing a good deal of her right up until her death.

Were you one of those children who were sent away to school very young?

Absolutely. One day when I was eight I was dressed in a tweed suit with long trousers, a shirt with a stiff collar and a black tie. A blue overcoat was put over me, a bowler hat was put on my head, and an umbrella was hung on my arm. 'You're now a gentleman,' I was told, 'and you're going off to lead your own life at school.' I was absolutely petrified.

Oh, no, of course one didn't feel hard done by. All the other children I knew were having exactly the same thing happen to them, and the average person doesn't resent what he sees happening to everybody else around him. So off one went, dreading the thought of going to school but assuming that it was quite inevitable and one was simply doing what everybody else was doing, so it must be all right.

On the whole it was all right. Of course, one used to be terribly homesick for a few days at the beginning of the term, but then things settled down and I enjoyed learning and got a lot of pleasure from it. I loved being with other children. I didn't much like playing football or cricket, and I used to get very bored and rather cold in winter, but again you accepted that as inevitable. You just tried not to be humiliated by not playing very well.

From school you went straight to the Royal Naval College. Was that family tradition?

I suppose it was. It was also that I was becoming very independent. I'd read a great number of adventure books – things like *Mr Midshipman Easy, Peter Simple, Coral Island* and so on, and I believed that going into the navy somehow represented an escape. By then I had two younger half-brothers, the house was full of nannies and governesses, and I wanted to get away from all of that and saw the navy as a very dramatic way of escaping. Of course, my father had been in the navy, my stepfather was in the navy, my uncle had been in the navy, as had both my godfathers. I'd grown up in an officer-class family entirely devoted to the navy.

When you started at the Royal Naval College in 1932, did an eventual war with Germany seem inevitable?

Oh, we didn't think about it. One assumed that one day one would be fighting a war, and that wars just happened, but it didn't seem close in those days, not at all.

What took you up to Oxford in 1937? Had you decided the navy was not for you, or was it for in-service training?

Oxford wasn't in-service training. What happened was that my parents were living abroad and I spent a lot of my holidays with an aunt and a cousin who lived in Cornwall. My cousin was very intellectual. His friends were philosophy students and historians. He read a great deal, and under his influence I started to read from the age of fifteen onwards. By the time I was seventeen I had read an enormous amount and become very interested in contemporary affairs. By then I had got the message that we were heading fast towards a war, and I felt that my life in the navy, although I was proud of the navy, was going to be constricted and narrow. I passionately wanted to get a full education and to go to university. Before that, from Dartmouth, I went off to sea and joined the Mediterranean Fleet as a midshipman, but was already thinking, this can't be right, I must somehow get to Oxford.

Forgive me now if I spend a bit of time on this story, because it actually is rather fascinating. I went to my parents and said I wanted to leave the navy. My stepfather was horrified, though my mother thought that whatever I wanted must be right. Then we discovered that I was in a trap because when, at the age of twelve, you took your examination to get into the navy, your parents signed a declaration saying that, so long as you were still under the age of consent, they would not give their permission for you to leave the service. And in those days the age of consent was twenty-one. By the time you were that age as a sub-lieutenant, you were already in receipt of the King's commission and so could not resign. You had to ask permission of the Board of Admiralty to be allowed to resign, and the board was certainly not going to make concessions at that stage. The had mobilized every ship they could find. Every old hulk was being repaired at the dockyards. They needed every man and boy they could lay their hands on, and certainly didn't want to see me disappear. 'Certainly not,' they said. 'There's no question of this boy being allowed to go.' I had a perfectly good record – rather a good record, in fact – and they could see no reason why they should lose me. So there I was, having moved into a position of serfdom at the age of twelve when I made my decision. There seemed to be no way out of it.

I became very moody and difficult, and my stepfather got frightened and went to see the commander-in-chief. 'I'm afraid this boy will do something silly,' he said. An enchanting man called John Godfrey, who acquired a kind of anonymous fame because he became head of Naval Intelligence and was Ian Fleming's employer and the one used as a model for M in the Bond books, was then captain of the *Repulse*, a great battle cruiser which had just been refitted and come out to the Mediterranean. 'Well,' he said, 'send this boy to me and I will look after him for a year. If at the end of that year he still wants to leave the navy, I think you should use your influence to get him out, but I will do everything in

my power to keep him in.' So I and another midshipman were shipped to the *Repulse*, where we had the most marvellous time. We were treated as adults, and great effort was made to retain my curiosity and interest, but at the end of the year I still said no, I wanted to go to Oxford, and that was that. They didn't know how to get rid of me. There was no provision for it. So I was discharged from the navy as temperamentally unsuitable, and that was the end of my naval career.

What was the university atmosphere like at that time?

Very political. It was also the period when intellectuals tended to be very left, and there was the Left Book Club – all those books in yellow jackets, full of misinformation about world affairs, which we all read avidly and believed implicitly. It was a moment of political ferment and people were very indignant about what was happening in Spain. I was a small hero because I'd been to Spain in the navy and had been landed at Barcelona in charge of two sailors to maintain the weather station there when the fighting was going on in Catalonia.

Of course, we were nearly all good Conservatives at university, but we were all anti-appeasement, pro-Churchill and keen to see rearmament. At the end of that time there was a famous election at which Quintin Hogg, now Lord Hailsham, was defeated by Lindsay, the Master of Balliol, and because Quintin Hogg seemed to stand for appeasement and Lindsay seemed to stand for standing up to Germany, it was one issue on which left-wing and right-wing students could unite.

Your six years in motor torpedo boats with coastal command must have been very hazardous. Did you accept that you might have to die for your country?

Oh, yes, without question, and of course I very nearly did. I didn't start in coastal boats at all, but in a dreadful thing called an armed merchant cruiser, which was a passenger ship that had been on the Cape run. It had a few guns mounted on it and was supposed to protect convoys. The convoys gathered either at Sierra Leone or at Dakar in Senegal and we would escort them up and into the Clyde and then go back for another lot. We were totally incapable of defending them, and on our third run inevitably we got torpedoed. I was fast asleep at the time. I rushed up on deck in my black silk pyjamas, most unsuitably clad for battle, and no sooner did I arrive on the upper deck than I saw another torpedo coming towards me and *woof* – up it went, and I was enveloped in a huge water spout. I just rolled up as if playing in a rugger match, was carried over to the other side of the ship and into the water and nearly came to a bad end. It was very very cold, and after about twenty minutes, when I felt I couldn't go on much longer, a lifeboat appeared. I shouted for help and the merchant service officer in charge said, 'We

can't take you in. The regulations only allow us to carry 110 and I've got 110 on board already.' So then there was a tremendous rebellion in the boat, and they all started shouting, 'Let him in, let him in! Come on, pull him out!' I was pulled out of the water by a couple of sailors and whopped into the bottom of the boat, and so survived that one.

After that I joined coastal forces, and in 1942 we went over an acoustic mine, and the following year were sunk by gunfire off the coast of Elba. That was a real disaster. It was after Salerno, and we were three vessels attacking a German coastal convoy that was carrying supplies south to Ostia to where the Germans were trying to contain our forces at Anzio. We went in and fired our torpedoes, but there was a terrific amount of return fire. My boat was totally destroyed. I got into the water, having been shot through both legs, and held on to a raft which I pushed around for an hour or two until we were picked up and taken to Corsica. It was still occupied by the Italians, though the Germans had withdrawn, and I was taken to hospital in Bastia. The Italians were desperate, having been left behind by the Germans, though they were very kind to me. They had no anaesthetics, but they operated on my legs to take the shell splinters out while four Arabs held me down. (God knows what they were doing there.) Then I was put into one of the wards in a nunnery.

One day as I was lying there, we suddenly heard screams and an Italian soldier was brought in. Since I spoke very good Italian I could understand him, and he was shouting, 'My stomach's been blown away! A pig threw a hand grenade at me, a pig threw a hand grenade.' We all thought he was mad, but he wasn't. When the Germans abandoned their camp, they left a lot of hand grenades lying about, and a pig that wandered into the camp picked up a hand grenade, started to chew it, decided it wasn't very good and spat it out. But the ring caught on its tooth, so the hand grenade fell to the ground, fully charged. The Italian soldier was standing near by and got it full blast.

What sort of duties were attached to your post in Moscow after the war?

What did a diplomat do? Well, I was in what is called the Chancery; that is to say, the political section of the embassy. My job was to report on what was going on in the Soviet Union. It was a very difficult thing to do. You could report what they said was going on in the Soviet Union, but you also had to know how to interpret that, and this immediately raised the whole issue of espionage and so on. When you go to another country, you expect to be able to walk around, look at things and form your own conclusions. In the Soviet Union, you were not allowed to walk around. You were not allowed to travel, except in very limited ways, or to ask questions of a Soviet citizen. In their eyes, that was an act of espionage. The result was that, instead of asking

questions and getting answers, you had to build up very slowly a layer of knowledge from hundreds and thousands of tiny little facts that were rather like dust circling in an attic. Tiny little observations and facts would drift into one's range of vision and settle down, and after a while you would have some kind of soil in which your knowledge could grow. However, eventually I came to the conclusion it wasn't just that the Russians weren't allowed to tell you anything; most of them didn't know anything.

There was a great temptation to travel since one wanted to see as much of the Soviet Union as possible. Although most of the country was out of bounds to foreigners, about a third of it was open in theory, except, of course, that they didn't want you to go there, so you couldn't get railway tickets. We developed the most extraordinary techniques to travel and get a feeling for what was really going on. In the end one saw a great deal more of the Soviet Union than they would perhaps have wished.

I was terribly conscious of the poverty and persecution. It was really very obvious. They couldn't isolate you. My friends and I spent a lot of time going into what were called *stolovye* – popular restaurants, usually in basements or ground floors of office blocks, where you'd go in, sit at a table and keep quite quiet. All around you people were getting drunk, because that's what happened. Every evening, wherever you were in the Soviet Union, you were surrounded by men getting drunk. You also knew that you were the focus of interest for everybody in the room, but nobody was going to talk to you because it was too dangerous. Equally you knew that, after a while, someone would get so drunk that he would lose his sense of caution. You would look at somebody and suddenly hook him, and he'd come shambling over and sit down and start talking. After twenty minutes the waiters would grow very agitated and come and say, 'Move away from this table. You are bothering these foreign gentlemen. They do not want trouble with someone like you.' Another twenty minutes on, a policeman would be seen hovering in the door and a waiter would come and whisper to the man, 'The police want you,' and the man would disappear and you'd never see him again.

In this way, and in railway carriages and station buffets, where so much of Soviet life went on, and still does for all I know – Tolstoy died in a station buffet, people got married in them and so on – you would talk to people. But eventually I realized that my view of the Soviet Union was seen entirely through the eyes of people who were drunk. Railway carriages seemed to have a very loosening effect on the Russians. Trains went so slowly that it took three days to get somewhere like Tiflis, or four days to Tomsk. People boarded the train in Moscow, and everybody took off their clothes and put on pyjamas over their

underwear, and this somehow seemed to make you all friends. You'd roll slowly across the flat landscape for hour after hour, day after day, and get to know each other rather well.

Did the Russians have preferences among Western governments?

I wouldn't say so, but they were really interested in what the Americans thought, because they saw the Americans as a great danger, both as an obstacle to their plans for overrunning the rest of Europe and genuinely as a force which might attack them. They were much less interested in us, and only considered European countries as a way of putting leverage on the Americans or getting information about American intentions.

I think the Russians were on the defensive because the whole of their ideological background led them to suppose that, if the capitalist powers ever felt strong enough, they would attack. But they believed equally that capitalism was doomed and in its last stages, and that if they played their hand right, one by one the capitalist countries would fall. By 1950, Stalin had understood something very important, and he enunciated a principle which was based on experience of what happened in Yugoslavia, where Tito worked his own revolution then began to defy the Russians. Stalin said that true revolution could only take place in the presence of Soviet armies. What he meant was, you were only a truly revolutionary country if you were in the orbit of the Soviet Empire.

Stalin saw this very clearly, and I don't think he was particularly anxious to have revolution sparked off somewhere like Portugal, where he couldn't deal with it. What he really wanted was to upset Germany first, exactly as Lenin had always done, Germany being the real target for the next advance of Soviet power. At the same time, the idea was slowly to strangle the capitalist powers by cutting them off from their sources of raw materials. In other words, you went to Africa and Asia, you encouraged the Vietnamese, got at such régimes as the Gold Coast (as Ghana then was), Somalia, Tanzania or wherever, and tried to create in that part of the world socialist states that would deny supplies. Very unrealistic, but the Russians believed in the tactic strongly and pursued it under the banner of peaceful coexistence.

Russia has clearly used its embassies as spy bases. What has been the relationship between our own embassies and the security services?

The Russians, of course, used everybody and everything, not only their embassies. They used trade offices, TASS, cultural missions. The proportion of members on Soviet delegations to the United Nations who are really there simply to use it as a marvellous base for operations in the United States is huge. Having been a diplomat, I'm still bound by the Official Secrets Act, and it's not a matter I can discuss, but

certainly I can tell you that the relationship between Britain's foreign service and Intelligence services bears no resemblance to the Russian equivalent.

Was the great flirtation with communism on the part of many of your contemporaries because democracy hadn't seemed to offer adequate resistance during the rise of fascism?

Among educated people there was a sizeable number who felt, on the one hand, that the Russians were the only ones who were seriously opposing the rise of fascism and were, on the other, shocked by the great depression and unemployment. Quite a few had, by the end of the war, been through that stage, but it was those who hung on, or who got themselves so deeply implicated during the war that they were unable to give it up and escape, who caused so much trouble later.

How shocked were you when it became apparent that Maclean, Philby and Burgess were Russian agents?

Terribly because, although I didn't know Maclean and Philby, I knew Burgess quite well. I once shared an office with him for something like eighteen months. He was rather a human wreck. No, wreck is the wrong word – a sort of human disaster. He was untidy and slovenly and his habits were bad, but nevertheless he didn't appear to be more left wing than many members of parliament and ministers in various Labour governments at that time. He seemed vaguely a slightly left-of-centre socialist. He was certainly fascinated by the 1917 revolution, but then he was an historian and that, after all, was a great historical event. Otherwise he never wasted time glorifying the Soviet Union or seemed obsessed by Russia or even particularly interested in it. I can't remember us ever discussing it much, except in historical terms, but he did use to make a tremendous case for the advanced liberal view of human relations and politics. I remember his quoting that thing of E. M. Forster's about rather betraying your country than one of your friends. I said, 'But Guy, your're absolutely mad, don't you realize it is the motto of every corrupt Greek politician, and you're supposed to be an idealist.' In the end, of course, he betrayed both his country and his friends. I was shocked by that.

Burgess was a very clever man, but one with so little self-discipline and a life so badly co-ordinated that his talents were completely wasted. Hector McNeil, Minister of State for the Foreign Office, originally engaged him because he had known him as a journalist and found him rather fascinating. His very educated style of conversation, his knowledge of English history, his ability to quote and so on all attracted Hector, who engaged him to write speeches. Not that he wrote very

good speeches, but he got the stuff down and then Hector would do it in his own words. It was in that capacity that he worked in Hector's office during the year and a half I knew him. I wouldn't have said he was a great intellectual. I believe he had been a brilliant student at Eton, and started off very well at Cambridge, but I would say his whole private life became so disorganized that he never made much of whatever talents he had.

What was your feeling about Germany when you returned from Moscow to help with running the German desk?

That we needed the Germans very badly; that we needed a stable, strong but not an overpowering Germany. In any case, the British are not a very vengeful people. They certainly used not to be, and by then the past was the past and people were ready to forget and forgive. My duty during the four years I was in that department was to negotiate a peace treaty with Germany. Of course, we couldn't negotiate a peace treaty because the Russians wouldn't agree to one, so instead we negotiated the Bonn agreements whereby Britain, the United States and France terminated the occupation of Western Germany and settled all outstanding matters left over from the war between themselves. I spent several years negotiating these, and carried them right through to the end. It was a very important chapter in post-war history, and I was glad to have been deeply involved.

It's not true to say that Germany was then being run by the Allies. We had occupation troops there, and we still have, and we had high commissioners rather than ambassadors. The high commissioners did have certain powers, but they weren't used to run Germany. By then these were being used simply to warn the Germans and stop them if they appeared about to do something against Allied interests or policy. In fact the three Western Allies had great confidence in Adenauer and his government, felt they were doing the right thing and were quite prepared to leave the running of Germany to them. But the reserve powers which they exercised from time to time later became absolutely essential during the Berlin Blockade.

After Russia and Germany there was Burma and Greece. It seems strange to an outsider how anyone can, at the drop of a hat, switch attention between such different cultures.

I didn't do it at the drop of a hat. I was in Burma nearly two years, and quite honestly there wasn't a great deal of political work. The Burmese had got their independence and there wasn't much you could do to influence or help them at that stage other than develop aid programmes. I spent a great deal of time travelling around, trying to

understand the country, and I did get a deep knowledge of Burma. When I was there, there were something like forty-nine different administrative districts and I visited forty-eight of them. I sailed right down the coast and back in a schooner; I crossed the frontier into India and spent a fortnight with the chief of the biggest tribe in the Chin hills, walking with him among his people. I went right across from the house of one princeling to another in each of their little semi-independent fiefdoms; I lived in monasteries with priests. I became very much bound up with Burmese broadcasting and made musical and English programmes for them.

By the time I left I knew as much about Burma as any foreigner could. I loved Burma. It's the most beautiful place. I found the people extremely engaging. But the night before I left I gave a huge party. There were all sorts of people there – government officials, professors from the university, schoolteachers, civil servants, students, businessmen. One guest was a professor of history. He took me by the arm, sat me down on the back step and said, 'You're going away tomorrow, Fred, and I will never see you again, I'm sure. I'd love to do something for you, but I'm poor and I've nothing to give you, so I'm going to give you a piece of knowledge. I can tell you that Ne Win is determined to take over this country, and it'll be very shortly after you leave, more likely a matter of weeks than of months. There will be a military *coup* and we are going to take over the government.'

Before I left I said to the British ambassador, 'Ne Win is going to take over this country,' and he replied, 'What absolute rubbish. Why do you listen to that kind of thing?' But of course the professor had been right. The thing which saddened me was that I had been rather close to Ne Win through being tremendous friends with his wife Kitty, who was a terrifically attractive and lively girl. I used to go and play tennis with her two or three times a week and rather got to know him too. He didn't seem like a man of destiny, nor like the cruel tyrant he was to turn into. He seemed an ambitious and headstrong but not a particularly remarkable officer who had been a post office clerk and, through the insurgent brigades, finally arrived as commander-in-chief of the Burma army. The last time I saw him was the day after the party, and I never met him or Kitty again. I was surprised and distressed when I saw the way things were going. Of course, he immediately arrested all my friends and put them into gaol.

In 1962, Averell Harriman went to Vienna to see Ne Win about helping with an Indo-China settlement. When he returned he said to me, 'General Ne Win is unbelievable. I simply can't make him out.' Averell had gone to his hotel and been met by his head of security, who took him aside and said, 'Before you see the general, Mrs Ne Win wants to see you.' So he was taken into a little sitting room, and there was

Kitty, who said, 'Oh, I'm so glad to see you, Mr Ambassador, because I'm very worried about the general. He says he's here for political reasons, but I will let you into a secret. We're actually here so that we can have psychiatric treatment. He's going to a very celebrated Burmese doctor, and we're hoping it's going to help. Be very careful what you say to him and don't ask too many questions.' Averell thought that pretty odd, and then went in to see the general, who said, 'Mr Ambassador, before we start discussing our business, there's one thing I want to say to you. Later Kitty's going to come and join us, and if you think she's a bit strange, I have to tell you that the real reason we're here is not for politics. We are all very worried about her. She's going to see a psychiatrist, and we're hoping she's going to be all right.'

Hasn't the diplomatic service become a lot less safe as an occupation over the past twenty years?

There is much less respect and terrorists sometimes think of diplomats as obvious targets. But I don't think we should fool ourselves into thinking that embassies have always led a sacrosanct life. It's always been a tremendous struggle to preserve the idea of diplomatic immunity, and if you read any history at all, you will see the terrible things that have happened to ambassadors from earliest times. Old Regulus went as an ambassador to Carthage and ended up rolling downhill in a barrel full of stones.

Do you envisage a time when the rules on diplomatic immunity will have to be different?

I think the rules have rather changed. For instance, in the old days the police just used to collect parking tickets. Now they clamp diplomatic cars if they have a sufficient number of charges against them. It's very difficult to know what to do about diplomatic bags where, say, drug smuggling is suspected. If you open somebody else's diplomatic bags, then you must expect that they're going to open yours. I personally think the whole concept of diplomatic secrecy is highly exaggerated. There are very few political or diplomatic secrets which are real secrets. I've always found that if you want to know what's going on in a country, the best way to find out is to cultivate very good relationships with sufficient numbers of people so that you can go to somebody and ask, 'What on earth is going on?' Very often they will tell you. To spend hundreds of thousands of pounds on maintaining an elaborate system of agents to try and find out what's happening in a ministry of foreign affairs is a total waste of time.

When you were in Laos, were you sympathetic to American difficulties in the Vietnam War?

Yes, very sympathetic, because they were obviously making such a mess of it. We had managed a very difficult situation in Malaysia successfully, had dealt with it and put down a dangerous rebellion by military means. We had also dealt with a very unpleasant emergency in Borneo, though it attracted little attention in the press. I was in charge of the South-East Asian policy, and we had ten brigades out there. We had confronted Sukarno and been largely instrumental in his final downfall, so I felt that we really knew a bit about how to deal with that sort of situation.

The Americans had no way of winning by just flying around in aeroplanes. The war needed to be won on the ground, not up in the air. Nowadays we see masses of films which portray Americans involved in ground warfare. I can only tell you that, during my time, I saw very little of it. Most of the ground fighting was being done by Vietnamese or by hill tribesmen. I thought the Americans mishandled the whole war. A lot of their officers and representatives were crassly stupid. The people I admired were young Americans – boys and girls – who went out to Vietnam on the various aid and support programmes and whom you'd find in small Vietnamese villages trying to run an agricultural programme – very exposed, in some danger of their lives. These were marvellous people. If the thing had been in their hands there might have been some solution.

One of the reasons why the Americans couldn't deal with the war was because they couldn't distinguish who were the enemy and who were their friends. That was one of the advantages we had in Malaya: the enemy were Chinese, our friends were Malays, and they don't look much alike. But the Americans could never distinguish, and of course, even if you can, once you're blanket bombing, the distinction becomes irrelevant anyway. You're going to hit everybody. The Americans never seemed to understand that this was not a part of the great advance of international communism, not one of those *Time* magazine things where huge arrows show communists advancing to the heart of Thailand and that kind of thing. The war was about the Vietnamese; it was about the régime in Hanoi being the successor to the French régime they had defeated at Dien Bien Phu. Their policy was to restore the hegemony of Hanoi over the whole of Indo-China: not just over South Vietnam, but over Cambodia and Laos as well.

When I was in Laos, the Vietnamese invaded and occupied half the country. They made constant excursions down into the Mekong river valley. The Lao hated the Vietnamese, and therefore were happy enough to accept American protection and see American bombers going over

to bomb Laotian territory, aiming for the Vietnamese and the Ho Chi Min Trail. The Lao weren't very good fighters and not very interested, while the hill people were serious fighters. But forgetting all the mistakes, the horrors, the cruelties, what always makes me smile is the absurd contradiction of the war. The communists in Hanoi were there to extend the concept of an industrial socialist society to the whole of Indo-China. The Americans were there to protect the way of life of the indigenous farming community, to help them to maintain their village identity and their livelihoods as prosperous farmers. And what was the outcome? The Vietnamese in the north, far from industrializing, gave up all attempts at it and were left at the end of the war with an extremely poor peasant economy in the Red River delta and no industry of any kind. The Americans created an enormous semi-literate industrial proletariat around their ports and bases, which meant that, when they left, all the skilled workers were in the south, sitting unemployed round abandoned American bases, with all the peasants undisturbed up in the north. It was a ridiculous contradiction, and it shows how very little control people have over their destiny once they set out on great causes. Who knows where it'll land them?

After Laos you became a minister with NATO, then went to the United Nations in New York. To which did you feel able to contribute most?

I probably contributed more to the United Nations than at NATO. The NATO Council had very limited powers. Its strength is in its military forces, and the council simply provides political guidance. I have to say that, when I was there, I don't think it was functioning properly. Its most interesting work went on in the nuclear policy group, which was trying to develop some intelligible nuclear strategy. But, as a means of influencing Allied policy, I thought the NATO Council rather a sham. When the Russians invaded Prague, our response was particularly feeble.

The United Nations is really a terrible body. By the time I got there, it had 125 members, I think, and was incredibly expensive. Every year it would meet for three or four months. An enormous amount of rubbish would be talked and it would pass a lot of resolutions calling for vastly greater expenditure. Every time the United Nations passed a resolution, somebody had to carry it out, which meant a lot more money, while most of its efforts were wildly misdirected. I used to lead in the General Assembly against the annual Russian so-called 'peace offensive' – always a major bit of rubbishy propaganda and always rather fun to expose. Generally speaking, the General Assembly was just something which had to be done. It was a great international institution, and it was better to keep it going than turn your back on it, but

what was worth while was the work of the Security Council. In those days it had a genuine peace-keeping role.

I got very involved in the Middle Eastern dispute – specifically the Israeli-Palestinian conflict – and became quite convinced (which you may say was defeatist and bad), that there was no present solution. The best thing to do was therefore simply to go on pretending that there was a solution and to keep looking for it. But though I could see no possible signs of an agreement at that stage, it didn't mean that you couldn't go into all the details of what an agreement could comprehend. There was a four-power committee on which I was the British representative, and we would go along the frontier, village by village, well by well, tree by tree, looking at what the settlement might one day comprise. That's very different from, and a long way away from getting a settlement.

Today I wouldn't say that there's no solution. Of course there's a solution. All problems get solved historically eventually. What one hopes is that they're not solved by some disaster like Titus destroying the Temple in Jerusalem, sending the Jews into exile, or anything of that sort – like the Mongols suddenly arising and destroying the whole of Middle Eastern civilization.

You have always been a keen traveller. What drives you to it?

Curiosity. I want to go and see. I find it impossible to pass an open door and not look in to see what's happening inside. I have a great feeling for society, for how people behave, the way in which they lead their lives. I like very much to sit among people who are leading their lives in their way, which isn't mine, and watch them, talk to them, listen to them. I love to be out in the forest, miles from anywhere, to be in the mountains, to be floating down a river. All of that gives me immense excitement and pleasure. I don't mind discomfort; don't mind the heat at all. I'm the eleventh generation of a family who lived in the tropics for three hundred years. My ancestor, Thomas Warner, founded the first settlement in the Lesser Antilles, and went to St Kitts in 1623. My family were there from then until my father's death in 1917.

Is it possible to single out one or two remarkable memories from your countless journeys?

Oh yes, many. Things like managing to throw off the dozens of policemen on one's trail in the Soviet Union; nipping into a taxi and making it drive across the steppes to some other town, and knowing that you were away from all the oppressive régime for a few hours before they caught up with you again. Or catching a train right up into the mountains of Georgia to a little mining town and sleeping in the miners' doss

house, knowing that everybody was looking for you down below in the valley.

Moments of great beauty in Burma, walking in the Chin hills with rhododendrons and magnolias all in flower; whole valleys full of golden blossoming trees. Walking day after day from village to village, sitting down at night while they danced and played their pipes. It was so beautiful, so peaceful, so utterly remote in these great forests.

Or, in Laos, going on picnics. Laotians love picnics, it's one art form they've developed to the highest standard. You go up the river and come round a bend, and there will be a great limestone crag rising out of the jungle where they'll have built a little pavilion of bamboo standing in the water at the base of the mountain. It will be all decked with orchids and flowers, and there will be an orchestra playing and ox carts bringing in the girls from the local villages, and great fires roasting hens and pigs. Marvellous. Music, rice wine, girls, excitement, beautiful landscapes. A great life that.

But I'll also tell you one very strange story. Wherever I've been I've always involved myself with the local religion because it has always played a great part in the life of the sort of countries I'm used to. When I was in Laos, I became very interested in Buddhism, although I'm a Christian, and I got to know a lot of Buddhist priests and spent time in monasteries. I was eventually consecrated as something I don't know how to describe. It involved a ceremony which is really reserved for princes, politicians and leaders, but they were anxious that I should do this before I left. The service went on for three or four hours and was conducted by the nine principal abbots of the country. At the end of it I had obviously acquired a certain sanctity, and the day before I left Laos I had a big party in my garden. Everybody was there: the cabinet, the military chiefs of staff, diplomats and civil servants. My butler came out and said, 'There's a venerable gentleman at the door who wants to speak to you.' I went out and there indeed in the doorway was this abbot I knew, someone whom I had always treated with great respect. I flopped down and asked, 'To what do I owe the honour of your venerable visit?' He replied, 'I've come to tell you about yourself.'

We went into a room where he sat down on the sofa and I sat on the mat in front of him. He asked if I had ever seen television. I said, yes, often. 'Well,' he said, 'this evening I suddenly saw the whole of your life stretching out as if on a television screen. Is there anything you want to know?' I thought I should treat it seriously, so I said, 'I'm now well into my forties, and I'm not married, and this is a sad mess in a way, but I've never met anybody I really felt I wanted to share my life with. I've got too much that I still want to do. Will I ever be married? Will I have children?' He said, 'Oh, yes, that is all very clear. You're going

to marry somebody much younger than yourself. She has blonde hair and is something to do with the university.'

Oh, my God, I thought, I'm going to marry one of those history dons and have a miserable life, so then I said, 'There's one other question I'd like to ask you. I love my home, I adore my farm in the West Country. Will I be able to pass part of my life there and end my days there?' He told me, 'No, I'm afraid not. You're going to leave your home and travel all over the world, doing things for your country.'

Now, two or three years after that I married my wife, who was twenty years younger than me and had blonde hair; and the first thing we did within a month of marrying was enrol as undergraduates at Sheffield University, where we spent the first year of our married life and where our first child was conceived. As for my place in Dorset, very sadly, in 1982, we decided that we ought to sell up and leave, because I then knew a great deal about agriculture, not only from having farmed for twenty-eight years but also through having been a spokesman on agriculture in the European Parliament. Therefore I could see that European agriculture was in for a terrible time, that while my children were still tiny I was going to have to keep the farm running in the face of falling prices and increasing difficulties until I was nearly eighty. It seemed to me to be senseless, so I sold at the top of the market. The abbot was right.

I have many such other stories. For example, there's one I call 'The Albany Ghost Story'. I had been wanting to live in Albany, and one day I read in the newspaper that a man I'd never heard of, called Sir John Phillips, had died in his bath in his flat in Albany. I immediately rang up the secretary, who said, 'You'll have to deal with his sister, but come round and look at the rooms.' When I got back from Paris two days later, I went round and rang the doorbell. The door opened and a woman who was obviously the housekeeper looked out and said, 'You'll be Fred Warner. Sir John was expecting you just before he died.' I said, 'But I never met Sir John.'

At all events, I moved in and shortly after was posted to Moscow. I let the apartment to a businessman, a young fellow who was a volunteer air pilot. Home on leave after a year, I was staying with friends down in Kent, and we were sitting on the lawn one Sunday afternoon when a lot of aeroplanes started doing gyrations overhead. They were taking part in a race. Suddenly one of them started to come closer and closer and we realized it was going to hit us. My hostess seized the children and rushed indoors and we flung ourselves in the bushes. *Woomph*, the plane hit the bottom of the lawn and blew up. Police arrived and looked down the hole. I asked if anything was left of the pilot and a policeman said, 'About a bucketful, sir, that's all,' and that was that. Next day I

opened my paper to discover that it was my tenant in Albany who had been killed.

Back again after another year, I decided to move in at last and found a decorator, a nice little Dutchman called Hermann Schreiber. The first thing to happen was that one of the workmen ran up a ladder, fell off the top and broke his pelvis. Then another dropped a hammer on his foot and went off work. I then went on holiday myself, and when I came back asked for Hermann Schreiber, but nobody had seen him. I rang his flat only to be told, 'He's at death's door.'

As soon as I did move in, things started to go wrong for me. I had a lot of personal troubles and things really were going very badly. I began to think, this damned fellow is haunting my flat, and asked Philip de Zulueta, a deep Catholic and a great friend, if he could get the place exorcized. He said, 'I've just the man.' I rang the priest, told him I was going to Venice for a couple of weeks and asked him if he'd exorcize the place when I got back. He said, 'I'd love to do it.' When I returned, I found the priest had died suddenly while I was away. At this I really took fright and said to Philip, 'For God's sake, get a priest into the place for me, will you?' He said, 'All right, I'll get my cousin, Father de Zulueta.'

Twenty-four hours later, Father Zulueta arrived with an aspirin bottle full of holy water, said the right prayers and sprinkled the flat. He asked if he'd done the whole flat, and I said, 'Well, no, there's upstairs. There's my housekeeper's room. She won't mind.' But when we went up the door was locked and she wouldn't let us in. Not wanting to make a scene, I said to Father de Zulueta that it didn't matter, and we went back down and drank a bottle of sherry.

Next morning, the housekeeper, Martine, didn't appear with my breakfast. Starting to get worried, I went upstairs, but although I could hear her moving about, she wouldn't answer. She was a country woman who could be very moody and who occasionally played rather silly tricks, so I left her to it. That evening my door opened and she came in. 'Now you've done it, haven't you?' she said. 'You've driven Sir John away. He never really left this place, you know. He trusted you to look after it for him, and you've driven him out, you and that clergyman. While you were dancing around down here, he came up into my kitchen, went straight to the fridge, took his milk and drank it, then flew out through the window wearing a halo.' She never mentioned him again.

When you were appointed to Japan, were you able to master enough Japanese in a short time for it to be useful to you?

Not at all. I spent a year studying Japanese and got a long way – eleven

or twelve hundred characters – but you need at least twice that number. You need to have them absolutely firmly fixed in your mind. I was over fifty, and you can't learn languages that fast at that age – or very few people can, and I'm not one of them. What I learned was a great deal about the structure of the language and how they use it, and it did help me to understand their thoughts and how they went about things.

My feeling about the Japanese today is that they've embraced democracy because it turned out to suit very well the national path on which they had embarked. They decided after the war that their previous path of military conquest had been disastrous and had demonstrably failed them. The people who formed Japan immediately after the war were businessmen and civil servants who saw a completely new Japan whose strength would be economic; and what's more, it would be a different sort of economic strength from what had gone before. It was to be based on high technology and high skills, and they knew that their people were incredibly skilful. The democratic system seemed to serve that well, but even so they had no choice because the Americans were sitting there in occupation. By the time the Americans left after two or three years, the thing had taken root and nobody wanted to disturb it.

By the time I was there, democracy was a natural way of conduct. Of course there were those who regretted the old days, whose minds couldn't grasp this way of doing things. Of course there were, as in any community, small cliques of people with violent or absurd ideas. But that has been enormously exaggerated by the press and by left-wing opinion. The fact is that people between the 1950s and the 1970s who followed the mainstream of left-wing thinking – Marxist and extreme liberal thinking – hated to see any capitalist country being truly successful. The two really economically successful countries were the United States and Japan, and this was hated because it was in complete contradiction to everything they believed in. They needed to represent America as a bullying, imperialist, drug-ridden, crime-ridden desperate society, and Japan as an absurd, automated, fascistic-leaning society that was about to return to militarism at any moment. They've consistently represented it in this way on television and in the press. If you live there, it's not what you get at all. It simply doesn't strike you in that way.

Does it seem strange to you that the Japanese and the Germans, having lost the war, should be the biggest economic powers in the world today?

It doesn't seem strange to me at all. People get what they set out to achieve. They've really worked at it. I've watched the Germans and the Japanese working at it, and I've watched many of my fellow countrymen failing to work at it. It may be partly a matter of tradition and national

culture, but it's also very much a product of education. If you look at the German and Japanese educational systems, they are very much designed to produce efficient working people. That has never, I'm afraid, been true of Britain.

I have two intelligent, enchanting young sons, who are very thoughtful about the world and about society, but I find it distressing that it's never occurred to either of them to equip themselves really to work. They like reading English literature, they like painting or music or whatever. They like having a good time, they like travelling, but it's never occurred to them that education is a period during which you equip yourself for life, and that your life isn't only your own life but also belongs to the community. I try to suggest this to them, but they look quite surprised. You mustn't think I'm complaining about them. I love and admire them both very much.

In 1975 you resigned from the diplomatic service after twenty-eight years. What prompted you?

It was a chapter of accidents. What happened was that I was appointed UK representative to the Common Market in Brussels. It was a wonderful, absolutely fascinating and marvellous job, but there were two snags. The first was that I had married very late in life, had tiny children and was really worried. I knew that life in those endless committees in the Community started at breakfast meetings and went on till ten o'clock at night, and I felt that this was to risk the whole of my family life when it had just come to me. These kids, who should have been my grandchildren, were my children and the only children I was going to know. So that was one important consideration. The other consideration was a difficult one to put to the government, but as a passionate European I frankly didn't think that Callaghan and Silkin, who were conducting European policy at the time, were in any way committed to the idea of keeping us in Europe. Indeed, we had just announced we were going to hold a referendum.

It had never mattered to me before in my career whether we had a Labour or a Conservative government in power, but now, for the first time, there was a policy which I profoundly distrusted and disliked. I could see that I was going to make myself absolutely miserable carrying out instructions which I just didn't disagree with – we can all do things from time to time we disagree with – but which went absolutely counter to the whole of what I conceived to be the history of my period and my life's mission. I knew I was going to get into trouble. Furthermore, I was not prepared to stay there if, as appeared likely at the time, we did not win the referendum for remaining. So what I did first was to say I just couldn't stay there under these circumstances. I got a tart

rejoinder from the permanent under-secretary, who said that if I wasn't prepared to do it, he supposed they'd have to accept my resignation, in which case I wouldn't get my pension. So I went straight over to the house and said to Simone, my wife, 'Are you prepared to start a new life with me, because I'm simply not going to put up with this.' She said, 'Yes,' and I went back and said, 'I resign and I will leave here immediately after the Queen's visit.' She was due in about three weeks.

I'd mishandled it obviously, and been haughty, but I didn't regret it. It seemed to me absolutely right. When I came back, I waited to be summoned by Callaghan, who was then Foreign Secretary. Not a word. Eventually I rang the private secretary and said, 'I wish to see the Foreign Secretary because I presume he may faintly be interested in what is going on in Japan and I must tell you that, if I don't see him, I'm going to give the whole of my story to the newspapers. Twenty-four hours later I was seeing the Foreign Secretary, who was very disagreeable. He said, 'You can't determine your own career.' I said, 'Look, I've never determined my own career. I've been sent to the most God-awful places where there have been wars raging. I've been to Laos, which is the kind of place most people would pay a million pounds not to go to, but I loved it and served very well there. I've always been in the thick of the trouble, and now you tell me I'm trying to make my own career. I'm not. I'm just telling you what the limits are.' He said it was quite unacceptable to him. I told him it would be quite illegal to stop my pension. He said he wasn't able to stop it, but that I wouldn't get it till I was sixty. I said, 'But you're paying people to leave the service. Why not me? Judging by your attitude, you should be pleased to see me go.'

Can you tell me something about the relationships ambassadors have with the governments they represent nowadays?

Governments are much more involved than they used to be in the old days. The vast range of subjects with which an embassy deals today in minute detail was unknown to a nineteenth-century embassy. Then they just talked about very general things: matters of peace and war, dynastic marriages or whatever. You didn't need a lot of instructions to deal with that. It's the infinite detail in which governments get involved today which leads to this mass of communication. When Mrs Thatcher came to power, we were told that government was going to intervene much less in the life of the nation. This hasn't happened. There seems to be a deep tide in modern events which leads governments to interfere in every bloody little thing. Hence all this correspondence.

But, of course, in an embassy like Washington there's bound to be an endless stream of close instructions because that's what modern

technology provides. When I was ambassador in Laos, on the other hand, nobody could care less what I was doing. It was an entirely nineteenth-century situation. Cabinet ministers would drop in for a drink on their way home from a meeting, tell me exactly what had happened, who'd said what to whom. Chiefs of staff would lay out their plans on my dining-room table before their spring offensive and ask, did I think this a good idea? People would tell you about everything. Once, when there was a rebellion in the air force, the American ambassador and I jumped into a plane, went down to Savannakhet on the Mekon River and, with the aid of Prince Boun Oum, persuaded the rebels to remove themselves and seek asylum in Thailand. We were really conducting old-fashioned diplomacy, but you can only do that in very small places in which nobody's particularly interested. Anywhere else you're a front for a huge technical machine. But despite all that, the character of the ambassador is of overwhelming importance, and his personal influence is great. See how effective, for instance, Nico Henderson was in Washington during the Falklands campaign, or Anthony Parsons in the United Nations during that same period; or the enormous influence which Christopher Soames exercised when he was ambassador in Paris. The man is still of enormous importance.

Did you find the transition from the public service into commerce difficult?

It's a very different world. You see, diplomacy and public service thrive on knowledge and communication. The idea that diplomats keep everything secret, and that when they do speak they speak only lies, is idiotic. The whole of diplomacy is based on confidence. You have to create a situation of confidence in which you can negotiate. Everything depends on communication and frankness. The moment you're into business, by contrast, you realize that nobody is going to tell you what on earth they're up to. At first I found that very strange, I must say, and I thought that banks particularly lost out a lot by it. I could see them again and again missing opportunities which they would not have missed if they'd spoken to each other.

The firm I went to first, Guinness, was most unsatisfactory. It went through a series of internal convulsions and there were a lot of very disagreeable personal factors in the equation. It went from one disaster and crisis to another, and I found it all very tiresome and distasteful. In contrast, I soon joined and became a director of an American company, which I'm still a director of after twelve years – a brilliantly successful company, and one I've thoroughly enjoyed.

I would say the standard of management in Britain is weak in two ways. First of all, I'm not satisfied that enough managers are adequately qualified. They simply haven't got the technical knowledge and

understanding of their subject to look ahead. The other great weakness is that they're terribly bad at communicating with their work force. One of the reasons I went into European politics for a short while was that, for twenty-eight years as a civil servant, I had had to put up with listening to members of parliament and ministers pretending to be jovial and friendly and saying, 'Well, of course, you wouldn't understand that kind of thing, you're just a civil servant. You don't know about the real guts of politics, whereas I'm a man who's in touch with the grass roots. You civil servants are fine at your job, you come up with ideas, but you've got no real feel.'

After a while I thought this was all phoney. So when I left the Foreign Office I thought I'd go into politics and see what it was really like. I got myself selected as candidate for Somerset with no difficulty at all and fought a tremendous campaign three times as long as any member at Westminster has ever fought. Their campaigns last twelve days; mine lasted thirty-six. Every bloody village, the whole of Somerset and South Avon. I loved it, and discovered after a while that all this stuff about grass roots is very often a cover-up. There's nothing special about being a politician. It's a matter of communication. Can you make people listen to you? Can you make them feel you're on their side?

Many people are disillusioned with Mrs Thatcher after ten years. Do you share that feeling?

No. I think she's done a fabulous number of things for the country. But one is entitled sometimes to be disappointed. I'm disappointed, for example, by her attitude towards Europe, because although I quite see what she's saying – that you mustn't allow yourself to be swept along on a tidal wave and must feel the ground carefully before going into new territory – I think her whole attitude is designed to increase the difficulties of Britain's integration rather than to smooth the path for it. But I can never forget how much she has done to try and make British people face up to the problems they've been running away from for years.

Successive British governments have spent little on the arts, believing that funding should come increasingly from the private sector. What do you feel about that policy?

I think it's a very bad policy. Of course funding should come from the private sector; it ought to be a pleasure and a duty for anybody who's made a lot of money to help the arts. I entirely agree with that, but there are some things which the government needs to do, and I don't think they do enough in this area. The people who make the decisions are frankly not very interested. Most members of parliament and

ministers seem to think that it is not a proper field of government expenditure; that it's money thrown down the drain and that if people want art, they should pay for it. The fact that there are many kinds of art which you're never going to get without some financial provision seems to escape them. They acknowledge it grudgingly, but the arts budget is very small compared to what it probably ought to be.

Take the Institute of Contemporary Arts, the ICA. It's a remarkable organization because it's the only one that brings in really contemporary films, plays, music, events, jazz, ideas, absurdities from all over the world. Yet only one third of its funding comes from the government. And very few people have the imagination to contribute towards it.

When I first came to this country at eighteen, I noticed that a majority of Englishmen, even though they were heterosexual and seemed to need women physically, ultimately preferred to relax with other men.

I do agree with that. I think that most Englishmen are very bad at talking to women. I get a great deal of this feedback from my wife. Men in this country have devised a kind of converse which is agreeable, undemanding, easy and satisfying to them, and is incubated at their prep and public schools. People say that the public-school system could be eliminated by the stroke of a pen, but the attitudes it represents will not be so easily eliminated. Men have a kind of convenience that avoids too much emotion, and when they're with women they feel that something is demanded of them. You see, sex can be a torment as well as a pleasure. Sometimes, when you're driving along the Spanish coast and you go through Benidorm, you see these vast hotels, and they're torture machines in a way, because everybody who has gone there thinks that, if they're on holiday, they've got to perform. The women are expecting a tremendous performance every night and the men are too tired and sunburned to give it. English people protect themselves from this kind of thing by the sort of society we've been talking about.

Did marriage and family responsibilities, coming to you comparatively late in life, alter you very much?

Oh, yes. I don't quite know how to put it, but they must have stirred me up a bit. I never knew how to say no to anything before I married. If somebody asked if I wanted to go to Portugal for a weekend, to go to a party up in Scotland or to go to an exhibition, the answer was always, why not? It alters you in that way, and makes you more human. I love and adore my wife, and I absolutely adore my children, and that does alter you. It makes me, I hope, a gentler person. Marriage, of course, brings many exasperations as well as as many consolations, but you do change, yes.

Have women been very important in your life?

I've always had very close relations with women. It comes down to the whole question of sex. We're all different. Some people need it two or three times a day. (You yourself, if I may say so, have quite a reputation round the town.) Other people, like Catholic priests, can virtually go without it or lose interest in a funny sort of way quite early in middle age. I suppose I am one of the typical middle-of-the-road Englishmen who enjoy it and think it fun, but whose lives aren't governed by it in any way. I've always had very close women friends of all ages. I've been very close to older women and women of my own generation, and before I married I used to see a lot of very young girls and to spend a lot of time with women much younger than myself. I can't imagine living without having women to ring up, to talk to, to go out with, be with and flirt with, up to a point, and have affairs with.

Why are people with a lot of energy and zest often also very active sexually?

I don't really know. Energy may be a by-product of sexual drive. Perhaps they are both expressions of appetite. I know I have a huge appetite for doing things – seeing, hearing, eating, drinking, feeling.

What temptations are you most subject to?

Doing too much, eating, drinking and talking too much, staying up too late, taking on too many jobs, wanting to be doing two or three things simultaneously and therefore not concentrating. It's an excess of appetite and not enough control.

If you were to live your life again, what lessons would you have learned and what mistakes would you be unlikely to repeat?

One lesson I would have learned is that, if you want something, it's no good waiting for it to come to you. It may seem more elegant to sit around waiting to be asked to dance, but if you want to dance with somebody, you've got to go and do it. I've also reinforced my view that, the less you complain and the more you show yourself ready to do what you're asked to do, the better you'll be thanked for it. That's something very important. It's a lesson I would have to learn and learn again, because it's sometimes difficult. I would also avoid bad company. That's a very hard lesson to learn, and a very difficult one to teach to young people. I know that if I were to say to either of my sons, 'I don't like that fellow you brought home,' then it's not going to work or help at all.

I have sometimes had difficulty extricating myself from bad company. I became very friendly with Guy Burgess. Feeling sorry for him and

wanting to help him, I saw a lot of him and used to try and encourage him to be sensible. I would laugh at his silly jokes, and of course it all rubbed off. It wasn't a good thing to do. There was no point in it.

Then, when I was in New York, I found I had a passionate, vibrating civilization all around me that I wanted to get to know. Although I was supposed to be the ambassador to the United Nations, the moment an official reception was over I would disappear, change and go to Greenwich Village or some hostess's salon; or I would be up at Elaine's on Second Avenue or 98th Street. I knew poets, painters, all sorts of people, and got into some disreputable situations. But I'm very good at stepping quickly out of those, so it never caused me any trouble. Nevertheless it was questionable. One ought to think very carefully before one does that sort of thing.

A last question: do you still have unfulfilled ambitions or desires?

Not serious ones. My desires now are all end-of-the-road ones. Certain things I regret. I feel I could have made more of my life, that I could have gone much farther than I did if I had been a little bit more single-minded – hadn't tried to do so many things at once and been a little less scrupulous and a little more pushy. I feel I haven't altogether realized my talents and that I've spent too much of my life driving in third instead of top gear, but that's nothing serious. I've had a wonderful life. There's not much I regret there.

I would like now to see my children happy and settled, I would like to feel that I've given my wife happiness and I would like to see some of my work published. But since I fail to produce it or submit it for publication, who am I to complain? I've got the most boring book ever written coming out this year. It's a history of financial relations between Japan and Europe, a sort of handbook for yuppies to tell them what Schroeder's were doing during the Russo-Japanese War in 1898. I don't consider that to be real work. I need to persuade myself that I actually write interesting poetry, that it's acceptable. That would be a good thing.

AUBERON WAUGH

Auberon Waugh was born the eldest son of Evelyn Waugh in Somerset in 1939. He went to Downside and Christ Church, Oxford, with an exhibition in English, but read PPE. He was commissioned a subaltern in the Royal Horse Guards and served in Cyprus where he was badly injured in an accident. He is a prolific journalist and has worked on *Private Eye* (1970–86), *The Times* (1970–1), the *Spectator* (chief fiction reviewer 1967–70), the *Evening Standard* (1973–80), the *Daily Mail* (1981–6) and the *New Statesman* (1973–6). He continues to write a column in the *Spectator*, is chief book reviewer at the *Independent* and since 1986 has been editor of the *Literary Review*. He has written several novels, including *The Foxglove Saga* and *A Bed of Flowers*, and his non-fiction includes *Biafra: Britain's Shame* (1969), *An Eyewitness Account of the Thorpe Trial* (1980) and *Waugh on Wine* (1986). In 1961 he married Teresa, daughter of the Earl of Onslow. They have two sons and two daughters.

I do not think my father was famous in the sense that people are famous nowadays. It was not as if he were a television personality, and none of my schoolmates had ever heard of Evelyn Waugh. To begin with, his celebrity affected me very little, but as I grew up and started to be a writer then obviously it did have an effect. People inevitably compared me with my father, since even if they had only read three books in their lives, one of those was probably an Evelyn Waugh. Journalism is a jealous profession and anyone thought to be getting in by the back door, starting a few steps up the ladder, comes in for backbiting. In the long run, even so, I feel that having a well-known father has been more of an advantage than a disadvantage. People are interested to meet you when they would not be interested otherwise, and when they do meet you they already know something about you, so you don't have to start from nothing in creating your own image. On balance a lot of sons of famous fathers seem to be upset by the circumstance, even destroyed by it, but I don't think they need be. It entirely depends on the personality, and if you are someone who enjoys showing off, then you profit from it.

My father was very much of a non-interferer in our lives, his great strength being that, although we were a large family, so long as we weren't getting in his way or making a noise outside his room, he didn't mind what we were up to. We had a much livelier social life than would have been the case with a father who was for ever participating, but if he wasn't supportive he wasn't obstructive either. I was a particularly difficult child and always on the point of being expelled from school, and he did occasionally appear and show an interest. But among his children he was really in touch with only one of his daughters, and he wasn't the sort of father who was in touch with any of his sons. That is something I understand. It is much easier for fathers to get on with daughters than with sons.

My mother was a very private person indeed who lived her own life entirely and never emerged into the public arena. In many ways, she was a more remarkable personality than my father in that, although she came from an aristocratic background, which might have been expected to give her a great self-assurance, she was never interested in social life, had no social confidence and lived almost entirely for her family. Her great peculiarity was that she really lived just for jokes – a trait most of her children have inherited. She saw the funny side of everything, mocked everything, and was a natural subversive. This was partly because she was socially unconfident, partly because she hated and despised the world at large and saw it as something inviting jokes. She held up her own end of the marriage and could be very withering and scornful of my father. Perhaps she should on the whole have asserted herself more, but she didn't particularly wish to, or to lead a separate life of her own. She didn't have favourites among her children. Like any proper mother she was always hottest for the lamest, the one least likely to get on at any particular moment.

Certainly it was nothing to do with piety or privilege or outdatedness that made me loathe the public school I was sent to. It was just that it was bloody horrible, like being in prison. Perhaps I minded more than most. I hated games, which formed a large part of the ethos, but it was the restriction, the idea of being kept there, which I found so awful. I automatically saw any rule as something to break. Even if it were an absurd rule, such as that no one must go to such and such a farmhouse, I would go there to make sure the rule was broken. I didn't like the hierarchical system. The idea of deferring to other boys simply because they had been made prefects was deeply repugnant to me. The discipline, the discomfort, the horrible food, the lack of privacy – there was really nothing I liked about it.

My Catholic education did not leave me hot on sin, certainly not in the sense of being plagued by guilt. A lot of people try to make me feel guilty, but on the whole I have a robust resistance to that. As for the seven deadly sins, I don't think I'm especially guilty of lust; more than some, perhaps, but less than others. You can't expect me to be too frank about it. I'm not covetous at all, I'm not slothful in my work, since I love it, though I am slothful about doing things I don't want to do.

My only regret is my fatness, or stoutness rather. I'm acutely aware of my figure and what a very ridiculous figure it is. If I were on the lookout for new women to conquer I might have a slightly uphill task, but as I'm well settled I don't let it worry me. I'm sure I've missed many opportunities, but not so as to find it oppressive.

I sometimes wish I didn't eat, smoke and drink quite as much as I do. I'm certainly not prepared to do anything about it, but I will regre

it a lot if I have some sort of collapse and become senile or simple. Of course, I can think of embarrassing things, even a few shameful things, I've done, but they don't depress me and I don't think of them often. Generally speaking, I view my life with a sort of odious self-satisfaction.

I verge more nowadays on being a sort of lazy Anglican than a proper Catholic. Catholic services have become very depressing and I find myself filled with anti-religious sentiment whenever I go to Mass. There are one or two exceptions in the Catholic Church, such as Father Caraman in Dulverton, who holds a pleasant, dignified and proper service, and when one has glimpses of the old Church one feels a sense of loyalty; when one sings the Creed in Latin, for example.

I think, in any case, that the Church had the skids under it before the reforms of the Second Vatican Council because the old Church was appealing to fewer and fewer people. They made a drastic mistake, though, in trying to come up with a new Church which had a more popular appeal since all they have done is upset the old Catholics without attracting new ones. Religion was inevitably going to contract into a small nucleus of enthusiasts, and all they've achieved is to change the enthusiasts; the new enthusiasts happen to be the ones who like clapping their hands and looking soppy. They repel me.

I had a bad accident in the army and was in hospital for nine months, but it may have saved me in a way in that it brought me down to reality. I was a very wild young man, and lying helpless for nine months in a hospital bed made me much more accepting of life. It probably saved me from a rather short and shameful career. One of the ways in which I was rather wild was being tremendously against the government, very anarchic. The army itself helped to cure that bit, but it might not have done so indefinitely on its own.

At Oxford I only stayed a year, but have never regretted not taking a degree since I thought there was really no further benefit to be derived from all that. I made many friends, whom I am happy to have kept, but I wasn't learning anything. I was studying PPE (philosophy, politics and economics), a silly combined subject which bored me stiff. Besides, I was unhappy in love and really wanted to move on to the next thing.

Then I married at twenty-one. I had been wild in the sense that most young bachelors are wild, getting their way when they can, but I had never had the sort of experience that young people have today, never had a living-in relationship with any woman. My motive for marrying was really just wanting to move on. I've always been rather impatient to move on to the next thing, and I'd grown bored with being a bachelor. I was quite rich by then, having written a successful novel, and had a good job and a very smart flat. I just decided to lay down some roots.

If I am a chauvinist in certain respects, it's because I'm a very lazy man. I don't like washing up, I don't like making beds, and I'm extremely gratified to find women who can do that for me. But in the sense of thinking women less intelligent, then I honestly don't believe I'm a chauvinist. Women are also more naturally compassionate than men, have much greater sympathy, and sympathy is what one really likes in people. By that I don't mean saying, 'Poor thing!' but a kind of understanding, accepting, forgiving. Not all men are unforgiving, of course, but it is a very feminine quality.

On the whole, I prefer the company of women to that of men. It isn't exactly a sexual tension but more an awareness of the difference between the sexes. Intelligence is very high up on the list of the qualities I look for in women, but they must be attractive, too. Susan Crosland and Tina Brown are examples of women I admire. Susan has beautiful manners, is highly intelligent, takes in everything you say, and is very attractive. Tina is extremely funny, very attractive and unusual and so determined and brave. I find it hard to get on with an ugly woman, even with a woman who has bad legs. I don't know why that should be so, but I find one jolly well marks them down, which is wrong and somehow fascist, but I do it just the same.

Women also have this nesting instinct which men don't have, and where careers are concerned there is a disadvantage simply because once a month they suffer from premenstrual tension and go slightly wonky. The cards are therefore stacked against them a bit when they try to do things they are not cut out for. You also have to realize that there is a sort of female logic which is based upon feeling rather than reason, and it can be quite frightening if ever it is allowed to govern what happens in the world. Mrs Thatcher is not typical since she is probably more male than many men, but there is always a madness in women that one should be aware of.

To the extent that the women's movement denies the woman's role in child rearing and the need for marriage, it has been quite a wicked and pernicious thing. Human society has been going on for 5,000 years, and with the exception of a few half-witted South Sea islanders, every society has decided that to raise children you need a husband and wife and that it's a great all-round misfortune for a mother and child where she becomes a single parent through being widowed, divorced or seduced. Those silly women who think that the smart new thing is to have children without a husband are being extremely selfish, arrogant and anti-social. On the other hand, I don't see any harm in women having economic independence and feel it is probably quite a good idea, though it's nothing especially new or progressive. The fact of the matter is that the need to earn has been imposed on them, the price of housing being such that you have to have two earners before the mortgage can

be paid. Women have been forced into working when they would often prefer to raise children and not to work.

People who break up their marriage when they have young children are doing something pretty bad. If they break up when they're older, I still think it's pretty bad since, although one of them might be all right, the other one is almost certainly going to suffer agonies. Under those circumstances, it's quite wicked to break it up, but when you get two people who don't like each other, don't give each other any pleasure and who can manage on their own, then I don't see any harm in it by the time their children are grown. Personally I think I'll see my own marriage out.

When you work for sixteen years on *Private Eye* you really do need enemies. I don't have many, but on the whole I cherish those I've got and go on building them up. My attacks on Lord Gowrie certainly have their origins at Oxford and my being unhappy in love there, but my feelings towards him today are more tied up with my hatred of modern art. If I keep the attack going it is partly out of force of habit, because once you savage the enemy you might as well carry on. I don't really bear grudges. It is only copy, and these things are more like public feuds. I used to have a nightmare, particularly when I worked for *Private Eye*, of entering a room and finding all those I'd insulted there, mostly politicians I've been rude about, such as Wedgie Benn, or that disgusting man Eldon Griffiths, or of course Lord Hailsham, whom I've always mistrusted. That had its origins when I was about fourteen and Hailsham came to Downside to give a lecture. I thought then what an appalling, affected man he was. Much later I learned about his behaviour to P. G. Wodehouse and decided to go for him, and I've been doing it ever since.

My equally famous dislike of Shirley Williams was prompted by her bossiness. I'm afraid she produced a kind of mysogyny in me which is reserved for a certain type of bossy woman whom she epitomizes and whom I simply can't take at all. It was sparked off at the time when Rees-Mogg was adulating her and saying she would make a good prime minister, and suddenly I thought, no, this won't do, and made a rash vow I would devote my life to humiliating her and afterwards kept it on out of habit, though she is now removed from any possibility of further damage.

I think the best sort of education was what we had before Shirley Williams went to work on the educational system: the secondary modern and the grammar schools, the grammar school being devoted to classical education and the secondary modern to skills. Comprehensive schooling only deepened class divisions and was disastrous. Under the old system, at least if you were competent, hardworking and intelligent, you could have a leg up and get out of the pit. Comprehensives, with their large

classes and indifferent standards, have been a tragedy in that sense. It's almost impossible for an intelligent child of the working class to come out of it, and side by side with that we have had a general lowering of standards which has brought about a more proletarianized society. But then, in a society in which long-distance lorry drivers are paid more than university professors, there is no particular reason to be well educated.

It's not so much the working class I feel distaste for as the sort of proletarian culture which the *Sun* newspaper epitomizes. There is a great pretence that it would be a wonderful world if only it were run by the workers, but it would be absolutely horrible since the workers, by which I mean the proletariat, are much too stupid to run it. There are those who find the idea of élitism anathema, but I say boo to them. If you don't have the best people doing the jobs they can do best, then you have a rotten, incompetent and impoverished society.

I wouldn't agree that journalists make opinions or shape people's attitudes. All we can do is help other people discover their own opinions. Our role is no more than to divert, amuse and stimulate. People either agree with you by nature, or they disagree with you by nature, and on the whole you are read by those who agree with you. One likes to imagine that anything one says is stimulating and therefore, even if not original, at any rate provocative. If you then meet a really boring person producing your own views back at you, you suddenly realize what very boring views they are. I'm not saying that you therefore cease to hold such views, it's only that, having discovered how boring they are, you no longer write about them or express them.

All writing needs to be a bit provocative because you want to make people think and to stimulate their brain cells. Occasionally one does use vituperation and insult since it's a device that's there to be used, but if you do it too often or too boorishly it doesn't work. It needs to be done with skill. It is, after all, only one of the tools of the trade and one would be a fool not to use it. Besides, it's always fun to steer close to the wind, to chance your arm and see what you can get away with. I enjoy a scrap – a written one, not a spoken one – but I think that possibly you need to be fairly conceited to be unaffected by criticism.

As for causing hurt, I'm a great believer in the saying, 'Sticks and stone may break my bones, but words can never hurt me.' People are only hurt if they think you like them and you suddenly reveal you don't. People are not hurt if it is merely an insult; they may be angry and wish for revenge, but they're not hurt. Our libel laws, however, have got much worse since the Sutcliffe action against *Private Eye* and the Tolstoy libel. Nobody in his senses will dare to defend a libel action in court because there is simply no knowing what the jury is going to bring home. It's absolutely terrifying. These juries are very much biased

on the plaintiff's behalf, and where you have a libel action being brought by an individual who is not even staking his own money but is backed by an employer, then it's absolute hell because you have to give in every time. I'm not speaking here about being able to expose commercial scandals, though that comes into it as well, but of having the sort of freedom of expression to say that somebody stinks. Nobody will dare to do it now. The gutter press can survive for a while, but if every single libel action is going to produce an award of half a million pounds, then that will be the end of it. I feel sure that the tabloids have become much less acerbic of late.

One would never write against one's own convictions for there would be no point in doing so, but convictions are such rare things anyway. To pretend I'm totally convinced by everything I write would be mad because I'm saying eight different things in every article and writing three articles a week. You try things on to see how they work, and you might write with conviction where there is none. My writing certainly doesn't set out to conceal my true feelings. Naturally I posture and attitudinize because that's what it's all about when you're writing a column. You strike attitudes and try them out, and people will say, 'Good old Waugh,' or they'll throw a rotten egg at you.

I never deliberately take the opposite view from everyone else, but there has to be some mileage in the tactic. For instance, if I said I think Hitler had a point really, don't you, then that would be fatuous and a waste of time. You only use the device if you sense there's some sloppy thinking going on. When it comes to a subject such as child abuse, which has been turned into a ghastly soppy crusade by Esther Ranzen, you suddenly start to think no, this can't be right, it's too facile, it simply isn't true that child abuse is as rampant as she pretends; and so one niggles away at it, certainly in a spirit of contradiction but also because you feel there's something phoney there and you need to define what it is. It's the same with drunken driving. In point of fact we have the lowest rate of road casualties in Europe and it's going down, so what's the reason for this huge campaign against drunk drivers?

I'm accused of holding strong views against homosexuality, but it's not really true. I don't like having homosexuality flaunted, nor do I like the idea that everybody, if true to their natures, would be homosexual, but I don't think they should be teased or persecuted. I am fairly tolerant of homosexuals, except that if two of them come and stay with us then I don't put them in the same bedroom. It's not as if there were any servants to be shocked, it's simply that I don't think it's what one does. It would be difficult, I admit, for me to have a homosexual as a close friend. I don't know why. It's not because I hate or despise them, but only because they make me uneasy. I can't think why homosexuals

should suppose I despise them. I imagine they assume it because I'm vaguely right wing, which only goes to show that they are slightly paranoid.

I do have a distaste for louts and boors whoever they may be, and I occasionally make jokes about Jews, but I am in no sense a racist. Polly Toynbee tried to perceive anti-Semitism and racism in me in an interview she did some time ago, but Polly Toynbee is a silly woman. She has one ghastly little set of opinions which are all the standard left-wing ones, and so assumes that anyone who doesn't agree with her must have the alternative set, which equals anti-Semitism and racism. It just isn't true, it doesn't apply. The article annoyed me, but I decided it wasn't worth answering or paying attention to since it was a straight-down-the-line ghastly stupid left-wing woman's view. I thought: let her hold it.

Are moral convictions the privilege of affluence and can our inherited moral schemes survive huge population increases, you ask. A lot of questions there. Where the Catholic Church's stand on contraception is concerned, the truth is that no Catholics pay it any attention except for the backward ones; and this has an effect, not only on the Church but on everybody, since it is only the lowest stratum of society which breeds while all educated Catholics practise contraception like nobody's business. The fact is that if the Church were to change its doctrine it would have egg all over its face.

I wouldn't in any case accept that morality has been the preserve of the upper classes. I think that wherever you had religion, whether it was Methodist, Catholic or whatever, there you had firm morals among some if not all of the working classes. The privileged are perhaps more aware of the need for morality, but that is in part to protect their own position, in part because they need a pattern and a system to their lives in a way that the working class and the unemployed do not.

Political morality invariably involves a lot of humbug and I certainly do not think that all charity should be left in the hands of the state. I consider private charity to be essential. Even if there were government hand-outs to everyone, you would still find people in need of help. I don't feel under any particular obligation to go out looking for the poor and to give them soup, but if there is anyone within your circle of acquaintance who is in trouble then you will try to help. Charities have become big business, and once you get on to a particular charity's list then you have a great deal of stuff sent to you. But I am very choosey. I send money occasionally to the Salvation Army, and some to the Commonwealth Institute for the Blind. If you are told that for £10, £30 or whatever they can save someone's sight, then you have to give something, and very occasionally one of the other charities touches a

chord. I never give money to the Royal Society for the Prevention of Cruelty to Animals, though, or to the Protection of Birds and things like that, because I feel they are a load of rubbishy busybodies.

The conservative half of me is one which rejoices in privilege, comfort, the good things of life, and it doesn't particularly mind that other people can't enjoy the same things. I also happen to like old things – old houses, old pictures. I would much prefer to preserve them than, for example, put up a new building. I like to keep things as they are, partly because they seem to be run rather to my advantage at present.

One of the reasons why I don't involve myself in any political movement or any of the great campaigns for change, like that against South Africa, for instance, is that any change always involves upsetting apple carts. It's only bossy and self-important people who interest themselves in that sort of thing. Take the obvious example of thinking how wonderful it would be if everyone had the same amount of money: you try it and all you do is create total misery, oppression, incompetence, poverty.

Only fools believe in the millennium, of creating heaven on earth. By definition you cannot create heaven on earth; there will always be evil people and those who are less well off and envious and filled with hatred. I consider we should see the religious fanaticism which now affects the whole of the Middle East as the enemy and that we should fight it. There is no point in being mealy-mouthed about this. These people are out to spread a brand of religion which is disgusting and unsympathetic and they should be resisted. Quiet, calm religion is excellent, but fanatical or ecstatic religion is almost always unhealthy and bad and leads to excess.

One should try just to make one's own little world and live in it; try not to interfere with other people and make sure they don't interfere with you. That's my philosophy of life. Government interference should be confined to public-order constraints, as when you have a lot of drunken yobs making a nuisance of themselves; then the police should remove them. On the whole the private pleasures of people should be left alone, which was John Stuart Mill's attitude.

I would agree with you that it is possible to be a libertarian on the pattern of John Stuart Mill while also embracing conservative political views, though many would think otherwise. Someone like Michael Foot, for instance, whom I regard as a worthless tribune, would consider himself to be a disciple of Mill when in fact he isn't anything of the kind because he believes in a bossy socialist society. I can see how people who have read their Mill may reach the conclusion that socialism offers a promise of greater freedom, but as soon as you examine the matter you realize it doesn't. Of course, the ranks of the Conservatives are full of ghastly authoritarian pigs as well. It seems to me that libertarians

won't on the whole be particularly interested in modern politics, the struggle being to keep government off your back, to keep away from it as best you can and not become involved.

I don't like Mrs Thatcher, don't admire her, but she has done wonders for Britain, there's no good pretending she hasn't. We really were in a terrible state when she took over. But having been her party's greatest asset she is now its greatest liability, and if they had the guts they would get rid of her before the next election; but they haven't the guts so they won't. She is naturally a very bossy woman, and the fact that she has been bossing the country in the right direction for ten years is something we should all be grateful for. The truth of the matter is that the bossiness is now coming out on top and she is, in my view, pretty well crazed with her own power and importance. I would not even trust her not to use terrorism against the IRA, which would be the most stupid and wicked thing anyone could do. She has so many ideas now that are silly and wrong, and her suspicion of Europe is pathetic.

You say the Left is in the ascendant in Europe, but it has to be realized that the European Left isn't like our Left. France is a much more conservative country than Britain, even though it has for many years had a socialist government. France is a much better place in which to be rich than Britain. They would never pay a rate of 98 per cent income tax as we had in England for years, so when you speak of the Left being ascendant in Europe you are really talking about Thatcherite conservatives being in the ascendant there. In Italy, even the Communist Party is miles to the right of the Tories on things like inheritance tax.

The idea of a United States of Europe quite pleases me as I don't trust English politicians at all, and since the English electorate is one of the stupidest in Europe, we'd probably be better off with the Dutch, German and French people having a say in our affairs. The main trouble is that you go on getting these ghastly xenophobic rivalries which the French always win. We would no doubt see the same kind of problems between Thatcher and Mitterrand within a united Europe as we have without it.

Where culture is concerned, one of the things we have had in England is a general retreat from cultural interests. Somebody like Prince Charles is doing a great job, trailing his coat in front of the builders and architects who are guilty of perpetrating more damage on this country than the Germans ever did in the Second World War. You do occasionally get a successful modern building in England, but they are jolly few, and quite apart from what is known as modern architecture, the design of ordinary shops, houses or whatever on the domestic side is always ugly in itself. It always seems to be making a statement that beauty doesn't matter.

Architects are the great enemies, and who is fighting against them, apart from Prince Charles?

If you talk about poetry as part of our cultural life, then I don't think anyone is doing anything useful for it apart from the *Literary Review*. The novel still occasionally has some vitality, but fewer and fewer people are really interested in novels. When I was a young man, everyone you met at dinner would have read whatever the smart novel was that week. Nowadays you have to go into literary circles to find such conversations, and as a result writers are writing for each other and not really for a wider public. The whole situation is reinforced by the system of prizes, novels being judged not by how enjoyable they are, but by whether they break new technical ground and that sort of thing. I think that's all a mistake.

Money spent on culture is not generally well spent in England because it is all given to a handful of charlatans. In the case of literature, when there was a department of literature in the Arts Council, the funds were always cornered by a set of friends who bolstered themselves against the others. Nor do I believe that you can trust the government to supply money usefully to culture. It's true that in France they do spend a great deal of money on the arts, but then they have more common sense than we have. Having said that, I wouldn't go out on a limb and claim the Pompidou Centre justified all the money that's been spent on it. I suppose I'm so much out of sympathy with almost everything going on in the pictorial and plastic arts, that I do not really think they should be encouraged.

Where friendship is concerned, it's true that I don't like talking about people's feelings. If they've got problems, then I'm happy to discuss them and to give advice, but whenever the problems turn out to be inside themselves, then I become bored by it all. When people say they are depressed and life doesn't seem worth living, then I find myself wishing they would take an aspirin.

I'm more a gregarious than a solitary person, and I have friends whom I like. When I'm not working I very much like and expect to have company and I love to be with people. But my life is such that I don't see my friends all that often. You can only see people if you ask them down for the weekend, and that means a lot of work for Teresa. In any case, I'm always working at the weekend and just don't have the time.

The other thing I find as I grow deafer and can't hear what people say is that I enjoy parties less and less. I sometimes hanker after solitude, but never for long. One day on my own is quite enough. I wouldn't mind if I were reading or working, or even had an interesting television programme to watch, but I hardly ever do watch television. One needs to keep the mind active and I find that solitude is not good in that

respect. Moreover, I am not at all self-sufficient. I couldn't begin to keep a house tidy, serve meals for myself, make the bed and do all that. I rely upon an enormous number of people – admittedly mostly paid – to make my life run smoothly.

I need them in part because my memory has for a long time been shockingly bad. One reason for this may be the drink, but it is also because I write at least three articles a week, and every time I finish an article I have to wipe the slate clean or else I wouldn't be able to move on to writing the next. Luckily I have a storage system, so that I know where I can look something up, but when it comes to remembering anything I'm hopeless. I worry about having a stroke or something of the kind, then living on as a sort of vegetable. I couldn't bear it. I couldn't bear not to be able to work on all four cylinders. The thought scares me stiff.

One of the reasons why I work so hard is because I've got expensive habits. Until recently we had three houses. We've just given one to Sophie, but the other two still involve large overheads. My secretary has been through my accounts and discovered I've got £3,000 a month going out in bankers' orders, and you have to work quite hard to keep up with that. Another reason for working so hard is that I like the challenge of doing something new. If you stop welcoming new experiences, then you're done for and might as well die.

I think I'd like to be judged by what I've written rather than by what I've done, but it's nearly all journalism and nobody's going to read it in the future – it's all totally forgotten by the next day. I have been asked to write my autobiography, though, and offered a lot of money to do it, and since, apart from anything else, I have a slight feeling that I'm probably not going to live as long as other people because of having only one lung, I'd like to get it down. It's a very easy thing to write compared with a novel. In fact it writes itself.

I don't really feel by this stage that I live in the shadow of my father, though I might if I were still writing novels. His generation is more or less gone, you see. A few of them are still around, like Harold Acton, but mostly they're dead or senile. Besides, my own generation has known me now for quite a long time. When I look back I remember my father as a very funny man, witty, reckless and likeable in some aspects. It was true that he could sometimes be terribly rude to people if he didn't like them, but among friends he was extremely funny and lovable.

After he died I missed him, simply because he was a great gossip and I had always, whenever anything happened in my life, written him a letter and described it. For years I used to think of the things which would have amused him although he was no longer there to tell them to. His death was also quite a relief, however, in the sense that I was

then twenty-eight or so and he was a looming presence. He had the power of making people very much want to be approved of by him, and so it was all quite oppressive. He was much more firm in his faith than I am, but I don't really envy that. I quite like being wobbly. Towards the end of his life he was distressed by what was happening in the Catholic Church, but he never wavered in his belief.

I don't fear death myself, but the thought of it makes me angry. I don't want to die but I see I'm going to have to, which makes me furious not frightened. What I find repugnant about death is the thought of not being able to know what's going on with the children, not being able to read the gossip columns. I find it completely against reason that an intelligence just dies out like that. I'd be quite happy to accept being born again in the slums of Liverpool, but I can't see it as right that an intelligence, an awareness, a perception should suddenly stop. It's entirely egomaniac, but I can't bear the thought of not existing.

If I'm going to be born again in the next world, I'd like to be a better novelist. I'd also love to be a great grandee with palaces dotted all over the country, surrounded by grateful people. It's a silly, babyish wish, and I wouldn't lift a finger to achieve it on earth, but I'd like to be a king, a prince, a duke.

EDMUND WHITE

Edmund White was born in Cincinnati in 1940 and graduated BA from the University of Michigan. Between 1962 and 1970 he worked for Time-Life Books and in 1982 he became executive director of the New York Institute for the Humanities. Between 1981 and 1983 he taught creative writing at Columbia University. *Le Monde* called him the most accomplished American novelist since Henry James. He is best known for his books about the gay experience, especially the non-fiction *States of Desire: Travels in Gay America* (1980) and the novels *Nocturnes for the King of Naples* (1978) and *A Boy's Own Story* (1982).

What are your earliest memories, and what emotions do they stir?

My earliest memory is of my third birthday party during the war. My mother forced me to wear an aviator's cap and a pilot's uniform for children, and I hated the feeling of the cap and the idea of having to play with other children my own age. I much preferred being with adults. I didn't like the idea of being forced to do anything.

I was extremely attached to my mother, though she was a rather melodramatic and emotional person at that time. Now I think she is much more mature, but then she was going through the difficult end to her marriage, a very naïve woman who had been handed by her father to her husband. She had always been rather spoilt and didn't even know how to write a cheque. Being aware that her husband was leaving her for another woman made it a painful period for her.

Both my parents are Texans. My father was a cowboy when he was a boy and then became a self-made businessman. He was a person almost frightened of fantasy. He despised talking about people or ideas, about anything imaginary. He preferred to talk about stocks and bonds, or measurements or scientific processes. The one exception he made was for classical music, which he adored. When I was very young, we lived in Cincinatti, Ohio, which was a town settled by Germans in the 1840s and so a very musical city. My father loved all that. We went to the symphony every week and often had musicians play in the house. My sister and I both had to learn several instruments, the harpsichord, the recorder, the piano, the violin and so on.

No, I didn't get on well with my father. I was afraid of him. He was very violent. If you spoke at table he would throw a spoon across and knock you out with it. He was a very eccentric man who disliked people, who slept all day and awoke at six in the evening when he'd sit down to a massive breakfast. He then stayed up all night playing

harpsichord music till dawn when he'd go back to bed. Since he owned his own business, he was able to do the work at home, then pass everything out under the door to his secretary – which is rather an efficient way to work, but not a very human one. He did it expressly that way because he didn't like to come into contact with people. With me he was always disappointed that I wasn't more athletic, more aggressive; that I didn't want to take over his engineering business; that I was too cissy, too artistic, too attached to my mother.

When your parents divorced, did it make for great insecurity?

At first it was a great feeling of release because I didn't like my father. The idea that we were rid of him, and that my mother, my sister and I could move to another, bigger city like Chicago – which is where we went – was very exciting. I also knew that it was easier for me to manipulate my mother than my father. But the second reaction was a feeling of guilt, because, I suppose, I had wanted to get rid of him. It was almost a classic Oedipal feeling that I had succeeded in killing off my father, or at least in disposing of him. At the time of the divorce we moved into a hotel before moving to Chicago, and while in that hotel I went through a terrible crisis of guilt. I locked myself in the toilet and kept shouting, 'I did it, I did it! It's my fault.' Finally they had to get the doorman to take down the door to get me out. About that time, when I was seven, I had an ink-blot test, and the person who gave the test said the results pointed to somebody psychotic. I didn't see any human beings in the test, only diamonds and graveyards. Those were my two great obsessions.

How far were those early years and experiences formative of your adult persona, or can these links be exaggerated?

The links can definitely be exaggerated. I feel not very much attachment to the child I once was. I have been extremely conscious of childhood influences, but have exorcized them through writing about them. I now feel quite detached from my childhood. One of the wonderful things about being a reader is that it puts you in touch with other lives and standards of behaviour. My own family was quite brutal and given to violence, and it was through novels that I learned about more decent ways of behaving. I wanted to aspire to that, to be like a person in a Henry James novel, not like someone in *Tobacco Road* by Erskine Caldwell. I didn't want to be violent. You have to remember that my Texas relatives were homesteaders, were pioneers who, as late as the end of the nineteenth century, moved to Texas with their rifles, still fighting off Indians. So we were not very remote from a state of real violence. One of my great-grandfathers was a preacher, and when he

was denouncing somebody from his pulpit, the person he was denouncing shot him.

You always insist that you do not conform to the standard Freudian theory: the product of dominant mother and absent father.

When I wrote *Nocturnes for the King of Naples*, people said this book has a dominant mother and an absent father, therefore, Mr White, you subscribe to the Freudian pattern, don't you? I replied I had not written the book as an illustration of a psychoanalytic period, but as an artistic reflection of my own experience, which may conform to certain Freudian dynamics but which I didn't feel was universally true for homosexuals. When I first started writing in the early 1970s, people would read a novel which was openly homosexual as though it was a blueprint for all homosexuals, as if it was a statement of principle. I was eager to defend the individual's right to tell his own story without generalizing about others.

Wasn't the first draft of A Boy's Own Story *written when you were fifteen? Did you write it in diary form, or as a kind of therapy to help you face the difficulties of adolescence?*

It was written as a real novel. I began to write it in the first person and in a confessional mode, but I quickly found the book was running away from me and being swamped in detail. I didn't know how to make it go forward, so decided to go to the opposite extreme and to write it not only in the third person, but with a third-person narrator who had no access to the boy's thoughts. So it was all described in an objective way. It didn't really work, but it was written as a form of therapy because I felt I was drowning. I had been sent away, or had chosen to go away, to a boarding school, and every night we had two hours' enforced study. I would get my homework done in the afternoon and then in the evening, between eight and ten, when we had to be at our desks, I wrote my novel furiously until the bell rang. It was always exhilarating. I loved writing it and I felt it was an example of Freud's idea of the repetition compulsion.

Freud noticed that children playing with dolls would often times repeat with a doll the same terrible things that had happened to them. The mother doll would spank the baby doll. Why would they do that, why re-create the pain, why not make a happy story? He realized that, in repeating the pain, there was pleasure when they became the ones doing the manipulating. They enjoyed their mastery over a painful situation. At that time of my life, to write about the very events which were happening to me but to be the one who controlled them artistically, gave me a feeling of mastery over the situation.

At that time of my life I was extremely unhappy. I was besieged by violent, even obsessional, sexual urges that I didn't like or approve of. There are young homosexuals who have strong desires but never act on them, and who only begin to do something about it later when they are twenty or twenty-two. There are others who become sexual very young, but are very unupset about it and find it easy to deal with. But I was both sexually precocious and guilt-ridden; I had a strong drive to do something about it, but also terrible feelings of guilt. It made me feel I was going crazy.

In the same book you say, 'It's the particular curse of adolescence that its events are never adequate to the feelings they inspire.'

I think what I meant is that one often has a big tragic feeling, a feeling that one has lived through bitter and dramatic events, and when, for instance, you read a novel like *Wuthering Heights*, it is adequate to such feelings; but in the case of the typical teenager, especially for one like me who was rather lonely, who was neglected, who didn't do much, who just walked around through beautiful grounds filled with mist feeling lonely and melancholy but also tragic, you tend to ask, but what's so tragic? What have you done? Nothing. Nothing has happened to you, you haven't done anything. In other words, you have this very strong Hamlet-like response but not to strong events. T. S. Eliot talked about the objective correlative: that you have to have objective events adequate to the emotions you hope to elicit. When you write about adolescence, often times the feelings are extremely strong, but it's hard to communicate that to a third person, a reader, because the events don't in themselves trigger such a powerful response for them.

The writing itself, though, came all too easily. I wrote from a kind of obsessive interest in confession and with very little interest in artistic expression, so most of my writing of that period is worthless. In fact it was only towards the end of my twenties, after I had written four or five books, that I began to understand that you couldn't simply babble, that you had to stop and think and arrange things. In other words, when I began to resolve some of my psychological problems and no longer wrote quite so much from the need to confess, I began to have a certain inner calm. I was able to fashion a text like *Forgetting Elena*, my first published novel, though the fifth or sixth I wrote.

The hero of A Boy's Own Story *says, 'I feel sorry for a man who has never wanted to go to bed with his father.' Isn't that just the Oedipus complex in reverse?*

I don't know. If I read Freud right, he says the boy wants to sleep with his mother and kill his father, but is so frightened of his father and his

father's revenge that he becomes homosexual as a way of distracting his father's rage – of convincing his father that he doesn't really want to seduce the mother and doesn't even like women. That was Freud's idea, more or less, but he doesn't talk about a boy's sexual interest in the father so much. Yet many of the homosexuals I have known and spoken with intimately have had strong erotic fantasies about their fathers, and have often even slept with their fathers or brothers. It's not unusual. A psychiatrist once told me that people have a very difficult time talking about incest with members of the opposite sex, such as a boy with his mother, or even a boy with his sister, but between two brothers or two sisters, it's not very difficult to talk about. Father-son, yes. In others words, between generations it's difficult, or between two sexes it's difficult, but the same sex, the same generation, is very easy to talk about. People don't have strong guilt feelings about that. Anyway, I definitely had strong erotic feelings towards my father, though, as I say, I don't feel they're classically Freudian.

I think the idea was that whoever was sleeping in my father's bed was in a privileged position in the family and would gain power. In other words, my father was a tyrant, and at first my mother was in his bed and therefore a privileged person; then my stepmother became a privileged person; then my father had an affair with my sister, and my sister was elevated in the family because of it. I didn't know about it at the time, but I sensed it because I once walked in on them when my father was brushing my sister's hair. She had very long blonde hair, and looked quite a bit like his mother, who was very pretty. My father, my sister and my father's mother were all blonde, whereas I resembled my mother and my mother's side of the family, the paternal side of the family being considered the more beautiful.

Anyway, my father was brushing my sister's hair, standing behind her and crying while he did so. It was the only time I saw my father cry. I sensed there was something going on, but I wasn't certain to what extent. It was only years later, after my sister had a complete breakdown and was in a mental hospital, that I knew for sure. She had tried to kill herself and it all came out, but that was many many years later. I guessed she had always had strong guilt feelings about this relationship with my father, maybe partly because she liked it.

I think she had loved him very much. It was extremely dramatic when my father died, because we had a farm in the north of Ohio where he wanted to be buried, and that was terribly inconvenient for everybody because it took hours to get there. We finally arrived in the small town with its little farmers' church, and there he was in an open coffin, which I hate. But my sister went up to the coffin and talked to my father a long time, rather angrily and crying. Then she took off her wedding ring and put it on his finger. She was forty something at the time.

She became a lesbian, you think, because of the affair with your father?

I think maybe. She was married and had three children with her husband, but always had strong lesbian feelings. Finally, maybe, she was able to express it after her breakdown. She seems quite happy now.

You wrote an introduction to Genet's posthumous Prisoner of Love, *but it struck me as rather ambiguous. Did you admire Genet?*

Very much. I'm sorry if it was ambiguous. It's not an obvious book for an English reader, and I am very naïve politically, so I wouldn't feel too comfortable in saying what I thought about his politics towards the end of his life. But for me his novels are some of the greatest literature written this century. Next come his plays, then his essays, and least of all the poetry.

I never met him. I could have, but by the time I moved to Paris in 1982, he didn't like to meet white or middle-class people, nor Americans. I was all three, so figured it was pointless even to try. Of course, one of the good things about being a biographer today is that you can watch hours and hours of somebody on video. I've seen forty hours of him. You get the feeling of how somebody moved and talked and so on.

You are sympathetic to Genet's idea that any novel which doesn't set itself up as an Aunt Sally is a fake, but isn't twentieth-century literature riddled with enough irony? Is there no reason at all for commitment, or must every idea self-destruct?

I can't see any philosophical reason why he should be right, but if you look at the novels you actually like, it turns out he is right. The novels that are very *engagée politiquement*, like Sartre's, have become very difficult to like – even Malraux I find almost unreadable now. Whereas novels which are deeply ambiguous, like Genet's, are still readable and seem to have a universal interest.

In your introduction you excuse Genet's acknowledged admiration for treachery by thinking of it as a code word for an incorrigible subjective voice. Do you think that treachery can really be excused by a semantic shift?

Personally, no. But it's very interesting, now that I know so much about his life, to find he was actually deeply loyal to the people around him. For instance, he had a lover in the 1960s, a high-wire artist called Abdullah, who committed suicide. Abdullah's best friend, though Genet never slept with him and didn't even particularly know him, was given money by Genet every month till the end of his life – that is, from 1964 to 1986. Even then Genet made him one of his three principal heirs.

And in many other instances you find tenacious loyalty on the part of Genet to his early friends, though he would also excommunicate certain intellectuals, usually women, who tried to dominate him too much. He had terrible fallings-out with friends, but I don't think you can call that treachery, just an eruption of rage.

He liked to present himself as a traitor and to suggest in a dark way, in *A Thief's Journal*, that he betrayed people, but when you look for real instances in his life, it's hard too find them. If you say he admired treachery, though, then I do think that it is a philosophical position, that he had a kind of love for the unsalvageable person. When he wrote his last play, *The Screens*, he chose as his hero not a loyal militant Algerian soldier fighting against the French, but the most miserable proletarian Algerian who betrays even the revolution though he doesn't like the French either. Again and again Genet was attracted to the person everyone else despised, the lowest person. That's the person he speaks for finally: the person he wants to redeem. I'm not defending him, but I think it's interesting how his mind works. In *Pompe Funèbre* there is Jean, a real person, a real friend, his real lover, a Communist killed by the *milice* in 1944 during the liberation of Paris. Then Genet, in mourning, sits down to finish this novel as a monument for Jean, but what does he do? In the novel he glorifies Hitler, glorifies especially a young character called Riton who is in the *milice*, one of the very people who killed Jean.

This idea of embracing evil, of honouring people who are more or less unsalvageable, was very strong in him. It's partly philosophical choice; he's partly a Nietzschean. He was certainly very influenced by Nietzsche, and he loved the idea of the transvaluation of all values. Most criminals, when they write, present themselves as wonderful, kind, intelligent and moral. The usual thing for a prisoner who writes is to justify himself in terms of the most conventional morality. What is daring about Genet is that he not only writes about the real evil he's committed, but exaggerates it and doesn't apologize at all. From the point of view of homosexual history, that turns out to be something fascinating, because he is probably the first homosexual ever to write without any sense of apology or trying to give a diagnosis of how this strange medical state of affairs came about. Unlike Gide, for instance, who is fairly liberated; or Proust, who distances himself completely from homosexuals so that all the characters in his book are homosexual except him, Genet spoke as a homosexual about actual homosexual life in the ghetto, and it was something brand-new.

In A Boy's Own Story *you say, 'I was appalled by my own majesty . . . I wanted someone to betray.' Many people who are not homosexual might therefore be tempted to think that the urge to betray is characteristic of homosexuals.*

My feeling is that everything about homosexuality can be explained by two things. One is that it is an all-male culture. In other words, in heterosexual life men are always adjusting to the expectations and values of women, but in homosexual life they are, at least on the sexual plane, interacting only with other men. The other thing is that they are a persecuted minority group.

In *A Boy's Own Story*, the boy's urge to betray at the end of the book is morally ambiguous because, on the one hand, the reader applauds, this being the first time the worm turns, the first time this rather persecuted boy, usually passive and always suffering things at others' hands, decides to do something himself. It's a revenge on the adult world, a kind of self-assertion. It's certainly the end of innocence, but the bad thing, on the other hand, is that the object of this attack is another homosexual. The person he chooses to persecute is one of the few people who has actually been nice to him and who to some degree shares his sexual taste.

But that was very characteristic of that period, because homosexuals who belonged to it hated themselves. How could they not? There was no favourable picture of homosexuality available in that culture. A homosexual was either ill, criminal or a sinner. There were only the medical, the legal or psychological models. There was no other way of justifying them sexually. All three of those images are quite pejorative, and so the boy suffers the usual self-hate. Attacking another homosexual was, in a way, proving one wasn't oneself so homosexual. The one he attacked was the scapegoat.

But, today, do you still find that homosexuals have special characteristics?

I don't. I know most people do say that, but I think it's much like anti-Semitism. Anti-Semitism and anti-homosexuality resemble each other closely because they tend to look for a unity that doesn't exist. In his little book on Jews, *Sur la question juif*, Sartre suggests that the anti-Semite regards the Jew as a synthesis. So if one man says a Jew is not courageous, and another says yes, but here is a Gentile who is not courageous, the first rejoins, ah yes, but the lack of courage of a Jew is different from the lack of courage of a Christian. In the same way, people search for a kind of mystical unity in homosexuals. We all share something which is our condition, but the condition shifts from time to time, so while homosexuals do share something which is their particular social condition at a particular historical moment, I always find it ridiculous when homosexuals talk about 'we homosexuals' and mention Plato or Michelangelo. Even if they had homosexual sexual practices, the nature, formation and contours of their personalities, their mentality, must be entirely different from now. A homosexual living on a Greek

island today is entirely different from a homosexual living in Manhattan. So which homosexual are we talking about? I suppose you could say that certain middle-class homosexuals living in London at the moment bear certain resemblances to each other because their condition is a shared one, but only to that degree.

Do you think of your work as political in the sense, as you explain in the Genet introduction, of heightening consciousness by making people more aware of different convictions and lifestyles?

Yes, I think my books are political in the sense that they put you in the shoes of another person, but I also think that my most recent work, *The Beautiful Room is Empty*, is political in an even more direct sense in that I wanted to show the beginning of homosexual liberation and the period of oppression just before it happened in 1969. There are many people who have grown up or become homosexual since then, and I wanted to show them what things were like before, and to end on a very positive note with the idea, the feeling of liberation. Therefore I chose as my hero someone who is extremely middle class, quite repressed, rather self-hating and a reluctant revolutionary. I wanted even the heterosexual reader to say to himself or herself, oh come on, get on with your life, stop tormenting yourself about all these ridiculous scruples. It pleased me very much to see a review by a *New York Times* reviewer, a heterosexual male who said in effect, I am heterosexual and I barely understand all this stuff, but for Christ's sake, Mr White, get on with your life. That is exactly what I wanted the reaction of the reader to be. I wanted the reader to be more liberal than the boy himself.

And do you find the ordinary reader today more liberal?

It depends. You see, I'm from the United States, which is a very religious country, and I have all these Texan relatives who are Baptist and are convinced I'm going directly to hell. The ordinary literary reader, living in Paris, London or New York, is quite liberal, as they have been for a long time. But I've had people from America writing letters denouncing me, telling me I'm going to hell and so on. America is an extremely religious country.

I feel more like an outsider in America than I do in Europe. That's the odd thing. In London I have so many friends who are writers, and I feel so warmly accepted that I don't feel like an outsider at all. If I have a new book out in London, maybe the *Independent* will do a review, *The Times* will do a review and the *Literary Review* will say this is one of the best books of the year and so on, which is very thrilling; whereas in America, if they review me at all, it's almost entirely in the context of where are homosexuals now and what's happening to them in this

age of Aids? In France, if they were taking a poll of important people, asking what do you think of nuclear power, they might ask 100 people and I might be one of them, but in America *The New York Times* would never ask me about nuclear power, only about homosexual rights. I feel very ghettoized in America, but that's not a problem peculiar to me, it's peculiar to American life. America is nothing but ghettoes. There is no general reader in America, no general culture. It's all lobbies, ghettoes and special-interest groups.

The reason I'm returning to America now is partly because I was offered a very good job. I'm about to be fifty and I support my mother, and if she didn't have me I think she would be in the gutter. If I work fifteen years, then I can have a retirement plan and all those nice things, but also, as a writer, it's dangerous to be out of contact with your country too long. It'll be interesting to go back, at least for a few years. If I like it, I'll stay; if I don't, I'll come back here. But it was a wonderful offer: a full professor with tenure in Brown University, one of the best universities in America. I couldn't refuse. I'm going with a friend, who has just got divorced and wants to start a new life. He's French, and the idea of moving is exciting for him too, so it's just a good moment to be going back.

But do you feel more appreciated in Europe than in America as a writer?

Definitely in Europe; specially in England. But also in France. And five of my books are coming out at the same time in Italy now, and five more or less at the same time in Germany, so I feel there's a big push going on.

But why should that be? After all, you're American.

Yeah. Well, I asked Alison Lurie once why she was more famous in England than in America, and she said, 'Because in America I'm writing about familiar subject matter in an unfamiliar style, that is in an English style, whereas for English people I'm writing about unfamiliar subject matter, that is American life, in a familiar, that is English, style.' I think that's true of me too to some degree. In other words, there is something exotic about those rich American children that I write about, but it's in a reflective, more European, more literary style of writing. It's not the sort of Raymond Carver minimalism that people have come to expect from Americans.

In A Boy's Own Story *you say: 'It seemed to me then that beauty was the highest good, the one thing we all want to be or have, or failing that, destroy.' Why should a young homosexual feel like that? Is it a thoughtlessness of youth which imagines it will never be old, or is it a more specifically homosexual fear?*

I don't think it's a fear, and I don't think it's homosexual. I think it's artistic. Artists are susceptible to beauty, including physical beauty, which in real life we all react to. Yesterday I had a party where there was a beautiful young man, twenty-two years old, and all the men and women were reacting. He is also an aristocrat, so that helps, but, you know, he's blond and his father is the governor of Bermuda and so on. He didn't have to say a word and everybody found him enchanting, everyone one was giving him their phone number, men and women both. People do respond to physical beauty very strongly, but when they write, they pretend they're much more moralistic, that they have better values; that is, that they prize nothing but intellect and virtue. But artists are people who love beauty, and one of the forms of beauty, maybe the main form, is physical, human beauty. It's not any accident that the Greeks made statues of beautiful athletes and goddesses.

I've had Americans criticize me, saying, 'Oh, you're always talking about physical beauty,' because oft-times I'll say about somebody, she is very intelligent, this and that, and beautiful. 'Oh', they say, 'why do you mention beauty?' Feminists especially, of course, hate that. Yet I mention male beauty as much as female beauty, so it's not that I'm specially keen on female beauty. Anyway, I do think that physical beauty is an important thing that artists respond to.

How do you view feminists?

Having lived in France now, where feminism is scoffed at and completely over as a movement, it's hard for me to remember it's still taken so seriously in England. Recently, when I was a judge on the Booker Prize, there were two women on the panel who had strong feminist sentiments. I found it difficult. I was even shocked by some of the things they said. For instance, to be against a novel because one of the characters is female, masochistic and shown as liking to be mistreated, seemed to me a very shocking response. On the other hand, I consider myself a feminist, but I think of myself as not applying those principles to novels but to actual life.

For instance, after a long debate in my mind, I feel I'm against the idea that Moslem girls should wear the *fular* here in France, because it is mainly men who are deciding that women should wear them. The women have not been asked at all. It is a way of separating those girls from other girls, marking them and oppressing them. It really is a continuation of male domination. I think that's all right within the context of the Moslem world, but here in France it goes against two things: the secular aspect of the schools and the idea of women's rights, which is very important if you are a member of French society. If you were a highly devout Catholic, you would have a hard time living in

Syria, just as if you were a highly devout Moslem, you would probably have a hard time living in France. So I would say I am a feminist on questions of economics and legal rights, but I don't like feminism much when it's applied to art.

Has women's liberation helped gay liberation?

What we've witnessed in this century is a shift away from an ethic of responsibility to an ethic of pleasure. I'm not talking about aristocrats, because aristocrats have always behaved according to their ideas of personal pleasure, but in other centuries 95 per cent of people were farmers. They needed children to work in the fields, they were watched closely by their neighbours, they were obliged to conform and were obsessed with performing their duty to their Church, their family, their parents, their children. The whole idea was of self-sacrifice to help the next generation and fulfil your duty, which was clearly defined and ordained by God; nobody doubted it. You still see that in Third World cultures, but once it shifts you have a kind of aristocraticization of middle-class life, hence the vast armies of people in the major cities of Europe and America who have adopted the ethic of self-satisfaction and pleasure. They divorce when they're no longer in love, get rid of their children if they feel it's cramping their style. They do exactly as they please, treat their lives as a work of art, and are mainly interesting in self-fulfilment. That's when homosexuality becomes much more important, because if those are your real feelings, then you are going to act on them.

But hasn't feminism driven some men towards homosexuality?

I don't think so. That suggests that men have more choice than they really have. If a man is really attracted to a woman physically, so that he gets an erection when he looks at her, then even if she's a difficult bitch, he's not going to become excited by a man. Oddly enough, I think women have more choice than men. I do feel that there are women who, for political reasons, have decided to be lesbians, but I don't feel that there are many heterosexual men who, for political reasons, have decided to be homosexual.

Is homosexuality on the increase, or is it that people are now liberated and have come out of the closet?

It's that it's more visible, but there might have been many before who, if they were marginal cases, would have worked very hard, with their psychoanalyst or their priest, to remain heterosexual if at all possible. I know of several examples in my father's generation of women who

married men who really were homosexual, but the men did not act out their homosexuality. They lived with their wives and were sadists. They tortured their whole family. They were alcoholic, disagreeable, wife-beating monsters because of their repressed homosexuality.

Has American society yet absorbed the idea of homosexuality? Can it now be regarded as part of the make-up of the nation, or is it accepted de jure *but not* de facto*?*

It's accepted neither *de jure* nor *de facto*. It's become a powerful special-interest group in certain cities, especially in the West where there aren't other ethnic groups to compete. In New York, where strong Jewish, Italian, Polish and Irish ethnic groups, and now Puerto Ricans, control the city, gays do not represent a very powerful vote even though they are numerous. But in places like Houston, Texas, or Los Angeles, which are newer cities and where ethnic groups are less well organized and the largest ethnic groups are comprised of either blacks or Mexicans, who tend not to vote very much, gays have become powerful in local government and have even helped to elect a woman mayor in Houston. So in certain regions, gays have gained a lot of clout.

In response to Aids, gays have become very well organized, and activist groups, like ACT UP in New York, have done a lot to change legislation, to streamline the availability of new medicines for the critically ill. Before, people who were ill were being told that they couldn't try a new drug because it hadn't been tested long enough to see if it was safe, but if you are going to be dead in a month, what difference does it make? Now all that's been streamlined and there is much quicker access to the drugs, even to dangerous ones, if one wants to try. This has been something achieved by ACT UP, and they've gotten much better funding for people who are ill, for home care, for medical bills and so on. So gays do represent a powerful special-interest group in certain regions and certain aspects of American life. But whereas in France a recent poll showed that 60 per cent of heterosexual French people regard homosexuality as a normal variation of sexual behaviour, probably less than 10 per cent of Americans would say the same.

Why could no publisher be found initially for A Boy's Own Story *in Britain? Was the country simply not yet receptive enough for gay literature?*

Well, *A Boy's Own Story* was quickly accepted in the United States, but in Britain, where I had already had one or two books published by André Deutsch, they didn't like the book. Deutsch rejected it, and then it went to several other publishers and was rejected. It was finally accepted by Picador, who decided it was good and made a big fuss over it.

As a title, A Boy's Own Story *looks deliberately provocative, Did you feel it necessary to provoke a response when you wrote it?*

Actually, you know, the title has slightly different echoes for an American. For the British, of course, it's clearly provocative because it makes you think of *A Boy's Own King Arthur,* a *Boy's Own History of England,* the *Boy's Own Paper,* but in America, at the turn of the century, there was a series of first-hand oral reports given by juvenile delinquents to an important Chicago sociologist that were printed in a book called *A Boy's Own Story,* which was the context in which I first thought of it as a title. I wasn't really thinking of British books so much. Later I thought it would be amusing to take this very strange boy and place his story, which was anything but the typical Boy Scout's story, in this very traditional context. Susan Sondheim, who was a very good friend of mine at the time, hated the title because she felt it made light of the book, that the book was better than the title and the title was ironic in a light way, but I liked it.

Is she no longer a friend?

She's no longer a friend because she felt I portrayed her as a character in one of my books, which I didn't mean to do, but she's been angry with me every since, though I still admire her and like her. I felt she was over-sensitive, and for somebody who has always been an advocate of the freedom of speech, she reacted in an odd way.

Much of your work, I think you acknowledge, is autobiographical. Can you tell me something of the relationship between the life and the fiction?

First of all, I'd like to say that a book like *Caracole,* which is not at all autobiographical in the obvious sense since it has no first-person narrator and no character obviously based on me, is, I feel, my most autobiographical novel. This is because it's the only novel I have written in the third person in which the narrator has the ability to get into the minds of all six of the characters: three women and three men. I felt fully expressed in that book, in the sense that I felt I could exaggerate different aspects of my own personality and project them on to those six characters and dramatize my own inner conflicts in the bi-play between them. If you write a so-called autobiographical story, like *A Boy's Own Story* or *The Beautiful Room is Empty,* then you are stuck with only one character, the narrator, and you don't really have that kind of full expressivity. Certainly in any autobiographical novel you're always shaping it primarily for novelistic purposes. A real autobiography, written by, let's say, a famous general like Eisenhower, is written by somebody you can assume the public is already interested in. He doesn't need

to create interest, he can assume it on the part of the reader. But a novelist, and especially a novelist who is not well known or who is only well known for his novels, has to create interest in the book. Therefore it has to operate as a piece of literary machinery to create interest and satisfy the reader's normal anticipations.

A lot of shaping has to go on. Say, for instance, that you have had three boyfriends in a six-month period. It's much better to have them become one boyfriend, because otherwise the reader gets confused with too many names, too much coming and going, too much shifting of stage machinery. I also tended with *A Boy's Own Story* to make the character more normal than I actually was, because in real life I was more competent than the boy. I was less timid, had had more sexual experience and more artistic success at an earlier age. My boy in the book tends to be a bit timid, unsure of himself; more, I think, like most gay people that I've interviewed and talked to. I spent years and years in group therapy with other gay men, listening to their stories. The psychiatrist once said to me, 'Don't tell your story to this group because it upsets them too much.'

I had poems published when I was young, I had a play produced on Broadway when I was twenty-two. In other words, I was not quite as defeated, retarded or slow as the boy in my book, but I wanted to create somebody I thought the reader could identify with, somebody a little more timid. The brassiness in Americans seems very foreign to English readers, especially to English children, who tend to be rather more supervised, but even though I changed all those things, many English readers still said to me, 'I find the amount of freedom the boy had absolutely astonishing.' That shocked me, because I had thought of him as being rather oppressed, but English children, brought up in a traditional way, tend to think that the boy has an enormous amount of freedom. So, to return to your question, I've changed many things to simplify them, to make them more shapely, to make them more novelistic, but also to make the character more representative.

'I never doubted that homosexuality was a sickness,' says the boy in A Boy's Own Story. *How long was it before you began to feel differently? Is it just social programming, or does it represent some deeper and more permanent fear?*

Many Americans are phobic about sex itself, not just homosexuality, so many times, when American homosexuals are coming out and trying to accept their homosexuality, they find they have an even bigger problem, which is to accept their sexuality at all. And it's a universal problem, it seems, among certain kinds of Protestant and Irish Catholic Americans. That's one thing, but I feel myself to be very involved with the history of Gay Liberation, and deeply indebted to it because the kind of self-

assertion, the kind of political activisim that emerged in 1969, was liberating for me personally.

Oddly enough, I was the co-author of a book called *The Joy of Gay Sex* in 1976, published by the English publisher Mitchell Beazley. I wrote it with my own psychotherapist, but that was pure accident. He had already been chosen to be the doctor half of the team when they were looking for a writer. They auditioned ten writers, who all had to write sample entries. They liked mine the best, so chose me, and then I found it would be with my own psychotherapist. He said to me, 'You must choose either to continue to be my patient or to be my collaborator, but you can't be both.' I chose to be his collaborator because I needed the money badly and felt it was towards the end of my therapy anyway. But I told Mitchell Beazley that I didn't want to sign my own name because I thought it wasn't a work of any literary interest and would hurt my literary career.

The book, though it had some rather juicy sexual drawings in it, wasn't in fact very sexual in the end, but tended to be more about life-style than sexual activity. More than half of the entries were about such things as coming out, dealing with your parents, taking a lover, telling a fellow office worker you were gay and all that kind of stuff. And the more I worked on it the more I said to myself, 'It's completely hypocritical for you to urge everybody else to be honest and open and then sign a false name.' So I put my own name to the book, and it was the first major thing I had written that was specifically and openly homosexual. That had a tremendous liberating influence on me. I was rather old, I was thirty-six, and it is shocking to admit how many years of therapy and struggle it took me before I could accept myself. Now I really do.

I can't imagine myself going to a therapist and talking to him about a problem. Why did you find it necessary and were you helped?

It was very destructive at the beginning because the therapist acted as an agent of repression rather than liberation. It was only when I was in my late twenties and I chose to go to a homosexual therapist – a therapist who was, I knew, openly homosexual and felt relaxed about it – that I began actually to make some progress. But, you see, in choosing him I already made progress. In other words, up to that point, as late as the age of twenty-nine, I was still engaged to a woman, trying to go straight and get married.

But you needed therapy because of your homosexuality?

Yeah.

Nothing else?

Nothing else. Although it had such consequences that it made me quite crazed in other ways too. I mean, I was full of nervous tics, constantly shaking my head and bobbing. I couldn't sleep at night. I would eat too much or too little. I had all kinds of anxiety attacks where I would hyperventilate and almost pass out, all kinds of strange psychological and psychosomatic symptoms. My sister too. Then in both of our cases, when we came to accept, really accept, our homosexuality, we relaxed and all these other psychological problems disappeared.

Did your father know that you had homosexual tendencies?

Uh-huh, yes. And he hated it. He hated it and wanted me to stop.

Did you ever go through a period of your life when you could make love to a woman and enjoy it?

Yes. I was always afraid, though, of being somehow captured by women, maybe because I had a mother who depended on me very much when I was a child. After my father left us, even before, my mother would often say things like, 'Oh, I wish you were grown up, I would marry you.' I felt suffocated by her need for me. After that, I would tend to choose similar women, women who were very needy, partly because I didn't have very much self-confidence. So a woman who was overweight, or who had extreme psychological problems and who was very dependent on me, reassured me in one way though in another it reminded me too much of my mother and I felt suffocated by that very need that I liked and trusted. It was all rather upsetting to me. I have the feeling that if I had been able to work out those problems, I might have had a more bisexual life. Certainly the interest in men was very early and strong, but there was a real genuine interest in women that got stifled at some point along the line, mainly because I was afraid of them, afraid of failing sexually myself; because oftentimes I would be impotent with women. Never with men.

You spoke of A Boy's Own Story *as 'the laying to rest of a section of my life'. It suggests a sort of therapy in which you speak to a public, arranging and qualifying your life for inspection. Would that be a fair analysis?*

Yes. I suppose it's a very American and especially a very Protestant thing, the idea of bearing witness to your life. In America we have revival meetings where everyone becomes hysterical and saved through Jesus. They run to the altar and confess their whole lives. Europeans find it very amusing that Americans have this tendency to confess, but I think I'm typically American in that sense. I can only say in my defence that I feel that very few people have ever made this particular confession

before in this particular way, and that it has meant a lot to a lot of readers. I still get letters from readers, and it's reassuring for people to realize that someone else has had the same experience.

When A Boy's Own Story *was published, the* New York Times *review claimed you had 'crossed* The Catcher in the Rye *with* De Profundis *– J. D. Salinger with Oscar Wilde'. Was that a claim you were happy with?*

I found it an odd remark because it seems to me that, from a technical point of view, the trick of *The Catcher in the Rye* is that he is still an adolescent, so it is a brilliant act of ventriloquism, whereas with *A Boy's Own Story* I felt it was important to have the narrator much older than the protagonist. In other words, the same man is speaking, but he is speaking about himself twenty years before. I felt that the life portrayed in *A Boy's Own Story* was that of somebody who was in such pain and who hated himself so much that, if the reader was to come away with a feeling of consolation, he could only get that through an indirect contact with an adult narrator who did accept himself.

In fact, somewhere in the book the narrator says that even though he hated himself, he now loved the boy he was, and it is almost as though it's autobiographical paedophilia. We love the self we once were, but that self-acceptance trails behind our actual life by about twenty years. And it is true that I do now feel a kind of pity and sympathy with that boy who at the time thought of himself – as I thought of myself – as a kind of monster. But now I see that, given his situation, he wasn't so bad, he was rather normal. In that sense my book had an entirely different strategy from *The Catcher in the Rye*, which is a teenage boy speaking to you in his own voice, which was not at all my goal.

As far as Oscar Wilde's *De Profundis* is concerned, I feel it's a very elegant piece of blackmail directed at Lord Alfred Douglas. He wants to wring his heart and preach at him, and finally punish the ideal reader of this long letter, who was Lord Alfred Douglas. I don't feel that my book is at all interested in targeting, punishing or manipulating a particular reader. I suppose what the reviewer had in mind is that it is a cross between a teenage narrative and a homosexual narrative, but then it would have been simpler to say it.

If you were to relive your youth, how differently would you relive it?

Given the circumstances then, I was fairly courageous and probably did as best I could, but I would like to live now and lose less time feeling guilty; to have more fun, having sex and being more self-accepting sooner. I don't feel I was deprived of sex, because I had a lot of sexual experiences, but I feel I was deprived of love, because I was unable to sustain a long-term relationship – even a six-month relationship –

because I hated myself too much. In other words, many homosexuals from that period, and even homosexuals now who hate themselves, can perform individual sexual acts, but don't want to have the piece of evidence that proves they're gay sitting round day and night. If you have no lover around, then you can say to yourself each morning, well, today's a new day, everything's indeterminate and maybe I'll be heterosexual later, who knows? So the kind of commitment to homosexuality that an actual lover represents was very hard for me then, and if I had to live everything again now, I hope that I would come to self-acceptance earlier and be able to experience love younger.

Many reviewers point to a vein of poetry running through your prose. Is that a deliberate or unconscious device?

Oh, like many writers of prose I started off writing poetry, and I probably still read more poetry than most prose writers. I read French poetry, English poetry and American poetry. Ezra Pound said poets should be at least as good as prose writers, and I feel that prose writers should be at least as good as poets. There's a great deal of careless prose writing, especially now in the age of the word processor. A lot of people have a good plot which is destined ultimately for the movies, and the style is ramshackle, just a way of conveying the plot as quickly as possible. That's a betrayal of the artistic possibilities of prose. I like a finely worked style. It's where the English oftentimes lose patience with me, because they'll say it's too self-conscious or over the top or arty. That's why I'm happy that Quartet is publishing so many foreign works, especially French, because I find English prose a little sterile in its sociological preoccupations with class, with region and its obsession with realism, especially in showing small pictures of small lives. I find all that tiresome.

You have taught a lot of creative writing. Is it really possible to teach people to be creative?

I'm about to start teaching creative writing again, so I've been thinking about it a lot, and one of the things I've been thinking is that when I was a boy beginning to write, the only idea that one had of serious literature was the *New Yorker*. The *New Yorker* story was a kind of formula that aspiring young writers held in mind as a goal. Of course, now it seems terribly *démodé*, and I think it would have been useful if somebody had put Proust in my hand at that age – read this, forget about the *New Yorker*. Young writers now have Raymond Carver and other minimalist writers. I love Ray Carver, by the way. He was a good friend of mine and I admire him as a writer, but he pulled those stories out of his guts and invented the style. He was a working-class man who

was an alcoholic, who suffered tremendously but who finally tore those wonderful stories out of himself. But because it is a very plain-spoken style, it is an easy one for people to imitate, and now you see rather spoiled middle-class kids who want to be writers but have never suffered a second in their lives, writing as though they're tortured. They don't know any other way of writing because it's all they see around them.

So one thing the creative writing teacher can do is expose the student to world literature. I always ask students, 'What have you read, and what are you reading now,' and it's very interesting. Many of them don't read at all, and I can say in my whole long life of knowing writers, and I've known hundreds, I never met any good writers who didn't read, except Tennessee Williams and Truman Capote. And they both read when they were young. Every other writer I know reads all the time – maybe not always fiction, maybe autobiography, history, or whatever they're interested in. Every writer worth his salt is interested in innovation, and there are two sources: one is by imitating life, that is to say writing about situations that have never been written about before in ways that have never been used before; the other is through parody of other literature. That is a deliberate act of influence and I think you choose your influences very carefully.

There is a school of thought which says there are profound links between homosexuality and artistic talent. Indeed, some people would claim it is difficult to find one without the other.

I think that's ridiculous. Clearly you can find many great writers and painters who are heterosexual. It does tend to vary according to the arts, and to the period. For instance, very few architects are homosexual, but maybe it's partly because the engineering, technical aspect of architecture has become so important. I find that most homosexuals don't like spending years and years studying maths, science and engineering. When I was a boy in the 1950s, the whole world of American painting was extremely macho, and if you were a homosexual you had to hide it because you wouldn't be considered a serious artist. If you think of the generation of De Kooning, Pollock, Franz Kline, Hans Hofmann, they were all heterosexual. You barely find a woman and certainly not a gay man. Now, with the Hockney generation, you find many homosexuals, but I think it varies according to the period and the ethic of the period.

If gay men tend to be sensitive in the arts, it's partly because they are participatory outsiders. If you are a complete outsider, like a gipsy who doesn't ever get into the inner structure of society but lives as a complete marginal, it's rather difficult to be a writer, or you can only write about that small world. If you're a complete insider or a successful Wall Street

broker who was head prefect at Eton, it's hard to question the mechanics of your world, but if you're a Jew who passes as Gentile or a gay who sometimes passes as heterosexual, you can enter into the world without ever feeling completely part of it. You feel very much like an outsider, but are a participatory outsider; you participate in the system. It's no accident that Proust, who was half-Jewish and at least half-homosexual, should be the person really to have written about the mechanics of the inner world of the French ruling class.

But people with great artistic talent nowadays often are homosexual.

There are many exceptions. For example, of the 102 books we read for the Booker Prize, I think only two had any overt homosexual content. It was a shockingly low proportion, and the only one that was good was Sybil Bedford's *Jigsaw*, where she was quite open about her own lesbianism. Just numerically, there you have a spread of all the best English fiction of one whole year, and very very little of it was homosexual at all.

Would you want to claim heightened sensibility, as many homosexuals do, and if so, is it cause or effect?

I think you could claim heightened sensibility, which is the heightened sensibility of an outsider, and it's definitely an effect. It's an effect of being homosexual, nothing mystical, nothing innate.

From what you have written, the various psychological explanations for homosexuality seem inadequate to you. Can you suggest any reason why people should be divided in this way? Lesbians often point to the brutality and self-regard of men, but presumably a different explanation is needed for male homosexuals.

I think, as I said earlier, that women can choose to be lesbians. There are many women who felt they never had a choice, that they were born lesbian, but I've also known many who have actually chosen to be lesbian for political reasons – disappointment in marriage or disappointment in contact with men, or because of their political feminist convictions. But I have never known a man make a similar claim. I read a poll that *Playboy* magazine conducted of their readers, asking what is your secret fantasy, what would you like to explore that you've never had the courage to explore? Many women readers responded that they would like to explore lesbianism, but no heterosexual male reader said they wanted to explore homosexuality. So either they're not admitting it or, as I suspect, it's much more clear-cut for men.

I think it's linked to masturbation. I think that when you masturbate

alone, you have fantasies, and those fantasies guide you to what your real desires are. In that sense masturbation is psychologically productive, because it allows you to locate what you actually want to do sexually. But many women, especially of your generation and mine, did not masturbate until they were in their thirties or early forties, and it's only at that point that they discover they're having persistent lesbian fantasies. It's a very interesting phenomenon.

You mean that boys masturbate at an early age, women don't.

I don't think that's the case now, but it was the case before, at least among traditional cultures or people who were from a religious background. Many girls simply didn't touch themselves until they were older. As a political statement, I would say that no explanation is necessary, and that just as we don't search for explanations for heterosexuality, so we shouldn't search for explanations for homosexuality. To search for an explanation is to fall into the trap of regarding it as a pathology that needs an explanation. Curiously enough, the translator who is translating Genet material of mine into French, and who is heterosexual, said, 'I find reading your work so odd because you name heterosexuality as a condition, and every time you present a new man, you say he's a heterosexual. Heterosexuals themselves never think in those terms. They think of themselves as being a kind of universal nameless class, and then everybody else gets names as exceptions.'

But don't people want to know more about homosexuality because it's perverse?

Yes, because it's different and because it can be threatening. They begin to think, maybe this will happen to me or my children, and what are the early signs? How can I be sure I'm not that way? It's interesting. My friend who is just getting divorced – I'm his first male friend – has always lived as a heterosexual, with the wedding ring and so on, and he was telling me that in his milieu, which is architecture, many men joke about wanting to have homosexual adventures. It is constantly on their minds, always being brought up but in a joking fashion. They don't act on it, but is is a thought that passes rather frequently through their heads.

In my own case, homosexuality struck me as a source of freedom. I knew I didn't want to be bourgeois, didn't want to have a family or the expenses of a family, didn't want to have a wife or children dependent on me, didn't want to need a full-time job. I wanted to be a writer. I never felt I was rich enough to have children, nor did I want to be rich enough to have children. I wanted to be free as the wind and not to re-create the same kind of stifling manly situation that I suffered from as a child. When my father would come to visit me at university, the minute he

left I would rush off to pick somebody up to have sex with. I needed to touch flesh, to prove to myself that I wasn't like him, that I wasn't going to be like him. In other words, I was fleeing into a kind of freedom that, for me, homosexuality stood for: the opposite of everything my family stood for.

If you had a choice, would you opt for homosexuality or heterosexuality?

I would opt for bisexuality, because it would be very exciting to be able to experience everybody and everything. I wish I had more flexibility as a heterosexual. I mean, I wish that part of me were developed because first of all I love women and the company of women and think it would be fun to explore that more. Also, women are very tolerant towards older men if they're successful, but men are not very tolerant, so I think that if the world were ideally arranged, you would, if you're a man, be homosexual when you're young and heterosexual when you're old; and the exact contrary if you're a woman, because lesbians tend to like older women and heterosexual men like younger women, so a woman should go from being heterosexual to being lesbian.

With people's awareness and acceptance, however partial, of more sexually explicit writing, a certain kind of literature, which might be called the literature of concealment, has disappeared. Do you think that more relaxed attitudes have always been good for literature?

Yes and no. One of the most exciting homosexual stories ever written is one that's not at all homosexual, 'The Secret Shower' by Conrad; or another, 'The Pupil' by Henry James. Those writers wrote about highly charged erotic situations that were never specific. Even, let's say, the paedophilia that is concealed in *The Turn of the Screw* by Henry James is absolutely thrilling and hair-raising, so it's true that that has a kind of artistic value which is no longer quite so possible; though in my own novel, *Forgetting Elena* – even though there's no specific homosexuality – the atmosphere is heavily charged with a kind of mysterious and repressed homosexuality and I think the book works perfectly all right, although it was written after Gay Liberation. So it's still an option if one wants to write about things in that way. I'm now editing an anthology of homosexual fiction for Faber, and the contribution by the youngest of all the writers is a throwback to this earlier period. In other words, it is about the relationship between a white man and an American Indian out West, and there's a strong homoerotic pull between them, but neither of them appears to be conscious of it. It works as a very exciting homosexual story of a friendship, but definitely physical.

In The Darker Proof, *the volume of short stories you wrote with Adam Mars-*

Jones, there seems to be a note of defiance in the face of Aids. Is this defiance aimed at those who would smugly and piously claim that Aids has nothing to do with them, or is it perhaps stalking the spectre of death itself?

I think both. I have a very peculiar reaction to Aids that nobody else I know has, and that is a feeling of rage and humiliation. I'm a very proud person and I hate to have people condescend to me, but I have felt since Aids came along that many well-intentioned and perfectly nice heterosexual people look at me pityingly. I was very early in coming out as somebody who was HIV positive. I gave interviews early on, and I even wrote in *Life Magazine* recently that I am HIV positive. Now I find that many people have this way of looking at me as though they know I'm going to be dead in two years, and it's as though that proves that everything I was saying earlier about the importance of expressing yourself homosexually was a mistake. It's as if the Establishment, or heterosexuals or square normal people, are having the last laugh, and it absolutely infuriates me. So in these stories I'm interested partly in showing the kind of heroism, and even the high spirits, with which homosexuals are sometimes responding to the disease. I'm also very interested in showing that it's not just people who are always at the baths having sex twenty times a day who are getting it. In fact it's a single exposure that causes it. The viral nature of the disease wasn't known till 1984, and by that point the disease had already been very widely spread.

It first started appearing, as far as we know, in 1981, so there were three or four years of sexual activity when we didn't know what safe sex was. Now we know how the disease is transmitted, and of the younger generation, the people who have come out since 1984, only 1 per cent has reported being positive in the United States. It's a very low percentage. In other words, safe sex is really working, while for the older group there was no such thing as safe sex. People said you shouldn't use poppers. Now it turns out that that had nothing to do with it. People said you shouldn't have too much sex, or you should know the name of your partner. All of which is ludicrous, since it's a question of a single exposure and you can get it as easily from your lover in bed at night in your home as you can at the baths or in the back room. It had nothing to do with the promiscuity, it had to do with the nature of sexual contact.

How much does it worry you?

It worries me constantly. Every time I make plans I make them with a double accounting system. In other words, I can tell you in one breath that I'm going to go teach so that I can have a retirement plan in fifteen years, but the other system of accounting says I'll probably be dead in

four years, which is a statistical possibility, and a very strong one, because I know I've been positive since 1985, which is from the beginning of the tests. The view now is that 90 to 100 per cent of the people who are positive will develop the disease. They used to say 10 per cent, then it was 25 per cent. All you can hope for is either that they're wrong or there will be a vaccine for people who are positive but don't yet have the disease.

Does that fear make you reject sex, or doesn't it make any difference?

I never have non-safe sex, but that's for the other person's benefit, not for mine. I continue to have a lot of sex, so it doesn't make any difference that way, but it makes you wake up in the middle of the night thinking you're going to die. I've lost some forty friends, you know – almost my whole generation. We were a group of gay writers, in New York together, and now I'm trying to organize all of their papers for Yale University before the last of us die, so they can have something to study for the future.

Why is it that homosexuals get the virus, and lesbians don't on the whole?

It's the nature of the sexual contact. It's spread by blood and sperm. A homosexual man, or any man, can get fucked in the ass, so he receives sperm, and the nature of the anus is to absorb fluid to make a hard stool, so it absorbs instantly anything that's put in it. Drug addicts, for instance, will often put drugs up their ass to get high quickly, or if you give yourself a wine enema you will get high very quickly because it doesn't pass through your liver first. It's very vulnerable tissue, whereas the nature of the vagina is not to absorb but to conduct the sperm all the way to the uterus.

The anus being highly absorptive, a man can get fucked in the ass, can get Aids that way, and then can turn around and fuck somebody else in the ass. The nature of homosexual men is that they can both receive sperm and give sperm. The nature of a heterosexual man is that he can give sperm but can't receive it. The nature of a woman is that she can receive sperm but can't give it. So it's almost a fact that, mathematically, a homosexual man plays this pivot role of both giving and receiving sperm, and it's that which makes a homosexual especially vulnerable.

What has been the social impact of Aids? I know what liberal response is proper, but is it not time to curb freedoms as Aids spreads through the population? The Soviet Union, for example, has a very small-scale problem, seemingly because homosexual acts are still illegal there and are heavily punished.

Western Europe, at least, is not likely to be very repressive about Aids

because there was a period when the disease was heterosexualized, that is to say, it was being presented as a strong heterosexual possibility and people started getting very frightened. Now it appears that the target populations are black Africans, mainly heterosexual, gay men and intravenous drug-users, and the ruling class in Western Europe isn't very interested in any of these three groups. If they all die, nobody cares. That's the ignoble side of it. The noble side is that people like the Minister of Health here in France have realized that forbidding homosexuality or closing bath-houses is not really very efficacious in stopping the spread of the disease.

It can take up to ten years before it manifests itself, but there's no way of knowing who has it. For a while, the Bavarians were trying to give people instantaneous tests before they crossed the border, and other people, like the Finns, were insisting you had a blood test before you went to their country; and India was saying that to have longer than a six-month visa, you had to have blood tests. All of that was quite ridiculous, and in Western Europe it was decided it was against human rights, so now the European Community, with the reluctant acceptance of Britain, which is always more primitive in these matters, has decided it is unenforceable and we must first spread health information to encourage prevention, and secondly pay for research. Trying to stop people from having sex is pointless.

It's almost twenty-five years since Viscount Montgomery said of homosexuality: This sort of thing may be tolerated by the French, but we are British, thank God.' Presumably you would agree we have moved on since then, but do you think that the underlying attitude of the majority of British people remains the same?

Yes, I think England is especially backward in the acceptance of homosexuality. But again it extends to sexuality in general. For instance, all the business that was going on two or three years ago with small children, the witch-hunting of parents in Cleveland and all. In France people laughed. They couldn't believe something like that could possibly happen. One of the main reasons why England is so primitive is its press. In France we don't have a popular press, a gutter press. There are no headlines saying 'Mother Tortures Baby'. In Britain you have almost nothing but. Even *The Times* runs sensational headlines. The level of British journalism is appalling, and it's interesting, going back to the question of Aids, to find the countries that have behaved the worst have been the United States, England and Germany, those being the three countries which have a great gutter press. The countries that have behaved the best have been those in the Latin world – Spain, Italy

and France – which don't have a gutter press to stir up all this anxiety and craziness.

And aren't we in Britain much more hypocritical about sex in general than people in Europe?

Absolutely. In France, if you go to a dinner party among middle-class or educated people and you start whispering about somebody's divorce or somebody's adultery, everyone looks at you askance. But in England I'm shocked even by my friends about how much they gossip, especially about sex. Somebody said something very amusing recently: that in America people talk about money in order to avoid talking about the real secret, which is sex, whereas in France everybody talks about sex in order to avoid talking about the real secret, which is money.

In your view, are you born homosexual or do you become homosexual? Is it nature or nurture?

In my own case I feel it was nature, because one of my earliest memories, during the war, when I was less than five years old, was of sitting on the lap of a pilot who was a friend of our family and being absolutely enthralled by him as a man – I mean feeling weak at the knees with admiration for this huge man with golden wings on his shirt. It wasn't the usual little boy's desire to want to be the man. It was the desire to have him, somehow. Admiration of a little boy for a soldier is perfectly normal, but this was something slightly different. Certain societies favour the expression of homosexuality, but the urge towards homosexuality may well be determined biologically.

Now for the important question. What is it about the homosexual that makes him generally more promiscuous than the heterosexual? Where does the compulsion spring from? It's something everyone wants to know.

It goes back to what I said earlier. Almost everything about homosexuality can be explained by its status as an all-male world. For instance, a study done of lesbian couples, gay male couples and heterosexual couples, showed that if you took a certain age group, say thirty to thirty-five, the lesbian couple had sex once a week, the gay male couple had sex three times a week, and the heterosexual couple had sex twice a week. In other words, heterosexuality is what needs to be explained in that it is a compromise between a powerful male sexuality and a weaker or more restrained sexuality. Many heterosexual men used to say to me before Aids, you guys are really lucky because you can get laid all the time and don't have to spend a fortune taking somebody out to dinner four or five times, then sitting around waiting and hoping she

might put out. You see somebody in the street, you ask him for a light, you go home with him and you have sex immediately. That was the great advantage of homosexuality before Aids. You didn't have the braking effect of female socialization, but you had the affectionately enhancing effect of male on male. Men were doing exactly what they wanted to do, and what they would be doing with women if they could. I think very few heterosexual men, if they're honest, would say oh, I like having to court a woman for a month before I can go to bed with her. If you read erotic fantasies by heterosexual men, it's oftentimes where women are on heat. Many erotic movies are about women who have hungry pussies – they are on heat, they can't have enough. In fact they don't exist very often. There are nymphomaniacs, of course, but never enough.

But there's another thing which is inexplicable. However heterosexual I may be, it's unlikely I will go to a public lavatory and wait outside for a woman to come out and proposition her. But there are very distinguished men who, before sexual liberation, ran the risk of arrest by visiting lavatories. There's a compulsion there.

That has partly to do with the repression of homosexuality. Many of those men were married and did not have a homosexual lifestyle, but did have strong homosexual urges and no normal channels for expressing them. They were afraid to be seen in a homosexual bar or pub; they couldn't take a lover because they had a wife. I have in those furtive situations met men who turned out to be married. I used to cruise all the time, but found I was most compulsive before I accepted my homosexuality, which was when I went to a Freudian woman Viennese psychiatrist when I was twenty years old. My biggest problem was that I was so sexually compulsive, and I asked, 'What can I do to cure this?' She said, 'If you can speak to your heterosexual friends a little bit about why you are homosexual, and if you could be more open about it and could integrate it into your life, you would find you would become less compulsive.'

So in your present settled situation, would you never dream of cruising?

Yes, of course I would cruise. Just as I can imagine how it would be if you were in an airport bar and a very attractive woman sat down next to you and you bought her a drink and started talking to her; and then it was announced that all the planes were cancelled and that you would have to stay in Paris another night. If she invited you back to her apartment or you invited her to your hotel for another drink, what happens next?

Yes, but I wouldn't go looking for it.

Well, I don't go to bars and I live with somebody, but I can't say I would resist temptation 100 per cent if it presented itself.

You say in A Boy's Own Story: *'Sex seemed a strange thing to me, a social rite that registered, even brought about, shifts in the balance of power.' What is the relationship between sex and power?*

A sub-text in many sexual acts, even ones that seem quite affectionate, can be sado-masochism. There was a famous American psychiatrist called Stoller who began to record the sado-masochistic fantasies of patients who called themselves sado-masochistic, but he was a good enough scientist to realize that he should record the sexual fantasies of regular people too, and found that they also had fantasies of submission and domination to a shocking extent. The truth is that, even when the sex act, viewed by a camera or a voyeur, looks fairly peaceful, if you were reading the text going on in the head of the man or the woman or the two men or the two women you might find there were themes of submission and domination; that they were very fluid in that sometimes one might begin as the submissive one and end as the dominant one. Many of the themes of childhood, the feelings of wanting control and fear of losing control, get played out in the adult sexual act. It's part of what makes it exciting. Stoller found that the reason couples get bored with each other is that they get to know each other too well and know that the other doesn't really represent any threat. The ideal sexual moment is when people are comfortable enough with each other to feel free to express their fantasies but don't know each other so well that there's no longer a mystery.

That's true. Can you suggest something of the homosexual attitude towards women? It must be a different kind of relationship in general from that which obtains between heterosexuals, even when there is no overt liaison, nor any liklihood of one.

Friendships between heterosexual women and homosexual men can be some of the strongest in the world. It approaches Hegel's idea of the brother/sister relationship, because it's a sister that you've chosen. It's one of the purest relationships because it is completely disinterested. There's no sexual tension. You don't want anything from the woman and she doesn't want anything from you. What you want is each other's friendship. That can be very complex too, and it can be involved with social ambition, working together, all kinds of things, but nevertheless I would say it approaches a state of purity, because for homosexual men every other man is potentially a sexual partner.

Has it ever happened that you befriended a woman and she fell for you?

Yes. That's painful. I try to be very clear from the very beginning, though now that I'm well known as a gay writer I don't even have to. But before I would always try to be very clear that I was exclusively homosexual so that at least I was being fair and honest about what was possible. It does happen, but less often I find because I tend not to make a mystery of my life and I will often introduce a woman friend to my boy-friend very early on. Therefore it would have to be somebody very unbalanced and strange who would let herself go so far.

I understand that you are also occasionally attracted to heterosexuals. How do you deal with that. Is it possible for you to seduce the heterosexual?

[*Laughs*] Yes, well, that's maybe one reason why I like Genet, because Genet never had sex with homosexual men, only with heterosexual men. They were always working-class boys who were in some way dependent on him for money, but he would always arrange for them to have girl-friends. He would even choose their wives and so on. It was the sort of thing that used to happen a lot in the Mediterranean world, especially Greece; the older man who had the younger boy, then set the younger boy up in the world. Many younger heterosexual men admire me as a writer. They're curious and they want to have an edge on you. I've been seduced more by heterosexual men than I have seduced. I don't think I've seduced them very often. But if they want to seduce me, it's OK.

To come back to Genet and the subject of Prisoner of Love. *How do you feel about the Palestinian cause. Are you sympathetic?*

It's a very awkward question. I'll tell you why. It's because American publishing is entirely pro-Israel. Recently I was asked if Genet was anti-Semitic, and I said yes and no, but yes to some degree. The publisher said, 'Well, why are we even bothering to publish your book? Nobody will read it in America.' So there's a commercial part of me that thinks I have to be very careful how I respond to your question, but the truth is I'm very sympathetic to the Palestinians.

You can be sympathetic to the Palestinians without being anti-Semitic. I'm certainly not anti-Semitic.

Nor am I. I'm not even anti-Zionist, but all the contact I have had with Palestinians has been very good. I find the Arab people that I've met are most cultured, and even their attitude towards literature is extremely sophisticated. For instance, a book like *Prisoner of Love* would have been a very easy one for the Palestinians to claim and try to use as a political

weapon, but in fact, when I was recently at the Institute of the Arab World here in Paris, on a panel with the head of the *Palestinian Review*, he said that he thought the book should be considered a work of art and not as a political text; that, of course, it did have a political aspect, but it would be very difficult to decode a clear political message. It's very ambiguous politically. The thing about Genet is that he himself was a homeless person and hated France. He though that he was an orphan. He was always rejected by everybody, and the two political groups he identified with were the Black Panthers and the Palestinians, both of whom had a government but no country. He once said that the day the Palestinians recovered their land, then he would no longer love them. It was very important to him that they were marginal homeless people like himself.

He identified with them.

Absolutely. He hated France and never thought he was French. When he was a child, he had a persistent fantasy that he was Polish. He loved it when people told him he looked Polish.

Could you write a novel without any trace of homosexuality in it?

I've already done it, and that's *Caracole* where there are no homosexual characters. Mind you, it's been a very difficult book to sell because our society is one which packages everyone, and so people were very puzzled by it, especially in the English-speaking world. Why would a homosexual writer write a book where there are no homosexual characters?

I found it exciting and liberating to write. For one thing, in this book I wrote compulsively about heterosexual sex, which I have very little experience of, so it was all my fantasies, and I found that very exciting. Several heterosexual readers have told me they found it exciting too. It was a pure act of imagination, projection and voyeurism.

What's the greatest ambition left to you?

I want to finish the cycle that has begun with *A Boy's Own Story* and *The Beautiful Room Is Empty*. I want to write two more volumes, one about the 1970s, the heyday of gay life, then one about the 1980s, about the Aids period. So I want to finish that as a cycle, and I certainly want to finish the Genet book. After that we'll see.

SIR GORDON WHITE

Gordon White was born in Yorkshire in 1923 and was educated at De Aston School in Lincolnshire. After serving with the Special Operations Executive in the Far East from 1942 to 1946, he started his business career in the family publishing firm. He and James Hanson began their partnership on the board of Oswald Tillotson, a company which sold and distributed vehicles. It merged with the Wiles group in 1964 and the following year Hanson became chairman of the group and White deputy chairman. The Hanson Trust was founded in 1969 and four years later Gordon White moved to the United States and founded Hanson Industries, becoming chairman in 1983. In 1979 he received the KBE in recognition of services to British commercial and community interests in the USA. He has been married twice and has a son and two daughters. His interests include flying helicopters and horse-racing.

Was your childhood a happy one and did your early years in the North of England stand you in good stead?

My formative years were very happy. I had two brothers and a close family life. My father was away a lot of the time because he had a publishing business that involved him travelling around England. We were ten or eleven before my mother found she could no longer cope with us and sent us off to boarding school. My mother and father were a devoted couple. Once married, they lived together all of their lives and died within two years of each other. I got on well with my father. He was a wonderful man, a great character, but we never got anything for nothing. If we wanted pocket money, we had to earn it. If we played cards, he would win our pocket money from us and not give it back.

I was a terrible rebel in my schooldays, and after I set the school on fire I was asked to leave. I would have gone to another school, but my father said, 'If you can get a job, you're leaving. I won't send you to another one.' So the only job I ever had to look for in my life was as an office boy. I worked for six months and then asked for an increase in salary. They didn't give it to me, so I left and joined my father in his advertising business.

I was always a rebel against authority, always looking for reasons why things had to be done, and if the reasons didn't seem to make sense, I didn't see why I should do them. But I was always very positive. I think perhaps one of the major influences in my life was working in my father's advertising business, and then the war broke out and I went off into the services. I was away for four years in an organization known as Special Operations Executive, a clandestine outfit. I stayed on in Siam after the war and didn't get back to England till the beginning of 1947. So, by the time I returned, the war had already been over for about two years. There were no bands playing, no welcoming garlands, no

rejoicing, no feeling of a conquering hero returning. I arrived on a dull day in Liverpool, and it was quite a shock to come back and find everything so dismal.

My father's business had gone. There was nothing to sell and therefore nothing to advertise. He'd started another business making toys, but that became moribund. So I restarted his advertising business, and that rolled along for a number of years.

Did you know, as a young man, that you were going to succeed?

I did really. I knew that I wanted to make a lot of money. I think I was motivated primarily by that need. I was a very romantic individual, steeped in the whole British thing – Bulldog Drummond, romance, knights in armour. The whole of a certain type of civilized living was exemplified in that kind of book. That's what I thought I would achieve. Money was important because, if you wanted fast cars, if you wanted a great lifestyle, you had to pay for it, and the only way you could pay for it was with money.

The gossip columnists continue to write about the film stars you escorted back in the 1950s, which rather suggests you were well of by then.

I was. I had a lot of fun, because beautiful movie stars are usually very lonely people. I knew a lot about the film industry and had started a company called Artists Personal Appearances. I had also won an air race and become quite famous in my own way as a pilot, and that led to an advertising campaign using me as the star. They asked me if I would do a number of commercials with leading actresses. I met a lot of actresses, and after working hard for a period, I would take a holiday in the watering holes of the world and have fun. If one had been thinking about getting married, one might have found it rather difficult, but I wasn't really interested in getting married at the time. I just loved being in the company of famous, beautiful women. It was very flattering to one's ego. When I did get married, I couldn't believe it as I came out of the church. There must have been sixty photographers as well as the television cameras. It was headline news. The most eligible bachelor in the world, I was called.

You left Britain in 1973 because of what you saw as the encroachment of socialist bias in government.

If someone had said to me in the summer of 1973 that I would soon leave England, emigrate to the United States and live in New York, I would have told them, 'You had better go along and see your local shrink because you're crazy.' Until then I could never bear to be out of

England for more than two weeks without getting homesick. I'd been to America many times, I'd travelled all over the world, but I'd always come back to England. It was going to war that made it like that for me. My father had been the first volunteer in Grimsby in the First World War and spent four years in the trenches in the Coldstream Guards. He was wounded seven times and lost three brothers. One of my own brothers was killed in the Second World War. The whole thing to me was what one had to give to England: the blood, sweat, toil and tears of Churchill's promise to the British people. It appealed to me and I thought that this was the way it should be. When I came back, the fruits of victory were something I had anticipated, and they weren't there. But I was young, enthusiastic and ambitious, and so I put up with the 2 oz. of butter and 4 oz. of meat a week, and the fact that you couldn't get this and that, and the strikes, and the ghastly winter of 1947. All of those things would get better, or so I thought. But as we rolled on from government to government, Conservative and Labour, nothing ever changed. A touch on the accelerator, a bang on the brake. The economy never got going.

During all this time I remained optimistic about the future of England, but finally it came to that period in the 1970s when we were facing the prospect of another socialist régime. James Hanson and I put together a deal to merge with Bowater, and the Office of Fair Trading stopped it. In other words, the entrepreneur was not to be allowed to operate within the economic climate of Britain. At that time, you may recall, Edward Heath came up with the statement about the unacceptable face of capitalism. And what was the unacceptable face of capitalism? Was it Mr Tiny Rowland's having a house on the company? Having read up the subject now, I realize that what we have today is radical. Margaret Thatcher is not a Conservative, she's a radical. And she is determined to change the paternalism that has ruled and ruined this country. You have to create wealth. Unless you create wealth you can't spend it. Communism doesn't work, socialism doesn't work, and, in my view, liberalism doesn't work either.

The Japanese will eventually prove that they can become a superpower by growing to be the richest nation in the world, without even an army, because capitalism works. There's no doubt about it. In this country, as happened to Lester Piggot, you get arrested if you have more than £35 in your pocket. What sort of a country were we living in where you could have Customs officials stopping you to see how much money you had on you? Our profits the year I went to America were £8 million. The first thing I did was employ the *Economist* intelligence unit to do a paper to find out the exact value of the exchange control regulations. The regulations turned out to be absolutely valueless. In fact they were restricting the growth of the country.

I turned copies of that report over to Harold Wilson as well as to Margaret Thatcher. That summer of 1973 I felt crushed by the Heath government. They had unlocked the doors of the banks, lowered interest rates to some ridiculous level, and shovelled out money. Then the crash came. At fifty-one years of age I suddenly found that all my shares were practically worthless, that the market had collapsed. So I left.

You describe yourself as 'ridiculously patriotic'. Didn't that make it hard for you to leave England in the middle of such a crisis?

It wasn't a crisis. It was a weakness: the abdication of the right to manage. People had abdicated that right and the whole system was negative. They had become so used to saying you couldn't have this, or that was rationed, or you had to be on a three-year waiting list to buy a motor car. National servicemen, when they were fighting a war in Korea, used to see in Japan, when they went on rest and recuperation, the Japanese driving round in English cars which they couldn't buy. The habit of mind became permanent.

Legend has it that you arrived in New York with $3,000 and turned it into a vast fortune, but wasn't the Hanson Trust already an established company in Britain?

We were a tiny little nothing: £8 million pre-tax profit. When I arrived in the United States and went to see my first bank manager there, he kept me waiting a long time. He'd never heard of me. The English were a joke. If you made the mistake of taking sterling travellers' cheques, you couldn't get them cashed in a bank. No one realizes how Britain at that time was gone, finished. We were considered a tourist country. I couldn't borrow money on the balance sheet or bring money out of Britain, but I was very lucky in that the first deal I ever did there I did on paper. A miracle. I found a business which they didn't want cash for immediately. It suddenly became highly successful because of the OPEC crisis, when the product went through the roof. The business cost $30 million to be paid over two years, and the first year's pre-tax profit was $17 million.

I admit I was lost when I first went to America. But I believed in and was steeped in integrity. When somebody asked me how I was going to pay back the money I'd borrowed, I was actually affronted and said, 'I always pay back the money I borrow.' I said it with such conviction that it became a bit of a legend. James Hanson and I both think identically about the business of borrowing money and paying it back. We were brought up the same way – both Yorkshiremen. I even used to believe naïvely that you could do a deal with a handshake.

Would you have an absolutely laissez-faire *economy or should the state take some responsibility in certain areas of social welfare?*

I believe there is a major responsibility in a capitalist system for it to provide for the mentally handicapped, the old, the crippled, the disadvantaged. I believe that the classless society is obviously the right way to go, but I believe that the strong, the more intelligent and the more commercial will rise to the top. It's frightening to see a welfare system that can be abused by people who don't want to work, a system that will create areas of no-go, a system of misery that creates the muggers, and robbers and killers. I don't think you can lay down a line and say that's the fault of the rich, therefore the rich should throw money at those problems. You get young active people on welfare because the system will pay them. Right now the major problem in the United States is one-parent families. On CBS they interviewed black women who were mothers of fatherless children. Each child represented an additional welfare payment.

But success does carry with it an enormous responsibility. I believe that the people who amass great wealth, flaunt it but give nothing back to the community are wrong. I believe that the more wealth you accumulate, the more power you accumulate, and the more responsibility. I would call myself a generous man in this respect, though when it comes to socialist ideas, I don't believe that socialism has a chance. It's unnatural. In my view, it's an invention of the intellectually arrogant, and intellectuals do have an enormous arrogance. They believe they can think for the rest of us. The Labour party is 50 per cent working class people and 50 per cent intellectuals. But they have done nothing to change the face of England in terms of providing for a society that is going to move upwards.

Out of this little country was created the biggest empire the world has ever seen, and colonialism, as produced by the British, was not what the popular image of colonialism in the United States would have it be. American ignorance about world affairs can sometimes be devastatingly profound. The country which united under the British – India – in fact produced railways, universities, schools, a civil service, but it couldn't cope with the religious problems that existed at Independence. Then you had the Moslems running one way and the Hindus running the other. It was one of the biggest slaughters in history, with something like three million people being killed. That was what happened when the British scuttled out of India under American pressure.

They're trying to do to the same in South Africa right now. They would hand the country over to the blacks to rule it without any possible opportunity for them to create, over the years of evolution, the type of

people who could rule South Africa. Should they just take over because they have black skins? You've also got racism among the blacks. The Zulus are not going to agree to be ruled by another black race. It's an example of the confusion which surrounds the American desire to have so-called democracy. Where does democracy exist in Africa, outside South Africa? Every other African country is ruled by a one-party state. They immediately wipe out the opposition, like the Nigerians did when they were slaughtering the Ibos.

So how would you solve the South African problem?

What they should do is give every black man over fifty a vote. That way they could slowly carry the country over a period of years into an evolution of one man, one vote. But as soon as you give all the blacks a vote, they will immediately vote on colour of the skin. They're not politically intelligent enough to say, well, just a second, we've got a choice here – this white man might be a good guy. They just vote black. Politically Africa is perhaps two hundred years behind South America, and South America has a long way to go.

You said in an interview with Alan Whicker in 1985 that you felt that business was like boarding a ship, robbing all the men and raping all the women.

I never said that. At least, not in that context. Undoubtedly there is a tremendous thrill in the chase, the fight. It's a war to win control of a company, a war in the market place. And you can be hurt financially if you make mistakes. I've always believed that one should be ruthless in decision but compassionate in execution. People talk about chucking people out and closing factories down. Absolute rubbish. We pay high compensation and severance pay. Life is all about winning, and you can consider that you've won every time you cross the street without getting run down by a vehicle; that you've survived.

But haven't you generated a lot of hostility in your remarkable career?

I feel very strongly about companies that have allowed themselves to become quaint, who have allowed themselves to be overtaken by nepotism and bureaucracy, by committees they've created themselves. Today Hanson PLC is unique in its lack of protocol. There are no politics in this company, no intrigue. It is wide open. There is no one within the company who can't get us on the telephone if they want to talk to James Hanson or myself. I'm very accessible.

I would claim that we predators have done a tremendous job, not only in this country but in the United States as well, because a company cannot, by and large, be God. You find the most extraordinary things

when you take over a company. You cannot believe the departments that get created. Sometimes you take over a company with 250 people and find it needs only ten. Imagine the dead hand of that bureaucracy.

We're not asset strippers. Absolutely not. What we've done is sell off divisions. Selling off a division is part of the operational philosophy. We believe that we are guardians of a portfolio of businesses. If someone else can see, in one of our companies, value in excess of what we can see in it, then it's worth a lot more to them and I sell. That's not asset stripping. We've sold many businesses in our time, and all of them have flourished as they've gone on to better homes. Asset stripping would happen if you had a factory making goods and decided you could get more money for the factory than for the business; in which case you fire all the people, strip out the equipment and flog the building.

I've been told that I'm a legend in the United States for having, within fifteen years, created a company worth $6 billion from nothing. That is to my mind one of the greatest compliments that can be paid to the capitalist system. Hanson's has a solid background. It's not a get-rich-quick organization. Both Hanson and I are primarily industrialists. I was brought up at ground-floor level to run a company. When I worked for my father, I sometimes had to sweep the floors.

In your view, is the stick and carrot technique basic to management?

There is a lot more to it than the carrot and the stick. There has to be enormous satisfaction and happiness in going to work. You have to feel happy about dealing with your colleagues. You mustn't be frustrated by bureaucracy. There must be an atmosphere. We had a dinner the other night at the Hyde Park Hotel for our American and British executives, and the atmosphere there was so good, I wish I'd had it on video. We don't take ourselves too seriously. Our corporate lawyer, the head of our legal department in America, did a humorous piece on each of our British executives, and it had everybody in fits of laughter. It was very irreverent, but that's the spirit of the company. I don't believe in the stick. I believe that you put a man in charge of his own destiny. That is the difference between Hanson and any other company. We say to a man running a division, 'You have to come to us for your capital expenditure, and we in turn want to see your budgets. First of all, you will be paid the salary for the job, and then comes your incentivization. You are incentivized to produce a return on your capital, because your capital is under your control. Beyond that, it's your business, you run it.' If we were to use the carrot and the stick and say, 'We'll give you some more money if you do well but if you don't do well we'll fire you,' that would produce nothing. The American system is, of course,

very tough. And American workers are very pragmatic about it. They don't expect a free lunch.

You never visit factories or businesses you control.

I believe that the manager is in charge of his business. He doesn't need the chairman. The manager should run the business as if it were his own and make it work for him. I'm just there to support him. If you take away from a man the right to manage, he is able to abdicate his responsibility. It might not be a bad thing if I visited factories, said hello and showed my face, but really it isn't going to make them any more efficient. I'm a distant, corporate figure, which is why I don't insist that all of our divisional companies have a Hanson name on them.

I understand that there is a low proportion of American investors in Hanson.

We've got the largest number of American investors of any industrial company of our size in the world, so the opposite is true. We've been floated on the American market for only three years, and nearly 20 per cent of our shares are owned in the United States. ICI have been selling their shares in America for over twenty years and only about 7 per cent are owned in America. I believe that ultimately we will be owned 50–50 by the United States and the United Kingdom.

You must find lawyers' fees a terrible irritant, given the way you feel about top-heavy management.

I think they're obscene. I feel even more strongly about the legal fees in the United States, and the merchant banking fees too. They are absolutely ridiculous. They bear no relation to the amount of work done. I believe that one of the great disasters of the United States is the legal system. It's totally and utterly wrong for lawyers to follow ambulances. It's totally wrong for lawyers to be able to work on a contingency basis and take law suits in order to get money for themselves. When I took over one company, Smith Corona, it involved a long legal battle. At the end of the day we got their legal bills, banking fees and everything. It came to $50 million. Our legal bills and banking fees were $12 million.

I have heard it said that your greatest ambition is to buy back in the United States the amount lost as a consequence of the Second World War.

I wanted to feel that Britain would once again have a major economic presence in the United States. But we've got it now – not just the 20 per cent, which we had before the war, but as the biggest foreign

investor in the United States. Britain is bigger than the Japanese, bigger than anybody.

What is it you so admire about the United States compared to Britain?

I admire the environment of freedom enormously. I could never have come from America to Britain and built a business of the size I did in fifteen years, nor could I have gone to Germany or France and done it.

To what do you attribute the success of the Japanese?

The Japanese discovered the weakness of the major companies, first of all in electronics. They saw that they could copy things, but then they realized that, if they did a bit more work, they could make them better. The television business is a perfect example of the manufacturer's abdication of his rights to supply the customer. Here the thing to do for years was rent your television set. Why did you rent your television set? Well, if it broke down they'd come and fix it. So why didn't the dealer come and fix it? The Japanese entered this market with the Sony Twinatone, half the size of the first colour television, created a network of dealers and guaranteed the sets. If anybody brought a television set back, it was exchanged and Sony picked up the bill. The Japanese forte was to spot loopholes and exploit them; and to listen to the customer.

I know how much you admire Mrs Thatcher, but what is it you so admire about her?

She had to change a whole way of thinking. Lots of people, even in the Conservative party, were very against wealth. The 'us and them' syndrome existed in the Conservative party as much as in the Labour party. Both parties conducted government in a paternal fashion. Macmillan, in his last run for election, said, 'You have never had it so good.' He didn't say, '*We* have never had it so good.' When Mrs Thatcher took over, the union barons didn't want democracy. They had the lads. I've been addressed by a major union leader who said, 'The lads will never agree to this.' The lads? Who were these lads? Some of them were seventy years old. Margaret Thatcher needed to tackle the grass roots.

I admire her for seeing the arrogance of intellectuals who believe they should tell you how to live. There again, she doesn't believe in big government. When you think about the state Britain was in when she took over – the unions were totally in control of the country. Harold Wilson at one point considered running the country with the help of the unions, and they used to turn up at 10 Downing Street. But Margaret Thatcher stuck to her guns. She would not be deviated.

To secure our economic future, we're going to have to work a lot

harder and follow the dictates laid down by Margaret Thatcher, which are basic common sense: don't spend more money than you've got, and you have to do a day's work for a day's pay.

When it comes to the next General Election, I'm no prophet, but I can't see that clown Kinnock getting in. He reminds me of an old English comedian called Tommy Trinder. He's just not prime minister material. I think the Labour party is totally and utterly discredited. It's been proven socialism doesn't work. Nationalized industries don't work. Bit state enterprise doesn't work. Even nationalized medicine isn't working. They'd be far better off if they pelted money into private medicine, gave everybody insurance and commercial clinics were built. I was talking recently to a professor of medicine at a major English hospital who has been there fifteen years. He told me that, when he first started, the administrative staff in his department numbered six, and now there were eighty-five. The drones of bureaucracy had multiplied.

David Steel once suggested it could be thought that the fact that the Hanson bid for Imperial was allowed to go ahead was a reward for helping Mrs Thatcher over the Westland helicopter affair. Why did you buy so many shares at well over the market price?

David Steel is absolutely full of rubbish. I've never found in my experience that there has been any help from the government. The only government that has a certain power in this way is the US government. You can approach a congressman and a senator, and he has influence, but I don't think a British politician, by and large, has much influence. I'm a helicopter pilot. I no more wanted to see Westland go to the French than the man in the moon. Nothing to do with the political aspect of it at all. Westland was a British company, and I don't believe that the French would have had Westland grow. That was my opinion and I still believe it. Mr Steel is full of baloney.

Most Englishmen who have been to public school, including those who are heterosexual, don't actually enjoy the company of women, but prefer the company of other men.

I guess I'm the same as all the rest of the Englishmen. I prefer the company of men. There are so many different aspects of a man's life that women just don't seem to be able to get involved in, like sport. Dangerous things have always quite appealed to me. All my flying career was littered with instances of near death, and on the whole it's not easy for a woman to relate to danger the way a man does.

You once said you loved beautiful women, but they had to be achievers too. What counts as achievement in the case of women?

A woman can be a marvellous mother, for example. I admire Princess Diana enormously as a woman and as a mother. I admire Margaret Thatcher enormously for what she has achieved in what has always been considered a man's world. I admire a woman who does anything exceptionally well. If you see the Queen Mother across a crowded room, she radiates warmth.

On the subject of what attracts me to a woman, I suppose one has to say that a beautiful woman is a challenge. Men are afraid of beautiful women. Did you know that? It's quite extraordinary. Every man has his type. *Playboy* magazine was created on big boobs, so obviously you have to believe that the world's men adore big breasts. Quite frankly, that's never what appealed to me. During my days in the theatrical world, I always admired a great actress. If a woman was not only beautiful but talented, then there was an attraction. But the most important thing to me is femininity. There is enormous sensuality in certain women. I once saw a black girl walking down Piccadilly, and I didn't know she was black, but, from the back, I have never seen a walk like that in my life. She barely touched the ground as she walked. It was the most sensual thing I'd ever seen. It wasn't an exaggerated swing of the hips, or anything like that, but a flow. I'm not attracted to women who are highly competitive and have lost their femininity because of their competitive nature.

Are you sympathetic to the feminist movement?

I deplore the feminist movement. These women are crazy. The whole lot of them are absolutely crackers. Women are being destroyed by the feminist movement. All male chauvinist pigs have mothers. It's the mother who brings the boy up to be a chauvinist, who says open the door, carry this, stand back, ladies first. My mother brought me up to believe that, if I was in an aeroplane which was about to crash and there was only one parachute, I should give the parachute to the girl and should go down with the plane – exactly what happened with the *Titanic*. The men went down with the ship. The band played, and officers stood by with guns and pistols in case men tried to get into the lifeboats ahead of the women and children.

Men used to respect women, but the way a young man treats a young woman today is as an equal. Do they stand up and give their seats to a woman? Do they take their hats off in an elevator? Of course they don't. All men are led by their cock. A man will lie, cheat and steal to get a woman into bed. He's now discovering that all he has to say is, 'Do you want a fuck? My place or your place? You want to argue about it? Forget it. I'll find somebody else.' After the war, the most difficult girls to get into bed were American, because American mothers brought

their daughters up to believe they should be virgins and that, if they ever gave their body, they'd hate it. Now *Cosmopolitan* magazine tells you how a woman should have multiple orgasms, how she should do this, do that, do the other. It's full of bullshit. Now they've got to find the man to give them all of this.

I would certainly be considered a male chauvinist. I believe it is my duty to protect women, I really do, and I'm quite sure I would have gone down with the ship too. The thing I object to very strongly is, of course, the token woman who is forced on people. People say we must have a woman for vice president, so they pull a woman out of the block and she becomes a token vice president. Her qualifications are zero, but she is a woman. This is an insult to women.

The secret of my success with women? I don't know. I love to spoil women. I appreciate women. I respect women. I never treat a woman lightly. I've got enormous respect for women, and I think that probably shows. I'm thoughtful, and I think I'm a romantic.

Would you agree that, when one is young, one likes to go out with older women, but as one grows older, one wants to go out with younger women?

Absolutely. There's a book called *The Jennifer Syndrome* about why older men are attracted to younger girls, and why young homosexuals are attracted to older homosexuals. It's a question of youth and age. The older man is tremendously flattered by the admiration a girl shows him, and in addition is in a position to use his great experience to teach her, in many different ways, many different things. I've got a very young girlfriend at the moment, and I'm motivated by her in the most incredible fashion. I've just found one of the biggest challenges of my life, which is getting fit. This particular girl happens to be very much interested in the body, and what you put into your body. So it starts off with food, and the second part of it is exercise. Years ago there was never any need for a man to worry about his body. But we're in the 1990s now, and it does matter. My feeling was, God, it's impossible, I could never get myself into physical condition, I couldn't do it. I smoked, drank, put lots of butter on the bread. But then, two years ago, I stopped smoking, cut my liquor intake to almost nothing, and stopped taking butter, sugar and salt. Then I started to work out and got myself an exercise teacher. My girlfriend didn't make me do it, but the challenge was there.

You have been divorced twice. Do you see the failure of your marriages as in any way the price of success?

Yes. The ending of my last marriage was the price of success. My wife had a terribly tough time. My lifestyle, in the course of the build-up of

my American interests, was just a nightmare. The hours, the travelling, the whole thing. We lived in a hotel room for a year or eighteen months. The whole enterprise started in a room in the Hotel Pierre, till they sent a lawyer's letter to stop me blocking their switchboard with telephone calls.

I have always made a point of having my children with me in the holidays during the formative years. Not any longer with my two girls, but still by and large with my son. I was divorced when he was four, and he is now fifteen, and I would say that, during the intervening years, eighty per cent of the holidays he spent with me. Obviously I would like to have spent more time with them.

As for remarrying, I don't know. That's a question I couldn't even begin to answer. I'm uncertain whether marriage is as important today as it was when I was a young man.

Apart from your business interests, what has most caught your imagination in life?

I would love to have been a major figure in the sporting world. There is something fascinating about somebody being the best in the world at something. All my life I've been attracted to something that has a large element of danger. When I flew, I challenged the weather practically all the time. I was a perfect fool. The challenge of beating something is a compulsion. I'll never forget my brother arranging to pick me up at the airport when I was flying from London to Yorkshire in an aeroplane without a radio and there was a thick fog. My brother drove out to the airfield at Brough, near Hull, where he ran into the chief test pilot of Blackman aircraft and told him he'd come to meet me. The man said, 'Not even that idiot brother of yours would be flying today.'

What might you have taken up as a career if your business interests hadn't prospered?

If I'd had any nerve, if I'd had real courage, I would never have gone into business at all. I would have been an actor. I was once offered a screen test but didn't have the courage to do it. I was afraid of failure. You see, I looked right. I was a very good-looking guy when I was younger.

A N WILSON

Andrew Wilson was born in 1950 and educated at Rugby and New College, Oxford. Between 1976 and 1981 he lectured at St Hugh's College and New College before becoming literary editor of the *Spectator*. His novels include *The Sweets of Pimlico (1977), Unguarded Hours* (1978), *Kindly Light* (1979), *The Healing Art* (1980 – Somerset Maugham Award, Arts Council National Book Award), *Wise Virgin* (1982 – W. H. Smith Literary Award), *Incline our Hearts* (1988) and *A Bottle in the Smoke* (1990). He has also written biographies of John Milton, Hilaire Belloc, and Tolstoy (for which he won the Whitbread Biography Award). He is currently engaged on a biography of Iris Murdoch.

You nicknamed your prep school the Gulag, but do you look back on your childhood as a time of happiness in other respects?

I don't look back on it very much. It's strange. I certainly hated going away to school, and I don't now regard it as a time of happiness. I didn't know until very recently that I was an impossible child – hyperactive, screaming all the time. I didn't seem to have a happy temperament. I was moody, I cried and shouted a lot, and I'm sure I was spoilt. So it was a terrible wrench being sent away to that boarding school. It was called Hillstone, in Malden, and was a crummy, hateful little place.

You've described the fact of being too young to do National Service as a source of 'wistful regret'. Did you have a romantic idea of yourself as an officer on the parade ground, or was there some other basis for regret?

My regret wasn't very serious. It might have been fun, but I certainly didn't think of myself as officer material. I imagine I'd never have risen through the ranks. People don't regard me as a figure of authority and I have never accepted the idea of authority myself. I have been a rebel since early childhood. It probably has something to do with relations with my father. He was about fifty when I was born, and although I got on with him well, it was quite a distant relationship. He was a bit of a disciplinarian, my mother being much softer. I can confide in my mother now, though I never did as a child. It's this awful boarding school thing that the English have: they send their children away so a child doesn't form a relationship with its parents. It's a hopeless preparation for life.

Do you think that's part of the problem later on in life, when Englishmen in general feel uncomfortable in the presence of women?

Yes, it must have to do with it – and with their being uncomfortable with the emotions generally.

You married when you were in your second year at Oxford. Did that have the effect of segregating you from your contemporaries or diluting the experience of being a student?

Yes.

Why did you marry so young?

No comment.

But did you want to settle down?

I don't think so. No.

Are you prone to depression?

I have been in the past. And if you've known depression, you touch wood and hope it won't come swirling back. I have known great waves of debilitating misery that have made it impossible for me to get out of bed or do anything, and where the world has seemed a very black place and sleep was impossible. But I think these times have passed for me. I'm not talking about unhappy circumstances, but about irrational descents of gloom. I've never had analysis, but I've undergone hypnosis and I found that helped. I was hypnotized because I couldn't eat during one depression, and having become more or less anorexic and paralysed with hatred of food, I emerged ravenously hungry and happy as a bird.

To move straight on to your writing, have you felt flattered when reviewers have claimed to detect the influence of Evelyn Waugh in your novels?

I wrote a couple of early books that were pastiches of Evelyn Waugh, and very bad ones. I don't like Evelyn Waugh's novels, probably because I read them too much when I was young. I don't mean that he isn't a brilliant writer and a wonderful stylist, but I like the sort of novels that tell you what it's like to be inside people, inside their minds, or what it feels like to be them. You never get inside an Evelyn Waugh character. The only exception among his novels is *The Ordeal of Gilbert Pinfold*, which I love, and think is a wonderful book.

You have said that, for a novel to work, all the characters must come from an 'unconscious source'. Surely the material has to be empirical in some sense? What exactly is this unconscious source?

If you know what you're up to when you're writing a novel, then it

doesn't work. I've tried dozens of novels written from the top bit of my brain – a surface thing – and they have never got beyond three or four chapters. At some stage – and in my case it's sometimes before I even start to write – you've got to organize the material and you've got to use your mind and think what kind of shape it's going to take. To that extent an empirical source exists, but if it doesn't come from somewhere deep down, if you don't feel you've got to write it, then it's so much easier to write something else or not to write it at all. The whole thing with me is finished before I start to write, either in my head or in notebooks. Having said that, once you start you sometimes realize you've got it all wrong. Normally I take six months to write a novel, but the one I am on at the moment has taken eighteen months. I had to unpick it all in the middle and start again. It becomes a technical and rather boring process in some ways.

So you might sometimes create a whole character from your imagination?

Of course. Characters come from all kinds of sources. Some of mine do appear to have been invented. They are not all based on real anecdotes or incidents or combinations of people I know. Some really do seem to have come from nowhere, others are derived from my feelings about actual people, or they might be combinations of real people. That's not to say they're portraits, for if you try to do that then it doesn't last beyond about four chapters but becomes dead wood in your hands. There are, however, some very good writers – Nancy Mitford being one – who can simply draw portraits of friends, or enemies, and do it completely successfully. But I think they're rather rare.

So do you think novelists are right to use all the information and experience they accumulate, including their acquaintances?

That area is very interesting. If you haven't ever written a novel, you tend to assume that the way to do it is simply to put all your friends in, and change the names and the colour of their hair, or something of the sort. In fact the whole process, except in a very few rare cases, isn't like that at all. It's to do with thinking of a group of people, some of whom might be loosely or even closely based on real life, others of whom wouldn't be, and seeing the way the story and the whole situation takes shape. If you are contemplating real-life originals, which I've seldom done myself, they very quickly get transformed into something else anyway.

In terms of putting one's own experience into books, I should think it was something to do rather sparingly. I've seen it happen, either in novelists I've read about or novelists I've known. I don't know why it should be, but if you do it it's a kind of death. For some reason, writing

novels uses something up inside you. It's terribly tiring. If I write a biography, I can work for eight hours a day and not feel tired at the end. If I do journalism, I don't feel particularly tired. But after three hours of writing a novel I feel absolutely exhausted. Something or other is going out of you, I don't know what. You have to learn not to use up your experience.

As a novelist, do you make a point of respecting confidences?

Obviously one tries to respect confidences, but I'm not at all sure I've received many confidences. Writing biographies is a different matter. If you are specifically talking to somebody about a biography you're writing, then of course you don't respect confidences because you are trying to find things out. Similarly, if I were doing a newspaper article about somebody, I wouldn't be very scrupulous about what I included so long as it was all on the record. Novels are completely different. I don't think I would mind appearing in someone else's novel. If it were bad, it would probably sink without trace, and if it were a good novel, I might feel rather flattered. Evelyn Waugh said that you could put anybody in a novel so long as you made them attractive to women. Probably true.

Your second novel, Unguarded Hours *is a wonderfully funny account of a young man preparing for the priesthood. How far was it based on your own experience in a seminary?*

That was one of the Evelyn Waugh style novels and I don't like it very much. It was loosely based on the seminary I attended, yes, but, as always, when you put real life into books, you have to tone it down rather than the other way about. Nobody would believe what that place was like if I were to write it down accurately. It was a madhouse. It was the only time I've ever been in a wholly, or almost wholly, homosexual world. That was interesting and amusing, but it was a homosexual world of a particularly high-camp kind – a girls' names and feather dusters sort of world. There were about forty men in this seminary, and there were five or so who were either like me, married and living out, or for some reason or other didn't want to take part in it. The thirty-five others had all been to bed with each other. It was beyond belief.

Homosexuals do seem to be talented in the artistic sphere.

I think all that's rubbish. The idea that poets or painters are predominantly gay just isn't borne out by experience. I can think of refined homosexuals and lots of very coarse, boring homosexuals whom I know, who are, as it were, chartered accountants or bank managers.

There is a certain degree of self-congratulation in certain quarters of the gay world – oh, look at me, I'm gay, therefore I must be talented. It just doesn't follow.

Do you think of yourself first as novelist or biographer?

I think of myself primarily as a novelist, but I do find I get tremendously absorbed in the biographies I write, as I did particularly with the Tolstoy. There's a point in that book where I meditate on what it is to be a novelist. Obviously I wasn't writing about myself, but the two things overlapped tremendously. I probably get most satisfaction and pleasure from writing fiction, but in either case one is contemplating human character, so they're not completely different exercises. It's not as if I were writing novels on the one hand and, say, gardening books or books about horses on the other.

Your biography of Tolstoy in 1988 was well received and you were widely praised for your analysis. Tolstoy is well known to have been a mass of contradictions, obsessions and paradoxes, combined with an almost unrestrained ego. Was it because you to some extent share a similar make-up that you were able to write such a penetrating biography?

No. It's a brilliant question, but I'm really very unlike him. It's a lovely idea. If I thought it was true I'd grow a beard. But I'm not a very clever self-analyst and I don't think I'm like Tolstoy.

You wrote of Tolstoy's horror on discovering that marriage was the enemy of egoism and how angry he was to have his self become gradually eroded. Is that a common experience?

That's my suspicion, but who can know about marriages? I suspect it's true of any sort of love relationship; it does rather depend on a kind of losing of the self.

Your literary output is prolific by any standards. How do you manage to do so much in the time available?

The funny thing is, if I've taken on a great big book like Tolstoy, I tell myself that unless I work eight hours a day it's never going to get finished and I make myself do it. But most of the time I don't work very hard. Certainly not nowadays.

The word philistine occurs from time to time in your articles and reviews. Does it convey anything more than disapproval of a particular view or attitude?

I try to use it in the generally accepted sense of the term, that is, of

somebody who either disapproves of the life of the mind or art, or who in some way or another is in a position where they might appreciate it, but don't appreciate it or won't appreciate it. It's a pretty common phenomenon in English life. It's hard to approve of philistine views, wouldn't you say?

Doesn't writing for the popular press promote philistinism?

Yes, probably. But it's hard to be snobbish about the popular press. Why shouldn't there be a popular press, and if there is one, why shouldn't people write for it? I don't know quite what Philip Howard meant when he wrote of my 'fogeyish fulminations', but I can think of instances where that criticism might be justified. The *Daily Mail* once asked me to rubbish Graham Greene, and for some reason I thought it would be an amusing thing to do, but I felt ashamed afterwards.

But why exactly do you write for the popular press?

Money. Just money.

Isn't reviewing a bit incestuous in this country in the sense that you see the same author's book reviewed over and over by the same sort of people?

If you're a literary editor, which I was for a couple of years, you sit despondently by the telephone thinking, who can I get to review this book? You have a brilliant idea for breaking out of the boring old mould of sending it to the kind of reviewer people will expect, and decide to send it to somebody new. You ring them up. They don't want to do it. You ring up some other brilliant person. They don't want to do it either. Eventually you find some new person who you know is brilliant, and they say they will do it, and you post the thing off; and, of course, since they aren't professional reviewers, they lose the book or they ring you back in about two months and say they've read it but can't think of anything to say about it. Literary editors, like anybody else, want an easy life, and you tend to send a book to the person you know will hand in their copy on time, do the right number of words and all that. I'm sure that's partly why it happens. If you're a literary editor, you develop a little stable of well-loved reviewers – well-loved to you. It doesn't matter if the readers like them or not.

You were reported in a review as thinking fairness boring and tolerance stodgy, but can such views bear serious examination, or is this just posturing on your part?

No. It is very difficult to devise any criterion by which to judge a good book. I was talking about fairness in a review. In the end, particularly

in something like a review in a newspaper, where you're not given thousands of words as you might be, say, in the *New York Review of Books*, you've just got to give your own impression. And if you're bending over backwards to be fair, it's bound to be boring, that's all. I'm not an intolerant person, if we're speaking of behaviour. I am intolerant on idiocy. When I hear people saying foolish things I always want to say that they're foolish.

Does the idea of hurting people with trenchant reviews worry you?

Well, somebody said a gentleman was someone who never caused pain, except intentionally. Quite honestly, I used to mind. When you're young, you write what you think, and you write what you hope might be funny. Then you discover somebody's spent all night sobbing into the Kleenex because you haven't liked their lousy book. After that, if you're me, you feel awful and experience terrible guilt. I now think a bit differently about it because writers are such appalling egotists for the most part that it won't do them very much harm to be told occasionally their book's no bloody good. If you know somebody is going to be awfully annoyed by something you write, that's obviously very satisfying, and if they howl with rage or cry, that's honey.

You apologized publicly for calling Marina Warner 'a charlatan and a bore' in a waspish review, but, questioned subsequently, have always insisted that your review was fair. Exactly what were you therefore apologizing for?

I was apologizing for the fact, told to me by her godfather, that she had been snivelling into the Kleenex, and I didn't want to think of an apparently nice person – though I don't know Marina Warner – crying because of something I'd said. I wasn't suggesting that everything about her was boring. I simply found that particular book boring. Perhaps it was unkind of me to say so in public.

You explained at one point in relation to leaving the Spectator*: 'I'm very silly to think that my acts don't have consequences.' You made it sound as though acknowledging a fault is the proper alternative to avoiding it. Is it?*

What a moral philosopher you are, Naim. It sounds like a question at some Jesuit confessional. In that particular case I think I was very naïve, and I'm much less naïve now. In my twenties I very often thought that anything was good for a laugh. Well, I still think that, but I didn't realize then that not everybody would find it screamingly amusing. It wasn't a sin.

Your view of the Established Church seems at best ambivalent. Are you an adherent?

Not a serious one. I don't really take the Church seriously any longer.

What has changed your views?

Well, one changes. I find myself less religious as I grow older.

Isn't there a case for saying that the sort of laxity in doctrine and organization you have complained of from time to time may actually represent perfectly honest attempts to make faith possible in the late twentieth century?

Where have I done all this complaining? I'm always reading in papers that I've complained about this and that, but the articles being referred to are nearly always written by Charles Moore or Gavin Stamp. I did a book with them which started out with ten contributors until seven dropped out. Because only three of us were left, it looked as though we were all thinking the same way. The others might have complained about laxity of doctrine, but I don't remember doing so myself. The question is an interesting one, however, because obviously it is widely supposed among intelligent people that Christianity is frankly incredible, which it is now. There's no particular scientific reason to suppose that the universe is a created thing, for example. People used to think it had to have origin, but there's now no logical reason to suppose it did. We also know much more than we used to about how the Bible came into being. There are many reasons why people might lose their belief in Christianity altogether, and I would have thought the only way you could sustain Christianity at all would be along the lines of a more liberal attitude; to try to accept these new modern scientific or philosophical developments and reconcile them to the old structures. But whether that can be done, or whether it wouldn't in the end destroy the essence of the Christian religion, I don't know.

Isn't religion a force for good in our society?

Not necessarily. Not when it's taken too seriously by stupid people. Religion has been a mixed blessing to the human race. It encourages stupidity, intolerance and cruelty. Look at the large portions of the world that are dominated by Islam and Roman Catholicism in different forms. I know you're a Catholic, but you know what I mean. Yet can one live without faith? One can live without belief in organized religion certainly. Plenty of people do.

But don't many people as they grow older become more serene because they believe they are going to have an after-life?

The reason people become more serene has nothing to do with their views of the after-life. Life for young people is very painful. Everything is potentially painful for a young person. Falling in love is never a pleasurable experience for a young person, but always painful. Everything gets on your nerves, you're worried all the time, and gradually those things change and one becomes blander and probably more boring. But life becomes happier and you develop a capacity for enjoying things like food, and nature, and friendship. That's why people are happier in their middle age. It's not because they think they're going to go to some imaginary place in the sky.

So what do you think will happen to you when you die?

It wouldn't make sense to have a thought about that. By definition, we don't know. We can't possibly know what's going to happen to us when we're dead. Of course, I have thoughts about death, but they don't involve thoughts about the after-life. They involve thoughts about being parted from people I love, of the timing of the death and so on.

I'm still unclear about your own theological position. You say, for example, that there is no evidence in the New Testament to suggest that Christ claimed to be God, but it's not clear whether or not you think that significant. Do you in fact believe that Christ was God?

No.

'If Christ be not risen, our faith is vain,' St Paul said. But you seem equally unwilling to allow for the evidence of the New Testament on the question of the Resurrection. Is it just an elaborate way of saying that faith is all and that one must not look for truth?

Well, faith is all. Lots of other truths come to us by means other than thinking, and that's how the ideas about Christ arose. It is a matter of empirical fact that there's no historical evidence that Christ claimed to be God, but the Resurrection is a different question because there are documents. They're all contradictory, so you have to make up your own mind about them. The creeds saying that Christ was the same person as Almighty God were formulated years after his death. But that's not something you can make up your mind about without what we call faith.

Christianity seems on the whole to disapprove of sex. Some Eastern religions believe it to be a gift from God, to be enjoyed not just for the purpose of procreation.

Good for the Eastern religions, if that's what they're saying. But why

does it have to be a gift from anybody? Christianity came to us through a filter of Platonism and Plato, and his followers thought that matter itself was wicked, and therefore anything to do with the flesh or matter was wrong. Then that great genius but ghastly and tormented man, St Augustine, invented the idea that original sin actually came into the world through semen, so that any manifestation of sexuality was inextricably and unavoidably wicked. He had a good foundation to build on, since St Paul hated sex, as did all the other Christian writers in between. Only think of the pointless misery that it's caused the human race to think that sex is wicked.

You mean suppression of sex itself can be very harmful?

That's a different question. If everybody led an unbridled sexual life, there would be chaos, but the idea that one's sexual feelings, quite apart from anything you do with them, are wicked – which is a fundamentally Christian idea – strikes me as disastrous.

Some puritans would argue that sex is addictive, and from addiction comes perversion.

I don't know who they are, so it's rather easy to knock down these Aunt Sallies, these puritans. Obviously, if you're a healthy grown-up person, your sexual impulses go on, but that's not the same as saying that something is addictive. To say that is like saying food is addictive, which it isn't. The fact that you want to have it all the time doesn't mean it's addictive.

But wouldn't it be true that, if you suddenly had three or four women, and you started having sex with them, you'd want to have more and more?

What an adventurous life you must have led, Naim. I'm not qualified to answer that question. What I disagree with the puritans about is that excess is somehow the same as perversion. There isn't such a thing as too much or too little sex. If you don't want to have sex, fine. Plenty of people don't. If you want it and you're not making a public nuisance of yourself and the person concerned wants it too, fine as well. I'm certainly not stopping anybody.

What do you think of the proposal to ordain women, bearing in mind that some dioceses in communion with the Church of England have already done so?

As I said, I'm less interested than I once was in the Church, but I'm very much in favour of ordaining women. There's no logical or theological reason why they shouldn't be ordained, especially if you're thinking of the Christian Church as something more than the sum of its parts,

something that influences the whole of society, which it still does in a marginal way. The Christian Church is where most of us in the West came from; it's the origin, to a large degree, of Western civilization. And one of the ghastly legacies of old-fashioned Christianity is the suppression and degradation of women, which is not necessarily a truthful extrapolation from the New Testament. I think Christ was rather revolutionary in many ways. He talked to women who were strangers, and that was forbidden by the laws of his religion. There is a definite though very minor and much-suppressed feminist tradition buried in the New Testament. It would be a good thing if, in its latter stages, Christianity could admit it and have a few women bishops and lots of women priests. St Paul wouldn't have wanted it, but then St Paul wouldn't have wanted a lot of things.

What are your views on feminism and the women's movement? Do they extend beyond contraception and economic independence?

Those two things are jolly important, because without them it's quite hard to keep the feminist thing going. I'm a through and through feminist and support the movement totally.

Even if the movement discourages family life?

Many good things have discouraged family life, or, at least, many supposedly good things have, like early Christianity or academic life. Until the nineteenth century all academics were celibates. In effect, all kinds of professions and areas of expertise discourage family life, as does the feminist movement occasionally, but only because women have had such a raw deal out of it. I know it's a cliché, but take clever women like the Brontë sisters who spent most of their lives making apple pies in a parsonage rather than being able to go and be educated. It's astonishing to think how long it's taken women to rebel against the assumptions of a male-dominated world.

Of course we all believe in equal rights, we all believe in independence.

We don't all believe. A lot of people pay lip service, but I don't think they believe in equal rights and independence by any manner of means. Ask around the married couples you know, where both parties work, whether they actually take an equal share in shopping or cleaning the house or looking after the children. I know that's rather basic stuff, but you'll find they don't. A lot of men say they believe in equal opportunities for women, but what they mean is that they believe in having a double income and still expect their wives to iron their socks. We all know, if we're honest, that women are better off without men in many

respects. In an ideal set-up, men and women are complementary. But how many ideal set-ups are there? If I were a woman, I would hold out against falling in love with a man as long as I possibly could.

But you might be miserable in the process?

I might not be. Men aren't the only thing in life.

But don't women need men in the same way as men need women?

Well, obviously, and that's how the whole problem arose in the first place. I support feminism in all its forms, with the obvious proviso that any political movement is complicated by human nature. You might fall in love with somebody or derive tremendous satisfaction from a personal relationship, and that obviously makes the whole business more complex. I have two daughters, and I would want them to have a completely independent life with all the opportunities they would have had if they had been men. But, of course, I wouldn't want them to think that work is the be-all and end-all of life. And that's where the trouble begins. Because, as a woman – partly because of the biological fact that you're the one that carries the babies as they come along – if you're not careful it's going to be quietly assumed, not just by your man but by the other mums and all these other insidious and terrible groups, that you must put being a mother first. It's very difficult from a practical point of view to lead a completely emotionally fulfilled life with a man and a child, and be responsible for a lot of the practical things, like running the household, and yet pursue your career.

Your novels don't fall at all into the fashionable modes of magic realism or post-modernism or faction and so on. Have you ever felt an urge to experiment with the novel form?

My novels are fundamentally comic realist, and they haven't been very adventurous. Without wishing to be boring about it, I'm changing slightly. The one I'm writing at the moment is a bit different. It's a long novel, a sort of multi-volume approach, and the first volume starts off as a conventional comic tale and then, as you get deeper into this labyrinth, there is going to be something of what I suppose some people might think of as the experimental. If a novel is mainly designed as an entertainment, though, there is a limit to what you can do with it. Salman Rushdie may be very brilliant for all we know, but if you can't read him, what's the point in his being brilliant? That's the trouble with some of these experiments. Look at James Joyce. He's wonderful in *Portrait of the Artist as a Young Man*, wonderful in *Ulysses*, though far less wonderful in *Finnegans Wake*, which is full of gobbledegook that

only Joyce scholars can read. That's been the fundamental difficulty of so-called modernism ever since it was invented.

The narrator of Incline Our Hearts *says: 'Of all liars, the most arrogant are biographers.' Is that a reflection of your own view?*

No, he's a different character from me, though we have things in common. That statement is meant to be within the context of that story, which involves a lying biographer. But I suppose what lies behind the remark is the knowledge which comes to someone who has written biographies, that however truthful you try to be, you can't tell something as finished and bald as *the* truth about a human life; that there's no such thing. You have to interpret a life. However full it is and however serious it is, it is going to be a sort of caricature. That's why writing novels is, in a sense, an easier way to the truth about human nature.

So you'd feel there's something to be said for recent critical arguments that literature is superior to history or biography because, there being no way of establishing truth, whatever is clearly labelled 'fiction' is more honest than fictions labelled 'history' or 'biography'.

I certainly think there is something to be said for that. Most history, so called, is only an interpretation of facts, and quite a lot of it is an interpretation of falsehoods, most historical facts not being, in fact, true at all. Take the storming of the Bastille. The storming happened, but the Bastille held about six people; it wasn't full of wailing starving prisoners, as in the first act of *Fidelio*. Almost everyone thinks that the French Revolution happened because there was a prison called the Bastille full of unhappy people. Most great historical events are myths. All of that's true, and yet there is a bit of me which is a kind of English empiricist, common-sense character. You'd go mad if you took it too far, and a lot of these post-structuralist critics are certifiably insane, particularly the French ones. There has to be at least a convention that there is some reality outside ourselves, some reality that can be investigated. If we lose sight of that, then we've lost something terribly important. To say there's a kind of creative truth in historical falsehood may be the great myth, the great opera, and although it is a boring thing to do, one has a duty to point this out. Lenin created a great myth, based on the Marxist myth and fleshed out by all kinds of stories that most Soviet citizens, until very recently, believed to be the same as historical fact. Then it's the patient task of a historian to sit down and say, 'Well, it didn't actually happen like that.' It's true that such a patient boring task doesn't fire the imagination, but without it people can be led up the garden path.

Can there be any sort of objective standard in literature?

That's quite deep stuff. We've got to say that there is a standard, I think. We've got to say that Jane Austen is, in some sense of the word, a better novelist than Barbara Cartland – in a world where you can't distinguish between those two. Great as the merits of Barbara Cartland may be, there is something missing, something lost. On the other hand, once you enter into what it is that makes Jane Austen better than Barbara Cartland, you've entered a very nebulous area, and philosophers of aesthetics can never agree about anything. I would want to think it was possible, in a rough and ready way, to say, yes, there are things other than enjoyment or purely commercial considerations, but you have to be a very good critic to be able to put your finger on what they are. With most of us, it's an irrational gut feeling.

As a nation, are we as literary as we claim to be?

I'd have thought we were very unliterary. In France, if you go on the arts programme *Apostrophe*, and say you've just written some rather highbrow novel, the next day you'll sell 80,000 copies. But in this country, if you write a rather clever highbrow novel and try to get on the *Terry Wogan Show*, let us say, they won't even have you. A good example is Iris Murdoch, who was billed by her agent to go on the *Terry Wogan Show*. In the end it was decided that Terry Wogan wouldn't have anything to say to her, so she was withdrawn from the programme. We're a thunderingly philistine nation, but it's also one of our saving graces, which is the paradox. If you value the things of the mind, it's depressing to contemplate the fact that the English don't take literature or, indeed, anything else very seriously. On the other hand, it means that they're less likely to be interested in, and therefore hoodwinked by, ideologues. Historically that's been the case. Thinking has always been the preserve of a tiny little minority of people in England. The generality of clever people in this country never think. They don't dare to. They have jobs in the civil service or the universities, where thought is almost unknown.

What is most important to you in friendship?

I certainly can't imagine having a very happy friendship with anybody who didn't have a shared sense of humour. I can imagine other sorts of relationship. One could fall in love with somebody's beauty or something of the kind, but I can't imagine wanting to see a lot of somebody who didn't laugh at the same things as I do. You could take the view that sexual tension is there all the time in everything, and that if a man and a woman get together and make a friendship, sex therefore plays

some part, even if it's not a sexual relationship. But there are many, many cases where the sexual aspect is somehow minimalized. One can easily be friends with one's lover, but what I'm saying is that it may well be that, in platonic friendships between men and women, there is a sexual element, but the friendship will be spoiled if you pause to examine what or how strong that sexual element is. Once you get into bed together, you might stop being friends. It's happened a lot in the history of the world, for all the usual old boring reasons. People have completely different expectations of a relationship once they've been to bed together, and the expectations usually become unequal. In a platonic relationship, the level of emotion between the two people may not be the same – one person may like the other to a greater or lesser extent – but it doesn't really matter very much if all you're doing is having lunch or playing cards. It suddenly starts to matter terribly once you go to bed with somebody. Or so I've read.

But seriously, your novels are champions of irony and paradox, so don't you think that, while these elements may be amusing from time to time, their continuous use is bound to undermine substantial response to both life and art, becoming so easily a way of avoiding serious reflection or commitment?

I'm tempted just to say yes. The trouble with serious reflection and commitment is that it can so often be boring and wrong-headed. And irony and paradox aren't necessarily false responses to so-called serious questions. So not necessarily yes.

David Sexton said in a review of your book Stray *that the view of human beings as coarse, smelly, ugly creatures was pretty much the message of your previous nine novels.*

Some human beings are, aren't they? I'm not a misanthrope, but I do think the human race is a mixed blessing. I'd be happier if it was just the birds and the bees and the pussy cats. Obviously human beings are the most interesting creatures on the planet, but one hardly needs to labour the point that they are also vile, stupid and cruel.

But would you say that the fact that you fill your novels with people with contemptible habits, joyless marriages, physical imperfections and so on, is simply because it is difficult to make interest out of harmony, or because you aim at an honest attempt to portray the world as it is?

I think it's the second. Complete harmony would obviously be difficult and perhaps not very interesting to write about. I don't know, but I would say my books are meant to be comedies rather than anything else. Comedy doesn't exactly thrive on human perfection and, anyway,

where is human perfection? The genre is much more attuned to imperfection.

Some people I have spoken to, while acknowledging your considerable talent, have suggested that you are idiosyncratic almost to the point of madness.

I didn't know that was a generally held view. I'd regard myself as one of the most luminously sane beings in the universe.

Is there anything you've regretted when you look back?

There are things I've regretted in my personal life, but I wouldn't necessarily want to say what they are. Naturally one could have taken lots of different courses, but it wouldn't necessarily have been any better.

How do you see the future for yourself? Are you ready for any change of direction?

One is changing all the time. 'To live is to change,' as Cardinal Newman says, and if you're not changing to a certain extent, I think it's a sign you're dead, although there are many constants in my life. Looking back, I am aware of many changes in my attitude to life. I certainly feel I understand more about human nature and about my own nature, and I think I am much more tolerant as a result. I've become miles nicer, too.